Advanced Information and Knowledge Processing

Series Editors

Professor Lakhmi Jain
Lakhmi.jain@unisa.edu.au

Professor Xindong Wu
xwu@cs.uvm.edu

For other titles published in this series, go to
http://www.springer.com/

Alexandra Okada
Simon Buckingham Shum
Tony Sherborne (Eds)

Knowledge Cartography

Software Tools and Mapping Techniques

Alexandra Okada, BSc, MA, PhD
Knowledge Media Institute,
The Open University, Milton Keynes, UK

Simon Buckingham Shum, BSc, MSc, PhD
Knowledge Media Institute,
The Open University, Milton Keynes, UK

Tony Sherborne, BSc, MA, PhD
The Centre for Science Education,
Sheffield Hallam University, Sheffield, UK

AI&KP ISSN 1610-3947
ISBN: 978-1-84800-148-0   e-ISBN: 978-1-84800-149-7
DOI 10.1007/978-1-84800-149-7

British Library Cataloguing in Publication Data
A catalogue record for this book is available from the British Library

Library of Congress Control Number: 2008923184

© Springer-Verlag London Limited 2008

Apart from any fair dealing for the purposes of research or private study, or criticism or review, as permitted under the Copyright, Designs and Patents Act 1988, this publication may only be reproduced, stored or transmitted, in any form or by any means, with the prior permission in writing of the publishers, or in the case of reprographic reproduction in accordance with the terms of licences issued by the Copyright Licensing Agency. Enquiries concerning reproduction outside those terms should be sent to the publishers.

The use of registered names, trademarks, etc. in this publication does not imply, even in the absence of a specific statement, that such names are exempt from the relevant laws and regulations and therefore free for general use.

The publisher makes no representation, express or implied, with regard to the accuracy of the information contained in this book and cannot accept any legal responsibility or liability for any errors or omissions that may be made.

Printed on acid-free paper

9 8 7 6 5 4 3 2 1

Springer Science+Business Media
springer.com

Contents

Preface vii

Contributors xxi

1. **Empirical Studies of the Value of Conceptually Explicit Notations in Collaborative Learning** 1
   Daniel D. Suthers

2. **Concept Mapping Using CmapTools to Enhance Meaningful Learning** 25
   Alberto J. Cañas and Joseph D. Novak

3. **Enhancing Collaborative and Meaningful Language Learning Through Concept Mapping** 47
   Rita de Cássia Veiga Marriott and Patrícia Lupion Torres

4. **Thinking Maps®: A Visual Language for Learning** 73
   David Hyerle

5. **The Constructivist Mapping of Internet Information at Work with Nestor** 89
   Romain Zeiliger and Liliane Esnault

6. **Cognitive and Pedagogical Benefits of Argument Mapping: LAMP Guides the Way to Better Thinking** 113
   Yanna Rider and Neil Thomason

7. **Scaffolding School Pupils' Scientific Argumentation with Evidence-Based Dialogue Maps** 131
   Alexandra Okada

8. **Argument Diagramming: The Araucaria Project** 163
   Glenn Rowe and Chris Reed

9. Mapping the Curriculum: How Concept Maps can Improve the Effectiveness of Course Development 183
Tony Sherborne

10. Using Compendium as a Tool to Support the Design of Learning Activities 199
Gráinne Conole

11. Performing Knowledge Art: Understanding Collaborative Cartography 223
Albert M. Selvin

12. Knowledge Cartography for Controversies: The Iraq Debate 249
Simon Buckingham Shum and Alexandra Okada

13. Computer Supported Argument Visualisation: Modelling in Consultative Democracy Around Wicked Problems 267
Ricky Ohl

14. Human-Agent Knowledge Cartography for e-Science: NASA Field Trials at the Mars Desert Research Station 287
Maarten Sierhuis and Simon Buckingham Shum

15. Template-Based Structured Argumentation 307
John Lowrance, Ian Harrison, Andres Rodriguez, Eric Yeh, Tom Boyce, Janet Murdock, Jerome Thomere, and Ken Murray

16. An Experience of the Use of the Cognitive Mapping Method in Qualitative Research 335
Mário Vasconcellos

17. Collaborative Knowledge Modelling with a Graphical Knowledge Representation Tool: A Strategy to Support the Transfer of Expertise in Organisations 357
Josianne Basque, Gilbert Paquette, Beatrice Pudelko, and Michel Leonard

Author Biographies 383

Index 391

Knowledge Cartography: Preface

The eyes are not responsible when the mind does the seeing.
Publilius Syrus (85–43 BC)

Maps are one of the oldest forms of human communication. Map-making, like painting, pre-dates both number systems and written language. Primitive people made maps to orientate themselves in both the living environment and the spiritual worlds. Mapping enabled them to transcend the limitations of private, individual representations of terrain in order to augment group planning, reasoning, and memory. Shared, visual representations opened new possibilities for focusing collective attention, re-living the past, envisaging new scenarios, coordinating actions, and making decisions.

Maps mediate the inner mental world and outer physical world. They help us make sense of the universe at different scales, from galaxies to DNA, and connect the abstract with the concrete by overlaying meanings onto that world, from astrological deities to signatures for diseases. They help us remember what is important, and explore possible configurations of the unknown. Cartography – the discipline and art of making maps – has of course evolved radically. From stone, wood, and animal skins, we now wield software tools that control maps as views generated from live data feeds, with flexible layering and annotation.[1]

"*Foundational concept, fragmented thinking, line of argument, blue skies research, peripheral work*": We spatialize the world of ideas all the time with such expressions. *Maps* can be used to make such configurations tangible, whether sketched on a napkin or modeled in software. In this book we bring together many of the leading researchers and practitioners who are creating and evaluating such software for mapping intellectual worlds. We see these as new tools for reading and writing in an age of information overload, when we need to extract and construct meaningful configurations, around which we can tell different kinds of narrative.

For a visual generation of children who have never known a world without ubiquitous information networks, we might hypothesize that knowledge maps could have particular attraction as portals into the world of ideas. Moreover, *the network* is not only dominant when we think about our social and technical infrastructures, but almost an ontological stance in postmodernity, where we hold our viewpoints to be precisely that: always partial and contextualized. Weaving connections between nodes in the network is the most flexible way to bring ideas and information into locally coherent relationships with each other, knowing that there is always another viewpoint on the validity of these patterns. Modeled in software, the vision is that intellectual continents, islands, and borders can be invoked and dissolved at different scales, as required.

---

[1] Our sister volume in this series, *The Geospatial Web*, explores the convergence of spatial data, mapping tools and the social web (Scharl and Tochtermann, 2006).

Knowledge Cartography can be defined as:

The art, craft, science, design, and engineering of different *genres of map* to describe intellectual landscapes – answering the question *how can we create knowledge maps?*

And the study of *cartographic practices* in both beginners and experts as they make and use such maps – answering the question *how effective are knowledge maps for different kinds of user?*

The particular focus of the authors in this volume is on *sensemaking*: The process by which externalizing one's understanding clarifies one's own grasp of the situation, as well as communicates it to others – literally, the *making* of *sense* (Weick, 1995: p. 4). While "sense" can be expressed in many ways (nonverbally in gesture, facial expression and dance, and in prose, speech, statistics, film…), knowledge cartography as construed here places particular emphasis on digital representations of connected ideas, specifically designed to:

I. *Clarify the intellectual moves and commitments at different levels.* (e.g., Which concepts are seen as more abstract? What relationships are legitimate? What are the key issues? What evidence is being appealed to?)
II. *Incorporate further contributions from others, whether in agreement or not.* The map is not closed, but rather, has affordances designed to make it easy for others to extend and restructure it.
III. *Provoke, mediate, capture, and improve constructive discourse.* This is central to sensemaking in unfamiliar or contested domains, in which the primary challenge is to construct plausible narratives about how the world was, is, or might be, often in the absence of complete, unambiguous data.

Our intention with this book is to provide a report on the state of the art from leaders in their respective fields, identify the important challenges as they are currently seen in this relatively young field, and inspire readers to test and extend the techniques described – hopefully, to think more critically and creatively. Many of the tools described are not sitting in research labs, but are finding application in diverse walks of life, with active communities of practice. These communities represent the readership we hope for: learners, educators, and researchers in all fields, policy analysts, scenario planners, knowledge managers, and team facilitators. We hope that practitioners will find new perspectives and tools to expand their repertoire, while researchers will find rich enough conceptual grounding for further scholarship.

Genres of Knowledge Map

A range of mapping techniques and support tools has evolved, shaped by the problems being tackled, the skill of mappers, and the sophistication of software available. We briefly characterize below the main genres of map. The Appendix summarizes at a glance which mapping approaches and software tools are presented in each chapter.

Mind Mapping was developed by Tony Buzan (Fig. 1) in the early 1970s when he published his popular book "*Use Your Head*." Mind Mapping requires the user to map keywords, sentences, and pictures radiating from a central idea. The relatively low constraints on how elements can be labeled or linked makes it well suited for visual notetaking and brainstorming.

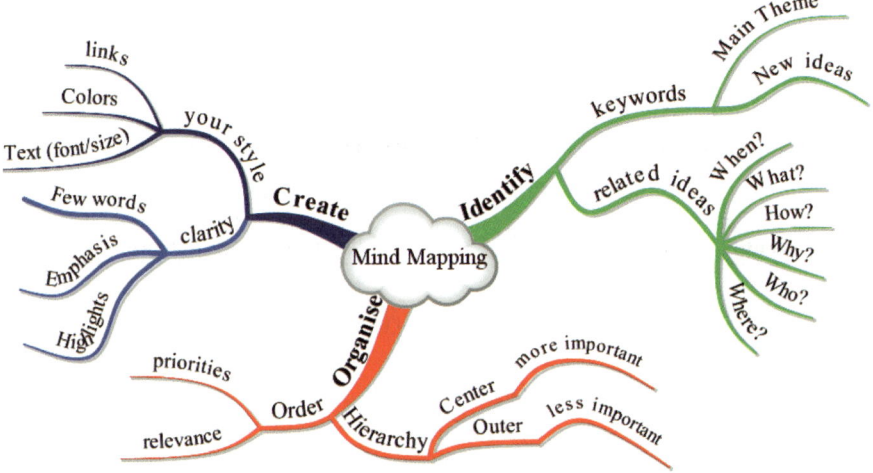

Fig. 1. Mind Map created with Buzan's iMindmap.

Concept Mapping (Fig. 2) was developed by Joseph Novak around 1972, based on Ausubel's theory that meaningful learning only takes place when new concepts are connected to what is already known. Concept maps are hierarchical trees, in which concepts are connected with labeled, graphical links, most general at the top. Novak and many others have reported empirical evidence of the effectiveness of this technique, with an international conference dedicated to the approach.

Argument and Evidence Mapping (Fig. 3) was first proposed by J.H. Wigmore in the early 1900s to help in the teaching and analysis of court cases. The objective is to expose the structure of an argument, in particular how evidence is being used, in order to clarify the status of the debate. Still used in legal education today, the idea has been extended, formalized (and reinvented) in many ways (Buckingham Shum, 2003; Reed et al., 2007), but all focused on elements such as *Claims, Evidence, Premises* and supporting/challenging relations.

Issue Mapping (Fig. 4) derives from the "Issue-Based Information System" (IBIS) developed by Horst Rittel in the 1970s to scaffold groups tackling "wicked" socio-technical problems. IBIS structures deliberation by connecting *Issues, Positions, and*

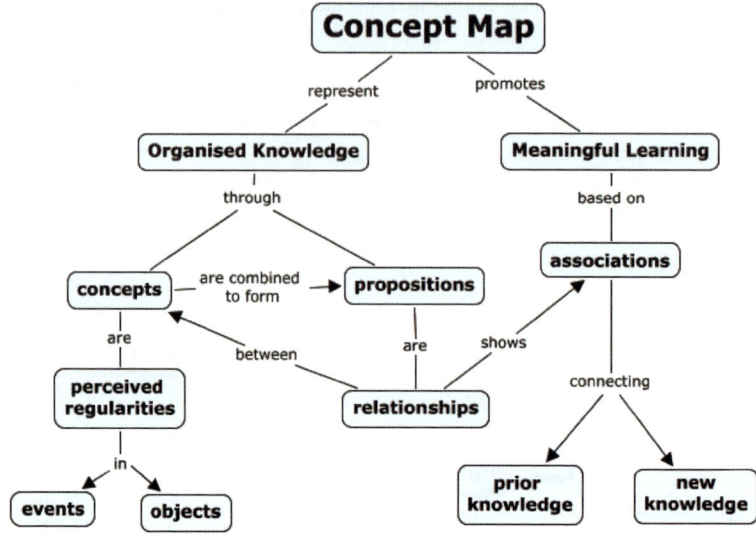

Fig. 2. Concept Map created with CMap Tools.

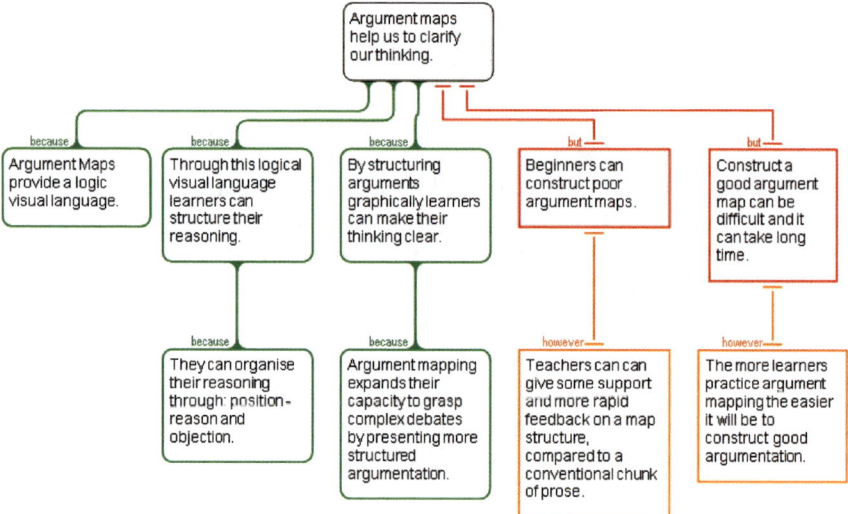

Fig. 3. Argument Map created with Rationale.

Arguments in consistent ways, which can be rendered as textual outlines and graphical maps. "Dialogue Mapping" was developed by Conklin (2006) for using IBIS in meetings, extended as "Conversational Modelling" by Sierhuis and Selvin (1999) to integrate formal modeling and interoperability with other tools.

Preface xi

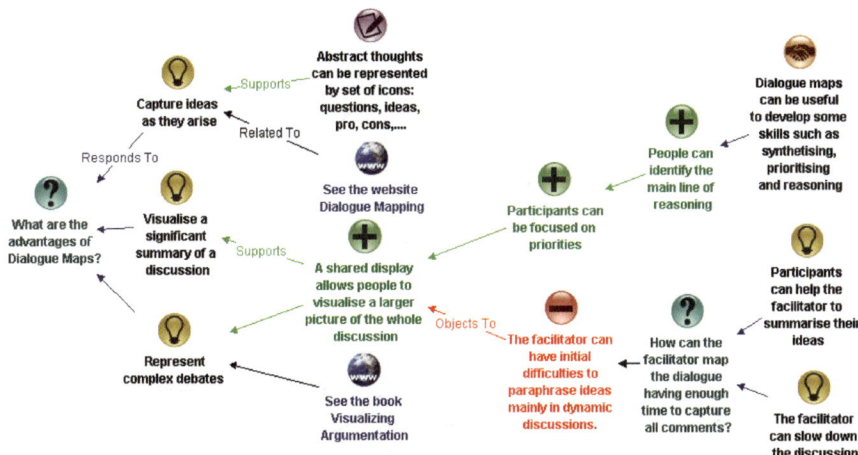

Fig. 4. Issue Map created with Compendium.

Web Mapping (Fig. 5) appeared relatively recently as a result of the rapid growth of the internet. Software tools provide a way for users to capture, position, iconify, link, and annotate hyperlinks in a visual space as they navigate, creating a richer trail which comes to have more personal meaning than a simple bookmark list.

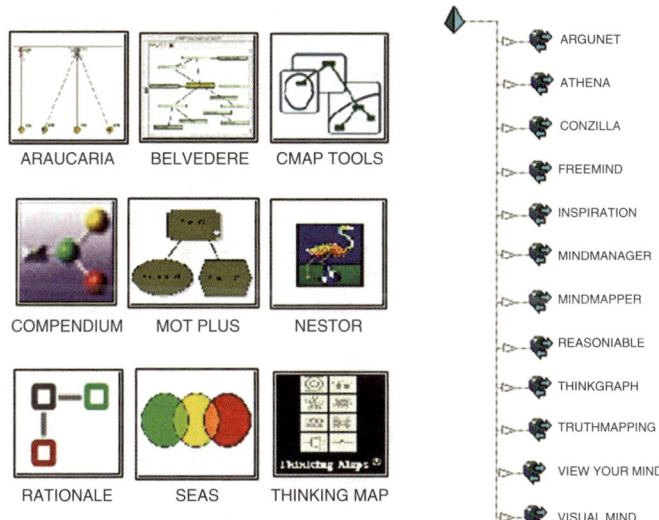

Fig. 5. Web Map about mapping tools with Nestor Web Cartographer.

Thinking Maps (Fig. 6) as defined by Hyerle (Chap. 4) contrasts all of the above with a set of abstract visual conventions designed to support core cognitive skills. Hyerle's eight graphic primitives (expressing basic reasoning about, e.g., *causality, sequence, whole-part*) are designed to be combined to express higher order reasoning (e.g., *metaphor, induction, systems dynamics*).

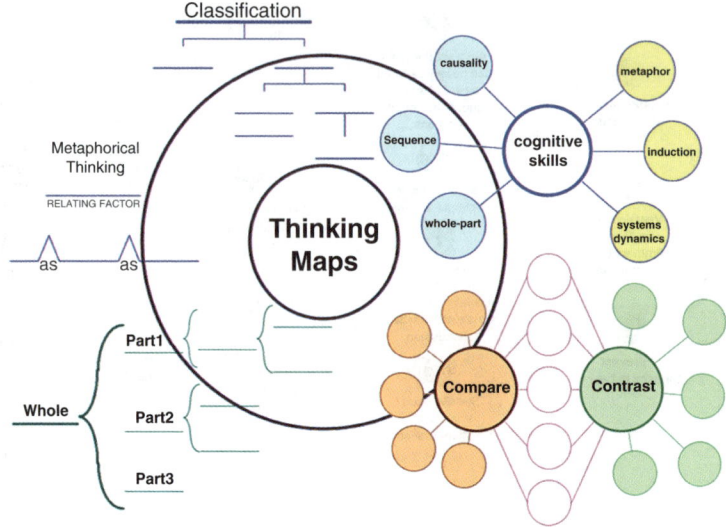

Fig. 6. Thinking Maps created with Thinking Maps © tool.

Finally, a note on what we might term *Visual Specification Languages*, which are designed for software interpretation by imposing constraints on how links and often nodes are labeled and combined. This is a huge field in its own right, with schemes such as Unified Modeling Language (UML) supporting user communities far larger than any of the others listed here, plus innumerable other notations and tools that exploit the power of visualization for modeling processes, ontologies, and organizations. These are not, however, heavily represented in this book (though see Chaps. 14 [Sierhuis] and 17 [Basque]) for the simple reason that this book's interest in sensemaking focuses on the analytical work required at the upstream phases in problem solving, or in domains where formal modeling is contentious because of the assumptions it requires. Once the problem, assumptions, and solution criteria are agreed and bounded, there is a clearer cost/benefit tradeoff for detailed modeling.

Overview of the Book

This book has 17 chapters organized in two parts, defined by whether the primary application is in formal learning or the workplace. However, while this distinction reflects two large audiences, readers will find ideas cross-fertilizing healthily between chapters. The first half, *Knowledge Maps for Learning and Teaching*, focuses on applications in schools and universities. We start with tools for learners, opening with a literature survey, followed by examples of different approaches (concept mapping, information mapping, argument mapping). Attention then turns to the kinds of maps that educators need. In the second half we broaden the scope to *Knowledge Maps for Information Analysis and Knowledge Management*, examining the role that these tools are playing in professional communities – but with great relevance also to more formal learning contexts. We start with an analysis of the knowledge cartographer's skill set, followed by three case studies around issue mapping, one on evidence mapping, concluding with case studies on two additional approaches.

1. Suthers in *"Empirical Studies of the Value of Conceptually Explicit Notations in Collaborative Learning"* reports on a series of studies which show that differences of notations or representational biases can lead to differences in processes of collaborative inquiry. The studies span face-to-face, synchronous online, and asynchronous online media in both classroom and laboratory settings.
2. Canas and Novak present *"Concept Mapping Using CmapTools to Enhance Meaningful Learning."* After briefly introducing the pioneering concept mapping approach and CmapTools software, they provide an update to what is probably the world's largest systematic deployment of concept mapping, the "Proyecto Conéctate al Conocimiento" in Panama, reflecting on their experiences introducing concept mapping in hundreds of schools to enhance meaningful learning.
3. Marriott and Torres in *"Enhancing Collaborative and Meaningful Language Learning Through Concept Mapping"* describe how concept mapping can help develop students' reading, writing, and oral skills as part of a blended methodology for language teaching called LAPLI. Their research was first implemented with a group of preservice students studying for a degree in English and Portuguese languages at the Catholic University of Parana (PUCPR) in Brazil.
4. Hyerle in *"Thinking Maps®: A Visual Language for Learning"* summarizes a graphical language comprising eight cognitive maps called Thinking Maps® and Thinking Maps® Software. These tools have been used from early grades to college courses to foster cognitive development and content learning, across all disciplines.
5. Zeiliger and Esnault in *"The Constructivist Mapping of Internet Information at Work with Nestor"* present the Nestor Web Cartographer software and the constructivist approach to mapping Internet information. They analyze a case study in Lyon School of Management (EM LYON), to show how the features of the software, such as a hybrid representational system, visual widgets, and collaboration, help in constructing formalized knowledge.
6. Rider and Thomason in *"Cognitive and Pedagogical benefits of Argument Mapping: LAMP Guides the Way to Better Thinking"* show that in dedicated Critical Thinking courses "Lots of Argument Mapping Practice" (LAMP) using a software tool like *Rationale* considerably improves students' critical thinking skills. They present preliminary evidence and discussion concerning how LAMP confers these benefits, and call for proper experimental and educational research.
7. Okada in *"Scaffolding School Pupils' Scientific Argumentation with Evidence-Based Dialogue Maps"* reports pilot work investigating the potential of Evidence-based Dialogue Mapping to foster young teenagers' scientific

argumentation. Her study comprises multiple data sources: Pupils' maps in Compendium, their writings in science and reflective comments about the uses of mapping for writing. Her qualitative analysis highlights the diversity of ways, both successful and unsuccessful, in which dialogue mapping was used by these young teenagers to write scientific explanations.

8. Rowe and Reed in "*Argument Diagramming: The Araucaria Project*" describe the software package Araucaria, which allows textual arguments to be annotated to create argument diagrams conforming to different schemes such as Toulmin or Wigmore diagrams. Since each of these diagramming techniques was devised for a particular domain or argumentation, they discuss some of the issues involved in translating between the schemes.

9. Sherborne in his chapter "*Mapping the Curriculum: How Concept Maps can Improve the Effectivness of Course Development*" argues that "curriculum development" is a process that naturally lends itself to visualization through concept mapping. He reviews the evidence for how mapping can help curriculum developers and teachers, by promoting more collaborative, learner-centric designs.

10. Conole in "*Using Compendium as a Tool to Support the Design of Learning Activities*," reports work to help multimedia designers and university academics create and share e-learning activities, by creating a visual language for learning design patterns. She discusses how learning activities can be represented, and how the maps provide a mechanism to supporting decision making in creating new activities.

11. Opening the second half, Selvin in "*Performing Knowledge Art: Understanding Collaborative Cartography*" focuses on the special skills and considerations involved in constructing knowledge maps with and for groups. He provides concepts and frameworks useful in analyzing collaborative practice, illustrating them with a case study.

12. Buckingham Shum and Okada in "*Knowledge Cartography for Controversies: The Iraq Debate*" use the debate around the invasion of Iraq to demonstrate a knowledge mapping methodology to extract key ideas from source materials, in order to classify and connect them within and across a set of perspectives. They reflect on the value of this approach, and how it can be extended with finer-grained argument mapping techniques.

13. Ohl in "*Computer Supported Argument Visualization: Modeling in Consultative Democracy Around Wicked Problems*," presents a case study where a mapping methodology supported the analysis and representation of the discourse surrounding the draft South East Queensland Regional Plan Consultation. He argues that argument mapping can help deliver the transparency and accountability required in participatory democracy.

14. Sierhuis and Buckingham Shum in "*Human-Agent Knowledge Cartography for e-Science: NASA Field Trials at the Mars Desert Research Station*," describe the sociotechnical embedding of a knowledge cartography approach (Conversational Modeling) within a prototype e-science work system. They demonstrates how human and agent plans, data, multimedia documents, metadata, discussions, interpretations and arguments can be mapped in an integrated manner, and

successfully deployed in field trials which simulated aspects of mission workload pressure.
15. Lowrance et al. in *"Template-Based Structured Argumentation"* present a semi-automated approach to evidential reasoning, which uses template-based structured argumentation. These graphical depictions convey lines of reasoning, from evidence through to conclusions. Their structured arguments are based on a hierarchy of questions (a tree) that is used to assess a situation. This hierarchy of questions is called the argument template (as opposed to the argument, which answers the questions posed by a template).
16. Vasconcelos in *"An Experience of the Use of the Cognitive Mapping Method in Qualitative Research,"* analyzes concept mapping as a tool for supporting qualitative research, particularly to carry out literature reviews, concept analysis, and qualitative data examination. He uses his own experience in applying CmapTools software to understand the concept of partnership.
17. Basque et al. in *"Collaborative Knowledge Modeling with a Graphical Knowledge Representation Tool MOT: A Strategy to Support the Transfer of Expertise in Organizations"* present a strategy for collaborative knowledge modeling between experts and novices in order to support the transfer of expertise within organizations. They use an object-typed knowledge modeling software tool called MOT, to elaborate knowledge models in small groups composed of experienced and less experienced employees.

Toward Human–Machine Knowledge Cartography

To summarize, *Knowledge Cartography* is a specific form of information visualization, seeking to represent spatially intellectual worlds that have no intrinsic spatial properties. We have emphasized the challenge of helping analysts craft maps of information resources, concepts, issues, ideas and arguments as an intrinsic part of their *personal and collective sensemaking*. As with all artistry and craft, the *process and product* should interweave: The discipline required to craft a good map should clarify thinking and discourse in a way that augments the analytic task at hand, and the emerging map should in turn provoke further reflection on the rigor of the analysis. We are interested in mapping the structure of *physical phenomena* (e.g., a biological process), of *intellectual artifacts* (e.g., a curriculum), and *intellectual processes* of inquiry (e.g., a meeting discussion, or a scientific, or public debate).

This orientation complements the work that has emerged in recent years in Domain Visualization within the information retrieval community, and Meeting Capture from the multimedia analysis community. In Domain Visualization (e.g., Chen, 2003; Shiffrin and Börner, 2004), "maps of science" are generated from the analysis of text corpora and related scientometric indices (e.g., cocitation patterns in literature databases), with the analyst then able to tune parameters to expose meaningful patterns (e.g., emerging research fronts; turning points in the literature), and interactively navigate the visualization as they browse trails of interest. In Meeting Capture research (e.g., the European AMI and US CALO Projects), the analogous goal is to extract significant moments from audio and video meeting records (e.g., decisions; action items; disagreements), including generating argument maps (e.g., Rienks, et al., 2006) in order to index the meeting and support follow-on activity.

We envisage that human and machine knowledge mapping will eventually converge. Software agents will work continuously in the background and on demand, generating maps and alerts that expose potentially significant patterns in discussions and publications (e.g., term clusters; hub nodes; pivotal papers; emerging research fronts; supporting/challenging evidence; candidate solutions). Analysts will assess, further annotate, and add new interpretive layers. While some of the authors in this book focus on mapping domains where objective, "hard" science data can be used to decide whether a map is correct or not, other authors are interested in how maps can support modes of interpretation and discourse across "softer" disciplines within the arts and humanities, and for teams confronted with wicked problems in policy deliberation and strategic planning, where there is no single, knowable solution.

The layers that analysts will add to machine generated maps will, therefore, also reflect the community's deliberations – whether in meetings or the literature – adding important connections and summaries that are not in the source documents/datasets. Human and machine mapping should be synergistic. Machines will play a critical role by filtering the data ocean, extracting increasingly higher level patterns, and acting on those semiautonomously. People will, however, sense connections between experiences and ideas, and constantly read new connotations into their physical and information environments, in ways that are hard to imagine in machines. Crafting maps by hand will, in this view, continue to be an important discipline for sensemaking, even as our tools expand exponentially in computational power.

We are confronted today by ever more complex challenges at community, national and global levels. As we learn almost daily of new, unexpected connections between natural and designed phenomena, we have to find ways to teach these rich, multi-layered Webs to our children. More than ever, we need to find ways to build common ground between diverse groups as they seek to make sense of the past, the immediate challenges of the present and possible futures. It would trivialize the dilemmas we face to declare a technological silver bullet. However, we cautiously propose that rigor and artistry in Knowledge Cartography has a significant role to play in shaping how stakeholders, young and old, learn to think, listen, and debate.

Alexandra Okada, Simon Buckingham Shum and Tony Sherborne

Milton Keynes, October 2007
Companion website with supplementary resources:
kmi.open.ac.uk/books/knowledge-cartography

References

AMI: *Augmented Multimodal Interaction project*: publications.amiproject.org

Bowker, G. and Star, S.L. (2000) *Sorting Things Out: Classification and Its Consequences.* Cambridge, MA: MIT Press.

Buckingham Shum, S. (2003) The Roots of Computer Supported Argument Visualization. In *Visualizing Argumentation*, (Eds.) P. Kirschner, S. Buckingham Shum, and C. Carr. Berlin Heidelberg New York: Springer.

CALO: *Cognitive Assistant that Learns and Organizes*: caloproject.sri.com

Chen, C. (2003) *Mapping Scientific Frontiers.* Berlin Heidelberg New York: Springer.

Conklin, J. (2006) *Dialogue Mapping.* Chichester: Wiley.

Reed, C., Walton, D., and Macagno, F. (2007) Argument Diagramming in Logic, Law and Artificial Intelligence. *The Knowledge Engineering Review*, 22 (1), pp. 87–109

Rienks, R., Verbree, D., and Heylen, D. (2006) First Steps Towards Automatic Construction of Argument-Diagrams from Real Discussions. *Proceedings of COMMA'06: First International Conference on Computational Models of Argument,* Liverpool, September 2006. Amsterdam: IOS Press.

Scharl, A. and Tochtermann, K. (2006) *The Geospatial Web.* Berlin Heidelberg New York: Springer.

Selvin, A., (1999) Supporting Collaborative Analysis and Design with Hypertext Functionality. *Journal of Digital Information*, 1 (4), Article No. 16, 1999-01-14

Shiffrin, R.M. and Börner, K. (2004) Mapping Knowledge Domains. *Proceedings of the National Academy of Sciences*, 101, pp. 5183–5185. (Special Issue Editorial)

Weick, K.E. (1995) *Sensemaking in Organizations.* Thousand Oaks: Sage Publications.

Appendix: Mapping approaches and software by chapter

Part 1: Knowledge Maps for Learning and Teaching

Chapter		Tool	Technique	Use Context
01	Empirical Studies of the value of Conceptually Explicit Notations in Collaborative Learning	Belvedere	Argument Mapping	Undergraduate Science
02	Concept Mapping Using CmapTools to Enhance Meaningful Learning	CmapTools	Concept Mapping	Schools
03	Enhancing Collaborative and Meaningful Languages Learning Through Concept Mapping	CmapTools	Concept Mapping	Undergraduate Language
04	Thinking Maps®: A Visual Language for Learning	Thinking Maps	Thinking Maps	Schools
05	The Constructivist Mapping of Internet Information at Work with Nestor	Nestor	Web Mapping	Web Learners
06	Cognitive and Pedagogical Benefits of Argument Mapping: LAMP Guides the Way to Better Thinking	Rationale	Argument Mapping	Undergraduate Philosophy
07	Scaffolding School Pupils' Scientific Argumentation with Evidence-Based Dialogue Maps	Compendium	Dialogue Mapping	Schools
08	Argument Diagramming: The Araucaria Project	Araucaria	Argument Mapping	Undergraduate Philosophy
09	Mapping the Curriculum: How Concept Maps can Improve the Effectiveness of Course Development	CmapTools	Concept Mapping	Schools
10	Using Compendium as a Tool to Support the Design of Learning Activities	Compendium	Mind Mapping	Learning Designers

Part 2: Knowledge Maps for Information Analysis and Knowledge Management

Chapter		Tool	Technique	Use Context
11	Performing Knowledge Art: Understanding Collaborative Cartography	Compendium	Conversational Modeling	e-Science and other mission operations
12	Knowledge Cartography for Controversies: The Iraq Debate"	Compendium	Dialogue Mapping	Policy Analysis
13	Computer Supported Argument Visualization: Modeling in Consultative Democracy Around Wicked Problems	Compendium	Modeling Mapping	Government Public Consultation
14	Human-Agent Knowledge Cartography for e-Science: NASA Field Trials at the Mars Desert Research Station	Compendium	Conversational Modeling	e-Science for space exploration
15	Template-Based Structured Argumentation	SEAS	Evidence Mapping	Intelligence and other Evidence Analysis
16	An Experience of the Use of the Cognitive Mapping Method in Qualitative Research	CmapTools	Concept Mapping	Postgraduate Research
17	Collaborative Knowledge Modeling with a Graphical Knowledge Representation Tool MOT: A Strategy to Support the Transfer of Expertise in Organizations	MOT	Conceptual Modeling	Organizational Knowledge Sharing

Contributors

Josianne Basque
LICEF Research Center, Tele-universite, West Montreal, QC, Canada,
basque.josianne@teluq.uqam.ca

Tom Boyce
Artificial Intelligence Center, SRI International, Menlo Park, CA 94025, USA,
tom.boyce@sri.com

Alberto J. Cañas
Florida Institute for Human and Machine Cognition (IHMC), Pensacola, FL, USA,
acanas@ihmc.us

Gráinne Conole
Knowledge Media Institute, The Open University, Milton Keynes,
Buckinghamshire MK7 6AA, UK,
g.c.conole@open.ac.uk

Liliane Esnault
Ecole de Management de Lyon, Lyon, France,
esnault@em-lyon.com

Ian Harrison
Artificial Intelligence Center, SRI International, Menlo Park, CA 94025, USA,
ian.harrison@sri.com

David Hyerle
Plymouth State University, Plymouth, NH, USA

Michel Leonard
LICEF Research Center, Tele-universite, West Montreal, QC, Canada,
leonard.michel@licef.teluq.uqam.ca

John Lowrance
Artificial Intelligence Center, SRI International, Menlo Park, CA 94025, USA,
john.lowrance@sri.com

Rita de Cássia Veiga Marriott
Department of Hispanic Studies & Centre for Modern Languages,
University of Birmingham, UK,
r.marriott@bham.ac.uk

Janet Murdock
Artificial Intelligence Center, SRI International, Menlo Park, CA 94025, USA,
janet.murdock@sri.com

Ken Murray
Artificial Intelligence Center, SRI International, Menlo Park, CA 94025, USA,
ken.murray@sri.com

Joseph D. Novak
Florida Institute for Human and Machine Cognition (IHMC), Pensacola, FL, USA,
jnovak@ihmc.us

Ricky Ohl
Department of Management, Griffith University, Queensland,
R.Ohl@griffith.edu.au

Alexandra Okada
Knowledge Media Institute, The Open University, Milton Keynes,
Buckinghamshire MK7 6AA, UK,
a.l.p.okada@open.ac.uk

Gilbert Paquette
LICEF Research Center, Tele-universite, West Montreal, QC, Canada,
paquette.gilbert@teluq.uqam.ca

Beatrice Pudelko
LICEF Research Center, Tele-universite, West Montreal, QC, Canada,
pudelko.beatrice@licef.teluq.uqam.ca

Chris Reed
School of Computing, University of Dundee, Dundee, UK,
chris@computing.dundee.ac.uk

Yanna Rider
School of Philosophy, University of Melbourne, Melbourne, VIC,
yannarider@gmail.com

Andres Rodriguez
Artificial Intelligence Center, SRI International, Menlo Park, CA 94025, USA,
andres.rodriguez@sri.com

Glenn Rowe
School of Computing, University of Dundee, Dundee, UK,
growe@computing.dundee.ac.uk

Albert M. Selvin
Knowledge Media Institute, The Open University, Milton Keynes,
Buckinghamshire MK7 6AA, UK,
alselvin@gmail.com

Tony Sherborne
Centre for Science Education, Sheffield Hallam University, Sheffield, UK,
t.sherborne@shu.ac.uk

Simon Buckingham Shum
Knowledge Media Institute, The Open University, Milton Keynes,
Buckinghamshire MK7 6AA, UK,
sbs@acm.org

Maarten Sierhuis
NASA/Ames Research Center, Moffett Field, CA 94035, USA,
Maarten.Sierhuis-1@nasa.gov

Daniel D. Suthers
Department of Information and Computer Sciences,
University of Hawaii at Manoa, Honolulu, HI, USA,
suthers@hawaii.edu

Neil Thomason
School of Philosophy, University of Melbourne, Melbourne, VIC,
neilt@unimelb.edu.au

Jerome Thomere
Artificial Intelligence Center, SRI International, Menlo Park, CA 94025, USA,
jerome.thomere@sri.com

Patrícia Lupion Torres
Department of Education, Universidade Católica do Paraná, Curitiba, Brazil,
patorres@terra.com.br

Mário Vasconcellos
Centre of Applied Social Studies, University of Amazonia (UNAMA), Brazil,
mariovasc@unama.br
Centre of Environment, Federal University of Pará (UFPA), Brazil,
mariovasc@ufpa.br

Eric Yeh
Artificial Intelligence Center, SRI International, Menlo Park, CA 94025, USA,
eric.yeh@sri.com

Romain Zeiliger
Centre National de la Recherche Scientifique, GATE, France,
zeiliger@gate.cnrs.fr

1. Empirical Studies of the Value of Conceptually Explicit Notations in Collaborative Learning

Daniel D. Suthers

University of Hawaii at Manoa, Department of Information and Computer Sciences, suthers@hawaii.edu

Abstract. "Knowledge Cartography" is concerned with a diversity of notations that all make certain conceptual structures explicit, but may differ from each other and from conceptually implicit notations in what they make salient. This chapter reports on a series of studies that investigated the idea that these differences or *representational biases* might lead to differences in processes of collaborative inquiry. The studies span face-to-face, synchronous online and asynchronous online media in both classroom and laboratory settings. An understanding of the observed effects can help both designers and practitioners think more deeply about the pedagogical implications of their representational tools and how these tools are embedded in a learning situation; i.e., how to convert representational *biases* to representational *guidance*.

1.1 Introduction

The variety of representational tools discussed in this volume – argument maps, concept maps, evidence maps, knowledge maps, mind maps, etc. – all offer the common advantage of being explicit about some conceptual structure or model: their notations are for constructing *conceptually explicit* representational artifacts. (See Suthers, 2001b for discussion of the distinction between notation, tool and artifact). In contrast written language is far more expressive yet as a notation does not make any particular conceptual structure visually salient. Researchers have claimed that explicit representations of conceptual structure encourage participants to clarify their thinking (Brna et al., 2001), make this thinking visible to others (Bell, 1997), provide resources for conversation (Roschelle, 1996), can guide students' argumentation to include disconfirming as well as confirming evidence (Toth et al., 2002; Veerman, 2003), and can function as a "convergence artifact" that expresses the group's emerging consensus (Hewitt, 2001; Suthers, 2001a). The present chapter summarizes a series of studies undertaken to test hypothesized advantages of conceptually explicit notations, and that led to further discovery and explorations in the roles of representational tools in mediating interaction. The chapter begins with the historical context and motivation for the work and some theoretical considerations that led to the studies. The bulk of the chapter summarizes a series of classroom and laboratory studies comparing evidence maps to other representational notations, before concluding with some implications for practitioners.

1.2 Background

This section summarizes the practical and theoretical motivations for the studies that will be described in the next section.

1.2.1 Belvedere and Kin

This line of work had its origins in the *Belvedere* project at the University of Pittsburgh. The project was intended to support secondary school children's learning of critical inquiry skills in the context of science, particularly at the scale of scientific discourse that spans multiple studies and authors (Cavalli-Sforza et al., 1994). Belvedere was intended to enable the construction of node-and-link style diagrams using a complex visual language that could capture the nuances of scientific argumentation, and an intelligent tutoring system that would help the student reason about the arguments. The name "Belvedere" was chosen by Alan Lesgold to convey both the "beautiful views" of arguments that it would enable, and the guidance it offered children like the butler "Mr. Belvedere" in a locally set television show.[1]

A prototype that included a portion of the visual language and a simple pattern matching advisor was implemented (Paolucci et al., 1996; Suthers & Weiner, 1995; Suthers et al., 1995). Belvedere's diagrammatic language was later simplified in version 2 (Fig. 1.1) to focus on evidential relations between data and hypotheses (Suthers et al., 2001).[2] This change was driven in part by a refocus on collaborative learning, which led to a reconceptualization of the role of the diagrammatic representations. When more than one student was working with Bevledere, much of students' argumentation took place verbally between them rather than in the representations, and was concerned with manipulations and interpretations of the representations. Rather than viewing the representations as medium of communication or a formal record of an argumentation process, the author came to view them as resources (stimuli and guides) for conversation (Roschelle, 1996) among co-located learners concerning issues of evidence.

---

[1] Personal communication, Alan Lesgold.
[2] Version 4 of Belvedere is available at http://belvedere.sourceforge.net/. It supports multiple views on an evidence model, but does not support networked collaboration or include the prototype coach found in version 2. Version 2 is available from the author, but is based on 1990's technology.

1. Studies of the Value of Conceptually Explicit Representations 3

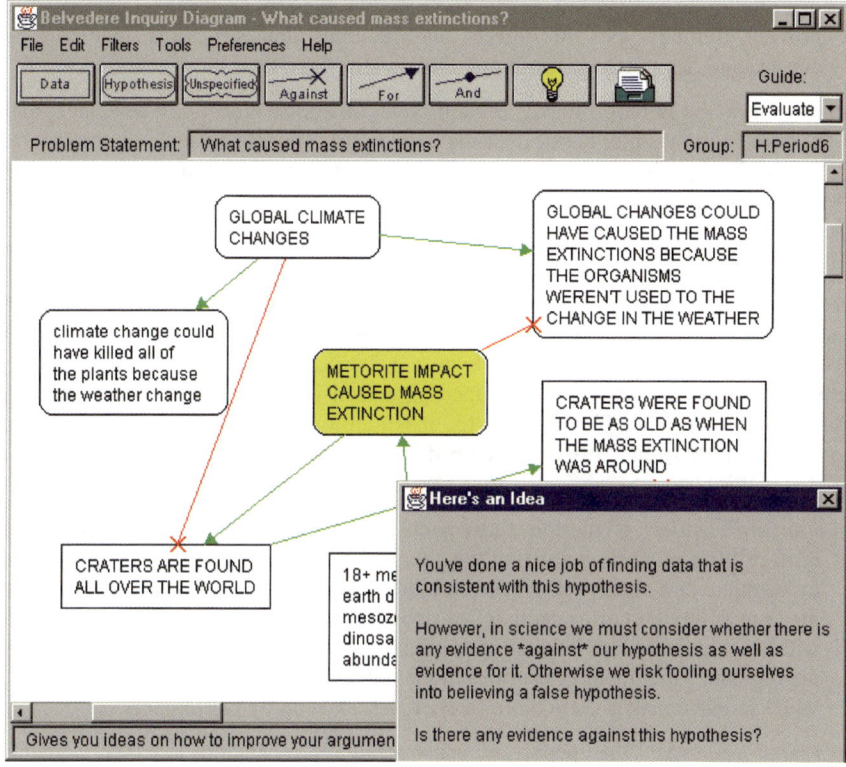

Fig. 1.1. Belvedere 2, with prototype coach.

Meanwhile, it was apparent that various projects with similar goals (i.e., critical inquiry in a collaborative learning context) were using radically different representational systems. These included various forms of hypertext/hypermedia (Guzdial et al., 1997; O'Neill & Gomez, 1994; Scardamalia et al., 1992), node-link graphs representing rhetorical, logical, or evidential relationships between assertions (Ranney et al., 1995; Smolensky et al., 1987; Suthers & Weiner, 1995), containment of evidence within theory boxes (Bell, 1997), and evidence or criteria matrices (Puntambekar et al., 1997). The obvious question arose: if representations are resources for conversation, does it matter which representation one uses?

1.2.2 Theoretical Background

In response to this question, the author postulated two broad ways in which representational notations influence learning (Suthers, 2001b):

Constraints: limits on expressiveness, for example, the representational system may provide limited types of objects and relations and structures that can be constructed from them (Stenning & Oberlander, 1995).

Salience: how the notation makes certain types of information (such as conceptual relationships) visible, possibly at the expense of others (Larkin & Simon, 1987; Lohse, 1997). The absence of information where it is expected is also a form of salience (e.g., the empty cells of a matrix suggest that they might be filled).

These two fundamental expressive features of notations play out in many ways, including influences on individual (cognitive/perceptual) reasoning and learning (e.g., Kotovsky & Simon, 1990; Novick & Hmelo, 1994; Zhang, 1997), but here we are concerned with collaborative learning. Of the various influences that representations have on collaborative processes, which are intrinsic to collaborative processes themselves rather than being due to the aggregated influence of representations on individuals? Three possible answers to this question, first outlined in Suthers & Hundhausen (2003) and further developed in Suthers (2006b), motivated the work reported in this chapter:

Negotiation Potentials. If multiple participants can add to or change a representational artifact that they are constructing together, the participants may feel an obligation to negotiate and obtain agreement on modifications to those representations. Any medium offers certain potentials for action (affordances). The ideas associated with these potential actions are more likely to be discussed in the course of this negotiation. Notational constraints limit but focus these negotiation potentials, while salience makes them more likely to be taken up by participants.

Referential Resource. When people are constructing representations together, elements of the representational artifact become imbued with meanings for the participants by virtue of having been produced through the process of negotiation discussed above. These elements then enable participants to reinvoke these meanings through language, gesture, or direct manipulation. In this manner, collaboratively constructed external representations facilitate subsequent negotiations, increasing elaboration on previous conceptions and the conceptual complexity that can be handled in group interactions. Constraints on expressiveness will focus what is available for reference, and salience will affect the immediacy of its availability for reference.

Mutual Awareness. Computational media can be designed to foster group awareness (Kreijns & Kirschner, 2004). The mere awareness that others are present and will evaluate one's actions may influence one's choice of actions (Erickson & Kellogg, 2000). An individual working in a group must constantly refer back to the shared external representation while coordinating activities with others: information about the attentional status of group members and their attitudes towards previously proposed ideas may influence the actions of individuals in the group.

Following this reasoning, the author constructed a taxonomy of the various representations in use by researchers at the time, and made predictions such as the following:

- A *plain text* environment (e.g., a word processor) does not constrain expressiveness in any particular way (written language is very expressive), but nor does it make any particular relationships salient (e.g., one cannot tell "at a glance" the overall argumentative, conceptual, or evidential structure of a text).
- A *graphical* (node-link) tool such as Belvedere (e.g., Fig. 1.1) will prompt users to make connections: all new contributions will be related to something else. Since participants talk about what they will do, this means, for example, that users of an evidence map are more likely to talk about evidence (as well as represent it) when using a graphical representation than plain text. Statements and the evidential relationships between them will be visually salient, so are more likely to be referenced in subsequent discussion, again leading to more talk about evidence.
- The salience of all the empty cells of a *matrix* (tabular) representation (e.g., to be shown in Fig. 1.2) will prompt users to consider many possible relationships that can be expressed in those cells. For example, if hypotheses label the columns and data label the rows, users are more likely to talk about evidential relationships between the two, even more so than with a graph representation.

Predictions were made for other representational notations as well, but due to limited resources and the desire to sample diverse points in the design space of notations, the research to be discussed below was undertaken with these three notations. It should be understood that the research was not concerned with demonstrating the efficacy of these specific notations for learning. Rather, it sought to evaluate the idea that representations influence interaction in predictable ways that can be leveraged to influence the quality of collaborative learning. That is, we sought to show that *representational bias* exists (i.e., notational differences influence collaborative processes), which can be leveraged for *representational guidance* of learning.

1.3 A Summary of the Research

A series of studies were undertaken with various versions of software derived from Belvedere to test the effects of selected representations on collaborative inquiry. These studies include a classroom study and laboratory studies. The classroom study provided evidence that representational bias influences students' work in classroom settings. The laboratory studies provided a closer look at the effects of representational bias on learning *processes* under controlled conditions, with a particular focus on the predictions just stated. Subsequently we shifted our focus to online settings.

1.3.1 Guidance for Inquiry in a Classroom Setting

Eva Toth, Arlene Weiner and the author developed a comprehensive method for implementing Belvedere-supported collaborative inquiry in the classroom (Suthers et al., 1997; Toth et al., 2002). Students work in teams to investigate "science challenge problems" that present a phenomenon to be explained (e.g., the Cretaceous mass extinctions; the cause of a disease on the island of Guam), along with indices to relevant resources. The teams plan their investigation, perform hands-on experiments, analyze their results, and report their conclusions to others. Investigator roles are rotated between hands-on experiments, tabletop data analysis, computer-based literature review, and use of modeling tools such as Belvedere (we used the version of Fig. 1.1). Assessment rubrics are given to the students at the beginning of their project as criteria to guide their activities. The rubrics guide peer review, and help the teacher assess learning objectives pertaining to inquiry in science. For further information on this integrated approach to classroom implementation, see Suthers et al. (1997) and Toth et al. (2002).[3]

As part of this work, we conducted a classroom study comparing two forms of guidance for inquiry with respect to quality of inquiry process and conclusions (Toth et al., 2002). The forms of guidance included Belvedere's graphical representations of evidential relations, and assessment rubrics. The Belvedere graphs relate data and hypothesis objects (represented by distinct shapes) with *consistency* and *inconsistency* relations (represented by links labeled "+" and "−"). The assessment rubrics were paper-based charts that included detailed criteria for progress in data collection, evaluation of information collected, quality of reports, and quality of peer presentations. Criteria used in the rubrics included the following:

- The teams' work is composed of information found in multiple sources.
- The content of the information the team used is related to the question asked.
- The team considered multiple hypotheses that are appropriate to explain the scientific problem in question.
- The team lists data for each hypothesis they have.
- The team lists data against each hypothesis they have.
- The team's work includes a conclusion summarizing the results of inquiry from various sources.
- The report describes how the artifacts of investigations were used to analyze data and to formulate explanations and draw conclusions.
- The presentation was clear, well organized and easy to follow.

The rubrics were provided to students at the outset of the study with explicit instructions to use them during the activity to guide inquiry. A 2 × 2 design crossed *Belvedere* versus *Microsoft Word*™ conditions with *Rubric* versus *No-Rubric* conditions across four 9th grade science classes in U.S. Department of Defense Dependent Schools in Würzburg, Germany. Students spent about 2 weeks on each of three science challenge problems.

---

[3] Supporting materials, including science challenge problems and assessment rubrics, are archived at http://lilt.ics.hawaii.edu/belvedere/index.html.

The data analysis was based primarily on artifacts produced by groups of students, namely their Belvedere graphs or Word documents, and their final report essays. The amount of information recorded did not differ significantly between groups. Significant results were obtained on the categorization of information and the number of evidential relationships recorded. An interaction between the type of representational tool and the use of rubrics prompted a post-hoc comparison. We found that the combination of graphing and rubrics resulted in a larger number of evidential relations recorded compared to all other conditions. Further analysis showed that this interaction was primarily due to the Belvedere/Rubrics students having recorded significantly more *inconsistency* relations. Thus, there appears to be a synergistic effect between effective representations and guidelines for their use, particularly with respect to attending to discrepant evidence. The best results were obtained with the combination of rubrics encouraging students to look for and record disconfirming as well as confirming information and explicit representational devices for recording such inferences. This result is consistent with other work on "distributed scaffolding" (Tabak, 2004). These results suggest that representational tools be designed together with other instructional interventions.

1.3.2 Comparing Three Representations in a Laboratory Setting

Subsequent laboratory studies were undertaken to document representational guidance in a controlled setting and to observe *processes* of representational guidance (we were not present during the classroom implementation in Germany). With the assistance of Christopher Hundhausen and Laura Girardeau, the author conducted a study comparing three alternative notations for recording evidential relationships between data and hypotheses with respect to participants' amount of talk about evidential relations (Suthers & Hundhausen, 2003). We employed a single-factor, between-subjects design with three participant groups defined by the notation they used. Participants in the control group, *Text*, were given a simple word processor offering control over font characteristics and basic formatting. Participants in the *Matrix* condition used a tabular representation in which hypotheses were recorded as column headers, data were recorded as row headers, and each cell provided a menu for selecting symbols ("+," "−," "?," or a blank space) to indicate the relationship between the data item labeling the row and the hypothesis labeling the column (Fig. 1.2). Participants in the *Graph* condition used a Belvedere-like evidence-mapping tool (similar to Fig. 1.3, but without the chat). Dependent measures included: (a) categorization of utterances and participant actions in the software; (b) ability to recall the data, hypotheses, and evidential relations explored in a multiple-choice test; and (c) ability to identify, in a written essay, the important evidential relations between the data and hypotheses presented.

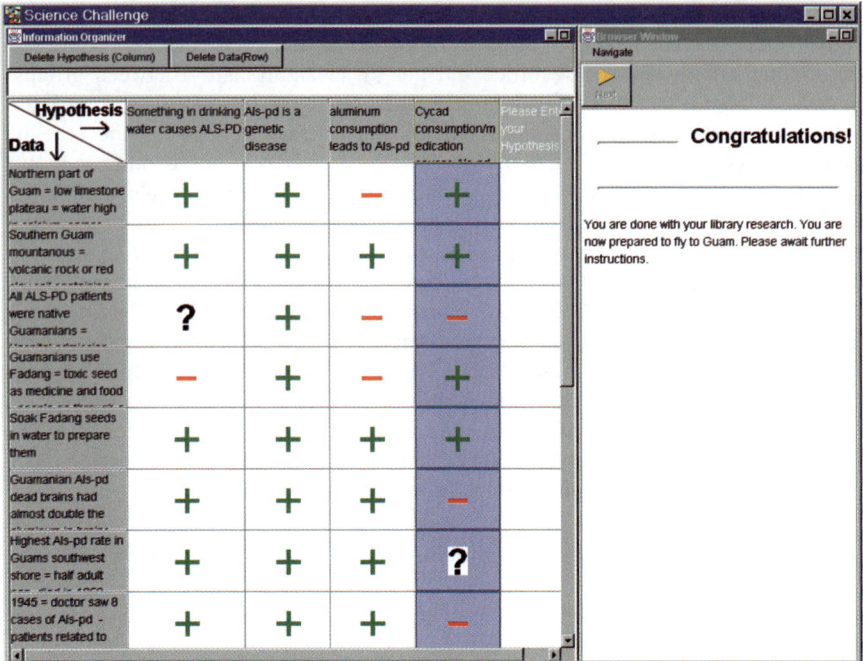

Fig. 1.2. "Matrix" software, face-to-face study.

Sixty students (in addition to students for a pilot study) were recruited out of introductory undergraduate science courses in same-gender pairs of self-selected acquaintances and randomly assigned to the three treatment groups under the constraint that the treatment groups were gender balanced with respect to Female/Female, Female/Male and Male/Male pairs. The experimental software had two main windows, one containing a workspace for creating either text, graph, or matrix representations, and the other presenting a science problem (e.g., to identify the cause mass extinctions, or of a neurological disease on the island of Guam) as a fixed sequence of 15 information pages available to both participants. Participants were instructed to visit each page in the sequence, and to record data, hypotheses, and evidential relations in their workspace. Once finished, they were individually given a post-test, and then asked to work together on an essay summarizing their findings.

All 30 sessions were videotaped and transcribed, including both verbal utterances and actions performed with the software. Transcript segments were coded on several dimensions, including content categories such as whether participants were discussing issues of evidence or using empirical or theoretical concepts. Essays were scored according to the strength and inferential difficulty of the evidential relations they cited.

Although no significant differences were found on outcome measures related to the post-test and essays, there were definitive process differences. Results confirmed our prediction that notation significantly impacts learners' discussion of evidential relations. Analyses focused on the contents of participants' representations and their elaborations on (revisitations and reuse of) information and beliefs once they are represented. The results of these analyses indicated that visually structured and constrained representations provide guidance that is not afforded by plain text. Users of Matrix and Graph revisited previously discussed ideas more often than users of Text, as was predicted from the greater salience of ideas and prompting for missing relations in the more structured representations. However, not all guidance is equal, and more prompting is not necessarily better. Text and Matrix users represented more hypotheses and Matrix users represented far more evidential relations than were considered relevant by our own analysis of the problem. Matrix users revisited prior data and hypotheses mainly to fill in the matrix cells that relate them. They revisited relations far more often than Text or Graph users, but often appeared to be doing this because they were attempting to make relationships between weakly or equivocally related items due to the exhaustive prompting of the matrix. A representation such as Graph may guide students to consider evidence without making them unfocused.

We found no significant differences between the groups' post-test scores (recognition of factual information) and essay scores (using various measures of quality of inference), although all trends were in the predicted direction. These results were disappointing, but not surprising. Participants spent less than an hour on task, and this may not have been enough time for learning outcomes to develop fully. We did find that the contents of the Graph representations overlapped with the content of those participants' essays more than the corresponding representations overlapped in the Text or Matrix conditions. This result suggests that the work done using evidence maps had greater influence on participants' views of the problem as expressed in the essays.

1.3.3 Appropriation of Representations for Online Collaboration

All of the foregoing studies were undertaken with face-to-face collaboration of participants, yet online learning is becoming increasingly important, especially in higher education. We conducted a follow-up study designed to explore how the roles of representations in online learning might shift, with possible implications for the relevance of representational guidance (Suthers et al., 2003b). Although asynchronous learning environments are most prevalent, we chose to begin with a study of synchronous online collaboration so that the data would be comparable to our synchronous face-to-face data. This study was undertaken with a version of the Belvedere 3.0 research software that supported synchronous computer-mediated communication (CMC) with a textual "chat" provided in addition to the graph representation and information pages (Fig. 1.3).

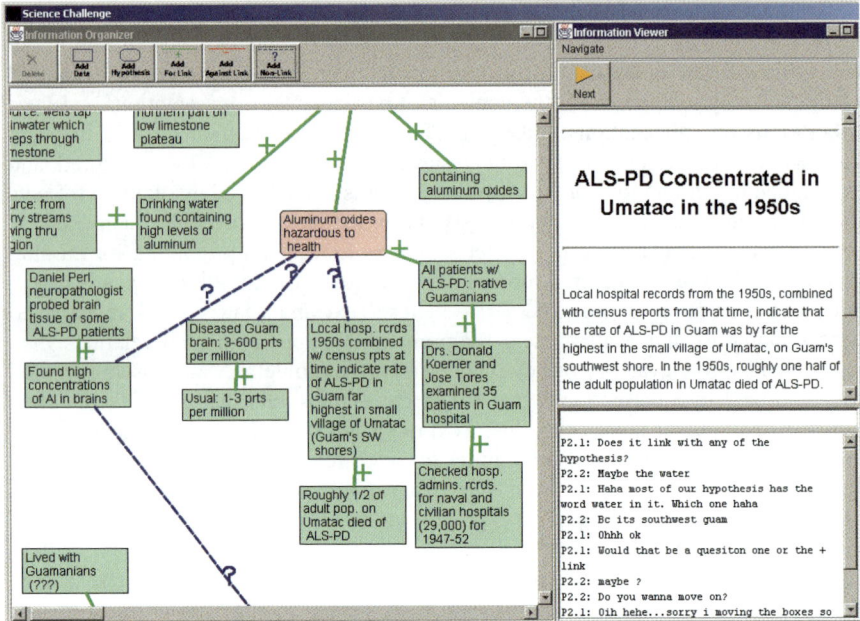

Fig. 1.3. "Graph" software, synchronous CMC study.

Extensive prior research has compared the performance of face-to-face collaborators with the performance of users of various forms of technology-mediated communication. Many of these studies show degradation of both problem-solving performance and interpersonal communication due to the reduced modes of interaction associated with technology-mediated communication (Doerry, 1996; Olson & Olson, 2000). However, other studies show that people can compensate for and even benefit from restricted interaction (Burgoon et al., 2002; Herring, 1999), and that factors extrinsic to the technology itself may play a role (Walther, 1994). It was not our intent to replicate these results: our focus was on how the roles of external representations in supporting collaboration might change when going online, especially in ways that might affect the relevance of representational guidance. Two hypotheses were considered without prejudice:

(H1) Visual knowledge representations will play *less* of a role in guiding discourse online because without co-presence the representations do not as easily function to convey "taken as shared" information, and gestural references are more difficult online (Olson & Olson, 2000).

(H2) Visual knowledge representations will play a *greater* role in supporting discourse online because participants will make use of them to make up for the reduced bandwidth of the chat tool as compared to speech.

We conducted sessions with ten pairs of students using the CMC version of Belvedere 3.0, and compared these sessions to the face-to-face graph sessions from the previous study in order to identify how the roles of representations in supporting collaboration might change. Other than the use of CMC, the protocols and measures were identical to the previous study.

Our quantitative results provided adequate evidence for the second hypothesis (Suthers et al., 2003). In the online condition, a greater proportion of communicative acts relevant to the problem domain were undertaken in the graphical knowledge representation as opposed to spoken or chat communications. (Examples of communicative acts in the shared graphical medium include creating new data or hypothesis objects or linking two such objects together). This was related to a shift in the role of the graph representation from *object of discourse* in the face-to-face condition to *medium of discourse* in the CMC condition. Online participants introduced new ideas directly in the graph medium (rather than in the chat) by modifying the representation far more often than face-to-face participants, who almost always introduced and discussed new ideas verbally before modifying the graph representation. As a consequence, in the online condition there was greater use of categories supported by the software (i.e., evidential relations and epistemic classifications). The chat was used primarily for social banter and task management (e.g., coordinating access to information pages and allocating responsibility for graph edits), and occasionally for problem-related discussion that was not supported by the graph representations (e.g., deciding how to interpret problematic information).

However, there was also qualitative evidence for the first hypothesis. Our informal review of the transcripts shows many examples of poorly coordinated activity in the online groups, such as disconnects between the activity in the workspace and the verbal activity in the chat. Also, we observed less use of gestural deixis[4] and less rich discussion in the online condition. A subsequent analysis provided further evidence for H1 (Suthers et al., 2003a). In face-to-face collaboration, deixis was accomplished quite effectively through gesture. Gesture is *spatially indexical*: it can select any information in the shared visual space, regardless of when that information was previously encountered or introduced, making it an effective device for integrating old and new information. We did an analysis to determine what filled the functional role of gesture in the online environment. Online collaborators accomplished reference through verbal deixis and direct manipulation rather than gestural deixis. (See also Gergle et al., 2004). As participants used it, verbal deixis in the chat tool was *temporally indexical*: it most often selected recently manipulated items (e.g., typing "what do you think?" after modifying the representation).

These results raised the question of whether and how online participants revisited prior information. Direct manipulation of the representations seemed to play this role most effectively, and indeed constituted an alternative means through which some aspects of communication about problem solution took place. However, communication in an evidence map is limited to propositions in the domain and the evidential

---

[4] Deictic referencing, or deixis, is a reference to an entity in the extra-linguistic context. Deixis can be accomplished verbally with indexical terms such as "this," "it," and/or with gestures such as pointing or computer-aided highlighting.

relations between them.[5] Direct manipulation is in a sense "first order." Higher order reflections such as discussion of possible interpretations of the information available are undertaken more often in the verbal media (speech or chat). Putting these observations together, there is a danger that online discourse may be less reflective, especially in its integration of new and prior information, because the more expressive and reflective mode of interaction – chat – focuses on recent (temporally indexed) items; while the easiest means of reintroducing prior information is through direct manipulation. This reasoning is consistent with our finding that online participants had lower scores on measures of information integration in their essays.

Having evidence for both hypotheses, we concluded that they are not in direct conflict, and may be synthesized as follows: Lack of mutual awareness of orientation towards shared representations may result in poorer coordination of immediate activity and the thinking behind it (H1). At the same time, greater reliance may be placed on those very representations as the medium through which activity takes place, biasing activity towards actions best supported by the representations (H2). From this work we learned that online discourse will not be confined to the medium provided for natural language interaction: it will be distributed across all mutable representations and influenced by the properties of those representations. Therefore, close attention must be paid to the design of affordances for argumentation in all representations provided to online collaborators. We also learned that the role of external representations as aids for integrating old and new information in an interactive, conversational manner could be weakened online due to the awkwardness of or lack of deictic affordances. Designers of online learning environments are advised to seek more natural means of referencing the contents of shared representations, particularly in conjunction with verbal communication. For example, chat or discussion tools might be designed to enable easy insertion of visual references to elements of other representations being discussed. Designers might also investigate other methods for helping online collaborators mutually attend to prior information, such as redisplay of prior information along with reflection prompts provided after a period of time.

1.3.4 Enhancing Knowledge Construction in Asynchronous Collaboration

The most recent experimental study in this line of work was conducted in an asynchronous setting to inform this common form of online learning (Mayadas, 1997). This study focused on the question of whether conceptually explicit representations such as evidence maps can improve on the prevalent tool for online learning, namely threaded discussions. Although the lack of time-pressure in discussion forums may support more reflective contributions than synchronous communication (e.g., Hawkes & Romiszowski, 2001), online interaction can also suffer from *incoherence* due to the violation of adjacency conventions for topic

---

[5] The phenomenon discussed here may be independent of what is represented. Other researchers have observed an initial resistance to formalization, even in representations that are intended to map discussion or argumentation rather than evidence. See for example Shipman & McCall (1994).

maintenance (Herring, 1999) and the coarse granularity of referencing (Reyes & Tchounikine, 2003). Furthermore, there can be a *lack of convergence* due to the intrinsically divergent representations used in threaded discussion (Hewitt, 2001) and a bias towards addressing recently posted messages (Hewitt, 2003). The shared knowledge being constructed is not made explicit by typical CMC tools, and hence it is difficult to find relevant contributions, place one's own contribution in the relevant context, or quickly assess the outcome of the discussion (Suthers, 2001a; Turoff et al., 1999). Suthers (2001a) argued that if the conceptual development of the conversation can be made explicit and each contribution to the discussion can be referenced to a component of this conceptual representation, interactional coherence may improve because the conceptual relevance of each contribution is clear (see also van der Pol et al., 2006), and convergence may improve because multiple contributions referencing a given topic are collected together. We conducted an experimental test of these ideas in which two forms of conceptually-enhanced support were compared to each other and to a threaded discussion control condition (Suthers et al., 2007c; Suthers et al., 2008).

Based on reasons outlined at the beginning of this chapter, our primary hypothesis claimed:

(H1) Collaborative knowledge construction is more effectively supported by environments that make conceptual objects and relations explicit.

This primary hypothesis does not specify the relationship between knowledge representations and the conversation that accompanies the creation of those representations. Our secondary hypotheses are alternative elaborations of H1, arguing for either maintaining the distinction between discussion and knowledge representations or combining the two, as detailed next.

One could argue that discussion representations should be embedded in or mixed with the conceptual representations to contextualize the discussion and facilitate ease of reference (e.g., by simple attachment of notes to the objects to which they refer). A usability argument can also be made: it may be easier to manage a single workspace than interactions distributed across multiple tools. This reasoning led to the second hypothesis:

(H2) Collaborative knowledge construction is more effectively supported if conversational and conceptual representations are tightly integrated.

The third hypothesis is motivated by the observation that conversational structures and conceptual structures are different: conversation relies on regularities in adjacency and focus shifts for coherence (Grosz & Sidner, 1986; Sacks et al., 1974), while conceptualizations may be organized according to diverse ways of modeling or systematizing knowledge about the world. Therefore, separate tools will enable designers to optimize representations to meet the distinct structural needs of conversation and conceptualization in a given domain of discourse. Explicit referencing can be used to make the connection between the two representations (Mühlpfordt & Wessner, 2005; Suthers, 2001a). This reasoning leads us to the third hypothesis, which is in opposition to the second:

(H3) Collaborative knowledge construction is more effectively supported if the distinction between discussion and conceptual models is reflected in the representations provided.

We constructed three software environments in order to test these hypotheses. All three of the environments had an information browser on the upper left side in which materials relevant to the task were displayed, and a shared on the right hand side in which participants could share information they gather from the problem materials as well as their own interpretations and other ideas (Fig. 1.4). Changes made to the workspace by each participant were propagated to other participant's displays under an asynchronous update protocol to simulate asynchronous interaction common in online learning. An action taken by one participant did not appear in the other participant's workspace until after the receiving participant "took a break" by playing a game of Tetris™.

The three environments differed on the nature of the shared workspace. The shared workspace in the *Text* condition was a conventional threaded discussion tool. This is the control condition for testing the above hypotheses, since the workspace only provided explicit support for representation of discussion structure (subject headings and reply relations). Motivated by H2, the shared workspace for the *Graph* condition was based on the same Belvedere-derived evidence map representation as the previous studies with the addition of an embedded *note* object that supported a simple linear (unthreaded) discussion that was interactionally asynchronous and could be linked in the evidence map like any other object. Motivated by H3, the shared workspace of the *Mixed* condition (Fig. 1.4) included both a threaded discussion tool (lower left) and an evidence-mapping tool for representing conceptual structure in the same manner as the Graph condition, except that there were no embedded notes in the Mixed version of the evidence map. Instead, one could embed references to evidence map objects in the threaded discussion messages by clicking on the relevant graph object while composing the message. The references showed up as small icons in the message that could be clicked on to highlight the corresponding object in the evidence map (as exemplified in Fig. 1.4).

Materials were prepared based on the professional literature concerning a complex public health problem: a disease that historically occurred in the native population on the island of Guam. The materials suggested several distinct possible causes of the disease, and provided mixed evidence for and against each cause. Relevant evidence was distributed in a hidden profile such that if participants did not share any information each participant would have evidence favoring a suboptimal disease hypothesis. Sharing was required to reject these hypotheses and construct a more complex explanation. In each dyad, Participant 1 (P1) received evidence for aluminum in the water and against genetic causes; Participant 2 (P2) received evidence against aluminum and for genetic causes; and both participants received evidence for and against cycad seeds as the source of a neurotoxin as well as crucial information about native diets that, when brought together, points to seed-eating bats as the vector by which this toxin gets into humans. The articles included distracter information as well as relevant evidence.[6]

---

[6] Archived at http://lilt.ics.hawaii.edu/lilt/papers/2006/Suthers-et-al-CE-2006/.

1. Studies of the Value of Conceptually Explicit Representations 15

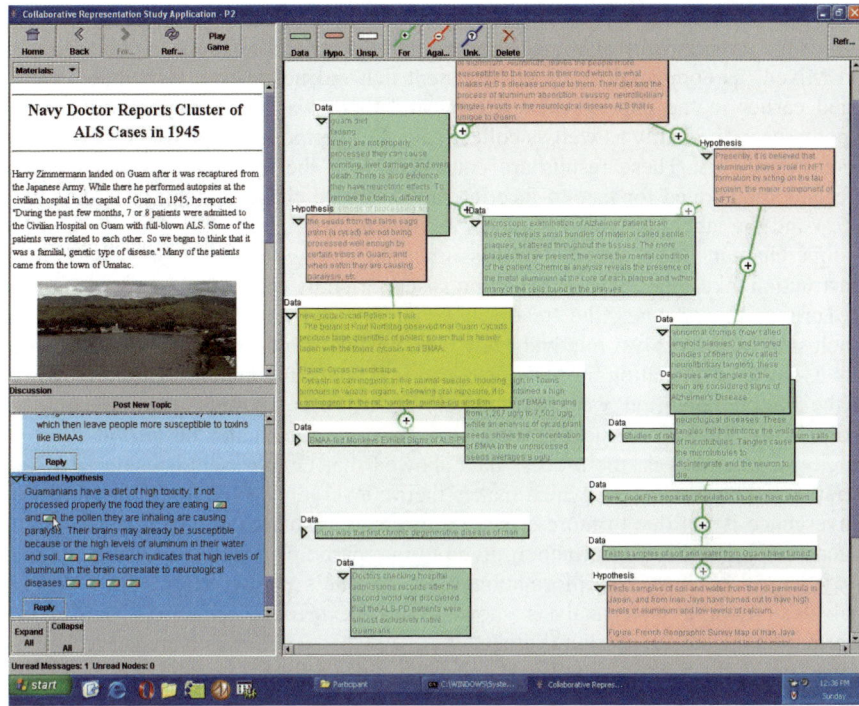

Fig. 1.4. "Mixed" software from the asynchronous CMC study.

Participants were directed to use the computer workspace to share information with their partner, and were told that this was necessary to identify the correct cause of the disease and to perform well on the essay and post-test to be given at the end. At the conclusion of their problem solving, each individual was asked to write an essay detailing the disease hypotheses considered and the evidence for and against those hypotheses, and to identify the best explanation for the disease. One week after their session, participants were directed to take an online post-test. This test included questions that tested participants' memory for distracter information, memory for relevant information, and facts that required integration of multiple items of relevant information. "High integration" questions required integration of information that occurred far apart in the materials (in Suthers & Hundhausen's (2003) terms, there is a large "inferential span"). The questions were based on information given uniquely to one or the other participant, enabling us to assess the residue of information sharing.

Our analyses addressed *outcomes*, based on content analyses of the essays and scoring of the post-test; and *session processes*, based on quantitative analyses of elaboration on hypotheses. Two lines of evidence support H1, based on process and outcome data, as detailed below.

The *process* data shows clearly that there was more elaboration on hypotheses in both of the environments that made conceptual objects and relations explicit (Graph and Mixed) as compared to the environment that did not (Text). Hypotheses were stated earlier in the experimental session and there was more elaboration on the hypotheses individually as well as collectively. Furthermore, Graph users considered more hypotheses. These results are consistent with the representational guidance effects demonstrated for face-to-face interaction in the classroom study (Toth et al., 2002) and the laboratory study (Suthers & Hundhausen, 2003) discussed previously in this chapter. In summary, process measures suggest that more knowledge construction takes place when interaction is supported by conceptual representations.

Turning to *outcomes*, the treatment conditions did not differ in optimality of conclusion in the essays: relatively few participants in all conditions identified the bats-as-vector explanation for how the cycad toxin gets into humans. However, pairs in the Graph condition were more likely to express the same (not necessarily optimal) conclusions in their essays. This convergence cannot be attributed to a paucity of alternatives: the process data showed that Graph users considered *more* hypotheses than the others, which makes their convergence even more notable. The convergence is not due to more effective information sharing per se: there were no differences on whether information given to one participant appeared in the other's essay, or on memory for information given to one's partner (from the post-test analysis). Also, a later analysis showed that Text users actually shared more information during the session (Suthers et al., 2007b). (There was a greater tendency of the Text participants to simply cut and paste entire articles into their text messages and leave discussion for the end). Technologies that enable people to share more information do not necessarily lead to effective use of that information (Dennis, 1996). Given the process data just reviewed, it is plausible that something beyond information sharing, such as collaborative consideration of hypotheses *during* the study sessions had an effect on convergence of the participants' conclusions.

On the other hand, the lack of differences on quality of solution may be counted as evidence against H1. Also, the failure of the Mixed condition in some analyses to display the advantages claimed by H1 may also be considered as evidence against H1, but the dual workspace is a confounding factor, as it requires managing two representations (Ainsworth et al., 1998). Participants in the Mixed condition may have converged the least because the dual workspaces provide more variation in strategies for using the workspaces, increasing the possibility that members of a pair will look at different material.

Turning to the comparison between H2 (in favor of integrated representations such as Graph) and H3 (in favor of distinct discussion and conceptual representations such as Mixed), significant differences on direct comparisons between Graph and Mixed are limited to the result that Graph users scored higher than Mixed users on post-test questions requiring integration of information that was distributed across the materials. The distribution of information across two media in Mixed may have posed a barrier to integration of that information, obscuring the advantage of Mixed's evidence map. However, there is indirect evidence bearing on the choice between H2 and H3. All other statistical analyses in which there was a significant advantage for one of the conditions over the others included an advantage of Graph over Text. In contrast, Mixed was sometimes advantageous to Text, sometimes not, but never was advantageous to Graph, and sometimes yielded the worst results. Since Graph and Matrix were introduced as competing alternatives to threaded discussions, support for H2 (Graph) is stronger than for H3 (Mixed).

The primary conclusion of this study – that collaborative knowledge construction is fostered by conceptual representations – not only adds to the growing literature on representational guidance for collaborative learning, but also has practical implications. Should threaded discussion tools be replaced with knowledge mapping tools in online learning? Although that is the direction in which the results point, it would be a brash conclusion to draw from this experiment alone, as it is limited in many ways. We studied dyads interacting over a relatively short period of 2 h. Dozens of students interacting over the course of a semester (even if divided into smaller groups as is generally recommended in ALN implementations) would generate much more complex artifacts. Any workspace has a limited useful life before it becomes important to "rise above" the clutter and start fresh (Scardamalia, 2004). The subject matter, task structure, and nature of the representations used could also affect results. However, in conjunction with previous work the present results merit extending the research program beyond the laboratory by undertaking action research in which richer interactive representations are studied in settings of educational practice.

1.4 Related Work

During this time, other researchers have undertaken related studies of representational effects using conceptually explicit representations. For example, Veerman (2003) compared Allaire Forums (asynchronous online discussion), Belvedere 2.0 (using synchronous discussion with a chat tool) and NetMeeting (internet videoconferencing) in a heterogeneous design (the activities were not identical). Among other differences, Veerman observed a greater percentage of argumentation related content, particularly counter-arguments, in Belvedere, a result that seems consistent with the Toth et al. (2002) result on discrepant evidence. Schwarz et al. (2002) showed that argument maps were superior to pro-con tables in supporting students' collaborative argumentation and essay writing, but these differences were not internalized individually during the relatively short study. Others have studied alternative instructional strategies for using conceptually explicit representations in collaborative learning (e.g., Lund et al., 2007; Stoyanova & Kommers, 2002). Related work may be found in (Andriessen et al., 2003).

The studies reported above were conducted using experimental manipulations and quantitative analyses. This methodology is valuable for hypothesis testing, but is weaker for discovery of the actual practices by which participants make use of resources to accomplish their goals. Coding and statistical aggregation obscures what participants are doing as they try to make sense of the problem and the situation at multiple levels. For these reasons (Suthers, 2006b), following (Koschmann et al., 2005; Stahl, 2006), argued for a turn towards the study of practices of individual and intersubjective *meaning-making* through which learning is ultimately accomplished, and suggested that sequential analyses of interaction are more appropriate for understanding how the cognitive and social affordances of technologies such as knowledge maps are appropriated by participants as well as influencing their interaction. Pursuing this agenda, the author re-examined the data from the synchronous laboratory study using the concept of *uptake* as the fundamental unit of analysis (Suthers, 2006a). Subsequently, we have explicated a formal and theoretically motivated basis for such analysis (Suthers et al., 2007a). Early results from associated studies include an apparent pattern of successful collaboration in which information sharing is followed by subsequent "round trips" of negotiation of agreement, and the observation that while information sharing takes place in the knowledge map, parallel linguistic channels are used for these subsequent negotiations. Other recent analyses of meaning-making with conceptually explicit representations include Mirza et al. (2007) and Schwarz & De Groot (2007).

1.5 Conclusions

The studies of representational guidance for collaborative learning summarized in this chapter were motivated by the idea that some roles of representations in supporting learning are endemic to collaborative situations and that logical and perceptual differences between representations may influence how they fill these roles. A laboratory study confirmed several predicted process differences, including discussion of evidence and revisitation of prior information, as well as suggestive results indicating that the work done with graphs had greatest impact on participants' understanding of the problem. A study of the products of students' classroom work showed similar effects of representation on consideration of discrepant evidence, this effect being amplified by a coordinated set of peer-evaluation rubrics calling for evaluation of discrepant evidence. The online study showed that all actionable/mutable representations will be appropriated as part of the discourse medium (not just the intended discussion tools), and therefore we may expect representational guidance to be enhanced in online discourse. This work was continued in a study of asynchronous interaction, which confirmed the influences of conceptually explicit representations on collaborative processes, leading to greater integration of information by individuals and greater convergence of conclusions by pairs (even after they considered a diversity of alternatives).

The immediate implication of this work is that system designers should treat representational design as design of resources for conversation between learners. A designer or teacher might ask: What activities does a given representational notation suggest or prompt for? Do the actions that can be performed on a shared representation in this notation correspond to the potential ideas that we want learners to negotiate and distinctions we want them to attend to? Do the resulting representations express and make salient the ideas and relationships that learners should revisit and relate to new information? Are the needs that should be addressed by subsequent activity, such the lack of information, made obvious? Do the representations capture important aspects of learners' thinking and expose conflicts between alternative solutions or perspectives? Stepping beyond the scope of the studies reported here, one might ask: does the notation provide the preferred vocabularies and representational perspectives that constitute both the target skill to be learned as an aspiring member of a community, and focus learning activity on ways of approaching a problem that are productive? Representational notations are not determinants of behavior, but when the features of representations are coordinated with the design of other elements of a learning situation they can guide behavior. Activity theory (Cole & Engeström, 1993; Wertsch, 1998) tells us that tools and artifacts (among other things) mediate the influences of various learning resources on the learner, such as other individuals, community norms and roles. Therefore, the impact of the representational choices we make in designing these tools is not limited merely to the direct effects of representations. The impact of these choices will be amplified to the extent that the representations mediate how other resources in the human–computer system bear upon the learning activity.

Acknowledgement

This work was supported by the National Science Foundation grants #9873516 (Knowledge and Distributed Intelligence) and #0093505 (CAREER), and was conducted in collaboration with numerous individuals acknowledged in the author's cited publications.

References

Ainsworth, S.E., Bibby, P.A., & Wood, D.J. (1998). Analyzing the costs and benefits of multi-representational learning environments. In M.W. van Someren, P. Reimann, H.P.A. Boshuizen, & T. de Jong (Eds.), *Learning with Multiple Representations* (pp. 120–134). Amsterdam: Elsevier.

Andriessen, J., Baker, M., & Suthers, D.D. (2003). Arguing to Learn: Confronting Cognitions in Computer-Supported Collaborative Learning Environments. Dordrecht: Kluwer.

Bell, P. (1997). Using argument representations to make thinking visible for individuals and groups. In *Proceedings of the 2nd International Conference on Computer Supported Collaborative Learning (CSCL'97)* (pp. 10–19). Toronto: University of Toronto.

Brna, P., Cox, R., & Good, J. (2001). Learning to think and communicate with diagrams: 14 questions to consider. *Artificial Intelligence Review, 15*(1–2), 115–134.

Burgoon, J.K., Bonito, J.A., Ramirez Jr., A., Dunbar, N.E., Kam, K., & Fischer, J. (2002). Testing the interactivity principle: Effects of mediation, propinquity, and verbal and nonverbal modalities in interpersonal interaction. *Journal of Communication, 52*(3), 657–677.

Cavalli-Sforza, V., Weiner, A.W., & Lesgold, A.M. (1994). Software support for students engaging in scientific activity and scientific controversy. *Science Education, 78*(6), 577–599.

Cole, M., & Engeström, Y. (1993). A cultural-historical approach to distributed cognition. In G. Salomon (Ed.), *Distributed Cognitions: Psychological and Educational Considerations* (pp. 1–46). Cambridge: Cambridge University Press.

Dennis, A.R. (1996). Information exchange and use in group decision making: You can lead a group to information, but you can't make it think. *MIS Quarterly, 20*(4), 433–457.

Doerry, E. (1996). An Empirical Comparison of Copresent and Technologically-Mediated Interaction based on Communicative Breakdown. Oregon: University of Oregon.

Erickson, T., & Kellogg, W.A. (2000). Social translucence: An approach to cesigning systems that support social processes. *ACM Transactions on Computer–Human Interaction, 7*(1), 59–83.

Gergle, D., Kraut, R.E., & Fussell, S.R. (2004). Action as language in a shared visual space. In *Proceedings of the 2004 ACM Conference on Computer Supported Cooperative Work* (pp. 487–496). Chicago, Illinois: ACM Press.

Grosz, B.J., & Sidner, C.L. (1986). Attention, intentions, and the structure of discourse. *Computational Linguistics, 12*(3), 175–204.

Guzdial, M., Hmelo, C., Hubscher, R., Newstetter, W., Puntambekar, S., Shabo, A. et al. (1997). Integrating and guiding collaboration: Lessons learned in computer-supported collaboration learning research at Georgia Tech. In *Computer-Supported Collaborative Learning* (pp. 91–100). Toronto, Ontario.

Hawkes, M., & Romiszowski, A. (2001). Examining the reflective outcomes of asynchronous computer-mediated communication on inservice teacher development. *Journal of Technology and Teacher Education, 9*(2), 285–308.

Herring, S.C. (1999). Interactional coherence in CMC. *Journal of Computer Mediated Communication, 4*(4).

Hewitt, J. (2001). Beyond threaded discourse. *International Journal of Educational Telecommunications, 7*(3), 207–221.

Hewitt, J. (2003). How habitual online practices affect the development of asynchronous discussion threads. *Journal of Educational Computing Research, 28*(1), 31–45.

Koschmann, T., Zemel, A., Conlee-Stevens, M., Young, N., Robbs, J., & Barnhart, A. (2005). How *do* people learn: Member's methods and communicative mediation. In R. Bromme, F.W. Hesse, & H. Spada (Eds.), *Barriers and Biases in Computer-Mediated Knowledge Communication (and How They may be Overcome)* (pp. 265–294). Amsterdam: Kluwer.

Kotovsky, K., & Simon, H.A. (1990). What makes some problems really hard: Explorations in the problem space of difficulty. *Cognitive Psychology, 22*, 143–183.

Kreijns, K., & Kirschner, P.A. (2004). Designing sociable CSCL environments. In J.-W. Strijbos, P.A. Kirschner, & R.L. Martens (Eds.), *What We Know about CSCL and Implementing It in Higher Education* (pp. 221–243). Berlin Heidelberg New York: Springer.

Larkin, J.H., & Simon, H.A. (1987). Why a diagram is (sometimes) worth ten thousand words. *Cognitive Science, 11*, 65–99.

Lohse, G.L. (1997). Models of graphical perception. In M. Helander, T.K. Landauer, & P. Prabhu (Eds.), *Handbook of Human–Computer Interaction* (pp. 107–135). Amsterdam: Elsevier.

Lund, K., Molinari, G., Séjourné, A., & Baker, M. (2007). How do argumentation diagrams compare when student pairs use them as a means for debate or as a tool for representing debate? *International Journal of Computer Supported Collaborative Learning, 2*(2).

Mayadas, F. (1997). Asynchronous learning networks: A Sloan Foundation perspective. *Journal of Asynchronous Learning Networks, 1*, http://www.aln.org/alnweb/journal/jaln_issue1.htm#mayadas.

Mirza, N.M., Tartas, V., Perret-Clermont, A.-N., & de Pietro, J.-F. (2007). Using graphical tools in a phased activity for enhancing dialogical skills: An example with Digalo. *International Journal of Computer Supported Collaborative Learning, 2*(2).

Mühlpfordt, M., & Wessner, M. (2005). Explicit referencing in chat supports collaborative learning. In T. Koschmann, D.D. Suthers, & T.-W. Chan (Eds.), *Computer Supported Collaborative Learning: The Next 10 Years!* (pp. 460–469). Mahwah, NJ: Lawrence Erlbaum.

Novick, L.R., & Hmelo, C.E. (1994). Transferring symbolic representations across nonisomorphic problems. *Journal of Experimental Psychology: Learning, Memory and Cognition, 20*(6), 1296–1321.

O'Neill, D.K., & Gomez, L.M. (1994). The collaboratory notebook: A distributed knowledge-building environment for project-enhanced learning. In *Proceedings of Ed-Media '94*. Charlottesville, VA AACE.

Olson, G.M., & Olson, J.S. (2000). Distance matters. *Human–Computer Interaction, 15*(2/3).

Paolucci, M., Suthers, D.D., & Weiner, A. (1996). Automated advice-giving strategies for scientific inquiry. In C. Frasson, G. Gauthier, & A. Lesgold (Eds.), *3rd International Conference on Intelligent Tutoring Systems (ITS'96)* (1086 ed., pp. 372–381). Montreal: Berlin Heidelberg New York: Springer.

Puntambekar, S., Nagel, K., Hübscher, R., Guzdial, M., & Kolodner, J. (1997). Intra-group and intergroup: An exploration of learning with complementary collaboration tools. In *Proceedings of the 2nd International Conference on Computer Supported Collaborative Learning (CSCL'97)* (pp. 207–214). Toronto: University of Toronto.

Ranney, M., Schank, P., & Diehl, C. (1995). Competence versus performance in critical reasoning: Reducing the gap by using Convince Me. *Psychological Teaching Review, 4*(2), 151–164.

Reyes, P., & Tchounikine, P. (2003). Supporting emergence of threaded learning conversations through augmenting interactional and sequential coherence. In B. Wasson, S. Ludvigsen, & U. Hoppe (Eds.), *Designing for Change in Networked Learning Environments-Proceedings of Conference CSCL 2003* (pp. 83–92). Dordrecht: Kluwer.

Roschelle, J. (1996). Designing for cognitive communication: Epistemic fidelity or mediating collaborating inquiry. In D.L. Day, & D.K. Kovacs (Eds.), *Computers, Communication & Mental Models* (pp. 13–25). London: Taylor & Francis.

Sacks, H., Schegloff, E.A., & Jefferson, G. (1974). A simplest systematics for the organization of turn-taking for conversation. *Language, 50*(4), 696–735.

Scardamalia, M. (2004). CSILE/Knowledge Forum®. In *Education and Technology: An Encyclopedia.* (pp. 183–193). Santa Barbara: ABC-CLIO.

Scardamalia, M., Bereiter, C., Brett, C., Burtis, P.J., Calhoun, C., & Smith Lea, N. (1992). Eductional applications of a networked communal database. *Interactive Learning Environments, 2*(1), 45–71.

Schwarz, B., & De Groot, R. (2007). Argumentation in a changing world. *International Journal of Computer Supported Collaborative Learning, 2*(2).

Schwarz, B., Neuman, Y., Gil, Y., & Ilya, M. (2002). Construction of collective and individual knowledge in argumentative activities: An experimental study. *Journal of the Learning Sciences, 12*(2).

Shipman, F.M., III, & McCall, R. (1994). *Supporting Knowledge-base Evolution with Incremental Formalization, Chi94* (pp. 285–291). Boston, MA: ACM Press.

Smolensky, P., Fox, B., King, R., & Lewis, C. (1987). Computer-aided reasoned discourse, or, how to argue with a computer. In R. Guindon (Ed.), *Cognitive Science and Its Implications for Human–Computer Interaction.* Mahwah, NJ: Lawrence Erlbaum.

Stahl, G. (2006). Group Cognition: Computer Support for Collaborative Knowledge Building. Cambridge, MA: MIT Press.

Stenning, K., & Oberlander, J. (1995). A cognitive theory of graphical and linguistic reasoning: logic and implementation. *Cognitive Science, 19*, 97–140.

Stoyanova, N., & Kommers, P. (2002). Concept mapping as a medium of shared cognition in computer-supported collaborative problem solving. *Journal of Interactive Learning Research, 13*(5), 111–134.

Suthers, D.D. (2001a). Collaborative representations: Supporting gace to face and online knowledge-building discourse. In Proceedings of the 34th Hawai`i International

Conference on the System Sciences (HICSS-34), January 3–6, 2001, Maui, Hawai`i (CD-ROM): Institute of Electrical and Electronics Engineers, Inc. (IEEE).

Suthers, D.D. (2001b). Towards a systematic study of representational guidance for collaborative learning discourse. *Journal of Universal Computer Science, 7*(3).

Suthers, D.D. (2006a). A qualitative analysis of collaborative knowledge construction through shared representations. *Research and Practice in Technology Enhanced Learning, 1*(2), 1–28.

Suthers, D.D. (2006b). Technology affordances for intersubjective meaning-making: A research agenda for CSCL. *International Journal of Computers Supported Collaborative Learning, 1*(3), 315–337.

Suthers, D.D., & Weiner, A. (1995, October 17–20). Groupware for Developing Critical Discussion Skills. Paper presented at the 1st International Conference on Computer Support for Cooperative Learning. Bloomington, IN.

Suthers, D.D., & Hundhausen, C. (2003). An experimental study of the effects of representational guidance on collaborative learning. *Journal of the Learning Sciences, 12*(2), 183–219.

Suthers, D.D., Weiner, A., Connelly, J., & Paolucci, M. (1995). Belvedere: Engaging students in critical discussion of science and public policy issues. In J. Greer (Ed.), *Proceedings of AI-ED 95 – World Conference on Artificial Intelligence in Education* (pp. 266–273). Washington, D.C.: AACE.

Suthers, D.D., Toth, E.E., & Weiner, A. (1997). An integrated approach to implementing collaborative inquiry in the classroom. In R. Hall, N. Miyake, & N. Enyedy (Eds.), *Proceedings of the 2nd International Conference on Computer Support for Collaborative Learning* (pp. 272–279). Toronto: University of Toronto.

Suthers, D.D., Connelly, J., Lesgold, A.M., Paolucci, M., Toth, E.E., Toth, J. et al. (2001). Representational and advisory guidance for students learning scientific inquiry. In K.D.F. a.P.J. Feltovich (Ed.), *Smart Machines in Education: The Coming Revolution in Educational Technology* (pp. 7–35). Cambridge, MA: AAAI Press, MIT Press.

Suthers, D.D., Girardeau, L.E., & Hundhausen, C.D. (2003a). Deictic roles of external representations in face-to-face and online collaboration. In B. Wasson, S. Ludvigsen, & U. Hoppe (Eds.), *International Conference on Computer Support for Collaborative Learning 2003* (pp. 173–182). Dordrecht: Kluwer.

Suthers, D.D., Hundhausen, C.D., & Girardeau, L.E. (2003b). Comparing the roles of representations in face-to-face and online computer supported collaborative learning. *Computers and Education, 41*, 335–351.

Suthers, D.D., Dwyer, N., Medina, R., & Vatrapu, R. (2007a). A framework for eclectic analysis of collaborative interaction. In C. Chinn, G. Erkens, & S. Puntambekar (Eds.), *The Computer Supported Collaborative Learning (CSCL) Conference 2007* (pp. 694–703). New Brunswick: International Society of the Learning Sciences.

Suthers, D.D., Medina, R., Vatrapu, R., & Dwyer, N. (2007b). Information sharing is incongruous with collaborative convergence: The case for interaction. In C. Chinn, G. Erkens, & S. Puntambekar (Eds.), *The Computer Supported Collaborative Learning (CSCL) Conference 2007* (pp. 714–716). New Brunswick: International Society of the Learning Sciences.

Suthers, D.D., Vatrapu, R., Medina, R., Joseph, S., & Dwyer, N. (2007c). Conceptual representations enhance knowledge construction in asynchronous collaboration. In C. Chinn, G. Erkens, & S. Puntambekar (Eds.), *The Computer Supported Collaborative Learning (CSCL) Conference 2007* (pp. 704–713). New Brunswick: International Society of the Learning Sciences.

Suthers, D.D., Vatrapu, R., Medina, R., Joseph, S., & Dwyer, N. (2008). Beyond threaded discussion: Representational guidance in asynchronous collaborative learning environments. *Computers and Education, doi:10.1016/j.compedu.2006.10.007, 50*(4), 1103–1127.

Tabak, I. (2004). Synergy: A complement to emerging patterns of distributed scaffolding. Journal of the Learning Sciences, *13*(3), 205–335.

Toth, E.E., Suthers, D.D., & Lesgold, A.M. (2002). "Mapping to know": The effects of representational guidance and reflective assessment on scientific inquiry. *Science Education, 86*(2), 264–286.

Turoff, M., Hiltz, S.R., Bieber, M., Fjermestad, J., & Rana, A. (1999). Collaborative discourse structures in computer mediated group communications. *Journal of Computer-Mediated Communication, 4*(4), Online: http://jcmc.huji.ac.il/

van der Pol, J., Admiraal, W., & Simons, P.R.J. (2006). The affordance of anchored discussion for the collaborative processing of academic texts. *Comptuer-Supported Collaborative Learning, 1*(3), 339–357.

Veerman, A. (2003). Constructive discussions through electronic dialogue. In J. Andriessen, M. Baker, & D.D. Suthers (Eds.), *Arguing to Learn: Confronting Cognitions in Computer-Supported Collaborative Learning Environments* (pp. 117–143). Dordrecht: Kluwer.

Walther, J.B. (1994). Anticipated ongoing interaction versus channel effects on relational communication in computer-mediated interaction. *Human Communication Research, 20*(4), 473–501.

Wertsch, J.V. (1998). *Mind as Action*. New York: Oxford University Press.

Zhang, J. (1997). The nature of external representations in problem solving. *Cognitive Science, 21*(2), 179–217.

2. Concept Mapping Using CmapTools to Enhance Meaningful Learning

Alberto J. Cañas[1] and Joseph D. Novak[2]

[1]Florida Institute for Human and Machine Cognition (IHMC), acanas@ihmc.us
[2]Florida Institute for Human and Machine Cognition (IHMC), jnovak@ihmc.us

Abstract. Concept maps are graphical tools that have been used in all facets of education and training for organizing and representing knowledge. When learners build concept maps, meaningful learning is facilitated. Computer-based concept mapping software such as CmapTools have further extended the use of concept mapping and greatly enhanced the potential of the tool, facilitating the implementation of a concept map-centered learning environment. In this chapter, we briefly present concept mapping and its theoretical foundation, and illustrate how it can lead to an improved learning environment when it is combined with CmapTools and the Internet. We present the nationwide "Proyecto Conéctate al Conocimiento" in Panama as an example of how concept mapping, together with technology, can be adopted by hundreds of schools as a means to enhance meaningful learning.

2.1 Introduction

Concept mapping has been shown to be an effective tool for learning at all levels, from preschool to graduate school and corporate training (Novak & Gowin, 1984). Its use has extended across all continents as can be inferred by the diversity of participation and applications presented at the two International Conferences on Concept Mapping that have taken place (Cañas et al., 2004; Cañas & Novak, 2006a).

In this chapter we demonstrate how, particularly when integrated with technology, concept mapping can be at the center of the learning process, and can function as an artifact through which the student demonstrates a growing understanding of a topic and its integration with other diverse topics, and through which collaborative knowledge building can take place. We then describe a nationwide effort by the Government of Panama to implement this concept map-based learning environment in hundreds of public elementary schools throughout the country. For the reader to understand the ideas presented, we begin the chapter with a summary of concept mapping, its underlying theory, and its integration with technology that allows the implementation of this concept map-based learning environment.

2.2 Concept Maps and Meaningful Learning

Various knowledge mapping techniques are covered throughout this book. Although superficially many of these techniques look alike, there are underlying differences that are key to understanding the potential uses of each. Therefore, we begin with a short summary of concept mapping and its underlying theory, in order to distinguish it from other mapping techniques.

2.2.1 Concept Maps

Novak's research group at Cornell University first developed concept maps in 1972 in a research project that sought to follow changes in children's understanding of basic science concepts after audio-tutorial instruction in Grades 1 and 2, and continuing through Grade 12 (Novak & Musonda, 1991; Novak & Cañas, 2006b). Concept maps proved to be an effective way to represent and contrast the students' understanding of various concepts throughout time. Since then, the ability to represent the knowledge structure held by an individual on any topic remains one of the most powerful aspects of this tool, and this has served many users for a wide range of applications. The tool also allows for collaborative sharing and building of knowledge, both to archive knowledge and to foster creative insights by individuals and groups (Novak, 1998).

Concept maps, as we use the term, refers to a knowledge representation form that shows individual concepts at nodes with linking words that connect two concepts and indicate the relationship between them, thus forming a proposition. Usually, concepts are arranged hierarchically, from most inclusive, most general at the top to least inclusive, most specific at the bottom. We define a *concept* as a perceived regularity or pattern in events or objects, or records of events or objects, designated by a symbol, usually a word. Linking phrases are usually verbs which, when read together with the two concepts they join, form a simple phrase or proposition. Figure 2.1 shows a concept map that portrays key features of concept maps. Observe that for the most part, two concepts (which are depicted within rectangles) together with their linking phrase can be read as individual "sentences" that "make sense;" for example, "Concept maps *represent* Organized Knowledge," and "Concepts *are* Perceived Regularities or Patterns." In some cases, the proposition includes more than two concepts; for example, "Concepts *are* Labeled *with* Symbols." There is no restricted list of linking phrases – the map builder is free to use whatever phrase he/she prefers, as long as the concept-linking phrase-concept triad forms a sensible proposition. It is recommended that concepts and linking phrases be kept to as few words as possible. This propositional nature of the concept map, together with the freedom to select linking phrases, distinguishes concept maps from other types of graphical representations such as mind maps, argumentation maps, decision maps, and process maps.

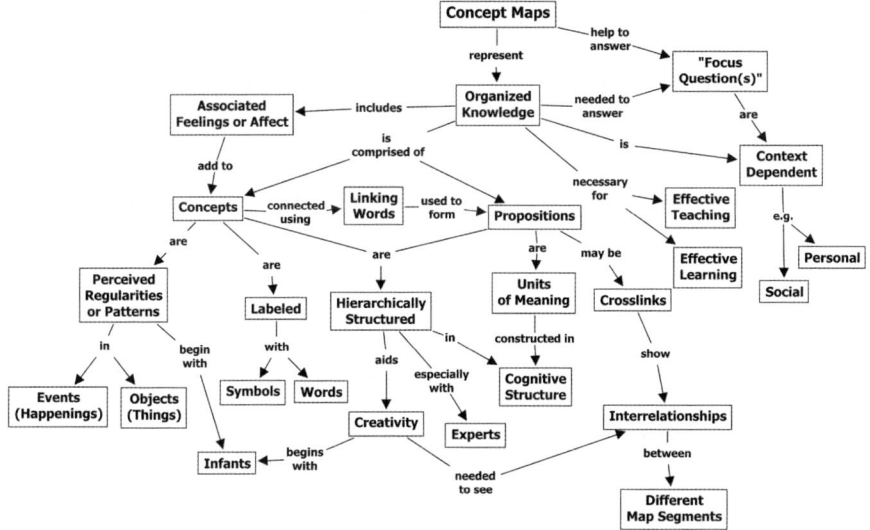

Fig. 2.1. A concept map that shows the key features of concept maps, as we define them.

2.2.2 Theory Underlying Concept Maps

Concept maps are also distinct from other mapping techniques in that they have a strong theoretical foundation. In 1963, David Ausubel published his theory of *cognitive* learning, and this became the psychological foundation for Novak and his research group's work on the concept map tool. Ausubel's theory puts forth several principles that explain how cognitive structure develops and elaborates. The most important principle is *meaningful learning*, a term that almost every researcher in education has used, but Ausubel (Ausubel, 1963; Ausubel et al., 1978; Ausubel, 2000) gives it explicit description. First, and in some ways most important, the *learner must choose* to seek ways to relate new concepts and propositions to existing relevant concepts and propositions she/he already knows. Second, the learner must *possess relevant concepts* and propositions with a sufficient degree of clarity and stability to anchor new, relevant concepts and propositions. Third, the material to be learned must be *potentially meaningful*; that is, it must be conceptually explicit and relatable to other ideas in this knowledge domain.

Meaningful learning represents one end of a continuum, with rote learning at the other end. Extreme rote learning occurs when the learner makes no attempt to integrate the new concepts and propositions to be learned into her/his cognitive structure and/or one or both of the two other conditions for meaningful learning are not met. Because motivation to integrate new knowledge with existing knowledge can vary and/or the learner may possess few or poorly organized relevant concepts and propositions, the same study materials may be learned by rote by one student and highly meaningfully by another. Several other principles of Ausubel's theory deal with processes involved in meaningful learning, and a discussion of these ideas can be found in Ausubel's writings or more succinctly in Novak & Gowin (1984), Novak (1998) and Novak & Cañas (2006b). Ausubel calls his cognitive learning theory *assimilation theory*, because new knowledge is assimilated into cognitive structure during meaningful learning, thereby modifying and enhancing the knowledge structure. *Constructivist* psychology and *constructivist teaching* are very popular terms in today's educational literature, recognizing that the learner must be actively engaged in the learning process. However, the literature on constructivist teaching often fails to recognize the subtle and important aspects of meaningful learning spelled out in Ausubel's psychology.

The theory of knowledge underlying concept mapping recognizes that knowledge is a human creation. We see knowledge creation primarily as the product of high levels of meaningful learning. Knowledge creation takes place by individuals embedded in a specific social milieu that changes over time. Consequently, knowledge evolves over time as the social milieu evolves. This *constructivist* view of knowledge stands in contrast to the *positivist* view of knowledge that dominated thinking during the first half of the twentieth century. Constructivist epistemology and constructivist psychology complement one another, and concept mapping serves to illustrate how this complementarity takes place.

2.2.3 Building Concept Maps

When learners build concept maps, meaningful learning is facilitated in several ways. The recommended procedure is to begin by first developing a good *focus question* that can be answered by understanding the knowledge that will be organized into the concept map. Focus questions that require explaining an event or the reasoning behind a procedure usually lead to better concept maps (Derbentseva et al., 2006), and concomitantly, better help to organize pertinent knowledge in cognitive structure (Cañas & Novak, 2006b). A question such as, "How does DNA code genetic information?" is better than one that asks, "What is the structure of DNA?" The process of developing the focus question requires that the mapmaker think about what she/he knows about a given topic; identifying what a person already knows that is pertinent is essential to meaningful learning. Next, we recommend that the mapmaker identify 10–20 concepts that are pertinent to the focus question and list these in a "Parking Lot" at the side of the paper (or window when using a computer). Reordering the concepts in the parking lot according to the most general, most inclusive for the question under consideration is the next step, and this begins to move the learner toward synthesis and evaluation of what she/he knows; two activities that Bloom (1956) identified as the highest levels of cognitive thinking. Moving concepts from the now hierarchical parking lot into a concept map, and selecting the best linking words to connect the concepts, further induces synthesis and evaluation of relationships between concepts and construction of good propositions. As the concept map is elaborated, it is also helpful to look for *crosslinks*, or relationships between two concepts in different sections of the concept map. Such crosslinks sometimes lead to creative insights. One should plan on three or four revisions of a concept map before achieving a satisfying structure with clarity of ideas. This need for revisions is one reason the use of computer software is so helpful, as it highly facilitates the revision process. Figure 2.2 shows a concept map made by Joan Novak, starting with the list of pertinent concepts on the left side.

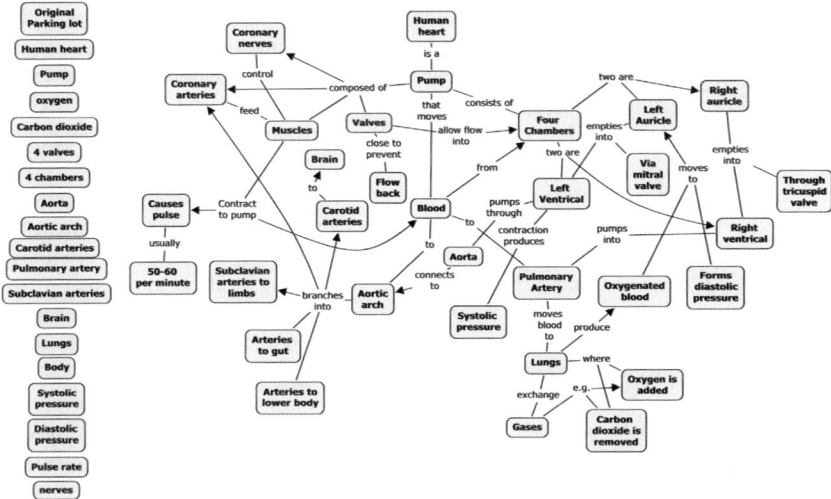

Fig. 2.2. Illustration of the end product in the construction of a concept map beginning with ordered concepts in a "parking lot." The map addresses the focus question: How does the normal heart function?

2.3 CmapTools: Integrating Concept Mapping with Technology

For many years, concept maps were drawn by hand. Iterating through revisions of a concept map was cumbersome and time consuming. Group concept mapping sessions were handled by using post-it notes. The introduction of personal computers enabled the development of software programs that facilitated the construction of concept maps. However, it was the marriage of the concept map and the Internet that launched a completely new world of applications and uses for concept mapping, as exemplified by the CmapTools (Cañas et al., 2004) software.[1] Based on this marriage of concept maps and technology, we propose the concept map-centered learning environment. To support this approach, CmapTools provides, among others, the following tools:

Network-based sharing and collaboration environment: Through a client-server architecture, students are given their own "space" where they can store their concept maps and associated resources. By providing this space long term, portfolios of each student's work can be collected and analyzed. Students control permissions over their space and they can create areas for group collaboration, publishing, and sharing. Alternatively, they can easily share concept maps by saving them in public shared servers. CmapTools was explicitly designed to support and facilitate collaboration.

---

[1] CmapTools can be downloaded from http://cmap.ihmc.us and is free for all to use.

Students can collaborate with peers using a variety of collaboration features including (a) shared folders (Cañas et al., 2004) described above, (b) synchronous real-time collaboration whereby two or more students from the same or different schools can simultaneously modify the same concept map, with the changes displaying in each student's screen in real time, (c) annotations and discussion threads, which provide a rich mechanism for peer review where students (and teachers) with appropriate permissions can annotate, critique, question, provide feedback, and comment on each others' maps, providing an environment for argumentation, and (d) "knowledge soups" (Cañas et al., 1995; Cañas et al., 2001) whereby students share propositions (not concept maps) that can be commented on and argued over by other students through annotations and discussion threads, leading to collaboration at the "knowledge level." Together, these tools provide a rich and versatile environment for team-based learning, and/or for students to collaborate at the "knowledge level" while each student constructs his/her own map. The variety of collaboration tools provides educators with the option of selecting those tools most appropriate for the objectives pursued.

Construction of knowledge models: A student can easily construct multimedia systems using concept maps as a means to organize all resources (e.g., drawings, pictures, WWW pages, videos, spreadsheets, documents, other concept maps, etc.; (Cañas et al., 2003) involved in his learning process. Teachers often complain that students "cut and paste" from the WWW and submit reports and projects that they don't fully understand or – in the extreme case – have not even read. Because it is extremely difficult and unlikely to construct a concept map for a topic one does not understand, by requiring students to use a concept map as the means of organizing information, the student is forced to understand the topic. These knowledge models can be of any size and have been used to build complete WWW sites (Briggs et al., 2004). These resources can belong to other students, and can be stored in CmapServers in other schools or countries, or on any accessible location on the Internet. Figure 2.3 shows a student-constructed concept map about birds, as well as associated resources that include images, videos, WWW pages, and a linked concept map about reptiles.

Publishing and Internet presence: Unfortunately, student-access to the Internet has become, in a large number of cases, an "objective" in itself. As with other technologies, the Internet, – or access to the WWW, which is usually what is meant by Internet access – by itself does not solve any of the problems we encounter in education. Although access to the information on the WWW is indeed valuable, as discussed below, we are concerned with the notion of students becoming "information pack rats" instead of "knowledge constructors." The CmapTools environment, therefore, supports easy "publishing" of knowledge models on the WWW. By storing a knowledge model in a CmapServer, it is automatically converted into a set of WWW pages, with links between resources including concept maps maintained through this conversion. If the CmapServer is accessible from Internet (that is, it can be accessed by users out on the Internet), and the appropriate permissions are set, the student's knowledge model is "published" out on the WWW. The CmapTools tools thus facilitate students (and teachers) selectively make their knowledge public and available to others.[2] We refer to the school as having a "presence" on the Internet, rather than being limited to just "access" to the Internet. For schools that do not have a CmapServer, IHMC provides public servers where any person can publish his/her knowledge models.

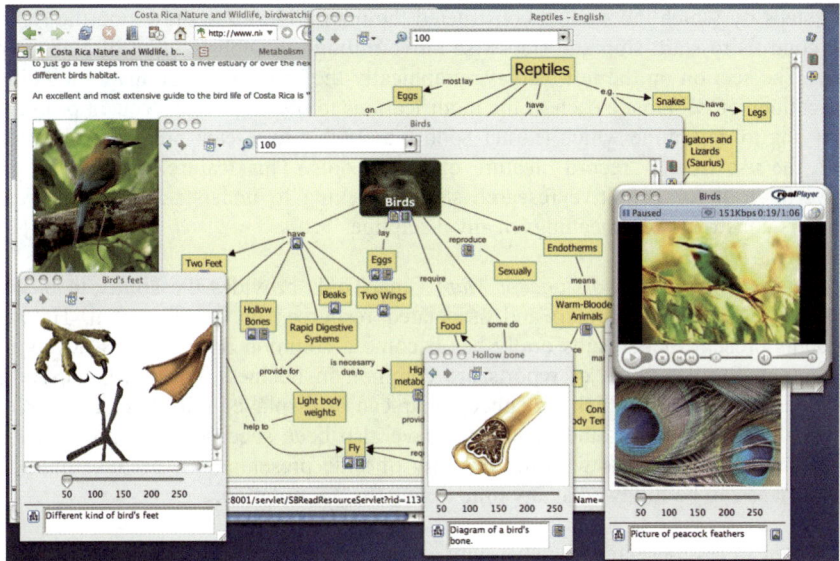

Fig. 2.3. Knowledge model about Birds constructed by a student. The various resources (images, videos, WWW pages, and other Cmaps) are linked to the Birds map and accessed through the icons underneath the concept. Notice that the student has integrated reptiles with birds, showing an understanding of the relationship between these. When saved on a CmapServer, this knowledge model automatically becomes a set of WWW pages browsable by others.

Searching for information based on a Concept Map: By taking advantage of the topology and semantics of concept maps, CmapTools enables the user to perform intelligent searches on the WWW and CmapServers, for information that is relevant to the map he/she is constructing (Carvalho et al., 2001). By starting with a simple map – possibly the result of a pretest – the student can use the map to search the WWW for information related to the map. The student can then delve deeper into the topic, improve his/her understanding, link the studied resources to the map as a reference, and carry out other activities related to the topic under study. The student uses these resources to enhance the map periodically, demonstrating the learning that has taken place, possibly linking other maps he/she constructs or making links to previous maps, and iteratively proceeding on another search. This way the student's knowledge model grows, reflecting an improved understanding of the topic.

---

[2]Recently, other environments such as Wikis and Blogs have also made it possible to publish information on the WWW easily.

Recording the process of constructing a Concept Map: CmapTools provides the ability to record and play back sequentially, steps in the process of constructing a concept map (Dutra et al., 2004). This feature provides support to the teacher in what is a key aspect of concept mapping: the process of constructing a map. We are very often confronted with a finalized map without the opportunity to examine the process and steps by which the student constructed the map. Figure 2.4 shows, on the right, the controls to start, stop and step-wise move through the construction of a concept map. The section on the left displays graphically the changes in the map, including indications of who made each of the modifications to the map. The frequent problem of trying to determine which learner contributed what to a team project is obviated with the use of the "record" feature of CmapTools. This feature also provides a powerful tool for cognitive research studies seeking to understand how different learners construct their meanings in any discipline.

Presentations based on a Concept Map: CmapTools provides the ability to piece-wise display a concept map and associated resources on a full screen. Having students present their results orally has become a common practice at all levels of education. Similar kinds of reports are common in business settings. CmapTools includes a module by which the concept map can be displayed full screen and piece-wise, allowing links to other maps that have also been specified with presentation information. This breaks with the linearity of slide presentations, because links to other maps can be followed at any time during the presentation.

The features presented, together with a number of additional tools available in the software suite, provide the technology infrastructure within which we can build the concept map-centered learning environment.

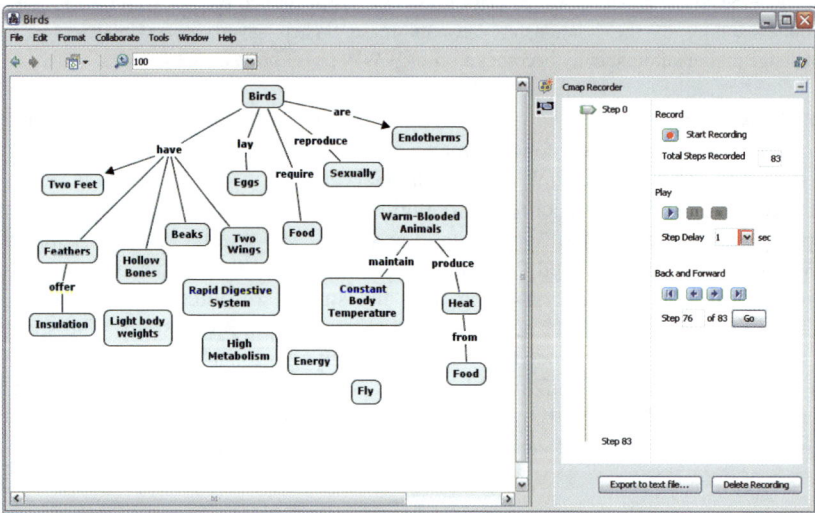

Fig. 2.4. An example of the recorder, which allows a step-by-step playback of the construction of a concept map.

2.4 A Concept Map-Centered Learning Environment

Educators have found a large variety of uses for concept mapping in terms of the types of use as well as the curriculum areas and age group of the learners. Coffey et al. (2003) reported on its use in a diversity of learning situations. Among these, we find lesson assignments, pretesting, readings, class discussions, practice or exercises, collaborative/cooperative work, comparing and contrasting views, research work, oral presentation, written reports, integration with other studies, post comprehensive test, and home/community presentations. In this chapter, we won't go into describing any of these uses, as they are well documented in the literature (Coffey et al., 2003). However, even though concept mapping is an effective tool that can be used in all the listed activities, in most cases it is used for only one of them. As an example, concept mapping has been shown to be very effective for pretesting of students; determining how much students know before the instruction begins. This use is particularly consistent with the main principle of the Ausubelian learning theory (Ausubel, 1968, Epitaph):

> *If I had to reduce all of educational psychology to just one principle, I would say this: The most important single factor influencing learning is what the learner already knows. Ascertain this and teach him or her accordingly.*

In most cases, however, the concept maps that the student constructs as a pretest are seldom used throughout the rest of the activities that take place on that same learning unit. This was understandable when concept maps were made by hand, as it was tedious to refine and reconstruct the map. We propose using the concept map as the artifact around which the various activities of the learning process are centered, as shown in Fig. 2.5. Based on the features provided by CmapTools described in the previous section, the student can use the concept map prepared as a pretest as a launching point toward his/her learning experience. As the student progresses through the learning unit, the concept map is enhanced to show his/her increased understanding. If the student engages in other activities (e.g., fieldwork, interviews, readings, writings, research, etc.), resources used and resources prepared by the student can be linked to the modified map. If the student is part of a team, concept maps can be built as a team or maps created by the various members can be linked together into a knowledge model. Unknown relationships between concepts generate questions for deliberation using annotations and discussion threads, and are a way to seed an issue-based IBIS discussion using Compendium, as described in chapters 7, 11 and 14 (Okada; Selvin; Sierhuis). Answers to unknown relationships can be researched using the search mechanism included in CmapTools, which takes advantage of the context provided by the concept map to generate smarter queries to Google and Yahoo, and to help locate other concept maps and attached resources that could be relevant to the concept map. Collaboration can take place among students within the class, within the school, or at other schools through the sharing mechanism provided by the CmapTools suite.

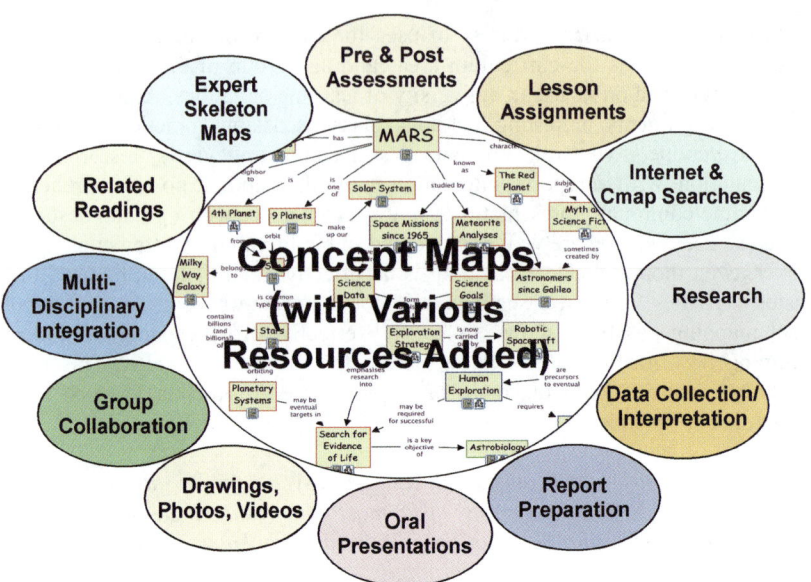

Fig. 2.5. This diagram illustrates how a concept map can be at the center of the various learning activities at school. As the student engages in the various activities shown, a concept map can show the student's increased understanding together with links to the resources involved in the activity.

Throughout the learning activity, the student uses the concept map to reflect his/her increased understanding. Key in this learning environment is the fact that the process of constructing the concept map has more importance than the final map. Educators familiar with concept mapping understand that its power lies in the process of constructing the map, of reflecting on which concepts should be included and how they should be organized, and, more important, what the linking phrases should be. The key task is trying not only to express one's knowledge explicitly, but also to do so in a way that is clearly understood by others. The negotiation and argumentation that takes place between team members constructing a common map, whether working together on the same computer or collaborating using CmapTools, has more value than the final map. Throughout the whole process, the CmapTools Recorder is able to capture all the steps taken during the construction of the knowledge models, and provides the possibility of reproducing the complete sequence of steps graphically.

As the student completes a learning unit, the knowledge model constructed, together with attached resources and other tangible products resulting from the student's effort, should reflect the level of understanding and knowledge the student has achieved. We propose that these knowledge models be kept throughout the student's years in school, and that students be encouraged not only to link knowledge models from different learning units to demonstrate how they integrate knowledge that normally is fragmented, but also to go back and enhance knowledge models previously built. Knowledge models a student begins in elementary school can become highly elaborated by high school or college, providing a visible record of her/his intellectual growth.

Students are often asked to present their work to their peers, and often they do so through PowerPoint slides. Although we don't have anything against using PowerPoint, in the great majority of cases PowerPoint slides consist of bullets that don't make much sense unless somebody presents them to you. We feel that it's a pity when a student has a set of concept maps that are a concise and highly organized representation of his/her understanding that he/she be asked to convert them into a list of bullets in PowerPoint slides. As an alternative, as described earlier, CmapTools offers the user the capability of a full-screen presentation of concept maps that can be displayed piece-wise according to instructions set by the user. The user can make links to other concept maps with presentations and to resources of all types. This way, the knowledge model resulting from the student's efforts becomes in itself the presentation to his/her peers. By taking advantage of the links between concept maps and to resources, the presentation can show what the speaker feels is desirable without having to follow a linear sequence as in traditional PowerPoint presentations.

To complete their efforts, students can publish their knowledge models on the WWW. If their work was performed on a CmapServer that can be accessed from the Internet, then all that needs to be done is to make sure visitors have "read" access to the maps and resources. The students' work is published and accessible by others (e.g., family and friends) through any WWW browser, and with most CmapServers, is accessible through search engines such as Google after they re-index, usually within a few weeks.

2.5 Adopting the Concept Map-Centered Learning Environment

The concept map-centered learning environment is a moving target that has evolved as schools adopt the use of concept mapping as a process and take greater advantage of the capabilities offered by CmapTools and other new technologies. In fact, many of the features that have been added to the software (e.g., the Presentation Module, the List View of propositions) are the result of schools providing us feedback for other uses of concept mapping that could be supported by technologies (e.g., student presentations).

The ideas that we have described in the previous sections have been implemented to varying degrees by schools in different countries. For example, the picture on the left of Fig. 2.6 shows high school students from Costa Rica at the Instituto de Educación Integral analyzing meteorological data that will be compared with data from other countries. At this high school, students use laptops in their subjects to construct concept maps, which are the center of their learning experience, both individually and in groups (Alonso-Delgado & Silesky-Agüero, 2004). Through the conceptual understanding derived from using concept mapping in their mathematics courses, students have been able to go beyond memorizing procedures and operations, and have significantly increased their grades in standardized national exams. The picture on the right of Fig. 2.6 shows elementary school children in Northeastern Italy, where a pilot project with 150 teachers is underway to improve science education in preschool, elementary, and high school under the leadership of Prof. G. Valitutti (2007) from the University of Urbino. These results have been reported in various publications (e.g., Berionni & Baldón, 2006; Mancinelli, 2006). Similarly, there are schools in other countries that are implementing or testing particular aspects of the concept map-centered learning environment. We prefer to concentrate on describing a large scale, nationwide effort that is taking place in Panama, where the concept map-centered learning environment is part of a project whose objective is to transform the public education system.

Fig. 2.6. On the left, high school students from the Instituto de Educación Integral, in Costa Rica, are observing meteorological data on their laptop that they will compare with data from other countries using the WWW. Their work, including the data collected, is integrated through concept maps. The picture on the right shows Italian elementary school students conducting studies with plants to learn how plants grow and reproduce. Their school is part of a larger pilot effort that includes 150 teachers in Northeastern Italy.

2.5.1 Proyecto Conéctate al Conocimiento[3]

In 2004, under the leadership of the then recently elected President Martín Torrijos, Panama adopted a national strategy based on meaningful learning for the public elementary school system through the project "Conéctate al Conocimiento" (Connect to Knowledge; Tarté, 2006). With the aid of technology, the objective of Conéctate is to create a computer network that interconnects the schools, creating a space that allows the construction, sharing, and publishing of knowledge, development of new learning skills in individuals and groups, and preparation of the national capacity for the country's development as a knowledge-based society. This implies aiding in the

---

[3]Even though the authors, particularly Cañas, have been heavily involved with Proyecto Conéctate al Conocimiento, the views presented in this chapter should be interpreted as those of a third party. Credit for the success of the project belongs to the Facilitators, technical team and leaders of the project.

transformation of elementary public education, from a traditional rote-learning system to one emphasizing knowledge construction and the development of skills according to the needs of the twenty-first century. The project's goal is to include teachers and students from 1,000 schools from all regions of the country over a 5-year period, with particular emphasis on reaching remote, rural schools. At the heart of the Conéctate project is the concept map-centered learning environment described earlier in this chapter. Thus, Conéctate provides a unique opportunity to observe and test on a national scale the ideas presented earlier.

2.5.1.1 Background Information

Before Conéctate, very few Panamanian public elementary schools had computers. Whereas in many other countries schools have had experience with technology for years or decades, and teachers have at least some familiarity with the use of computers, our studies showed that approximately 47% of the Panamanian teachers had never used a computer before (Miller et al., 2006). In those cases where the schools had computers, a specialty teacher, usually with some computer technology degree, used them for a course on "Informatics" that is part of the elementary school curriculum. Miller (*Ibid*) reports that practically all teachers surveyed were familiar with concept maps, but that the most common practice was for teachers to construct a concept map in class for students to memorize. Fewer than 5% allowed students to construct their own concept maps. Furthermore, there were a number of misconceptions among the teachers regarding concept mapping.

Even though Panama is a small country, rural villages are often very hard to reach, requiring many hours of travel over bad or nonexistent roads. In many cases, the schools that were to be included in the project did not have electricity, or the electricity distribution was such that installing computers in the school would leave the rest of the village without electricity. In many of the schools, both urban and rural, a new classroom needed to be built to install the computers. As a result, there are schools in Conéctate with electricity from a local power plant, a satellite connection to the Internet, and computers in a new classroom.

Rote learning and students copying from the blackboard characterized the Panamanian classroom before Conéctate, as is the case in many Latin American countries. For the most part, the teacher does not have many resources to use in the classroom, and libraries are lacking or poorly stocked. However, teachers, particularly in rural areas, are highly motivated and committed to their students, and embrace new opportunities like those offered by Conéctate.

2.5.1.2 The Project

Housing the Project

Conéctate presents challenges both in the technological arena – given the location and infrastructure of many schools – as well as in the methodological aspects of how to transform the way learning takes place in the classroom. The main challenge, however, is scalability. Building a new classroom to install computers and training the teachers for one, two, or a few schools is a very different proposition than doing so for hundreds of schools involving thousands of teachers.

Transformations such as those sought by Conéctate are difficult to implement within the bureaucracy of a Ministry of Education. These large government organizations have so many issues to resolve just in terms of personnel (e.g. dealing with teachers' salaries), that there is little room for innovation, let alone at the speed and scale that Conéctate required. For this reason, Conéctate was temporarily situated under a newly created Secretariat for Governmental Innovation, whose objective is to modernize the Panamanian government through technology. For the long run, a not-for-profit organization is being created that will house the Project. Meanwhile, the agility of the newly created Secretariat enabled Conéctate to get going in a much shorter time period than would have been possible otherwise. Financial resources, however, still come from the Ministry of Education, and a very close coordination is maintained with education authorities.

The Technology

Given the physical infrastructure of schools and the scale of the Project, it was determined that it would be impossible to install computers (i.e., desktops) in each of the classrooms. The high temperatures throughout most of the country year round make it necessary to install air conditioning units wherever desktops are installed, which, combined with the need for electrical infrastructure in the schools, would make the cost of this alternative prohibitive. Therefore, computers are installed in a special room that is referred to as the Innovation Classroom. However, our experience has taught us that in most technology-in-education projects that have a computer lab, what takes place in the lab is usually not reflected in what takes place in the classroom. That is, training teachers on how to use new technologies, particularly if the computers are not in the classroom, does not achieve changing the way learning takes place in the classroom. In other words, training teachers on how to construct concept maps using CmapTools would not lead to the concept map-centered learning environment where the various activities that occur in the classroom take advantage of concept mapping. Furthermore, given the rote-learning environment we found in most classrooms, training teachers on the use of the technology would most likely have no effect on the way they manage their classroom. In each of the Innovation Classrooms there would be a computer aid (formerly the Informatics teacher), a specially trained teacher that would help the classroom teachers take advantage of the technology. However, we knew that we couldn't rely on training these aids and having them train the teachers – cascade training gets watered-down pretty fast. Thus, it was decided that to the extent possible, all classroom teachers would be trained not only in new methodologies needed to implement a meaningful learning environment in the classroom, but also in the use of technology.

Conéctate was designed to be a network of schools that facilitates collaboration, publishing, and sharing. To achieve this goal, the whole set of participating schools is seen as being part of the same community, as a single organization, with all schools interconnected and connected to the Internet. Within each school, a

CmapServer is installed with a public IP address, which means that the server can be reached from other schools and from anywhere on the Internet. This leads, of course, to the school having a "presence" on the Web, not only access to it. Students and teachers can share and collaborate, and students can access their concept maps and resources from home or through an Internet Cafe (CmapServers in the Conéctate schools can be reached through the Places View in CmapTools or through a WWW browser). Within the CmapServer, each student and teacher has his/her own area for files, maps, and resources. The Project is in the process of implementing Nicho, a piece of software designed at IHMC that facilitates assigning each student an email address (managed by Google, teachers already have their email address) and implements a chat service. Nicho enables the use of the same userid for email, chat, CmapTools, and Web browsing, and additionally provides space in the school's file server. Through Nicho, students can use any of the computers in the school to access their resources and tailored environment. They are assigned a unique userid for their years at a school, and the "space" with its resources will migrate with her/him if she/he switches schools. The goal is for the technology to fully support and facilitate the sharing and collaborating environment needed to implement the concept map-centered learning environment described in this chapter.

Teacher Training

The scale of teacher training, together with the need to make personal visits to follow up on the teachers after the training, required the creation of a group of full-time Facilitators: professionals from a wide variety of disciplines that were trained to take on the tasks of training teachers, visiting schools, and preparing resources needed (e.g., documentation, videos, etc.), and in some cases carrying on research. The selection of the group was exhaustive, with more than 1,000 resumes reviewed to come up with a group currently of just over 30 Facilitators.

The teacher training workshops consist of 2 weeks of full time, intensive work. Training is also provided to the school principal (a principal that supports and understands the Project is one of the key factors needed for success) and Ministry of Education supervisors. Conéctate has the facilities to carry on 10 of these workshops concurrently, with 20 teachers in each group, for a total capacity to train 200 teachers every 2 weeks. Part-time substitute teachers teach in the classroom of participating teachers for the duration of the workshops. As was indicated earlier, most teachers have never used a computer before attending the workshop, and many have never used a keyboard. The decision was made, however, to have the teachers learn to use the computer through CmapTools as opposed to using Windows and/or Office as is often done. Within a few minutes, teachers are constructing their own concept maps, maybe with some difficulty in manipulating the mouse, but are engaged in representing their understanding, an effort that they can immediately identify with and that they perceive will be useful with their students. Suárez & Villareal-Bermúdez (2006) report that after a few days into the workshop, there is no distinction in the quality of the concept maps constructed by teachers who had or had not used a computer previously. That is, the use of the computer has become, to a certain extent, transparent. The workshops are completely constructivist in nature. In addition to concept mapping and meaningful learning, the workshop covers additional topics such as project based learning and collaborative projects, emphasizing the use of concept maps both as a way to integrate the projects' activities and to integrate diverse disciplines. Given that the teachers will not have computers in their classrooms, it is important that they feel comfortable with the idea of working with concept maps, both with and without computers. Figure 2.7 shows two examples of teachers using other materials to construct their concept maps. This experience carries on in the classroom as can be seen in Fig. 2.8, where the picture on the left shows students collaborating on the construction of a concept map with cardboard, and the display in the picture on the right shows some of the end products of a project, with a couple of concept maps on the wall. Overall, the objective of the workshop is to provide a basic understanding of constructivist environments, meaningful learning, concept mapping, and proper use of the technology so that teachers further along can take advantage of any resource, whether it is technology based (software, sensors, etc.) or not, in a constructivist way.

Fig. 2.7. Pictures showing teachers during workshops learning to use concept maps without a computer, as would take place in the classroom.

Fig. 2.8. The picture above shows students collaborating on the construction of concept maps in the classroom. On the right is a partial display of the material developed by students as part of a project.

Among the activities that take place during the workshop, there is one in particular that demonstrates how different aspects of the Project fit together, and how the work from the workshop continues when the teachers return to their schools. One of the first concept maps that teachers construct is themed "Who Am I?" – a concept map about themselves. Further along during the workshop, teachers from the same school together with their Principal prepare a "Who Am I?" concept map for the school. Along the way, teachers bring in pictures (family pictures, for example) that they wish to scan and link to the map, or borrow a digital camera to take pictures of their school when they go back for the weekend between the two weeks of training. The resulting concept maps are quite interesting, as teachers get quite personal in both their concept maps and their school's map, particularly when trying to describe what is to them important in their school (e.g., those from a remote rural school may emphasize that they have a boat with a motor, others emphasize that children receive free lunch, or list the names of the employees that clean the school). The teacher's maps are linked to the school's map, and when they are saved on the school's CmapServer, become the "web page" for the school. The school's map is then linked to a geographical map of Panama. Figure 2.9 shows a Web browser with three windows. The top left window is the main concept map for the Project, its WWW page (www.conectate.gob.pa). This map has a link to a geographical map of Panama, shown in the lower left window. For each province, there are links to each of the schools' "Who Am I?" maps, as is shown in the partial display of the schools of the province of Chiriquí. In the top right window is displayed the concept map for the school "El Limón," which describes details about this school. This school consists of only a computer aid and two teachers, one covering first, third and fifth grade, and the second covering second, fourth and sixth (these are referred to as multigrade schools, and are very common in rural areas where the student population is low). There are links to the teachers' "Who Am I?" map, from which there are links to the different grade's "Who Am I?" map. The intention is that from each of the grade's maps there will be links to each student's "Who Am I?" map, and links to projects the grade is engaged in. Each student can have links from his/her map to knowledge models that he/she wants to publish and share with others. As the Project progresses, students will be able to navigate to the concept maps of any other student in the Project, creating a sense of community. When students start collaborating with other students, they can easily search for their peer's concept maps and learn who they are, what their interests are, and so forth. This work is still in progress, of course, but the schools are moving toward this goal. The web pages for the school also provide a sense of pride and belongingness to the Project. Remember that most teachers had never used a computer. They return from the workshop with their school's web page as well as their own personal web page, and with their school having a "presence" on the Internet. They now have pages that they constructed by themselves, and more important, that they can modify at any time without the need of any webmaster or technician. This is a source of pride. As Google indexes the html versions of the concept maps, it is very common to see in the logs searches by teacher name – most likely teachers searching for themselves (or for a colleague). They also feel that having their maps linked to the main Project's map provides a sense of belonging – their school is now *part* of Conéctate.

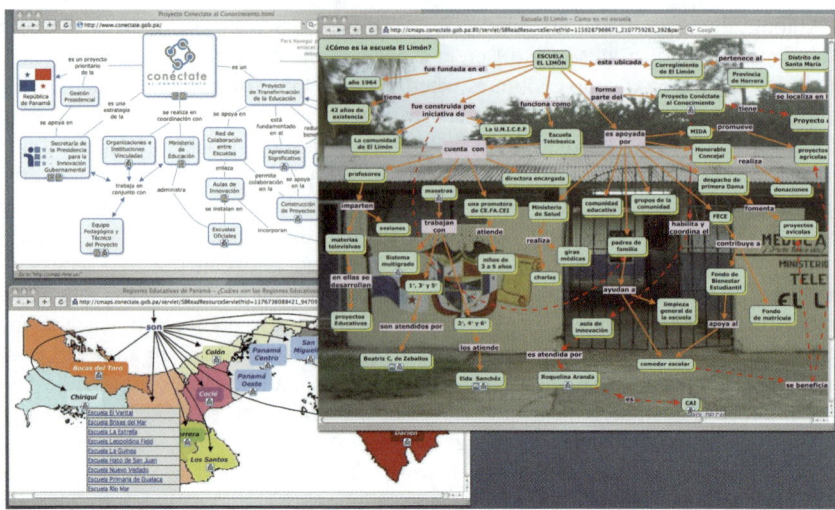

Fig. 2.9. These three browser windows show the linkage from Conéctate's Web page map (*top left*) to the geographical map of Panama (*lower left*) where there are links to each of the school's "Who Am I?," as shown in the right for the school El Limón. From the school's map, links can be followed to teachers' maps, student's maps, etc.

Follow-Up Visits and Support

Nobody expects teachers to "change" during a 2-week workshop. It is clear that for many of them, the workshop opens up many opportunities and provides a multitude of ideas, but reality sets in when they return to their classroom. That is why the Facilitators periodically visit each of the teachers to provide support, help, and advice. The visits are conceived of as a continuation of the workshop, a means by which the learning process can continue. These visits, together with the workshops, consume a large portion of the Facilitators' time. However, it is clear that their visits make a huge difference in whether the teachers take the initial steps necessary to change the way learning takes place in their classrooms. With the Facilitators' support, many teachers that were afraid to move ahead have been able to rise to the challenge. As a support within the schools, the Facilitators rely on the computer aid to provide daily help to teachers when using the technology.

Given the scale of the Project, as the number of schools increases it becomes physically impossible to continue to visit each of the teachers personally. Furthermore, it is also impossible to bring all the teachers back for follow-up workshops. To continue providing training and support to the teachers long term, Conéctate is currently moving quickly toward an online support and training platform. Once a school has reached a certain level of performance, online support will help reduce the frequency of personal visits. The Project has developed a set of tools, including a topological taxonomy (Cañas et al., 2006) and a semantic rubric for concept maps, to determine the level of advancement of the schools.

Current Status

Conéctate now includes more than 300 schools installed with computers and Internet connection. By the end of 2007, 500 elementary schools will be part of the Project. As discussed earlier, this has meant, depending on the school's setting, construction of new classrooms, electrical infrastructure, local electrical power plants, satellite Internet connections, and all kinds of problems that are encountered when dealing with a large number of schools in remote and difficult access areas. More impressive, over 5,000 fourth-, fifth-, and sixth-grade teachers have been trained in the 2-week workshops, reaching approximately 100,000 students. The Project intended to train only the upper grade level teachers initially, but in a large number of schools, these teachers have already involved and trained the first- and second- and third-grade teachers on their own initiative.

It is illusory to expect that all 5,000 teachers will adopt the concept map-based learning environment in their classrooms. We understand that it is a long-term process, and that it will be years before the real effects of the Project can be determined. However, in the large number of cases where the teachers have adopted the proposed model, the changes are clear and measurable in terms of the environment in the classroom, the students' participation, interests and questions, and in the students' grades (cf. Rodríguez & Coloma, 2006).

President Torrijos has announced Panama's participation in the One Laptop Per Child (OLPC) initiative, with an initial purchase of 100,000 laptops. Thus, the Project may soon be moving toward a model where the students will have their own laptop in the classroom.

Some Lessons Learned

Lessons are learned daily in such a large Project. In this section, we try to summarize some key observations. Readers will find some of them to be confirmations of results seen in other projects:

- Even in a Project that is conceived of initially as a technology-in-education effort, it is possible to transform the way learning takes place in the classroom, even when technology is not involved. (There were cases where, for various reasons, the installation of the computers was delayed way beyond the training of the teachers. However, there were teachers in this situation who, even without the technology, transformed their classroom based on the methodologies learned during the workshop).
- The school's Principal is a key player in the Project. If the Principal believes in the Project and supports it, the chance for success is much higher. Including the Principal in the training workshops was, therefore, an important decision, even though it is difficult to implement as most Principals firmly believe their school will collapse if they go away for 2 weeks.
- It is important to synchronize the arrival of technology with the teacher training; otherwise retraining may be needed.

- Teachers do not need to have previous training in the use of computers to be introduced to programs with a low threshold such as CmapTools.
- A sense of belonging and a sense of pride (e.g., the "Who Am I?" maps) can go a long way toward getting principals and teachers involved in the effort.
- Follow-up visits to the teachers, particularly shortly after they return from the workshop to the classroom, increase the chances of the teacher succeeding with the Project.
- Not all teachers are willing to change, thus one must accept that one may have to give up on trying to change many of them.
- In order to change the educational system permanently, the change needs to take place at the source: that is, the universities and institutes teachers graduate from need to change.

2.6 Conclusion

We have presented a concept map-based learning environment, where the concept map becomes an artifact through which the students demonstrate changes in their understanding of a topic. With the use of technology such as CmapTools, the concept map becomes a way to integrate various learning resources, and can be used as an artifact through which students can collaborate both locally and remotely. By organizing the knowledge models resulting from concept maps and attached resources, digital portfolios can be built that show the students' changes in cognitive structure throughout the years. Schools throughout various countries have reported successes with implementing some of these ideas. The large scale, countrywide implementation of this environment in Panama provides the opportunity to examine and test these ideas. The initial results are encouraging, as Conéctate al Conocimiento will have grown to 500 schools by the end of 2007. The experience being generated in Panama will undoubtedly help other countries in their efforts to adopt the concept map-based learning environment.

References

Alonso-Delgado, J. and O. Silesky-Agüero (2004) Los Mapas Conceptuales en Costa Rica: Ideas Nuevas, Odres Nuevos. Concept Maps: Theory, Methodology, Technology. Proceedings of the First International Conference on Concept Mapping. A. J. Cañas, J. D. Novak and F. M. González. Pamplona, Spain: Universidad Pública de Navarra. **2**: 33–36

Ausubel, D. P. (1963) The Psychology of Meaningful Verbal Learning. New York: Grune and Stratton

Ausubel, D. P. (1968) Educational Psychology: A Cognitive View. New York: Holt, Rinehart and Winston

Ausubel, D. P. (2000) The Acquisition and Retention of Knowledge: A Cognitive View. Dordrecht, Boston: Kluwer

Ausubel, D. P., J. D. Novak, et al. (1978) Educational Psychology: A Cognitive View. New York, Holt, Rinehart and Winston

Berionni, A. and M. O. Baldón (2006) Models of Social Constructivism, Laboratory Teaching and Concept Maps to Build Scientific Knowledge and Organize Concept Network. Teaching Experiences in First Level Education in Italian Schools. Concept Maps: Theory, Methodology, Technology. Proceedings of the Second International Conference on Concept Mapping. A. J. Cañas and J. D. Novak. San José, Costa Rica: Universidad de Costa Rica. **1**: 449–456

Bloom, B. S. (1956) Taxonomy of Educational Objectives; the Classification of Educational Goals. New York: Longmans Green

Briggs, G., D. A. Shamma, et al. (2004) Concept Maps Applied to Mars Exploration Public Outreach. Concept Maps: Theory, Methodology, Technology. Proceedings of the First International Conference on Concept Mapping. A. J. Cañas, J. D. Novak and F. González. Pamplona, Spain: Universidad Pública de Navarra. **1**: 109–116

Cañas, A. J., K. M. Ford, et al. (1995) Knowledge Construction and Sharing in Quorum. Seventh World Conference on Artificial Intelligence in Education, Washington DC: Association for the Advancement of Computing in Education

Cañas, A. J., K. M. Ford, et al. (2001) Online Concept Maps: Enhancing Collaborative Learning by Using Technology with Concept Maps. *The Science Teacher* **68**(4): 49–51

Cañas, A. J., G. Hill, et al. (2003) Support for Constructing Knowledge Models in CmapTools. Pensacola, FL: Institute for Human and Machine Cognition

Cañas, A. J., G. Hill, et al. (2004) CmapTools: A Knowledge Modeling and Sharing Environment. Concept Maps: Theory, Methodology, Technology. Proceedings of the First International Conference on Concept Mapping. A. J. Cañas, J. D. Novak and F. M. González. Pamplona, Spain: Universidad Pública de Navarra. **I**: 125–133

Cañas, A. J., J. D. Novak, et al. (2004) Concept Maps: Theory, Methodology, Technology. First International Conference on Concept Mapping. Pamplona, Spain: Universidad Pública de Navarra

Cañas, A. J. and J. D. Novak (2006a) Concept Maps: Theory, Methodology, Technology. Second International Conference on Concept Mapping. San José, Costa Rica: Editorial Universidad de Costa Rica

Cañas, A. J. and J. D. Novak (2006b) Re-Examining the Foundations for Effective Use of Concept Maps. Concept Maps: Theory, Methodology, Technology. Proceedings of the Second International Conference on Concept Mapping. A. J. Cañas and J. D. Novak. San Jose, Costa Rica: Universidad de Costa Rica. **1**: 494–502

Cañas, A. J., J. D. Novak, et al. (2006) Confiabilidad de una Taxonomía Topológica para Mapas Conceptuales. Concept Maps: Theory, Methodology, Technology. Proceedings of the Second International Conference on Concept Mapping. A. J. Cañas and J. D. Novak. San Jose, Costa Rica: Universidad de Costa Rica. **1**: 153–161

Carvalho, M. R., R. Hewett, et al. (2001) Enhancing Web Searches from Concept Map-Based Knowledge Models. Proceedings of SCI 2001: Fifth Multiconference on Systems, Cybernetics and Informatics. N. Callaos, F. G. Tinetti, J. M. Champarnaud and J. K. Lee. Orlando, FL: International Institute of Informatics and Systemics: 69–73

Coffey, J. W., M. J. Carnot, et al. (2003) A Summary of Literature Pertaining to the Use of Concept Mapping Techniques and Technologies for Education and Performance Support. Pensacola, FL: Institute for Human and Machine Cognition

Derbentseva, N., F. Safayeni, and A. J. Cañas (2006) Concept Maps: Experiments on Dynamic Thinking. *Journal of Research in Science Teaching* **44**(3): 448–465

Dutra, I., L. Fagundes, et al. (2004) Un Enfoque Constructivista para Uso de Mapas Conceptuales en Educación a Distancia de Profesores. Concept Maps: Theory, Methodology, Technology. Proceedings of the First International Conference on Concept Mapping. A. J. Cañas, J. D. Novak and F. M. González. Pamplona: Universidad Pública de Navarra

Mancinelli, C. (2006) Learning While Having Fun: Conceptualization Itineraries in Kindergarten Children Experiences with C-Maps in an Italian School. Concept Maps: Theory, Methodology, Technology. Proceedings of the Second International Conference on Concept Mapping. A. J. Cañas and J. D. Novak. San Jose, Costa Rica: Universidad de Costa Rica. **1**: 343–350

Miller, N., A. J. Cañas, et al. (2006) Preconceptions Regarding Concept Maps Held by Panamanian Teachers. Concept Maps: Theory, Methodology, Technology. Proceedings of the Second International Conference on Concept Mapping. A. J. Cañas and J. D. Novak. San José, Costa Rica: Universidad de Costa Rica. **1**: 469–476

Novak, J. D. (1998) Learning, Creating, and Using Knowledge: Concept Maps as Facilitative Tools in Schools and Corporations. Mahwah, NJ: Lawrence Erlbaum Associates

Novak, J. D. and A. J. Cañas (2006a) The Origins of the Concept Mapping Tool and the Continuing Evolution of the Tool. *Information Visualization Journal* **5**(3): 175–184

Novak, J. D. and A. J. Cañas (2006b) The Theory Underlying Concept Maps and How to Construct Them. Pensacola, FL: Florida Institute for Human and Machine Cognition

Novak, J. D. and D. B. Gowin (1984) Learning How to Learn. New York, NY: Cambridge University Press

Novak, J. D. and D. Musonda (1991) A Twelve-Year Longitudinal Study of Science Concept Learning. *American Educational Research Journal* **28**(1): 117–153

Rodríguez, M. Á. and E. d. Coloma (2006) Mapas Conceptuales en las Aulas Panameñas: Aptitud para Cambiar Actitud. Concept Maps: Theory, Methodology, Technology. Proceedings of the Second International Conference on Concept Mapping. A. J. Cañas and J. D. Novak. San José, Costa Rica: Universidad de Costa Rica. **1**: 391–398

Suárez, L. and K. Villareal-Bermúdez (2006) Hace Falta Una Alfabetización Computacional Antes de la Inmersión de los Maestros a la Tecnología en la Escuela? Una Respuesta usando CmapTools. Concept Maps: Theory, Methodology, Technology. Proceedings of the Second International Conference on Concept Mapping. A. J. Cañas and J. D. Novak. San José, Costa Rica: University of Costa Rica. **2**: 122–125

Tarté, G. (2006) Conéctate al Conocimiento: Una Estrategia Nacional de Panamá basada en Mapas Conceptuales. Concept Maps: Theory, Methodology, Technology. Proceedings of the Second International Conference on Concept Mapping. A. J. Cañas and J. D. Novak. San José, Costa Rica: Universidad de Costa Rica. **1**: 144–152

Valitutti, G. (2007) "Il Progetto "Le Parole della Scienza"." Retrieved August 23, 2007, from http://85.47.105.117/Le%20parole%20della%20scienza.doc

3. Enhancing Collaborative and Meaningful Language Learning Through Concept Mapping

Rita de Cássia Veiga Marriott[1] and Patrícia Lupion Torres[2]

[1]University of Birmingham, UK, Department of Hispanic Studies & Centre for Modern Languages, r.marriott@bham.ac.uk
[2]Universidade Católica do Paraná, Brazil, Department of Education, patorres@terra.com.br

Abstract. This chapter aims to investigate new ways of foreign-language teaching/learning via a study of how concept mapping can help develop a student's reading, writing and oral skills as part of a blended methodology for language teaching known as LAPLI (*Laboratorio de Aprendizagem de LInguas*: The Language Learning Lab). LAPLI is a student-centred and collaborative methodology which encourages students to challenge their limitations and expand their current knowledge whilst developing their linguistic and interpersonal skills. We explore the theories that underpin LAPLI and detail the 12 activities comprising its programme with specify reference to the use of "concept mapping". An innovative table enabling a formative and summative assessment of the concept maps is formulated. Also presented are some of the qualitative and quantitative results achieved when this methodology was first implemented with a group of pre-service students studying for a degree in English and Portuguese languages at the Catholic University of Parana (PUCPR) in Brazil. The contribution of concept mapping and LAPLI to an under standing of language learning along with a consideration of the difficulties encountered in its implementation with student groups is discussed and suggestions made for future research.

3.1 Introduction: The Use of Concept Mapping in Lapli

Concept mapping is widely known as a tool to facilitate meaningful learning. For Novak (2003), if this technique is to favour meaningful learning, it needs to fulfil three conditions (1) the subject matter to be learnt must be presented clearly, and the language and examples used must relate to the learner's previous knowledge; (2) the learner must have some relevant prior knowledge; and (3) the learner must choose to learn meaningfully in order to incorporate new meanings rather than just memorize them.

It also constitutes a very useful tool in helping students to reflect on their learning process, on the structure of knowledge and on its production; in other words, on meta-knowledge (Novak & Gowin, 1999). Telebinezhad (2007) describes these benefits in an experiment with a group of English Language Proficiency students, stating that "concept mapping [...] helped students attend to writing tasks, and control their learning more effectively. It helped students facilitate their learning by organizing key concepts into visual representation. They simply represented visually their understanding of ideas and their relationships. This created a much more tangible evidence of the quality of both the learning process and concept understanding."

According to Gonzáles et al. (2004), concept maps have been extensively used to plan didactical units and curricular material, to aid study, to represent students' knowledge structures about a wide range of issues and subjects at various levels, and to identify, analyze and intervene in students' ideas (Gonzáles et al., 2004; Morón, 2004; Novak, 2003).

Arbea & Campos (2004), however, noted a significant difference in students' concept maps when they were or were not engaged in learning meaningfully. This is expressed in Table 3.1 below:

Table 3.1. Learning Indicators in a concept map (Arbea & Campos, 2004).

More meaningful learning	More memoristic/mechanical learning
All concepts are used	Not all concepts are used
Concepts are organized hierarchically, and the more inclusive concepts are identified	There is an incorrect hierarchical organization, with the more inclusive concept not being identified
The most inclusive concepts have a complex progressive differentiation. Few linear relationships between concepts appear	Linear relationships and chain structures between concepts appear
Numerous cross-links indicative of integrative reconciliation	Few cross-links or wrong cross-links between concepts are established

The implementation of concept mapping into the foreign language classroom can promote a significant change in the teaching methodology and students' and teacher's level of participation in the learning process. As noted by Telebinezhad (2007) "Students maximize their learning by using concept mapping in their essay writing; hence they feel more independent and feel more responsibility for their own learning."

By concept mapping on selected texts of personal interest and level of understanding of the target language, we wanted our LAPLI students to break away from the following activities:

1. Teacher-centred approaches
2. The "cut and paste" philosophy of language production which has become easier to implement by use of computers with access to a wide range of material on the Internet
3. Ready-made materials for language teaching which usually come with exercises to "tick" off the correct answer

We wanted to encourage them to firstly become more active and responsible for their own learning; secondly to start practising the analysis of information on hierarchical levels of detail and thirdly to start thinking about how concepts can be linked together to convey one's own ideas; as well as finally to enjoy the benefits of this technique in their learning process.

Moreover, from a linguistic point of view, we also wanted to stimulate students to re-read the text in order to formulate questions and create the concept map using various reading techniques such as intensive reading, extensive reading, skimming, scanning and top-down reading, in order to:

- Identify the keywords in the text
- Predict or infer the meaning of keywords and how they are related
- Identify the structure and sub-structure of the text and use this knowledge to help create their own texts
- Learn new "vocabulary"
- Prepare a synthesis of the source texts
- Assemble an article
- Seek to extend an active vocabulary, and thus raise the level of their foreign language acquisition by using these keywords during the process of rebuilding phrases to create their own articles

Concept mapping is an activity that takes time, mainly when working collaboratively (Muirhead, 2006), and the teacher needs to give students a lot of support and guidance when it is first implemented. Additionally, the building of concept maps requires a change of attitude to learning. As Muirhead (2006) points out "Integrating cognitive activities into the online setting is a practical way to promote relevant interactivity while effectively meeting course objectives." By adopting concept mapping as one of LAPLI's activities, our aim was to challenge the students to develop their linguistic skills and creativity while they grew together and became more active and responsible for their learning.

3.2 Theories Underpining the Language Learning Lab

3.2.1 Collaborative Learning

Collaborative learning (CL) represents a significant shift away from the typical classroom, where the teacher places him/herself at the centre of the process. In collaborative learning, students and teachers combine their intellectual efforts and generally work in groups of two or more people to seek to understand, solve, create or determine the meaning of a product together. Activities revolve around the exploration or use of course material by students rather than a simple presentation or explanation by the teacher. Teachers who use this methodology tend to regard themselves not as experts in a subject and its transmission to students, but rather as intellectual creators of collaborative experiences in a process of emerging learning.

Involved in collaborative activities, students create something new by exchanging information and ideas with their peers. These intellectual acts of processing and constructing meaning or of creating something new are crucial to learning. Students, absorbed in challenging tasks or questions, bring many different perspectives to the classroom as well as different cultures, learning styles, experiences and aspirations.

This mutual exploration, creation of meaning and feedback result in a better understanding by the student and the creation of new meaning for all of us since, as teachers, we can no longer follow the "one-size-fits-all" approach. (Smith & MacGregor, 1992, p. 2)

In collaborative work, students are inevitably faced with differences and must make an effort to work with these. Developing the ability to tolerate and resolve differences, to come to agreements that respect all members of the group and to take an interest in colleagues' progress are crucial skills for community life. Development of these values and skills is generally relegated to the student's life "outside" the school environment. Encouraging teamwork, a sense of community and leadership skills are legitimate, valuable aims for both inside and outside the classroom. (Smith & MacGregor, 1992, p. 2)

For Silva (2001, p. 70–71), students must interact if there is to be collaborative learning, as interactivity is related to communication. In one-way teaching the student is a passive assimilator whereas in interactive teaching he/she is a "user who manipulates the message as co-author and co-creator" and reinvents it.

The interactive classroom thus emphasizes student-student interaction, which is the basis of collaborative learning. Peer exchange, emphasis on the process and emphasis on a proactive and enquiring attitude on the part of the students make each student responsible for his/her learning and that of other colleagues. Each team member has something to contribute, be it their personal experience, information, perspective, insight, skills or attitude, as these make an important contribution to problem solving or the development of a project or case study. The aim is to help with everybody's learning process. For a student to be able to make a contribution, the teacher must structure the classes and the learning so that all the students are involved in the process. They "do" something together to achieve a common goal. In this relationship between the students, collaborative learning encourages the development of critical thinking, such as analyzing, evaluating, synthesizing and applying information as well as stimulating social relationship skills.

3.2.2 Meaningful Learning

The concept of meaningful learning is associated with David Ausubel, Professor Emeritus at the University of Columbia, and his colleague Joseph D. Novak, of the same university. The main concept in Ausubel's theory bases meaningful learning on the social-interactionist constructivist approach, which is in opposition to rote-mode learning. For Novak & Gowin (1999, p. 23), to learn meaningfully, the individual needs to relate new concepts to propositions and concepts that he or she already possesses. In meaningful learning the teaching "ceases to be knowledge transmission (fixed truths) but is rather a process of creating didactical and pedagogical situations that facilitate learning, i.e., that favour the construction of meaningful relationships between components of a symbolic universe" (Moreto, 2002, p. 103).

Ausubel contrasts meaningful learning to rote-mode learning (Hassard, 2004) arguing that it takes place deductively, i.e., from top to bottom, with new concepts being related to concepts that have already been learnt. It is not enough for the student to learn isolated pieces of information, he/she must establish relationships between these and give meaning to the learning itself.

Ausubel is considered to be a representative of cognitivism because his theory focuses more on cognitive learning than on affective or psychomotor learning. Meaningful learning for Ausubel therefore is "the organization and integration of material within the cognitive structure" (Moreira, 1999, p. 152), and this takes place when new information anchors itself in relevant existing concepts or propositions in the subject's cognitive structure, increasing and modifying the subsuming concept. A subsuming concept, idea or proposition is one that already exists in the learner's cognitive structure and acts as an anchorage for new information. However, for this to happen, he states two conditions: the student must want to learn the subject matter in question, and the subject matter to be learnt must be "potentially meaningful", i.e., it must be capable of being related (or incorporated into) the learner's cognitive structure in a non-arbitrary and non-literal fashion." (Moreira, 1999, p. 156).

According to Hassard (2004) Ausubel proposes a number of learning phases, which can be divided into three stages: the use of advance organizers (an explanation of what is to be done); presentation of learning task or material (organised explicitly, following a logical order, and engaging students in meaningful learning); and reinforcement of cognitive organization by relating new information to the advance organizers referred to earlier and encouraging active learning. The word "organization" is a keyword in meaningful learning, both in terms of storing new data and recovering data to use it or to anchor new information; concept maps can potentially be used as strategies to facilitate meaningful learning and as instruments to evaluate this learning.

3.3 Lapli Methodology

LAPLI is a methodology for a hybrid course in a virtual learning environment aimed at foreign-language students who have already completed basic and intermediate-level courses (Marriott, 2004). It uses the activities linked to integrative Computer Assisted Language Learning (CALL), which promote a shift from rote-mode to meaningful-mode learning, involving concept mapping, collaborative and meaningful learning, Computer Mediated Communication (CMC), the Internet and a virtual learning environment (VLE). It was first implemented with 23 pre-service teachers taking a fourth semester towards a degree in English and Portuguese languages at the Catholic University of Parana (PUCPR) in Brazil from August to December, 2003.

LAPLI is a carefully planned course in which the framework is provided by the teacher but the material is produced by the students. It is based on LOLA (The Online Learning Lab), a distance learning methodology proposed by Torres (2002) which consists of 12 activities in which the emphasis is placed primarily on reading and writing but also on the development of oral skills. The 12 activities in LAPLI come together as a process which balances individual and group work whilst at the same time allowing students to interact. Whenever students meet either face-to-face or virtually, to produce a piece of written text or to work in pairs or groups to brainstorm or to revise a fellow student's concept map or article, for example, they must interact and exchange information either in written form (synchronously or asynchronously) or orally, during these face-to-face classes.

While they are carrying out research, selecting reading texts using LAPLI activities, students are activating their previous knowledge and background information. They are also practicing scanning, skimming, extensive and intensive reading (Brown, 1994) and developing cognitive and meta-cognitive strategies such as predicting and inferring the meaning of new words and structures (Nicholls, 2001; Bastos, 1998). Meaningful learning is stimulated when students select their topic for research, pair up with colleagues who have the same area of interest, when they construct and add details to concept maps of their choice as well as when they get involved in the construction of group articles and the final presentation of their selected topic. As Brown (1994, p. 340) states "much of what is required to make a good writer can be learnt more effectively in a community of students". This process of activities is intended to arouse the interest of students and challenge them to overcome their limitations and make full use of their potential, while at the same time motivating them to work interactively and collaboratively.

The intellectual acts of processing and constructing meaning and of creating something different and new collaboratively are important to learning and to LAPLI. Its activities form the process that underpins this approach, and the target language is the instrument that the students use to develop the activities. Working contextually with the language, students practise fluency and communicative skills in Stage 1 (Message Oriented) and accuracy in Stage 2 (Language Oriented) by first working individually (in cycle 1) and then collaboratively (in cycle 2), bringing many different perspectives and sharing their experiences in the foreign language classroom. All LAPLI activities are repeated in cycles determined by the course duration. In the experiment described in this chapter, we carried out three cycles of activities.

3.3.1 Lapli Activities

Using LAPLI, students need to work collaboratively and meaningfully and to interact in the foreign language to take decisions about subjects, timescales and teams, using the foreign language as a tool to achieve goals while they develop fluency (in activities 1–8) and accuracy (activities 9, 10 and 12) (Marriott & Torres, 2006). They communicate both face-to-face and via the use of synchronous and asynchronous tools, such as Chat, Forum or E-mail, available in their VLE. In this paper we discuss all LAPLI activities, illustrating them around the theme "Raising Bilingual Children" as developed by one of the groups researched. However, it is the activities directly linked with the use of concept maps which are be described in greater detail for our research purposes.

3.3.1.1 Activity 1: Inserting Links and Comments

The first LAPLI activity is called Inserting Links and Comments. This activity defines the topics/content that will be studied, discussed and developed by the students throughout the 12 activities in LAPLI. Students are free to choose their

3. Collaborative and Meaningful Language Learning Through Concept Mapping 53

topic of interest by doing research on the Internet on subjects relevant to their course work, selecting interesting material from trustworthy sites. Figure 3.1 presents the links students published in the VLE. In Cycle 1 (in August) students worked individually through the activities whereas in Cycle 2 (in September) the links had to be chosen in pairs or groups, working collaboratively. Figure 3.1 also illustrates the research interests of this particular LAPLI group.

Teaching Literature - Fiction and Non-Fiction	04/08/2003
Children's book	04/08/2003
ENGLISH LANGUAGE	04/08/2003
HOME EDUCATION	04/08/2003
Learnig English	04/08/2003
Educating children with autism	04/08/2003
"education+children"	04/08/2003
Family Involvement in Children Education	04/08/2003
Teacher's help	04/08/2003
young children education	04/08/2003
Educating Children and Youth in Homeless Situation	04/08/2003
Education	04/08/2003
Cardiac Children	04/08/2003
Music at Fox Chapel	04/08/2003
Teaching English	05/08/2003
Bilingual children understand written language ...	06/08/2003
Quality of Teaching	06/08/2003
Learning English at home	06/08/2003
Home education for your child	06/08/2003
Deaf and Music.	12/08/2003
How to be an English teacher	21/08/2003
Resources for involving families in Education	01/09/2003
Beethoven life (before and after his deafness)	01/09/2003
Resources for involving families in Education	01/09/2003
Deafness Resource Foundation	01/09/2003
About Learning English	01/09/2003
Internet Grammar	01/09/2003
About Learning English 2	01/09/2003
Picture Books by Dandi Pa...	01/09/2003
Bilingual children	04/09/2003
Bilingual Children 2	04/09/2003
Bilingual Children with Down Syndromes	04/09/2003

Fig. 3.1. Links selected by students in cycles 1 and 2.

When assessing material for its suitability, students have to scan several texts, brainstorming and comparing previous knowledge against the "new information" on screen for content and for a level of vocabulary and grammar appropriate to their level of understanding (meaningful learning), making a decision in the end to either keep this link or discard it. They make judgments and inferences, develop reading techniques (Brown, 1994) and linguistic skills. To publish their selection in the VLE, they need to write a brief comment on the text selected firstly by indicating the reason for their choice and secondly by persuading colleagues to read it and join them in their research (Fig. 3.2).

Torres (2007) emphasizes that material chosen by students for teachers and students is just as useful as that chosen by teachers. Teachers and students thus establish a true partnership which helps them play a collaborative, active and mainly reflective role in the process of knowledge acquisition and production.

Links		
	Título:	Bilingual Children 2
	URL:	http://iteslj.org/Articles/Rosenberg-Bilingual.html
	Autor:	Student 11
	Data:	04/09/2003 21:22:18
	That is a very good site about the subject. I hope you all like.	

Fig. 3.2. Bilingual Children 2.

The following three activities (Activities 2, 3 and 4) form part of a mini-sequence of collaborative activities in which students work on each other's topics, texts and materials, sharing their point of view and stimulating their colleagues' linguistic and communicative development.

3.3.1.2 Activity 2: Questioning Existing Knowledge

The second activity is Questioning Existing Knowledge. By preparing questions, the students become active and reflective participants in the process. Students review the links selected by their colleagues in the VLE and are free to choose any text/article to elaborate two or three questions on, provided these questions are made from another's contribution. The purpose of these questions is to (a) stimulate colleague(s) to think more deeply about the topic being researched; (b) encourage the development of his/her/their skills as a researcher; and (c) encourage the development of linguistic and communicative skills in a meaningful way. They work either individually (Fig. 3.3) or in groups (Fig. 3.4) and publish the questions on the VLE Forum tool. After reading literature uploaded by the teacher on "What makes a good question?" and discussing this topic in the Forum, students interested in the topic of Bilingual Children formulated the following questions, as illustrated in Figs. 3.3 and 3.4 below:

11/8/2003 21:43:55	Student 15	Bilingual children understand written language...	1
Questions about Student 11's link: 1. What called your attention to this site? 2. Where can we find more information about bilingual children? 3. Do you agree that a child "who is exposed to two languages at an early age, and simultaneously, will naturally learn to use both languages?" Why?			

Fig. 3.3. The questioning activity – Cycle 1.

4/9/2003 22:09:21	Students 13, 18 and 22	Bilingual children 2	1
1. Why does a family decide to raise their kids with 2 or more languages? 2. How do you define "bilingualism"? 3. What is the proper age to start developing bilingualism?			

Fig. 3.4. The questioning activity – Cycle 2.

The theme "Bilingual Children" attracted the attention of other students, who chose this topic to elaborate their questions (links that are not interesting or inviting may not attract any questions). Question 2 (Fig. 3.3) and question 3 (Fig. 3.4) are more factual questions, whereas Questions 1 and 3 (Fig. 3.3) and 1 and 2 (Fig. 3.4) are more conceptual and encourage students to interpret, compare issues, analyse, synthesise and evaluate. The answers to these questions require students to elaborate their own thoughts, challenging them to go beyond their linguistic and communicative limitations, encouraging them to express themselves.

3.3.1.3 Activity 3: Construction of the Concept Map

The construction of a Concept Map is the third LAPLI activity. This is where the students work with a text proposed by a colleague in the inserting-links activity. In the face-to-face lesson previously, students received some introduction to the benefits of using concept maps (CM) for language acquisition. It would help them (a) to develop their reading strategies; (b) to practise an analysis of the big picture as well as the supporting level of details in a text; (c) to incorporate new language and link new concepts expressing their understanding/thoughts of how those concepts relate to each other; (d) to improve oral skills when working collaboratively and linguistic skills in the exercise of selecting verbs/prepositions/linking words to connect the selected concepts; and (e) to use the CMs as a guide for the development of their own articles later on. To learn more about concept mapping, students were encouraged to explore links made available to them in the Links section and to do some more research on the topic. A PowerPoint presentation explaining the benefits of concept maps and how they can be created was also prepared and made available to them for consultation. The maps produced by the students for their colleagues were published by the students who produced them in the VLE. One of the maps produced in Cycle 1 is presented below:

This is the first time this group of students had experienced making concept maps and most of them faced some difficulties. In the example in Fig. 3.5 (Text from: The Internet TESL Journal, Vol. II, No. 6, June 1996, available at http://iteslj.org/ Articles/Rosenberg-Bilingual.html), although the main concepts were used and were organised hierarchically, showing that to some extent meaningful learning had taken place (Arbea & Campos, 2004), the student was unable to link the concepts.

Although s/he could identify some key words in the text and incorporate them into the map, a relationship is not made clear because of a lack of linking words. Therefore the reader can not quite understand how the concepts are related, nor can s/he be sure if this student has quite understood what s/he has read. These aspects were re-addressed and discussed with him/her during the feedback with the Summative and Formative Assessment Table (SFAT – presented in Sect. 3.6) and s/he was encouraged to implement the necessary changes to the map. As a matter of fact, students were encouraged to edit their maps and resubmit them for assessment until they were happy with them, but were reminded that they needed to publish their

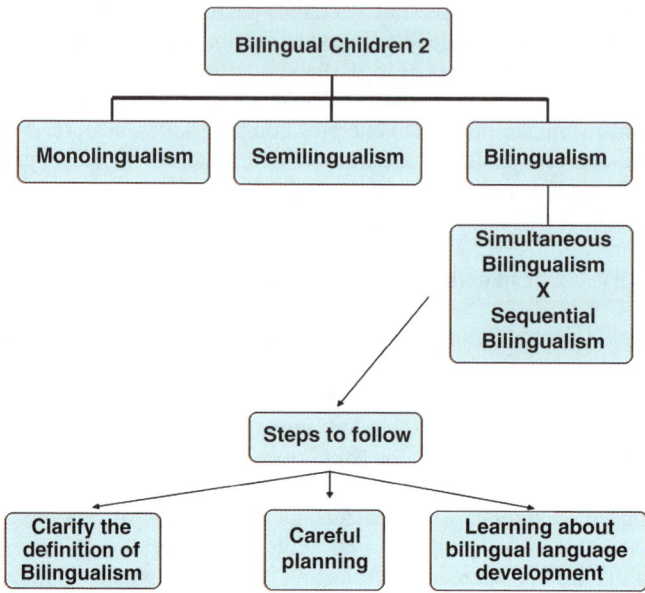

Fig. 3.5. Map produced individually by student 8 on the link selected and published by student 11 (Fig. 3.2 – Bilingual Children 2).

most recent version onto the VLE for future use (a revised version of this map is presented in Activity 6). Students were also advised to make use of a proper tool to build concept maps (such as CmapTools) which automatically prompts for the use of a linking word to join concepts.

With more practice and as a result of feedback given with the SFAT and making use of a proper tool, the quality of the students' maps improved, as can be seen in the map shown in Fig. 3.6, which was produced collaboratively by another group of students (3, 8 and 17). Nevertheless, before discussing this map an explanation is necessary on how students formed groups according to similar interests.

Until Activity 9 in cycle 1, students worked individually exchanging ideas and communicating but with no real need to defend opinions, negotiate meaning or justify choices. However, to engage in the tasks in Activity 10, Production of Group Article, they needed to decide on who they would be working with to form groups of similar interests. To do so, they could either use the Chat, Forum or e-mail facilities in their VLE. This class of students decided that making this decision synchronously via Chat would be the best option. The following Table 3.2 represents the conversation developed by students 5, 9 and 11 in the theme under study "Raising Bilingual Children". The sentences in yellow denote private exchanges between two students.

The choices considered by the three students was to work with either "bilingual children" or "home education" (although "children literature" was also considered by student 9 (21:31)). However, to make up their minds they decided to revisit the Links section (21:20 and 21:31) to check on the new links made available. After debating

3. Collaborative and Meaningful Language Learning Through Concept Mapping

on the topic in a very democratic way (21:12, 21:23, 21:2821:29), student 11 decides on "bilingual children" (21:29) and student 5 agrees to this, saying that it will be possible to incorporate "home education" under the same umbrella (21:32). Having formed groups at this stage, students worked together whenever possible in cycle 2.

Table 3.2. Chat to select research topic and group colleagues.

21:11 *Student 09 speaks to all*: *Student 05 and Student 11*: what are you going to write about? I liked the topics: bilingual children and home education but now there are so many new topics that I'll have to take a look at them
21:12 *Student 09 speaks to all*: *Student 11 and Student 05*: What are your interests?
21:13 *Student 09 speaks to all*: My link was about bilingual children but I chose Student 10's link about home education to do the questions, concept map and lexical list
21:15 *Student 05 speaks to all*: I also like the topic home education, it's so interesting
21:16 *Student 11 speaks to Student 09*: Hi, Student 09. Ok We can talk about your link, home education, or ....
21:20 *Student 11 speaks to Student 09*: I'll go to the Links section and take a look, ok?
21:23 *Student 05 speaks to Student 09*: What is your topic? I want to read and so to decide what we can write
21:28 *Student 09 speaks to all*: Student 05 and Student 11, What do we choose? Home education or bilingual children?
21:29 *Student 09 speak to Student 05*: Student 05 and Student 11: as far as I understood you liked the links I mentioned, are they ok? So, which one do we choose?
21:29 *Student 11 speaks to Student 09*: bilingual children
21:30 *Student 09 speaks to Student 05*: So Student 05, do you agree about bilingual children?
21:31 *Student 09 speaks to Student 11*: Student 11, let's wait to hear from Student 05
21:31 *Student 09 speaks to Student 11*: I like this topic very much. But I also wanted to study about children literature
21:32 *Student 05 speaks to Student 09*: Yes, for me is ok because I can speak about my link too. My link is about home education and home education includes bilingual children
21:32 *Student 09 speaks to Student 05*: So my group is Student 05 and Student 11, so we form 3

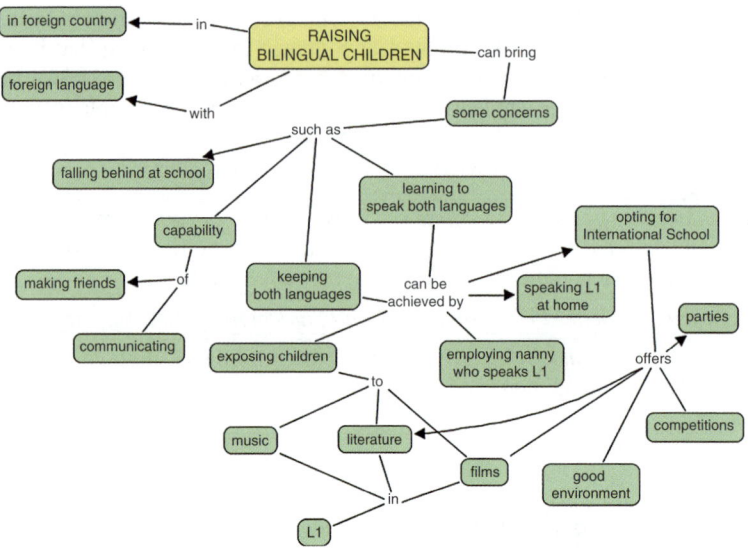

Fig. 3.6. First version of map built collaboratively (in cycle 2) by students 3, 8 and 17.

The activity of building a concept map in cycle 2 is more challenging than in cycle 1. Students have to work together, face-to-face or at a distance, synchronously or asynchronously to meet the deadline. However, the practice and formative feedback in the previous cycle has provided them with some knowledge and experience to face the challenges of building a map collaboratively. Figure 3.6 illustrates the map produced by students 3, 8 and 17 as part of the mini-cycle of collaborative activities in cycle 2.

The map produced above, on a new link published in cycle 2, is the students' first version. However, it is already possible to notice an improvement (as compared to the maps in cycle 1) in the map's whole structure, with some proper links, concepts in boxes, and propositions.

At this stage, the biggest difficulty experienced by the students was to work collaboratively. When working individually (map in Fig. 3.5), students are free to choose what to include and how to link the concepts, there is no need to negotiate, justify or defend a point of view. On the other hand, when working in groups, students need to negotiate and come to a consensus on every single concept/linking word used. Thus, they practise not only their linguistic skills but also their argumentative and persuasive skills. They need to come to a consensus on what to include and on how to express their thoughts in the map.

Although their maps show successful propositions ("Raising Bilingual Children"/ "can bring"/"some concerns"/"such as"/"falling behind at school") to come to this result was "not easy". They reported that, when editing the map asynchronously, some of their contributions had been changed or disappeared and that they had difficulty making themselves understood. Moreover, some students complained that they needed more time to work on the map. By overcoming their fears when trying something new and unfamiliar to them (Muirhead, 2006) they develop their communicative, social, problem solving and critical thinking skills as well as their self-trust and autonomy.

Nevertheless, in spite of all the difficulties faced, the feedback to us about the usefulness of working with concept maps was that "It's a clear way to visualize all the pieces of information that you need but working with others is sometimes frustrating" (student 19), "Concept maps help us organise ideas and working online was a very interesting experience" (student 12), "It is very important nowadays to work with visual things and working with the proper tool really helped" (student 8) and "Concept maps help us see the subject better, and then we can learn and understand faster and more easily" (student 23). Moreover, when asked if they considered concept mapping a meaningful activity in LAPLI, 60% of students said Yes (with 26.67% of them saying "very useful") (Marriott, 2004, p. 256).

It should be pointed out that the students faced three challenges in this activity: 1) learning to make the maps; 2) understanding how to build them in hybrid classes; and 3) making them as part of a collaborative activity, i.e., helping fellow students understand the text/link and write their own article.

The students' contributions reflected both the effort made by some of them to summarise the information extracted from the articles and the evolution of the maps during the cycles. At the beginning, some of the students only used keywords and phrases and no linking words (as in the map by Student 8 illustrated earlier) whereas others made use of very long sentences connected in a non-systematic way. However, after revising their maps, they started using verbs, prepositions and conjunctions to link concepts and the concepts themselves had no more than 5 words (a challenging skill to master for some students). Nevertheless, participation in this activity, taking into account individual and team contributions, was 88.67%. (Marriott, 2004, p. 166).

Creating a concept map requires time, concentration and an understanding of the material being studied so that the student can identify and relate the concepts being worked upon. Students who are used to ticking off answers and doing exercises that do not challenge them usually find this technique difficult, as it requires them to adopt a different approach. Once again, the student must take responsibility for his/her learning and behave proactively. As far as learning a foreign language is concerned, the exercise involving placing nouns in boxes and connecting them logically and coherently with verbs, prepositions and linking words makes the student work with the language, changing verbs into nouns, adjectives and adverbs to establish relevant connections.

3.3.1.4 Activity 4: Construction of Lexical List

The activity of constructing a Lexical List consists of preparing a list of vocabulary related to the subject that appears in the text. It is the student's responsibility to identify the vocabulary related to the subject, prepare a list and look for the meaning of the vocabulary (if s/he/they feel it necessary). In the following cycle, this list is retrieved and expanded with the new terms/nouns and verbs that appear in the text of the newly inserted links made available in that cycle. Table 3.3 illustrates some of the terms in this groups' Lexical List compiled in cycle 2.

Table 3.3. Lexical list in cycle 2.

Teacher, this our Lexical List:	
Bilingualism – Monolingual – Semilingualism – Simultaneous Bilingualism – Sequential Bilingualism – Borrowing – Reading abilities – Literacy – Bilingual schools – Bilingual environment – literature	More likely to – To raise – To keep both languages – To employ – To mix two languages – To recognise – To give into temptation

This progressive compilation into a single list during the work cycles provides information for the students to write individual and group texts, and the relationships between the terms can (sometimes) be visualized on the corresponding concept map.

3.3.1.5 Activity 5: Answering Questions

In this activity, students answer questions drawn up by their colleagues from the second activity. In this answering activity, students must choose, either individually (cycle 1) or in groups (cycle 2), the questions in the VLE Forum tool they want to answer in this task (not necessarily the questions asked on their link). To help prepare answers, the students can make use of all the texts and concept maps that they, their fellow students or teacher have published in the virtual environment. They can also make use of other sources, which must be made available to their peers. Some answers to the questions formulated in Activity 2 are provided in Table 3.3.

Table 3.4. The answering activity.

1. What called your attention to this site?
This site called our attention because it can answer very interesting question, like: "What is Bilingualism" or "How can we teach a child to be Bilingual" and etc
2. Where can we find more information about bilingual children?
You can look for specific books that will bring you good information about this topic
3. How do you define "bilingualism"?
It is difficult to define bilingualism, because there is not only one closed definition, for some people it is the ability to understand two languages but speak in only one and for others to understand and speak in both languages. As we are discussing about children, parents or teachers have lots of expectations about them, so there is a chain that considers bilingualism as knowing also the literature in both languages
4. What is the proper age to start developing bilingualism?
Actually, we think that any age is good to learn, but a good bilingual person could be created since he/she starts to speak. We can work first with single words in the middle of the sentences, and then start reading them bedtime stories... But the main thing is, we have to make this with pleasure, to show the kids that it is good learn other things

The freedom to choose which questions to answer poses some difficulties (Table 3.4). Should students choose an easy to answer question or a more difficult one? According to Torres (2002), students select the questions based on two criteria (1) interest or usefulness; or (2) ease or difficulty. Choosing to answer question 2 just gets the job done, but compromises their learning. On the other hand, questions 1 and 3 forces the student to elaborate an answer and to practise the new vocabulary in a meaningful and communicative way. Question 4 could have been simply answered "From birth", but this student understands that giving a short answer will not help practise or develop his linguistic skills and instead develops quite a nice answer bringing in new vocabulary such as "bedtime stories" and "make this with pleasure".

Giving students choices empower them, makes them more critical and responsible for their learning as well as encouraging them to develop linguistic and communicative skills in a meaningful way.

3.3.1.6 Activity 6: Adding Details to Concept Maps (CM+)

In this activity, students revisit their original links/texts and identify all the work that has been done on it by fellow colleagues (concept map, questions and answers). They then familiarise themselves with all this material and update their maps, thus creating *CM+*. (In the event that no concept map has been created on his/her link/text, the student creates his/her own.) In addition to completing the map itself, the aim of this activity is to develop the student's analytical and critical abilities by stimulating a comparison of the map with the text. According to Reynolds (2004), editor of *Prentice Hall Writing Center*, activities involving revision by fellow students encourage students to develop their own skills rather than depend on the teacher's trained eye. Nonetheless, this process of concentrating helps internalise grammatical structures and more advanced vocabulary, thereby enabling the student's foreign-language learning to advance to another level, both in terms of content (ideas) and form (language).

To illustrate this activity, we present CM+ below, created by students 7 and 14, which was constructed based on a revised version submitted by student 8 (the first version being introduced in Activity 3, Fig. 3.5).

It is possible to see that to construct CM+ (additions in green) presented above, students had to revisit the original text to read it more intensely. They identified more key supporting ideas to define "simultaneous bilingualism" and to define what a "bilingual" has the ability to do, linking one or two concepts in the box by a preposition or a verb with a preposition, making the map clearer and easier to follow. (The changes implemented by student 8 onto her/his revised version are discussed in section 4, Formative and Summative Assessment of Concept Maps.)

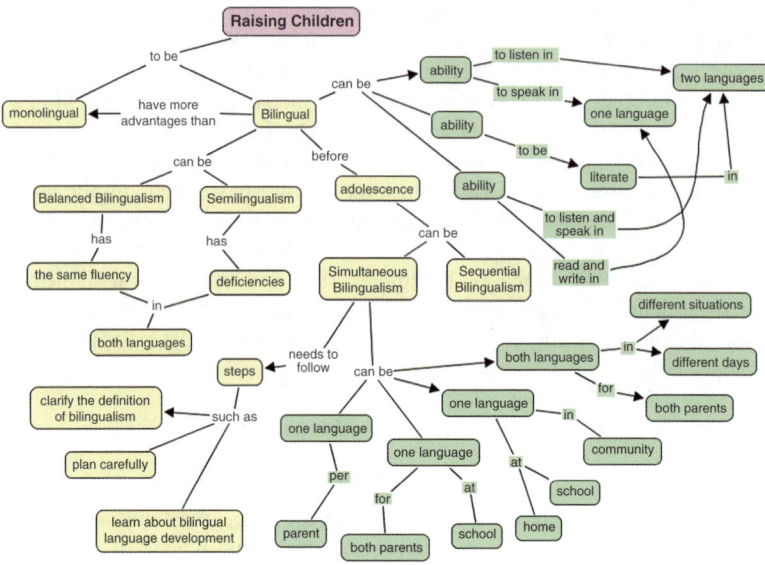

Fig. 3.7. CM+ created collaboratively by students 7 and 14 in cycle 2, built upon revised version of map presented in Fig. 3.5.

3.3.1.7 Activity 7: Elaborating a List of Linking Words

Elaborating a list of linking words involves identifying and listing conjunctions/linking words that the author has used to express a point of view, give an opposite opinion, explain, list, or, in short, ensure that the text is cohesive from the beginning to the end so that the students could use it later to write their own articles.

Some Linking words identified by this group of students were:

And / As / But / While / Yet / In general / At any rate / Another

3.3.1.8 Activity 8: Commented Reading

Commented reading offers students an opportunity for the development of oral skills. It involves having a group discussion (face-to-face or via videoconference) of the texts selected by the teacher. In this activity, each team is responsible for reading a text, which must then be discussed. After the discussion, the team must write a commentary on the text they read. This must be published and may be the subject of new commentaries by other teams. During this collective process of critical analysis of the contents of the text, the students manage heterogeneity. The texts read and discussed by this group of students were related to "Learning English on the Internet" and "How to write an article" as preparation for Activities 9 and 10.

3. Collaborative and Meaningful Language Learning Through Concept Mapping

3.3.1.9 Activity 9: Research on Grammar Topics

In the Internet-based research into Grammar Topics, preparation of material and presentation to fellow students, students consider their own experienced limitations when expressing themselves in the foreign language. These limitations were previously identified during the negotiations and opportunities created to develop fluency with fellow students. They then look for theoretical and grammatical explanations for ways of expressing themselves unambiguously. In order to help colleagues with learning in relation to this grammar point, they then prepare a short explanation and interactive exercise (using the VLE and PowerPoint resources), which they present to the other students. Once again, students are given the opportunity in this activity to practise their oral skills and to act as "researcher-creator of the current history" (Torres & Bochniak, 2003).

3.3.1.10 Activity 10: Production of Group Article

In this activity, Production of Group Article, the objective is for students to produce an article on a topic that is relevant to the overall subject. Just before this activity starts, the students need to form groups and define the topic for the article that is to be produced. This choice is the result of a dialogue between all the members of the group. A process of negotiation is thus started between members of the team who must exchange ideas, overcoming conflicts, resistance and communication problems to produce knowledge collectively.

The Production of Group Article is divided into 3 stages. The first (Ind_R) and second (Ind_RGR) stages of this activity are carried out individually. Students are encouraged to refer back to all material produced, (concept maps and CM+, lists of linking words, lexical lists, questions and answers) and write an article on the topic/link from a personal point of view, from a personal perspective. Table 3.5 illustrates this stage with Ind_R1 from one of the students from our focus group.

Table 3.5. Ind_R1 by Student 11.

Raising Bilingual Children
Bilingualism isn't something simple. Raising kids to be bilingual requires careful planning and learning about bilingual development. Bilingualism doesn't simply happen and one language is usually dominant. There may be periods when one language is more used than the other but the opposite occurs with a change in the environment. The term *balanced bilingualism* describes those that possess about the same fluency in two languages and *semilingualism* those who have deficiencies in both compared to a monolingual. Each child learns a language at his/her own speed. Some problems may occur to children when they were exposed to sequential bilingualism. In this case, parents should contact a bilingual speech-language pathologist to have an appropriate evaluation of their kids languages skills.

After receiving feedback from the teacher, implementing the necessary changes and uploading the revised version in the VLE, students are ready to prepare their second piece of text, which is a reflection on the groups' articles, Ind_RGR (Table 3.6). They do this by putting together all the individual articles produced by members of their group, combining all different perspectives and data into one article.

Table 3.6. Ind_RGR1 by Student 9.

Raising Bilingual Children

Bilingualism isn't something simple. Raising kids to be bilingual requires careful planning and learning about bilingual development. Bilingualism doesn't simply happen and a good thing to do first is to define bilingualism. For some people bilingualism means to have an equal ability to communicate and to be literate in both languages. For others having the ability to listen in two languages but speak or have greater skills in just one. In today's global world it's certainly advantageous to be bilingual. Because of today's appeal to accept and celebrate cultural differences, people feel freer and more willing to promote bilingualism presenting their kids with this opportunity. Parents, and teachers have lots of expectation but first there must be a discussion about it.

One language is usually dominant. There may be periods when one language is more used than the other but the opposite occurs with a change in the environment. The term *balanced bilingualism* describes those that possess about the same fluency in two languages and *semilingualism* those who have deficiencies in both compared to a monolingual. Each child learns a language at his/her own speed. Some problems may occur to children when they were exposed to sequential bilingualism. In this case, parents should contact a bilingual speech-language pathologist to have an appropriate evaluation of their kids languages skills.

Finally, the third and final piece of writing (Group_Art) is in fact one of the pieces of text written in stage two which is selected by the group as the best example, i.e., the one that presents the information more clearly, is better structured, and has more examples and quotes. This piece of text is then expanded to include more information, the Group_Art from previous cycles and the groups' opinion on the subject, making it a truly collective piece of work. Table 3.7 below (part 1 and 2) illustrates the students Group_Art2 (from cycle 2).

From the texts illustrated above, it is possible to see how the process of LAPLI activities have contributed to their creation. The words highlighted in different colours demonstrate the activities from which these parts of the text originate. The bits of text highlighted in yellow illustrate concepts and linking words found in the concept maps in Activities 3 and 6. The words in pink are from the students' Lexical List in Activity 4. The words in blue relate to one of the answers given in Activity 5. Finally, the words in green are Linking Words, from Activity 7.

The pieces of text presented above were also evaluated in a formative and summative way by the teacher, and these are the revised versions. The major difficulty with this activity is the revision process (submitting, revising, resubmitting, re-revising, resubmitting) and the publishing of the latest revised version within the deadline for it to be used by colleagues in subsequent stages. As mentioned in the introduction, this group worked though the specific activities three times (three cycles) and their final Group_Art3 production was 4 pages long, including front cover and references.

In this section we have examined examples of text produced by a group of students working around the theme "Raising Bilingual Children". Topics developed by the other groups in this class were: "The Education of Young Children with Downs Syndrome", "CALL – Computer Assisted Language Learning", "Different Ways to Learn English", "Deafness, Education and Family" and "Learning English on the Web".

Table 3.7. Group_Art2 – by Students 5, 9 and 11 (Part 1/2).

Raising Bilingual Children

    Bilingualism isn't something simple. Raising kids to be bilingual requires careful planning and learning about bilingual development. Bilingualism doesn't simply happen and a good thing to do first is to define bilingualism. For some people bilingualism means to have an equal ability to communicate and to be literate in both languages. For others having the ability to listen in two languages but speak or have greater skills in just one. In today's global world it's certainly advantageous to be bilingual. Because of today's appeal to accept and celebrate cultural differences, people feel freer and more willing to promote bilingualism presenting their kids with this opportunity. Parents, and teachers have lots of expectation but first there must be a discussion about it.

    Family goals vary. Some families want to maintain and share their primary language while others want to provide better possibilities for work in the future. For Marsha Rosenberg[1] it doesn't really matter what the goal is. What makes successful bilingual raise is a language plan, taking time to consider the kids' development in the two languages and making the necessary commitments to bilingual language development. One of Rosenberg's suggestion's is to evaluate kids in speech language besides the other languages proficiency (listening, speaking, reading, writing). However, some parents are concerned sometimes that child will fall behind at school, will not be able to make friends or communicate well.

    Psychologist Ellen Bialystok research tells us that bilingual children are more likely to learn how to read faster than monolingual ones. Knowing two languages helps them recognize a word by its characters and its sound without the help of pictures. Bilingual children understand symbolic relations and recognize that the writing carries a meaning and that the picture is irrelevant with it. This will help children learn how to read. Bialystok's recent research proves that being a bilingual at a very young age will help reading abilities.

    Parents can provide a bilingual education for their kids so that they can achieve good reading abilities while also exposing them to stories and literature in both languages and employing a nanny that speaks their language.

Marsha Rosenberg. In her article from The Ambassador, The American School in Japan Alumni & Community Magazine Spring – 1996. Taken from internet: http://iteslj.org/Articles/Rosenberg-Bilingual.html

Table 3.7. Group_Art2 – by Students 5, 9 and 11 (Part 2/2).

Another way of doing this is opting for a bilingual school, sometimes called International School. Bilingual schools are concerned about globalization and want to prepare their students to think in both languages so that they can do well professionally. They are also worried about the whole group so they employ the best teachers in town. The school provides a good bilingual cultural background through discussions, competitions, parties, exchange programs besides offering a good environment with sports, literature, and sightseeing tours. This could be a good possibility in providing a bilingual environment for the children.

    In her article, Marsha Rosenberg cites the two types of bilingualism: simultaneous learning and sequential or successive bilingualism. Kids that are exposed to two languages simultaneously at an early age will learn to use both languages. Sequential bilingualism happens when a child is exposed to a second language after having one established language already. There's no critical age to develop a second language but kids tend to develop more native-like pronunciation before adolescence.

    One language is usually dominant. There may be periods when one language is more used than the other but the opposite occurs with a change in the environment. The term *balanced bilingualism* describes those that possess about the same fluency in two languages and *semilingualism* those who have deficiencies in both compared to a monolingual. Each child learns a language at his/her own speed. Some problems may occur to children when they were exposed to sequential bilingualism. In this case, parents should contact a bilingual speech-language pathologist to have an appropriate evaluation of their kids languages skills.

    Raising bilingual children should be carefully considered to be successfully achieved by kids. Consistency, balance between the languages and good quality of the languages interactions are factors that need to be taken in consideration by parents. If the plans are made and the parents are committed, raising their children to be bilingual will be a successful task.

3.3.1.11 Activity 11: Evaluation

The Evaluation activity is a moment of self-reflection. It is carried out within the large group at the end of every cycle. It is an informal session that can be carried out orally (via videoconferencing or face-to-face) or in a written format (by means of a questionnaire) in the Forum. In these evaluation sessions, students are encouraged to think about the process, and not the product, of learning a foreign language using this methodology. The teacher talks to all the students as a group about their progress in the exercises, their experience of working collaboratively and at a distance, the obstacles they have faced and how they have coped with and overcome these difficulties, as well as the successes achieved in terms of why they think they have achieved these and what they did to achieve them.

3.3.1.12 Activity 12: Production of a PowerPoint Presentation

In the final activity, which is carried out only in the last cycle, students are asked to produce a PowerPoint Presentation on their findings. Their job now is to summarise their work into about 10 slides. The objective of this last exercise is to create a formal opportunity for the students to practise their new vocabulary and structures orally, concentrating both on fluency and on accuracy.

3.4 Concept Map Activity: Formative and Summative Assessment

As the building of a concept map can potentially be an activity that challenges not only a student's linguistic and creative skills but also taps into their world knowledge, the criterion for correcting these maps should not just be simply whether or not they are *right* or *wrong*. A map reflects the knowledge of what has been understood and the point of view of the student who created it, so that it is a unique form of expression. Therefore, when evaluating these maps, we must take into account how the student expresses these relationships. For example, whether s/he builds propositions (two nouns linked by a verb(s), linking word(s) or preposition) that are scientifically correct, if these propositions reflect the student's understanding of the subject matter being studied at that particular moment and if they associate it with the student's previous knowledge, as it is essential that the map provide "evidence that the student is learning the material meaningfully" (Moreira, 1999, p. 7).

In order to assess our students' concept maps, we sat down with them and revised what the characteristics of a good map were and how they had used these principles to build their map. A good map is one that has a hierarchical structure, with correct and concise links between concepts and cross-links relating concepts that are further apart (Novak (2003). Furthermore, in terms of language use, we also recapped on how to link two concepts (by a verb(s), preposition or linking word(s)). Finally, we talked about the importance of creativity when making the map and how students felt about their finished map.

Table 3.8 below constitutes our assessment table and details on the assessment of the first version of the map produced by student 8 (presented in Activity 3, Fig. 3.5):

3. Collaborative and Meaningful Language Learning Through Concept Mapping   67

Table 3.8. Formative and Summative Assessment Table (FSAT).

Criterion	2.5 points	1.5 points	1 points	0 points	Number of points
Subject studied	Includes all the main concepts studied	Includes most of the important concepts studied	Many important concepts are missing, but the map shows that an effort was made	No effort made	1,5
Are links between concepts scientifically established? Do they show an understanding of the subject studied?	Shows relevant and significant links between concepts and an understanding of the content	Shows some relevant and significant links and an average understanding of the content	Shows little effort to link concepts in a relevant manner and poor understanding of the content	No effort made	1,0
Presentation, ramifications and hierarchy	Easy to read, clear and accurate, with ramifications and relevant structural hierarchy	An acceptable effort, but a bit difficult to read although the ramifications and hierarchy are shown	Very difficult to read, with few ramifications and showing difficulty in arranging concepts hierarchically	No effort made	1
Creativity	Shows a high level of creativity, with five or more relevant concepts and five or more cross-links, some distant, included	Shows average creativity with about three relevant concepts and three cross-links, some distant, included	Shows minimal creativity with only one relevant concept included and about one cross-link established	No effort made	0
Total number of points	3,5 / 10				
General comments on the map (with suggestions and questions)	In your map, you have included some key words from the text in a hierarchical way. Well done! However, you have not used any linking words to express how these concepts are linked. Do you think you could include them in your revised map? Also, could you establish a cross-link in your map?				
Result of the student / teacher discussion, with self-assessment	I will re-read the text and try and understand how the concepts are linked and I will try to establish at least one cross-link.				

In the table above (based on the a prepared by the Department of Continuing Education, Faculty of Nursing, South Dakota State University, http://learn.sdstate.edu/nursing/ConceptMap.html), our aim is to combine and satisfy the need for two types of assessment, namely, formative and summative assessment. With constructive comments and suggestion of alternatives, the teacher attempts to get students to think about their map in terms of content, form and creativity. During this self-assessment, the student must try to reflect on the map-building process, taking into account the teacher's comments, and thus developing his/her metacognition.

Taking into consideration this assessment, students then reflected on their maps and re-submitted them. Therefore, comparing the first map in Fig. 3.5 (by student 8) with the concepts in yellow as presented in Fig. 3.7, it is possible to see how this map has evolved. In the final version presented by student 8, one can notice that:

- Concepts are now liked meaningfully by a verb, preposition or linking word
- The item "Simultaneous Bilingualism X Sequential Bilingualism" was broken down into two separate concepts "Simultaneous Bilingualism" and "Sequential Bilingualism"
- The concept "adolescence" was added to join "Simultaneous Bilingualism" and "Sequential Bilingualism" to "Bilingual", forming the propositions "Bilingual"/"before"/"adolescence", "adolescence"/"can be"/"Simultaneous Bilingualism" and "adolescence"/"can be"/"Sequential Bilingualism"
- A cross-link was established between the legs "Bilingual" and "monolingual", producing the proposition "Bilingual"/"has more advantages than"/"monolingual"

This exercise of reducing phrases into concepts and of linking them appropriately make students think more on the linguistic level of the maps and the reusability of concepts, which in turn assists them when trying to establish cross-links. The changes made not only contributed to the text's overall flow and presentation but also, importantly, made the student work on the vocabulary level while also thinking of the content of the propositions and on the overall message of the map. His/her revised version was also assessed using the same criteria and this time his/her score was higher and also importantly, this student reported feeling "very proud" of the revised map and now "having a much better idea of how to construct them". Comparing this student's production in both versions, it is possible to draw the conclusion that the assessment carried out has contributed to develop of his/her linguistic skills and meta-cognition.

This assessment table is shown to future students before they build their first concept map so that they can become familiar with the evaluation system and know not only what is expected of them but also how the teacher will assist them in the process. This sharing of responsibility in the learning process helps to shift the focus from teacher-centred teaching (transmissive pedagogy) to student-centred teaching (constructivist pedagogy) and greatly helps to develop autonomy and self-confidence.

The process of building a concept map is more important than the product (Novak & Canas, 2004). It is by reflecting on content and form in the search for a more concise way of expressing old and newly acquired knowledge that students develop their linguistic, critical and creative skills.

3.5 Results and Discussion

Learning a foreign language with the LAPLI methodology can be a challenging journey for students. In the group of students investigated, concept mapping, collaborative learning, a mixture of face-to-face with distance learning lessons, the use of a VLE and research on the Internet (as a fundamental part in the process) were all innovations in their syllabus.

Of all these innovations, the ones that took students the most out of their comfort zone were concept mapping and collaborative learning. The activity of concept mapping did this because at first they did not have access to the right tool (firewall at the university). Once this was not an issue, it was possible to concentrate on mastering how to build a concept map. However, this required an understanding of the text which in turn had to be read as many times as necessary. Once the message was understood, reducing phrases into key words proved difficult for some of the group. For others, linking the concepts meaningfully was more challenging and establishing cross-links involved "seeing the map from the top". In spite of these difficulties, when responding to our end-of-term questionnaire, 93% of those taking part recognised the contribution of concept maps to the development of their reading comprehension and writing skills (Marriott, 2004, p. 253–254).

As regards collaborative learning, 60% found this difficult (14% found it very difficult). (Marriott, 2004, p. 251). What caused the most problems was having to wait for colleagues to produce own work and upload the most updated version onto the VLE so that they could then proceed, as there were deadlines to be met. Other points mentioned were "I had difficulty getting my opinion across - I didn't have much space for that"; "It's difficult to accept and be accepted by others"; "It's difficult to accept our mistakes" and finally a student very honestly wrote "I need to

3. Collaborative and Meaningful Language Learning Through Concept Mapping

learn to accept different opinions". Other general difficulties faced were regarding access to the Internet and missing the presence of the teacher in all the lessons.

One very important aspect of working collaboratively with students in a VLE and with multiple tasks and files is the management and naming of all the files. The teacher must give clear guidelines for the naming of work as in Fig. 3.8 below:

```
Remember to follow these guidelines for naming your files:
CM_Name_of_link_yourname
LexL_Name_of_link_yourname
Ind_R1_yourname
Ind_RGR1_yourname
Group_Art1_Yourname_yourfriendsname(_yourfriendsname)
```

Fig. 3.8. Guidelines to students for naming files.

Moreover, clearly named folders must be provided for work to be uploaded and found for future reference as in Fig. 3.9:

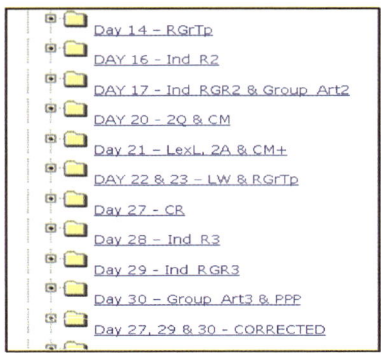

Fig. 3.9. File management in VLE.

Therefore, "Peter's" Concept Map in cycle 2 should be named "CM_Bilingual-Children2_Peter", and should be uploaded onto the File "Day 20_2Q_&_CM". The teacher's feedback would be marked "CM_BilingualChildren2_Peter_OKRs" meaning "marked but needs resubmission" and "CM_BilingualChildren2_Peter_OKPb" meaning "marked and can be published". A revised version of his work would be named "CM_BilingualChildren2_Peter_OKRs_2" and the teacher's evaluation would then be "CM_BilingualChildren2_Peter_OKRs_2_OKPb". This explicit organisation and following of a logical order encourages students to learn meaningfully (Hassard, 2004).

It is therefore possible to conclude, from an analysis of the students' work in Activity 10, that the aims of the 12 activities in LAPLI have been met and that a gradual linguistic development can be seen in the texts produced. Students worked meaningfully around a topic of their own choice; they interacted and worked collaboratively with colleagues; they developed their linguistic and communicative competence in informal situations (activities 1 to 8 – to develop fluency) and worked in more formal situations (activities 9, 10 and 12) to develop their reading, writing and oral skills. When working synchronously or asynchronously in the various activities 100% of students felt their vocabulary had increased, 20% felt it had increased significantly, and that they had developed their critical, analytical and evaluative skills when searching for texts and working collaboratively in a fellow's text or map. Additionally, they felt they had developed responsibility, autonomy and timekeeping skills by exercising their freedom of choice and meeting deadlines, as per Marriott (2004, p. 255).

3.6 Closing, but Not Final, Comments

Having aroused an interest in the collaborative approach to research and the aim of meaningful learning in language acquisition through the use of concept maps and continuous evaluation of the learning process, we offer by way of conclusion, and particularly for reflection, a few comments, which can never be conclusive; hence, the above title "Closing, but not final, comments".

Teachers and educators have long sought teaching/learning techniques that could not only help students understand the meaning of a text more easily and summarise and represent the information more quickly, but would also allow them to reflect on their experiences, build complete new meanings and develop strategies for creative and intelligent thinking.

Concept mapping is a way of achieving this goal. By concept mapping, students use their background knowledge and work on content and form while they are invited to use their creative and metalinguistic skills. However, this activity can prove a challenge to students used to more traditional teaching methods as it demands concentration and perseverance in finding the correct way (in terms of form and content) to convey their ideas. It is very suited to the foreign language classroom as it encourages students to work with the target language in a responsible and critical way, primarily if used collaboratively with a means of formative assessment such as we have proposed in the LAPLI methodology presented here.

As educators, we must sow the seeds of responsibility and critical analysis, encouraging research and knowledge production using computers and the Internet, as well as promoting interaction and collaboration among students to improve the quality of education. However, we must also face the challenge brought about by technology, for example the implementation of concept mapping and CALL methodologies such as LAPLI in virtual reality worlds such as Second Life and Web 2.0 technology (O'Reilly, 2005). Portable, wireless and pocket-size handheld devices such as mobile phones, palmtops, tablets and iPods and media files i.e. podcasts and mobilecasts are also challenges. According to Chinnery (2006) MALL - Mobile Assisted Language Learning is an emerging trend together with concepts of m-learning (mobile learning) or m-Education (Bull, 2006, p. 33), and research must continue on how to better implement these new technologies into the foreign language classroom.

References

Arbea, J. e Campo, F. D. (2004) Mapas Conceptuales Y Aprendizaje Significativo de Lãs Ciências Naturales: Análisis de Los Mapas Conceptuales Realizados Antes Y Después de La Implementación de Un Módulo Intruccional sobre La Energía. In: Cañas, A.J., Novak, J. D. and González, F. M., *Concept Maps: Theory, Methodology, Technology.* (pp. 45–48). Proceedings of the First International Conference on Concept Mapping. Vol. 2, Pamplona

Bastos, H. H. (1998) A escrita no ensino de uma língua estrangeira: Reflexão e prática. In V. L. M. Paiva (Ed.) *Ensino de Língua Inglesa: Reflexões e expressões.* Campinas:Pontes

Brown, D. (1994) Teaching by Principles: an Interactive approach to Language Pedagogy, New Jersey: Prentice Hall Regents

Bull, G. (2006) mLearning. *Beyond eLearning: practical insights from the USA – Global Watch Mission Report*, 31–34. Available at http://www.oti.globalwatchonline.com/online_pdfs/36688MR.pdf, retrieved in 25.07.2007

Chinnery, G. M. (2006). Emerging technologies: Going to the MALL: Mobile Assisted Language Learning. *Language Learning and Technology*, 10(1), 9–16. Available at http://llt.msu.edu/vol10num1/pdf/emerging.pdf, retrieved in 25.07.2007

Gonzáles, T., Bermejo, M. L. e Mellado, V. (2004) Los Mapas Cognitivos Elaborados a Partir de Entrevistas, Un Procedimiento de Análisis para Comprar Las Concepciones Del Profesorado Sobre La Enseñanza de Las Ciencias. In: Cañas, A.J., Novak, J. D. and González, F. M., *Concept Maps: Theory, Methodology, Technology.* (pp. 201–205). Proceedings of the First International Conference on Concept Mapping. Vol. 2, Pamplona

Hassard, J. (2004) *Meaningful Learning Model* – Georgia State University. Available at http://scied.gsu.edu/Hassard/mos/2.10.html retrieved in 08.03.2004

Marriott, R. C. V. (2004). Do LOLA – Laboratorio On-Line de Aprendizagem ao LAPLI – Laboratorio de Aprendizagem de Linguas: uma Proposta Metodologica para o Ensino Semi-Presencial em Ambiente Virtual. (From LOLA – The Online Learning Lab – to LAPLI – The Language Learning Lab: a Methodological Proposal for a Hybrid Course in a Virtual Environment) Curitiba, PUCPR. (Masters Thesis)

Marriott, R. and Torres, P. (2006) LAPLI – The Languages Learning Lab: A methodological proposal for a hybrid course in a virtual environment. In: P. Zaphiris and G. Zacharia (Eds.), *User-Centered Computer Aided Language Learning.* (pp. 133–151). USA: Idea Group

Moreira, M. A. (1999) *Aprendizagem significativa*. Brasilia: Editora da UnB

Moreto, V. P. (2002) *Construtivismo – a produção do conhecimento em aula*. 3rd edition, Rio de Janeiro:DP&A

Morón, C. M. A. (2004) Los Mapas Conceptuales en Humanidades: *El* Quijote, La Cultura. In: Cañas, A.J., Novak, J. D. and González, F. M., *Concept Maps: Theory, Methodology, Technology.* (pp. 447–455). Proceedings of the First International Conference on Concept Mapping. Vol. 1, Pamplona

Muirhead, B. (2006) Creating Concept Maps: Integrating Constructivism Principles into Online Classes. *International Journal of Instructional Technology and Distance Learning* 3(1). Available at http://itdl.org/Journal/jan_06/article02.htm, retrieved in 25.07.2007

Nicholls, S. M. (2001) Aspectos pedagógicos e metodológicos do ensino de inglês. Maceió/EDUFAL

Novak, J. D. (2003) *The Theory Underlying Concept Maps and How To Construct Them.* Cornell University. Available at http://cmap.coginst.uwf.edu/info/ retrieved in 20.08.2003

Novak, J. D. and Canas, A. J. (2004) Building on new constructivist ideas and Cmap tools to create a new Model for Education. In Canas, A. J., Novak, J. D. and Gonzales, F. M. (Eds.), *Concept maps: Theory, methodology, technology*. Proceedings of the First International Conference on Concept Mapping. Pamplona, Spain: Universidad Publica de Navarra

Novak, J. D. and Gowin, D. B. (1999) *Aprender a aprender*. Lisboa: Plátano Edições Técnicas

O'Reilly, T. (2005) *What is Web 2.0 – Design Patterns and Business Models for the Next Generation of Software.* Available at http://www.oreillynet.com/pub/a/oreilly/tim/news/2005/09/30/what-is-web-20.html retrieved in 25.07.2007

Reynolds, J. (2004) *Collaborative Learning*. Writing Center – Prentice Hall, Pearson, 2004. Available at http://wps.prenhall.com/hss_reynolds_phwrite_1/0,8308,1034767-site_search_frame,00.html retrieved in 03.03.2004

Silva, M. (2001) *Sala de Aula Interativa*. Rio de Janeiro:Quartet, 2ª. ed.

Smith, B. L., and MacGregor, J. T. (1992) What is collaborative learning? In: *Collaborative learning: A sourcebook for higher education*. University Park: National Center on Postsecondary Teaching, Learning, and Assessment, Pennsylvania: Pennsylvania State University

Telebinezhad, M. R. (2007) The Effect of Explicit Teaching of Concept Mapping in Expository Writing on EFL Students' Self-regulation. *The Linguistics Journal* 2(1). Available from http://www.linguistics-journal.com/April_2007_mrt&gmn.php, retrieved in 25.07.2007

Torres, P. L. (2002) O Laboratório On line de Aprendizagem: uma proposta crítica de aprendizagem colaborativa para a educação. Florianópolis, UFSC (Doctoral Thesis)

Torres, P. L. (2007) Trama do conhecimento. In: Torres, P.L. (org.) *Alguns fios para entretecer o pensar e o agir*. Curitiba: SENAR-PR

Torres, P. L. and Bochniak, R. (2003) Na Pedagogia da Pesquisa a resposta para os temas transversais. In: Torres, P.L. (org.) *Uma leitura para os temas transversais*. Curitiba: SENAR-PR

4. Thinking Maps®: A Visual Language for Learning

David Hyerle

Thinking Foundation, Founding Director www.thinkingfoundation.org;
Plymouth State University, Plymouth, New Hampshire, USA, Visiting Scholar

Abstract. There have been a range of different types of visual tools used in schools over the past 50 years such as "graphic organizers," mind mapping, and concept mapping. These tools are grounded in the mapping metaphor, reflecting our capacities to network information and create cognitive maps of content knowledge and concepts. This writing investigates a language of eight cognitive maps called Thinking Maps® and Thinking Maps® Software, used from early grades through college courses to foster cognitive development and content learning across disciplines by all students across entire schools.

4.1 The Mapping Metaphor

Mapping is the overarching metaphor for teaching, learning, and the representation of knowledge in the twenty-first century. This rich conceptual metaphor has a role in helping us understand how visual tools and technologies support learners in their capacity to transform information into knowledge in the "flat world" of communication technologies working 24/7. The common vocabulary of our time – *networking, connectivity, world wide web, interdependence, systems, integrated*, and *internet* – are expressions of the mapping metaphor. Mapping is both a metaphor for connecting and overlapping knowledge structures and also the name for practical visual tools for mental fluency. Mapping is a rich synthesis of thinking processes, mental strategies, techniques and technologies, and knowledge that enables humans to investigate unknowns, show patterns of information, and then use the map to express, build, and assess new knowledge.

The mapping metaphor is understandable and intriguing in a technological sense, yet ultimately this is about power sharing in the creation of knowledge. The gulf between our students' relatively high technological expertise and underdeveloped mental fluency is one of the key barriers we must move beyond in order to enact positive change through knowledge sharing in schools, the workplace, and in global communication. So the mapping metaphor also opens up a central dilemma: our students may be networked to information webs, yet few have developed congruent thinking tools that enable them to consciously pattern information into meaningful, integrated, networked knowledge. At this time in classrooms and workplaces, in lesson plans and meetings, memos and voice/text messages, our communication is often dominated by the one dimensional thread of linear language, a narrow representation that keeps our ideas hidden away in rich but unknown mental spaces, a *terra incognita*.

4.2 Cartography and Cognition

Historically, the unique representations derived from map making are best expressed through the history of cartographic links to cognition and communication, which reveals that this invention was a turning point for human understanding:

> The act of mapping was as profound as the invention of a number system. The combination of the reduction of reality and the construction of an analogical space is an attainment in abstract thinking of a very high order indeed, for it enables one to discover structures that would remain unknown if not mapped (Robinson, 1982, p. 1).

This quotation is drawn from James H. Wandersee's (1990) insightful analysis of the connection between cartography and cognition. He argued persuasively that cartography links perception, interpretation, cognitive transformations, and creativity serving four basic purposes: to challenge one's assumptions, to recognize new patterns, to make new connections, and to visualize the unknown.

Cartography has always been a central form of storing vital information about our surroundings and distant shores, from the ancient mappings of the earth and sky. Humankind has always sought ways to discover and map new frontiers and find our way home by land and sea and, most recently, by air. Cartography has been both a science and a gateway to new learning, but until the last few decades the term "mapping" has stayed within the intellectual domains of astronomers and geographers. Actually, from Africa to the Mayan astronomers, maps have been the documents of discoverers and ownership, and then, often, of domination. If a "discoverer" could map a region, then ownership was established. Planting a flag was a symbolic gesture, but mapping the region was the act of establishing physical boundaries and territories.

The attempt to discover longitude in the eighteenth century was foremost in the minds of seafarers, traders, and governments, as latitude and longitude lines crossed and established the relationships between time and space that could guide adventurers and conquerors alike to unknown lands. The Lewis and Clarke expedition across the western region of North America, like any other journeys into new landscapes, was an attempt to map territories unknown to a new republic so that commerce and land holdings could expand. The "map" that Lewis brought back to President Thomas Jefferson was technical in the geographic sense, commercial in the description of resources, and ethnographic in depicting cultures new to the adventurers:

> Lewis studied maps in Jefferson's collection. He also conferred with Albert Gallatin, a serious map collector; the problem was that west of the Mandans nearly to the coast was terra *incognita*. And the best scientists in the world could not begin to fill in that map until someone had walked across the land (Ambrose, 1996, p. 80).

Now we send captainless ships to distant planets to map and in some cases "own" new territories off the curvature of the earth. The "four corners" of our globe are known, and our technical expertise is often hopscotching over our immediate needs. We have access to electronically mapped terrain through GPS, or global positioning systems. We may be in our car with a map on a screen, guiding us around the corner or into another state. Likewise, and using similar technology for networking information, some of our children, are now interactively using computer screen portals from wireless connections, accessing linked data from points around the world, thus from different points of view. Those views may range from electronic explorers of knowledge on "the net" to mass marketers of goods to exploiters of graphic violence and other morally repugnant materials. They have few filters for all of this information packaged as knowledge.

Our technologies offer exponentially increasing quantities of downloadable information, but few ways of filtering information into practical knowledge. There are few unknown territories in the physical world: the new territories are of human imagination, interaction, communication. We are mapping the human genome system as well as all the systems of the body and mind. The brain is based on pattern seeking and mapping and thus we use cartographic means to discover how we think: we use fMRI's to map that organ of our body that is continuously and unconsciously remapping reality for us every moment.

Educators are now seeing in practice and in the research that visual tools such as MindMapping® (Buzan, 1979), Concept Mapping™ (Novak & Gowin, 1984) and Thinking Maps® (Hyerle, 2004) are supporting students to transform information into useful knowledge. These tools are also facilitating diverse learners from across a range of multiple intelligences (Gardner, 1983) and dispositions of thinking, or Habits of Mind (Costa, 2001) Students are transforming information into knowledge using these applied "mapping" languages in seeming congruence with the unconscious, associative networking of the brain. Pat Wolfe, a leader in the translation of evolving brain research for practitioners offers this connection: "Neuroscientists tell us that the brain organizes information in networks and maps." (Wolfe, Forward in Hyerle, 2004).

4.3 The Cognitive Dissonance of Linear Representations

High-quality visual tools are used for surfacing dynamic schemas, graphic representations that externalize in dynamic blueprint form the conceptual information structures, within the architecture of the brain. This is why visual tools are a breakthrough in education and not just another tool on the sagging toolbelt of endless and uncoordinated "best practices" for teachers. It is now clear that the traditional linear strings of words students see in textbooks and hear from teachers in dominantly "auditory" classrooms do not even come close to approximating the complex visual-verbal-spatial patterning of what is going on in their heads.

Our minds consciously create patterns, our emotions are driven by layers of interconnected patterns of experience, our media thrives on the communication of patterns, and nature – that which we are a part of and surrounds us – is a complex weave of patterns. Some of these patterns are linear and procedural, but the foundation of knowledge from the basic factual knowledge record to decision making borne of evaluative processes are nonlinear patterns. Are thoughts linear? Emotions? An ecosystem? Our values?

Put in the most stark terms, our educational *system* and educational leaders can no longer lag behind the children who sit before handheld computers and access, download and create a complex interweaving of information as we stand before them and speak and write and numerate in linear strings of words and numbers. There is *cognitive* dissonance between the highly constrained linear presentation of information in classrooms as text blocks and the multidimensional, mapping of mental models that the brain-mind naturally *performs* when processing and crafting information into knowledge. I believe that this dissonance is *the* fundamental barrier to improving students' thinking and teachers' capacities to convey and facilitate basic and complex content and conceptual learning for all students.

The double meaning in the term "cognitive" dissonance is clear: *cognitively* we process beyond the linear mindset but we asked students to show their thinking primarily in linear terms. This is disorienting at a most fundamental level. Visual tools *do not* offer a replacement of traditional forms of literacy but an additional way of "showing what you know" that is shifting our perception of knowledge on the most basic level. Why? Because visual tools of every kind, from brainstorming webs and graphic organizers to thinking process mapping are all based on the metaphor of the visual-spatial-verbal *mapping of knowledge*. Like any breakthrough technology, this transformational technology of the mind – the hand drawn and technology based mapping of mental models – includes that which came before. The visual mapping of information into knowledge is what the brain does already and emerges in an historical sense of mapping physical space.

From the point of view of how knowledge is represented, there is a fundamental disconnect between how students and educators SEE and understand knowledge. The primary reason for this is that most educators, as most educational researchers, are primarily text drive and auditory: we live not only by the idea of text books and the spoken word, but also that information is valid only when substantiated in linear text *blocks and strings of sentences*. To find out something we have traditionally read text out of books. To find out what students know we have them write text blocks to us or speak to us in strings of words. This has been our guiding definition of literacy for longer than we can remember. One of the main reasons that learners young and old often have writer's "block" or their thinking is "blocked" is that a guiding metaphor for information could be called the "wall of text." The linear wall of text does not explicitly show the rich networks and patterns of thinking that the author is attempting to present through the only form available: linear representations. When visual tools are presented along side text or used by learners to find the patterns embedded in the wall of text, then what is unveiled is the rich foundational structures of knowledge.

Recently I was working with teacher and administrator leaders from a school system in New York State and, after presenting an overview of visual tools within the context of some of the conclusive research and practice, the literacy coordinator for the district broke through the paradigm for defining "literacy" in classrooms and dramatically offered this epiphany: "For all of these years, I thought it was all about my students speaking and writing, but now I understand that what I really wanted to know was how my students were thinking." The breakthroughs in how we represent information, ideas, and concepts have been occurring over the past 20–30 years from the first uses of brainstorming webs for prewriting processes to concept mapping and systems to diagramming, to an additional, synthesis language of visual tools called Thinking Maps®.

4.4 A Summary Definition of Visual Tools

Visual tools are used by learners, teachers, and leaders for graphically linking mental and emotional associations to create and communicate rich patterns of thinking. These visual-spatial-verbal displays of understanding support learners in *transforming static information into active knowledge*, thus offering additional representational systems for integrating texts of different kinds into visual displays. These visual forms also support the processes of information in linear ways (such as traditional flow charts) and in nonlinear forms such as systems feedback loops and hierarchical category structures. These additional forms for generating, organizing, and reflecting on information offer metacognitive tools for self-assessment in each content area and for interdisciplinary learning that may unite linguistic, numerical, and scientific languages together on the same page.

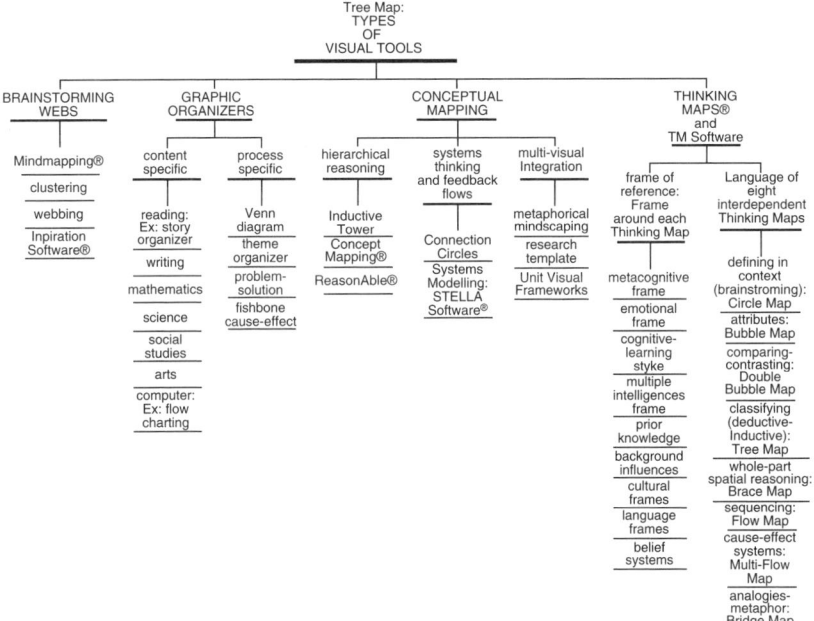

Fig. 4.1. Tree map of types of visual tools.

As shown in Fig. 4.1, I have identified three informal, sometimes overlapping categories of visual tools, each with specific purposes and congruent visual configurations:

Brainstorming webs for fostering creativity and open mindedness;
Graphic organizers for fostering analytical content and process-specific learning;
Conceptual mapping for fostering cognitive development and critical thinking.

A fourth category is a unique synthesis *language* of visual tools that has been used extensively across schools called Thinking Maps® since 1990 (Hyerle, 1993, 1996; Hyerle & Yeager, 2007). This common visual language of visual tools integrates the creative dynamism of webs, the analytical structures of content-specific learning, and the continuous cognitive development and reflections fostered through conceptual mapping. Over time, new visual languages may develop that integrate different visual tools and thus enabling a greater range of thinking, communication and reflection.

Visual tools are used for personal, collaborative, and social communication, negotiation of meaning, and networking of ideas. These graphics are constructed by individual or collaborative learners across media networks and mediums such as paper, white boards, and computer screens. Because of the visual accessibility and natural processes of "drawing out" ideas, many of these graphics are used from early childhood through adulthood, and across every dimension of learning, teaching, assessing, and leadership processes. Visual tools are also used across cultures and languages and may become keys to new levels of more democratic participation and communication in human systems. Across traditional cultures and new "virtual" cultures, visual languages ultimately may be used for uniting diverse and distant learning communities as people in schools, communities, businesses and in different countries *seek to understand* each other through *seeing* each others' thinking and perceptions through multiple frames of reference.

In reviews of practical applications of visual tools (Hyerle, 1996, 2000) it is clear that there are significant differences between student developed maps and what are common known as "graphic organizers." There are many published resource materials that include preformed, highly structured graphics for students to fill in, much like checklists and simple worksheets. Some of these resources are helpful as they guide students through particular processes in an orderly way. The downside becomes evident over time as students may never gain the capacity to map out their own thinking independently from these sturdy, but limiting scaffolds. In contrast, visual tools, that are generated from a blank paper or electronic page *by students* enable them to become the center of learning in order to create conceptually rich models of *their* meaning. While the processes of training students to become independent visual tools users takes time, once students gain basic mastery over the tools from they are able to transform concrete information and concepts bound by linear texts into maps that show patterns that add depth to their understanding of content knowledge. Visual tools offer a third way through the great false dichotomy which we as educators have endlessly debated since the time of John Dewey: *Should we focus more on content area facts or thinking process instruction*? I believe that dynamic visual tools offer a third way that triangulates this dichotomy, as visual tools are used for integrating content information and cognitive processes into *forms of knowledge*. Visual tools offer teachers and learners mental maps for trans*form*ing in*form*ation into knowledge using fundamental thinking patterns as the foundation.

4.5 Thinking Maps®: A Synthesis Language of Visual Tools

As shown in Fig. 4.1, a full range of visual tools has been developed and successfully used as pattern-tools for thinking creatively, organizationally, and conceptually. Some tools may focus more on one aspect of thinking and learning, or one form of representation, such as holistic, conceptual hierarchies or intricate feedback loops for representing dynamic systems over time. We can see through the use of these tools and extensive research how students are making sense of their own stored knowledge in displayed "visual schemata" and how they accommodate and assimilate new information and concepts through these richly developed visual tools: brainstorming webs foster creativity, graphic organizers explicitly model more analytical content processes, and conceptual mapping tools for explicitly focusing on conceptual understanding. The book detailing the theory, practice, and research on concept mapping, "Learning How to Learn" (Novak & Gowin, 1984) was an influential text as I began to see how a coherent language grounded in visual tools could be used to mediate learning and as new tools for assessment.

So it was reasonable – and practical as a classroom teacher – to consider and question how this wide range of tools could be synthesized, coordinated, and offered to students in a practical and meaningful way so that they could ultimately take control of their own patterns of thinking. Here are a few of the questions I asked myself as I was investigating and teaching with a range of visual tools in the mid-1980's when I was teaching middle school:

How could student centered visual tools be coordinated in way that they are generative like webs, analytic like organizers, and focused on conceptual learning? Could all learning be held in hierarchies or systems diagrams?

What would theoretically ground an organization of visual tools? How would we organize and link these visual tools?

How would this work in practical ways for students, teachers, and school leaders?

These questions were surfaced for me when I had an opportunity to use a program based on the explicit definition of fundamental cognitive skills – some displayed graphically – as the point of synthesis. The nexus of patterns of cognition and nonlinguistic representations became the theoretical and practical foundation of Thinking Maps as a language of eight nonlinguistic representations defined by fundamental cognitive skills.

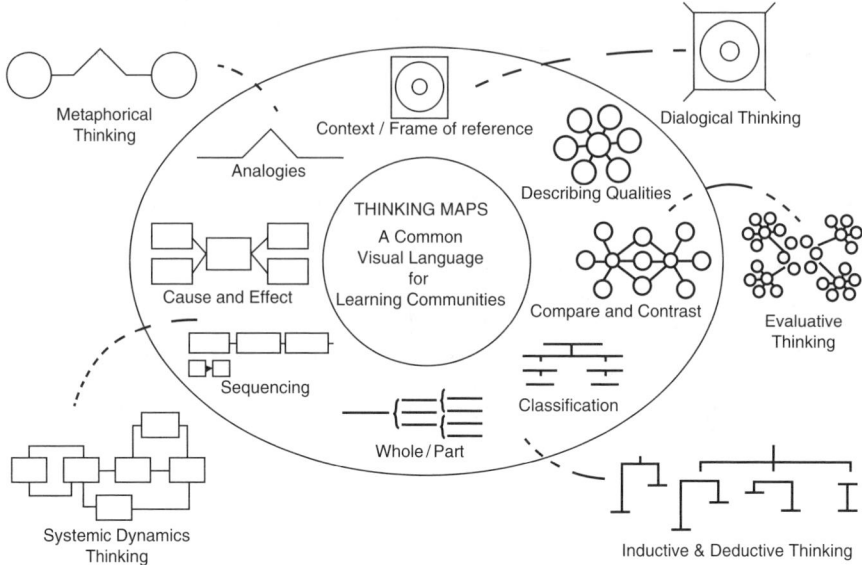

Fig. 4.2. Thinking Maps® as a common visual language.

Thinking Maps is a language for learning that has now been implemented through professional development training and systematic follow-up coaching in nearly 5,000 schools across the United States and internationally since 1990. Teachers, students, and administrators across entire elementary, middle, and high schools are introduced to this language in the first year of implementation through a professional development process that includes workshop training, follow-up coaching, and the development of deep applications in reading, writing, mathematics and technology. The primary outcome of the interactive professional development is that teachers work together over multiple years to *explicitly* teach all of their students across whole schools how to become fluent independent and collaborative users of this language for in depth content learning and transfer of the same language of thinking across all content areas and grades levels. This enables the continuous cognitive development for *all* students as a foundation for lifelong learning.

The effectiveness of Thinking Maps has been established through scientifically based research on nonlinguistic representations and graphic organizers, and extensively documented through test scores and qualitative evidence in academic publications since 1990. Most recently, over a dozen authors from the United States, New Zealand, and Singapore – from high to low achieving schools and from inner city to rural schools – presented the documented results and research on Thinking Maps implementation in the book "Student Successes with Thinking Maps: School based Research, Results and Models for Achievement Using Visual Tools" (Hyerle, 2004). At this time, the most common focus of use of the model, and the documented successes, come in the areas of reading comprehension and writing process. Ongoing research and development on Thinking Maps and other approaches to creating "Thinking Schools" is supported by the nonprofit organization, *Thinking Foundation* (www.thinkingfoundation.org) in order to document how these tools work across grade levels and content areas for a range of students with unique needs.

4.6 Thinking Maps as a Language

The language of Thinking Maps is first and foremost based on eight fundamental cognitive skills. These eight cognitive skills, as shown in the center two circles of Fig. 4.2 are based on a synthesis of cognitive science research, models of thinking developed for psychological testing and educational programs, and a transformation of Dr. Albert Upton's early work in book "Design for Thinking" (Upton, 1960). This model is neither linear nor hierarchical. The eight cognitive skills are: defining in context, describing attributes, comparing and contrasting, classification, part-whole spatial reasoning, sequencing, cause and effect reasoning, and reasoning by analogy. This "language" for thinking is not a comprehensive view of thinking: it identifies coherence and interdependency of eight *fundamental* cognitive skills that ground thinking and learning. Upton drew from his close study of the connection between thought and language and attempted to explain how underlying thinking patterns are intertwined with language. The first modern translation of the Upton Model as the foundation for Thinking Maps came when I systematically analyzed different thinking skills models, tests of cognitive skills, and the field of cognitive psychology. If you look within the outside rectangular frame, the extensions of the maps to more complex iterations are found. The essence of this model is that each tool (and the tools together) may be used at the most complex levels of the human mind.

This model is somewhat analogous to the primitives of any language, such as the eight parts of speech of the English language. The eight parts of speech, consisting of nouns, verbs, adjectives, etc. are used in an integrative, limitless way to produce phrases, sentences, and paragraphs. Of course, there is no hierarchy or procedural linearity in the use of the eight parts of speech. It is a language of eight graphic primitives, much like using the "legend" inset in most maps for reading the different graphic displays. While it is dangerous to proclaim universals – as possibly disrespectful to different cultures, language, and cognitive styles represented around the world – the eight cognitive primitives that ground Thinking Maps have found resonance and relevance as we have introduced the tools in places like Singapore, Japan, Mexico, and of course, in cities in the United States where large urban districts such as New York City work with at least 150 different student languages and dialects.

The claim offered here is that around the world, like universal human emotional patterns such as love, joy, and sadness, there are also basic universal cognitive processes: every child born into this world, for example, comes to learn how to *sequence* the day, *categorize* ideas and objects around them, break down objects *whole to parts* and parts to whole, survive by *causal* reasoning, and reason by *analogy*. For example, there is no doubt that every human being has a visceral if not always conscious understanding of the causes and effects of actions: we would not survive physically, socially, or emotionally in the world if we did not reflexively and reflectively use cause and effect reasoning. The challenging question for long term research is this: how are these cognitive processes mentally "mapped" within vastly different cultures?

Key to the understanding of the eight cognitive processes is the essential interdependence between and among each process, or pattern. The awareness by teachers and students of the *interdependency* of thinking skills is, I believe, a missing link in classrooms today. Educators at every level, and psychologists and researchers, simplify these processes by teaching and testing thinking skills in isolation from each other, implying the use of thinking skills rather than explicitly teaching the interdependency of the processes to students. Thus "thinking" is reduced to isolated skill development rather than as a complex of cognitive processes that must work together to enable students to think at the highest levels of creative and analytical thinking.

A central dimension of the Thinking Maps model is drawn from the field of frame semantics which describes how individuals and groups create personal, interpersonal, and social structures, or patterns, that drive perceptions, language, and behavior. In the context of the map, this means that everyone may understand and utilize the cognitive process of categorization, but the categories carry a different language, content, processes for development, and forms within and across cultures. After playing with and testing the eight maps in isolation and as a language of interdependent tools, I realized what was missing: a way for learners to name and visually represent what was influencing, or *framing* (Lakoff & Johnson, 1980) the thinking patterns they had developed using each Thinking Map. I realized that inherent in the metaphor of "frame" was the visual needed for facilitating reflection. I developed a simple rectangular frame that learners could draw, like a window frame, around any of the maps and thus ask many different reflective questions such as:

- What is influencing how I am seeing this information?
- What prior knowledge is helping or getting in the way of my understanding of this new content knowledge?
- Why did I chose this Thinking Map?
- Is there another or several other Thinking Maps I should use to understand this idea?

In retrospect, and from what we now know about the effectiveness of Thinking Maps from over 15 years of implementations in whole schools, the eight cognitive processes grounding the visual representations are most powerful when the learner adds this metacognitive frame of reference around the map being created. Once a students maps out their own thinking, we want the students to "frame" the map by asking themselves what may be influencing how they are mapping information. The frame offers a concrete visual for them to become self-assessing and metacognitive. When all learners in the classroom or school use the maps and frame, they see each others different ideas in different configurations and this has led to teachers and students having a deeper understanding and empathy for another person's point of view.

4.7 Five Qualities of Thinking Maps as a Language

While there are only eight maps – and the "metacognitive" frame that surfaces the culture, belief systems, and perspective of the maker of the maps – there is an infinite number of configurations of each map, much like the English language, which has only eight parts of speech but a vast number of combinations that create infinitely simple to complex variations. Five essential qualities of Thinking Maps are key to seeing how these tools are infinitely expandable and used simultaneously, as a carpenter would use multiple tools for constructing buildings. For example, using the Flow Map as an example, the map is

- Graphically consistent as the Flow is created with boxes and arrows only and can show substages;
- Flexible so as the graphic primitive expands, the flow can be linear and cyclical, or have multiple parallel flows connected;
- Developmental as it can be used at any age level and responsive to simple to complex applications;
- Integrative as it is used across disciplines and for interdisciplinary problem solving;
- Reflective as it is used by the learner to assess how they are thinking and share and compare the visual representations with one another and teachers.

These qualities of each tool and the tools used as a language lead to more complex orders of thinking, such as evaluating, thinking systemically, and thinking metaphorically. When students are given common graphic starting points, *every* learner is able to detect, construct, and communicate different types of patterns of thinking about content concepts.

Let's look at some examples of student work in order to highlight these key qualities of Thinking Maps. Some years ago I received a forty page document from a high school biology teacher outside of Chicago, IL, USA who, along with her colleagues, had systematically trained all of the students in the school to use Thinking Maps and software at a highly adaptable level. This document was a student's work that had been generated using Thinking Maps Software (Thinking Maps, Inc., 1997, 2007) developed over a year's course from a biology text. With most chapters she decided which maps best reflected the key information in the text, and with accuracy and great clarity displayed, for example, types of cells using a tree map and the properties of each, the cycle of cell, and dozens of intricate interrelated parts of a muscle using a brace map.

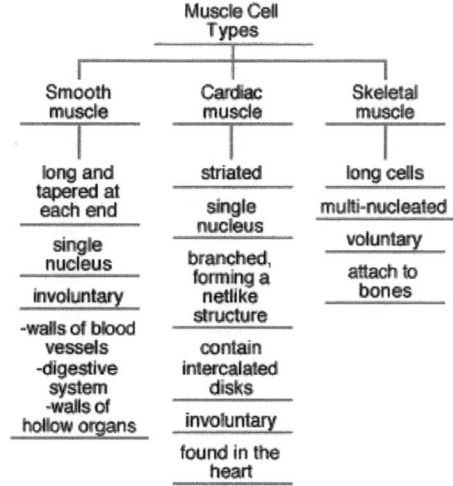

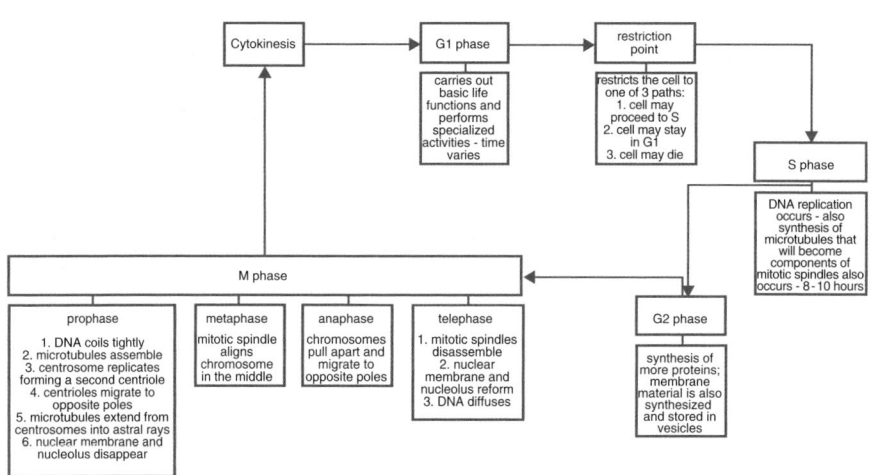

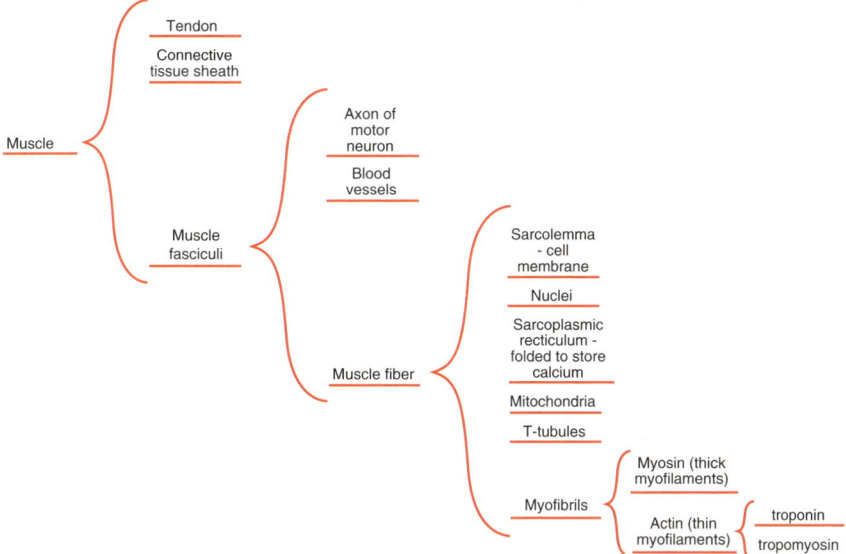

Fig. 4.3. Types of cells, cycle of cell, muscle parts.

She was also able to show in several maps that she could map out the feedback loops of different body systems, comparison of different processes, and properties of unique parts of the body. At the end of the year, with her notes contained in maps which reflected the conceptual content of the chapters, she was able to spread her documents out for review for exams. But her teacher was also able to assess how this student drew the information in the chapters together conceptually.

This student example also reveals aspects of the five qualities of the Thinking Maps language. The graphic consistency and flexibility of each tool enable this student to start with three different graphic primitives, expand each map, while holding onto the basic forms. Because of the common graphic unique to each thinking process, the student's teacher and peers could easily read and assess the map for factual content information, conceptual clarity, and interpretation. This student was also showing the advanced developmental progression from learning the basic elements of each map to complex applications, in this case using Thinking Maps Software. We see this developmental aspect of the maps as first grade students, college students, and school administrators alike are able to use each map in novel applications as they grow from novice to expert users of the tools. Given a full view of the forty pages of Thinking Maps developed by this student over the course of the year, we also witness both the integrative and reflective dimensions of the language. She was able to integrate multiple maps together (for example, information on types of cells and the cycle of a cell) and evolve a deeper understanding of how this information works together. This student also, along with her teacher, could use the maps as what Arthur Costa has called, "displayed metacognition." Teachers and students alike may use the maps for "bifocal" reflection by assessing the development of content/conceptual knowledge while also focusing on the cognitive development of the individual student. Most often in classrooms students' content knowledge is assessed through various means of assessment – including linear written responses and multiple choice items – but rarely are teachers and learners looking closely and over time at the development of thinking processes.

What is also interesting in the forty page document is that beyond the rich mapping of content knowledge, this student was able to work across different types of maps representing different knowledge structures. More specifically, she could map information hierarchically when needed, much like the dynamic form of Concept Mapping® developed by Novak and Gowin or the top-down design of software such as ReasonAble®. She was also able to surface and model feedbacks in systems much like the rich mapping of systems dynamics generated from using STELLA® software and other systems approaches. This reveals a unique characteristic of Thinking Maps as a language. Each visual tool comes with its own theoretical framework for *defining* how knowledge is constructed: concept mapping is based on holistic hierarchical logic and systems diagramming on interdependent feedback flows. This opens conversations in classrooms about how we *see* knowledge that does not surface often in the linear form of texts. Each visual tool thus offers students and teachers a theory of knowledge that is surfaced visually.

Thinking Maps, as a synthesis of different types of visual structures works together as a language based on eight different ways of seeing information, how knowledge is structured, and how these different forms may work together. The difficulties faced with the implementation of Thinking Maps in schools for faculty and students is the same as with many innovations. One of the most problematic issues is the concern teachers, administrators, and educational leaders have for staying focused on discipline specific learning and "content skills" such as, for example, reading comprehension, math, and science skills. Though there is a great degree of overlap, the idea of a generalized thinking and problem-solving model for students to use independently across disciplines is still antithetical to the existing structure of schools and common assessment factors. In this time of high-stakes testing in the United States, the pressure to focus on content specific skills overrides cognitive skills development and the facilitation of problem solving across disciplines. But the theoretical assumption that there is a common visual language for transferring "thinking skills" across disciplines also may be challenged by researchers and practitioners as a search for "fools gold." Thus, much of the professional development work that is conducted in order to sustain Thinking Maps across an entire faculty over multiple years is often driven by the need, as articulated by teachers and administrators, to continually find ways to refine the use of the maps to meet the specific assessments for passing a test or course. Where schools have sustained the use of Thinking Maps over multiple years to the point of students and teachers gaining fluency with the tools, the results show positive changes in student performance and teacher effectiveness. Where the tools are implemented with minimal follow-up support and without purposeful use as student centered tools, the work becomes merely an isolated set of graphics for isolated uses.

4.8 Whole System Change

The discussion of the range of different types of visual tools and the language of Thinking Maps presented in this chapter provides a new metaphor, and theory-embedded tools, for communication for students, teachers, administrators and the whole community of learners in a school. Through this we see that students develop essential Habits of Mind (Costa & Kallick, 2007): to be creative and flexible, to persevere and to be systematic, and to be reflective and self-aware of cognitive patterns to the degree that they can independently *and* interdependently apply these patterns to challenging performance. At any time learners can access this thinking language – using it on paper or through software – to construct and communicate networks of mental models of linear and nonlinear concepts. As students across whole schools become fluent with Thinking Maps, this array of eight visual tools becomes a common visual language in the classroom for communication, cooperative learning, and for facilitating a deep empathy for how others think as well as for the *continuous cognitive development* of every child over a lifespan of learning.

Yet, we also now know that our students must continue to grow and adapt over their lifespan. When we look forward into the decades of the twenty-first century with technology growing exponentially, we realize that explicitly supporting students in their capacities to think and problem solve independently and collaboratively across content areas, languages, and cultures may be one of the linchpins in an evolution in how we as human beings transform information into meaningful knowledge.

References

Ambrose, S.E. (1996). *Undaunted Courage*. New York: Simon & Schuster.
Buzan, T. (1979). *Use Both Sides of Your Brain*. London: Dutton.
Costa, A. and Kallick, B. (2001). *Discovering and Exploring Habits of Mind*. Alexandria, VA: Association for Supervision and Curriculum Development.
Gardner, H. (1983). *Frames of Mind: The theory of Multiple Intelligences*. New York: Basic Books.
Hyerle, D. (1993). "Thinking Maps as Tools for Multiple Modes of Understanding." Unpublished doctoral dissertation, University of California, Berkeley.
Hyerle, D. (1996). *Visual Tools for Constructing Knowledge*. Alexandria, VA: Association for Supervision and Curriculum Development.
Hyerle, D. (2000). *A Field Guide to Using Visual Tools*. Alexandria, VA: Association for Supervision and Curriculum Development.
Hyerle, D. (ed.) (2004). *Student Successes with Thinking Maps®*. Thousand Oaks, CA: Corwin Press.
Hyerle, D. (2008, in press). *Visual Tools for Transforming Information into Knowledge*. Thousand Oaks, CA: Corwin Press.
Hyerle, D. and Yeager, C. (2007). *Thinking Maps®: A Language for Learning Training Resource Manual*. Cary, NC: Thinking Maps, Inc.

Lakoff, G. and Johnson, M. (1980). *Metaphors We Live By*. Chicago: University of Chicago Press.

Novak, J. and Gowin, R. (1984). *Learning How to Learn*. Cambridge, MA: Cambridge University Press.

Robinson, A.H. (1982). *Early Thematic Mapping in the History of Cartography*. Chicago: University of Chicago Press.

Thinking Maps®: Technology for learning [Software]. (1997, 2007). Cary, NC: Thinking Maps, Inc.

Upton, A. (1960). *Design for Thinking*. Palo Alto, CA: Pacific Books.

Wandersee, J.H. (1990). Concept mapping and the cartography of cognition. *Journal of Research in Science Teaching, 27*(10), 923–936.

Wolfe, P. In Hyerle, D. (ed.) (2004). Forward. *Student Successes with Thinking Maps*®. Thousand Oaks, CA: Corwin Press.

5. The Constructivist Mapping of Internet Information at Work with Nestor

Romain Zeiliger[1] and Liliane Esnault[2]

[1]Centre National de la Recherche Scientifique, GATE, zeiliger@gate.cnrs.fr
[2]Ecole de Management de Lyon, EM LYON, esnault@em-lyon.com

Abstract. This paper presents the Nestor Web Cartographer software, its features, its user interface, the constructivist approach to mapping Internet information that guided its design and the experience gained after 10 years of use in academic contexts. We focus on five selected features such as the hybrid representation system, some original visual widgets, the groupware section, and we discuss their role within a constructivist approach. We argue that they favour the collaborative and incremental construction of formalized knowledge. A case study in Lyon School of Management (EM LYON) is discussed with more details.

5.1 Introduction

5.1.1 A Presentation of Nestor

NESTOR is a Web browser that draws interactive web-maps of the visited Web space during navigation: the objects that show on Nestor maps are the visited web documents and the links that have been used to reach them. The web-maps are hybrid in the sense that users can add objects of their own – concepts, links, personal documents, organizers – and progressively evolve the maps into concept-maps. The maps are interactive in the sense that they provide direct navigation back to the represented objects, and allow for a full set of drag-and-drop operations aimed at structuring the information extracted from the Web: Nestor combines graphical Web navigation and mind-mapping features. Nestor is also a collaborative software that enables small groups of people to share their navigation experience. To summarize we could say that Nestor promotes a constructionist approach to Web information mapping: "NESTOR's approach is to provide an interactive, stimulating environment where the learner's expertise is deployed, rather than drawing on knowledge held in some expert model as in a knowledge-based system" (Eklund et al., 1999).

5.1.2 A Brief History

Nestor was developed at CNRS-GATE laboratory. Its design started in 1996 and stretched over a period of 10 years with constant interaction with users mainly in academic settings: it was guided by Participatory Design and was developed according to Agile principles. In the late 1990s it was re-designed by a French company which sold it under the commercial name of "e-savoir", but this was no success. The French CNRS protected it and sold a few licenses until it declared it a freeware in 2004. Today it has been used by at least 42,000 people across 53 countries, mainly in academic settings. More than 1,000 maps are available on the Web.

5.1.3 Technical Information

Nestor is a 100,000 lines freeware. The client software runs on top of Microsoft Internet Explorer on Microsoft Windows platforms. It is written in Borland Delphi (2006). The server software which is used for collaborative work runs on Microsoft IIS Web Server as an ISAPI extension. The collaborative features use HTTP, FTP, SMTP and IRC Internet protocols. The peer-to-peer features use the TCP/IP protocol. Nestor download is available from the GATE-CNRS Web site at: http://www.gate.cnrs.fr/~zeiliger/nestor/nestor.htm. Nestor map files have a proprietary format, however Nestor can export the map in XML or HTML format. About 120 "html-maps" are available on the Web in HTML format which means they read with any browser.

5.2 Constructivism

Back in the 1996 when the design of Nestor started, the World Wide Web had just come out as an unlimited hypertext with amazing possibilities. From a usability perspective the growth of the WWW had revived the debate on the difficulties of navigating in hyperspace: the problem of disorientation coined by Conklin (1987) as "lost in hyperspace". It had revived also the debate about the "didacticizing" of hypertext (Hammond & Allinson, 1989): whether learning get plagued by the difficulty of making navigation decisions in an unknown domain or on the contrary is favoured by serendipity. The design of Nestor as a map enhanced browser was initially guided by the aim of easing navigation in hypermedia pedagogical contents: in the late 1990s the browser was becoming the standard interface for accessing pedagogical content, so it was meaningful to think of "dressing it up" with a graphical software layer that would enable learners to take more control over their navigation path.

One of the starting ideas that guided Nestor's design was to give users the means to solve their own navigation problems instead of "drawing on knowledge held in some expert model as in knowledge-based systems" (Eklund et al., 1999). This would be achieved in allowing users to visualize, reflect on, capitalize and share their navigation experience. This idea matches the idea that taking control of one's learning is a key issue for a successful learning. It is primarily a psychological issue, one that relate to activity, motives and consciousness. But nowadays, in the information age, in those times of distance education, of Web based learning and training, with "the expansion of the opportunities for learning after school" (Brown & Cole, 2000) and with the pervasive resorting to searching Web information, it is also a social and technological issue: a matter of which computerised tools we use, their usability, and the perspective and approach to information and knowledge that they convey. We want to stress here that software tools do not merely facilitate a few operations, they mediate activities, change practices and shape human thinking (Vygotsky, 1994). According to the tool mediation principle proposed by Vygotsky, tools change the range of the activities performed by their users; they "congeal" human experience in their properties; they eventually re-shape the mental activity and the social practices of their users. Thus the psychological, social and technical dimensions of tools are intertwined. In domains such as learning where the philosophical positions on information and knowledge are crucial, the computerised tools should be designed to be consistent with existing theories. In the late 1990s an important turn was made by the technology scholars who "look to social and organizational issues implicated in technology design and development" (Jackson et al., 2001). So the cognitive constructivism in learning and the social constructionism in technology at work with the growth of the Web – greatly influenced the design of Nestor. The real challenge was then to imagine the computer features that would support user's constructive activity.

Theories. There are many theories and principles which relate to constructivism and that influenced Nestor's design. Activity theory is the most important. "Activity theory (AT) is a commonly accepted name for a line of theorizing and research initiated by the founders of the cultural-historical school of Russian psychology, Vygotsky, Leont'ev, Luria, in the 1920s and 1930s" (Engestrom et al., 1999). Over the 15 past years the Activity Theory ideas had an increased impact on such fields as learning, human–computer interaction, distributed cognition and theories of practice. The basic principles that are constitutive of the Activity Theory conceptual system and that are relevant to the issues discussed here are: the principle of unity of consciousness and activity, the principle of object oriented-ness of activity, the duality of internalization and externalization processes, the principle of tool mediation, and the hierarchical structure of activity. We shall not recall those principles with more details here: a summary may be found in Kaptelinin et al. (1995). In the domain of technology for learning Activity Theory has been acknowledged as a framework that may help design constructivist learning environments (Jonassen & Rohrer-Murphy, 1999): these authors present a six steps analysis of the activity system in which a software tool is going to be embedded, an approach that helps defining the tool components. The navigation activity which is mediated by Nestor was considered according to this perspective.

We cannot present in this paper the debate and nuances that generally come along with the idea of constructivism in learning – an idea very often stated as an "umbrella" concept. The basic principle is that there exist not such thing as an objectively correct mental model; on the contrary each person has to construct her own knowledge building on her individual experience. Let us recall that Jean Piaget articulated the mechanisms (assimilation and accommodation) by which knowledge is internalized by learners. And Vygotsky contributed the complementary idea of "Zone of Proximal Development" (ZPD) referring to a situation made of challenging tasks where a novice learner can be expected to develop her own knowledge under the guidance of a knowledgeable tutor. Social constructivism – also referred as constructionism – emphasizes that individuals make meanings through the interactions with each other and with the environment they live in. Nestor collaborative features centred on maps were designed to support the construction of socially shared representations of navigation paths.

We make use in this paper of the term "enactional" in the sense of « driven by the course of interaction ». The term « enactive knowledge » was initially coined by Bruner to refer to a kind of non-symbolic knowledge which is gained through natural and intuitive interactions performed in some environments that support a close coupling of perception and action (Bruner, 1968; Varela et al., 1991). The concept of enaction has been used in the domain of Human–Computer Interaction to build "enactive interfaces": interfaces that engage the users in "sensory-motor interactions" with symbolic representations that have been specially designed to give a kind of physical object status to the screen elements. The manipulation of Nestor maps has been designed accordingly.

Design Decisions. Let us come back now to the challenge of designing Nestor as an "authentic constructivist tool". In our view there are two basic properties that characterise such tools: i) an appeal for action and activity – like in games, ii) a support for construction. A constructivist tool should be an "activity enabler" (Jonassen & Rohrer-Murphy, 1999): it should be able to engage novice users into effortless operations implementing transformative actions that fit into meaningful activities (operation, action and activity in the sense of AT). For example it should be easy, quick and constraint-free for any user to build a first "draft webmap" intended to focus a discussion with a remote peer. This simple activity should be as appealing as a game. Then, in further steps, when it comes to constructing more elaborated representations (for example conceptual or argumentative maps), "some of the cognitive responsibility (should be) off-loaded to the machine" i.e. the software tool should be able to "supplant some or all operations" in the constructive task so that the user "more intensely focus consciousness on actions and activities".

Both properties entail the design of a visual tool supporting the direct manipulation of symbols. We followed an Agile consistent principle: because tools mediate practice, it seemed a good idea to quickly implement mock-up features and let users play with it: appealing features would eventually emerge when confronted to users practices. Finally, we made a design decision that deeply shaped Nestor: no artificial intelligence. This statement should not be interpreted as rejecting the efficiency of IA based tools; but in the late 1990s, with the development of human–computer interaction (HCI) as a computer sciences research field, it was challenging to bring the demonstration that computers amazing capabilities could rely on something else than "computations". A promising alternative was clearly to try to use computers' visualization and manipulation techniques to give users the feeling that they were "immerged in a world of symbols", and that this immersion was the occasion for a full set of constructive activities.

5.3 Applied Constructivism at Work with Nestor

We will not describe here the detailed functionalities of Nestor; this has been done in previous papers (Zeiliger et al., 1999). We present a set of selected features that – in our view – exemplify the promoting of a constructive work with Internet information. We now discuss five examples of selected Nestor features and outline in which manner we think they contribute to a constructivist mapping of Internet information.

5.3.1 The Mapping Layout, a Mix of Machine and Human Contribution

The user interface of Nestor has two main components: a browser window and a map window. For every navigation operation (open, back, forward, query, home) done with the browser, a visual feedback is provided into the map window. The overall result of a navigation session is a web-map which is automatically drawn by Nestor. This computer-drawn web-map has a default layout. The objects on the map show with standard icons, computed size and default labels.

The default layout for example is drawn according to a model of "travel through hyperspace" which is consistent with the very metaphor of travel that founded the use of the word "navigation" to refer to traversing links in an hypertext. The default layout consists of nodes and arrows which appear as straight lines as long as the user follows links: a straight line represents a "travel". With the use of backward navigation followed by a sequence of link navigations, a new straight branch is drawn so that the default layout soon displays a tree (Fig. 5.1). The default layout is designed to convey a first visualization of the experience of navigation. It is a sort of "scaffolding". This representation of experience would not be complete (and it has not been designed with such goal) before an active re-organising of the layout by the user is done. The user is expected to manipulate this default representation – through direct manipulation and drag-and-drop operations – so that she constructs her own layout i.e. a layout that (i) congeals a thinking process supported by enaction (ii) has acquired a meaning (Fig. 5.2). A meaningful layout is what makes the web-map useful for a particular user in further re-use. Though the user is entirely free to fully re-arrange the layout, the final layout reflects a joint process of contribution between man and computer. The computer role is to propose a scaffolding and allow for easy re-constructing, the man just know what is meaningful for himself. We propose this joint process may be generalized and serve as a principle for guiding the design of some other constructive features.

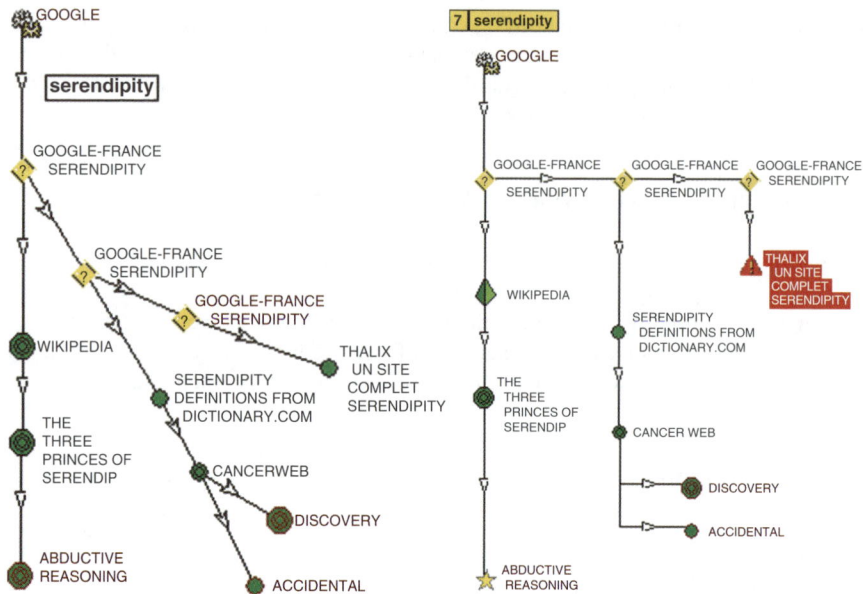

Fig. 5.1. Default layout.   **Fig. 5.2.** Re-arranged layout.

There are numerous features available in Nestor to further customize the Web-maps so that the produced maps display an amazing variety of styles; this seems to reveal the idiosyncrasy for what concerns the representing of experience in the mind of heterogeneous users. Samples may be found by querying Google-Images with the keyword "nestor-converted" (here is the Google query to be used: http://images.google.fr/images?hl=fr&q=nestor-converted). The consequences of the heterogeneity in those unconstrained representations will be discussed below in the example dedicated to the collaborative features.

To finish with this example we would like to add a remark: the default labels of Nestor's map Web sites are taken from the referrer link rather than from the Web site title. Of course the referrer labels are many, while the Web document title is unique. This choice was guided by a user centred view: we think a user expects that the document she reaches would have the label of the link she has followed to reach it. In other words the default labelling of the documents is an historical scaffolding. In that case as in the layout one, the user is free to change the full label.

5.3.2 Creating Intertwined Networks of Information

The idea that guided the design of this feature is inspired by considerations about the relation between reading and writing, transposed to the Web. As stated by Spivey: "Building meaning through reading entails organizing, selecting, and connecting. Readers use previously acquired knowledge to operate on textual cues, organizing mental representations that include material they select from the text and connect

5. The Constructivist Mapping of Internet Information at Work with Nestor 95

with material they generate. This constructivist characterization of the reading process extends also to literate acts in which people are writers as well as readers, those acts in which they compose texts by drawing from textual sources. To meet their discourse goals, writers perform textual transformations associated with the operations of organizing, selecting, and connecting as they appropriate source material for uses in different communicative contexts. They dismantle source texts and reconfigure content they select from these sources, and they interweave the source material with content they generate from stored knowledge" (Spivey, 1990).

The transposition of this constructivist approach to reading to the domain of mapping Internet information is achieved in Nestor by a radical change in the function of maps: at first maps were intended to represent an existing information space i.e. mapping the relevant documents found on the Web and the navigation links that relate them. In a further stage maps become a work space i.e. a new information space where users may create documents as well as links of their own, and where they may intertwine their personal documents with the public ones. They graphically construct a personal extension to the Web; this extension is consistent in its form and content with the Web structure: it is composed of html documents and

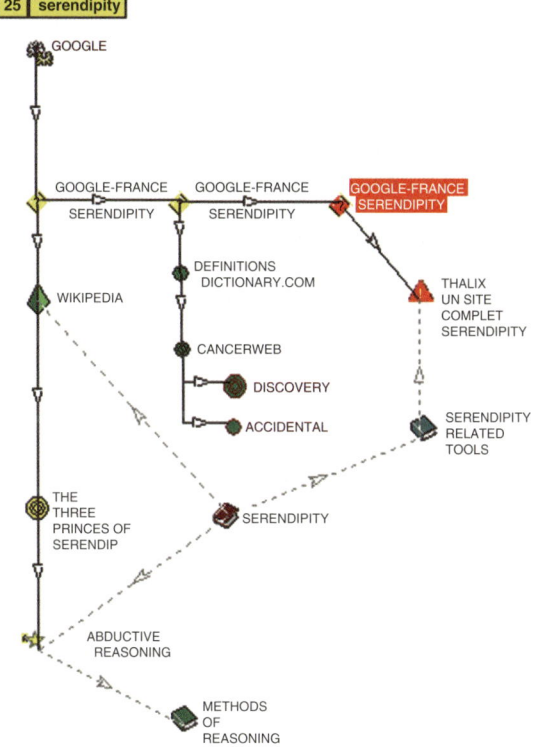

Fig. 5.3. Intertwined networks.

of new navigation links. Even if it is not yet a "real" contribution to the public Web (the user creations are stored on their hard disk), it is ready for publishing as we will see in the example N°5 below.

In that way Web readers become Web writers; they are encouraged in generating their own material and may organize, select and connect it to existing information. According to the work of Spivey they may even eventually improve their reading of Web documents. The activity which is supported by such features favours the internalisation/externalization loop process described by Vygotsky (1994). We think that those read/write and private/public dichotomies (dichotomies in the sense that they shape each other) are key components of a constructivist approach. Figure 5.3 illustrates this process: it shows the previous map augmented with user generated enhancements: documents that show with a "book" icon and that are related by dotted-arrows which figure new hypertext links.

5.3.3 Multi-Page Widgets

Our third example focuses on a widget that exemplify what we would call the "appeal for action" conveyed by an interactive software. The scenario of use which is supported by this widget is as follows: the user browse through documents and selects relevant information – text or image – that she pastes into the map window. We did not mention it yet, but the map window – now considered as a work space – may incorporate at the initiative of the user, a full set of new objects and relations: textual notes, images, concepts, conceptual-areas, grids. Those are the standard objects that usually appear in mind-mapping software. Some of these objects have been designed to play an information structuring role: this is the case for lists, grids and the so-called "multi-pages" objects we want to detail here. The structure which is imposed by the multi-page object resembles the structure of a book i.e. a sequence of pages. Each page may contain a text-memo, an image, and a set of checkboxes. Pages are arranged in a sequence and each page has a tab and a label (Fig. 5.4).

The page sequence may be easily re-ordered. The user is supposed to fill the pages through dragging the texts and the images to the different pages (Fig. 5.5). The result is a sort of book that structures the information extracted from the Web. A few remarks: each piece of information remain attached to the source document it comes from – a simple click navigates back to the source document; the pages may also embed some information generated by the user; the aim of the checkboxes will be discussed in the next example.

We reckon that this widget supports constructive activities in two ways: (i) it provides means of literally constructing meaningful information, in the sense that it allows to assemble pieces of information into a commonly used structure (the book structure) (ii) it allows to do so through the direct manipulation of symbols i.e. through an external activity that has a strong enactional dimension.

5. The Constructivist Mapping of Internet Information at Work with Nestor

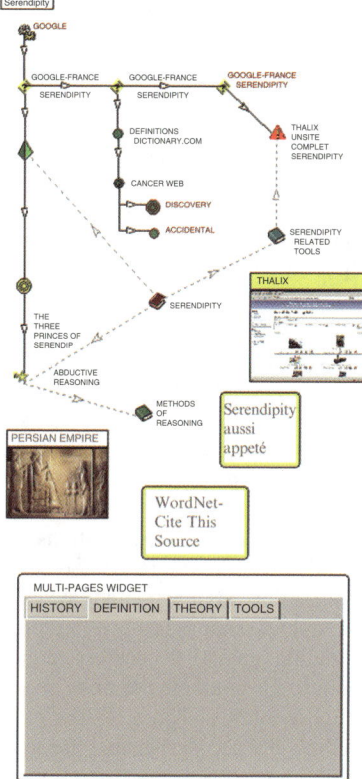

Fig. 5.4. A sample of the multi-page widget.

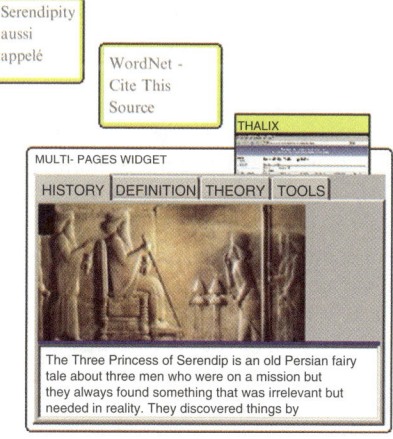

Fig. 5.5. Filling the pages through drag-and-drop.

5.3.4 The Hybrid Representation System

Nestor provides what we call an hybrid representation system: it mixes all the elements that are necessary to visualize surf-maps, mind-maps and concept-maps. Surf-maps represent the user navigation experience and are targeted at facilitating navigation; mind-maps can represent ideas and their associative relations; the aim of mind-maps is to support thought processes; concept-maps are a more abstract "system view" composed of concepts and typed relations destined to communicate complex ideas and arguments. Going from surf-map to concept-map is going through a reflective process which is rooted in experience and evolve toward abstraction. This process unfolds through de-constructing Internet information and re-constructing it for a given purpose linked to a particular context. The context may be for example a learning assignment on a specific theme. A certain degree of abstraction is required when one wants to communicate and negotiate ideas with others – the representation of raw experience is too idiosyncratic to be understood and valued by other users.

The inherent structure of the maps matches the de-construction/re-construction process: surf-maps have a quite strong structure which is determined by the recording of the history of a single user's navigations; mind-maps have a loose structure which supports the de-construction stage; the concept-maps structure fits a certain level of re-organising that is considered as characterizing a successful reflective process (Nestor hybrid maps have a structure compatible with the assimilation and accommodation mental processes); concept-maps – in Nestor – have a low formalized structure: for example the links may be typed or un-typed and there is no notion of concept hierarchy. Three classes of relations match the three kinds of maps: navigation link for the surf-maps, association links for the mind-maps; conceptual links for the concept-maps. This representing system is flexible: rather than imposing a clear distinction between the three classes of maps, Nestor design choice is to allow a smooth evolution – with possible backward and forward steps as well as loops – from raw experience to formalized abstraction. It intends to bring the practicalities of mind-mapping and conceptual-mapping to the domain of Internet information search. It aims at attracting Web "foragers" into a more reasoned information quest.

However this incremental formalization process is supported by a full set of visualisation techniques: (i) Nestor provides two classes of objects that have almost the same properties except that they differentiate through being system-created or user-created (ii) users may hide or show each class of object separately; this is targeted at allowing an easy switching back and forth from the hybrid representation to a plain-surf or plain-conceptual one; this is part of the smooth evolution scheme (iii) each map has two independent possible layouts (of the same objects) so that users can start building a new meaningful layout without loosing the previous one whose meaning is preserved (iv) maps may incorporate sub-maps; sub-maps do not differentiate from first-level maps i.e. every map may appear as a first-level map or as a sub-map or both; this is supposed to allow a smooth hierarchical structuring. Other visualization techniques such as hyperbolic view or variable level-of-detail view are provided by Nestor but not described here.

5. The Constructivist Mapping of Internet Information at Work with Nestor

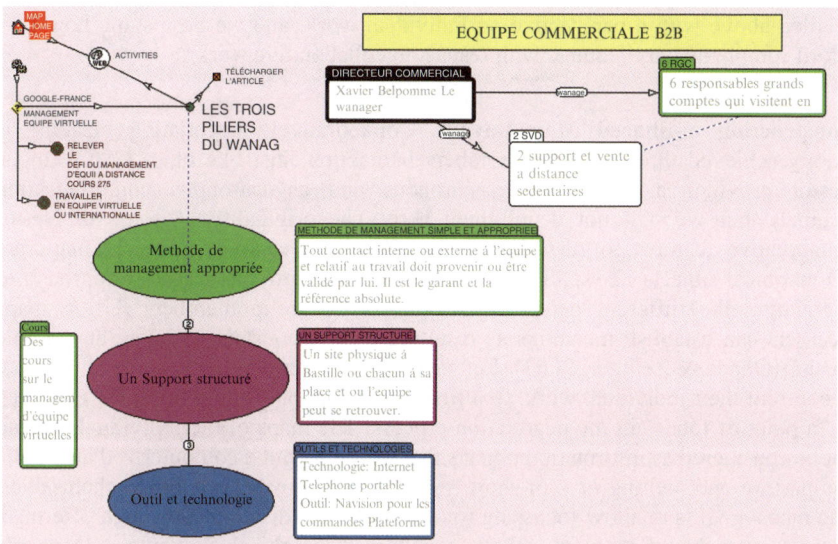

Fig. 5.6. A sample hybrid map (by Davoine, EM LYON, 2007).

Figure 5.6 illustrates this process of smooth evolution of the maps toward formalization; it is borrowed from a student at EM LYON. The work theme is "Virtual teams in organizations". Each student – during a training period within an organization – has to investigate the relevance of the given theme within her organization. The map in Fig. 5.6 corresponds to an early stage on the way to conceptual formalization: on the left we can see cues of a surf-map which has then been enhanced with three web-outsourced text memos that seem to correspond to three main ideas (coloured pies in the middle screen). On the right the student is sketching out a first conceptual schema. Currently the surf-map, the mind-map and the concept-map still cohabit. The layout from left to right even suggest that the evolving toward formalization is a process than unfolds overtime.

5.3.5 Constructive Collaborative Features

A set of constructivist features would not be complete without their counterpart in the domain of collaborative work. Further more we stress that every feature destined to support individual work should be designed to suit also a form of shared work that may eventually facilitate the process of negotiation of meaning that characterize group work. Lets recall what Wenger says about the process of reification in communities of practice: reification is "giving form to our experience by producing objects that congeal this experience into thingness", and reification is useful "for its capacity to create points of focus around which the negotiation of meaning becomes organized" (Wenger, 1998). This is exactly the idea that guided the design of Nestor reification functions. We now come back to the four examples which have been detailed above with a perspective on individual work, and we now show how they afford complementary features with respect to collaborative work.

Constructing a Shared Map Layout. Collaboratively negotiating meaning is mainly achieved through group members interaction; just like other CSCW tools, Nestor provides a palette of synchronous and asynchronous communication channels, but we will not detail them here. The originality of some of Nestor collaborative features follows directly from its map centred approach: maps are 2D-graphical objects i.e. spatial representations that provide a spatial approach to negotiating the different perspectives brought by group members. Using maps "learners can establish meanings as resulting from a constant updating at multiple levels" (Okada & Zeiliger, 2003). Let suppose for example that two members want to confront their individual work. In a first stage, each one would bring her own map as "a point of focus" in the negotiation process. The maps of the individuals should not be considered as information objects that would permit a computerized automatic comparison and melting or – in short – map to not convey meaning in themselves. The maps' goal is to allow focussing (or scaffolding) a discussion through offering a concrete start based in a first phase on concrete graphical elements: two people would bring of course two different maps and start talking about it. 2D-maps are more flexible than texts for supporting this process: (i) a first-step raw merging would consist in placing the two maps side by side on the same window, thus allowing for global comparison – to the contrary of text, maps may be read both at the local and global level; (ii) a second step could be the re-organizing of the juxtaposed maps along with the advancement of the discussion – it is much easier to manipulate a graphical layout on-the-fly while discussing than to re-writing a piece of text; (iii) the following steps would probably consist in collaboratively merging the two maps – once again this is much easier to do in a graphical space than in a text, because the elements of a schema may be re-organised progressively without breaking the consistency of the whole sketch. One could argue than a negotiated text is a more formal achievement that a loosely structured text. It is true indeed, but the collaborative construction of a shared map with Nestor is not a goal in it self; it is a means; it is a pretext, the occasion for a focussed joint activity in the course of which the process of negotiation of meaning may unfold. In further stages of more sophisticated collaborative work, the construction of a commonly agreed conceptual map may become an important achievement, an artefact that truly convey some meaning.

Constructivism "embodies the notion of constructive engagement understood as engagement in activities that facilitate learning" (Armitage & Wilson, 2004). Collaboratively managing "screen real estate" may be viewed as a constructive engagement:

5. The Constructivist Mapping of Internet Information at Work with Nestor 101

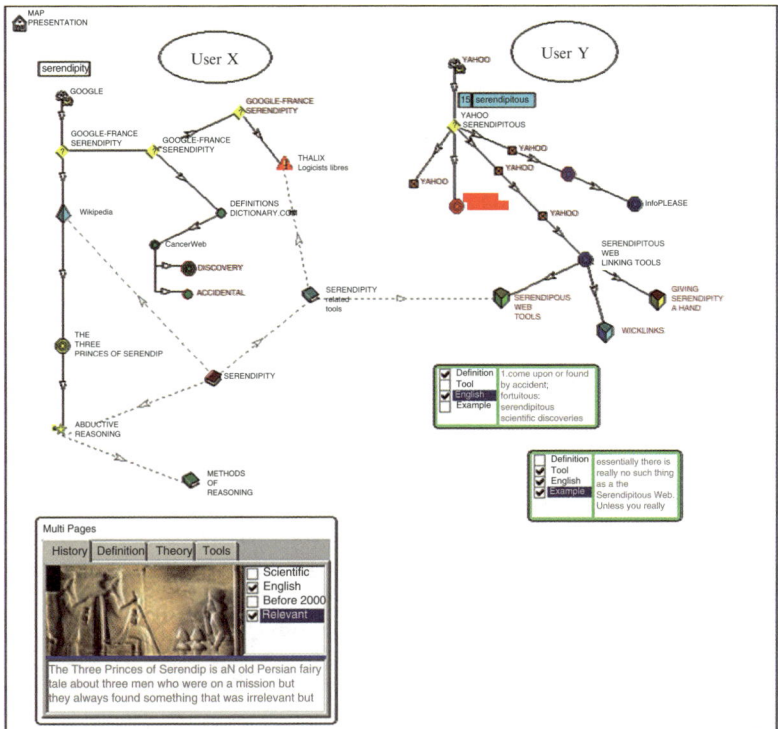

Fig. 5.7. Merging the maps of User X and User Y. The two maps which both focus on the concept of "serendipity" are still side by side. One user-created relation begins to "bridge" matching objects. There is a foreseen conflict because the text notes of user Y (*highlighted in green*) have a set of properties that could not match the properties attached to the multi-page widget of user X.

Intertwined Networks of Information. We have already mentioned above the appeal of Nestor hybrid maps for mixing private and public information (documents as well as relations). This very argument applies also to collaborative work; in the process of merging maps users tackle the negotiation of three classes of documents: private (contribution of member x), public (extracted from the Web), and agreed (congealing an agreement between participants). Changing the status of the documents involved in a map is likely to feed a discussion and a joint activity which focuses around what should stay a private contribution, what should become an agreed contribution, and what is destined to be published on the Web with the same status in the end that the documents that were originally extracted from it. Indeed, publishing a Nestor map not only make it publicly available as a stand alone interactive image (just as any Web document), but it also publishes its component documents and links i.e. while the documents that were already public keep their status, the documents and links constructed by the users are uploaded to a Web server and become part of the public Web. They can be accessed either separately – as any Web document they will be indexed by search engines – or through the map which then provides a context to the document.

Multi-page widget: the properties checkboxes. As mentioned above Nestor multi-page widget incorporates a simple device for beginning characterizing the content of the pages. Users may define a list of properties that apply to the content they have clustered in the widget pages. It shows on each page as a list of checkboxes labelled with the selected properties (Fig. 5.7). The properties are the same for every page, but their value (checked or unchecked) is attributed by the users depending on the content of each page. We can argue that this is a first step toward encouraging users to explicitly define the arguments they take into account for clustering information. With respect to individual work we could also say that this was designed to prepare an explicit formal object scheme applying to information objects. It may well serve this purpose, but the idea behind this device is better understood as triggering a collaborative process of negotiation of categories: in the case two (or more) users would want to merge their multi-page widgets, they have to agree on the list of properties. Again this is viewed as an occasion for joint activity.

Toward Incremental Formalization: Maps as Information Assets. The multi-page widget is not implemented in Nestor with the aim to let users prepare a sort of slide show, a poor substitute to Microsoft Power Point. It is destined to be used in collaborative work as a "boundary object". This is a term coined by sociologist Leigh Star to refer to objects "to-think-with" that "serve to coordinate the perspectives of various consistencies for some purpose" (Wenger, 1998). So it plays a provisional role in Nestor shared maps during the collaborative process through which two or more users "inscribe" their agreement ("alignment of their interests" in the wording of Actor Network Theory) into a more abstract representation. The ultimate stage in this process would lead to constructing a plain conceptual-map. "Plain conceptual" should be understood here as no longer bearing explicit signs of the user navigation experience (in short: bearing no navigation arrows). Which doesn't mean that objects referring to a Web site should not be used; they just have to appear as linked to some concept (see the blue dot arrows into Fig. 5.8 or 5.11).

An Overview of Nestor Collaborative Features. Going beyond the examples detailed above, we now give an overview of some other collaborative features in Nestor. They have been designed to support small groups of up to about twenty people. To enable the collaborative features a specific software – the Nestor ISAPI extension – has to be installed on a Web server. The Nestor client should also be configured to work with the selected Web server.

5. The Constructivist Mapping of Internet Information at Work with Nestor

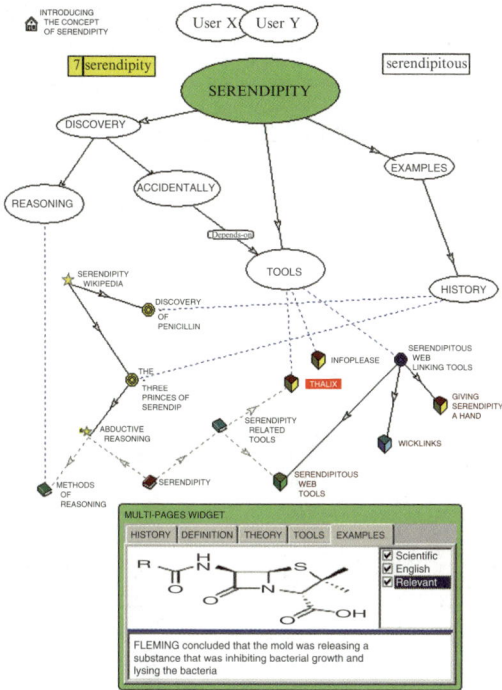

Fig. 5.8. Introducing some concepts (*top coloured pies*):upon agreement users resort to a more abstract schema: elements recalling their private experience tend to disappear; the multi-page widget is used as a "boundary object": a point of focus around which the negotiation process get organized. It is destined to disappear.

Each Nestor work group is provided with a private Web site. Every member of the group as the rights to edit any page of her group site (Nestor incorporates a simple html editor). The user rights management is limited to a very simple scheme; two roles corresponding to two levels of rights only are available: simple-participant and empowered-participant. This is part of an intended "minimalist" design. User participation in a Nestor work group get organized around three main Web pages: (i) the home page of the group, (ii) the resources page, and (iii) the activities page. The so-called "activities" page is assigned a central role in building up the group awareness (Fig. 5.9). It shows as a table where each group member has ownership over her own line in the table. The activities page is supposed to be fed by every group members so that at any time it reflects the advancement of the work of the group. It incorporates a minimalist task agenda as well as a simple argumentation system. It provides a single computer interface to be used in asynchronous as well as synchronous mode. Most joint activities supported by Nestor consist in sharing, exchanging and re-organising maps. A set of peer-to-peer features are also available, such as synchronous map-editing, joint navigation, and joint resource management. They are targeted at supporting the work of two people (only) in synchronous mode.

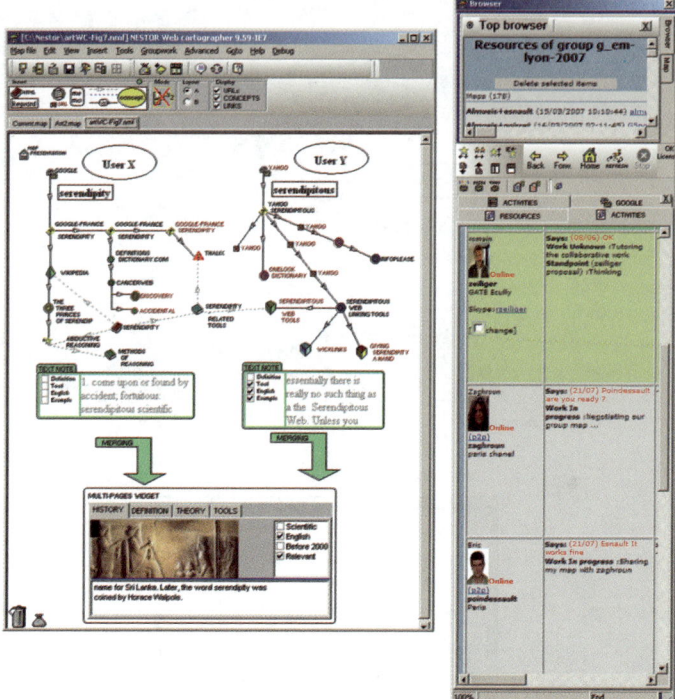

Fig. 5.9. A full screen shot of Nestor illustrating a collaborative work situation: the two maps to be merged appear on left; they have been downloaded from the group resources; the browser window (*on the right*) splits in two independent panels: the group resources Web page on top, and the group activities page below. The "activities" page currently shows three online members involved in the current task.

5.4 Lessons Learned from Nestor Use

From 1998 to 2007 Nestor has been used by numerous anonymous users (an estimated 42,000 individuals) who downloaded it from the Web. They probably used it exclusively for personal work although the peer-to-peer features were freely available; for ethical reasons we have almost no feedback on their activity. During the same period a lot of registered users also used it in organisations, mostly in academic settings. We are particularly grateful to some of them who participated actively in the participatory design approach that shaped today's release of the software. We want to thank them here, particularly the Service de Technologie de l'Education at ULG (Liege, Belgique), the Pontifica Universidade Catolica of Sao Paulo (Brasil) and EM LYON, France (for a more exhaustive list see http://koala.gate.cnrs.fr/groupware/community.htm). Most of the issues we discuss here stem from discussions with the teachers and the tutors in these Universities, and from the observation of the maps built by their students. They used Nestor work groups with small groups of students. Around 20 work groups are still publicly accessible on the Web (only the group members may upload maps, but the maps may be seen by everybody whatever the browser). One standard group – such as those running at EM LYON – holds 100–150 maps, so our observations were carried on more than 1,000 maps. Most maps are publicly accessible through the links to the Nestor work groups that appear in the "community page" mentioned above. We now give a more detailed presentation of the EM Lyon use case because (i) it is a typical example of Nestor use in academic context and (ii) most of our remarks stem from our 8-years experience there.

The EM LYON Use Case. The course, titled "the Net Company", gathers about 30 students (graduate level) each year. The main topic is Network Organisations and how to work in such organisations. The principle of the course is to learn by experiencing situations related to the topic of the course, articulating the "theory" and a field experience, and reflecting upon the learning process. All participants are in internship in different companies, thus the course is a blended one. The initial session, in classroom, is devoted to the presentation of the course and the pedagogical format, and the initiation to manipulating Nestor. The last session, also in classroom, enables the students to present the web pages they have developed and the maps connected to it. In between, there are two synchronous "rendez-vous", where students are supposed to be connected at the same time during 2–3 h. These synchronous meetings (called "synchronous on-line sessions"), are mainly devoted to answering questions, clarifying the work to do and the requirements, and experiencing the differences between asynchronous and synchronous work. Students work individually and by teams (56 students per team), with tutoring of two people (the professor in charge of the course regarding the course content and pedagogical scenario, and Nestor author regarding the ergonomic, communication and technical aspects). Individually they have to realise three maps (called field maps) about the situation in their company regarding three themes (this year, for example, the tree themes are: "Network Organisations", "Managing virtual teams", and "Communities"). Collectively they have to build one map on each theme (called "theoretical maps") presenting the results if their readings, in the "web literature" and through documents tat are given by the tutors. At the end, each group develops and presents, through Nestor, a web page which is their view of the course matter, and in which they articulate the different maps, individuals and collectives. The main communication is done through Nestor's synchronous and asynchronous communication facilities. Within groups, students may use whatever communication means they want (mostly instant messaging, mobile phones, and, starting this year, tools like Skype).

The main challenges for them is to cope with the software, not really on the technical side, but because it requires them to change their habits on how to produce what is required. They are very good at producing Word files and PowerPoint presentations, but they are not used to work "graphically" as it is required in Nestor. They are not used to mix the "navigation" part which is new (though it can be seen that they get more and more easily familiar with this) and the "traditional writing" (they should also write their own pages within the maps). Most of the time they spend their efforts on the map (re)presentation – the innovative part – and neglect the document writing.

They are not used to have to produce the main part of the course content by themselves, though they have documents posted and also have access to the previous years' web site.

About the Maps Graphics. The students' maps show a great variety of graphic styles. Of course the styles depend also on the graphical possibilities build in Nestor and are related to the lack of imposed formalism; but we observe that some users develop a style of their own, a style that pertains to all their maps: for example a square-based or round-based style. We find also a great variety in the layouts: tree-like, network-like, stack-like… Most layouts tend to occupy the full "map real estate" available. We interpret this observation as indicating that the maps exert an appeal for playing with the spatial distribution. A commonly found structure is based on triplets, just as if – whatever the matter – it could be decomposed into three main aspects. On the contrary, one particular user relies on sets of four items whatever her map. Map aesthetic seems important: it could be noticed for example in the choice of colours, or in the use of bended arrows (Fig. 5.10). We assume that a "beautiful" map is recognised and valued by other users; and because the subjective appreciation of the "beauty" of a map depends on the culture of the users, we can observe what we would call "cultural styles of information mapping".

About the constructive work. The theoretical evolving of the maps from surf-maps to concept-maps that we mentioned above as a central feature of Nestor is not clearly observable in the work of students. We can observe along the time that the students maps tend to become more sophisticated and more abstract. There is of course an initial learning effect, and there are also some usability problems. Then we do observe a clear evolution of the map composition over a period of work of 9 weeks as it is the case at EM LYON. We think we can notice an effort of the students to escape from an initial visualizing of their Web surfing experience, toward a more abstract form of representation that is valued in collaborative work: for example no student would propose a surf-map for collaborative editing after a period of 3 weeks. However the claimed specificity of Nestor – mixing a Web browser, a mind-mapping tool and a concept-mapping tool – is not well understood by the students; and not exploited. Most students build maps which are a mix of organisations flowchart and scattered concepts with related Web sites. In short, maps remain hybrids and fall steps behind a consistent formalism.

However for what concerns the use-case at EM LYON we should note that: (i) a final concept-map formalism was not required from the students, (ii) the maps themselves as well as some of their embedded widgets are destined to be used as "boundary objects", not as final products, (iii) the final product required from the students is a Web site presenting their work. We notice that these final Web sites are of high-quality; that the best maps are usually linked to the Web site; and we observe that the Web sites really stem from the maps in a bottom-up approach. A sample Web site may be found at: http://koala.gate.cnrs.fr/groupware/g_em-lyon-2004/groupe2.htm.

5. The Constructivist Mapping of Internet Information at Work with Nestor

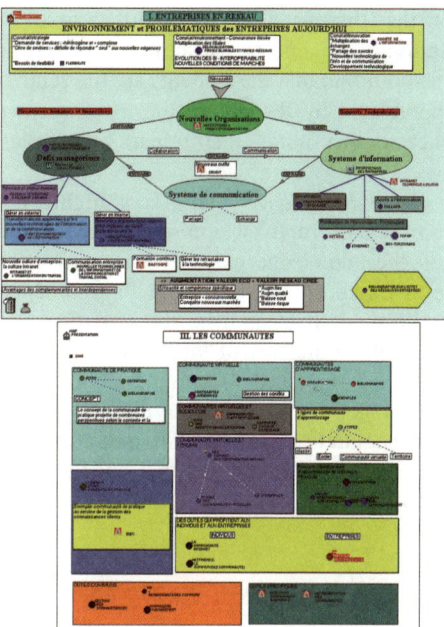

Fig. 5.10. Map samples – EM LYON use case.

About the Collaborative Work. The collaborative process at work during the construction of shared maps is seldom visible in the maps themselves. The reason is that the negotiation process takes place mainly on communication channels (IRC chat, Skype conversations or MSN) and the maps are used as "boundary objects" i.e. objects that focus the negotiation but do not necessarily keep tracks of it. In addition, for the EM LYON use-case the real product of the collaboration is the Web site. There are some exceptions such as the one described in a previous paper (Esnault et al., 2004) where the elements of a final map could be tracked back to the individual contributors. In that specific case we observed a refinement of the conceptual categories along the collaborative process, leading to an agreed highly-structured final map (Fig. 5.11).

Here are a few additional raw remarks we draw from the EM LYON use case:

- The students are not prepared to the practicalities of a Nestor-oriented collaborative work; they cannot anticipate early enough what kind of map will be valued in the collaborative stage. In other words, they tend to build stand alone maps that do not remain open to the negotiation process. We also observe that the building of a synthetic map if often delegated to one of the group members.

- The teachers reckon that they usually give high scores to students that: either constructed smart individual maps, or participated actively in the collaborative process. They very seldom find that the students are the same ones.
- Nestor maps are appreciated by the tutors: the maps seem to provide a space where the tutors can easily incorporate their remarks, examples or expectations.

Do the Maps Convey Some Knowledge? This is a highly controversial matter, specially when one claim a constructivist approach. However we do not want to escape the discussion on the knowledge management aspects, and we feel we can draw on our experience to enrich the controversy with arguments which are specific to the Nestor practice. We made it clear from the start that at EM LYON Nestor maps are not destined to hold some sort of knowledge: the group Web site is the document where students are supposed to summarize the knowledge they have acquired; the maps are used as (i) scaffoldings in the individual and joint activities (ii) point of focus in the negotiation process, (iii) monitoring instruments for the tutors. In short Nestor maps support activities that engage students in a reflexive process in the course of which they construct – with the help of tutors – their own knowledge representations.

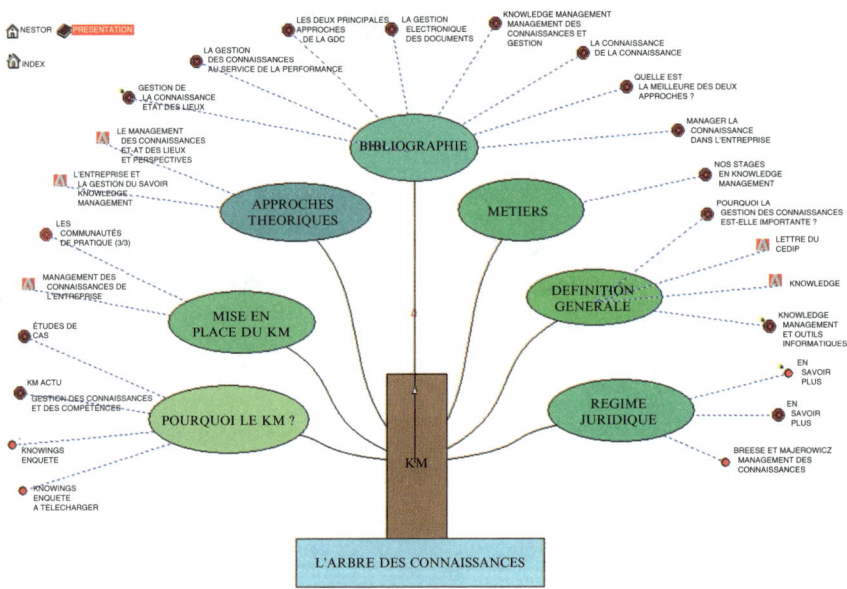

Fig. 5.11. KM final map by Group, DESS-IE University Lyon 2 Available at: http://koala.gate.cnrs.fr/groupware/g_DESS-IE-2004/ARBRE2.htm.

Nestor hybrid maps do not seem an appropriate media for knowledge management. However we shall bring some nuance to this assertion with a few remarks:

The teachers at EM LYON feel they are able to evaluate their students learning achievements from seeing the maps they have produced. The maps seem to reflect in some way their degree of deepening in the understanding of the domain, their capacity to articulate the domain elements and the span of their reflexive process.

The maps built by the students often contain information structures of some kind: sequences, categories, hierarchy, which do not directly exploit the corresponding widgets i.e. students use the spatial layout to structure information according to their mental model. In such cases we are sure that the information structure is not driven by the availability of some Nestor widget; it stems directly from the user intent.

In rare cases a Nestor map may convey some structure other people would find helpful for their own reflexive process. That is: such map do not directly embeds domain knowledge but nevertheless embeds some representation that is inspiring for acquiring that domain knowledge.

We cannot consider the Nestor maps produced at EM LYON as formalized concept-maps, nor as semantic Web documents. However when considering the Web pages the students finally produce after 9 weeks of work, we can acknowledge they bear a semantic dimension as the discourse they contain is explicitly referred to the maps from which it is drawn.

We are aware that these remarks need further investigation and do not bring a satisfactory contribution to the debate. A thorough analysis of the maps produced by the students at EM LYON has still to be done. Figure 5.10 shows a few map samples.

5.5 Conclusions

We have presented a summary of our design decisions and experience in implementing a concrete constructivist approach to Internet information mapping guided by theoretical principles. We have discussed the challenges that students as well as software designers have to face on their way toward the collaborative and incremental construction of formalized knowledge. We have proposed that computers may promote such an approach without resorting to artificial intelligence techniques: through the use of visualisation and symbol manipulation tools, the use of boundary objects, the engagement in joint activities.

The main lesson we draw from our case study is that over a period of 10 years, our students always met the assignments we gave them (their production is available at http://koala.gate.cnrs.fr/groupware/community.htm). They were smart students: they were not used to constructivist learning, they achieved their goal at the price of a substantial effort and they often criticized our approach; however we can testify that – given their limited learning time constraint – they reached through the practice of computer supported collaborative work a satisfactory understanding of the issues related to making sense of Internet information. This does not mean that Nestor is another smart software mapping tool, it just does *not* invalidate its design decisions: supporting user activity by tuned HCI techniques is a promising track of research for mapping software and AI techniques are not mandatory. Constructivist learning may be implemented when an "authentic" practice takes place within a group of students, and knowledge – although partly tacit – is produced in such context. The software tool plays an important role as a practice enabler, a quality that is reached eventually after a long process of refinement anchored in artful and participatory design.

We are aware that what we called knowledge in this paper may seem an elusive idea. Reconciling the contradictory visions of knowledge brought by constructivism and computing is not easy. However we trust we kept in line with the prophetic visions of early pioneers. Let us recall what Vannevar Bush stated years ago about the Memex in his famous paper "as we may think": "he (the user) builds a trail of interest through the maze of materials available to him" (Bush, 1945). And we feel we did not betray the constructivism central principle: "Knowledge is a conscious reading and re-writing of the world by the subjects themselves" (Freire, 1991).

References

Armitage, U., Wilson, S. (2004), Navigation and ownership for learning in electronic texts. An experimental study, EJEL, Vol 2.
Brown, C., Cole, M. (2000), Cultural historical activity theory and the expansion of opportunities for learning after school, http://lchc.ucsd.edu/People/Localz/MCole/browncole.html.
Bruner, J. (1968), Processes of cognitive growth: Infancy. Worcester, MA: Clark University Press.
Bush, V. (1945), As we may think, The Atlantic Monthly, July.
Conklin, J. (1987), Hypertext: an introduction and survey, Computer, September, 17–41.
Eklund, J., Sawers, J., Zeiliger, R. (1999), NESTOR navigator: a tool for the collaborative construction of knowledge through constructive navigation. In: R. Debreceny and A. Ellis (eds.). *Proceedings of Ausweb99, The Fifth Australian World Wide Web Conference.* Southern Cross University Press, Lismore, pp. 396–408.
Engestrom, Y., Miettinen, R., Punamaki, R.-L. (Eds). (1999), Perspectives on activity theory. Cambridge: Cambridge University Press.
Esnault, L., Ponti, M., Zeiliger, R. (2004), Constructing knowledge as a system of relations, In: *Proceedings of the Scandinavian Baltic Sea Conference: Motivation, Learning and Knowledge Building in the 21st Century*, Stockholm, June 18–21, Sweeden.
Freire, P. (1991), The importance of the act of reading. In C. Mitchell and K. Weiler (Eds.), Rewriting literacy: Culture and the discourse of the other. New York: Bergin & Garvey.
Hammond, N., Allinson, L. (1989), Extending hypertext for learning: an investigation of access and guidance tools. In: A. Sutcliffe and L. Macaulay (eds.), People and Computers V. Cambridge: Cambridge University Press.
Jackson, M., Poole, M., Kuhn, T. (2001), The social construction of technology in studies of the workplace. In: Lievrouw, L.; Livingstone, S., (Eds.), Handbook of new media. London: Sage.
Jonassen, D.H., Rohrer-Murphy, L. (1999), Activity theory as a framework for designing constructivst learning environments, ETR&D, Vol 47, N°1, 61–79.
Kaptelinin, V., Kuutti, K., Bannon, L.J. (1995), Activity Theory: Basic Concepts and Applications, Lecture Notes in Computer Science, Vol 1015, Berlin Heidelberg New York: Springer.

Okada, A.L.P., Zeiliger, R. (2003), The building of knowledge through virtual maps in collaborative learning environments, In: *Proceedings of the World Conféerence on Educational Multimedia, Hypermedia & Communistaions*, Hawaii. EDMEDIA, pp. 1625–1628

Spivey, N.N. (1990), Transforming texts: the constructive processes in reading and writing, Written Communication, Vol 7, N°2, 256–287, SAGE Publications.

Varela, F., Thompson, E., Rosch, E. (1991), The Embodied Mind: Cognitive Science and Human Experience, Cambridge, MA: MIT Press.

Vygotsky, L. (1994), Thought and Language, Kozulin (ed.), MIT Press.

Wenger, E. (1998), Communities of Practice: Learning, Meaning, and Identity, Cambridge: Cambridge University Press.

Zeiliger, R., Belisle, C., Cerratto, T. (1999), Implementing a constructivist approach to web navigation support, In: *Proceedings of the ED-MEDIA '99 Conference*, Collis, B. and Oliver, R. (eds.), June 19–24, AACE, Seattle,WA, USA.

6. Cognitive and Pedagogical Benefits of Argument Mapping: LAMP Guides the Way to Better Thinking

Yanna Rider[1] and Neil Thomason[2]

[1]Austhink Consulting and University of Melbourne, School of Philosophy, yannarider@gmail.com

[2]University of Melbourne, School of Philosophy, neilt@unimelb.edu.au

Abstract. Experimental evidence shows that in dedicated Critical Thinking courses "Lots of Argument Mapping Practice" (LAMP) using a software tool like *Rationale* considerably improves students' critical thinking skills. We believe that teaching with LAMP has additional cognitive and pedagogical benefits, even outside dedicated Critical Thinking subjects. Students learn to better understand and critique arguments, improve in their reading and writing, become clearer in their thinking and, perhaps, even gain meta-cognitive skills that ultimately make them better learners. We discuss some of the evidence for these claims, explain how, as we believe, LAMP confers these benefits, and call for proper experimental and educational research.

6.1 The Promise of LAMP

LAMP is a teaching method where students practise Argument Mapping often and rigorously, and receive timely feedback on their efforts. Evidence suggests that copious argument mapping practice confers substantial cognitive and pedagogical benefits. It clarifies thinking, deepens reading comprehension, improves critical thinking, and improves written argumentation. It can promote an enquiring classroom.

Students reaped these benefits from practising a particular kind of Argument Mapping, which we will outline here. If what our initial explorations suggest is correct, we are potentially looking at one of the most important innovations in learning, because LAMP can be used in many types of classroom, such as advanced secondary, gifted and talented education and standard university. We need rigorous, sustained research if we are to realize these possibilities.

6.2 The AM in LAMP

The Argument Mapping involved in LAMP – the kind of mapping we do with a software tool like *Rationale* – is driven by a single question: Given a claim, why should I believe it? What reasons (justification, evidence) do I have for and against it?

In this way, an Argument Map seeks to represent the best interpretation of the rational considerations brought out by the overall debate. In a sense, it aims to extract the logical essence of the arguments, leaving out the purely discursive elements and uninteresting past, failed moves, and inserting the hidden premises (unstated assumptions) necessary to make the inferences more explicit. Constructing a good argument map requires considerable thought about the claims and evidence and understanding the basic issues, and is far from a mechanical process following an inflexible set of rules. How a student (or anyone) goes from that understanding to assessing the argument itself is rarely taught at any educational level, even though it is crucial.

Although it has evolved to help people (whether academic, in business or other) think through complex issues and decisions, *Rationale* was originally designed to teach Critical Thinking. Its theoretical, cognitive and pedagogical principles spring from a formal understanding of argument, with its roots in Aristotelian syllogism, rather than from tracking the history of a debate. That said, *Rationale* is intended as a tool for representing real, everyday, "messy," informal arguments; but with a far greater rigour than they normally have. One aspect of this greater rigour is the articulation of unstated premises. Consider the following brief argument from a letter to the editor: "The public should be concerned about the rising rat population, because it is a public health risk." Even as simple an argument as this has literally hidden complexity.

Figure 6.1 is a *Rationale* diagram of the argument.[1] It shows a single reason, made up of three premises, supporting a conclusion. (In *Rationale*, reasons are colored green, objections are red and rebuttals – objections to objections – are orange. See the picture of a more complex map at the end of this article.) The letter explicitly stated only one of its premises, namely, that a rising rat population is a public health risk; but the Argument Map shows all the premises required to make the inference clear, whether stated or not. Unstated premises are put into square brackets, to indicate that this is the mapper's additions to what is explicitly stated in the text. Articulating the implicit, but crucial, unstated premises is an essential skill for reasoning carefully, particularly for responding to someone else's reasoning.

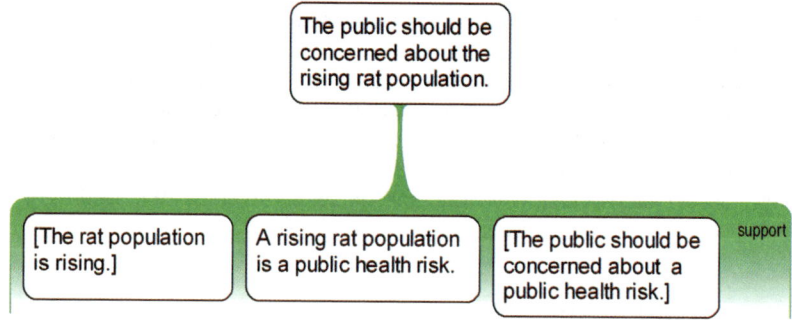

Fig. 6.1. Argument map of short letter to editor.

---

[1] For more details about *Rationale*™, including its conventions and more examples, see http://www.austhink.com/rationale/

Especially in political contexts, the explicit argument is often a string of unproblematic truisms, while the argumentative work (such as it is) is being done by things left unstated. Unless these are identified, it is near impossible to assess the argument – or even figure out what it is.

With Argument Mapping, most students do learn to recognize many of the unstated premises, challenging though learning it is. Several heuristics help students learn how to locate missing premises.

Holding Hands: The Holding Hands heuristic prompts the mapper to look for key concepts that just "dangle" – that is, are found in only one box. In a fully detailed map of a reason or objection, every key term appearing in a premise or in the conclusion must also appear in (hold hands with) either another premise or the conclusion. In Fig. 6.1, the key terms "rising rat population," "public," "should be concerned" and "public health risk" hold hands.

The most powerful application of Holding Hands is the "Rabbit Rule" – to pull a rabbit out of a hat, there must be a rabbit in the hat to begin with. "You can't conclude something about rabbits if you haven't been talking about rabbits." More generally, "Every important term in the conclusion must appear at least once (i.e. in at least one premise) in each reason bearing on that conclusion."[2] The Rabbit Rule proves to be remarkably helpful for students. It helps them notice the missing (unstated) premises that so often do so much of the argumentative work.

In very simple cases, students can easily provide the hidden premise(s). E.g., given "Socrates is a man, therefore Socrates is Mortal" they happily add "All men (or all people) are mortal." The Rabbit Rule takes this basic ability and helps the student to apply it to far more complex and subtle cases. The Rabbit Rule illustrates how a heuristic can help an argument map depict the logical structure of the prose original. Like the others below, the Rabbit Rule teaches how to read and write maps and how to distinguish a good map from a poor one – and, by extension, a good argument.

Still, observing Holding Hands exhaustively can be laborious and tedious, and in many cases the suppressed (unstated) premises uncovered are commonsensical and unproblematic. When mapping a complex argument, an experienced mapper need not represent every hidden premise. In fact, most of the time many (perhaps most) of the hidden premises should not be made explicit, otherwise one can't see the forest for the trees. And with reasonably complex arguments, too many trivial premises can result in a most intimidating map, of little use to anyone. Bram van Heuveln (2004) has proposed a "Forest Formula": one should only make explicit those claims with which the inference is sufficiently transparent. He continues, "However, it is not always clear what 'sufficiently transparent' is." Sufficient transparency is almost certainly audience-relative and this whole area needs much careful investigation.

So, students should learn both how to apply Holding Hands and when (and when not) to actually follow it in their maps. Thus, the best way to render an argument is often far from obvious.

---

[2] Footnote for logicians: Some arguments containing logical operators such as universal quantifiers (e.g. categorical syllogisms) legitimately contain such operators as danglers. For example, in "All men are mortal; Socrates is a man; therefore Socrates is mortal" the key term "All" is legitimately a dangler.

In addition to leaving out entire premises, people often also leave key qualifications out of their explicit premises. This brings us to our second heuristic.

How Many? How Much? Most of the time, people's explicit statements leave out key qualifications and, even worse, speakers don't reflect on the qualifications they leave out. Consider someone saying, "Harriet is bad tempered, since she is redheaded."[3] What is being assumed? That all redheaded people are bad tempered? That all redheaded women are bad tempered? That most redheaded people are bad tempered so, on balance, any redhead is more likely to be bad tempered than not? That most redheaded women....? That all redheaded people in my social circle, ...?? Etc., etc.

It is clear that students benefit from discovering how often they – and almost everyone else – drop these crucial quantifiers, making rational discussion that much harder. Training students to semi-automatically ask, "How many? How much?" helps with this discovery.

Going in Circles Doesn't Get you Anywhere is another useful heuristic. Overt, simple textbook-type examples of circular arguments are rare; people rarely say "Bill is at the store because Bill is at the store." But, by argument mapping, one soon discovers that circular arguments are remarkably common. Reconstructing arguments one often finds the only plausible way to put the argument into the map is to make it circular. One naturally tends to fight this temptation – "Surely all of those words couldn't just be going around in a circle!" But often enough it is. Hidden circular arguments illustrate once again Richard Whately's (1836) insight: "A very long discussion is one of the most effective veils of Fallacy;....a Fallacy which when stated barely would not deceive a child, may deceive half the world if diluted in a quarto volume."

The Principle of Charity is a crucial heuristic for counteracting the strong tendency to caricature the reasoning of those who disagree with us. While philosophers have several versions, we are happy with our simple one: Would the author agree that you have presented her claims fairly? The Principle of Charity requires that students try to identify the fairest interpretation possible.

These heuristics and principles do not automatically guarantee a good argument; a non-circular argument may have no danglers, have its quantifiers all in place and yet still be blatantly fallacious (e.g., "All balls are round; All oranges are round; therefore All balls are oranges"). Such heuristics simply help a student recognize what needs to be added to the explicit prose to produce a well-formed argument map. But, it is also true that students who master them will be far ahead of the general public in thinking clearly.

6.3 The L...P in LAMP

Naturally, Argument Mapping by itself will not automatically confer such Critical Thinking gains, any more than running for the bus every day will make one an Olympic sprinter. That's where "Lots of ... Practice" comes into LAMP. These results

---

[3] Based on an example from Scriven (1977).

were premised on the hypothesis that Critical Thinking is a very complex skill, and that maximum improvement, therefore, requires the same kind of training regime that improvement in any complex skill requires – be it fine-furniture making, Olympic swimming, or mathematical prowess. Based on the research by Ericsson et al. (2006),[4] the students' training regime involved extensive, deliberate practice with feedback in mapping and evaluating arguments.

In the dedicated Critical Thinking subjects, the students in the experimental groups did a range of exercises, but primarily mapped and evaluated other people's arguments. Most of these arguments were contained in short texts (around a paragraph long) drawn from the printed media. They were therefore real, messy texts, not texts that were contrived or specifically written to express arguments clearly, so mapping them required interpretation and comprehension. In all, each student tackled around 20–30 arguments in a semester for assessment with feedback. Around the same number of arguments again was available for non-assessable practice exercises, with model answers; but we do not know what proportion of students availed themselves of those.

Once they mapped each argument, students had to evaluate it by assessing the plausibility of the claims and the strength of inferences and record their judgments on their maps. (*Rationale* has an evaluation function that enabled them to do this. Figure 6.3 shows what an evaluated map looks like, using color variation to represent the strength of each inference.) Students then wrote a short (half page) critique of the argument.

In addition to these critiques, students also mapped their own arguments, such as arguments from their essays in other subjects.

In classes where we integrated LAMP into standard courses, students primarily mapped their own arguments for their essays and weekly mini-papers. These were argumentative responses to their weekly academic readings, so students read longer articles, drew their own conclusions and mapped their own case for those conclusions. Although they were encouraged to begin by mapping the arguments contained in the readings, they were not required to do so and those maps were not assessed. Academic authors' arguments were, however, mapped in class, with students either working in small groups or working as a whole group being led by the tutor.

An ideal dedicated LAMP subject would last for, say, 15 weeks meet 3 h per week for lectures as well as an hour of discussion groups. Students would have weekly assignments and would get immediate feedback as far as possible. That is, they would be able to turn in at least part of their weekly assignments and get useful feedback within, say 10 min. Computerized assessment of some aspects of the maps would make this possible.

This is the ideal LAMP and, of course, we have not had the resources or the students' time to reach the ideal. The experimental results above were obtained in classes that only lasted for 12 weeks (as opposed to the typical American 14 or 15 week teaching semester) and only had 2 h of lecture per week (as opposed to 3 h in

---

[4] For a recent comprehensive view of acquiring expertise, see Ericsson et al. (2006). The basic results can be found in Ericsson & Lehmann (1996).

many American universities). That is, American subjects have about twice as many lecture hours per semester as the Melbourne 24 lecture schedule. With only eleven 1-h discussion groups per semester, we only had about three-fourth of the American norm. That the students using LAMP so outperformed the typical American critical thinking subject is strong indication of how powerful LAMP is – we hope soon to run similar tests at an American university. We believe that such a full-semestered subject will easily break what we have been calling "the one-standard deviation improvement barrier."

Further, as most educators will appreciate, we could not give students rapid feedback on their maps – although Ericsson's and other research on expertise emphasizes the considerable advantages of immediate feedback. The computerized feedback is not yet available, but it is, we hope, just a matter of time before it becomes available.

Nor were the dedicated Critical Thinking LAMP classes able to provide weekly homework assignments with their marked papers returned a week later – there was not enough money to pay for such an intensive marking regime. This problem will be near universal in today's tertiary education world.

Given how far our experimental situation was from an ideal LAMP situation, the massive improvement found in these experiments is all the more impressive.

We do not yet know how much practice or feedback it takes to make a substantial difference for most non-university students or those in universities with students quite different from where the experiments were run; far more research is required. Presumably, the answer will differ considerably depending on how intellectually sophisticated the students are. One (unsurprising) possibility is that people vary in how long it takes for the penny to drop. We would then expect improvement to come in a series of "Aha!" moments rather than in a smooth curve, with the frequency of "Aha!" moments and the time it takes for the first "Aha!" varying from person to person. But this is just speculation for the moment.

6.4 Experimental Evidence for LAMP's Cognitive and Pedagogical Benefits in Dedicated Critical Thinking Courses

With regard to Critical Thinking courses, the evidence for LAMP is straightforward: university students doing a semester's subject with reasonably intensive practice in analyzing and evaluating short arguments improved in their ability to think critically two to three times more than students in traditionally-taught Critical Thinking courses, and three to four times more than in standard undergraduate courses.[5] These dramatic results were obtained from several hundred students and were consistent over several years and with different teachers.

---

[5] For reviews of the experimental evidence, see Twardy (2004) and van Gelder et al. (2004). Further research is being done and should be published shortly. All of the critical thinking studies were conducted with first year undergraduates and used standard, objective instruments to measure gains.

6.5 Evidence about LAMP in Standard Classrooms

What does this mean for the teacher in the regular university or secondary classroom where, except in the rarest of circumstances, intensive Critical Thinking training *per se* is not an option? Unlike the strong evidence for dedicated Critical thinking subjects, here the evidence is anecdotal. Although further research with extensive trials is very much needed, our own experiences are encouraging.[6]

All the data below comes from a first year philosophy subject, two second/third year subjects and two honours (fourth year) subjects. In total, there were about 500 students were taught over 3 years. In some subjects, argument maps were integrated into the lectures. In all subjects, students' homework required argument maps of the readings.

From our experience of integrating LAMP into standard university classes, it is clear that it can be done without sacrificing content, at least when the teacher and teaching assistants are sophisticated mappers.[7] We do believe that it confers broader cognitive and pedagogical benefits, though the evidence is much more informal than in the case of dedicated Critical Thinking classes. In the case of all of the following improvements, we strongly believe students using Argument Mapping progressed much further and much faster than in ordinary classes. Yet we must stress that the evidence here is anecdotal. In putting forward these claims, we aim at persuading readers not so much of their truth, as of the importance of subjecting them to proper experimental scrutiny. If there is substance to our observations, LAMP deserves much greater attention from educational researchers than it has hitherto received.

We perhaps should say something about doing careful scientific research in this area. It is difficult, expensive and time-consuming. It is not easy to get an adequate sample size of students in intervention and control groups. It is harder to get an appropriate control group of classes, ones taught by equally committed teachers using traditional methods. While there are several reasonably good standardized tests for Critical Thinking (the studies above used the California Critical Thinking Skills Test), they are really only useful for pre- and post-testing for a single subject. We know of no well-validated standardized subject related tests, such as a test of critical reasoning in history, or philosophy or political science.

In the absence of such tools, the researcher must rely on inter-subjective expert ratings of student papers. While valuable, such ratings can face several difficulties. First, the questions have to be such that the rater cannot distinguish pre-intervention from post-intervention material, except perhaps by the change in question. But, often after a LAMP subject, students use many more connective words such as "thus" and "because." Such words can inform the rater of which group the subject was in, thereby breaking the blind. Second, it is unfortunately not obvious that all experts in such disciplines really are experts in assessing the logical structure of the argument presented. i.e., not all well-established academic "experts," regardless of their other

---

[6] In one subject we gathered feedback half-way through the semester. The results of that feedback are given here whenever relevant.

[7] We have mostly used Argument Mapping in university subjects, though we have had some experience with senior secondary and with gifted primary school students.

qualifications, really have mastered argumentation in their discipline. This can become a tricky, socially awkward issue. Finally, it is not easy getting grants required to get robust data.

Still, these difficulties can be overcome and we intend, in the fullness of time, to overcome them. All offers of help gratefully received.

Let us now turn to specific ways students improved.

6.5.1 Students Became Better at Questioning Arguments

The written assignments and tutorial discussions increasingly showed that students understood objections and how to raise them. For example, they became far better at targeting their own criticisms to specific parts of a given argument, and began to see how to substantiate and justify their criticisms beyond simply stating their disagreement.

Students also became much better at distinguishing objections to a conclusion from objections to one of the reasons for that conclusion. We believe that Argument Mapping greatly helped learning this key distinction and applying it in practice. But we only have informal evidence for this, striking though the effect appeared to us.

6.5.2 Students Became Better at Reading

The quality of weekly tutorial discussions and of weekly written assignments, where students were required to read and comment on a small set of readings, improved as the semester progressed.[8] Discussions and assignments exhibited a greater understanding of the material and of its significance in the broader context of the weekly topics. Students read less for "general feel" and more for conclusions and arguments. They became much better at such crucial basic tasks as distinguishing premises from conclusions.

The difference can be dramatic. For example, before a semester of argument mapping in an introductory Philosophy of Science class, we asked students to identify the main conclusion in the first few pages of Popper's warhorse article, "Science: Conjectures and Refutations" (1952). Many pointed to something that was salient or interesting for them, such as "astrology is a pseudoscience." They did not seem aware of the role this claim played in Popper's argument. After a semester of argument mapping, they were much more likely to approximate the main contention – in Popper's case, along the lines that true science makes bold conjectures and then tries to falsify them.

6.5.3 Students Became Clearer in Their Own Thinking

Again, our impressions were formed primarily from the students' written work and from the tutorial discussions. What's more, students themselves seemed to think that Argument Mapping helped them think more clearly. In the mid-semester feedback,

---

[8] Their maps, also, reflected this shift, though it is difficult to separate their mapping skill from their understanding.

63% agreed with the statement "Argument Mapping helps me think more clearly"; 15% disagreed. In addition, 85% of students agreed with the statement, "Argument mapping makes me think harder about what I am arguing" (7% disagreed and the rest were uncertain). What we've gleaned is that LAMP clarifies students' thinking in regard to specific issues.

We also suspect that LAMP improves students' metacognitive skills because it would be surprising if the acquisition of the concepts of conclusion, reason, objection, etc., did not give students categories for understanding and reflecting on their own thinking; it would be odd if the process of identifying hidden premises both in others' arguments and in their own did not make them aware in general that their thoughts depend on unarticulated, often problematic, assumptions.

6.5.4 Students Became Better at Argumentative Writing

We saw considerable improvement in students' weekly mini-essays in two ways. First, there was a gradual shift from what we term "argument by association" to real arguments; i.e. a shift from "Here's everything I can think of to say about such-and-such" to "Here are the arguments for and against the claim that such-and-such." As one student wrote, Argument Mapping made writing papers "more difficult, because it seemed that all of my ideas had to somehow connect with each other"!

Second, students' later attempts were better structured, both in the order of presentation and in the use of indicators – expressions that clarify the evidential or inferential relationships between ideas. In one informal poll, about 60% of the students said Argument Mapping interfered with their ability to write BS rapidly, which we took as a good sign.[9] Ironically, 46% also thought that it interfered with their ability to express themselves clearly. It is unclear what the second, rather high, figure means. Are students simply complaining that their writings must be more logically coherent? In that case, we can happily live with the objection. Or is there some deeper concern being expressed? More research is needed.

Our listing these benefits of integrating LAMP into a standard subject is not to say that dedicated Critical Thinking classes using LAMP are not preferable. They almost certainly are. It is, however, to say that we believe that substantial improvements in critical thinking can happen in regular classrooms, if they regularly use argument maps both in lectures and class discussion groups. This should be tested in several ways, over a range of subjects from history to English, student levels, and teacher understanding of argument maps. Integrating argument maps into lectures as well as discussion groups is another dimension that needs much more exploration. We do not expect a simple picture to emerge from such research, but do expect considerable improvements in subjects where students are expected to learn how to reason on their own about the material. We also expect that our techniques would be considerably improved if not abandoned altogether for better ones.

---

[9] "BS" was code for bovine excrement.

6.6 How LAMP Confers These Benefits

Fundamentally, we believe that LAMP, whether taught in dedicated critical thinking subjects or in standard content subjects, works because of two interrelated factors. First, Argument Mapping clarifies students' inchoate concept of argument. Second, lots of quality practice ensures that students truly grasp the concepts in a practical and applied (as opposed to vague and theoretical) way.

We strongly suspect that these factors, in combination, produce much better results than either would produce in isolation. In other words, we suspect that students would not get the same substantial benefits either from occasional Argument Mapping alone or from lots of quality practice using a more discursive argumentative method.

It is unclear why LAMP is so effective. Perhaps it is because Argument Mapping makes highly abstract (inferential/evidential) relationships explicit by representing them as spatial relationships; perhaps also because the kind of practice it affords is very precise and constrained; perhaps also because in mapping one lays aside much of the words so one can better see the logical structure.

These are big questions for the psychologists and educationalists, and we can only gesture toward them here. Instead, in this section we will address some of the practical skill elements we think responsible for the benefits we have observed.

A key element in all of what follows is the ability Argument Maps confer on the instructor to give targeted and timely feedback. It goes without saying that students simply putting sentences in boxes does not automatically lead to any of the benefits above. Some students, when asked to accompany a written response with an Argument Map, write their response and then just cut-and-paste their vacuous prose into boxes – a practice with no value whatsoever. For the teacher, however, a lousy map immediately exposes the student's fuzzy thinking. It is less tempting to try reading sense into a map, perhaps simply because of the discrete nature of diagrams: we are not seduced by the apparent continuity of prose. If we fail to understand a paragraph, we may put it down to our own lack of concentration. Failure to understand a map, however, is a clear indication that mapping conventions have been sloppily applied and the failure to communicate clearly lies squarely with the student.

A map helps the teacher give very quick feedback on structure and clarity of thought. For example, a teacher's putting a question mark on an inference arrow, or identifying a term as a "Rabbit," immediately tells the student that that inference doesn't follow. If the task is to analyze someone else's argument the teacher can provide a model map to which students can compare their own. Disagreements in interpretation can focus subsequent debate. Educational research has shown that prompt feedback is much more effective than detailed comments received long after a student completes a task. The minimal and transparent nature of maps makes this feasible. An in-class mapping exercise allows the tutor – or indeed other students – to comment on maps as the students are engaged in constructing them and while the thoughts are fresh in their minds.[10] By contrast, imagine trying to give feedback while students are writing prose!

---

[10] For a glimpse at some of the benefits of fast feedback and collaborative learning see Mazur (1997).

We should note that marking is fastest and most useful once a student has learnt to map reasonably well, otherwise it can be difficult to distinguish problems with grasping mapping conventions and problems with thoughts. By the same token, the basic principles of mapping (with the possible exception of identifying hidden premises) are generally not difficult to understand; so if poor mapping persists beyond an initial introductory period it is not unreasonable to conclude that the difficulty is with the thinking rather than with mapping per se.

Maps make "moves" in argumentation highly visible. Both student and teacher can instantly see the strategies employed by the student in tackling an issue, just by looking at the configuration of red and green boxes on the map. Students can quickly learn that arguments containing objections (and rebuttals to those objections) are likely to be less vulnerable than arguments made up of mountains of green boxes. Because of the mapping conventions, a map will also quickly alert a student to an unrebutted objection, and hence to a weakness in their case. Again, see the sample map at the end of this article.

6.6.1 Improved Reading Comprehension

Reading and mapping an argumentative piece of prose is very complex. When they attempt to map someone else's argument, students must ask, "What is this person actually saying?", "What are the reasons given?". Students must determine what is part of an argument and what is irrelevant. They must distinguish an argument from additional, background information, rhetorical flourishes, repetitions, paraphrases, elaborations and illustrations. Beginners often try to fit onto the map every sentence of a text or every interesting point, whether or not it is germane to ascertaining the truth of the conclusion.

Students must also distinguish the main argument(s) from subsidiary or minor arguments. Then they must identify the different parts of an argument – the main conclusion (not always articulated by the author), reasons for and against, evidence, rebuttals and so on – and make explicit the roles different claims play in relation to one another. They must distinguish an author's rebutting an objection from an author's self-contradiction. They must be able to paraphrase the author's claims, refining them by simplifying, clarifying, making them easier to understand and more precise, eliminating vagueness and ambiguity where possible (e.g. by using quantifiers), and they must do all this without misrepresenting the author's intent. In addition, they must be able to fill in the blanks of all that is implicit in the prose presentation of an argument. They may need to extrapolate, abstract, and identify hidden premises sensibly and fairly. Students understand an argument more clearly to the extent that they manage to articulate its assumptions successfully. Attempting to articulate someone else's assumptions requires that mappers actively and consciously interpret texts in a way they are otherwise unlikely to pursue.

When all this is done in the context of the overall class topic, students can better see the connections between the arguments of different authors. It is easier for them to see the bigger picture when they have clarified its parts. Of course, seeing the bigger picture further enables them to grasp the significance of the detail, and this dynamic interplay between part and whole significantly enhances their understanding both of any particular author's perspective and of the overall issue or debate.[11]

How does LAMP help a student master all those "musts?" We think it is primarily that, by mapping an argument's logical structure, the student becomes aware of each of these tasks. The mapping process itself makes each requirement more salient, in no small part by eliminating those parts of the prose that do not contribute to answering the questions: What is the author saying? Is it true? Once the goal is clear, students begin to look for ways to achieve it; and perhaps the more they practise trying to meet these requirements, the better they become at meeting them.

6.6.2 Improved Questioning of Arguments

Once students understand that an Argument Map is driven by the question, "Why should I believe that?", they begin to better grasp the key notion that an argument is based on justification and evidence. This fundamental understanding enables them to query claims that lack support, and begin to spot inferential leaps.

Careful analysis makes an argument much easier to interrogate. Having identified the premises, including hidden ones, a student can question their reliability and raise objections. Having made the inferential relationships explicit, a student can evaluate their strength: "How well does this support that conclusion?" "Does this really follow?" Finally, having articulated all the arguments presented by an author, the student can ask, "Are there any important considerations missing?"

More generally, maps make thorough evaluation possible. Around four decades of psychological research has shown that there is a range of cognitive biases affecting judgment.[12]

One widespread bias is our tendency to forget or downplay evidence against our beliefs. Making all the arguments explicit prompts people to consider a greater number of relevant considerations, not just the most salient or favorable ones.

How would this work? Why would argument mapping get people to explicitly state otherwise unstated material? After all, crucial objections and awkward facts are not likely to be implicated by holding hands. The answer seems to have two parts. First is what appears to us to be a basic fact we have discovered: when writing prose, students strongly tend to just present the case for their position with, at most, a bit of a caricature of the opposition. They seem to have little appreciation for J.S. Mill's lovely insight in *On Liberty*: "He who knows only his own side of the case knows little of that."

Argument Mapping, when the map has not become too complex, seems to bring out students' recognition that often different people have differing positions, that those alternatives do not necessarily show that the other person is an idiot, and so they should be presented with at least some attempt at accuracy and fairness.

---

[11] The failure to truly understand what we're reading extends far beyond students. In one workshop, hardened bureaucrats were scandalised when they realised they were unable to articulate the argument in a memo. "And yet," they said, "this is so utterly familiar! I read things like this all the time!"

[12] There is a huge literature on these topics. For an accessible introduction, although now a little outdated, see Plous (1993). The classical anthology is Kahneman et al. (eds.) (1982). A recent excellent anthology is Schneider & Shanteau (eds.) (2003).

We suspect that there is a couple of reasons for the different attitudes toward argument maps and prose presentations. First, for reasons which remain obscure, putting arguments into an argument map tends to make students see the propositions more as a logician would, rather than as an advocate would. Perhaps it is because the argument maps stress the logical structure and considerably downplay rhetorical maneuvers. Second, with the pro-argument there in its logical clarity, somehow objections seem psychologically more accessible. But we really don't yet understand why this should be.

Students can learn to evaluate a map systematically. In the courses that achieved substantial gains in Critical Thinking skills, students were required to assess each claim for truth, reliability or credibility, as well as explicitly assessing the strength of each inference and, where appropriate, the extent to which the case presented was complete (i.e. to look for major considerations that might be missing). When these judgments are recorded on a map, weaknesses such as unreliable sources, dubious premises, questionable assumptions and fallacious reasoning are made highly visible, as is the way they infect a whole chain of argument. Only when they have carefully assessed every sub-argument and questioned the case's completeness can students assess the main contention and draw a reliable conclusion. Not only are such cumulative judgments more rigorous than any we perform by relying strictly on our memory; they also give a student a much deeper understanding of what it takes to be justified in holding a belief.

6.6.3 Greater Clarity of Thought

Good mapping requires students to put clear, concise statements in each box, which encourages them to "distill" the key ideas in an argument and express them through a precise sentence. This, combined with the fact that they may not insert extraneous information into a map, discourages waffle (a consequence many resent). When mapping their own arguments, students must keep answering the question, "What am I really trying to say?" They are constrained to be much more explicit about what they think. In order to map their own opinion, they must articulate it much more precisely and argue for it much more cogently than they are likely to do in prose, which has a much higher "fudge factor." Mapping also prompts students to support contentious claims and to anticipate and rebut objections. Further, articulating their own assumptions clarifies their own thinking.

When constructing maps collaboratively, students discover where they disagree with one another; and through their discussion they more deeply understand their own and their fellow students' positions.

6.6.4 Improved Writing

The box and arrow diagrams emphasize in students' minds how claims are evidentially related – what counts as evidence for or against what – since that is what the lines in argument mapping mean. Mapping prompts students to move away from the usual tendency to respond to questions in a vague and thematic way (what might be called the "keyword" or "essay-by-free-association" approach: here's everything I know/can think of saying about X) and try to construct an argument instead. We are convinced that even our bright university students' intuitive grasp of arguments is extremely poor.[13] Few can initially tell the difference between a conclusion arrived at by chains of inference and something simply paraphrased and repeated in the spirit of "What I say three times is true." For all too many students, "therefore" means "and here's another thing I've thought of."

A students' prose can easily obscure an argument's logical poverty, not least of all from a sympathetic teacher, since the teacher can intuitively construct connections between ideas that may not, in fact, be present in the student's head. By overly liberally interpreting what students write, we may be robbing students of the opportunity to learn both how to think clearly and how to articulate those thoughts clearly.[14] Argument mapping puts the onus back on the student to construct and communicate a cogent argument.

Even as they come to far better grasp the notion of an argument, still all too often students think as they write. Consequently, their prose is little more than the diary of their amorphous journey through a brainstorm of ideas. When students construct their map, reach their conclusion and so clarify their thoughts before starting to write, they can convey their reasoning more clearly and in a more structured way. This is not simply because they know what they think and what they want to say before they start writing – a significant benefit in itself. It is also because the map's structure suggests good ways of structuring the paper.[15]

Since mapping encourages a more careful reading of other people's texts, students are likely to treat other authors' opinions more fairly and with more insight. They can better detect vagueness both in their own and in others' ideas, and accordingly present tighter arguments. Rhetorical questions, caricatures and melodramatic overstatements may at best be cognitively vacuous and at worst actively limit or constrain subsequent thinking. They are more plausible in prose than in maps. For instance, if someone says "Textbooks are rubbish" they don't really mean it universally and categorically – it's clearly an exaggeration – but they may nevertheless feel subsequently constrained (by some psychological need to remain consistent) to dismiss all textbooks and so not do the hard work of engaging with such serious issues as whether or not, for example, the way textbooks often simplify topics is a good or bad thing educationally. Beginning with a map, the student can avoid heading in melodramatically overstated directions.

6.7 The Enquiring Classroom

Generally, we believe that employing LAMP in classes creates an atmosphere of enquiry. Because mapping is structured, students better understand the task before

---

[13] This is not surprising. As Deanna Kuhn (1991) showed, people's grasp of argument is poor in general. Kuhn's own studies were conducted in the US; but there is no need to assume the situation is better elsewhere.

[14] See Thomason (1990).

[15] There are ways for a teacher to focus on and scaffold this process of producing written prose from a map. We have constructed both a step-by-step guide for doing so and exercises to hone the skill.

them and so can benefit more by discussions with their fellows.[16] Further, maps often help some students who are reluctant to speak in class. Pointing to a map and saying, "Can you think of any evidence that this is or is not true?" or "Do you think this is a good reason to believe that?" can clarify the task for such students.

The bane of most classroom discussions is that they often meander all over the place, go off on tangents and miss the point. Maps help keep discussion on track. The teacher simply has to literally point to a contentious statement on the map and re-focus attention on it by asking such questions as: "How do you see that as bearing on this point?" "Do you mean that this statement is not true because...?" "Remember we're trying to decide whether or not to accept this statement (or whether or not this is a strong reason/objection). How does this discussion help us do that?" "How would can we put your point onto the map?" The visual representation of an argument makes it much easier to return the discussion back to where the meander started from.[17]

In our experience, mapping an argument helps depersonalize the argumentative process in a liberating way, increasing candour on sensitive issues and defusing tensions by making disagreements more impersonal. Jeff Conklin (2005) has reported a similar phenomenon in organizations, using his form of dialogue mapping. Mapping seems to make it easier to disassociate a point made from the person who made it. Objections are not inadvertently treated as *ad hominem*. Criticisms are seen as directed at statements or inferences on the map, not at their source. Students' views are given a certain validation or legitimacy by being added to the map; and once added, statements or judgments are part of the (abstract) argument and need not be seen as representing a particular person's point of view. The teacher can encourage this attitude further by saying things like, "What do you imagine someone who disagrees with this might say?" or "Can you think of something someone might say to support this point?", thereby prompting students to think of arguments as abstract links between ideas rather than as expressions of one's dearly held beliefs.[18] Still, more research is needed.

6.8 Conclusions

LAMP is Lots of Argument Mapping Practice (e.g. Fig. 6.2 and Fig. 6.3), where the students analyze and comment on the strength or weakness of arguments, receiving timely feedback from instructors. They map their own arguments, as well as arguments

---

[16] On the benefits of peer instruction, see Mazur (1997) and Thomason (1990).

[17] 13 out of 28 students (46%) agreed that argument maps helped keep tutorial discussions on topic, seven (25%) disagreed, while eight respondents were undecided.

[18] We have seen this not only in classroom situations but in the corporate world as well. When facilitating a meeting on a politically sensitive issue where no one was prepared to be seen to be breaking with the "party line," we found that genuine, valuable discussion got going only once someone said, "I don't actually think this, but someone might say...," whereupon others joined in and voiced much underlying anxiety in this way.

contained in real texts of varying lengths.[19] Students engaging in LAMP derive substantial cognitive and pedagogical benefits.

There is good evidence that LAMP, rigorously applied in a semester of a dedicated Critical Thinking subject, confers spectacular gains in critical thinking skills compared to standard courses. However, solid research on its benefits and costs when used in a standard classroom is not yet available. What we have offered here is a preliminary judgment based mostly on our experiences as instructors and partly on students' self-reports. Admittedly the evidence is thin. We need proper experimental and educational research. Are our judgments really justified? If we are right about LAMP and it can benefit younger students, how can it best be incorporated into classrooms? Is there an optimal age at which Argument Mapping should be introduced? Does LAMP work with all kinds of students? What are its effects on students less sophisticated than ours? Do other kinds of mapping confer similar benefits? What sorts of benefits might be derived from a simpler type of argument mapping, where students map reasoning but aren't required to identify hidden premises? How much practice makes a difference? How much training do instructors need in order to employ LAMP successfully? How and why does it really work? Far too many questions remain. Until they are answered our own conviction is the best we have.

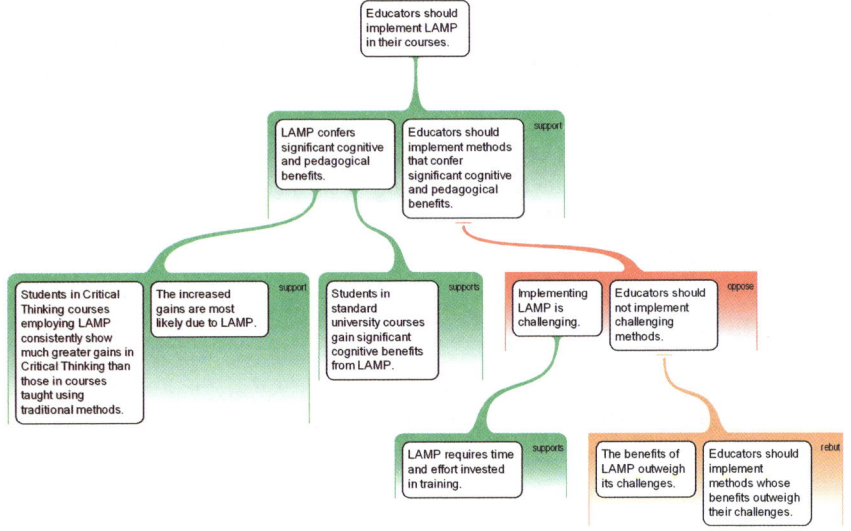

Fig. 6.2. Sample argument map showing some of the color conventions.

---

[19] By "real" texts we mean genuine texts derived from published sources, not artificially simple texts contrived by us. The task of understanding and mapping real examples of arguments is much harder, since such arguments are seldom clearly laid out in prose.

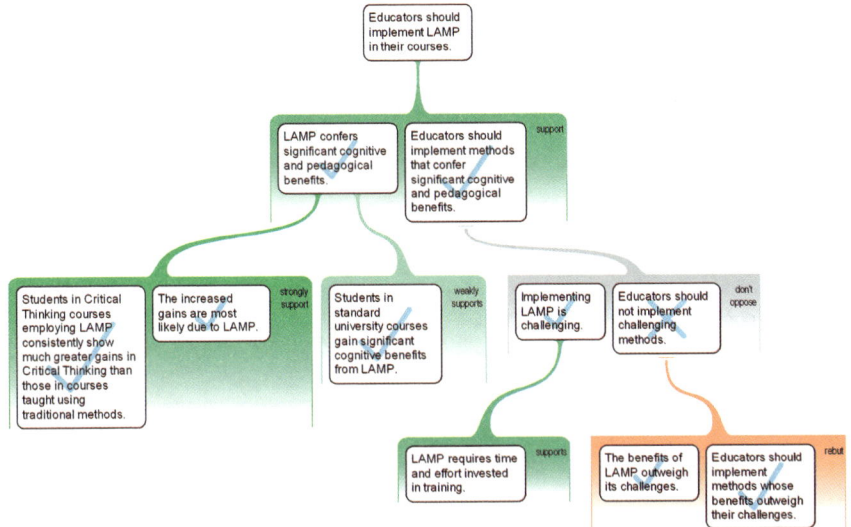

Fig. 6.3. Sample evaluated argument map showing some evaluation conventions.

Acknowledgment

We would like to thank Mark Daley, Steve Crowley, Olaf Ciolek, Tim van Gelder, the editors and anonymous reviewers for very helpful feedback.

References

Conklin, J. (2005) *Dialogue Mapping: Building Shared Understanding of Wicked Problems*. Chichester: Wiley.
Ericsson, K.A. and Lehmann, A.C. (1996) Expert and exceptional performance: evidence of maximal adaptation to task constraints. *Annual Review of Psychology*. 47, 273–305.
Ericsson, K.A., Charness, N., Feltovich, P.J. and Hoffman R.R. (Eds.) (2006) *The Cambridge Handbook of Expertise and Expert Performance*. Cambridge: Cambridge University Press.
Gilovich, T., Griffin, D., and Kahneman, D. (Eds.) (2002) *Heuristics and Biases: The Psychology of Intuitive Judgment*. Cambridge: Cambridge University Press.
Kahneman, D., Slovic, P., and Tversky, A. (Eds.) (1982) *Judgment under Uncertainty: Heuristics and Biases*. Cambridge: Cambridge University Press.
Kuhn, D. (1991) *The Skills of Argument*. Cambridge: Cambridge University Press.
Mill, J.S. (1859) On Liberty, in S. Collini (ed.), On Liberty and Other Writings, Cambridge: Cambridge University Press.
Mazur, E. (1997) *Peer Instruction: A User's Manual*. Upper Saddle River, New Jersey: Prentice-Hall.
Plous, S. (1993) *The Psychology of Judgment and Decision Making*. New York: McGraw-Hill.

Popper, K. (1952) Science: Conjectures and Refutations reprinted in Popper (1962) *Conjectures and Refutations: The Growth of Scientific Knowledge*. Harper.

Schneider, S.L. and J. Shanteau (2003) *Emerging Perspectives on Judgment and Decision Research*. Cambridge: Cambridge University Press.

Scriven, M. (1977) *Reasoning*. New York: McGraw-Hill.

Thomason, N.R. (1990) Making Student groups work: To teach is to learn twice. *Teaching Philosophy*. 13:2, 111–125.

Twardy, C. (2004) Argument maps improve critical thinking. *Teaching Philosophy*. 27:2, 95–116.

van Gelder, T.J., Bissett, M. and Cumming, G. (2004) cultivating expertise in informal reasoning. *Canadian Journal of Experimental Psychology*. 58, 142–152.

van Heuveln, B. (2004) Reasonable, an argument diagramming software package. *Teaching Philosophy*. 27:2, 167–172.

Whately, R. (1836) *Elements of Logic*. New York: Jackson.

7. Scaffolding School Pupils' Scientific Argumentation with Evidence-based Dialogue Maps

Alexandra Okada

The Open University – Knowledge Media Institute, a.l.p.okada@open.ac.uk

Abstract. This chapter reports pilot work investigating the potential of Evidence-based Dialogue Mapping to scaffold young teenagers' scientific argumentation. Our research objective is to better understand pupils' usage of dialogue maps created in Compendium to write scientific explanations. The participants were 20 pupils, 12–13 years old, in a summer science course for "gifted and talented" children in the UK. Through qualitative analysis of three case studies, we investigate the value of dialogue mapping as a mediating tool in the scientific reasoning process during a set of learning activities. These activities were published in an online learning environment to foster collaborative learning. Pupils mapped their discussions in pairs, shared maps via the online forum and in plenary discussions, and wrote essays based on their dialogue maps. This study draws on these multiple data sources: pupils' maps in Compendium, writings in science and reflective comments about the uses of mapping for writing. Our analysis highlights the diversity of ways, both successful and unsuccessful, in which dialogue mapping was used by these young teenagers.

7.1 Why is It so Hard to Argue Scientifically?

Within the school science education research community, there is increasing concern about the weakness of pupils' scientific thinking skills, particularly about the quality of argumentation. Teaching how to argue with evidence is essential for pupils to understand how scientific knowledge is constructed and validated. In many countries like the United Kingdom, the emphasis of the science curricula is shifting towards "scientific literacy". Teachers are now required to develop pupils' capabilities to engage with science-based technology and the socio-scientific issues they will encounter outside school, rather than just on grounding in knowledge or a preparation for a scientific career. As scientific issues continue to dominate public policy that impacts our lives (e.g. food safety, environment, genetic engineering) citizens need to have the skills to assess the reliability of information, the soundness of arguments, and the ethical implications. In order to be "scientifically literate" pupils need to know how to put together arguments coherently (Hodson, 2003). Teachers need to equip young teenagers with the ability to evaluate claims about science in the media.

Learning "scientific argumentation", which is defined by Suppe (1998) as the coordination of evidence and theory in order to support or refute an explanatory conclusion, model or prediction, is not an easy task for pupils. They find it difficult to apply their knowledge to construct scientific explanations. Recent studies show that many pupils are very poor at connecting data and theory in order to validate arguments (Kuhn, 1991; Means & Voss, 1996; Hogan & Maglienti, 2001). Schwarz & Glassner (2003:232) observed that pupils do not know how to connect, to check or challenge arguments and apply them in further activities. *"In science, children 'see' arguments; however they are 'paralytic' concerning the argumentative activities of which these scientific arguments may be the subject"*.

Scientific argumentation skills do not come naturally. Kuhn's studies (1991) motivate the view that presenting controversial socio-scientific issues for debate in the classroom is not sufficient on its own to foster good argumentation skills (Kuhn, 1991; Newton et al., 1999; Rider and Thomason, Chap. 6. Teachers need to assist pupils in making their thinking explicit, helping them to clarify and shape their reasoning around the norms and criteria which underpin scientific discourse (Hogan & Maglienti, 2001:683). Simon et al. (2002) emphasise scientific reasoning is a special form of discourse that needs to be developed and appropriated by pupils through suitable tasks, and through "structuring and modelling". In order to help pupils scaffold scientific argumentation teachers need to show how to set out strong components and establish good connections.

A good scientific argument is constituted by both domain knowledge and argumentative knowledge. Simon et al. (2002:2) point out *"scientific rationality requires a knowledge of scientific theories, a familiarity with their supporting evidence and the opportunity to construct and/or evaluate their inter-relationship"*. Means & Voss (1996) also highlight that subject knowledge and personal experience to elaborate arguments are two important components for argumentation. In order to argue, pupils need to use both scientific concepts and their own arguing skills to ground their reasoning. The more knowledge is integrated in their arguments, the richer is their argumentation (Schwarz & Glassner, 2003:230).

This pilot study is the first in a long term research programme to investigate how approaches like dialogue mapping can augment pupils' scientific reasoning, and critical thinking more broadly. This exploratory work analyses the potential of using dialogue mapping to scaffold young pupils' scientific argumentation. In this context, by scaffolding we mean constructing scientific argumentation graphically through a step-by-step process. We are currently framing this inquiry in terms of the following general questions, each of which has many possible sub-issues:

- *Scientific knowledge and mapping.* As noted, the current interest in deliberation and argumentation that we see amongst researchers and practitioners is driven by the recognition that beyond a good understanding of the domain, pupils also need the skills of being able to communicate and critique in an appropriate way their own reasoning, and that of peers. This question focuses on the interplay between domain and argumentation knowledge: how can each one sharpen the other?
- *Scientific writing and mapping.* What are the effects of translating between the non-linear graphical languages of maps, and linear presentations in speech or prose? Does translating their own or a peer's speech or writing into a map lead to

new insights? What is the effect of creating a dialogue map on derivative written and spoken presentations?
- *Cartographic literacy.* We know a lot from previous research about the cognitive skills of crafting good concept, dialogue and argument maps: it is hard work, but at its best is satisfying and fosters intellectual rigour. Which of these processes do pupils find easy or hard to attain, and can they be communicated in more age-appropriate, multimodal/media ways?
- *The teacher's role.* While highly motivated pupils may learn concept and dialogue mapping from a brief, solitary exposure, we are interested in its development as an intellectual discipline with wide application in the curriculum. How should dialogue mapping be introduced to different ages? What are the key roles for staff/peer interventions? What kinds of activities provide orientations that lead to better or worse deliberations?
- *Software design.* While brief, small scale mapping can be done with pen and paper, software clearly adds new possibilities, e.g. in terms of the unlimited canvas, iterative revision, reusable structures, customisable language, embedded multimedia, storage and retrieval, and working over the internet. What do trials with pupils and staff tell us about the digital tools we are offering them?

We will see these themes emerging as we analyse the case studies, and will revisit them in turn in our discussion. In Section 2, we introduce the idea of using diagrammatic representations to support the acquisition of scientific reasoning skills in secondary schools. Section 3 motivates the use of Dialogue Mapping as an approach, based on the hypothesis that its success in non-educational contexts may be transferable to gifted teenage pupils in the science classroom. In order to ensure quality of scientific argumentation, we introduce an "evidenced based dialogue mapping" approach, which integrates dialogue mapping with Toulmin's model of a scientific argument. In Section 4, we present the methodology applied to this research, which comprises a set of learning activities for applying dialogue mapping to arguing and writing in science, data collected and criteria for analysing extracts. Through three case studies, we describe pupils' achievements and difficulties in constructing scientific arguments. Section 5 presents our findings and our future work.

7.2 Could Argumentative Maps be Useful for Secondary School?

Clearly, no simplistic statements can be made about the merits of different media, ontologies and notations, since they each exert their own influence, and interact strongly with factors such as the learner's domain expertise, fluency with the tools, familiarity with each other, and the way in which their activity is designed (Veerman, 2003). However, based on some chapters in this volume, appropriately designed and deployed mapping tools can aid learning: to make sense of internet information (Zeiliger & Esnault, Chap. 5), clarify reasoning (Rider & Thomason, Chap. 6), develop conceptual understanding (Canas & Novak, Chap. 2; Mariott & Torres, Chap. 3), foster critical thinking (Reed & Rowe, Chap. 8), collaborative inquiry and affordances of different representations for learning (Suthers, Chap. 1).

As a practitioner working on science education for gifted school pupils, O'Brien (2003, p. 70) concludes that argument maps offer:

- A permanent record of thinking on a topic that contributes to a debate
- Clarity and rigour in thinking by improving the sharing of knowledge in a group leading to a deeper understanding of issues
- Efficient ways to present overviews indicating boundaries of current knowledge or debating in complex argumentation to another pupil
- Better decision making by ensuring that a higher proportion of relevant considerations are taken into account

Specifically, in science education, there are recent studies about using graphic representations to help students argue in science in high school and higher education. For instance, Schwarz & Glassner (2003) analysed argumentation as a central form of literacy with high school pupils in physics. Suthers (2003, Chap. 1) investigated scientific argumentation for collaborative inquiry with undergraduate pupils in physics. In the literature, several researchers have developed argumentation with younger pupils, but without computer support (i.e. Driver et al., 2000; Hogan & Maglienti, 2001; Jaubert & Rebiere, 2005; Manson & Boscolo, 2000; Means & Voss, 1996; Ratcliffe, 1997).

This is the first work to explore the potential of using a particular approach called Dialogue Mapping for young secondary school pupils to construct their scientific arguments. Children and teenagers frequently argue in home and at school, asking questions, giving answers and reasons for and against. They also have to give counterarguments to refute other's opinions. The components of their argumentative conversation – questions, answers, pros, cons, comments and conclusions – are similar to those used to represent dialogue maps, as described next.

7.3 Adapting Dialogue Mapping for Scientific Arguing

Dialogue mapping is a knowledge mapping technique developed by Conklin (2006) to build shared understanding during discussions. Dialogue mapping extends the Issue-based Information System (IBIS) created by Rittel in the 1970s to solve ill-structured problems – denominated "wicked problems". IBIS is a rhetorical grammar with three core elements, issues, positions and arguments, which can be rendered as textual outlines and as "graphical IBIS" (gIBIS) networks that grow with the conversation (Conklin & Begeman, 1988). Extended by Compendium visual hypermedia tool, this technique has been applied in organisations and companies by researchers, training facilitators, consultants and team leaders in support of collaborative sensemaking (Selvin, 2003, Chap. 11; Ohl, 2008, Chap. 13; Sierhuis & Buckingham Shum, 2008, Chap. 14). Given the success of Compendium in these sectors, and the growing need to begin instilling argumentation literacy at an early age (with a specific interest in science), the question arises: Could dialogue mapping be equally useful in the classroom, to help pupils argue scientifically?

In order to show how dialogue mapping can be used to represent the process of arguing, we selected this example below, which collates responses posted online at the summer school where pupils were asked: "what makes a good scientific argument?".

7. Scaffolding School Pupils' Scientific Argumentation with Dialogue Maps

> Teacher: What do you think makes a good scientific argument?
> Kim: It must include questions, answers and explanations of the reason why.
> Sara: Statistics are very useful and gives readers an idea of amount or what you are talking about
> Beth: Evidence and strong pros and cons and a good topic to base the argument on
> John: A good scientific argument consists of a good question, a good strong fact with an even better argument!
> Teacher: What is a strong argument?
> Peter: An argument showing both sides fairly with evidence for them and some biased comments for the side that you support but be careful you don't contradict yourself
> Alex: A logical, well thought out statement that works in putting your thought across in a few concise sentences
> Tina: Keep arguing and go over all evidence and always confirm it.
> However, nether be biased and expect to be surprised, not all discoveries are predictable.
> Lucy: The more facts the better

Extract 7.1 Responses from Totally Wild Science Course in Moodle.

In these maps, the Compendium icons were used to represent questions (question node), answers (answer node), arguments (pro node), counterarguments (con node) and data (note node). As we can see, this map could have different representations, depending on the interpretation of the group and mapper. If the discussion in Extract 7.1 was Dialogue Mapped by a beginner, they might capture contributions more or less as they were uttered, and linked to reflect the temporal sequence. However, Dialogue Mapping at its best helps to clarify the key Issues, thus illuminating how the other contributions relate to these in the form of Ideas responding to those Issues, and the relative Pros and Cons of each Idea in that context (Fig. 7.1).

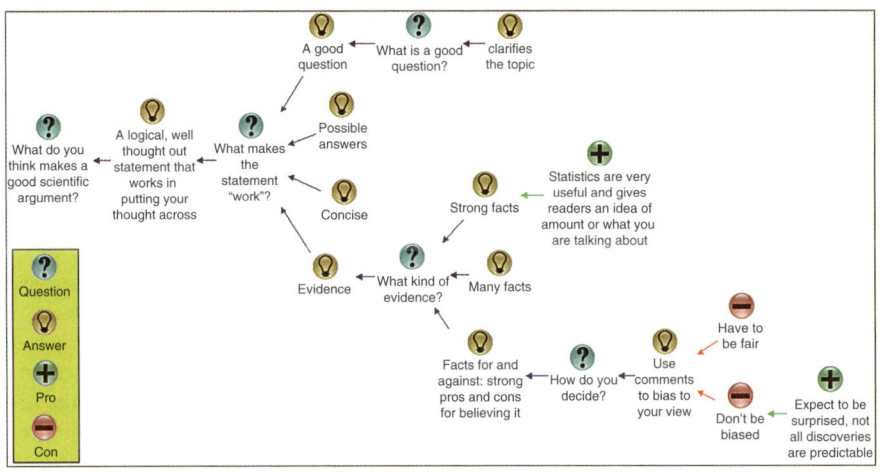

Fig. 7.1. Dialogue maps in Compendium (tool described in Chap. 14 by Sierhuis and Buckingham Shum).

The emphasis thus shifts from chronological structure to logical structure. The challenge is how teacher intervention, software tools and practice can effect this shift in students, from naturalistic reasoning/discourse to conceptual reconstruction.

While IBIS provides a relatively intuitive language, as we discuss next, it is missing a key element central to scientific argumentation: evidence.

7.3.1 Evidenced-based Dialogue Map

In scientific reasoning, it is important that the pupils can ground their claims in scientific concepts instead of personal convictions. The quality of their arguments is also better if they can connect not only supporting arguments, but also counter-arguments (thus resisting confirmation bias), and data as backing for claims.

In order to represent the components of a scientific argument for teachers, Simon et al. (2002) adopt the well known Toulmin (1958) model [shown in Fig. 7.2; also discussed in Chap. 8 by Rowe & Reed and Carr, (2003)]. In their research, Toulmin approach was applied for teachers to guide pupils in structuring their argumentation scientifically and assessing the quality of their argumentation.

Toulmin's model can be re-expressed in dialogue mapping's IBIS language as shown in Fig. 7.3 (Carr, 2003). Following dialogue mapping's conversational paradigm, the link arrows go from right to left since they respond to or otherwise build on prior contributions, as shown by the various link types (supports, challenges, etc.).

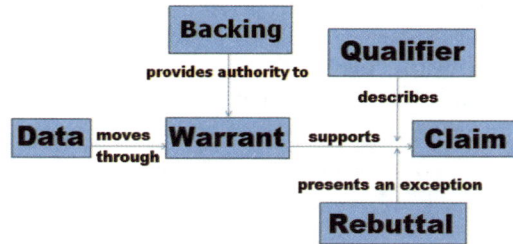

Fig. 7.2. Toulmin argumentation scheme.

In Toulmin form, there are six basic components of an argumentative move:

1. *Claim*: is the position on the issue and the essence of the argument. This represents the arguer's conclusion.
2. *Data*: i.e. initial grounds for the argument and evidence that can be accepted as factually true. This can be based on facts, events, examples and statistics.
3. *Warrant*: evidence used to support the connection between the data and the claim. It can be "authoritative" based on a reference by an expert; "motivational" based on convictions or "substantive" based on example, classification, generalisation or cause and consequence. In science, the quality of the warrant is based on scientific concepts (substantive) rather than own convictions (motivational).
4. *Rebuttal*: this states the exceptions to the claim and is an exception to the truthfulness of the argument. It illustrates instances where the argument may not be true.
5. *Qualifier*: this states the "strength" of the claim. It represents the validity of an argument and indicates the context or circumstances where the argument is "true".
6. *Backing*: a source of authority for the warrant…

7. Scaffolding School Pupils' Scientific Argumentation with Dialogue Maps   137

However, in this study we selected only four components of Toulmin's model – claim, warrant, rebuttal and data. These were considered by the science teacher to be the most relevant elements for pupils to incorporate into a scientific argument and a simple approach to scaffold their arguing skills.

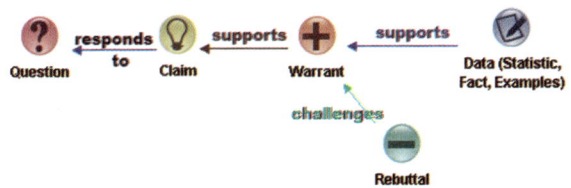

Fig. 7.3. Evidenced-based dialogue map.

Figure 7.3 shows the scientific argument structure created in Compendium which we call as "evidenced-based dialogue map". The connections between these components are not exactly as Toulmin's model. It is a simple structure for scientific explanations, whose a claim should be connected to one or more warrants, rebuttals and data in order to demonstrated the evidence for the claim. Considering the vocabulary of these 12–13 years old pupils, these four components refer to answers, pros, cons and data (shown in Extract 7.1).

In this context, we examine whether Compendium helps pupils write scientific arguments. Our hypothesis is that it does so by scaffolding the task, breaking down the process into a series of more manageable and visualisable steps for pupils:

1. Represent initial reasoning in the form of a map, using Compendium's icons to show the parts of the argument visually.
2. Use these visualised components to elicit further existing knowledge, and add this to the map.
3. Assess the strengths and weaknesses of the reasoning, by seeing if the claims are backed up with enough evidence.
4. Once the reasoning is strengthened, to transform the map into a linear text-based argument.

These four steps were used to plan the learning activities described in the following section.

7.4 Methodology: Constructing Scientific Arguments in Compendium

7.4.1 Context: A Science Summer School

In this research, we observed 20 "gifted and talented" pupils who volunteered to attend a summer course "Totally Wild Science" during their school holiday in 2006. "Gifted and talented" is a term used in the United Kingdom for pupils who are in the top 10% of the national average based on their performance in formative assessment and test scores. The educational science consultant who organised this course with the educational committee of Canterbury Christ Church University selected 12–13 year-old teenagers, from different schools in the United Kingdom, based on an essay that described why they wanted to take this course and why they were very good at learning science.

"Totally Wild Science" was a science course organised around three topical themes: Forensic Science, Space, and Environment, with the aim of engaging pupils to develop their science learning skills. The main approach of this course was to use a great variety of learning projects in the science and computer laboratory, virtual learning environments and events such as trips and workshops with scientists. The main aspect of this course was to help them apply their own knowledge in projects in order to develop their scientific skills, rather than teaching new science concepts.

This research focused on the Environment project: "Global Warming – what do you think will happen in the future?" We developed a set of activities using dialogue maps about global warming with the science teacher. The tasks were published in the Moodle virtual learning environment, which was used to support collaborative learning. Pupils recorded their discussion and dialogue maps in a Moodle Forum (threaded discussion tool). They also posted their essays based on their dialogue maps. During this process, they described their progress and reflected on their difficulties and improvement. Compendium was introduced by the author, who demonstrated how the discussion between the science teacher and pupils could be recorded by dragging and dropping Compendium icons: questions, answers, pro, cons and notes. Some examples (similar to Fig. 7.1) were presented to illustrate a dialogue mapping structure. The science teacher explained the importance of organising scientific arguments through these icons. Each answer should be connected to pros, cons and data. He showed some examples of maps based on Fig. 7.3.

Fig. 7.4. This picture illustrates a pupil working with Compendium (*left*), dragging into her map the results of web image searches (*right*).

Although pupils were using Moodle and Compendium for the first time, they did not encounter difficulties in manipulating these tools. Dragging and dropping information from the web and Moodle into Compendium (illustrated by Fig. 7.4) was straightforward. This level of digital literacy enabled us to start the project with new tools with a brief introduction.

7.4.2 Learning Activities

In this *Global Warming* project we organised seven activities (Table 7.1).

Table 7.1. Learning activities – using dialogue mapping for arguing and writing about global warming.

Learning activity	Tools
"*Reflecting on Writing in Science*": 1. How much do you like writing in science? (1 = not at all, 3 = OK, 5 = I really like it) Give a reason. 2. What do you think makes a good scientific argument?	Moodle – Forum I
"*Writing about Global Warming*": Elaborate a composition in pairs about "What will be the impact of Global Warming (crops, diseases, ecosystem, water or weather)?". Share it in the forum discussion.	Moodle – Forum II
"*Mapping Scientific Arguments*": Use Compendium for arguing about "What you think will happen in the future in the UK?" Represent your answers, arguments, "facts and evidence".	Compendium, Moodle – Forum III
"*Mapping data from the web*": Enrich the map with significant information from the internet and prepare a better argumentation structure.	Compendium, Internet, Moodle – Forum IV
"*Editing and improving map*": Improve scientific arguments in the map by using teacher's feedback and focussing on the strongest idea.	Compendium.
"*Writing from your map*". Export your map as an image or a list. Bring it into Word. Write your composition from this map and share your map and text	Compendium, Word, Moodle – Forum V
"*Reflecting on writing from maps*": Share your opinion about your learning, the use of Compendium and dialogue mapping applied to writing.	Moodle – Forum VI

7.4.3 Data Focus for This Study

The method of this qualitative research was case studies involving qualitative analysis. We collected discussions, maps, writing and notes posted by pupils and the teacher in Moodle, which served not only as a collaborative learning environment but also as a data archive for subsequent analysis. We also collected the teacher's private annotations during the project.

The analysis consisted of three stages: (1) preliminary consideration of all recorded data (40 maps, 40 messages and 20 writings); (2) detailed examination of each pair of pupils who worked together analysing what they have produced (three maps, four messages and two writings); (3) deep study of three cases which were selected because they were distinctive, as defined by Tables 7.2 and 7.3.

7.4.4 Criteria for Analysing the Extracts

We identified different levels of argumentation and writing. Based on the Toulmin argument scheme, we described four levels of argumentation and writing. These two tables were used as a reference to guide the analysis of the three case studies.

Table 7.2. Criteria for analysing level of arguing.

Level of argumentation	Description
(1) No argument	Only claims
(2) Weak	Claims and (weak) warrant (based on convictions)
(3) Simple	Claims (weak) warrants and rebuttals or data
(4) Strong	Good Claims, good warrants, rebuttals/data

Table 7.3. Criteria for analysing level of writing.

Level of writing	Description
Very weak	Few words, no sentences, weak argumentation
Weak	Few sentences with weak or simple argumentation
OK	Connected sentences with simple argumentation.
Good	Well connected sentences with strong argumentation.
Very good	Good paragraphs with strong argumentation and domain knowledge

We present data from three pairs of pupils for range of sources, since they represented different outcomes. Like the rest of the class, these six teenagers did not enjoy writing in science. None of them had problems in using Compendium, although they encountered difficulties in dialogue mapping which we will describe.

Case A analysed data from pupils who had difficulties in writing and arguing. Their writing in science was considered "weak" by the science teacher; because they did not apply enough science concepts and their arguments were based on personal convictions. The level of argumentation dropped in their first map (from level 2 to level 1), then it gradually improved (from level 1 to level 3). Their final essay showed that mapping did not help them construct significant arguments. Although it contributed to making their writing clearer – level "ok", their argumentation were not strong because they did not present enough data nor counterarguments. Here, we focus on analysing their difficulties.

Case B analysed data from pupils with poor skills for writing and arguing. Their first writing before mapping was classified as "very weak" with no arguments. In their maps, the level of argumentation gradually increased (from level 2 to level 4). At the end, their composition from maps was significantly improved – "good". They included data and counterarguments, but they were not able to include science concepts to ground every claim. Here, we focus on analysing their achievements.

Case C analysed pupils who were good at arguing and writing, but presented initial difficulties in mapping. At the beginning of their project mapping was neither easy nor useful for them. Their level of argumentation dropped from 4 (in their writing) to 2 (in their first map). During the mapping activities, their scientific arguments were gradually improved (from level 2 to level 4). At the end, they were also able to present significant improvements in their writing, which was considered "very good". Here we focus on mapping skills for constructing scientific arguments.

Table 7.4 summarises the level of argumentation and writing based on Tables 7.2 and 7.3 during their learning activities. In forum 2, they recorded their initial writing. In forum 3, they created their first map. In forum 4, they improved their map by bringing data from the web. In forum 5, they prepared the final version of their map, exported to web outline and from a sequential list of their map's components they elaborated their writing.

7. Scaffolding School Pupils' Scientific Argumentation with Dialogue Maps 141

Table 7.4. Level of argumentation and writing of three pairs of pupils.

Case	Pupil	Forum 2 first writing	Forum 2 arguing	Forum 3 first map	Forum 4 second map	Forum 2 third map	Forum 5 final writing	Would you use maps?
A	Alan	Weak	(2)	(1)	(2)	(3)	Ok	No
	Alex							Maybe
B	Beth	Very weak	(1)	(2)	(3)	(4)	Good	Probably not
	Ben							Yes
C	Chris	Good	(4)	(2)	(3)	(4)	Very good	Yes
	Carl							Yes

7.4.5 Case A

In Extract 7.2, two pupils who worked together explain why they don't like writing in science. For Alan, writing is "painful" and for Alex, "it helps for revision but is boring". Both were able to provide reasonable answer what makes a good scientific argument. They also constructed an argument about the future of the UK in the event of Global warming.

Teacher: How much do you like writing in science? (1 = not at all, 3 = OK, 5 = I really like it).
Alan: Not at all. Because I get cramp in my wrist easily, so it is actually painful to write large amounts by hand.
Alex: OK. It helps for revision but gets a bit boring. It is more fact than fiction. It is more remembering than imagining.
Teacher: What do you think makes a good scientific argument?
Alan: A good scientific argument consists of a good question with a good strong fact with an even better argument!
Alex: A theory and logical, well thought out statement that works in putting your thought across in a few concise sentences.

Extract 7.2 from the Forum I – Reflecting on Writing in Science.

Extract 7.3 shows these pupils' writing. Their answer was based on a long sentence, which presented their ideas, argument and a short science explanation.

Teacher: Write down for your topic: What you think will happen in the future in the UK? Give reasons.
Re: Writing about Global Warming – Group Water by Alan and Alex.
If the ice caps do melt and the product of the melting (the water) goes into the sea (which it will) it will make the water levels rise dramatically and flood villages, towns, cities and maybe even small countries! Shocking(!) The reasons for these ideas are really just logic.
Teacher: Why will water levels rise dramatically if the ice caps melt?

Extract 7.3 from the Forum II – Writing about Global Warming.

In order to analyse the level of argumentation of these pupils' writing, the author created the map below (Fig. 7.5) in Compendium. By interpreting their answers graphically based on Toulmin's model, we can see that they included a claim, a warrant and one piece of data. The level of this argumentation is 2. They were able to connect warrant and a concept to support their claim, but they were not able to apply knowledge scientifically. They presented strong conviction (which it will) to support their answer, but they did not provide enough justification. The argument is sound in structure. However, they were not able to explain how ice caps melt would make the water levels rise "dramatically". They did not include data showing the risk of flooding in the UK nor any rebuttals.

Fig. 7.5. Map created in Compendium based on Toulmin's models.

Extract 7.4 shows the first dialogue map this pair created in Compendium. They generated eight questions and six short answers. Although their questions were very relevant and imaginative, their answers were very short ("yes", "no", "probably not") and there were no arguments.

Re: Mapping scientific argument – Group Water by Alan and Alex

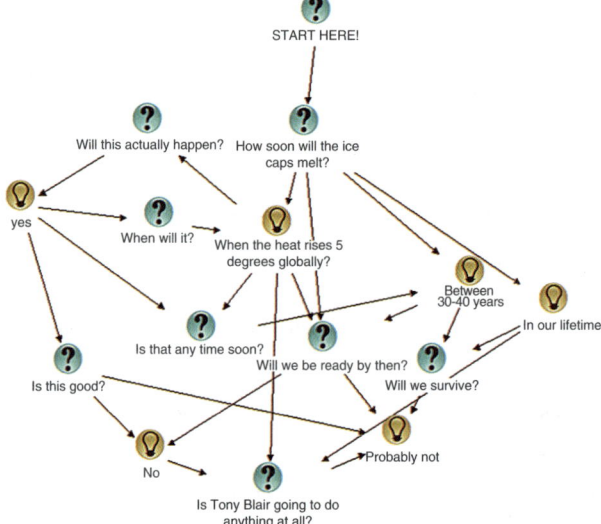

Teacher: What are your main questions? What pros and cons can you include?

Extract 7.4 from the Forum III – Mapping Scientific Arguments.

For these pupils, writing an argument in the discussion forum was quick, but representing an argument graphically was very hard. They spent a long time, and they were not able to structure clearly their reasoning. Reading the content of this mapping is a little distracting, and it is easy to be lost. In this intricate structure, connecting pros, cons and data for each answer is more difficult because the information is not well organised spatially. The level of their argumentation in this map is 1 – weak claims (e.g. "yes", "in our lifetime", "between 30 and 40 years",…) and no arguments (neither pros nor cons). Comparing the argumentation in their writing (Extract 7.3) to their first map, the quality dropped from level 2 to level 1. Looking at their short answers, it is hard to identify "well thought out statements",

7. Scaffolding School Pupils' Scientific Argumentation with Dialogue Maps   143

because they are incomplete sentences. These few words only make sense if we read the questions, but each answer addressed several questions.

In this case, Compendium functioned as a brainstorming medium which helped them to generate several interesting questions about implications for policy and action. They were able to go through a rich process of questioning. As Alex mentioned "a good scientific argument consists of a good question". However they were not able to connect warrants, rebuttals and data in their map. In this case, the challenge for teachers is to help pupils find ways to reorganise their map. Pupils who are not good visual thinkers and not familiar with mapping techniques will need more support for establishing good connections between components.

Extract 7.5 shows their map after teachers support. The pupils improved the structure and they were able to construct scientific claims through full sentences. This new structure suggests a sign of substantial cognitive change. This process is not quick; they spent a long time restructuring their map. In this activity, "Mapping data from the web", they did not access the internet because they were focussed on disentangling their "intricate web" and clarifying their thinking. They deleted many nodes; some of them were excluded accidentally (as described in Extract 7.7).

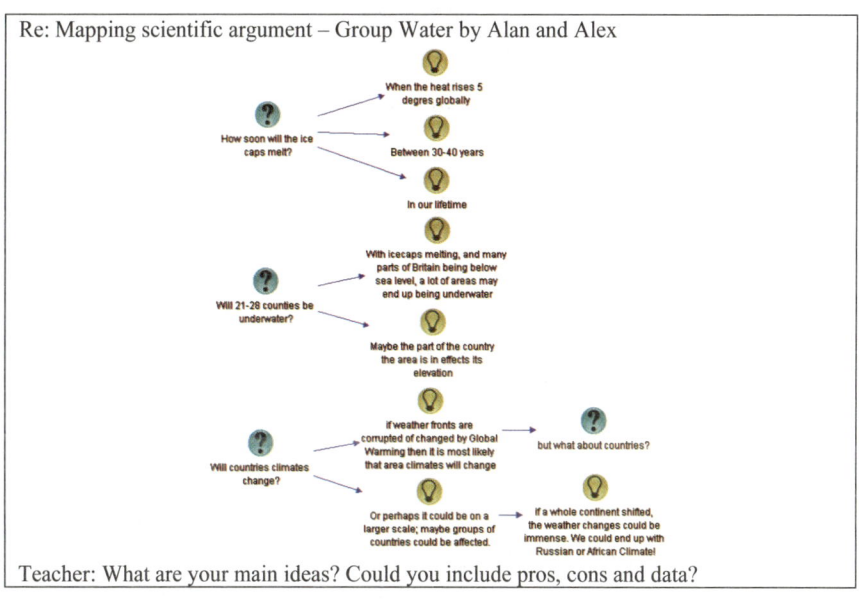

Extract 7.5 from the Forum IV – Mapping Data from the Web.

As we can see in the Extract 7.5, although the structure of their map is better, the level of argumentation was not significantly improved. They made some progress on the content of their claims, but the quality of their arguments in this new map is similar to their initial writing. Their warrants are not based on accurate knowledge. They did not give any evidence to support their arguments. Their argument is based on common sense knowledge (melting ice increases the volume of water) but if the ice is floating on the sea, the level of water will not rise. If they are talking about ice from land, then it will rise. From the science perspective it would be important to ask what science concepts ground their ideas, for instance, why would "the whole continent shift"? They tried to create arguments which make sense based on "logic" and suppositions. They did not support their claims with warrants based on science concepts, rebuttals or data.

Extract 7.6 presents their final map and composition. In the map, we can notice their difficulties again in organising the structure of nodes, in choosing icons and making connections. The arrows, again, were represented in different directions.

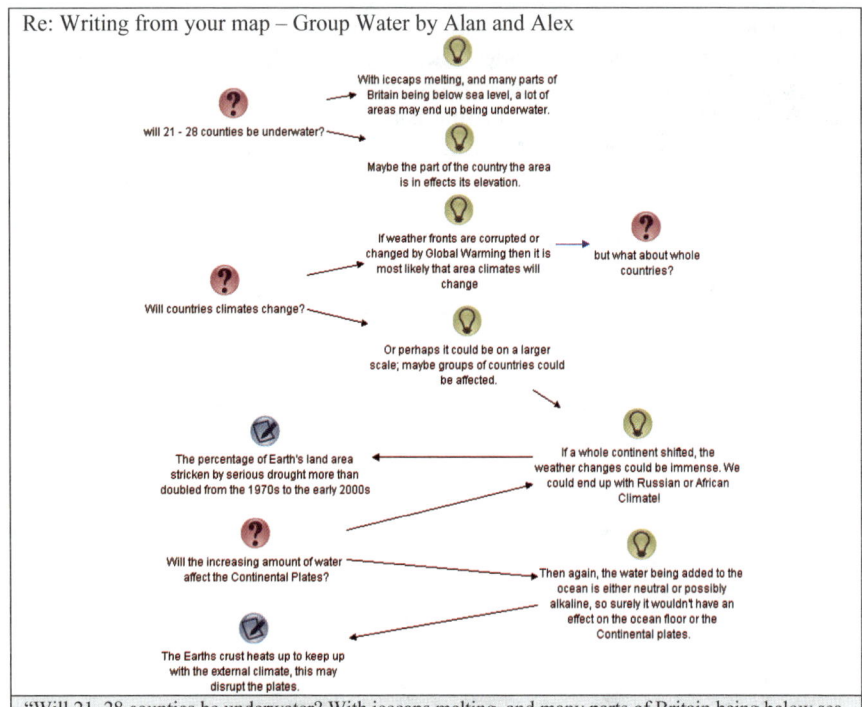

"Will 21–28 counties be underwater? With icecaps melting, and many parts of Britain being below sea level, a lot of areas may end up being underwater. Maybe the part of the country the area is in affects its elevation.
Will countries climates change? If weather fronts are corrupted or changed by Global Warming then it is most likely that area climates will change. It could be on a larger scale. Maybe groups of countries could be affected. If a whole continent shifted, the weather changes could be immense. We could end up with Russian or African Climate! The percentage of Earth's land area stricken by serious drought more than doubled from the 1970s to the early 2000s.
Will the increasing amount of water affect the Continental Plates? Then again, the water being added to the ocean is either neutral or possibly alkaline, so surely it wouldn't have an effect on the ocean floor or the Continental plates. The Earths crust heats up to keep up with the external climate, this may disrupt the plates.

Extract 7.6 from the Forum V – Writing from Your Map.

In their second paragraph, they came up with a series of plausible claims, but rarely included relevant data, and did not establish a relationship between the claim (e.g. "If a whole continent shifted, the weather changes could be immense") and the

7. Scaffolding School Pupils' Scientific Argumentation with Dialogue Maps   145

evidence (e.g. "The percentage of Earth's land area stricken by serious drought more than doubled from the 1970s to the early 2000s"). In their third paragraph, the argument is good, but the science knowledge (suggesting that climate change might alter the structure of the Earth's tectonic plates) does not make sense. Their argumentation did not improve significantly comparing the initial writing (level 2) with their final composition (level 3). There are more sentences organised in better sequences, they could visualise their strongest ideas, but they did not develop the quality of arguments, they were not able to identify where they should connect more evidence. They did not add strong warrants, rebuttals and enough data. There were no strong connections based on science concepts between their claims.

Extract 7.7 shows pupils confirming that mapping was not significant to construct arguments. "The map doesn't make things any easier". "A written explanation can be clearer" than a graphical representation of argumentation. For these pupils, "it is easier to just think through an argument than make one on compendium". About mapping for writing, Alan states "The map doesn't make things any easier". For Alex mapping "makes writing quick and efficient, but some good detail can be lost".

Teacher: How useful do you think maps are for constructing scientific arguments? Give reasons.
Alan: Little use. For me it is easier to just think through an argument than make one on Compendium.
Alex: Good, but a written explanation can be clearer
Teacher: Did you find any problems during the process of mapping?
Alan: It was a little bit fiddly, and I accidentally deleted things a few times.
Alex: Not really
Teacher: Would you use a map in future? If so, say why?
Alan: No.
Alex: maybe, it depends on what it would be used for
Teacher: Overall, does the map make the process of writing any easier? Why?
Alan: The map doesn't make things any easier.
Alex: It briefs things. that makes it quick and efficient but some good detail can be lost
---

Extract 7.7 from the Forum VI – Reflecting on Writing from Maps.

In summary, pupils turned dialogue mapping into a "brainstorm of questions". Constructively, the pupils generated several new interesting issues, but their argumentation remained poor. A good question was a good starting point for creating a scientific argument: incisive issues can presumably only help scientific inquiry. However, in the process of brainstorming in the "blank canvas" of Compendium – giving it flexibility to establish connections – one of pupils' difficulties was to organise icons and arrows on the screen. A strong visual template could probably help them develop their scientific arguments.

Selvin (2003, Chap. 11) points out that practitioners (Compendium users) need important skills for constructing good dialogue maps. Rider and Thomason (2008, Chap. 6) show the importance of developing lots of argument maps to create good argumentation.

Pupils need to learn how to structure all issues properly in the map to avoid a confusing layout. If pupils create an intricate web of ideas, than teachers need to help them disentangle it, because the more complex is the format of their map, the more difficult would be editing and improving it. It is important to teach how to establish good sequences and connections between components. At the same time it is good to have initially the flexibility to allow pupils shape their reasoning by creating nodes and connections without feeling attached to a particularly structure.

7.4.6 Case B

Case B shows quite structured mapping, which helped pupils generate evidence-based claims. Their maps provided visual guidance for them to identify for which claims they could develop arguments using their existing knowledge, and which they could not.

Extract 7.8 presents this pair of pupils who dislike writing in science as well. Beth "hardly ever does it and always gets stuck for an answer". For Ben "doing it fully and properly is V. Tedious and Tiresome". They were able to describe what makes a good scientific argument. However, they had serious difficulty in writing an argument.

> Teacher: How much do you like writing in science? (1 = not at all, 3 = OK, 5 = I really like it).
> Beth: 2. Because I hardly ever do it and I always get stuck for an answer
> Ben: 3. Writing is ok for me. I don't mind writing and sometimes it can be good, but doing it fully and properly is V. Tedious and Tiresome
> Teacher: What you think makes a good scientific argument?
> Beth: Evidence and strong pros and cons and a good topic to base the argument on.
> Ben: I think that good sturdy evidence is obviously the basis to a strong conclusion and also to try and disprove any other theories by any means possible

Extract 7.8 from the Forum I – Reflecting on Writing in Science.

In Extract 7.9, we can see their text posted in the forum. Their writing was based on short answers of a few words, with no sentences, and critically, no arguments. They did not give reasons for their answer and they were not able to justify their ideas using "evidence" or "pros and cons".

> Teacher: Write down for your topic: What you think will happen in the future in the UK? Give reasons.
> Re: Writing about Global Warming – Group Ecosystem by Beth and Ben
> Impacts on nature. Disappearance of many wetlands and extinction of some species.

Extract 7.9 from the Forum II – Writing about Global Warming.

Figure 7.6 shows a map created by the author to represent the level of argumentation of these pupils' writing. Based on Toulmin's model, we can see that all components are claims. They did not present any warrant, data or rebuttals. Their level of arguing and writing is very weak (level 1).

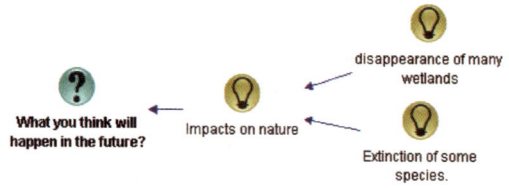

Fig. 7.6. Map created in Compendium based on Toulmin's models.

7. Scaffolding School Pupils' Scientific Argumentation with Dialogue Maps

Extract 7.10 shows their first dialogue map in Compendium. They generated a question, two answers, a pro and a con. Interestingly, for each answer, they represented a clear intention of supporting and challenging it by bringing pros and cons. For the second idea, they were able to bring an argument and a counterargument. However, they were not able to explain their claims properly or connect data to them. Looking at their map, it was possible for the teacher to see immediately from the "placeholder" Pro and Con nodes with question marks where they lacked information, and what role they saw this playing in their analysis (that is, how information fragments could become contextualised knowledge). By looking at the text of each node, the science teacher could also identify problematic assumptions in their argumentation (e.g. if it gets colder there will be no sun) and pose follow-on questions (Extract 7.10).

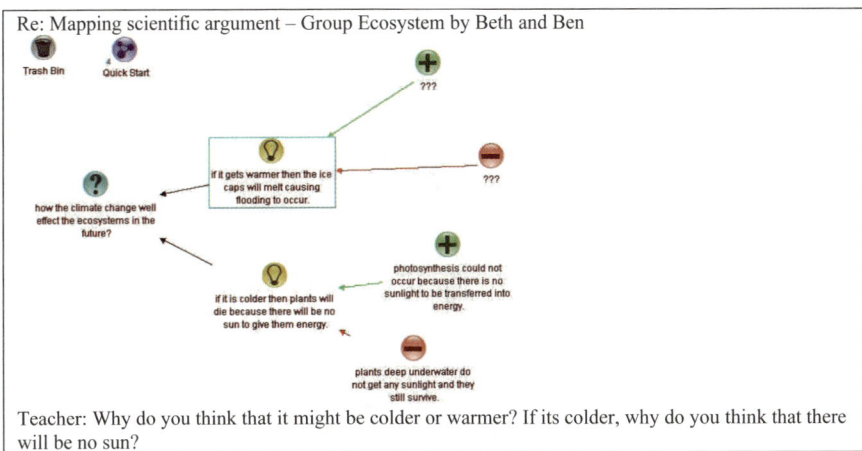

Extract 7.10 from the Forum III – Mapping Scientific Arguments.

In order to analyse the level of argumentation embedded in their dialogue map, we examined each component directly from their Compendium map. They represented two claims using proper sentences but they were not able to establish good connections. Their level of argumentation in their first map (2) is better in the map than in their writing (1) because they included warrant and rebuttals, but it was not significantly improved. Looking at their second claim they applied successfully the concept of photosynthesis in order to justify that "plants will die" in case of "there is no sunlight". However, this warrant was not substantive. They did not explain the connections between "climate change", "it might be colder" and "there will be no sun". This association was based on their own convictions. Their map suggests that they do not have clear understanding about the relationship between Global Warming and the Gulf Stream.

In this case, we would argue that while the visual IBIS language in dialogue mapping prompted them to bring warrant and rebuttals to ground each of their ideas, the nature of the argumentation did not show improvement, particularly due to the lack of science concepts presented in their map. They were not able to apply enough science concepts to support their main claims. The macrostructure of their reasoning was good (i.e. at the level of good IBIS form), but the microstructure was weak.

Extract 7.11 shows their maps extended with data from two websites during the activity to map data from the web. Pupils brought two notes from the internet. Mapping the web was neither easy nor fast. For them, bringing data into the map did not mean simply dragging and dropping sentences into Compendium. They had to think about what to select and where to connect it. It is easy to visualise in the map where "they got stuck for an answer". Although they could not answer the teacher's questions (Extract 7.10) to improve their two initial ideas, they selected two new pieces of information that helped them elaborate three arguments around a new answer.

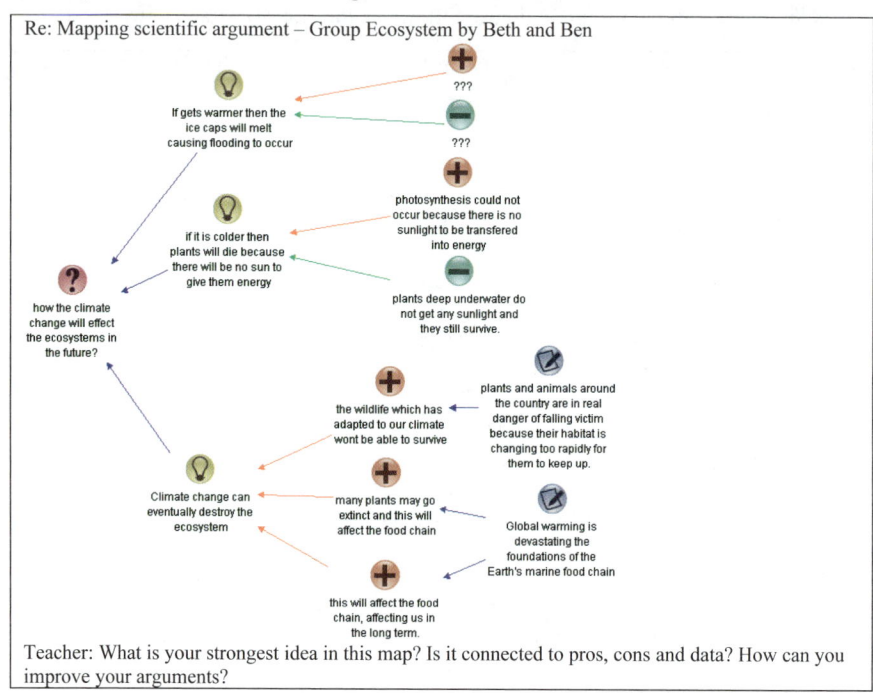

Extract 7.11 from the Forum IV – Mapping Data from the Web.

Considering their new claim "climate change can eventually destroy the ecosystem", their argumentation improved (from level 2 to level 3). They presented substantive warrants based on data collected on the web ("plants and animals ... are in real danger", "global warming is devastating..."). However, their argumentation falls short of the ideal through the lack of any rebuttals.

Extract 7.12 shows their map edited after comments from teacher. From this map they elaborated their writing. Comparing this map with their previous one, their main change was focussing on their strongest answer by bringing more arguments, counterarguments and notes. The part of the map that they "got stuck for an answer" they decided to delete.

7. Scaffolding School Pupils' Scientific Argumentation with Dialogue Maps

As we can see, there was a significant improvement of the level of argumentation in their map (at the beginning it was level 1, at the end it was level 4) and in their writing (from "very weak" to "good"). They were able to bring more science concepts and also include other perspectives such as social and ethical issues. The science teacher considered the first paragraph good, but the second one could be better if they had added more science concepts rather than personal opinion.

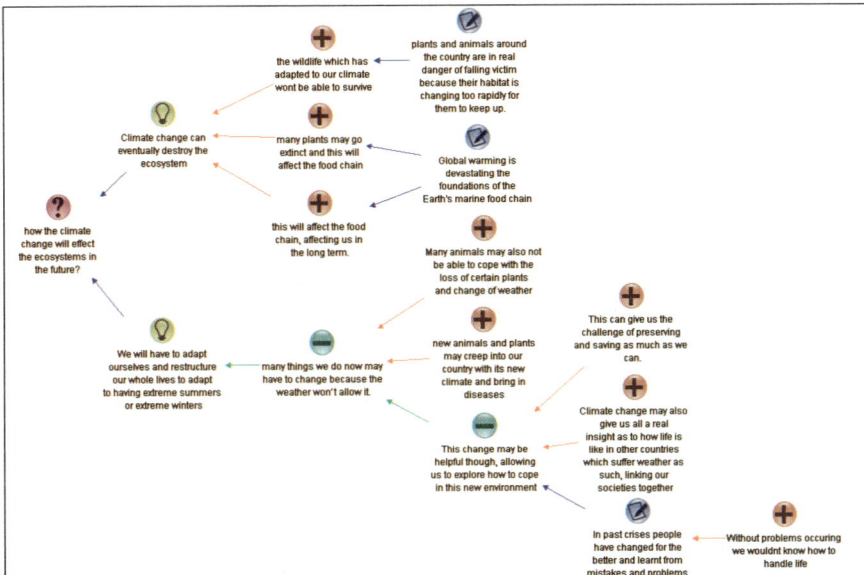

Re: Writing from your map – Group Ecosystem by Beth and Ben
"We think that the climate change will eventually destroy the system as we know it today because the wildlife which has adapted to our climate won't be able to survive, many plants may go extinct and this will affect the food chain, affecting us in the long term. As we know, "Global warming is devastating the foundations of the Earth's marine food chain". "Plants and animals around the country are in real danger of falling victim because their habitat is changing too rapidly for them to keep up".
We will have to adapt ourselves and restructure our whole lives to adapt to having extreme summers or extreme winters. However, many things we do now may have to change because the weather won't allow it. Many animals may also not be able to cope with the loss of certain plants and change of weather or new animals and plants may creep into our country with its new climate and bring in diseases. This change may be helpful though, allowing us to explore how to cope in this new environment and give us the challenge of preserving and saving as much as we can. Climate change may also give us all a real insight as to how life is like in other countries which suffer weather as such, linking our societies together.
"In past crises people have changed for the better and learnt from mistakes and problems". Without problems occurring we wouldn't know how to handle life."

Extract 7.12 from the Forum V – Writing from Your Map.

Figure 7.7 shows how Compendium was useful for pupils to structure their writing from their map. They exported it using the Web Outline View option which linearises the map into an indented list of nodes. They then edited the outline into more flowing prose.

Extract 7.13 shows how the pupils analysed this process. They had different opinions about how useful these maps were for constructing scientific argument. Ben found them "very useful" and "would use this type of map again". Beth considered "useful" but "probably wouldn't (use it again) because it took a bit too much time".

Both of them described how maps helped them in several ways: "prove up their point", "think of many ideas", "construct a good fair balanced scientific argument" and "link arguments together with words for their composition".

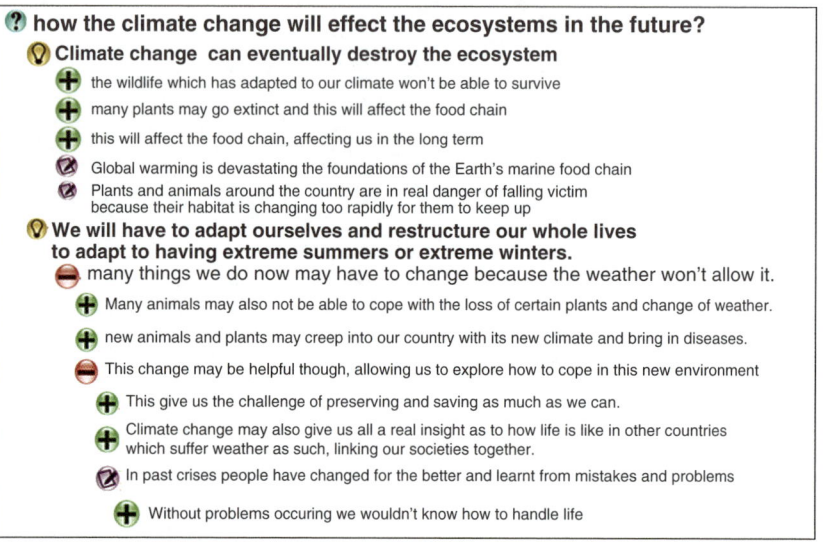

Fig. 7.7. List of topics generated by Compendium as a "web outline".

They did not have difficulties using Compendium, they considered "fairly easy", "it was fine". The "few problems" was "along the way like whether the nodes were right". The tool was easy, but the mapping was hard!

Teacher: How useful do you think maps are for constructing scientific arguments?
Beth: OK. They help prove up your point in a scientific argument. However, it takes a LONG time.
Ben: They are very good because they help you to think of many ideas connect them and not miss anything out then you can construct a good fair BALANCED scientific argument (s.p) by using all of the nodes you have created and linking them all together with words.
Teacher: Did you find any problems during the process of mapping?
Beth: I encountered a few problems like whether the nodes were right, but other than that it was fine.
Ben: No it was fairly easy
Teacher: Would you use a map in future? If so, say why?
Beth: I probably wouldn't because it took a bit too much time.
Ben: I think i would because it is an easy way to sum up ideas for a report.
Teacher: Overall, does the map make the process of writing any easier? Why?
Beth: It does. Everything is there easy to read, not in your head where it may slip away.
Ben: I think it does because it has all the information you need in the shortest formation possible. It is kind of like a sophisticated mind map. I AM DEAD.

Extract 7.13 from the Forum VI – Reflecting on Writing from Maps.

In summary, for these pupils, the process of thinking about the nodes is not trivial, nor quick. It takes a "LONG time" and one pupil declares at the end "I am dead". As Conklin (2006) states there is lots of interpretation involved in dialogue mapping. In Compendium, for each node that they dragged and dropped into the screen, they had to tackle several implicit questions, such as "Is this icon right?", "Is this text right?", "Is this connection right?" (see Buckingham Shum et al. (1997) for detailed analysis of these cognitive tasks). If the pupils can be engaged in this process of thinking, and of course supported by their colleagues and particularly by the teacher, then this analysis illustrates how dialogue mapping can serve as a new kind of scaffold for improving scientific argumentation.

Debating their map with colleagues and teachers requires them to address other relevant questions such as "Is this a strong idea?", "Is this idea supported by robust evidence?", "Is this idea connected to pros, cons and data?", "Are these arguments and counterarguments based on science concepts or on personal convictions?", "What is the source of this data?", "Is this a reliable source?". If pupils can be engaged in all these kinds of questions, then thinking about "the nodes", means thinking about the components of a scientific argumentation. Questioning "whether the nodes are right", means questioning if their scientific reasoning is right.

Dialogue mapping, from the perspective of these pupils, functions as a "sophisticated" strategy for argumentation. By visualising "all the information they need in the shortest form possible" they were able to use the most significant components to construct "a good fair BALANCED scientific argument". Dialogue mapping can also be an "easy way to sum up ideas for a report."

7.4.7 Case C

Case C presents another role for dialogue maps, "self assessment". Once pupils are able to visualise their arguments through the right icons, they can recognise easily what part should be clarified, deleted or extended. The good use of icons help them "make their points clearer and easier to understand" and also make it "easier for teacher to mark their ideas". This kind of "formative assessment" – feeding back information to the learner about their understanding – is widely recognised as a major factor in enhancing achievement.

In Extract 7.14, this pair of pupils explained that writing is neither as fun as practical nor as easy as presentations. For Chris "It is boring". For Carl "writing is ok", but "presentations to people you know are easier". They wrote fluently, addressing the topic set by the teacher's question, and giving good explanations of what makes a good scientific argument.

Extract 7.15 shows their writing with a good science argument. Their text was based on two short paragraphs, in few well-connected sentences. This text not only presents a good claim grounded in pros, cons and data, but also they were able to bring some science concepts to ground their answer.

152   Alexandra Okada

> Teacher: How much do you like writing in science? (1 = not at all, 3 = OK, 5 = I really like it). Give a reason
> Chris: 3. Because you can get want you want to say across quite easily, but presentations to people you know are easier
> Carl: 2. It is boring, I have more fun in practical.
> Teacher: What you think makes a good scientific argument?
> Chris: EVIDENCE!! you need evidence to back up your ideas and arguments otherwise you dont have a very good case. Finally you need to be able to argue both sides of a case
> Carl: A good scientific argument puts across what you mean simply and clearly, keeps attention and is not to complicated, but does not leave out important logic steps (it shows your thinking well).

Extract 7.14 from the Forum I – Reflecting on Writing in Science.

> Teacher: Write down for your topic: What you think will happen in the future in the UK? Give reasons.
> Re: Writing about Global Warming – Group Diseases by Chris and Carl
>
> Global warming will either make Britain (focusing here for now) a lot warmer, or shut down the gulf stream and make it a lot cooler. Either way, we will face a rise in disease as cold weakens the immune system and heat causes dehydration, heatstroke and other health problems.
> Of course, if you take into account the cause of global warming, pollution, you have even more problems. Pollution causes eye and lung diseases.

Extract 7.15 from the Forum II – Writing about Global Warming.

Figure 7.8 shows a map created by the author to represent the level of argumentation embedded in the pupils' writing. Based on Toulmin's model, we can see that they included the main components to ground their claim: claim, rebuttal, pros and "evidence to back up their ideas". The level of their argumentation and writing are very good.

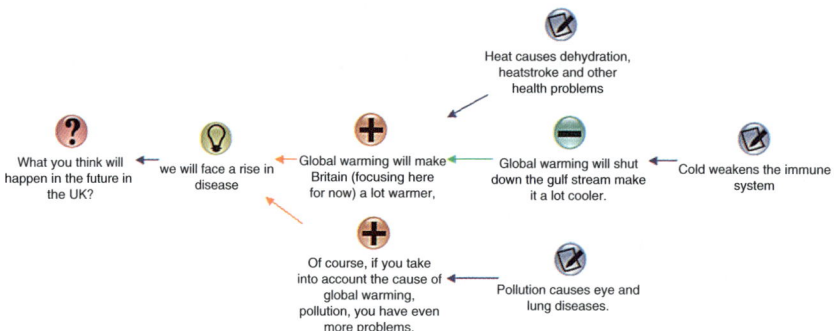

Fig. 7.8. Map created in Compendium based on Toulmin's model.

Extract 7.16 shows their first dialogue map in Compendium. They generated more questions and more claims. They extracted the different issues from their initial statements, and opened up discussion about them. They also described some science concepts giving more details. However, their arguments in the map were not as clear as in their writing (where they considered pros and cons and data for their main claim.) If they had included all these components of science argument, then the maps would be better. As they had difficulty in choosing the icons, they can not visualise what part could be improved. They represented all of them as answers in three linear sequences as if they were writing, which suggests that, in fact, they could have written these arguments without creating the map.

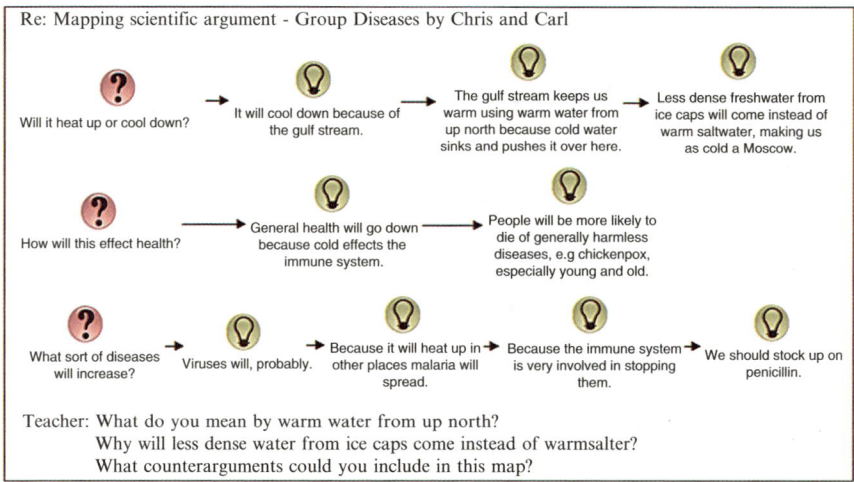

Extract 7.16 from the Forum III – Mapping Scientific Arguments.

Extract 7.16 shows pupils were able to present warrants based on their science knowledge. However, the science teacher noticed they did not show a clear understanding about why the UK might cool down. Moreover, they did not include any counterargument. They had also difficulties in representing data through proper icons. The level of argumentation dropped from level 4 to level 2.

Extract 7.17 represents their map with information from the web. They added more data, questions and arguments. They also represented the components through different icons and established more connections between them. However they still were not able to explain clearly the effect of Global Warming and Gulf Stream. They were also not sure about the difference between answers and pros.

154   Alexandra Okada

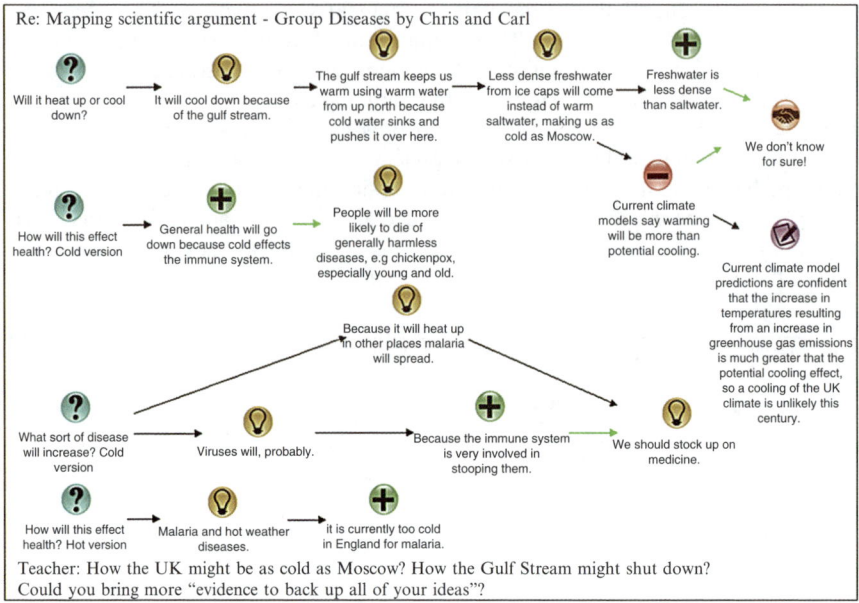

Extract 7.17 from the Forum IV – Mapping Data from the Web.

The level of argumentation in their mapping improved. However, it is not possible to conclude that mapping helped them to construct better arguments. They established good connections, not as linear as the previous map. However, their arguments in this map were not as well integrated as in their writing (Fig. 7.10) where we could see all of their arguments connected to data. In the writing Extract 7.15, as they mentioned, they were "focussed" on the main idea (Britain, a lot warmer) and they brought more components to ground that claim (Fig. 7.8). In the map in Extract 7.17, they raised more questions and open more statements, but they weren't able to put their arguments together in order to construct a good argumentation.

Extract 7.18 presents their final map and writing. After the teacher's feedback and explanation about the Compendium icons, pupils were able to improve their map significantly. With better understanding to visualise the components of their map, they were able to assess their strengths and limitations; and construct better arguments. They used the icons more systematically to express the roles played by each node:

- "Note" to represent facts, concepts and data. These are their evidence, which means statements that can be considered acceptable as truth based on science. Normally they are presented with simple tense verbs.
- "Answer" to indicate their main claims which address their questions. As their questions refer to the future, these sentences are in the simple future tense.
- "Pro" to show their arguments. This can also be in the future, but their function is to support or explain their main answer.
- "Con" to introduce exceptions, opposite ideas, statements against.

7. Scaffolding School Pupils' Scientific Argumentation with Dialogue Maps 155

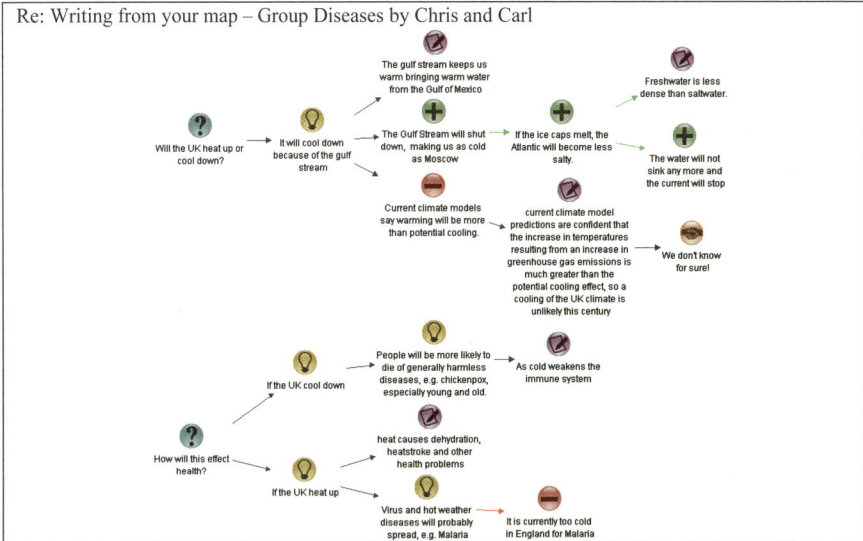

Re: Writing from your map – Group Diseases by Chris and Carl

"We think that the UK might cool down because of the gulf stream. The gulf stream keeps us warm bringing warm water from the Gulf of Mexico but the gulf stream might shut down, making us as cold as Moscow. This is because if the ice caps melt, the north Atlantic will become less salty. Freshwater is less dense than salt water so salt water normally would sink allowing the freshwater to pass above it. But if the water becomes less salty, the water will not sink anymore and the current will stop making the UK cool down rather than heat up.
However, current climate models say warming will be more than potential cooling. Current climate model predictions are confident that the increase in temperatures resulting from an increase in greenhouse gas emissions is much greater than the potential cooling effect, so a cooling of the UK climate is unlikely this century. We don't know for sure!
How will this effect health? If the UK cool down, people will be more likely to die of generally harmless diseases, e.g. chickenpox, especially young and old because cold weakens the immune system. If the UK heat up, heat causes dehydration, heatstroke and other health problems. Virus and hot weather diseases will probably spread, e.g. Malaria. However, it is currently too cold in England for Malaria".

Extract 7.18 from the Forum V – Writing from Your Map.

Once they were able to use the icons properly, they really improved their map with better and more consistent explanation of Gulf Stream. They also had a clearer visualisation about what their main viewpoint was, in order to support and challenge it. At the beginning they said that their focus was on "it will be warmer", then after better explanation, they changed to "it might be colder".

As they were able to construct strong argumentation on their map, and clear structure, it was easier for them to edit all the nodes from the map into a good composition. As they could clarify their understanding about the Gulf Stream, they could present better explanation in the composition which made it better than the previous writing. They were also able to visualise better what was their main proposition and describe it clearer on the text.

Extract 7.19 shows how these pupils reflected as mapping for writing. Both of them considered it useful. They presented several reasons: "helped me to sort out my ideas and arguments", "make my points clearer and easier to understand", "It also helps you to think through the facts and how they affect your arguments".

Although they considered it difficult to export and import maps in Moodle, they really showed interest in using mapping again. They also presented interesting reasons: "Writing from mapping "is more fun", "Argument is more logical and ordered", "It makes the whole thing a lot quicker". They could also identify significant benefits such as "it would also be easier for a teacher to mark my ideas".

> Teacher: How useful do you think maps are for constructing scientific arguments?
> Chris: 4 It's reasonably good because it helped me to sort out my ideas and arguments and make my points clearer and easier to understand. I presume it would also be easier for a teacher to mark my ideas.
> Carl: 5. It was a really good tool to sort out your ideas with and was very effective. It also helps you to think through the facts and how they affect your arguments.
> Teacher: Did you find any problems during the process of mapping?
> Chris: The only problem I found was that the process of saving the maps, opening, exporting etc. was very complicated and I would not be able to do it by memory, I would need the whole process written down for me to do it by
> Carl: Importing and exporting were quite tricky and it would be easier if you could just save and copy and paste the text.
> Teacher: Would you use a map in future? If so, say why?
> Chris: I might use the map in the future because it makes writing easier for me to do personally and for other people to understand. Overall it makes life a lot easier for everyone and it is definitely a very useful
> Carl: Of course, but I wish saving the work was easier.
> Teacher: Overall, does the map make the process of writing any easier? Why?
> Chris: You can get down the basic ideas and link them together, making connections and then edit the same text, which makes the whole thing a lot quicker because you can actually use the notes you make.
> Carl: yes its more fun. I find when it comes to writing up an essay that my argument is more logical and ordered.

Extract 7.19 From the Forum VI – Reflecting on Writing from Maps.

In summary, we observed in case C that when pupils present good knowledge and arguments in their initial writing, maps can acts as a tool for seeing whether they were able to apply their knowledge and formatively assessing their understanding. As pupils need to support their position in the map through connections, maps can reveal possible misunderstandings that their writing can not. Once pupils, through teachers' feedback, are able to clarify their connections, then they can enrich their argumentation and improve significantly their writing. Then, maps work as a tool for "sorting out their ideas and arguments". Their "arguments are more logical and ordered" and their "points are clearer and easier to understand".

7.5 Discussion: Returning to Our Research Questions

Encouraged by the success of Compendium-enabled dialogue mapping in non-educational contexts, we have presented the first step in our efforts to investigate its potential as a cognitive discipline, within a structured digital medium, to foster school pupils' scientific argumentation. We now discuss the preliminary answers that we can give to our opening research questions, based on the analyses of pupil pairs A–C.

7.5.1 Scientific Knowledge and Mapping

In our case study pairs, we saw examples of superficially well-structured maps with poor argumentation, and of poorly structured maps with good argumentation embedded in the labels of nodes. We saw how the visual language of IBIS can provide a template, for instance, cueing pupils that at least one Pro and Con are expected to be linked to each Position, even if they are not yet sure what these should be. We saw that the maps added depth to searching the Web: pupils may be seeking a specific kind of data to complete a map, or when unexpectedly encountering a potentially relevant page, they must now reflect on how to link it in coherently to their narrative.

Reviewing this work, O'Brien stated "mapping has its strength in that the pupils can determine for themselves the links that make the knowledge intelligible, through conceptual bridges they can make in their own minds, and in this way their learning skills are greatly enhanced. For these pupils, this allows them to develop strong strategies for learning like chunking, and skills to develop thinking in depth".

7.5.2 Scientific Writing and Mapping

The pupils we worked with clearly did not see writing as particularly enjoyable or central to science. It is likely that this naïve separation between what might be paraphrased as "doing the real science" versus "merely communicating it" is widely shared in the general public, but is directly challenged by the work we briefly reviewed at the start, in which science is constituted by its different discourses, which in turn actively shape the work that is undertaken. Sociological theories aside, we have the intensely practical task of raising a generation who want, and have the skills, to engage in public debate about science-related dilemmas. Pragmatics confronts us with the task of teaching pupils how to argue and reason critically, and convincing them that how and why scientists argue is deeply interwoven with what experiments they do and what can be concluded from them.

Since we are all schooled in writing prose from an early age, it is no surprise that writing essays or posting comments to a discussion forum came more easily to the pupils than mapping. This will always be the "path of least resistance" – but as all teachers and researchers know to their cost, fluency with the language and the fluidity of the digital medium can simply serve as a channel for unfocused verbiage. As historians of orality, literacy and digital media note, greater resistance in an information environment can foster greater reflection before ideas are committed (Ong, 1982, Heim, 1987).

We have described some of the translations that we observed from maps to prose, with some indicative results that a good IBIS tree structure in a map assisted the subsequent linearisation task by generating a coherent document outline. Sometimes pupils wrote maps in anticipation of conversion to prose, using connectives in node labels, while others added them after, in order to translate the nodes and links into more flowing prose. A closer analysis is needed to investigate specific questions about how graphical connections in a mapping language relate to appropriate use of connectives in prose.

Moving in the other direction, we translated pupils' prose into maps for analytical purposes, but there were no activities that specifically scaffolded this, e.g. through teaching the systematic annotation of texts, as is supported more directly by tools such as Araucaria (Chap. 8). Again, it is an open question as to whether young teenagers can be taught this, in the way that Reed et al. have worked with university undergraduates.

7.5.3 Cartographic Literacy

Prior work has documented the intellectual work involved in constructing dialogue and argument maps. The cognitive tasks (Buckingham Shum et al., 1997) include parsing the flow of ideas at an appropriate granularity, assigning a node type (icon), labelling them succinctly, and connecting them with meaningful links to an appropriate node. Doing this in real time to capture a discussion in the graphical IBIS language is a specific skill that Conklin (2006) terms Dialogue Mapping, which includes a collection of heuristics for recognising different kinds of conversations and creating coherent, balanced maps. Selvin (2008, Chap. 11) takes this even further, examining expert performance when formal modelling and multimedia assets are added to the mix. In sum, like any advanced intellectual or artistic discipline (as cartography surely is), one starts simple, but there is great scope for mastery and beauty.

To a practised dialogue mapper's eye, the pupils' maps leave much to be desired in terms of form and content, but these are equivalent to the first stammering phrases in a new language. The question is to what extent dialogue mapping can add value even at this stage, in order to maintain pupil (and staff) motivation to use this new way of reading and writing ideas. Our case studies provide qualitative indicators that we take to be promising, although the story is clearly not straightforward.

The tasks of parsing one's thoughts into discrete nodes, and classifying with appropriate icons are possibly the most demanding, and examination of the pupils' maps (or, indeed, any dialogue map) highlights that there are no hard rules. Whether a node is considered objectively reported Data or a personal Idea varies; whether an idea is a Pro/Con or an Idea depends on how the root Question is framed. Whether a complex idea is left as one node or decomposed into constituents is again context dependent. The point is that concepts such as Problem, Answer, Data, Evidence are merely roles that elements play in discourse. At one moment, an idea is an unproblematic assumption, folded into a Question. That same idea may become an explicit Idea node somewhere else, or a Pro/Con. Pedagogically, this is of course an extremely complex point to teach any teenager, but this abstract concept is made tangible in dialogue mapping through the icons: the message is implicit in the visual language, if taught correctly. This brings us to the teacher's role.

7.5.4 The Teacher's Role

In any context, teachers must provide appropriately constrained activities in which pupils can accomplish meaningful work. Knowledge cartography's process-orientation can provide a "window" into the workings of pupils' minds by showing the intellectual moves they are making more clearly than when it is embedded in prose. As one pupil commented, mapping makes it easier for the teacher to mark the work, and we saw a key role for teachers to provoke thinking by asking specific questions about maps. The science teacher working on the summer school commented, "Dialogue mapping can function as a teaching aid if this mapping technique is applied in a context of a project with a set of activities, where pupils can rethink of their mapping get feedback and improve it".

In terms of dialogue mapping, this translated in a number of ways, including drawing attention to a specific part of the map that lacks clarity (what are your key ideas?) or needs elaboration (where are the counter-arguments?); focusing pupils on substantiating reasoning with evidence from the Web; as well as domain knowledge checks (why will melted ice raise water levels?). We see huge scope for developing a "battery" of checks that both teachers and pupils could use to assess the quality of dialogue maps, adapting the works of Conklin (2006) and Selvin (2003) on the practitioner skillset to capture the heuristics in engaging, memorable ways.

7.5.5 Software Design

We have discussed at some length the nature of the resistance that a diagrammatic language like graphical IBIS presents to the expression of ideas. In contrast, the mechanics of driving Compendium were unproblematic, with pupils comfortable with a familiar direct manipulation user interface for dragging, dropping and linking nodes and websites. Greatest problems were encountered in exporting maps to outlines, and sharing maps via the Moodle web environment, a process that has been streamlined since this summer school: Compendium now has a custom Moodle export that integrates HTML Maps, Outlines and XML data versions, which can be uploaded as one file for processing by Moodle.

Of most interest to us is the match between how pupils give form to their thinking, and how this can be gradually structured, moving from an inchoate collection of thoughts equivalent to a sheet of sticky-notes, into a deliberation map that can be judged rigorous by scientific and argumentation standards. Central to Compendium's design has been a focus on avoiding "premature commitment" to inappropriate structure, and other key cognitive dimensions that determine the fluidity of tools for thought (Green, 1989; Cognitive Dimensions, 2007). We saw in the case studies the value of permitting freeform layouts of nodes, but also the danger that this low constraint condition can provide "enough rope to hang yourself" with spaghetti link structures. We are concluding that predefined visual patterns in the form of reusable templates could have an important role to play in seeding maps with useful structures, establishing a visual language that makes tangible important intellectual lenses that we want to instill.

To summarise, we might pull together the above threads in a vision as follows. We want to reach the point where pupils and teachers feel as confident with knowledge cartography as they do with other digital tools, and where the visual schemes provide an intuitive way to build and critique reasoning using the cartographic language of colour and space, e.g. Where's the purple? (=there's no data); Where's the red? (=there are no counter-arguments); Why do these nodes all say the same thing? (=there may be a clearer structure to this map which groups these nodes together more elegantly); Where's the root node? (=what's the core issue at stake?); Why is this node out here on the edge? (=are they irrelevant to the rest of the argument, or are you missing an important question that will bring them in?).

7.5.6 Conclusion and Future Work

Dialogue Mapping is a relatively mature knowledge cartography approach, with an established user community, technical base and codified training, with demonstrable value outside education. This chapter has discussed the results of a pilot investigation introducing it into a secondary school context, specifically in response to growing concern over pupils' poor scientific reasoning skills.

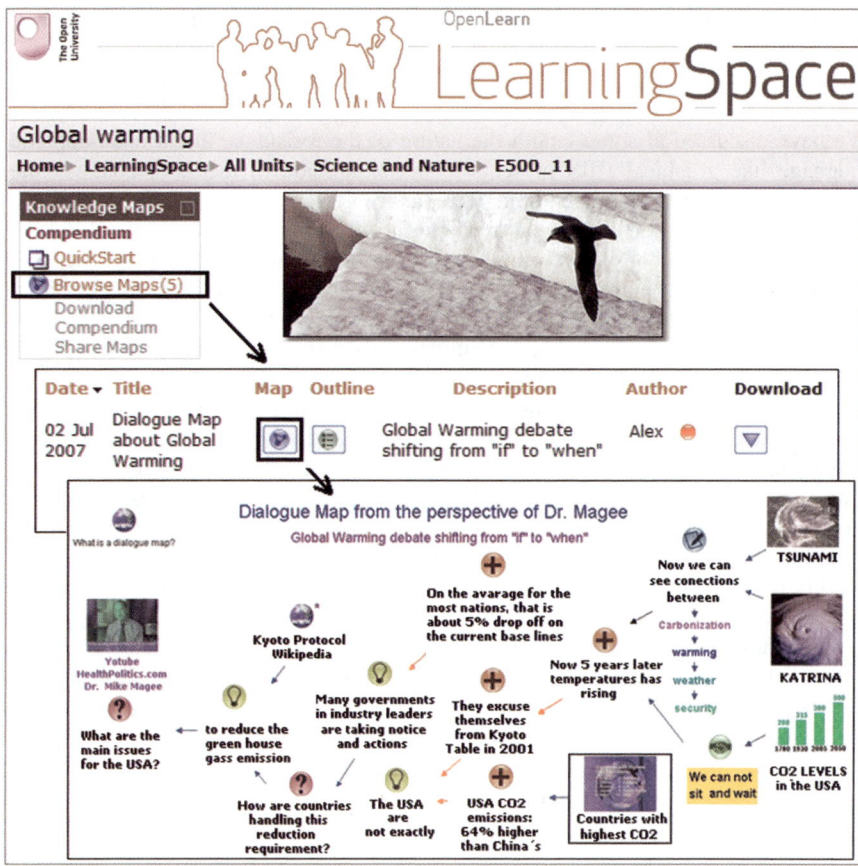

Fig. 7.9. OpenLearn Project was developed in Moodle, which integrates Compendium knowledge maps http://openlearn.open.ac.uk

We have explained the relationship of scientific argumentation and Dialogue Mapping, and presented qualitative analysis of three case studies from a UK summer school for teenagers aged 12–13 years. We aim to continue investigating the research questions introduced above with respect to how Dialogue Mapping and Argument Mapping can be used to improve pupils' critical thinking and argumentation skills in contemporary socio-scientific debates.

Our objective in terms of professional development is to foster a community of practice (in the OpenLearn project – Fig. 7.9) amongst educators and researchers (and perhaps even pupils), with its own focused workshops, online discussions and the sharing of curriculum ideas.

We welcome contact from all who would like to participate in such a network.

Acknowledgments

I am grateful to *Pat O'Brien* from the P&S Consultancy, whose work has been used by the National Academy for Gifted and Talented pupils in science and the National Learning Science Centre, for his very helpful feedback. I am grateful to *Tony Sherborne* from the Sheffield Hallam University, the author and coordinator of the Totally Wild Science Summer Course, for the opportunity to start this research. I am grateful to colleagues at the Open University: *Karen Littleton* from the Centre for Research in Education and Educational Technology for her significant comments, *Simon Buckingham Shum* for precious contributions, careful review and continuing supervision of this research, and *Michelle Bachler* (both from the Knowledge Media Institute) for technical support during this project.

References

Buckingham Shum, S., MacLean, A., Bellotti, V., Hammond, N. (1997). Graphical argumentation and design cognition. Human-Computer Interaction, 12(3), 267–300.

Carr, C. (2003). Using Computer Supported Argument Visualization to Teach Legal Argumentation. In: Kirschner, P., Buckingham Shum, S. and Carr, C. (Eds.) Visualizing Argumentation: Software Tools for Collaborative and Educational Sense-Making. Berlin Heidelberg New York London: Springer.

Cognitive Dimensions of Notations (2007). Resource Site <http://www.cl.cam.ac.uk/~afb21/CognitiveDimensions>

Conklin, J. (2006). Dialogue Mapping: Building Shared Understanding of Wicked Problems. Chichester: Wiley.

Conklin, J., Begeman, M.L. (1988). gIBIS: a hypertext tool for exploratory policy discussion. ACM Transactions on Office Information Systems, 6(4), 303–331.

Driver, R., Newton, P., Osborne, J. (2000). Establishing the norms of scientific argumentation in classrooms. Science Education, 84(3), 287–312.

Green, T. (1989). Cognitive Dimensions of Notations. In People and Computers V: Proc. HCI'91 Conference. (Eds.) A. Sutcliffe and L. Macaulay, 443–460.

Heim, M. (1987). Electric Language: A Philosophical Study of Word Processing. New Haven & London: Yale University Press.

Hodson, D. (2003). Science education for an alternative future. International Journal of Science Education, 25(6), 645–670.

Hogan, K., Maglienti, M. (2001). Comparing the epistemological underpinnings of pupils' and scientists' reasoning about conclusions. Journal of Research in Science Teaching, 38(6), 663–687.

Jaubert, M., Rebiere, M. (2005). Learning sciences by writing. In: Camps A. and Milian M. (coord.), L1 Educational Studies in Language and Literature, Amsterdam: Kluwer.

Kuhn, D. (1991). The Skills of Argument. Cambridge: Cambridge University Press.

Manson, L., Boscolo, P. (2000). Writing and conceptual change. What change? Instructional Science, 28, 199–226.

Means, M.L., Voss, J.F. (1996). Who reason well? Two studies of informal reasoning among children of different grade, ability and knowledge levels. Cognition and Instruction, 14(2), 139–179.

Newton, P., Driver, R., Osborne, J. (1999). The place of argumentation in the pedagogy of school science. International Journal of Science Education, 21(5), 553–576.

O'Brien, P. (2003) Using Science to Develop Thinking Skills at Key Stage 3. NACE/Fulton Publication.

Ong, W.J. (2002). Orality and Literacy, London: Routledge.

Ratcliffe, M. (1997). Pupil decision-making about socio-scientific issues within the science curriculum. International Journal of Science Education, 19(2).

Schwarz, B., Glassner, A. (2003) The blind and the paralytic: supporting argumentation in everyday and scientific issues. In: Andriessen, J., Baker, M. and Suthers, D. (Eds.) Arguing to Learn Confronting Cognitions in Computer-Supported Collaborative Learning Environments.

Selvin, A. (2003). Fostering collective intelligence: helping groups use visualized argumentation. In: Kirschner, P., Buckingham Shum, S. and Carr, C. (Eds.) Visualizing Argumentation: Software Tools for Collaborative and Educational Sense-Making. Berlin Heidelberg New York London: Springer.

Simon, S., Erduran S., Osborne J. (2002). Enhancing the quality of argumentation in school science Annual Meeting of the National Association for Research in Science Teaching, April 7–10, New Orleans, USA.

Suppe, F. (1998). The structure of a scientific paper. Philosophy of Science, 65(3), 381–405.

Toulmin, S. (1958). The Uses of Argument. Cambridge: Cambridge University Press.

Veerman, A. (2003). Constructive discussions through electronic dialog. In: Andriessen, J., Baker, M. and Suthers, D. (Eds.) Arguing to Learn Confronting Cognitions in Computer-Supported Collaborative Learning Environments. Dordrecht: Kluwer.

8. Argument Diagramming: The Araucaria Project

Glenn Rowe[1] and Chris Reed[2]

[1]University of Dundee, School of Computing, growe@computing.dundee.ac.uk,
[2]University of Dundee, School of Computing, chris@computing.dundee.ac.uk

Abstract. Formal arguments, such as those used in science, medicine and law to establish a conclusion by providing supporting evidence, are frequently represented by diagrams such as trees and graphs. We describe the software package *Araucaria* which allows textual arguments to be marked up and represented as *standard*, *Toulmin* or *Wigmore* diagrams. Since each of these diagramming techniques was devised for a particular domain or argumentation, we discuss some of the issues involved in translating between diagrams. The exercise of translating between different diagramming types illustrates that any one diagramming system often cannot capture all of the nuances inherent in an argument. Finally, we describe some areas, such as critical thinking courses in colleges and universities and the analysis of evidence in court cases, where Araucaria has been put to practical use.

8.1 Introduction

The technique of argument diagramming is widely used in informal logic (Hurley, 2003), and in the teaching of philosophy and critical thinking (Harrell, 2005). It also has a long history going back at least as far as the start of the nineteenth century (Walton, 2006). It has recently been attracting attention in both decision support and computational linguistics, and there are a wide range of software tools available targetted at different markets [see Kirschner et al. (2003) for a good review]. Perhaps surprisingly, most of these tools adopt a similar style of diagramming.

Araucaria (Reed & Rowe, 2004) is a freely available, open source software package developed over the last few years at the University of Dundee. (See http://araucaria.computing.dundee.ac.uk/ for downloading instructions.) Araucaria allows the text of an argument to be loaded from a file, and provides numerous tools for marking up this text and producing three types of diagram (standard, Toulmin and Wigmore; see below) illustrating the structure of the argument contained in the text. It also provides support for defining and marking up argumentation schemes (Walton, 1996).

Araucaria allows the user to select a block of text with the mouse and create a node corresponding to this text which can be inserted into a diagram in the main display area. These nodes can be edited and adorned in various ways to add properties such as a label stating the owner of a given proposition in the argument, symbols on the edges connecting the nodes stating the strength of the inference from support to conclusion, and so on.

Araucaria allows the saving and export of a marked up argument in the form of a text file using Argument Markup Language, or AML. AML is a form of XML which provides a standard by which argument can be stored and transmitted between software packages. Araucaria also provides an interface with the argument research corpus maintained at the University of Dundee (Katzav et al., 2004), allowing new arguments to be stored in the corpus and providing a search facility for retrieving arguments from the database.

Araucaria is amongst a small number of diagramming tools that actively support and encourage the use of widely different styles of analysis. The next three sections briefly review three popular and influential styles (each of which reflects a theoretical architecture for argument understanding).

8.2 Diagramming the Standard Account

The most common diagramming technique does not have an official name, so we will refer to it simply as a *standard* diagram. A standard diagram is a tree with the conclusion of the argument as the root node. Some authors draw the root node at the top of the tree, while others invert the tree so that the root node is at the bottom of the diagram. We will use the former convention, although Araucaria allows either type of diagram.

Each node in the diagram can be supported by one or more additional nodes, each of which represents a premise in the argument. Premises can be of two main types: *convergent* or *linked*. A convergent premise stands on its own as support for another node, while a linked premise must link with one or more other premises to form support. As an example, the argument "a cat makes a good pet because it is friendly and it can look after itself" consists of a conclusion (a cat makes a good pet) supported by two convergent premises ("it is friendly" and "it can look after itself"). Either premise provides support for the conclusion without the other, although the two together form a stronger argument than either on its own. A convergent premise is drawn as a node with a single arrow leading to the conclusion it supports. See Fig. 8.1.

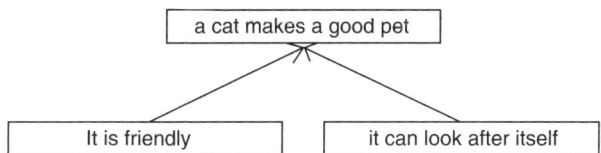

Fig. 8.1. A simple convergent argument in Araucaria.

An example of a linked argument would be the following. "Jon understands Newton's laws of motion because Jon got 90% in the first year physics course and the first year physics course covers Newton's laws of motion." Here the conclusion is that "Jon understands Newton's laws of motion" and this is supported by the premises "Jon got 90% in the first year physics course" and "the first year physics course covers Newton's laws of motion." These two premises are linked because neither on its own is sufficient evidence from which to draw the conclusion that Jon understands Newton's laws of motion. Linked premises are shown as connected by a horizontal line which in turn gives rise to a single arrow connecting all linked premises in that group to the conclusion they support. See Fig. 8.2.

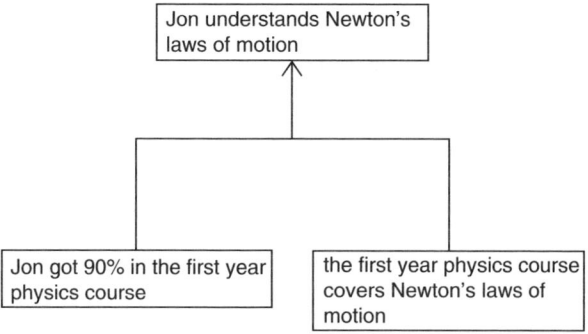

Fig. 8.2. A simple linked argument in Araucaria.

Standard diagrams support the notion of a *refutation*, which is an argument that refutes or argues against another node in the diagram. In propositional logic, the notion of refutation is that for a given statement P, there is a statement not-P which is the logical opposite of P. Since each statement can have only one logical opposite, the standard diagram allows only a single refutation for any given node. Of course, in a "real" argument, there could be a number of arguments against a given proposition. In the standard diagram, such a situation is represented by creating the single refutation node for the proposition which is to be refuted, and then to draw in the various arguments against the proposition as supports for the refutation. In the example above, the refutation to the conclusion "Jon understands Newton's laws of motion" is "Jon does not understand Newton's laws of motion." This refutation could be supported by the proposition "the first year physics course got a bad review from external assessors" as shown in Fig. 8.3.

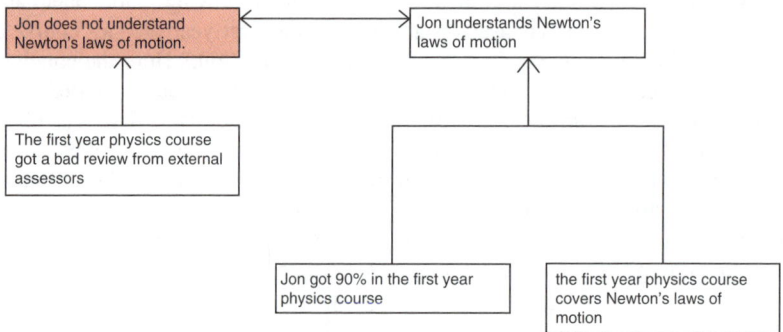

Fig. 8.3. An argument with a refutation.

In Araucaria, a refutation is drawn as a node to the left of the proposition it is refuting, and is connected to the proposition by line with arrows on both ends.

In addition to the basic structure of the tree in a standard diagram, Araucaria supports several other features. An argumentation scheme (Walton, 1996) is a pattern based on the types of premises used to support the conclusion. For example, the argument "global warming is real and is caused by human activity because a recent UN conference came to this conclusion" is an *argument from expert opinion* because the evidence supporting the conclusion is that a panel of experts says that the conclusion is true. Each argumentation scheme is usually associated with a set of *critical questions* which should be answered in order to verify the validity of the argument. In the case of argument from expert opinion, for example, critical questions could include: "does the presumed expert have experience in an area related to the conclusion?", "is the expert free of bias?" and so on. Numerous other schemes can be defined for arguments of other types.

In Araucaria, a scheme can be drawn by selecting several supports or nodes and then selecting the scheme to which they belong. This is shown in the diagram by a colored outline of the selected supports and nodes. Full information on the particular scheme can be obtained by bringing up a dialog box which displays the role of each premise in the scheme and which critical questions have been answered. In addition, Araucaria allows the editing and creation of sets of schemes, so the user can customize existing schemesets or create new ones. The software currently supports approaches to schemes advocated by Walton (1996), Grennan (1997), Perelman & Olbrechts-Tyteca (1969), Katzav & Reed (2004) and Pollock (1995).

In the example above, the refutation and its support could be an example of the scheme "argument from expert opinion," in which a conclusion is stated to be true because experts in the field say it is true. Figure 8.4 shows the scheme added to the diagram shown in Fig. 8.3.

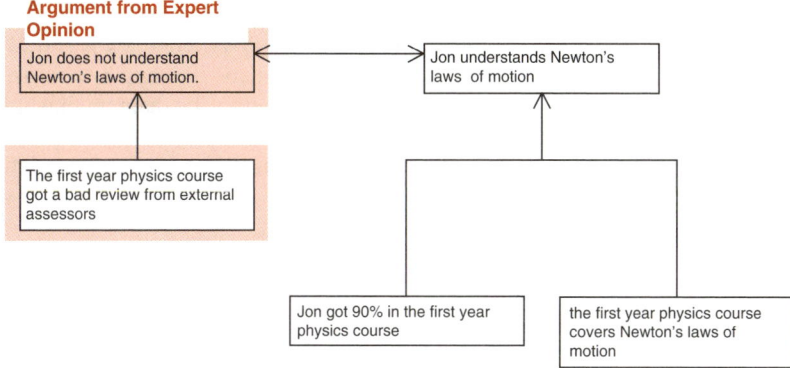

Fig. 8.4. The refutation and its support form an example of the scheme "argument from expert opinion".

In a natural argument, some propositions will have greater validity or force than others. In a standard diagram, a force can be represented as an *evaluation* of the support line connecting a proposition with its conclusion. Typically an evaluation is just a number such as a percentage value which indicates how strong the inference is between the two nodes. Araucaria allows evaluations to be defined for any support arrow, and evaluations can be any text (not just numbers).

When analyzing text, different propositions can be derived from different sources. For example, in the "cats make good pets" argument above, the various convergent arguments may have been obtained by a primary school teacher asking the class for reasons that cats make good pets, and each convergent argument may come from a different child. In such a case, a proposition can have an *owner*, which is someone who proposed that argument. Araucaria allows a given proposition to have one or more owners, which can be defined as text strings.

8.3 Diagramming the Toulmin Account

The Toulmin diagram (Toulmin, 1958) in its original form is based on the datum-warrant-claim (DWC) complex. The claim is the conclusion of the argument, which is supported by the datum. The warrant provides justification for the statement that the datum supports the claim. Thus the DWC seems closest to the notion of a linked argument in a standard diagram. We might say that Jon understands Newton's laws of motion (the claim) because he got 90% in the first year physics course (the datum). On its own, however, this could leave the reader wondering if the physics course's coverage of Newton's laws was sufficient to provide even a very good student with an understanding of them. Thus we provide the warrant which states that the first year course does indeed provide a through grounding in Newton's laws.

In Araucaria, a warrant is drawn as a green node with a link into the line connecting the datum and the claim.

A simple Toulmin diagram containing only a single DWC complex is shown in Fig. 8.5. The datum is on the left and connects to the claim on the right by a horizontal line. The warrant links into the line from below as shown. The diagram thus illustrates the idea that the warrant supports the inference from datum to claim, rather than the claim directly. This diagram is produced by Araucaria as a direct translation of the standard diagram shown in Fig. 8.2. See below for a discussion of the translation of diagrams.

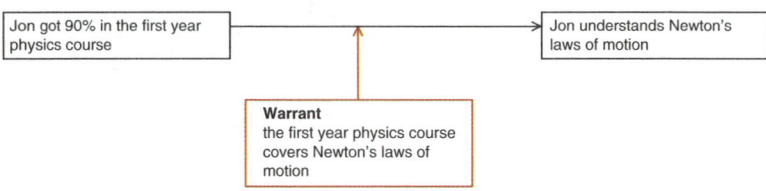

Fig. 8.5. A Toulmin diagram showing the basic datum-warrant-claim complex.

A Toulmin diagram provides the *rebuttal* as the mechanism for rebutting an argument. A rebuttal appears as another node that links into the DWC by a vertical line from below. The fact that the rebuttal also impacts on the link between datum and claim shows that it attacks the inference from datum to claim, rather than being a strict negation of the claim as is the case with the refutation node in the standard model. In the example above, we might add a rebuttal to the argument by saying "the first year physics course got a bad review from external assessors" which casts doubt on the value of getting a high mark in the course, thus undermining the implication that getting 90% in it would imply a sound knowledge of the material covered by the course. The correspondence between the Toulmin rebuttal and the standard refutation is discussed in more detail below in the section on translating Toulmin diagrams. In Araucaria, the Toulmin rebuttal is drawn as a red node connecting to the datum-claim link, as shown in Fig. 8.6.

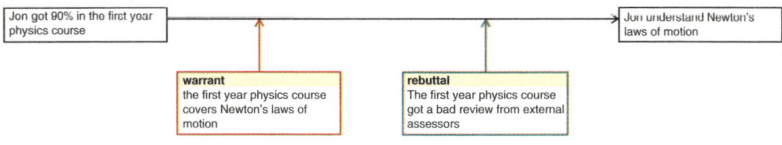

Fig. 8.6. A Toulmin diagram with a rebuttal.

The final feature in a Toulmin diagram is the *qualifier*. A qualifier plays roughly the same role as an evaluation in standard: it provides a measure of the confidence in the DWC complex. Qualifiers are also attached to the link between datum and claim, and are indicated in Araucaria as yellow triangular nodes.

8.4 Diagramming the Wigmore Account

A diagramming model was produced by Wigmore in the early twentieth century (Wigmore, 1913) to allow diagrams of legal arguments. The structure is superficially similar to the standard diagram in that the argument is drawn as a tree with the root node at the top, but there are some important differences. Usually, there are two main trees for a single court case: one for the argument from the prosecution and the other for the defense. Within each tree, the top level node is typically the central charge in the case which is either to be proved, in the case of the prosecution, or refuted, in the case of the defense. We will consider the prosecution's argument in what follows.

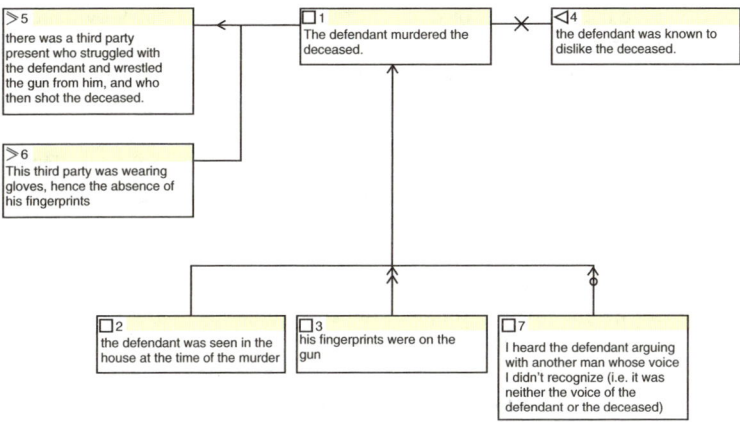

Fig. 8.7. A Wigmore diagram.

The root node can have three groups of nodes connected to it (see Fig. 8.7). The main evidence supporting the central charge is presented as a block of testimonial or circumstantial nodes. Testimonial evidence is evidence introduced as testimony by witnesses, so could consist of accounts of what the witnesses saw, or other evidence supposedly known as facts by the witnesses. Circumstantial evidence is evidence that is inferred from other facts, such as "the defendant was seen in the house at the time of the murder and his fingerprints were on the gun, so it can be inferred that he shot the deceased." This group of nodes thus corresponds to the basic facts (or statements that can be presumed to be facts since they were given under oath) pertaining to the charge. Nodes 2 and 3 in Fig. 8.7 represent these arguments (we will consider node 7 below).

The second group of nodes contains corroborative evidence. This is evidence introduced to support the central charge or testimonial/circumstantial evidence. Thus corroborative evidence is introduced on the side of the party attempting to establish the claim in the root node and would be seen as supportive evidence in the context of the argument. In the argument above, the claim that "the defendant was known to dislike the deceased" could be introduced as corroborative evidence since it establishes motive. The distinction between corroborative and testimonial evidence is not precise and is in many cases subjective. Node 4 in Fig. 8.7 shows the corroborative argument.

The third group of nodes contains explanatory evidence. This is evidence introduced by the opposite side in the case, and it attempts to lessen the credibility or deny outright the claim being made. In the above example, the defense may introduce the explanatory evidence that "there was a third party present who struggled with the defendant and wrestled the gun from him, and who then shot the deceased. This third party was wearing gloves, hence the absence of his fingerprints." Nodes 5 and 6 in Fig. 8.7 show the above evidence as two explanatory arguments.

In a Wigmore diagram, these three sets of nodes are placed in specific locations relative to the node they support (or deny, in the case of explanatory evidence). The testimonial/circumstantial nodes are placed below the central node, the explanatory nodes are on the left and the corroborative nodes are on the right. All nodes within each group are drawn as linked into a single support arrow, which in turn impinges on the central node.

The nodes and edges in a Wigmore diagram have a variety of symbols that are used to adorn them. We will not give a complete catalogue here, but an outline of the main categories of these symbols will be useful.

Each node itself can be evidence introduced either by the prosecution or defense, thus the symbols for the various nodes occur in pairs. The main symbol for each type of node is defined for the prosecution, and the corresponding symbol for the defense adds an extra horizontal bar within the symbol. Thus the symbol for testimonial evidence introduced by the prosecution is a square, and for similar evidence introduced by the defense, it is a square with a horizontal line drawn inside it. In Fig. 8.7, the symbols are shown to the left of the identifying number in the top line of each text box. The original Wigmore diagram showed only the symbol and associated number, and the analyst had to make reference to a separate text to provide the link between the diagram and the case notes. Araucaria allows both the full-text version of the Wigmore diagram (shown in Fig. 8.7) and the traditional version to be drawn.

The connections between nodes can have a variety of symbols added to them. An unadorned line indicates some "average" degree of support. Extra force in the support is indicated by adding various arrowhead or cross symbols (depending on the particular link), while a lessening of support, as might occur in with an explanatory node which argues against the claim, is indicated by a backwards pointing arrowhead. In Fig. 8.7, for example, the double arrowhead leading from node 3 indicates strong support for the conclusion. The backwards arrow on the link from node 5 indicates that node 5 detracts from the conclusion. The X on the line from node 4 indicates that corroborative node 4 reinforces the conclusion. There are a number of other symbols that can be used to indicate varying degrees of support between nodes.

Wigmore distinguishes between the support provided by individual nodes and the aggregate support provided by all the nodes in a particular group. For example, in the set of testimonial nodes, each node in the set can have its own influence on the claim by being assigned its own degree of force. Some nodes may have average force, some strong and others very strong force. Taken together, the net effect of all the nodes in the group may be judged by the analyst to have "strong" (as opposed to "average" or "very strong") force, so the single link leading from the line that groups all the nodes together can be assigned a symbol indicating what Wigmore calls the "net probative force" of all the testimonial nodes taken together. The line joining the set of nodes 2, 3 and 7 to the main conclusion is shown with a single arrow on it, which indicates that the net probative force of these three nodes is "provisional."

We have seen that the explanatory nodes provide a type of refutation or rebuttal mechanism in that they represent evidence provided by the opponent of the main claim. However, individual or aggregate links in a Wigmore diagram can be labeled as *negatory* nodes by placing a small circle on the line in the diagram. Wigmore is not entirely clear what this negatory symbol means, but it seems from the few examples he provides that it is intended to indicate that the evidence does not support the claim. Thus a testimonial node in the example given above might state "I heard the defendant arguing with another man whose voice I didn't recognize (i.e. it was neither the voice of the defendant or the deceased)." If this evidence was given by a prosecution witness, it would be included in the diagram as a testimonial node but given negatory force since it doesn't support the prosecution's claim that the defendant and deceased were alone in the room at the time of the shooting. This node is shown as node 7 in Fig. 8.7.

A hallmark of Wigmore diagrams is that many of the assignments of force or even the group into which a given bit of evidence is inserted can be quite subjective. The degree of force assigned to a particular node, or whether a node is testimonial or corroborative could vary from one analyst to another. The Araucaria representation of Wigmore diagrams is flexible enough to allow editing of the diagram to suit any taste.

8.5 Translation Between Diagram Types

8.5.1 Motivation and Desiderata

Argumentation theory enjoys a rich scholarly debate (see, e.g., Freeman (1991), Johnson (2000), Gilbert (1997) and van Eemeren (2004) for a representative sample of the range of this debate) about how best to conceive of, and then analyze real argumentation. There is no general consensus because different authors tend to focus on different aspects. The standard diagram is the style most commonly found in introductory texts on critical thinking and logic. It is probably the most intuitive, as it shows a single conclusion which is supported by a number of premises, with each premise in turn being supported by further premises. This is the sort of argumentation often used in daily conversation. Bob may state "Genetically modified food is perfectly safe." Anne will then ask him to defend his position, and he will provide points to support his original statement. Anne may decide to state her own position contrary to Bob's, which results in a refutation of Bob's position. Anne may then introduce her own premises to support her own position, and so on.

The Toulmin diagram introduces extra components to explain the structure of arguments in more detail. Toulmin's idea is that the proponent of a *claim* will produce a fact, called a *datum*, to support this claim. In order for the argument to make sense, a reason as to why this datum supports the claim may be needed; this is the Toulmin *warrant*. A warrant may thus be seen as extra information or justification that is not immediately obvious from the datum-claim link. The Toulmin rebuttal is seen not as a direct attack on the claim itself, but rather on the link between the datum and claim.

As we have seen above, the Wigmore diagram was designed exclusively for use in analyzing legal cases, so its language and structure are specific to that setting. Branches of the diagram are reserved for principle evidence presented by one side (usually the prosecution) of the case, explanatory evidence presented by the other side (usually the defense), and corroborative evidence from the first side. Wigmore diagrams put great emphasis on adding weights to the support lines between nodes.

As can be seen, these three diagramming styles emphasize different aspects of an argument. Translating between them is not straightforward and, just as with many natural human languages, frequently an exact translation from one style to another is not possible.

The approach taken by the Araucaria project has been to try to support this diversity whilst maintaining a core coherence, and to do so by engineering pragmatic solutions for translating between the different styles of theoretical and practical analysis.

Our experience working with these multiple theoretical approaches to argument analysis has yielded a wish list for the process:

(i) Translation should be deterministic, always providing the same output for any given input;
(ii) Translation should be "symmetrical," i.e. translation from A to B should be *one-to-one*, in the sense that any argument in A should have only one equivalent argument in B, and *onto*, in the sense that every argument in B has an equivalent argument in A. Backtranslation from B to A should possess the same properties, so that backtranslation from translation is always equivalent to identity;
(iii) Translation should make maximal use of a common interlingua where possible;
(iv) Where (iii) cannot be met, theory-specific analysis should be included by extending the interlingua.

The role of the interlingua here is taken on by the Argument Markup Language (AML). AML is a standard XML-based language which may be used to represent arguments, though in principle a more flexible system such as the AIF (Willmott et al., 2006) could be used. AML is designed around the concepts required to build standard diagrams, so tags for such things as convergent and linked premises are defined as part of the basic language. Specialized features of some nodes that are required in other diagram types such as Toulmin and Wigmore are introduced through a general "role" tag which allows one node to take on different roles in different diagrams. Thus an "added negation" role in a Toulmin diagram (see below) would be specified in AML as a role tag with a diagram type of "Toulmin" and a role description of "added_negation."

Here we explore the translation of Toulmin and Wigmore diagram types into standard notation, and back again. We have analyzed the translation of Toulmin diagrams (Reed & Rowe, 2006) and Wigmore diagrams (Rowe & Reed, 2006) in detail elsewhere, so we will present a summary of the main points here.

8.6 Translating Toulmin Analyses

In translating from a Toulmin diagram to a standard diagram, we need to consider the various components of a Toulmin diagram and how they correspond to features in a standard diagram. The elements of a Toulmin diagram we will consider are atoms, warrants, backings, qualifiers and rebuttals.

8.6.1 Atoms

Although the notion of what constitutes an argument or an atomic component of an argument (Katzav & Reed, 2004; Parsons, 1996; Wreen, 1998) is highly contentious, we will adopt the view that there is little difference between atomic statements in any of the models of argument. A standard premise can serve as a Toulmin datum or warrant, for example.

8.6.2 Warrants, Backings and Qualifiers

The simplest construct in a Toulmin diagram is the datum-warrant-claim (DWC) complex. The warrant can be interpreted (Freeman, 1991) as a reason for the datum being relevant to the claim. As such, it is reasonable to interpret the datum and warrant in a DWC as a pair of linked premises in the standard model. Figure 8 (Hansard, 2004) shows a typical translation.

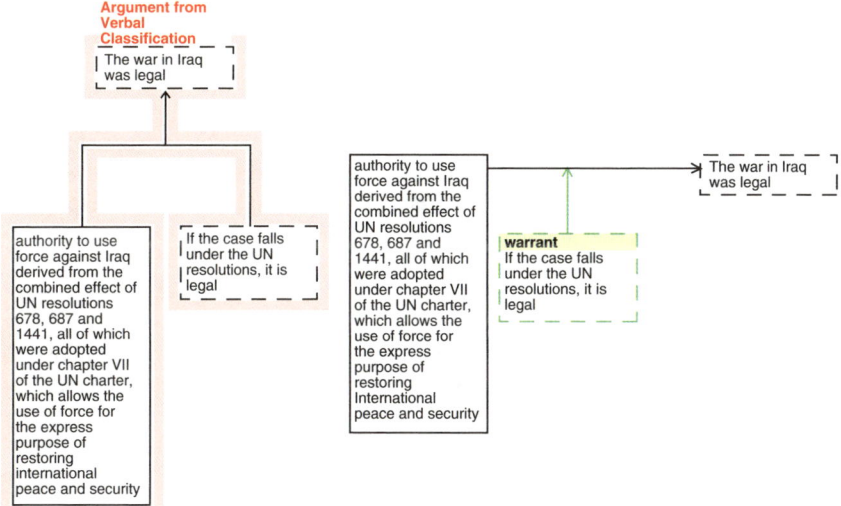

Fig. 8.8. A linked argument as a single DWC complex.

It is important not to read too much in to Fig. 8.8. We are not claiming that the diagram captures the full meaning of the particular argument structure; rather we are proposing a reasonable interpretation of one diagramming system in terms of the other, using those features of each system that are available. Some authors certainly do not regard a warrant as equivalent to a standard premise (Hitchcock, 2003) but since the standard system has no exact equivalent to the Toulmin warrant, the premise seems the best we can do. Figure 8.8 merely attempts to depict the argument so that it would make sense to workers using either system.

In the standard treatment, a linked argument can have any number of premises, while a Toulmin DWC complex typically contains only one datum and one warrant. Assuming we wish to preserve all the premises in the standard diagram when translating to Toulmin, we need to broaden the Toulmin diagram to allow either several data or several warrants, or both. Though taking liberties with the Toulmin picture, we allow several warrants to support a single datum-claim link. This meets objectives (iii) and (iv) from the introduction, and most importantly, means that as described in objective (iv), analysts working in either tradition needn't worry about the foibles of the other (just because Toulmin diagrams can be constructed in which more than one warrant supports the move from datum to claim does not mean that such analyses will be at all common for those working in the Toulmin framework).

In a similar way, we expand Toulmin's original concept by allowing diagrams of arbitrary depth, in the sense that each datum or warrant can, in turn, act as a claim for a nested DWC complex. In addition, a given claim can have more than one datum-warrant branch supporting it.

As mentioned above, the Toulmin qualifier is taken to be equivalent to the *evaluation* in the standard diagram, so we formally adopt this in translating from one to the other.

Finally, the Toulmin *backing* was defined originally as the only way a warrant could be supported. In our expanded view, a warrant may also be supported by a datum, so the distinction between the datum and backing is blurred somewhat. The distinction between the two is subtle and is discussed more fully in Reed & Rowe (2006). For the purposes of translation, both the backing and datum are interpreted as a normal premise in a standard diagram.

8.6.3 Rebuttals

The Toulmin rebuttal appears, from examples in Toulmin's original work (Toulmin, 1958), to provide a way of capturing exceptions to the statement that the datum supports the claim. The rebuttal is often denoted as an "unless" clause: "datum implies claim *unless* rebuttal." Translation from Toulmin to standard requires introducing a refutation into the standard diagram in a way which represents as accurately as possible the meaning of the rebuttal.

In Reed & Rowe (2006) we considered four possibilities in some depth. These are:

1. The rebuttal refutes the claim directly.
2. The rebuttal refutes the warrant directly.
3. The rebuttal supports a premise that refutes the claim.
4. The rebuttal refutes a premise that supports the claim.

Of these four possibilities, we argue in Reed & Rowe (2006) that the fourth comes closest to capturing Toulmin's intent. If the argument that the datum in a DWC supports the claim has an exception in a rebuttal R, then the opposite of R (not-R) should support the DWC argument. To use a popular example: an object that looks red (datum) may be assumed to be intrinsically red (claim) *unless* it is illuminated by red light (rebuttal). In this case, the premise not-R being refuted by the rebuttal is "the object is *not* illuminated by red light" which, in the context of the original datum and claim, clearly supports the claim. Since the not-R premise is usually not present in the original Toulmin diagram, Araucaria introduces it as an *added negation* when translating from Toulmin to standard. This node is normally not shown in the Toulmin diagram (although can be displayed if desired) but is displayed in the corresponding standard diagram.

8.7 Translating Wigmore Diagrams

We have considered the translation between Wigmore and standard diagrams in some depth in Rowe & Reed (2006). We will summarize here the main points to be considered in such translations.

A testimonial or circumstantial evidence node in a Wigmore diagram may have up to three supporting groups of nodes: other testimonial or circumstantial evidence, explanatory evidence and corroborative evidence. Each of these three groups of nodes is represented in the diagram by a set of nodes that has support edges converging on a single edge which then supports the parent node.

There is a superficial diagrammatic resemblance between the Wigmore notation for a group of supporting nodes and the linked argument structure in the standard diagram. It is tempting, therefore, to infer an equivalence between these two structures. However, we believe this correspondence is illusory. The linked argument in a standard diagram implies that all the premises making up the linked group of nodes are required for the connection between these nodes and the node they support. Common examples of linked arguments are found in argumentation schemes: the argument from expert opinion, for example, requires both that the expert have appropriate domain knowledge, and that the proposition they are advocating lies within that domain. In a Wigmore diagram, however, *all* nodes of a given type that support another node are grouped together, regardless of whether some of these nodes form linked arguments and others stand alone as support for the parent node.

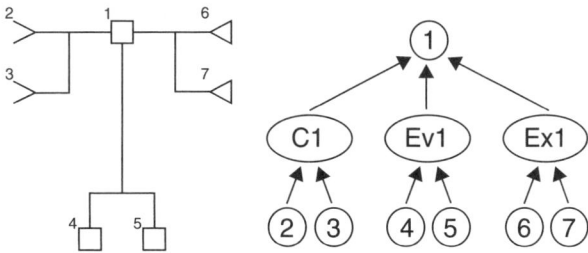

Fig. 8.9. A simple Wigmore diagram (*left*) and a possible deep structure representation (*right*).

A Wigmore diagram also strongly reinforces pictographically the tripartite grouping of all evidence. One possible way of representing a Wigmore analysis is therefore to introduce virtual "aggregation" nodes in the argument that aggregate all the corroborative evidence supporting a node, all the explanatory evidence supporting a node, and all the other (i.e. testimonial or circumstantial) evidence supporting a node. These intermediate nodes might then be further supported in their turn by convergent arguments from the various premises. The Wigmore diagram on the left of Fig. 8.9, for example, might be rendered at a deep level by the representation shown on the right of the same figure, with C1, Ev1 and Ex1 aggregating the corroborative, testimonial and explanatory evidence for claim 1, respectively. In this way, the ontological status of nodes in the Wigmore analysis (i.e. whether they are corroborative, explanatory or testimonial/circumstantial) is captured by structural features in the AML representation. Unfortunately, this misrepresents the arguments in an important way. The role of "corroborating" evidence is, as the terminology suggests, one of working with elements of testimonial and circumstantial evidence to support a claim. In this respect, it is most similar to traditional linked argumentation – but the linkage crosses the groupings in Fig. 8.9 – so, for example, it might be that 2 and 4 form a linked argument, and 3 and 5 form a linked argument. The analysis in Fig. 8.9 not only makes such relationships opaque, it absolutely proscribes the representation of such relationships.

The problem is compounded in that an analysis performed in the Wigmore style provides no mechanism for determining which premises of a claim are linked and which are not. Thus we have no choice but to represent all the nodes supporting another node in a Wigmore diagram as single, unlinked nodes in a standard diagram. Similarly, there is no distinction in a standard diagram between the concepts of explanatory, corroborative, testimonial or circumstantial evidence, so all nodes from all these groups must be treated equally when drawn in a standard diagram.

We can use similar considerations to translate in the reverse direction: from standard to Wigmore. A standard diagram does not contain any information on the type of evidence represented by a node, so we really have no choice but to represent all standard nodes, linked or convergent, as one node type in Wigmore. For convenience, Araucaria interprets all standard nodes as testimonial affirmatory nodes (represented by a plain square) in Wigmore.

The reader may be wondering how these rules conform to our desire to use the AML structure to represent all arguments as standard and then translate to other diagram types. If Wigmore diagrams contain properties not representable in standard, how do we store these properties in AML, thereby ensuring that our second desideratum is met? The answer is that no interchange format will be able, a priori, to cater for all possible representational and operational schemes that involve argument (Willmott et al., 2006). Instead, AML is designed to support extensibility through a simple "role" mechanism that allows new ontological categories to be catered for in the representation, without the representation having to revise existing analyses. Specifically, individual propositions within an analysis can be marked as taking on a particular role in a particular class. So, for example, in the Toulmin class, a proposition might be marked as a "warrant" – a concept that only makes sense in the context of Toulmin analyses. Of course, if these extensions are not only numerous but also individually significant, then the benefits of an interchange language such as AML are eroded. The exponentially expensive problem of translation between the different classes returns. AML takes a pragmatic solution, providing as much generic capability as possible, and supporting extensions that are intended to be small scale. If particular software systems aim to make use of these extensions in translation then they are not prohibited from doing so.

In the Wigmore case, the four basic types each represent different roles: corroborative, explanatory, testimonial and circumstantial.

The symbols in a Wigmore diagram also define the author of each premise (defense or prosecution). This can be translated directly into standard by using the *owner* property of a node. Clearly, a translation of ownership from standard to Wigmore only makes sense if the owner is specified as one of defense or prosecution.

Wigmore's concept of *negatory evidence* is rather unclear, as he never provides a definition of the term, and uses it only rarely in his own writings. The simplest assumption seems to be that negatory evidence argues against its parent in the diagram, and thus should be regarded as some form of refutation in a standard diagram. The problem with doing this is that a standard diagram allows only a single refutation for any one premise (based on the idea that a proposition p can have only a single opposite not-p), whereas in a Wigmore diagram, any number of negatory nodes can impinge on a single parent node. We can solve the problem of translation in a way similar to that employed with Toulmin rebuttals. We create an *added negation* as an extra node which contains a premise which is the opposite of that stated in the negatory node. The negatory node then has the added negation as its parent, and the added negation, in turn, supports the original parent of the negatory node.

The *forces* on the support edges in a Wigmore diagram have an obvious translation as *evaluations* in a standard diagram. However, Wigmore introduces one complication that is not present in a standard diagram: the set of testimonial evidence can also itself have a group evaluation that is distinct from those of each separate piece of testimony. Since this group evaluation pertains to the node supported by the collective testimony, it should be attached to that node rather than to any of the testimonial nodes (or, indeed, to some virtual node introduced for the purpose). We can, therefore, define a new role tag in AML to represent this group evaluation.

8.8 Applications

To underscore the importance of tying formal models of argumentation theory to applications with end users, we briefly review some of the application domains in which Araucaria has been deployed. As freely downloadable software, it is difficult to estimate the size of the current user group accurately; web server logs indicate between 1,000 and 2,000 downloads to unique IP addresses each year since 2001, and a further 1,000 or so package CDs have been distributed. The software has wide geographical appeal (a new version is under development which will support all Unicode languages) with known users in over 40 countries, but more surprising is the range of domains, including not just the academic and pedagogic domains that might be expected but requests have also been received demonstrating use of the software by engineers building safety cases, barristers preparing cases, doctors conducting complex diagnoses, statisticians representing test designs and more. Here we focus on a couple of the more significant user groups.

8.8.1 Applications in Education

The majority of Araucaria's users are probably instructors and their students. The development team has had close contact with three undergraduate courses, one in philosophy at Winnipeg, one in legal theory at Groningen, and one in argument and computation at Dundee. Student users – particularly those outside the computational sciences – make for demanding requirements on software, and it is through many hundreds of students' feedback that the software has been updated on a rolling basis. The ability to do simple graph matching automatically has been a great boon for instructors with large class sizes (which are characteristic of North American critical thinking courses in particular). For although complex arguments have too many potentially "right" analyses for completely automated marking to be feasible, smaller exercises with less variability and interpretability are well within the scope of Araucaria's automatic marking, and provide instructors with much more flexibility than is afforded by traditional multiple choice alternatives. Full classroom evaluations of critical thinking software is fraught with difficulties, but following the trailblazing of Reason!Able's assessments (Twardy, 2004), and the requirements for the process laid out in van den Braak et al. (2006), Araucaria will be undergoing controlled assessment as part of its longer term development. An experiment using Araucaria in the teaching of critical thinking at the University of Winnipeg (Rowe et al., 2006) shows that most (typically around 80%) students rate Araucaria as "high" or "medium" on eight usability criteria. However, the experiment also pointed out a few areas where Araucaria's usability could be improved, such as streamlining the installation process and providing facility for entering text directly rather than reading arguments in from files.

8.8.2 Applications in Legal Practice

In 2004, Araucaria was trialed by a number of magistrates in the Ontario Court of Justice. The remit of magistrates in Ontario is interesting because it covers a wide range of cases from the mundane to the headline-hitting. Specifically, at one end of the scale, magistrates are faced with processing traffic violations, and this represents and hugh majority of the caseload, with 60–70 cases requiring attention per day. Each case is small and follows a stereotypical pattern in which the number of alternative arguments and decisions is relatively small. On the other hand, there are much rarer, but much larger environmental law cases involving, from time to time, large, multi-national corporations. These cases can be protracted, lasting weeks or months, and can involve huge amounts of testimony and argument. Informal trials were set up by the magistrates themselves to explore the potential role of software in the process of preparing summing up arguments. The trials demonstrated that software tools, and Araucaria in particular, was found to be useful in the large complex cases – and that is exactly where a computer scientist's intuition would expect a tool to play a significant role. Much more interesting therefore, was the feedback that Araucaria was also being used extensively in processing the smaller cases, and specifically, that by setting up a small number of argumentation schemes, magistrates were able to very rapidly go through the associated critical questions as a kind of check list (and a number of minor modifications of the Araucaria interface were tailored to this process to streamline interaction). As a result, a program of roll-out has been initiated for all new appointments, which will eventually cover the entire magistracy in the province – over 400 individuals. Larger scale trials and feedback mechanisms are planned.

8.8.3 Applications in Autonomous Communications

There is a rich area of research in multi-agent systems exploring the uses to which argumentation can be put in structuring communication between agents (Rahwan et al., 2005). Sophisticated models of such interchange are starting to be developed, taking into account a wide range of argumentation-theoretic concepts (Norman et al., 2003). These models have, to date, been rarely implemented [though there are exceptions (Wells & Reed, 2005; Tolchinsky et al., 2006), for example]. One of the reasons for this relative scarcity is not only that it is time consuming to implement the protocols (which is the point made in Wells & Reed (2005)) but also that it is difficult to construct the knowledge that agents will use as the basis for their inter-agent arguments. For this, Araucaria and tools like it can be a great practical help (given that their output can be converted down into an appropriate framework style). Early evidence for this utility comes from initial assessments of argumentation scheme usage in agent communications in which patterns of data were constructed manually in Araucaria and then transformed automatically to produce many thousands of variants, with which to populate agent knowledge bases and thereby frame evaluation tests (Reed & Walton, 2005). With an increase in the number and flexibility of tools for argument creation, and the ability for those tools to produce framework-style output, this trend is set to continue.

8.9 Conclusion

We have introduced three popular styles (standard, Toulmin and Wigmore) for diagramming arguments and described the software package *Araucaria* which allows existing text to be marked up and converted into diagrams in these styles. We have explored some of the issues arising in the translation between these three diagramming methods. The translation exercise demonstrates that there are many subtle nuances involved in an argument, and that any single diagramming method captures only some of these. Araucaria introduces the Argument Markup Language or AML, which is an attempt to encapsulate these features in an interlingua and to allow automated translation between diagramming methods. Araucaria has become a popular system both for teaching and analyzing arguments in a variety of settings such as courses on critical thinking, legal analysis and communications.

References

Freeman, J. (1991) *Dialectics and the Macrostructure of Argument*, NY: Foris.
Gilbert, M.A. (1997) *Coalescent Argumentation*. New Jersey: Lawrence Erlbaum Associates.
Grennan, W. (1997) *Informal Logic*, Montreal: McGill Queens University Press.
Hansard (2004) *UK House of Commons Debates for 16 Sept 2004:* http://www.publications.parliament.uk/pa/cm200304/cmhansrd/vo040916/debtext/40916-06.htm
Harrell, M. (2005) Using argument diagramming software in the classroom, *Teaching Philosophy* 28(2).
Hitchcock, D. (2003) Toulmin's warrants, in: *Proceedings of the 5th International Conference of Argumentation (ISSA 2002)*, SicSat.
Hurley, P. (2003) *A Concise Introduction to Logic*, Belmont, CA: Wadsworth.
Johnson, R.H. (2000) *Manifest Rationality: A Pragmatic Theory of Argument*, Mahwah, NY: Lawrence Erlbaum.
Katzav, J. and C. Reed (2004) On argumentation schemes and the natural classification of argument, *Argumentation* 18(4), 239–259.
Katzav, J., C.A. Reed and G.W.A. Rowe (2004) Argument Research Corpus, in: B. Lewandowska-Tomaszczyk (ed) *Practical Applications in Language and Computers (Proceedings of the 2003 Conference)*, Peter Lang, Frankfurt, pp. 229–239.
Kirschner, P., S. Buckingham Shum and C. Carr (2003) *Visualizing Argumentation: Software Tools for Collaborative and Educational Sense-Making*, Berlin Heidelberg London New York: Springer.
Norman, T.J., D.V. Carbogim, E.C.W. Krabbe and D.N. Walton (2003) Argument and multi-agent systems, in: C. Reed and T. Norman (eds) *Argumentation Machines: New Frontiers in Argument and Computation*, Kluwer, pp. 15–54.
Parsons, T. (1996) What is argument? *Journal of Philosophy* 93.
Perelman C. and L. Olbrechts-Tyteca (1969) *The New Rhetoric: A Treatise on Argumentation*, Notre Dame: University of Notre Dame Press.
Pollock (1995) *Cognitive Carpentry*, Cambridge, MA: MIT Press.
Rahwan, I., P. Moraitis and C. Reed (2005) *Argumentation in Multi-Agent Systems (Proceedings of ArgMAS2004)*, no. 3366 in Lecture Notes in Artificial Intelligence, Springer.
Reed, C. and G. Rowe (2004) Araucaria: software for argument analysis, diagramming and representation, *International Journal of AI Tools* 13(4): 961–980.
Reed, C. and G. Rowe (2006) Translating Toulmin diagrams: theory neutrality in argument representation, *Argumentation* 19(3): 267–286.
Reed, C. and D. Walton (2005) Towards a formal and implemented model of argumentation schemes in agent communication, *Autonomous Agents and Multi-Agent Systems* 11(2): 172–188.
Rowe, G. and C. Reed (2006) Translating Wigmore diagrams, in: P.E. Dunne and T.J.M. Bench-Capon (eds) *Computational Models of Argument (Proceedings of COMMA 2006)*, Amsterdam: IOS Press, pp. 171–182.
Rowe, G., F. Macagno, C. Reed and D. Walton (2006) Araucaria as a tool for diagramming arguments in teaching and studying philosophy, *Teaching Philosophy* 29(2): 111–124.
Tolchinsky, P., S. Modgil, U. Cortes and M. Sanchez-Marre (2006) Cbr and argument schemes for collaborative decision making, in: P. Dunne and T. Bench-Capon (eds) *Computational Models of Argument (Proceedings of COMMA 2006)*, Amsterdam: IOS Press, pp. 171–182.
Toulmin, S. (1958) *The Uses of Argument*, Cambridge: Cambridge University Press.
Twardy, C. (2004) Argument maps improve critical thinking, *Teaching Philosophy* 27, 95–116.
van den Braak, S., H. van Oostendorp, H. Prakken and G. Vreeswijk (2006) A critical review of argument visualization tools: do users become better reasoners? in: *Working Notes of the 6th Workshop of Computational Models of Natural Argument (CMNA 2006)*.

van Eemeren, F.H. (ed) (2004) *Advances in Pragma-Dialectics*, Amsterdam: Vale Press.
Walton, D. (1996) *Argumentation Schemes for Presumptive Reasoning*, Lawrence Erlbaum Associates.
Walton, D. (2006) *Fundamentals of Critical Argumentation*, Cambridge: Cambridge University Press.
Wells, S. and C. Reed (2005) A drosophila for computational dialectics, in: *Proceedings of the International Conference on Autonomous Agents and Multi-Agent Systems (AAMAS 2005)*.
Wigmore, J. (1913) *The Principles of Judicial Proof*, Boston: Little Brown & Company.
Willmott, S., G. Vreeswijk, M. South, C. Chesñevar, G. Simari, J. McGinnis, I. Rahwan and C. Reed (2006) Towards an argument interchange format for multiagent systems, in: N. Maudet, S. Parsons and I. Rahwan (eds) *Proceedings of the 3rd International Workshop on Argumentation in Multi-Agent Systems (ArgMAS 2006)*, Springer.
Wreen, M. (1998) A few remarks on the individuation of arguments, in: *Proceedings of the 4th International Conference of Argumentation (ISSA 1998)*, SicSat.

9. Mapping the Curriculum: How Concept Maps can Improve the Effectiveness of Course Development

Tony Sherborne

Sheffield Hallam University, Centre for Science Education, t.sherborne@shu.ac.uk

Abstract. Every program of instruction taking place in schools, from French to physics, is the result of a complex process called "curriculum development." It begins with the setting of high level goals and then proceeds through successive stages of elaboration of the concepts, scoping and sequencing content. The design must then be communicated and adopted by the teachers who will implement it. Historically, curriculum reform efforts have not been consistently effective in delivering the desired improvements in student understanding. This chapter discusses how the use of concept mapping could help curriculum developers and teachers at various stages of the process. The ability of maps to focus on key ideas and their connections may help curriculum designs to survive better the translation into classroom experience, and promote collaborative working methods.

9.1 The Challenge of Developing Curricula

Change is a constant in education. In countries like the UK, the government responds to a rapidly changing society by conducting regular reviews of school provision. So the curriculum is like a motorway; you can always find one section being taken apart and rebuilt.

However, the path to successful curriculum change is a rocky road, littered with the "road kill" of new courses that have failed to make their intended impact in terms of pedagogic practice e.g. Stenhouse (1975) and Cornbleth (1990). Centrally initiated curricula have had particularly limited success (Skilbeck, 1984). A central aim of almost every modern school curricula must be to develop and deepen students' understanding. Yet, according to many critics, this remains an elusive goal, despite decades of curriculum development. Instead, critics characterize the knowledge most students emerge with as "isolated" (without a grasp of the underlying principles), "naïve" (where misconceptions remain after teaching), and "inert" – (not transferred to contexts beyond those being taught and examined), Perkins (1992).

There are of course main reasons why curriculum development may fail. We can group these problems into three broad areas:

- Curriculum design: the substance of the new curriculum design may be lacking in focus or clarity, or be too wide in scope or complex, or be insufficiently desirable or feasible.
- Curriculum communication: the design may not be effectively communicated, or attracts little commitment of those who will implement it – schools and teachers.
- Curriculum implementation: the original intentions become subverted or diluted as the design is transformed into a classroom experience.

This chapter will consider each of these areas in turn, and argue that concept maps possess features that could reduce the impact of these problems on curriculum development. Before this, we will make explicit certain assumptions about the curriculum and the process of development.

Although there is agreement that a curriculum broadly means "all the learning which is planned and guided by the school" (Kerr, quoted in Kelly, 1983) there are different viewpoints about the nature of curriculum.

9.1.1 Curriculum Philosophies

The traditional view is of "curriculum as a body of knowledge" to be transmitted: "organized, communicated, acted upon and in some sense reproduced by students" (Skilbeck, 1984). Here the syllabus is pre-eminent, a list of facts to be covered and examined. Although widely criticized by the educational philosopher John Dewey and the progressive movement, this theory has stayed alive, partly because of the professional values and skills of teachers, and partly because it is reinforced by institutional structures like examinations.

In terms of curriculum development, the dominant model in use today takes the philosophy of "scientific management" from business and applies it to education. Based on the work of Ralph Tyler (1949), what is most important is to define the educational objectives as clearly as possible at the outset. The curriculum is then the instrument by which pupils attain these learning objectives, taking the form of a program of activities (Grundy, 1987, Chap. 11). This philosophy is therefore often known as *"curriculum as technology."*

9.1.2 Concept Mapping

There are several kinds of mapping techniques that could be commandeered for the purpose of curriculum development. This chapter focuses on concept mapping, which has been the most thoroughly investigated. Almost as soon as concept mapping was developed for use by students, researchers began to recognize its potential for curriculum development (Stewart et al., 1979; Novak & Gowin, 1984). Just as concept maps can evolve from being static representations of knowledge into tools for more effective learning (see the chapter by Joseph Novak), it was suggested that curriculum maps can go beyond visualizing key objectives and become a tool for curriculum developers to achieve better quality designs (McDaniel et al., 2005). The rest of the chapter explores the use of concept mapping at each stage of the curriculum development process. The stages were formulated by Taba (1962) and for convenience have been grouped within the phases set out earlier: curriculum design, curriculum communication and curriculum implementation.

9.2 Mapping for Curriculum Design

According to the "curriculum as technology" model, the process begins by defining the main elements of the curriculum. This is a complex undertaking because so many elements have to be blended simultaneously (Harden, 2001): learning outcomes, course content, students' needs, interests and learning styles, teaching and learning strategies, assessment and evaluation. There are three stages involved (Taba, 1962; Ornstein & Hunkins, 1998):

- Conceptualization and legitimation
- Diagnosis of students needs
- Formulation of objectives

9.2.1 Conceptualization and Legitimation

First, curriculum designers need to answer the question "what educational purposes should the school seek to attain?" (Tyler, 1949). In other words, to become clear why a new curriculum is needed, and what its essential design features are. As with any design process, it is also important to identify what the constraints are – what Skilbeck (1984) calls "situational analysis."

This is in large part a creative, problem-solving process. It would often involve a group who brainstorm and organizing ideas, and so lends itself to a visualization technique like mapping. In this instance mind maps, rather than concept maps, have been studied by researchers. Paykoc et al. (2004) found mind maps increased both the quality and quantity of the issues and needs identified by the group. However, what appealed most to the participants was how "drawing a big picture" created a shared, meaningful experience for them. The benefit of mapping at this stage seems to be its "utility in building understanding and consensus within groups" (Brightman, 2003). Vilela et al. (2004) argues that visualizing the problem together secures more "active involvement" of a group of curriculum reformers than a standard textual presentation.

Curriculum designs that are interdisciplinary rather than single-subject based might benefit even more. Not only is it a greater challenge to gain involvement and consensus in a diverse group of planners, but by their very nature, concept maps help reveal connections between different topics. Edmondson (1995) found that using concept maps to design a course for veterinary students using interdisciplinary "problem-based learning" course allowed faculty planners to "trace common themes and concepts."

9.2.2 Diagnosis of Students' Needs

Any enlightened curriculum will be based on a consideration of students' needs. This is a question of building up a picture of the experiences and knowledge students possess before the course, along with any misconceptions they may hold. Concept maps can act as a diagnostic tool with which to probe students' existing knowledge, since they provide a visual mirror of one's mental structure (McAleese, 1998). Walker et al. (2002) compared the concept maps of novice biomedical engineering students with those of experts in the field. Each group was asked to visualize the 10–20 most important concepts in the subject and how they related together. They found the resulting maps provided a reliable indicator of differences in understanding between the novices and the experts. As Fig. 9.1 illustrates, there is a quantitative difference in "link density," with the students' maps showing less connectedness between the concepts. These objective measures of understanding were backed up by qualitative judgments: novices tended to emphasize the detailed domain content, whereas experts displayed deeper understanding by highlighting the underlying principles and their applications. Indeed several scholars (Aidman & Egan, 1998; Diekhoff, 1983) have suggested that the degree of similarity between the students' concept maps and those of expert concept maps is in fact a good predictor of examination performance.

Differences between the concept maps of expert maps and student maps can be used as a "game plan for teaching" (Jonassen, 1987). A teaching plan based on the philosophy that curriculum is about transferring knowledge, would aim to make the mental equivalent of students' concept maps resemble that of the experts as closely as possible.

However, more constructivist views of the learning process would aim less for convergence to an ideal state than to developing greater richness in each student's map, whilst still demonstrating features of sophisticated understanding. Students' concept maps could also provide starting points for individualized instruction.

Concept maps can help curriculum developers by opening a window into students' minds. However, they do only represent a snapshot of students' knowledge (Jonassen, 1996). In practice, understanding is heavily context dependent, so maps should not be used dogmatically as a measure of students' capabilities.

9.2.3 Formulation of Objectives

Most curricula are defined by lists of key objectives: what the students should know, understand, be able to do, etc. In choosing these objectives, an important considerations is the age or cognitive development level of the students, as this influences what kinds of understanding and skills are appropriate. For instance, one obviously cannot expect 11 year olds to think like researchers. The challenge for curriculum designers is to create an appropriate progression of objectives from one year to the next. Here concept mapping could be a valuable tool.

9. Using Maps for Curriculum Development 187

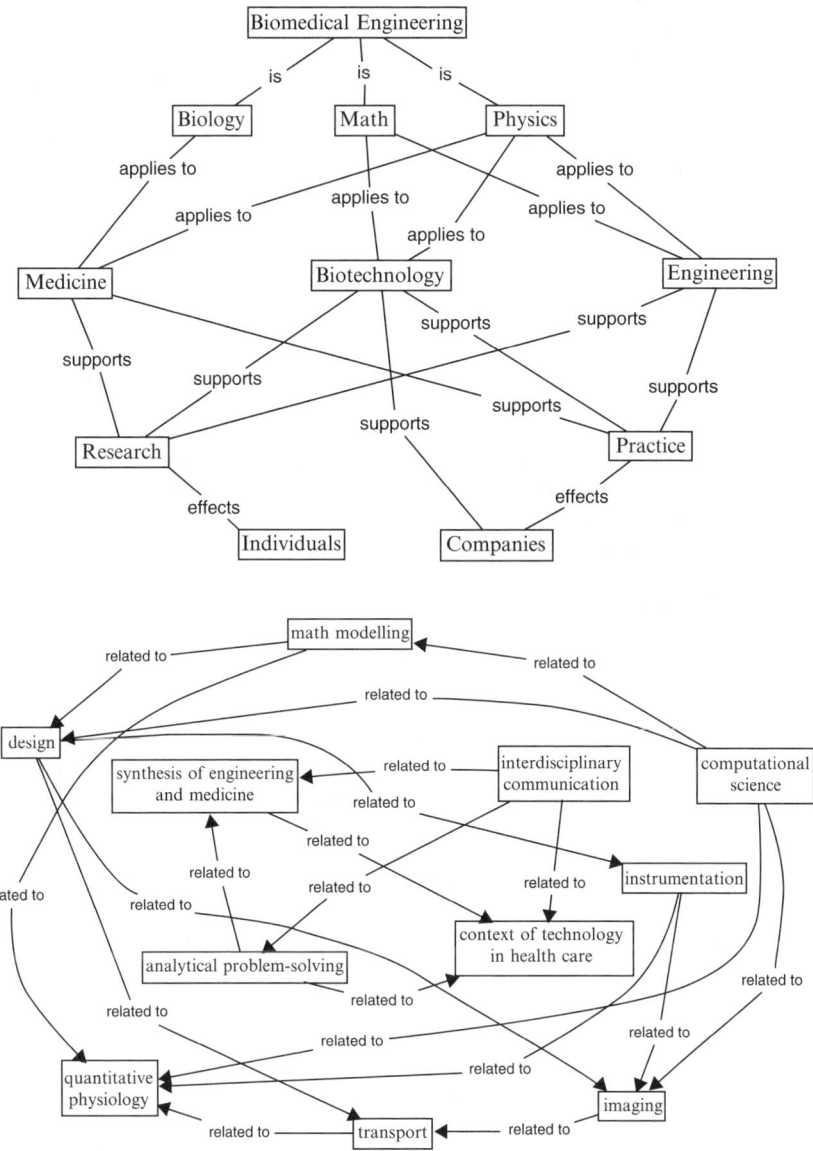

Fig. 9.1. The difference in link density of "novice" and "expert" concept maps (http://www.vanth.org/presentations/walker-asee02-1.pdf slide 11 and 12).

Table 9.1 shows in text form some of the key learning objectives for "Space" in the 11–14 English National Curriculum for science (Department for Education and Skills, 2002). The continuity, how objectives in later years build on those in earlier years, is not obvious. The objectives seem to be just different collections of ideas.

Table 9.1. National Curriculum learning objectives for Space, adapted by the author from the Qualification Curriculum Authority's schemes of work (QCA, 2000) http://www.standards.dfes.gov.uk/schemes2/secondary_science/

Year 7 learning objectives relating to Space	Year 9 learning objectives relating to Space
• To explain phenomena such as day and night, and the apparent movement of the Sun • That the Sun is a light source, but the Moon and Earth are seen by reflected light • To relate ideas about the Sun, Earth and Moon to familiar phenomena • That our solar system includes the Sun, its planets and asteroids and the natural satellites of the planets • That the planets orbit the Sun in similar ways to the Earth	• That gravity is an attractive force which acts on the Earth towards the centre of the planet • That gravity is an attractive force between objects with mass • That where the gravitational force is lower than on the Earth, the mass of an object remains the same, but its weight is less • That gravitational attraction between bodies decreases as the distance between them increases • That the Moon is a natural satellite of the Earth, whose orbit is maintained by the Earth's gravitational pull

Compare the table above to the map in Fig. 9.2. Here similar learning objectives have been organized into a hierarchical concept map. We can see the continuity clearly, in the connections between each concept and those underneath on which it depends on for its comprehension. The map gives a clear message about the desirable sequencing of concepts in the curriculum, which is difficult without using a two-dimensional layout. According to Prideaux (2003), a map is a better "structure for the systematic organization of the curriculum." Starr & Krajcik (1990) found that concept maps helped science teachers develop science curricula which were more hierarchically arranged, and thus highlighted and prioritized the more important objectives over the detail.

Another important consideration is the scope of the course. Typically, school curricula aim for breadth at the expense of depth of understanding. Because maps are visual and necessarily concise, they can help remind educators "of the areas of major emphasis" (Edmondson, 1995) and be more "conceptually driven" (Starr and Krajcik, 1990). One would also expect concept maps to help designers meet a further criterion of good design: "integration" (Tyler, 1949), which denotes the connectedness of the knowledge.

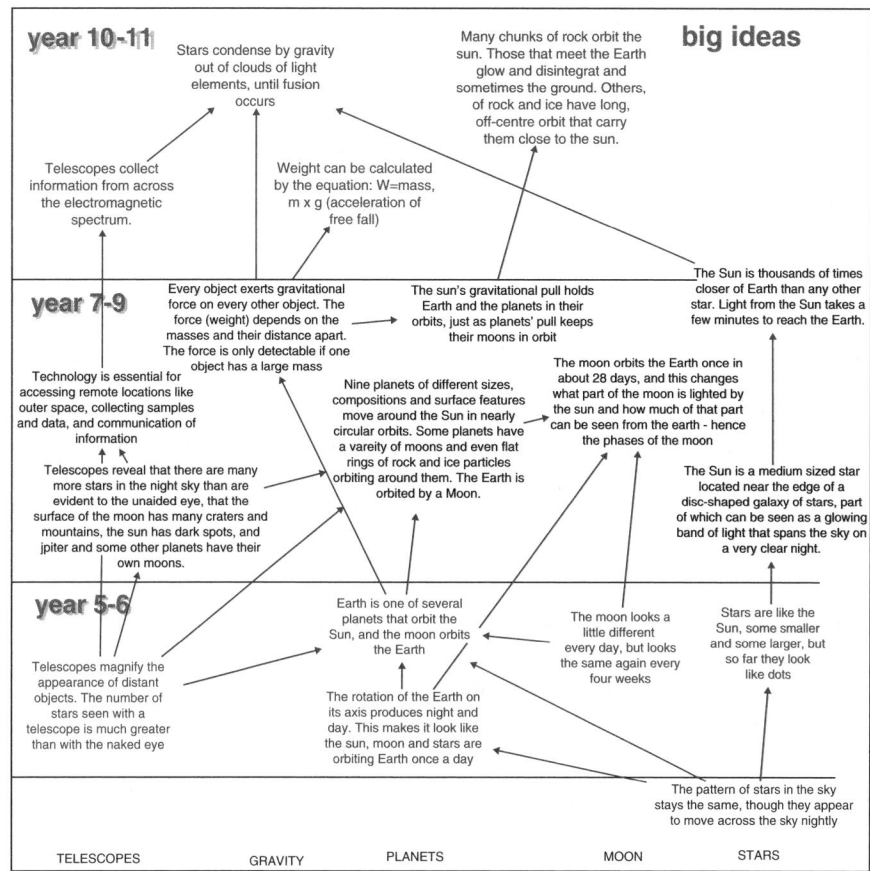

Fig. 9.2. Progression map for Space learning objectives, by the author, using Compendium.

9.3 Mapping for Curriculum Communication

After a curriculum is designed, it has to be communicated to the teachers who will plan and implement it. Teachers need to understand and become committed to a new design (Sparkes, 1991) if it is to be effectively implemented in the classroom. Both of these requirements are problematic. Curriculum documents are often so full of objectives and assessment criteria that the "design concept" appears opaque to teachers. "Schools cannot interpret what they do not value, appreciate and know" (Skilbeck, 1984). Therefore curriculum development agencies often fail to communicate the main features of a new design to teachers. It is a case of not seeing the wood for the trees, which take the form of pages of curriculum detail.

Maps may be a powerful way to communicating the essence of the curriculum to the important stakeholders, rather than overwhelm them. McDaniel et al. (2005) emphasize how the show important themes and conceptual relationships (Edmondson,

1995). It may be in recognition of this problem that the Qualifications and Curriculum Authority in England in 2006 chose a map-based model to communicate their "big picture" vision of the curriculum to stakeholders rather than a traditional text-based document.

The difficulty of getting teachers to feel committed to towards a curriculum change may be one of the biggest factors in why curriculum change so rarely succeeds. Teachers need to believe they have a role to play in the innovation (Brazee & Capelluti, 1995, p. 118).

Edmondson (1995) has suggested that the structure of maps seems to offer teachers more room to maneuver and shape their curriculum. So a curriculum presented as a maps may consequently engender less resistance from teachers than traditional text documents. Martin (1994) proposes that the adoption of curriculum concept maps by teachers can actually act as a catalyst for pedagogic change. He found that significant numbers of student teachers who had been through a curriculum development program, became committed to using the maps for concept-based planning and teaching afterwards. Edmondson (1995) also argues that extensive use of concept mapping by teachers gives them a more constructivist mindset, asking "what do I want students to learn?" more than "what do I want to teach?"

9.4 Mapping for Curriculum Implementation

Curriculum planning is the teacher's job: to translate an existing curriculum design into a teaching plan. Even with the help of curriculum documents, it takes considerable skill to ensure that the original intentions of the design survive this interpretation into detailed content and a sequence of learning experiences. Wiggins & McTighe (2003) describe two common pitfalls of curriculum planning they see in many classrooms, both of which might be addressed with mapping techniques. "Coverage" happens when teachers pressurized by testing obligations on a large body of knowledge, transform the design into a "march through the textbook irrespective of priorities, desired results, learner needs and interests." The other pitfall is an "activity-led" curriculum, that is, one organized around the hands-on experiences of the students. The danger here is the lack of focus on the key knowledge and skill objectives, which students are therefore less likely to achieve.

To consider the potential of mapping, we will divide implementation into its stages (Taba, 1962; Ornstein & Hunkins, 1998):

- Specification and organization of content
- Selection and organization of learning experiences
- Evaluation of the resulting curriculum

9.4.1 Specification and Organizing of Content

Hassard (2004, p. 268) recommends that all teachers construct a concept map in order to help them reflect on key question about the content, such as "are there too many abstract concepts?", "Should there be more concrete ones added?"

"What content do we teach?" and "in what order?" are the next decisions. Many school curricula suffer from the problem of "concept overload," leading to calls for reducing the amount of content. Clark & James (2004) found concept maps helped to keep the detail in check, by focusing on the key ideas and skills. In particular, creating maps-within-maps allows the developer to concentrate on first the overview, and then see how the content translates into successive levels of detail (Martin, 1994). A series of maps can also provide different "windows" (Harden, 2001) from which the developer can view the emerging curriculum, for example, showing how each part is to be assessed. Sharing the maps with students can have further benefits, in explaining "why a particular concept is worth knowing" (Allen et al., 1993) and showing relationships between important ideas, that can result in improved achievement (Willerman & Harg, 1991).

The problem of "isolated knowledge" referred to earlier, arises when content is taught as "one vertical hierarchy" after another (Martin, 1994). Topic maps, like that in Fig. 9.3 (Edmondson, 1995), might instead encourage teachers who can see the interconnections to teach in a more integrated fashion. According to Martin, creating horizontal relationships between the ideas give the learner greater meaningfulness, and therefore a coherent (not isolated) understanding.

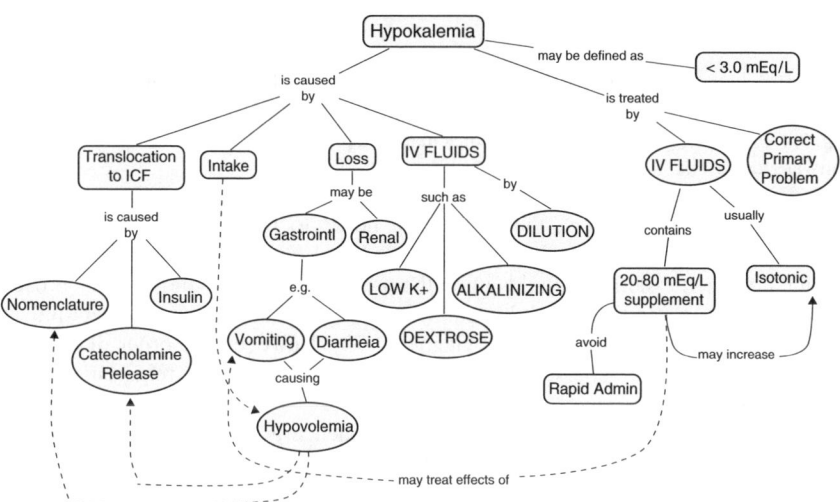

Fig. 9.3. A topic map for teaching veterinary students (note; from Edmondson, 1996 – http://adsabs.harvard.edu/abs/1995JRScT..32..777E).

There is a danger though that we forget that not all knowledge is alike. While most topics can be well represented in the hierarchical form of a concept map, there are others which demand to be understood as the interacting parts of a system (Hyerle, 1996). In these cases, a different kinds of map is required. In science, for instance, examples of such systems are food webs describing the relationships between predators and prey, and the hugely complex system of the Earth's climate.

These knowledge areas are better represented with a map like the one in Fig. 9.4. Its design clearly shows the causal relationships in terms of flows of numbers and feedbacks, that are needed to understand the dynamic nature of the system.

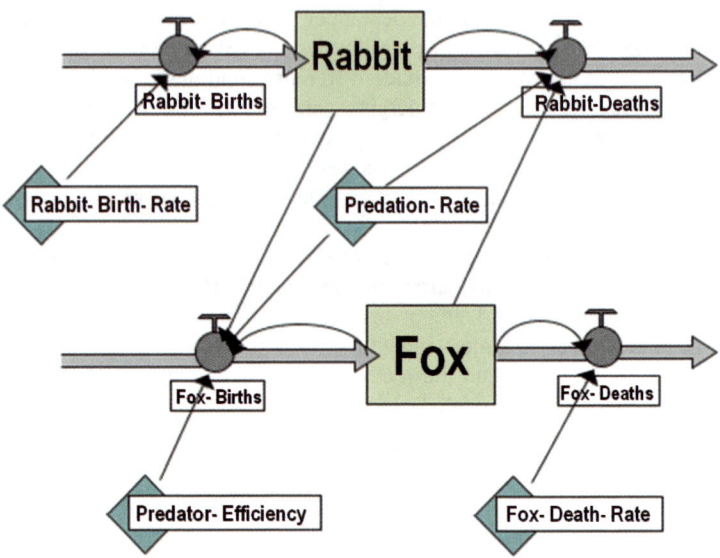

Fig. 9.4. Predation map – a system dynamics map of a predator prey relationship created in the software tool Stella.

After specifying content, the curriculum needs to be organized into a logical teaching order. This is called sequencing (Tyler, 1949), and in a well-developed curriculum, each experience builds upon the preceding one, moving towards broader and deeper understanding. Such logical sequencing can determine whether students perform well or otherwise (Okey & Gagne, 1970). However, the order of topics in many textbook-driven courses is often not based on learning requirements, but simply on tradition.

Concept mapping may be useful here to sequence a curriculum more from the students' perspective. Clark & James (2004) describe how making concept maps of their university geology course map led them to reject the conventional "series of unconnected vertical hierarchies" order of the textbook. The maps like that in Fig. 9.5, helped them see that the traditional order presented too many abstract ideas before pupils enough prior knowledge with which to connect them. So they re-sequenced the course, presenting concrete ideas at the bottom of the concept map first, and then moving onwards and upwards towards more general abstract concepts. The maps also allowed them to make the conceptual connections between different lectures more explicit to students. Figure 9.5 shows the connections between two lectures on joints and faults.

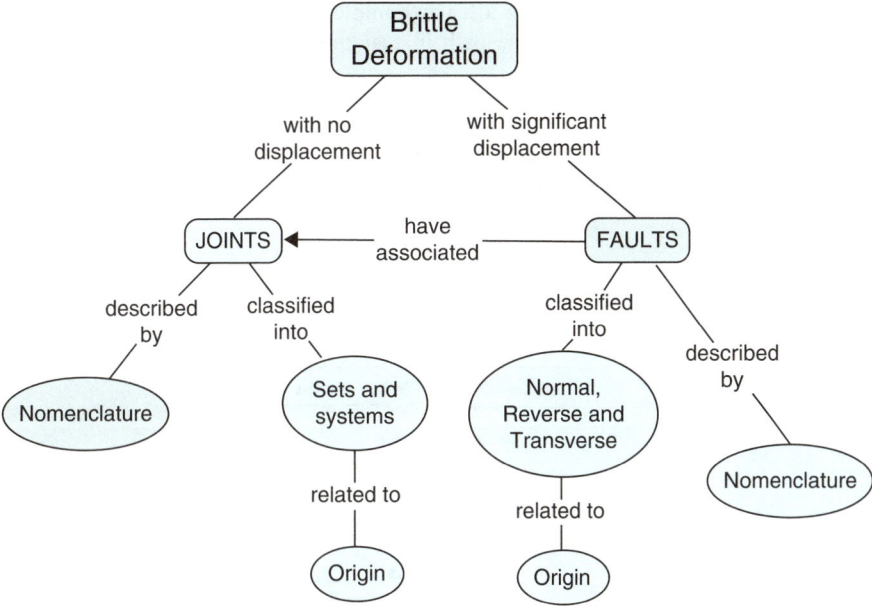

Fig. 9.5. Using concept maps to make connections between parts of a course. (Clark & James, 2004 http://www.nagt.org/files/nagt/jge/abstracts/Clark_v52n3p224.pdf).

Martin (1994) similarly describes the maps as helping to prevent "errors in sequencing" content. Although, as Novak & Gowin (1984) point out, concept maps are non-linear in form and cannot specify a linear teaching order, without some interpretation.

9.4.2 Selection and Organizing of Learning Experiences

A characteristic of the best teaching is that it customizes or "differentiates" a curriculum, addressing the range of abilities and needs of different students. One simple approach to differentiation is to distinguish between "foundation" concepts (for everyone) and "higher" concepts (only for those who make more progress). A concept map, or a flow chart for that matter, could be an effective format to help teachers plan and navigate differentiated routes through a curriculum.

Another relevant feature of exemplary teaching is "responsiveness," where teachers continually adapt lessons based on regular assessment of how the students are learning. The concept map of Fig. 9.6, showing a "route map" with several possible paths, was constructed by a teacher implementing a curriculum from the author. The idea was to choose the path in real time, depending on the students' responses.

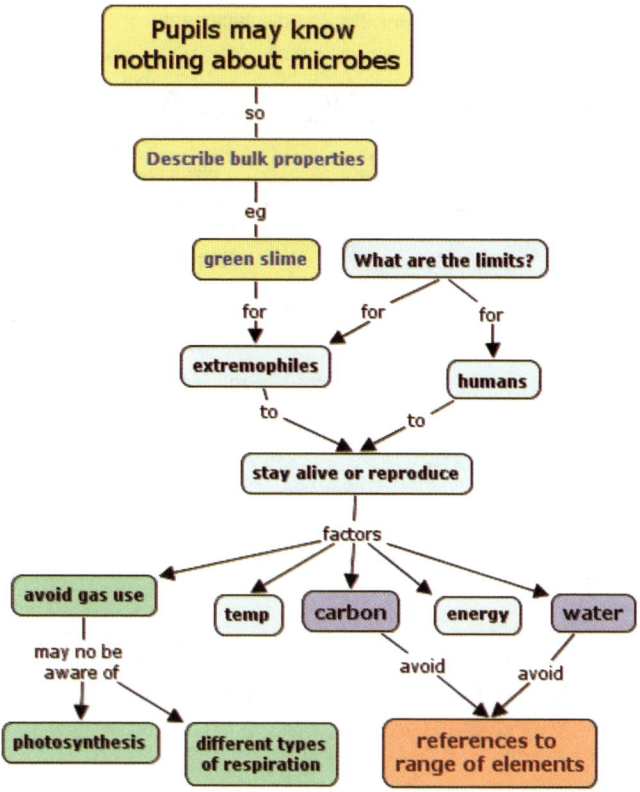

Fig. 9.6. A map showing a responsive learning plan for a "Space" topic (this map was developed by the author, using Cmap tools).

9.4.3 Evaluation of the Resulting Curriculum

Once a new course has been running for a while, it is often evaluated in terms of whether it is achieving its design objectives. Concept maps can play two roles here. First, the map can be used to assess how much the course has developed students' understanding. Analysis of the map in Fig. 9.7 revealed to the course instructors that certain misconceptions still persisted among veterinary students even after the course (Edmondson, 1995).

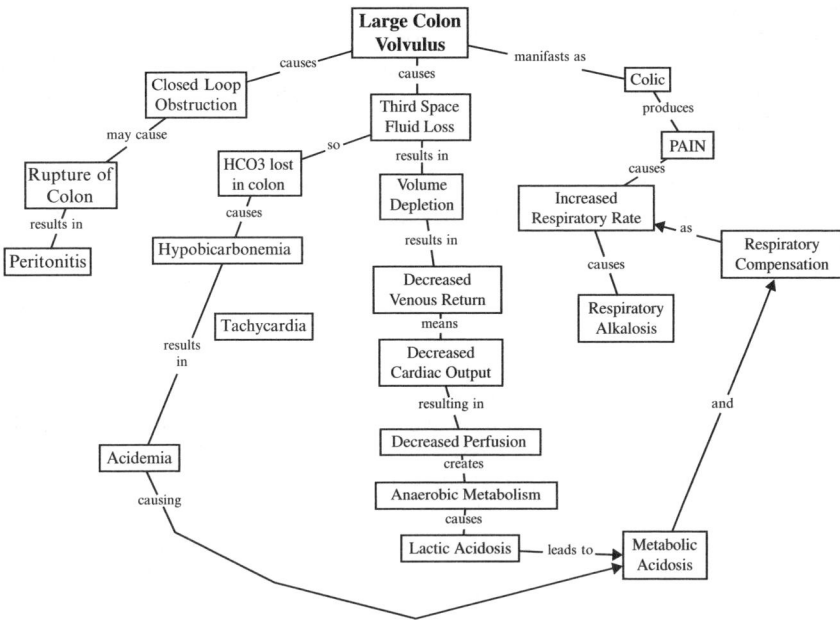

Fig. 9.7. Using concept maps to reveal misconceptions, for course evaluation (from Edmondson 1995 – http://adsabs.harvard.edu/abs/1995JRScT..32..777E).

A related use of the maps is to identify the causes of an under-achieving curriculum. This can be done by overlaying the course objectives and students' understanding maps, to highlight the outcomes which do not match up (McDaniel et al., 2005). Vilela et al. (2004) argue that curriculum mapping makes a curriculum more "transparent" to the planners, and helps identify faults such as "missing linkages, inconsistencies, false assumptions." If the curriculum has to be revised, instead of starting over from scratch, a good map structure can "anchor" an evolving sequence of iterative revisions (Edmondson, 1995).

9.5 Summing Up

There is evidence for the benefit of concept mapping at each stage of the curriculum development process. So far, maps have been used in small scale course development rather than large scale reform. Is it possible that consistent use of concept maps could help avoid the large number of curriculum failures noted at the beginning?

There are four main reasons for advocating the wider use of concept maps to design, communicated and implement curricula. The first is big picture thinking. If we are talking about curricula that aim at teaching for understanding, the focus needs to be on the big ideas rather than the detailed knowledge. Concept maps seem naturally suited to this style of thinking, by representing only most important concepts and their interrelationships. By contrast, long syllabus documents make it all too easy to lose focus on the key objectives.

Second, concept maps are "theory-embedded tools" (McTighe & Lyman, 1998). They embody the philosophy of constructivism, in which understanding is viewed as a network of interconnected ideas rather than isolated information. Presumably there is more likelihood that a learning philosophy will survive the transformation into classroom experience, if developers use a tool that embeds the paradigm.

Third is the power of shared visualization, allowing the design to benefit from many minds working together. An obstacle to collaborative planning is that everybody has a slightly different interpretation of what is being discussed. The visual representation of a concept map can reduce this ambiguity, by embodying the key features of a plan and their connections. It provides a reference point for discussion, and thus helps to draw the group closer together.

Finally concept maps may reduce the "cognitive load" inherent in the complex process of curriculum design. They relieve the mind of the task of organizing the most important factors. All in all, maps make "excellent heuristic devices" for more effective curriculum development (Wandersee, 1990).

However, there are significant obstacles to the widespread use of mapping by developers and teachers. Most educators are more used to communicating through text. It is fairly easy to become competence with the technique, or the computer software. But to gain the educational benefits requires a change of thinking, which takes much more time and persistence.

Perhaps a bigger problem is that many classrooms are instructivist rather than constructivist. Teachers who treat learning more as information transfer than as students constructing their own meaning are unlikely to make much use of concept maps in their planning.

We have also assumed that teachers take an active role in re-constructing the received curriculum design for their own needs. However, a consequences of having centrally determined curricula, with detailed specification of standards to be met, methods, is that many teachers instead see themselves as "deliverers," rather than as planners of their own curriculum. In this case, again they are unlikely to value the technique of concept mapping. Maps may have more potential where the model for developing curricula is less top-down and objective driven, and instead more "curriculum as process." This alternative model rejects the tight specification of objectives and methods. Instead teachers take a greater hand, "translating any educational idea into a hypothesis testable in practice" (Stenhouse, 1975, p. 142). Although this curriculum model is not in widespread use, mapping would be a powerful technique. The maps would allow individual teachers to plan and share their curricula with others, improving their joint practice through the medium of visual communication.

It is unlikely that a curriculum could be created entirely using maps. While some of the work rests on the big ideas, there also the need to elaboration more detailed descriptions of knowledge. Because a single map is limited in how much it can communicate clearly, this greater specificity could only be achieved through a series of maps at different levels of detail. It is doubtful in this case whether the maps would be any more effective than the traditional text documents. In other words, maps do not scale well. They are best when they confine themselves to showing the big picture.

Curriculum development is anyway much too complex an enterprise for one tool to guarantee success. However, some of the problems, such as teaching fragmented knowledge by following a syllabus, or mis-understanding the vision of a curriculum document, may be largely the result of choosing the wrong medium for communication. In such cases, the potential of a visual, economic form of communication, philosophically aligned to the intentions of the curriculum designers, surely deserves futher investigation.

References

Aidman, E.V. & Egan, G. (1998) Academic assessment through computerized concept mapping: validating a method of implicit map reconstruction. International Journal of Instructional Media, 25(3), 277–294.

Allen, B.S., Hoffman, R.P., Kompella, J., & Sticht, T.G. (1993) *Computer-based Mapping for Curriculum Development.* In: Proceedings of selected Research and Development Presentations Technology. New Orleans, LA.

Brazee, E.N. & Capelluti, J. (1995) *Dissolving Boundaries: Toward an Integrative Curriculum.* Columbus, OH: National Middle School Association.

Brightman, J. (2003) Mapping methods for qualitative data structuring. Present at "Strategies in Qualitative Research: Methodological issues and practices using QSR Nvivo and NUD*IST" conference: London.

Clark, I.F. & James, P.R. (2004) Using Concept maps to plan an introductory structural geology course, Journal of Geoscience Education, 52(3), 224–230.

Cornbleth, C. (1990) *Curriculum in Context.* Basingstoke: Falmer Press.

Department for Education and Skills (2002) *Framework for teaching science: Years 7, 8 and 9.* London: Crown.

Diekhoff, G.M. (1983) Relationship judgments in the evaluation of structural understanding. Journal of Educational Psychology, 75, 227–233.

Edmondson, K.M. (1995) Concept mapping for the development of medical curricula. Journal of Research in Science Teaching, 32(7), 777–793.

Grundy, S. (1987) *Curriculum: Product or Praxis?* Lewes: Falmer Press.

Harden, R.E. (2001) Curriculum mapping: a tool for transparent and authentic teaching and learning. Medical Teacher 23(2):123–137.

Hassard, J. (2004) *The Art of Teaching Science.* OUP, USA.

Hyerle, D. (1996) *Visual Tools for Constructing Knowledge.* Alexandria, VA: ASCD.

Jonassen, D.H. (1987) Assessing cognitive structure: Verifying a method using pattern notes. Journal of Research and Development in Education, 20(3), 1–14.

Jonassen, D.H. (1996) *Computers as Mindtools for Schools.* London: Prentice-Hall International.

Kelly, A.V. (1983, 1999) *The Curriculum. Theory and practice 4e.* London: Paul Chapman.

Martin, D.J. (1994) Concept Mapping as an aid to lesson planning: A longitudinal study. Journal of Elementary Science Education, 6(2), 11–30.

McAleese, R.A. (1998) The knowledge arena as an extension to the concept map: Reflection in Action. Interactive Learning Environments, 6(3), 251–272.

McDaniel, E., Roth, B., & Millar, M. (2005) Concept mapping as a tool for curriculum design, Issues in Informing Science and Information Technology Education Joint Conference, 505–513, Flagstaff, AZ, June 16–19, 2005.

McTighe, J. & F.T. Lyman Jr. (1988) Cueing thinking in the curriculum: the promise of theory-embedded tools. Educational Leadership, 45(7), 18–24.

Novak, J.D. & Gowin, D.B. (1984) *Learning How to Learn*. New York, NY: Cambridge University Press.

Okey, J.R. & Gagne, R.M. (1970) Revision of a science topic using evidence of performance on subordinate skills. Journal of Research in Science Teaching, 7(4), 321–325.

Ornstein, A.C. & Hunkins, F.P. (1998) *Curriculum – Foundations, Principles, and Issues*, Prentice Hall.

Paykoc, F et al. (2004) What are the major curriculum issues? The use of mindmapping as a brainstorming exercise. Proceedings of the First Int. Conference on Concept Mapping: Spain.

Perkins, D. (1992) *Smart Schools*. New York: The Free Press.

Prideaux, D. (2003) Curriculum design. BMJ. 326, 268–270 <http://bmj.bmjjournals.com/cgi/reprint/326/7383/268>

Project 2061 American Association for the advancement of science (2001) *Designs For Science Literacy*. Oxford: Oxford University Press.

QCA (2000) The Standards Site: Science at key stage 3. <http://www.standards.dfes.gov.uk/schemes2/secondary_science/>

Skilbeck, M. (1984) *School-based Curriculum Development*. London: Harper and Row.

Sparkes, A.C. (1991) Exploring the subjective dimensions of curriculum change. In: N. Armstrong and A.C. Sparkes (eds) *Issues in Physical Education*. London: Cassell.

Starr, M., and Krajcik, J. (1990) Concept maps as a heuristic for science curriculum development: Toward improvement in process and product. Journal of Research in Science Teaching, 27(9), 987–100.

Stenhouse, L. (1975) An Introduction to Curriculum Research and Development. London: Heineman.

Stewart, J., Van Kirk, J., & Rowell, R. (1979) Concept maps: A tool for use in biology teaching. American Biology Teacher, 41(3), 171–175.

Taba, H. (1962) *Curriculum Development: Theory and Practice*. San Francisco: Harcourt, Brace.

Tyler, R.W. (1949) *Basic Principles of Curriculum and Instruction*. Chicago, IL: The University of Chicago Press.

Vilela, R. et al. (2004) Using concept maps for collaborative curriculum development. Proceedings of the First International Conference on Concept Mapping: Spain.

Walker, J.M., Cordray, D.S., & King, P.H. (2002) Concept mapping as a form of student assessment and instruction. Proceedings of the American Society for Engineering Education Annual Conference.

Wandersee, J.H. (1990) Concept mapping and the cartography of cognition. Journal of Research in Science Teaching, 27(10), 923–936.

Wiggins, G. & McTighe, J. (2003) Understanding by design. New Jersey: Pearson Education.

Willerman, M. & Mac Harg, R.A. (1991) The concept map as an advance organizer. Journal of Research in Science Teaching, 28(8), 705–711.

10. Using Compendium as a Tool to Support the Design of Learning Activities

Gráinne Conole

The Institute of Educational Technology, The Open University, UK, g.c.conole@open.ac.uk

Abstract. This chapter describes how a mind mapping tool, Compendium, is being used to help designers and teachers create and share learning activities. Initial evaluation of the use of the tool for learning design has been positive; users report that it is easy to use and helps them organize and articulate their learning designs. Importantly the tool also enables them to share and discuss their design strategies. The chapter will ground this work within the wider literature on learning design, focusing in particular on how learning activities can be represented and mechanisms for supporting decision making in creating new learning activities.

10.1 Introduction

Technologies are now beginning to be used in a rich range of ways to support learning; beyond the simple didactic instructional approaches which dominated the early use of technologies in education. In particular social networking tools offer exciting possibilities in terms of supporting more distributed and collaborative learning activities (Alexander, 2006; Downes, 2006). Recent research on students' experience of using technologies shows that many are comfortable in this technology-enriched environment (Conole et al., 2006; Conole et al. 2008; Creanor et al., 2006). "Google," "Wikipedia," "Email," and "chat" emerge as core tools to support students' learning. They are sophisticated users who appropriate the technologies to their own needs. Coupled with this, current thinking in terms of effective learning, promotes active, engaging learning, where students construct knowledge, building on prior experience, often through collaboration with peers (Dyke et al., 2007). However despite these exciting possibilities examples of truly innovative forms of learning maximizing the potential affordances new technologies seem to offer, are still rare. Indeed recent research with practitioners on the creation of learning activities revealed that the most common design strategy was to mirror existing practice rather than exploit the opportunities and affordances of new technologies (Falconer & Conole, 2006; Falconer et al., 2007).

We have argued that there is a gap between the *potential* of technologies to support learning and the reality of how they are *actually* used and that this is due to a lack of understanding about how technologies can be used to afford specific learning advantages and to a lack of appropriate guidance at the design stage (Conole et al., 2007a). Its cause is due to a range of inter-connected issues: technological (immature tools, lack of interoperability etc.), organizational (barriers and enablers to uptake, cultural barriers) as well as pedagogical issues.

This chapter describes a project which is exploring the design for learning issues within a distance learning institutional context, the UK Open University. The initial focus of the work is reported elsewhere (Conole et al., 2007b), this chapter focuses on how we are using Compendium as a tool for aiding the design process. It will describe the rationale behind the work and initial findings from the evaluation of eight faculty-based workshops run using the software.

Our goal is to build on recent research on learning design to develop a tool that provides support in the course design process with an emphasis on the use of technology-enhanced learning. Users of the system might include individual teachers or course teams, as well as others involved in the design process such as learning technologists or those in our Learning and Teaching Solutions department tasked with helping course teams translate their ideas into technical solutions. The learning design tool will act as a bridge between good pedagogic practice and effective use of new technologies.

10.2 Learning Design

Design is a core part of any teaching or training role; i.e. how concepts can be presented to students to enable them to achieve a set of required learning outcomes. Educational text books might give the impression that there is a simple linear basis to the design process; starting with a set of learning outcomes, based on a particular pedagogical approach, appropriate resources, tools and activities are identified and linked together, assessment acting as the ultimate arbitrator in terms of success or failure. However in reality the design process is rarely so simple. In our previous research we observed a series of Geographers over a semester, noting their approaches to design and including any critical decision making points (Fill et al., 2008). More recently we have collated forty-four case studies through interviews with teachers across different subject disciplines within the Open University (Wilson et al., 2007). We focused on how they were using technologies in their courses and interrogated them on how they designed the courses and what support mechanisms (if any) they used. Both the Geography studies and the OU studies revealed that the design process is messy. Designers juggle a range of questions, focusing on different aspects of the design process at different points in time: "What do I want the students to be able to do having completed this learning activity (a focus on learning outcomes)?" "What tools and resources do I want to incorporate?" "What are the particular characteristics of this group of learners?" "How am I going to assess the activities?" "What specific discipline issues or problem does this address?" "How can I design the activity to promote: reflection, collaboration, application of theory to practice?" Therefore any form of support or tool for the design process needs to be cognisant of this messy, multifaceted and iterative approach.

10. Using Compendium as a Tool to Support the Design of Learning Activities   201

"Learning design" is a methodology that has emerged in recent years as a semi-formal process for support the curriculum design process. The term "learning design" came into common usage with the development of the IMS Learning Design specification, which sought to provide a means of formally representing (and thus reusing) learning sequences. Since then the term has gained a broader usage, and is often synonymous with "course design." Learning design has seen increased activity in the past few years, as researchers and developers have moved beyond a focus on creation and presentation of content (and hence associated concern with the management of "learning objects") to consideration of learning activities. Beetham & Sharpe (2007) provide a valuable overview of current work in learning design and provide a "critical discussion of the issues surrounding the design, sharing and reuse of learning activities, and tools that practitioners can apply to their own concerns and contexts." Learning design provides a formal methodology for describing learning activities and for formally representing (and hence potentially reusing) learning activities. Crucially it is seen as providing a way of representing learning activities so that they can be shared between tutors and designers and a scaffold to the process of creating new learning activities.

We have identified six main reasons why adopting a learning design approach is beneficial (Conole et al., 2007b):

- It can act as a means of eliciting designs from academics in a format that can be tested and reviewed with developers, i.e. a common vocabulary and understanding of learning activities.
- It provides a means by which designs can be reused, as opposed to just sharing content.
- It can guide individuals through the process of creating new learning activities.
- It creates an audit trail of academic design decisions.
- It can highlight policy implications for staff development, resource allocation, quality, etc.
- It aids learners in complex activities by guiding them through the activity sequence.

There are essentially two approaches to the design process: starting from existing practice or through a process of scaffolding the design process through a series of prompts and issues to be considered. Therefore the key research issues are:

- How can we gather and represent practice (and in particular innovative practice) (*capture and represent practice*)?
- How can we provide "scaffolds" or support for staff in creating learning activities which draw on good practice, making effective use of tools and pedagogies (*support learning design*)?

10.3 Capturing and Representing Practice

The Mod4L project[1] identified a range of representations that practitioners use to present practice. These included taxonomies and matrices, visual presentations (flow diagrams, mind maps), case studies, patterns and lesson plans. The project used these with practitioners in a series of workshops to identify their usage and perceived value. They concluded that use is complex and contextualized and that no one presentation is adequate (Falconer et al., 2007).

One of the most popular approaches to abstracting existing practice is in the form of a narrative-based case study. The Joint Information System Committee (JISC) in the UK gathered a range of effective and innovative practice case studies. Each case study was described in terms of the learning outcomes and problem being addressed and was aligned to a particular pedagogical approach (associative, cognitive or situative). In addition to the narrative description case studies included, where appropriate, additional resources such as video clips. The case studies are available as downloadable pdfs.[2] A similar exercise was carried out in Australia through the AUTC Learning Design project.[3] In addition to the case study narrative, the project developed a specific approach to presenting the core essence of the learning activities being described. In their approach learning activities are broken down into a series of tasks which students undertake, alongside these associated resources and support are illustrated. The project was a large-scale initiative which captured a wide range of learning activities and associated information. In addition to the visual "temporal sequences" for each learning activity there is a rich range of additional information about the design process.

An alternative to the descriptive case study approach is the application of the concepts of patterns derived from Alexander's work in Architecture (see for example Goodyear, 2005). This provides a more structured approach which starts with an intended pedagogical problem being addressed and moves on to provide a potential solution. The patterns approach is built on an underlying philosophy that there are a set of inherent "patterns" which, if identified, can be reused in a multitude of different ways. In addition these patterns combine to form a pattern language (see the Pedagogical Patterns project[4] and the EU-funded TELL pattern book (TELL, 2005) for examples).

10.4 Scaffolding the Learning Design

The alternative to presenting case studies or patterns is to provide some form of guided support or scaffold to the learning design process. A number of toolkits and

---

[1] http://www.academy.gcal.ac.uk/mod4l/
[2] Effective practice with e-learning – http://www.elearning.ac.uk/effprac/ and case studies of innovation – http://www.elearning.ac.uk/innoprac/
[3] http://www.learningdesigns.uow.edu.au/
[4] http://www.pedagogicalpatterns.org/

pedagogical planners have been developed in recent years which adopt different approaches to aiding the design process. The DialogPlus toolkit[5] guides users through the process of developing pedagogically informed learning activities (Conole & Fill, 2005). It is underpinned by a pedagogical taxonomy for learning activities (Conole, 2007). This includes a description of the types of tasks students might do as part of the learning activity; *assimilative* (attending and understanding content), *information handling* (gathering and classifying resources or manipulating data), *adaptive* (use of modeling or simulation software), *communicative* (dialogic activities, e.g. pair dialogues or group-based discussions), *productive* (construction of an artifact such as a written essay, new chemical compound or a sculpture) and *experiential* (practicing skills in a particular context or undertaking an investigation). Other examples of support for learning design include the pedagogic planner project[6] and the Phoebe project.[7] Phoebe adopts a similar approach to DialogPlus by attempting to provide a comprehensive online resource of tips and hints to support decision making. However it doesn't provide any directed guidance, acting more as a set of resources which users can work through. The pedagogic planner instead adopts more of a modeling perspective through mapping tasks to resources and attempting to align the design with specific pedagogical approaches. It is attempting to adopt a user-orientated approach and plans to integrate the tool with LAMS[8] a tool for managing and delivering learning activities.

Both from the experience of the Mod4l project and our own work with teachers and designers, it is evident that no one approach meets all needs. Case studies can provide useful ideas, but do not specifically guide users through the decision making process of their own design. Toolkits and planners on the other hand do provide this guidance but can be prescriptive in the approach adopted. With this in mind we decided to adopt a multi-faceted approach; by gathering case studies of good practice and using these as a basis for populating a learning design tool. Our approach was to enable users to be able to use the online tool in as flexible a means as possible, enabling multiple entry points and forms of guidance and support, trying as best as possible to mirror the real, messy process of design we identified by working with practitioners. The next section describes this work and progress to date.

10.5 The Role of Mediating Artifacts in Creating Learning Activities

Conole (2007, 2008) argues that practitioners use a wide range of processes and tools (mediating artifacts) to support and guide decision-making in creating

---

[5] http://www.nettle.soton.ac.uk/toolkit/
[6] http://www.wle.org.uk/d4l/
[7] http://phoebe-project.conted.ox.ac.uk/cgi-bin/trac.cgi
[8] http://www.lamsfoundation.org/

learning activities (Fig. 10.1). These are needed to guide various aspects of learning design: the context of a learning activity, the choice of pedagogy, the creation of associated learner tasks or any combination of these. They range from contextually rich illustrative examples of good practice (case studies, guidelines, narratives, etc.) to more abstract forms of representation that distil out the "essences" of good practice (such as vocabularies or educational models). Each mediating artifact abstracts different aspects of the existing learning activity. Individual mediating artifacts can then be grouped in a variety of different ways for example as a repository of case studies or a set of overarching tips and hints or they can be used as the basis for a more systematic tool such as a toolkit or planner which can then be used to guide the user through the design process.

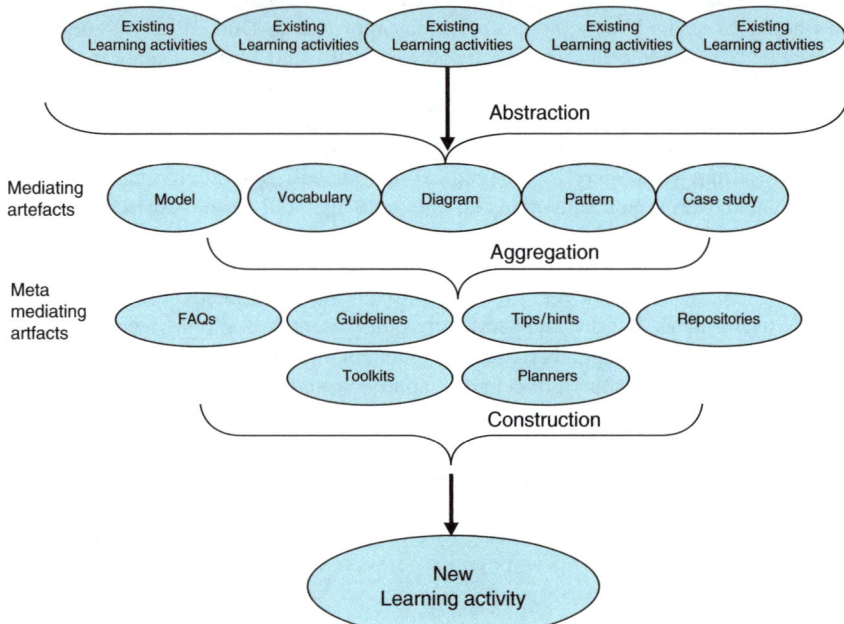

Fig. 10.1. The range of mediating artifacts which can be used to create learning activities.

10.5.1 The OU Learning Design Project

The OU is currently undertaking a cross-institutional Learning Design project. We are adopting an iterative methodology focusing on two areas of activity in parallel: a) capturing and representing practice – through user consultation and case studies and b) supporting learning design – through the development of an online tool and associated workshops.

10.5.2 Initial User Requirements Gathering

The initial phase was carried out as part of a broader program of work to introduce a MOODLE-based VLE environment.[9] During 2006, a series of user consultation exercises were undertaken to gather requirements for a learning design tool specification. These also highlighted a range of perceived barriers and enablers to adopting a learning design approach and to more effective use of technologies to support learning. From this a series of overarching factors emerged; designers and teachers wanted:

- Discipline specific case studies illustrating how others use technologies.
- Information about the tools available within the new VLE and how they could be used, along with ideas on innovative learning activities students could undertake using these tools.
- Step-by-step guidance through the process of creating learning activities.
- Pointers to further resources and named contacts within the institution.

A number of possible scenarios for use of a Learning Design tool emerged: by an individual to find examples of how different tools or pedagogical approaches can be used to undertake different tasks, to give them ideas, by a course team as part of the team design process, in discussions between an individual teacher and developer or as the basis for staff development workshops on effective use of the VLE. Following on from the user consultation exercise it was decided that it would be useful to explore some of the emergent issues in more detail and also to gather existing discipline specific examples of how the tools were being used. The focus was on examples which include some form of innovative use of technologies either to support a single learning activity within a course or to provide a scaffold or support across the course in relation to the development of a particular skill or towards a specified set of learning outcomes. The intention was to develop a tool that would act both as a repository of existing learning activities (such as the case studies) and as a design support tool for creating new learning activities.

10.6 Institutional Case Studies

Forty-four case studies were captured through in-depth interviews with course leaders (Table 10.1). The focus was on the pedagogies used to achieve specific learning outcomes and the use of tools (blogs, wikis, e-assessment, etc.) to support learning activities. Interviews were semi-structured around a number of core themes: contextual data (level, subject, etc.), details about the learning activity being described and the sub-tasks involved, pedagogical approaches adopted, and barriers and enablers to the creation of the activity (both technical and organizational). Each interview lasted ca. 1 hour and was recorded, transcribed, and content checked for accuracy with the interviewee.

---

[9] http://conclave.open.ac.uk/ouvlefaq/index.php?sid=1769&lang=en&action=artikel&cat=1&id=15&artlang=en

Table 10.1. Case studies by type.

Type	Number
Multimedia simulation/modeling/case study	9
Wiki group project	3
Wiki based dialogue	1
Online icebreaker	2
Online residential	2
Online tutorials (for global presentation)	1
Interactive assessment	4
Asynchronous discussion based collaborative learning	7
ePortfolio (Journal)	3
Group project	3
Resource based learning	4
Problem based learning	1
Synchronous audio based collaborative learning	1
"near – synchronous" collaborative group project	1
Podcasting (by students)	1
Reflective practice for tutors	1
Total	44

The case studies are already highlighting a number of overarching themes (Wilson, 2007). Disciplinary differences are evident – the reasons *why* and *how* tools are being used is often aligned with specific discipline needs. For example one case study focuses on the use of an e-Portfolio for a vocational practice-based course where it is a professional requirement to provide evidence of skills development. Some courses are using tools to mimic current practices which are known to be successful, for example a post-graduate course which has created a virtual "summer school." Comparative studies are also proving useful in terms of highlighting the way particular tools are used in different contexts. For example a number of courses are exploring the collaborative potential of wikis but the ways in which they are doing this are tied into the pedagogical needs and context of the course. In the Open University traditionally the main resource load is focused on the production aspects of course development, rather than during presentation (i.e. when courses are being delivered). However the case studies have revealed that this appears to be shifting, as new technologies enable teams to adapt and change course content and activities on a much shorter time frame. Use of technologies is also impacting on assessment methods and the forms of support and communication which are provided.

From our previous work, we were aware that representation of practice is notoriously difficult for a number of reasons. Firstly the degree or level of detail provided – too much is overwhelming, too little not informative enough. Secondly, the degree to which a case study is specific and contextualized. Thirdly the way in which a case study is presented (for example as a textual narrative, diagrammatically or through use of multi-media such as videos or interactive screen shots) has an impact on how much it is valued. We decided to adopt a multifaceted approach to presenting the case studies which would include the following elements: a clear and informative title, a short description of the learning activity and associated salient features, a detailed case study description, visual mapping using notational software and additional views, audio or videos, *etc.* as appropriate (Fig. 10.2).

Learning Activity Title:	
Summary	
Course context	This includes top level data to locate the learning activity including: title, the course code, course chair or activity lead academic, discipline, faculty, date first delivered, and time needed to complete the activity
Why are we doing this?	Brief description of the rationale behind the learning activity
What are the learning outcomes?	Brief outline of the learning outcomes – specifically in relation to the learning activity being described
How are the learning outcomes achieved?	Key steps associated with the learning activity. This ties into the associated visualisation of the activity
Enablers	List of any specific enablers which helped with designing or running the activity – sources of help or support for example
Barriers & Issues	List of any problems – technical, pedagogical or organizational
Pedagogic Models Used	Note of pedagogical models used, for example problem-based learning or resource-based learning
Technology Tools Used	Outline of tools used in the design and running of the activity
Diagram	
Diagram illustrating the key components of the learning activity, including the different roles of those involved and associated assets (tools, resources, outputs, etc)	
Outcomes	
Student evaluation	Brief description of any student feedback or evaluation results if available
Description/ Application	Suggestions of other disciplines or areas where an activity of this type might be useful

Fig. 10.2. Learning activity template.

10.7 Using Compendium to Visually Represent Learning Activities

In choosing a visual representation we adopted a similar column or "swim lane" approach to that used in UML modeling and the AUTC project, but with a central focus on tasks. We choose to distinguish between the different roles and the things associated with each task (tools, resources, *etc.*) by using different iconic representation. The diagram was built using a mind mapping tool Compendium[10] which enables you to provide hyperlinks between different parts of the diagram. It

---
[10] http://www.compendiuminstitute.org/

also enabled us to tag icons with appropriate metadata (such as roles, tools, tasks, resources, etc.) and to layer additional information about each element so that when the user hovers over an icon additional information appears. By clicking on an icon the user can either be linked to a specific URL, resource or tool, or to a sequence of layered additional information. Our development of the use of Compendium for learning design is described in more detail in this section.

Before describing the visualisation tool and how it is being used, it is worth giving a brief description of the underlying assumptions in terms of the development of the tool. In addition to gathering the institutional case studies, the other aspect of our learning design project is to develop an online learning design tool. This will be populated with both the information derived from the case studies, as well as selected resources and expertise drawn from our own experience in the field and the wider research literature. As discussed earlier the design process is messy and no one approach is likely to meet the needs of all users. Therefore part of our philosophy in terms of developing a specification for the online learning design tool is that it needs to accommodate a range of different ways in which it might be used. Our initial discussions included the development of a use case scenario of how such a tool might be used. Users could either begin by searching the database of case studies or start from a set of predefined templates. From their preferred starting point users could drag elements onto their workspace and start to build up their learning activity. Elements would relate to the different aspects of the learning activity (such as tools, resources, and roles of those involved). The system would provide adaptive help for each of the elements, for example, if the user has selected a collaborative activity, then tools such as asynchronous conferencing, wikis etc, would be shown, along with additional advice and examples. The user would then build up an activity sequence, adding in further layers of detail as required. We were aware that we needed to iteratively develop the prototype tool with the close involvement of the intended end users, so that we could learn from their use of the prototype and adapt accordingly. We felt such involvement would help us to identify how users might want to use an online tool and what kinds of support and advice they would find useful from the system.

The existing learning design tools discussed earlier (DialogPlus, Pheobe, the pedagogic planner and LAMS) were considered but rejected for a number of reasons. We felt each adopted a particular approach and were therefore not flexible in terms of how they could be used to support the design process. LAMS provided the greatest degree of flexibility but operates at the level of a set of pre-defined tool-focused learning activities (voting, discussion, etc.). We felt this straight-jacketed the design process by overemphasizing the importance of tools, to the detriment of the other elements involved in creating a learning activity. And by operating at the level of pre-defined tool-activities, we felt it did not enable the user to set their own criteria for the level of granularity of the activity they were designing. We wanted to use a more flexible tool as the basis for our initial prototype. We considered various drawing packages, as well as more specialized mind mapping tools (such as Inspiration and MindManager). In the end we choose to use Compendium, a visual representation tool, originally developed for enabling group argumentation, which was produced by researchers at our own institution. We selected Compendium for a number of reasons. Firstly because it was produced at the Open University, we felt there was more opportunity for further tool development specifically in terms of learning design requirements. Secondly, Compendium supports the creation of a range of visual mapping techniques, including mind maps, concept maps, web maps and argumentation maps (Okada & Buckingham Shum, 2006), which we felt offered the potential for a range of flexible approaches to the design process. Compendium comes with a predefined set of icons (question, answer, map, list, pros, cons, reference, notes, decision, and argumentation). The creation of a map is simple, users drag icons across and can start to build up relationships between these through connecting arrows. Each icon can have an associated name attached with more details contained inside the node, an asterisk appears next to the icon and if the user hovers their mouse over this the content inside the node is revealed. Other types of electronic files can also be easily incorporated into the map such as diagrams, Word files or PowerPoint presentations. The reference node enables you to link directly to external websites. Icons can also be meta-tagged using either a pre-defined set of key words or through user generated terms. Maps can be exported in a variety of ways from simple diagrammatic jpeg files through to inter-linked websites.

Our initial task was to agree a common format for representing learning activities visually. To begin with we worked only with the existing pre-defined icon set. Figure 10.3 shows an early example which attempted to visually represent a learning activity created by Oliver[11] in Australia as part of the AUTC learning design project. The figure shows a series of columns representing the key elements involved in the learning activity, which consisted of a simplified version of a learning activity taxonomy developed as part of the DialogPlus project (see Conole, 2007). The diagram shows the use of a number of the icon sets (notes, reference, list) and the inclusion of a series of external file types (a picture and word files). The note icons "Authors" and "Discipline" have asterisks by them showing that they contain additional information which is displayed when the mouse hovers over the icon.

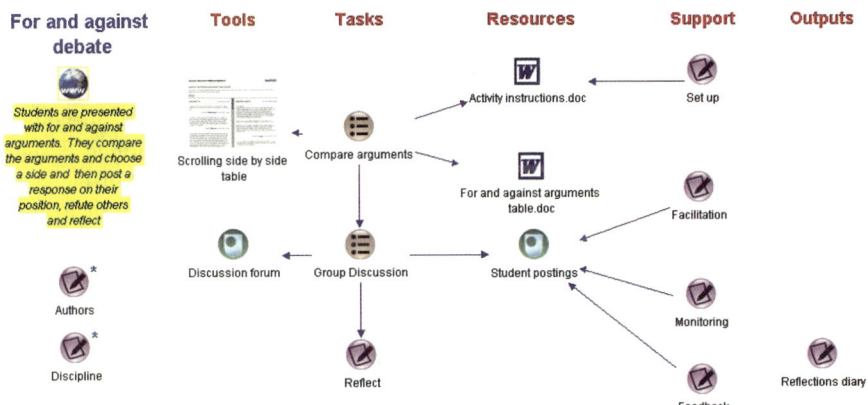

Fig. 10.3. Visual representation of Oliver's "for and against debate".

---

[11] http://www.learningdesigns.uow.edu.au/project/doc/GenericICTTools.pdf

The next stage in the process was to work with an individual academic on one of their own learning activities to try and elicit both their thought processes in the design process and their initial reaction to using the Compendium tool. A third-level environmental course, U316, was chosen for this purpose. This course was chosen for two main reasons. Firstly it was recognized to be an example of good practice and innovative use of technologies. Secondly, it had been the subject of an extensive research and evaluation project funded by the Mellon foundation and so a lot of detailed research data had been gathered on different aspects of the course and the design process (Thorpe & Godwin, 2006). Stewart Nixon, the main lead for the VLE-related learning design work, and I worked with the main researcher involved in evaluating U316 to represent the learning activity, we noted her reaction to interacting with the Compendium tool as well as her general thought processes in representing the key learning activities contained in the course. A number of interesting issues emerged in the discussion. Overall her reaction to the tool was positive, she felt that it helped her articulate and share the key aspects of the learning activity. The ability to provide layered aspects to the information represented was also deemed useful. What constituted an appropriate level of granulality of information was also considered and it was agreed that a pragmatic and contextual approach should be adopted. Interestingly she also felt it would be useful to include indications of time to complete against each task, a factor which we had not considered in our early design prototyping, which further supported our decision to adopt a user-centric and iterative approach to our prototyping and design of the tool. In describing her initial impressions of the tool, Thorpe notes the benefits of this approach as:

> Learning designs can be explained, as here, using narrative accounts but these are often not at a level of detail sufficient to enable a practitioner to capture the key elements in their own teaching. More detailed narratives also benefit from diagrammatic representations that teachers can use to clarify the activities involved. (Thorpe et al., 2007)

Armed with this initial positive feedback about the potential use of Compendium as a learning design tool we decided to create a dedicated set of learning design icons, to complement the generic set available within the tool. As part of the core functionality of the tool it is possible for users to create and incorporate their own "stencils" of icon sets. Once the appropriate set of icons have been identified, they are labeled with appropriate text and given an overarching stencil name set. We choose to focus on a simplified list of icons to represent what we felt were the key aspects of the design process, namely: task, role, tool, resource, output, group, assignment, and activity. All of the icons are of the same type except for the activity icon which is a variant of the generic map icon. As with the core Compendium icon set users are able to rename each of the icons to something more appropriate to their context. Once created the stencil set is opened via the tool drop-down menu. Figure 10.4 provides a screenshot of Compendium, showing the generic set of icons on the far left-hand side, along with the learning design stencil "LD2" we created.

10. Using Compendium as a Tool to Support the Design of Learning Activities 211

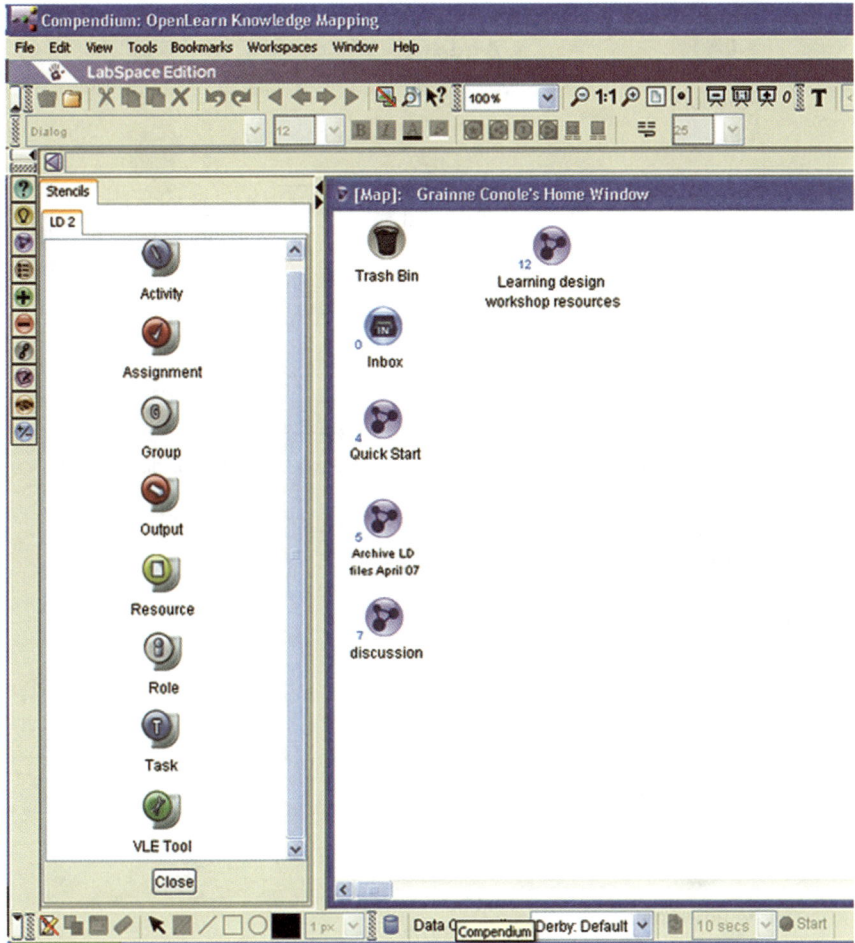

Fig. 10.4. Screenshot of Compendium with the LD2 learning design stencil set of icons.

We used the new stencil set as a means of representing the learning activities being described in the case studies. As we began to represent this and based on feedback from users we realized that our initial iconic representation (shown in Fig. 10.3) was overly complex and so we fixed on a simplified approach which consisted of a column for each role (student, tutor, *etc*) and an associated column for the "assets" associated with that role (i.e. any resources, tools or outputs).

Figure 10.5 represents a screen shot of part of the learning activity associated with the U316 course. Two roles are shown (student and tutor) along with their respective tasks. Tools, resources and outputs (i.e. assets) associated with each task are shown alongside, with arrows indicating connections.

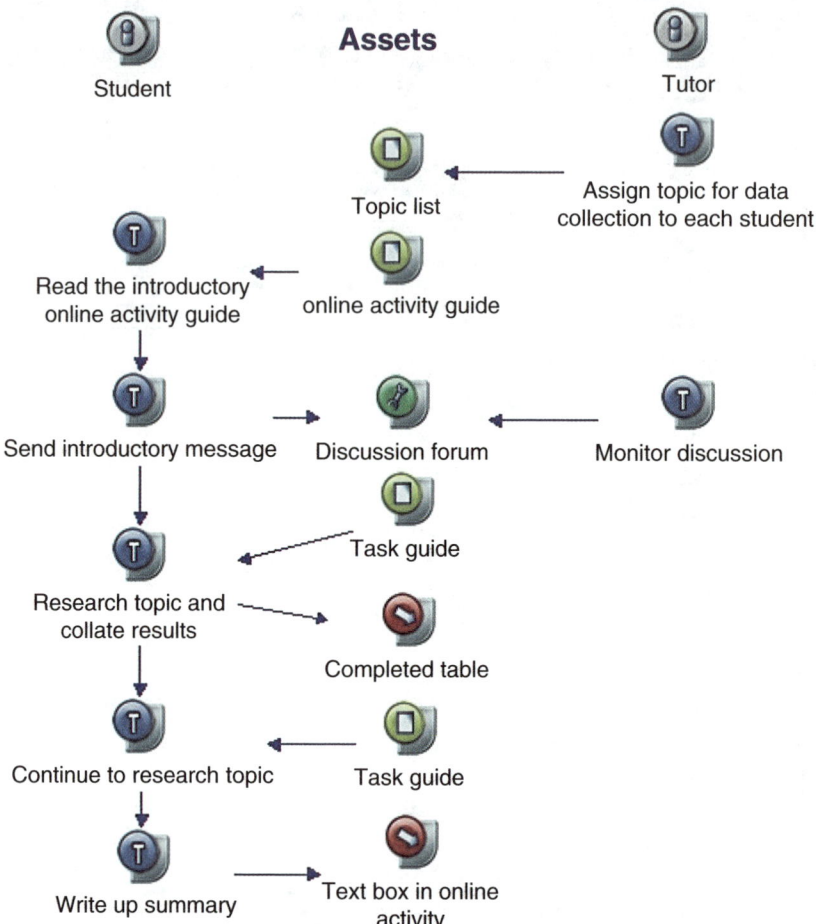

Fig. 10.5. Visual representation of part of a collaborative role play activity.

Our initial evaluation of the use of the tool to represent learning activities in a format similar to that shown in Fig. 10.5 proved positive and seemed to go some way towards addressing the first of our areas of research focus, i.e. how to capture and represent practice. The second aspect was to provide some form of intelligent scaffolding for the design process, in the form of guidance or additional support. As discussed earlier we were aware that no one approach to design would meet all users needs and hence the scaffolding needed to be adaptable and multi-faceted. Our ultimate goal is to provide adaptive and contextualized information on different aspects of the design process, tailored to individual needs and delivered on a just-in-time basis.

10. Using Compendium as a Tool to Support the Design of Learning Activities   213

As a first step to this, our review of related tools and planners identified a number of different approaches that helped the user think creativity about different aspects of the design process. For example, both the DialogPlus toolkit and the Pedagogic planner offered mechanisms for the designer to map learning outcomes, tasks and assessment. The Phoebe planner provided some useful tips on thinking about particular tools and which types of activities they might support. However feedback from users also showed that they valued having a simple step-by-step set of guiding questions to think about and guide them through the design process. The JISC effective practice with e-learning includes one example in the form of a learning design template. Beetham & Sharpe's (2007) recent book on learning design includes a series of Appendices which provide similar guidance. We wanted to experiment with using these different means of supporting the design process by creating a set of adaptable templates that users could work through and adapt to their own context. In addition to the creation of iconic stencil sets, Compendium also enables the user to create customisable templates. A template is a Compendium xml export file, which holds a set of maps/nodes which the user might use frequently. We used this template facility to create a series of learning design templates focusing on a core set of different approaches to the design process:

- Simple step-by-step guidance.
- Empty "swim line" style diagrams showing the key components for creating a diagram – as illustrated in Fig. 10.5.
- Two forms of mapping templates: a simple one linking learning outcomes, tasks and assessment and a more complex one incorporating tools, the discipline problems being addressed in the learning activity and topics covered.
- Two affordance-related templates: one to identify affordances of tools and the other to identify the affordances of different types of activity.
- Figure 10.6 provides a screen shot showing the LD template set on the side, along with the open "Step-by-step" template.

Finally we are beginning to draw together a comprehensive set of resources related to the learning design process. These we have collated in Compendium and exported to create a web-based version. The resources cover the following areas of support:

1. Learning design tools and resources – including the toolkits and planners described earlier, as well as repositories of case studies and patterns on learning design (Fig. 10.7).
2. Factors to think about – a series of guiding questions on the key issues to consider in the design process (Fig. 10.8).
3. Tools – brief descriptions of tools and the types of activities they support.
4. Activities – a growing database of iconic representations of learning activities grouped by discipline (Fig. 10.9).
5. Pedagogy – an outline of key pedagogical approaches and the forms of learning they foreground along with links to specific pedagogical models and frameworks.
6. Examples of using the learning design templates.
7. OU case studies – completed templates for the 44 OU-specific case studies.
8. Sandpit – an area where users can share rough learning activity designs.

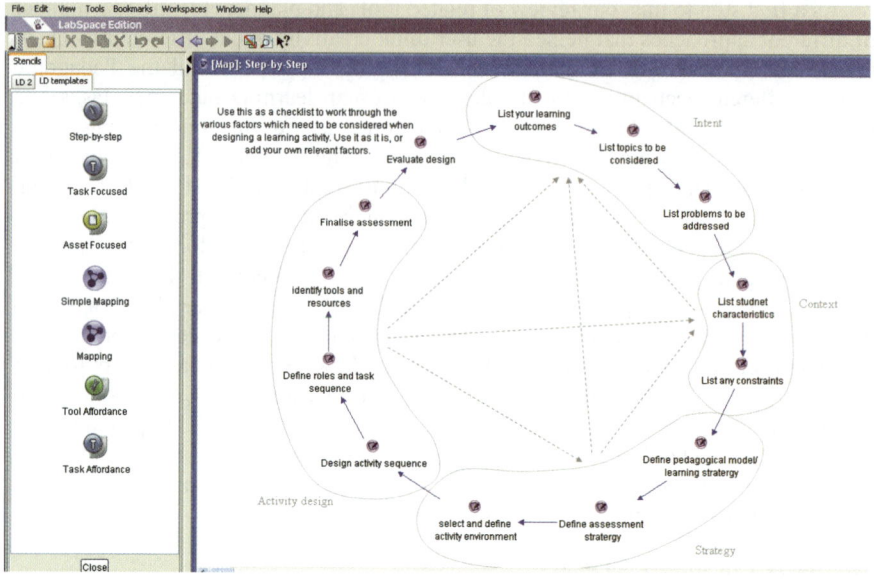

Fig. 10.6. The seven LD templates with the step-by-step template open.

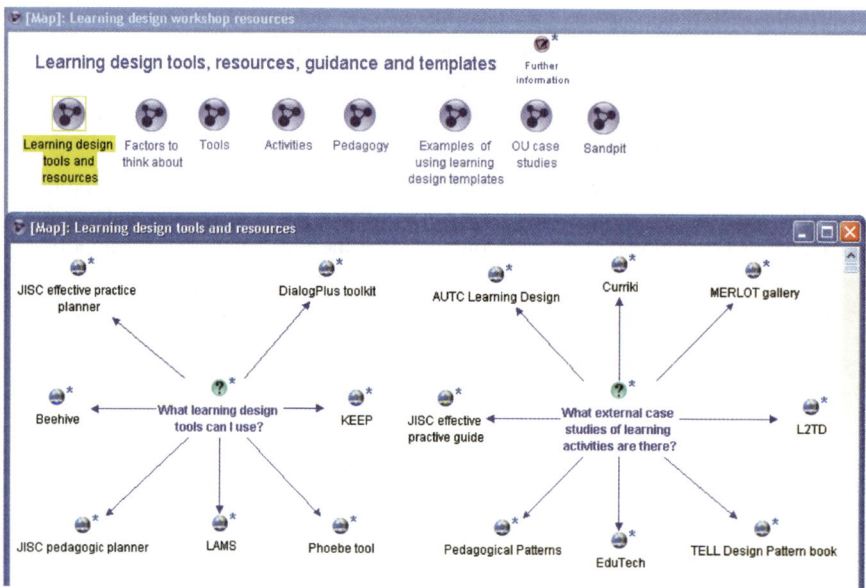

Fig. 10.7. Learning design tools, resources, guidance and templates.

10. Using Compendium as a Tool to Support the Design of Learning Activities   215

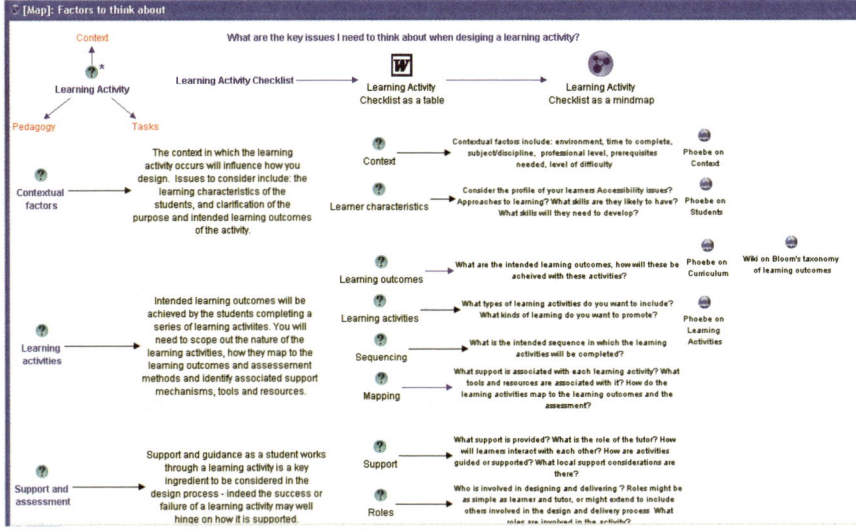

Fig. 10.8. Factors to think about in the design process.

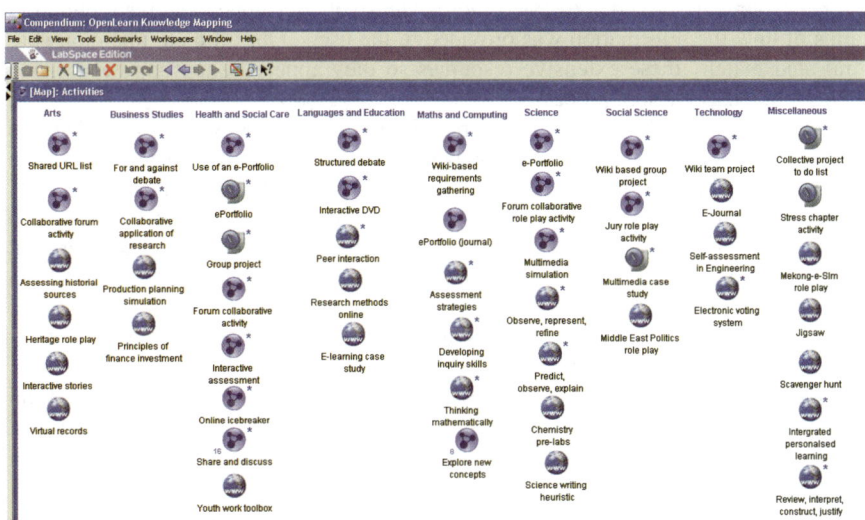

Fig. 10.9. Compendium maps of learning activities categorized by discipline.

10.8 Evaluation

During March and April 2007 these resources were trialed through a series of workshops. The first consisted of a group of critical friends made up of e-learning researchers and educational developers. The second was a workshop with 17 Engineers at the University of Porto in Portugal. As part of the workshop participants created designs using the DialogPlus, Phoebe and Pedagogic Planner tools described in this chapter, and one group using our first customized prototype version of the Compendium tool (which incorporated the specialized LD icon set). Feedback from the group confirmed that they did want some form of structured guidance to the design process, that they valued case study examples, particularly from their own subject area and that they valued the opportunity to articulate their design ideas with other colleagues. Encouragingly the group using the Compendium tool seemed to have the most positive experience and got furthest in terms of representing their learning activity:

(Compendium is) Very good to visually describe the activity itself and the actors, resources, *etc.* but it's not a planning tool in a sense it just describes the activity and it does not give you a framework. (University of Porto Workshop participants, 2nd–3rd April 2007)

They found the tool helpful in terms of developing a shared language and discussing and noting design decision making points. Based on this feedback the online resource described above was more extensively developed and restructured in terms of how the information was provided to the users. Our ultimate intention is to "mix and match" these extensive resources so they appear at appropriate decision points in the users design process.

During April 2007 eight faculty-based OU workshops were run using the improved learning design focused Compendium tool and associated resources. The workshops included an introduction to the concept of learning design and a series of exercises getting participants to reflect on their current strategies for design. The second part included a hands-on session where users worked in groups to present their own learning activities in Compendium. Figures 10.10 and 10.11 provide two different examples of designs that were produced in the sessions. What is interesting is the way in which the participants adapted the column-based role and asset structure we presented (for example see Fig. 10.5) to suit their own needs; importantly the flexibility of compendium as a tool enabled them to do this and did not stifle their creativity. We were surprised at how far the participants got in representing their designs and it did seem during the sessions that Compendium acted as a useful tool to help them articulate and share their thought processes. A few participants however commented that they did not find representing their designs visually helpful, stating that, for them, pencil and paper/discussion would be preferable. It is likely that such a focus on the visual aspects of the design process will not suit everyone, but overall most participants were positive both during the session and in their evaluation feedback.

10. Using Compendium as a Tool to Support the Design of Learning Activities 217

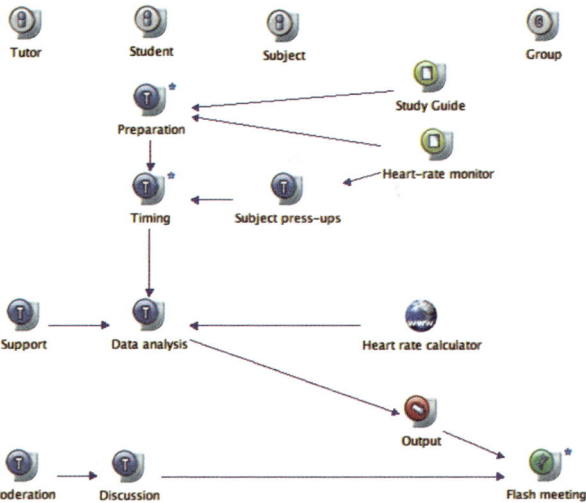

Fig. 10.10. A learning design showing four different roles.

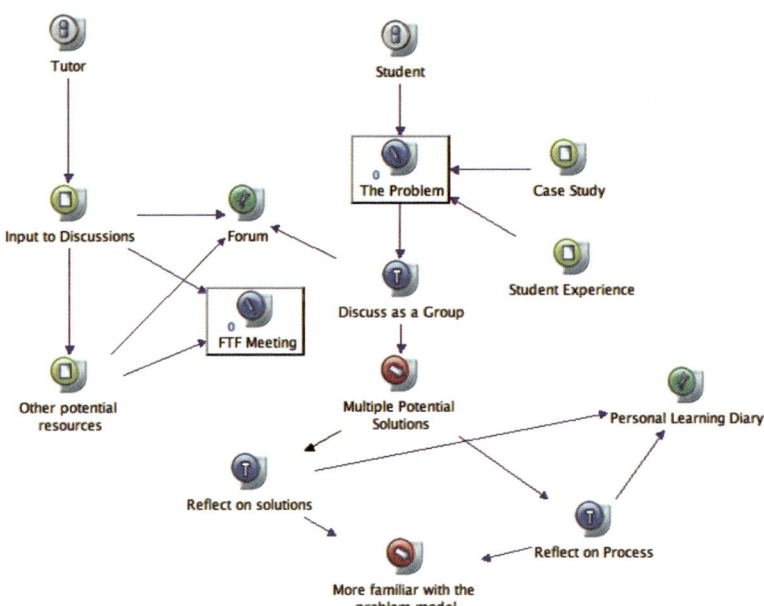

Fig. 10.11. A learning design emphasizing reflection.

Participants were asked to complete an evaluation at the end of the session. This was then used as the basis for a wrap up discussion highlighting what they found useful about the session and what they would like to see improved, along with an action list of "next steps" for their respective facilities. The questionnaire asked them a series of open-ended questions such as: what topics they would have included/excluded and why, and what they most liked/disliked about the workshop. More general questions about the length of the session, quality of the presentations and materials, and suggested follow up were also asked.

Feedback from the workshops has been very positive with all groups reporting that they liked Compendium, found it easy to use and a useful tool to help them not only think about and articulate their design process, but also as a means of representing and sharing their design. There were mixed views on the balance of theoretical and the practical hands-on aspects of the workshops:

Session would have been improved by getting into Compendium straight away and having less of the front end stuff. We need to grapple with the tools that will help us organize learning design rather than the "background to" LD.

I think the session held together as a whole with a good balance of input/discussion/activity. I feel like I have a handle on the basics of using a tool, access to a range of resources [sic] and has been thoroughly linked to my own practice – so I wouldn't want to change any of the content.

Similarly there were different views on how the material could have been ordered and the level of detail given to each sub-topic. Despite some negative comments about the amount of theory, as the workshop was introducing a new methodology and way of thinking about learning design we still feel that this theoretical underpinning is important and would want to include it in future workshops, however we will adapt this material and put more emphasis on the benefits to end users of adopting a learning design approach. Inherent in some of the negative feedback received is the fundamental problem that the concept of learning design on the surface appear very simple is in fact very complex. A classic example is the frequent call for examples or case studies, as users assume having access to these will be enough to give them ideas to create new designs.

Some more examples of good practice and their Compendium design.

Perhaps some more concrete examples – helps me relate the words to something concrete.

However, in our experience giving users a set of case studies can be overwhelming; they often don't know how to work through them or apply them to their own context. In fact as illustrated earlier a comprehensive set of resources (including links to several large databases of external case studies) was provided as part of the workshop material, but evidence to date suggests that few users are prepared to invest the time needed to work through these to extract the necessary information they require. Indeed this uncovers a further issue, that despite the overall positive evaluations for the workshops very few of the participants are continuing to use the materials as a basis for creating designs. This suggests that further work is needed to make use of the system intuitive alongside faculty-specific support.

In previous work a learning activity taxonomy was developed which identified the components associated with a learning activity (see Conole, 2007). The level of detail of the taxonomy (which includes for example 72 possible types of learning task) illustrates the complexity of the design process. However, the evidence from our previous work (Fill et al., 2008; Falconer & Conole, 2006; Jeffery et al., 2006) suggests that users are impatient and want/expect quick solutions and are not prepared to invest the time necessary to create learning activities which take account of all the different factors involved. This is the key challenge for research in learning design: how to provide simple and easy to use guidance and tools to support the design process, which users are prepared to use and can see the benefits to them of investing time in using these tools, which at the same time don't trivialize the process.

10.9 Conclusions

The project is timely as the OU is involved in two major initiatives on the use of technologies; the VLE program described earlier and the OpenLearn project[12] which is making OU content freely available. It is clear that there is a need for further research – practitioners are crying out for examples of good practice and guidance in design. However previous research shows that representing learning design practice and providing appropriate support for learning designers is both difficult and contested. By bringing together both narrative accounts of learning designs with notational maps showing the design visually, we hope to address and find practical ways of approaching the key issues in this area: How will users interact with the case studies and the learning design tool? Will practitioners find the tool useful? How will the tool be used in different contexts? What associated support mechanisms might be useful – such as individual expertise or interactive workshops?

Our initial evaluations of work to date is encouraging, Compendium seems to provide an easy to use visual tool to help represent different learning designs. The next stage in our work will be to try and structure the information emerging from our institutional case studies along with the wider set of resources on thinking about the different aspects of the learning design process into an adapted and contextualized set of scaffolds to guide users through the design process. If we can achieve this, we believe we will go some way towards addressing the problem outlined at the beginning of this chapter, namely the mismatch between the potential of new technologies in terms of how they can be used to create innovative and engaging learning activities and their actual use in practice.

Acknowledgement

The work described in this chapter is part of an institutional project on learning design. Others involved include: Stewart Nixon, Peter Wilson, Martin Weller, Simon Cross and Mary Thorpe.

---

[12] http://www.open.ac.uk/openlearn/home.php

References

Alexander, B. (2006), Web 2.0: A new wave of innovation for teaching and learning? *Educause review*, 41(2): 32–44.

Beetham, H. and Sharpe, R. (Eds) (2007), *Rethinking Pedagogy for a Digital Age*, Oxford: RoutledgeFalmer.

Conole, G. (2007), Describing learning activities: tools and resources to guide practice, in H. Beetham and R. Sharpe (Eds), *Rethinking Pedagogy for a Digital Age*, Oxford: RoutledgeFalmer.

Conole, G. (2008), Capturing practice: the role of mediating artefacts in learning design, in L. Lockyer, S. Bennett, S. Agostinho, and B. Harper (Eds), *Handbook of Research on Learning Design and Learning Objects: Issues, Applications and Technologies*.

Conole, G. and Fill, K. (2005), A learning design toolkit to create pedagogically effective learning activities, JIME, 8. www-jime.open.ac.uk/2005/08/> [28/08/06].

Conole, G. and Oliver, M. (Eds.) (2007), *Contemporary Perspectives in e-Learning Research: Themes, Tensions and Impact on Practice*, Oxford: RoutledgeFalmer.

Conole, G., de Laat, M., Darby, J. and Dillon, T. (2006), An in-depth case study of students' experiences of e-learning – how is learning changing? Final report of the JISC-funded LXP Learning Experiences Study project, Milton Keynes: Open University, www.jisc.ac.uk/mdia/documents/programmes/elearning_pedagogy/lxp%20project%20final%20report%20dec%2006.pdf [20/04/07].

Conole, G., deLaat, M., Dillon, T. and Darby, J. (2008), Disruptive technologies, pedagogical innovation: What's new? Findings from an in-depth study of students' use and perception of technology, Computers and Education, 50(2).

Conole, G., Oliver, M., Falconer, I., Littlejohn, A. and Harvey, J. (2007a), Designing for learning, in G. Conole and M. Oliver (Eds), *Contemporary Perspectives in E-Learning Research: Themes, Methods and Impact on Practice*, part of the Open and Distance Learning Series, F. Lockwood (Ed), RoutledgeFalmer.

Conole, G., Thorpe, M., Weller, M., Wilson, P., Nixon, S. and Grace, P. (2007b), Capturing practice and scaffolding learning design, Paper accepted for the EDEN conference, June, Naples.

Creanor, L., Trinder, K., Gowan, D. and Howells, C. (2006), LEX – The Learning Experience Project, Final report of the JISC-funded LEX project, Glasgow: Glasgow Caledonian University.

Downes, S. (2006), E-learning 2.0, eLearning magazine: education and technology in perspective, http://elearnmag.org/subpage.cfm?section=articles&article=29-1 [20/04/07].

Dyke, M., Conole, G., Ravenscroft, A. and de Freitas, S. (2007), Learning theories and their application to e-learning, in G. Conole and M. Oliver (ed), Contemporary perspectives in e-learning research: themes, methods and impact on practice, *part of the Open and Distance Learning Series*, F. Lockwood (ed), RoutledgeFalmer.

Falconer, I. and Conole, G. (2006), LADIE gap analysis, report for the JISC-funded LADIE project, available online at http://www.elframework.org/refmodels/ladie/guides/LADiE%20Gap%20Analysis.doc [22/02/07].

Falconer, I., Beetham, H., Oliver, R., Lockyer, L., and Littlejohn, A. (2007), Mod4L – final report: representing learning designs, Final report for the JISC-funded MOD4L project, Glasgow: Glasgow Caledonian University.

Fill, K., Conole, G. and Bailey, C. (2008, in press), A toolkit to guide the design of effective learning activities, in P. Rees, L. Mackay, K. Fill and H. Durham (Eds), *E-Learning for Geographers*, Idea Group Inc.: Hersey, Pennsylvania.

Goodyear, P. (2005), Educational design and networked learning: patterns, pattern languages & design practice, AJET 21.1, 82-101, www.ascilite.org.au/ajet/ajet21/goodyear.html [27/1/07].

Jeffery, A., Conole, G. and Falconer, I. (2006), *LADIE Project Final Report*, Southampton: University of Southampton.

Okada, A. and Buckingham Shum, S. (2006), 'Knowledge mapping with Compendium in academic research and online education' 22nd ICDE World Conference. Rio de Janeiro, Brazil http://kmi.open.ac.uk/projects/osc/docs/KnowledgeMapping_ICDE2006.pdf

TELL (2005), Design patterns for teachers and educational (system) designers, Pattern book, output of WP3, TELL project, available online at ttp://cosy.ted.unipi.gr/TELL/media/TELL_pattern_book.pdf [20/04/07].

Thorpe, M. and Godwin, S. (2006), Interaction and e-learning: the student experience, *Studies in Continuing Education*, 28(3), pp. 203–221.

Thorpe, M., Godwin, S. and Ferguson, R. (2007), Technoloiges in use: how context and design drive their effects, *Paper Accepted for the EDEN Conference*, June, Naples.

Wilson, P. (2007), Progress report on capturing eLearning case studies, Internal report, The Open University: Milton Keynes.

Wilson, P., Grace, P., Thorpe, M. (2007), Presentation at the CTSS Conference, The Open University, 1–2nd May.

11. Performing Knowledge Art: Understanding Collaborative Cartography

Albert M. Selvin

Open University, Knowledge Media Institute, alselvin@gmail.com

Abstract. This chapter focuses on the special skills and considerations involved in constructing knowledge maps for, and with, groups. Using knowledge cartography in a facilitative manner in such efforts as collaborative analysis, or simply trying to map discussions on the fly using knowledge mapping software, poses challenges and requires expertise beyond that which characterize individual practice. The chapter provides concepts and frameworks useful in analyzing such collaborative practice and illustrates them with a case study.

11.1 Introduction

Collective sensemaking in complex socio-technical situations is a constant feature of organizational life in science, government, business, and other institutions. Supporting sensemaking calls for both sophisticated tools and human expertise in their use. Examples include group decision support, process modeling, requirements analysis, argument mapping, strategic planning, and problem exploration. Such activities are increasingly widespread, and there are professional consultancies devoted to providing these kinds of services. The need for the kind of integrative, participatory thinking necessary to use these tools effectively is increasingly required by more than just specialists. However there has been surprisingly little research devoted to understanding and improving professional practice in this area. The absence of substantive analysis of the nature of human expertise in supporting this kind of work is striking.

My research studies practitioners who use software to provide sensemaking support to others through constructing graphical representations in real time. Having worked as a practitioner in this area for a number of years, I am interested in how the human experience of both practitioners and participants culminates in what happens at their shared interface – the representations they create with the software. Understanding expertise in this domain will help lead to better education for reflective practitioners. This requires developing a descriptive language that does justice to the complexity of the phenomenon, incorporating but extending the sphere of research in areas such as the nature and development of expertise, the role of human sensemaking around information visualizations, the intelligibility and usefulness of representations, and the construction of narrative coherence over multimedia and document repositories. Creation of representations in a collaborative or participatory environment also draws on work in design rationale, concept mapping, hypermedia, reflective practice, and participatory design. Key research questions include:

- What is the nature of the skills required to construct graphical knowledge representations in real-time, participatory settings?
- What are the kinds of choices practitioners face, especially at sensemaking moments in the course of conducting sessions?
- How does the context of the service being provided affect the choices a practitioner makes?
- What are the differences between novice and expert practitioners of such forms?
- How can practitioner skills be more effectively scaffolded and supported through improved software tools and training approaches?

Much of this book focuses on the creation of knowledge maps by individuals, who craft their maps as authors working by themselves. In contrast, this chapter looks at the particular considerations and skills involved when knowledge cartography is performed by a person (a "practitioner"; for a definition, see Table 11.1) working with a group of people building maps in collaborative sessions. I examine collaborative knowledge cartography from the perspective of the practitioner's *experience*. If we can characterize that experience, we may be better able to inculcate improved effectiveness through training, tools, examples and exercises. I will describe some concepts that help provide a framework for understanding collaborative knowledge mapping practice. I'll then provide a case study that uses the framework to understand the choices made by a practitioner in a collaborative session. At the conclusion of this chapter, I'll describe how the framework can be used to help practitioners see and reflect on aspects of their practice normally left implicit or unquestioned.

The aim of this chapter is to provide descriptive language and tools to characterize the practitioner experience in such a way as to be analytically useful across the spectrum of knowledge cartography applications. What are the thinking skills, competencies, and stances that a practitioner takes to the participants, materials, artifacts, tools, subject matter, and audience (recipients of the group's output) in a collaborative effort? What are the considerations common to such efforts, which can be used as lenses with which to view and describe the practitioner experience? In what ways do these considerations differ when looking at individual vs. collaborative practice?

I look at knowledge mapping practice from the vantage point of those who have developed some degree of fluency with the tools and techniques, rather than examining novices just beginning to use a mapping tool. For beginners, performing even basic actions presents obstacles, until they develop familiarity. Once fluency is attained, however, the challenges to, as well as the potential for, effective practice are just starting. It is in experienced practitioners that we are able to discern the aspects of expressiveness, style, creative choice, and performance under pressure that are required for effective knowledge mapping practice in collaborative settings.

My interest in studying collaborative knowledge cartography practice stems from more than fifteen years of professional work in the discipline in a variety of settings, acting both as an individual working alone to author knowledge maps as well as a collaborative practitioner, putting my mapping skills in service of a group of people. In some cases the maps themselves were the focus of the collaborative effort – that is, the group worked exclusively on the maps, often in an analysis effort of some sort, such as creating a process model or risk assessment. In other cases, the maps were part of a set of artifacts or materials the group worked with, where they served as one of the vehicles for group decision capture, note-taking, or issue exploration along with other tools, such as spreadsheets. In still other cases, the knowledge maps were a backdrop to group activities such as discussions, serving as repositories for notes and meeting minutes. Sometimes the maps were used at a single meeting or event, while at other times many maps were created, added to and interlinked over months or even years of a large-scale collaborative effort. Each kind of use brings with it different sorts of practitioner (as well as participant) experiences.

Knowledge mapping practitioners working in service to others must make moment-to-moment choices so that their actions are most appropriate and helpful to the group and its aims. Looking at expert practice in knowledge cartography in this way shifts the focus from rationalized, prescribed methods to the ways in which practitioners faced with an anomalous or unique situations make instantaneous, improvised choices and new combinations from their repertoire of possible actions and techniques (Schön, 1983). For Schön these are unquestionably artistic performances, in which a practitioner "responds to the complexity, which confuses the student, in what seems like a simple, spontaneous way. His artistry is evident in his selective management of large amounts of information, his ability to spin out long lines of invention and inference, and his capacity to hold several ways of looking at things at once without disrupting the flow of inquiry." (Schön, 1983:130) In this chapter I'll explore various dimensions of this artistry and performance as it can take place in collaborative knowledge mapping situations.

Table 11.1 outlines some general terminology that will be used throughout this chapter to refer to aspects of collaborative knowledge cartography in instances of actual practice.

In the next section, I discuss how some of the central considerations I use to analyze collaborative knowledge cartography are treated in other fields.

Table 11.1. Aspects of collaborative knowledge cartography.

Aspect	Description
Effort	The overall project in which collaborative knowledge mapping is taking place
Practitioner	The person who is using the knowledge mapping tool itself, whether as an individual user working alone, or as the person with their "hands on the keyboard" working with a group to create a knowledge map. The person taking primary responsibility for the form and content of the maps
Participants	People "in the room" (whether a real or virtual space) taking part in a collaborative knowledge mapping session
Session	An individual occurrence of mapping within an effort, such as a specific meeting. Some efforts may consist of a single session, where some comprise many sessions (which may include individual mapping sessions as well as collaborative ones)
Episode	For analytical purposes, every session can be seen to consist of individual episodes, subsections of the session each of which has a recognizable beginning, middle, and end. They can last from under a minute to several minutes or more
Event	Each episode is made up of several events, usually delineated by a particular set of moves made around an immediate task or goal
Choice	Choices made by the practitioner during the course of an event
Move	Individual operations or actions, such as verbal moves (statements, questions, exclamations) made by either participants or practitioner, and representational moves made by the practitioner within the knowledge mapping software

11.2 Related Work

As an emerging field, there is little research on the practitioner experience, or practice aspects in general, of collaborative knowledge cartography. However, aspects central to the framework presented in this chapter, such as ethics, aesthetics and improvisation, as well as treatment of the skills required to perform knowledge cartography in groups, are found in a number of related fields including hypermedia, group support systems, and aesthetic facilitation.

11.2.1 Hypermedia

Although there has been interest in knowledge mapping using hypermedia tools for group support and facilitation for many years (Conklin & Yakemovich, 1991), as well much work in using hypermedia in artistic contexts and as a literary and art form itself, there has been little research that directly addresses what it means to perform such practices from a practitioner point of view. Most work that touches on practice issues looks at concerns about novices learning to use hypermedia tools[1] (e.g. Bromme & Stahl, 2002), or examines the artifacts themselves, focusing on the "intellectual work" (Marshall, 2001) dimensions of hypermedia practice, with a relatively functionalist view of what skills such work encompasses.

Although there is much hypermedia research focusing on highly complex domains such as software engineering (Scacchi, 2002; Noll & Scacchi, 1999), library science (Nnadi & Bieber, 2004), and legal argumentation (Carr, 2003), in which few would dispute that a high level of skill, training, and experience is required to be successful, the specifically hypertextual aspects of the skills required are given little attention. It is almost as if to do so would be to admit some gap or deficiency on the part of the support technologies involved. Although many of these approaches implicitly assume a high degree of hypermedia literacy, skill, and even artistry on the part of their users, rarely if ever do such studies treat these matters explicitly. Indeed, promising hypertext approaches, such as the design rationale field in the 1980s and 90s (Fischer et al., 1996), have been dismissed or abandoned precisely because they appeared to require a high level of skill to perform effectively (which no one would begrudge the practitioners of the non-hypertextual aspects of those fields – e.g., no one would expect an architect or kitchen designer to move from novice to expert use of the tools of their trade in a couple of days).

Even within the realm of hypertext literature research, there is little attention paid to practitioner and practice issues. Most research in the field focuses on textual criticism of the artifacts themselves (Koskimaa, 2000; Miles, 2003), or on the navigation and reading of them, rather than on the process of construction or the skills involved.

---

[1] This is also true for other disciplines looking at professional practice. For example, Cross (2003) observed this for studies of professional designers: "Most studies of designer behaviour have been based on novices (e.g. students) or, at best, designers of relatively modest talents... if studies of designer behaviour are limited to studies of rather inexpert designers, then ... our understanding of expert designers will also be limited. In order to understand expertise in design, we must study expert designers."

When hypertext authoring skills are treated head on, it is most often in terms contrasting them with conventional notions of writing and reading (Landow, 1991; Barnes, 1994). These, while often valuable, only paint a portion of the picture. This is especially so when referring to the practice of constructing hypermedia representations for groups in real time, with the active participation of the members, rather than in building stand-alone hypertexts as a solitary activity, meant for readers to review and navigate, at a later time. For example, Emmet and Cleland's study (2002) of a hypermedia tool used for constructing narrative and graphical representations of safety issues focuses solely on tool features as the means to address issues of authoring and representational complexity and sufficiency.

Some researchers have touched on the skills required, and challenges faced, in building knowledge maps such as those depicting design rationale. Buckingham Shum (1996:21) cites "the difficulty of representing useful design rationale while engaging in artifact construction ... rapid testing and changing of the [design] artifact, coupled with a reluctance or even inability to interrupt and articulate one's process" results in either incomplete design rationale or incomplete design, as well as some degree of user (designer) frustration. Other researchers alluded to the role of a practitioner in such efforts, mostly indirectly and in a negative light, pointing to the large degree of time and effort involved to capture and represent design rationale, often involving third parties and considerable expense. Olson et al., (1996) noted, trying to capture the design rationales of our meeting discussion takes an enormous amount of coder time off line. Conklin & Yakemovich (1991) reported that the graphical Issue-Based Information System gIBIS approach seemed to work in actual project settings only with a scribe taking an enormous amount of time to capture and analyze rationale information.

11.2.2 Group Support Systems (GSS)

A large strain of GSS research has focused on the role of the facilitator (Bostrom et al., 1993), who operates the software and runs the sessions with groups. Facilitators play a key role by helping teams understand and work with the tools and conceptual frameworks, as well as by paying attention to "individual personalities, emerging group norms, and political realities" (Niederman et al., 1996:2) and ensuring that conditions are suitable for continuing development of shared understanding among the team. While there have been ethnographic studies of facilitators such as Yoong's (Yoong & Gallupe, 2002; Yoong & Pauleen, 2004), much of this research possesses a "technocratic" orientation, "generally framed and studied as rational planning and instrumental action in the service of client goals" (Aakhus & Jackson, 2004), versus a more grounded stance that treats such "expert servicing" as products of the "communicative imagination" (as well as degrees of "moral" decision-making) of such practitioners (Aakhus, 2001). In order to understand collaborative knowledge cartography practice, we may well need to study the often invisible "crafting and shaping" work such practitioners do (Aakhus, 2003). Studies emphasizing outcome-based measures, such as participant satisfaction, may reveal important aspects of their tools, but they often miss or obscure the role of practitioner skill and agency (Aakhus, 2002).

11.2.3 Situated Activity and Collaborative Work

The nature of expert practice has been a focus for the distributed cognition, social constructionist and situated activity schools in computer-supported collaborative work (CSCW), human-computer interaction (HCI), and related fields (Rogers, 2004). These researchers, such as Engestrom (1993), look at the various levels of interaction occurring in an actual life situation (as opposed to an idealized or laboratory setting), paying special attention to the ways in which social and historical context, interpersonal interactions, artifact creation, and tool use interrelate in a particular setting. These approaches illuminate such dimensions of expert practice such as problems and breakdowns, interdependencies between the actors, and the situatedness of practice (Rogers, 2004).

Work such as Keller and Keller's analysis (1993) of an expert blacksmith's execution of a custom-ordered spoon for a museum, focus on the "open-ended processes of improvisation" that such a practitioner employs, providing rich descriptions of not only the individual's actions and thought processes, but the way in which those processes interweave with other aspects of the context, such as cultural expectations and contractual relationships that inform and shape the apparently "individual" work of the practitioner. Much work in these fields also focuses on the "complex and demanding" coordination required in collaborative work settings, highlighting the need for people to perform "articulation work" (Schmidt & Bannon, 1992). They rarely, though, look at the skills of particular roles and individuals, preferring to focus on the distributed nature of such work as well as the social context of the work practices involved. An exception is research that examines the role of individual technology experts or "mediators" in making articulation work in new system implementations effective (e.g. Okamura et al., 1994).

11.2.4 Aesthetic Facilitation

There are a number of facilitative practices involving the use of art and art-based methods to help organizations effect change, whether via individual leadership development, workshops focusing on developing strategies, or other approaches. Nissley (1999) employed a wide variety of art practices in organizational change settings (theater, stained glass making, and music among others). He used these experiences to develop an epistemology of "aesthetic ways of knowing in organizational life" (Palus & Horth, 2005). Orr (2003) developed a "process in which artistic media are used to engage organizational members in collaborative learning, sensemaking and change," which she referred to as "aesthetic practice." Palus and Horth describe six types of "aesthetic competencies" discerned among participants in their work incorporating art-making in leadership development workshops:

> paying attention, personalizing, imaging, serious play, collaborative inquiry, and crafting... [these] aesthetic competencies are shown to support the sensemaking and meaning-making functions of leadership, and are particularly relevant in conditions of uncertainty and complexity.

Taken together the preceding lay the foundation for the concepts in the following sections, which outline a framework that more explicitly addresses the experience of collaborative knowledge cartography practitioners.

11.3 An Experiential Perspective

This section examines "experience" as a framing concept for collaborative knowledge cartography practice. Looking at this practice from an experiential perspective means foregrounding phenomenological aspects, such as what a practitioner sees, feels, and must contend with in the act of actually creating the knowledge maps. What obstacles do they face? What personal, intellectual, and technical considerations do they bring to the choices they make?

11.3.1 Aspects of Experience

McCarthy & Wright (2004) propose that an individual's "felt experience," as well as Dewey and Bakhtin's ideas of aesthetics, narrative, and subjectivity, provide a richer and more generative account of design moves and choices than that available from technorational, cognitivist or social constructionist approaches. Centrally for McCarthy & Wright are emotion and the "felt life" as omnipresent in any human experience. Emotions, which are always individual (that is, they are felt by individual people, not by masses or groups), are the elements of how humans actually experience any encounter with their environment and with other people. Emotions are always completely situated – that is, as felt, they don't exist in the abstract, apart from their object, the situation in which they arise. Affection, hope, fear, frustration, anxiety, sensuality, doubt, ambiguity, engagement, suffering, and other emotions arise and contend with each other in all our encounters as well as in our memories of previous situations and anticipations of future ones. They permeate and inform our more intellectual and "cognitive" thoughts and responses as well as the physicality of our actions, sensations, and perceptions. McCarthy & Wright claim that adopting felt experience as an observational stance reveals aspects of in situ human technology use that other approaches miss, such as the situated creativity individuals exhibit in making sense of or personal use of a technology. They look for the potential inherent in any situation where a person encounters or adopts a tool or methods; the room for surprise, how one deals with the opportunistic and unexpected. Using experience as a lens on practice foregrounds the "answerable engagement" a practitioner has with the other people in the situation of practice, which has both aesthetic and ethical dimensions. Such an orientation moves the focus of inquiry from objective and instrumental considerations to relational and creative ones.

McCarthy & Wright point out that as individuals our interactions with technology can be understood through the prism of roles like "author," "character," "protagonist" and "co-producer" – that is, that we are always actively engaging with technology as individuals with our own aims, history, emotions, and creativity, as much as we are also embedded in a socio-historical context or attempting to perform some kind of task or composite activity. They argue that this is a more generative approach than concepts like "user."

As aids to characterizing experiences, McCarthy & Wright suggest four "threads" discernible in any situation: *sensual*, which pertains to "sensory engagement with a situation"; *emotional*, which as described above provides the human "quality" of any experience; *compositional*, which addresses the "relationships between the parts and the whole of an experience," and *spatio-temporal*, which describes the experience of space and time in an event. I adapt these to help describe both the situations of practice themselves, and what a practitioner brings to them in their actions, interventions, and uses of the knowledge mapping artifacts. In Table 11.2 I summarize how these aspects are used in this analysis. Following that, I expand on how the notions of aesthetics, ethics, narrative, sensemaking and improvisation integral to an experiential approach apply to collaborative knowledge cartography practice.

Table 11.2. Experiential aspects used in this analysis.

Experiential Aspect	Definition
Time	Time informs and constrains all practitioner choice-making. Critical aspects include how much time is allotted for an effort as well as individual sessions and activities within the sessions, as well as how time is spent within each of these
Purposes and Goals	Any human effort can be characterized by the purposes that the people involved in it bring to it, or are imposed on it from without. Purpose describes the "why" of participant and practitioner actions, what they hope or need to accomplish
Interpersonal Relations	The ways in which the people involved in an effort relate to each other, feel about each other and experience their interactions
Engagement	What a practitioner engages with and focuses on at any moment, such as the participants, the subject matter of the session, the technical environment, or the maps themselves
Velocity and Pressure	How the speed and pressures of the events and interactions happen in the course of an effort, whether externally imposed (such as the short time and high urgency which managers may impose on a collaborative knowledge cartography task) or internally driven (such as the intensity that individual participants may bring into the sessions)

11.3.2 Aesthetics

One of McCarthy & Wright's main goals is to restore the "continuity between aesthetic and prosaic experience." They point to Bakhtin's and Dewey's theories as evidence that there are untapped and unexplored dimensions of the human experience of technology for which more conventional approaches fail to provide tools for understanding. Using felt experience and an aesthetic viewpoint onto technology use, they argue, would open up new possibilities for both analysis and design.

Aesthetics has to do with what human beings, in the moments when they are acting as artists (Arnheim, 1967), are actually doing. What distinguishes artistic actions from other sorts? What are the uniquely aesthetic characteristics of such actions, especially in the work of a collaborative knowledge cartography practitioner? For practitioners, aesthetics has to do with the ability to pull together aspects of experience into a new whole that itself provides a (shaped) experience (Dewey, 2005). When working with groups, the boundaries of the world of experience are closely aligned with the situation in which they are operating – the people, goals, interests, and constraints of the project or team they are working with. Even within this bounded world, the dimensions and particulars of experience can be vast and diverse, so the problem – and hence the artfulness – of pulling them together into an "integrated structure of the whole" (Arnheim, 1967).

The aesthetic dimension of practice is concerned with the shaping and crafting of knowledge maps in response to both immediate and context-specific imperatives (things that must be done to help achieve participant and project goals), as well as to implicit and explicit concepts of right form. Using the lens of aesthetics can offer a unique perspective on the relationship of a practitioner to the participants in a situation, emphasizing process, collective and participatory expressive forms, even ethical and political concerns (Cohen, 1997). Understanding the aesthetic dimension of a collaborative practitioner's work emphasizes how the encounter between participants, maps, and practitioner unfolds, the extent to which map-building engages participants, and the ways in which participants are affected by the proceedings.

The term "aesthetics" has until recently been relatively foreign to studies of human-computer interaction (Bertelsen & Pold, 2002), except with reference to graphic design. Traditionally, the focus of HCI and CSCW tends towards the functional – how best to support particular kinds of work, to better fit the tool(s) to the purpose(s), and to understand the purposes and tools themselves better, in all their social and cognitive dimensions. More recently, there has been renewed interest in the aesthetic and emotional dimensions to HCI (e.g. Fishwick et al., 2005).

11.3.3 Ethics

The ethical dimension is concerned with the responsibilities of the practitioner to the other people involved, and to their various individual and collective needs, interests, goals, and sensibilities. In some situations, these responsibilities can be weighty in nature – for example, in situations of conflict or dispute, where every action and statement on the part of participants or practitioner holds the possibility of worsening the situation. In less fraught settings, consequences of action or inaction may be less severe, but each action or inaction has effects of various types on the concerns of the direct participants or other stakeholders. Of particular concern are practitioner actions that affect the engagement of participants with each other, with the subject matter of their work, and with the nature and shaping of the collaborative knowledge maps. These can take the form of questions such as "Should I do action *x* or action *y*? What effect will it have on these participants if I do *x*? Should I intervene in their conversational flow?" "Should I expend the effort to capture everything that person A is saying at this moment, or is the time better spent in cleaning up the map or preparing for the next activity?"

Aakhus (2001) advocates research into the communicative actions of GSS facilitators, so as to "advance the normative level of communication practice." He stresses that facilitators' work is not just a neutral enabler of participants' decision-making, or a simple "unfolding" of a priori processes, but contains many "instrumental" aspects in which practitioner choices directly affect participants and the course of events during sessions of their work. He also (Aakhus, 2002) examines the "transparency work" performed by GSS facilitators in an ethical light. This work, the result of "active crafting" on the part of the facilitator, is often invisible in accounts of GSS practice. Aakhus (2003) further critiques frameworks that de-emphasize the ethical "obligations and responsibilities" of particular mediation and GSS practices, arguing that "objectivity" is an inaccurate way to frame practitioner actions. Facilitators do in fact intervene in their clients' situations. Schön (1983) argues for practitioners to take active and conscious ethical stances, recommending reflection-in-action as the means to achieve this.

11.3.4 Narrative

The narrative dimension concerns the connecting together of diverse moments and statements over time. Practitioner actions which have a narrative dimension – that serve to connect elements of the story being built in the knowledge maps for later "telling" and "reading" by others – contribute to the narrative shaping of both the effort itself and the knowledge maps that are the primary focus of their actions. Narrative is both a basic human psychological mechanism independent of any particular embodiment, and an aesthetic form that can be represented in verbal, written, performed, or other forms. Narrative functions as a key human strategy for exploring and overcoming unexpected turns of events. Stories and story-making form a key psychological strategy for connecting disparate occurrences. This is particularly so when there is a break or disruption from an expected course of action. "The function of the story is to find an intentional state that mitigates or at least makes comprehensible a deviation from a canonical cultural pattern." (Bruner, 1990) The skill of the storyteller lies in the artfulness and effectiveness with which they can craft an artifact that makes sense of the "breaches in the ordinariness of life." Narrative is a central means by which we are able to glue together bits of experience to construct a new understanding, and a key part of human development, a way that we learn to construct and communicated understanding of events and environments. Narrative is also an intentional form – things that are created, with varying degrees of skill, to serve various purposes. Narrative analysis provides a frame for understanding practitioner efforts to maintain the coherence and integrity of knowledge maps even in the face of interruptions and potential derailments of their sessions.

11.3.5 Sensemaking

In many collaborative mapping sessions, there are moments where forward progress is blocked because of unforeseen, uncontrolled, or otherwise problematic obstacles. The sensemaking dimension concerns the actions and consequences for what takes place at such moments. They call for creative and skilled responses, since programmed or prescribed responses and rote actions are rarely sufficient in such situations. What is the particular character of practitioner sensemaking at those moments, especially as it is expressed through, and manifested in, mapping moves, explorations of and changes to the maps, and interactions with participants about them? In what ways do knowledge maps and the practitioners' interactions with them contain both a source of obstacles and impasses, and a means of resolving or addressing them?

Dervin's (1983) model of individual sensemaking posits that a person is always attempting to reach a goal, or set of goals. Goals themselves shift in priority and nature, in time and place. Some are explicit where others are tacit. Individuals move toward these goals until an obstacle stops them. The obstacle impedes their progress and stymies their efforts to continue. In order to resume their progress, they need to design a movement around, through, over, or away from the obstacle. This can be as simple as asking someone for directions or help, or a more complicated set of actions that may have a trial-and-error character. These sensemaking actions can be understood as attempting to answer a set of questions: What's stopping me? What can I do about it? Where can I look for assistance in choosing and taking an action? Weick & Meader (1993) define sensemaking as the process of constructing "moderately consensual definitions that cohere long enough for people to be able to infer some idea of what they have, what they want, why they can't get it, and why it may not be worth getting in the first place."

Although in some ways sensemaking can be thought of as a perpetual, ongoing process (Weick, 1995:14), it is also something placed in sharp relief by the encountering of a surprise, interruption, or "whenever an expectation is disconfirmed." Schön (1987:19) characterizes such moments in professional practice as situations of "complexity, instability, and uncertainty," laden with "indeterminacies and value conflicts." Such moments are further defined by a "density of decision points" (Sawyer, 1996). In professional practice, the moments where sensemaking comes to the fore can have the character of impasses (Aakhus, 2003) or what Aakhus terms "dilemmatic situations" (2001). Collaborative knowledge cartography practice can include many such moments. We will see one described below in the Case Study section.

11.3.6 Improvisation

While some aspects of collaborative knowledge cartography practice follow predetermined patterns and draw on techniques and methods planned in advance, skilled practitioners often find themselves improvising. As with aesthetics, improvisation is rarely a focus for research in the HCI, CSCW, hypermedia, and GSS fields. Even in fields like teaching or semiotics, despite their focus on the highly improvisational world of human speech, studies of improvisational aspects are relatively rare (Sawyer, 1996). Improvisation is difficult to control for, or measure in, laboratory or outcome-based studies of software tool use. GSS research often regularizes the practices surrounding the technology, analogous to similar moves to "script" teacher-student interactions (Sawyer, 2004) and otherwise de-skill or de-emphasize the creative aspects of many sorts of professional practices (Schön, 1983). Yet improvisation is central to understanding what truly occurs in real-world software use situations.

Sawyer (1999) discerns three levels at which to understand improvisation: individual (improvisation on the part of particular actors), group (improvised interactions within a bounded, particular situation), and cultural ("the pre-existing structures available to performers – these often emerge over historical time, from broader cultural processes"). The cultural level supplies the elements of a practitioner's repertoire, the bag of pre-existing techniques and concepts (whether learned in school, or from work or other experiences) that collectively determine the "scope of choice" (Schön, 1983) that the practitioner draws from, combines, and invokes in the heat of an encounter. Practitioners of exceptional skill often possess repertoires of great "range and variety" (Schön, 1983:140) which they are capable of drawing on and combining in innovative, expressive, and subtle ways. This kind of characterization is particularly apt when a practitioner is confronted with a situation of confusion or uncertainty, where they can no longer continue on with a single pre-existing method or technique (though they may return to it later) and must make a high number of rapid decisions about what actions to take, ways to inflect those actions, or risk losing the coherence of the session, thus jeopardizing its goals.

Maintaining an awareness of the emergent aspects of a situation, however, does not mean that all is left to chance. Sawyer (2004) emphasizes the concept of "disciplined improvisation," which juxtaposes improvisational aspects of practice (dialogue, sensemaking responses, spontaneous and creative acts) with "overall task and participation structures," such as "scripts, scaffolds, and activity formats." Skilled practitioners are able to navigate judiciously between moments when they can rely on pre-existing structure and scripted actions, and moments when fresh responses and combinations are called for.

11.3.7 Summary

In this section I've outlined the main dimensions I use to characterize the practitioner experience of collaborative knowledge cartography. Table 11.3 provides a summary of these.

Table 11.3. Dimensions of collaborative knowledge mapping practice.

Practice Dimension	Definition
Ethics	How a practitioner's actions will affect the interests and well-being of participants, audience, and stakeholders
Aesthetics	How the form that artifacts and utterances take in the process of constructing knowledge maps, and the shaping and crafting that practitioners apply
Narrative	How the ways people understand and connect events together; the meanings they bring to events, especially the explanations for when something breaches the expected flow of events
Sensemaking	The ways in which practitioners deal with situations of doubt or instability, particularly when an obstacle blocks forward progress
Improvisation	The spontaneous moves that practitioners make, involving creative divergences from rote or prescribed methods or behaviors

11.4 Comparing Individual and Collaborative Practice

While all knowledge mapping practitioners who have progressed beyond the novice stage encounter the dimensions discussed above, the way the dimensions are experienced is different (and intensified) when the dimension of mapping live with a group (referred to as "collaborative mapping") is added. Table 11.4 provides a comparison of several of these differences.

Table 11.4. Comparison of individual and collaborative practitioner experience.

Dimension or Aspect	Individual Mapping Practice	Collaborative Mapping Practice
Aesthetics	Working individually, a practitioner can spend as much time, effort, and focus on shaping and refining maps as desired. Such "tweaking" often consumes much of the practitioner's attention and crafting. Continual refinement of every dimension, whether appearance (the form, look, wording, colors) technical (how well maps fit into the overall technical context of an effort, such as integration with other tools, tagging of elements), or hypertextual (elegance of linking and transclusions) is often the hallmark of individual practice and a core reflection of the expertise displayed	In collaborative sessions, the practitioner must trade off aesthetic shaping in the service of interruptions, obstacles, and shifts in emphasis. Participant contributions can and usually do come "fast and furious," so shaping activities tend to occur either on the fly or in the moments in between other activities. In such moments, equivalent to musical rests, the practitioner (if they are fast enough) can adjust the placement of a few nodes or links, create a transclusion, change a node type, or other small actions that enhance the elegance (and hopefully therefore, the coherence) of the maps
Ethics	For individual practice, ethics follow several levels. Practitioners should be aware of how their product (knowledge maps) can affect audiences and stakeholders, how it might be taken up or used to serve different purposes, as well as follow general ethical guidelines such as truthful handling of facts and evidence	All of the same considerations that guide ethical individual practice are in play, with the added weight of sensitivity to participant goals, interests, feelings, relationships, and the ways in which the practitioner's own actions, even on the moment-to-moment level, can affect these
Time	Within the context of the time allotted for the overall effort, time is generally open-ended for work sessions in individual practice. The practitioner can start, stop, explore, and work over details without worrying about the effect on others, interruptions, or squandering too much of the overall time budget	Practitioners can only act within the constraints of a session's time budget, which poses considerable sensemaking challenges. They must be judicious about taking the group's time to arrange maps, fix problems, and deal with technical issues. They must divide their attention between the maps, the participants, the tools, and the content as well as the goals of the session.
Purposes and Goals	In individual practice, the goals that guide the practitioner's work are generally external to the work session itself. They exist as ideas that motivate the work but do not generally shift within the work sessions themselves (except, of course, for new ideas that occur to the practitioner in the course of their work).	Practitioners in collaborative sessions must be sensitive to the goals of the participants as well as of external stakeholders. They shift (and sometimes adjudicate) between them, which can require delicate and painstaking attention. Practitioners need to be aware of divergent as well as emergent goals, and how their own actions can serve different goals and purposes

Now that we have outlined aspects of the special character of collaborative knowledge cartography practice, we can bring them together in an analytical framework. The next section describes this framework.

11.4.1 A Framework for Analyzing Collaborative Practice

If we bring these practice components together with the experiential aspects discussed above, we get the beginnings of an analytical framework that can be used to describe instances of collaborative knowledge cartography practice. Table 11.5 brings the above aspects together.

Table 11.5. A matrix of practice dimensions and experiential aspects.

Dimension	Time	Interpersonal Relations	Purposes / Goals	Engagement	Velocity / Pressure
Ethics	Choices about use of time, allotting time to various tasks, discussions, sidebars; each choice affects interests of various participants	Decisions about when and how to intervene in interpersonal dynamics; choices about a practitioner's own relations to participants	In any effort there will be multiple and sometimes conflicting purposes; choices about the attention and weight to give each	Practitioners must choose what to engage with. Any choice of focus removes attention from something else	Choices about how fast or slow to go, e.g. in making sure there is sufficient group ownership of a map through validation
Aesthetics	Time is nearly always a gating factor for how much one is able to perfect the form of a knowledge map. During sessions there is often little time for careful crafting and making small adjustments	Interpersonal considerations can come into play when deciding about what form to give a map, such as which participant ideas or feelings to reflect in what ways	The form of any map must be guided by what the map is "for"; implicit or explicit purposes have direct implications on aesthetic choices	The main focus for aesthetic engagement is with the form and content of the maps. This has many dimensions (partially a function of the software tool used), including text, color, layout, images, node typing, etc	The speed and pressure of a session has a direct bearing on the form a map takes; e.g. often practitioners must "slow down" in order to ensure quality and/or validation
Narrative	Narratives unfold over time. One of the central functions of narrative is to explain why one event follows another, cause and effect. Practitioners make choices of how to connect events to each other and how to reflect that in maps	Interpersonal relationships themselves can be understood as narratives, with breaches occurring in which the practitioner must choose whether, and how, to intervene. At times, these can even become subject matter for the maps themselves	Purposes drive and frame the experience of sessions and efforts for both participants and practitioners. Obstacles are experienced as interruptions in purposes	Engagement with narrative aspects can mean actions that help show how elements on one knowledge map connect to and relate to those on others, or how to shape a map so as to clearly indicate causation and explanation	The speed and pressure of a session can limit or enhance a practitioner's ability to make connections within and among knowledge elements in the maps

11. Performing Knowledge Art: Understanding Collaborative Cartography 237

Dimension	Time	Interpersonal Relations	Purposes / Goals	Engagement	Velocity / Pressure
Sensemaking	Time presents a wide variety of sensemaking challenges and obstacles to the practitioner, such as trying to complete a task without enough time to do it properly	Interpersonal relations often create sensemaking moments, such as conflict or disagreement about form, subject matter, or process	As with interpersonal conflicts, collisions of purpose can disrupt progress and create sensemaking moments	A practitioner engages with the sensemaking dimension when they realize a breach or obstacle has occurred and they must deal directly with it	The pressures bearing on a session can result in "too much too fast" for both participants and practitioners
Improvisation	A practitioner often has to improvise especially when there is not enough time to do a task in the prescribed way, or when sudden events cause the need to do something unplanned	Dealing with interpersonal issues in the course of a session usually requires effective improvisation; practitioners must find creative ways to deal with such events	Practitioners must often, in effect, shift between the different purposes, or even suddenly develop or articulate new purposes and new actions to support them	Choosing to improvise, rather than sticking to planned or prescribed methods and techniques, requires a level of engagement in the "here and now" that can be missing from more rote performance	The mark of an expert practitioner is often the speed with which they can act, in particular coming up with "instant" improvised solutions to problems

238   Albert M. Selvin

The above analysis is abstracted from a number of close studies of actual sessions and practitioners. The next step is to apply these considerations to actual practice and practitioners. The following section presents a short example of this excerpted from a longer case study.

11.5 Applying the Framework to an Example of Practice

To illustrate how the above framework can be applied to instances of actual practice, in this section we take a look at practitioner choices made in a session taken from a longer case study of collaborative knowledge cartography. Space does not permit a full analysis here, which would show the rich interplay of interactions, choices, moves, and artifacts over the course of an entire session, placed in context of the overall effort (for a longer treatment see Selvin (2005)). Rather, I will highlight a few such choices and moves and discuss them in terms of the aspects and dimensions presented above.

11.5.1 Background

The case was drawn from a video analysis of expert practitioners using the Compendium knowledge mapping software in the context of a NASA experiment in scientific collaboration as part of the Mobile Agents project (See Chapter 14, Sierhuis and Buckingham Shum). One team of scientists spent two weeks at the Mars Desert Research Station in Utah (USA). Each day these "astronauts" simulated portions of a Mars mission. They would plan and carry out an Extra Vehicular Activity (EVA) to gather science data, work with robotic rovers, and other activities, then upload via satellite their plans, data, and analyses (assembled via both manual and automated means into a Compendium database). Following a time delay, members of the Remote Science Team (RST) would download the Compendium database then gather in virtual meetings to analyze the data and form recommendations for the next day's EVA. In both settings, one team member acted as the team's knowledge mapper (referred in the analysis below as the "practitioner"), facilitating the meeting and capturing the discussion and analysis in Compendium.

The analysis focused on the changes to the Compendium representation during the sessions. I created annotated transcripts of the participant and practitioner conversation as well as all representational "moves" made within the software. Using a grounded theory (Strauss & Corbin, 1990) approach, I coded each move in descriptive categories, developing progressively more refined and expressive concepts. I then used critical incident analysis (Tripp, 1993) to focus more tightly on practitioner choices made when faced with obstacles or challenges, identifying the sensemaking, improvisation, aesthetic, narrative, and ethical trade-offs and consequences of the choices. The general characteristics of the case study are summarized in Table 11.6.

Table 11.6. Summary of this case study.

Aspect	Description
Effort	The 2004 NASA Mobile Agents field trial. Compendium knowledge mapping software was used as a principal mechanism to support Remote Science Team and Hab crew interactions, particularly the analysis of science data and the formulation of EVA plans
Practitioner	For each session, a single member of the Hab crew or RST would act as practitioner, crafting the knowledge maps in live interaction with the other participants
Participants	The other members of the Hab crew or RST members. Hab crew mapping sessions were performed face-to-face within the Hab; RST sessions were performed in live virtual meetings
Session	The particular session analyzed here was an RST mapping session held on 6 May 2004 and lasting 135 min. Participants met over a phone teleconference held simultaneously with a web conferencing tool so all could view the Compendium practitioner's computer display. All four people were in different physical locations, in California, Arizona, New York, and the United Kingdom
Episode	The episode studied here happened about an hour into the session and lasted three minutes. In the course of the planned analysis of the previous day's science data maps sent from the Hab crew, the RST discovered missing information that impeded their further progress. Since the missing information concerned geographical "waypoints" data, the episode is named "Finding Waypoints"
Event	Seven events are studied in the Finding Waypoints episode, from the discovery of the missing data to a provisional resolution recorded on the map
Choice	In the course of the seven events described here, the practitioner made a variety of choices that will be characterized below in terms of improvisational, engagement, aesthetic, and ethical dimensions
Move	There were 29 practitioner moves during the episode, 6 verbal and 23 mapping moves (the entire session consisted of 646 moves). Specific moves of interest will be detailed below

11.5.2 Overview of the Episode

Fig. 11.1 summarizes key moments in the Finding Waypoints episode. It shows the trajectory from sensemaking trigger through improvised investigation, consideration of alternatives, construction and aesthetic refinement, culminating in direct verbal engagement between participants and practitioner and further refinement.

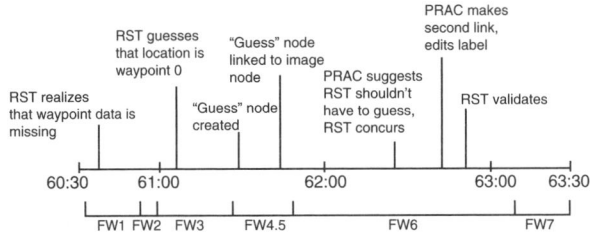

Fig. 11.1. Timeline of finding waypoints episode.

The RST's realization that critical information was missing from the imported science data created a dilemmatic moment which spawned sensemaking behaviors for both the practitioner and the participants. The practitioner's responses combined specifically hypertextual actions, such as navigating through the views in the Compendium database looking for helpful clues and creating new hypertext content (nodes and links), with facilitative behaviors, such as listening closely to the participants conversation (even while engaged with his own hypertextual actions), making helpful suggestions, paraphrasing participant statements, and gaining validation from the participants for how he had represented their thinking on the shared display.

Table 11.7. Events in the finding waypoints episode.

Event	Time	Description
FW1: (Trigger) Recognition that waypoint data is missing	60:37–60:50	The participants notice that a photo from the robotic rover does not have the expected location data (see Fig. 11.2). This is the sensemaking trigger for the episode. The participants experience the lack of waypoint information as a surprise and can't move forward with the analysis. Simultaneously the practitioner realizes that something is wrong and needs to take action
FW2: Looking for the missing data	60:50–61:00	The practitioner independently navigates to, opens and searches through various maps to look for the missing data, while the participants discuss various possibilities amongst themselves and consult external artifacts and notes
FW3: Diagnosing cause, making guess	60:58–61:24	The participants and the practitioner partially come together again, considering what they've just seen and trying to determine a way forward
FW4: Putting in the guess	61:27–61:46	The practitioner creates a Question node with the Label "RST guessing that this is at Waypoint 0," capturing the preceding few seconds' deliberation from the RST members. The node creation is impromptu, not directed from the RST, and not in response to any particular coda in the conversation. He also draws an associative link from the new node to the image node, emphasizing that the Question is in reference to the image node itself
FW5: Continuing diagnosis and discussion	61:27–61:46	Continuation of the discussion that continues between the RST members while the practitioner is engaged with the actions in event FW4
FW6: Augmenting guess node with diagnosis	61:45–63:12	The practitioner engages the participants to examine what he has done on the representation. See the detailed description below
FW7: Augmenting guess node with filename	63:14–63:29	The practitioner makes a final refinement to the "RST guessing…" node on his own volition, while the participants wait for him to navigate to the next image in the series. There is no further interaction between practitioner and the participants during FW7. The event concludes with his navigation to the next photographic image

The episode proceeded in seven short events, only one of which (FW6) will be described in depth here. In the following, PRAC is the practitioner. RST1, RST2, and RST3 are the RST scientists participating in the session. Table 11.7 summarizes the events. Timings sometimes overlap because an action from a previous event may still be occurring when the new event begins.

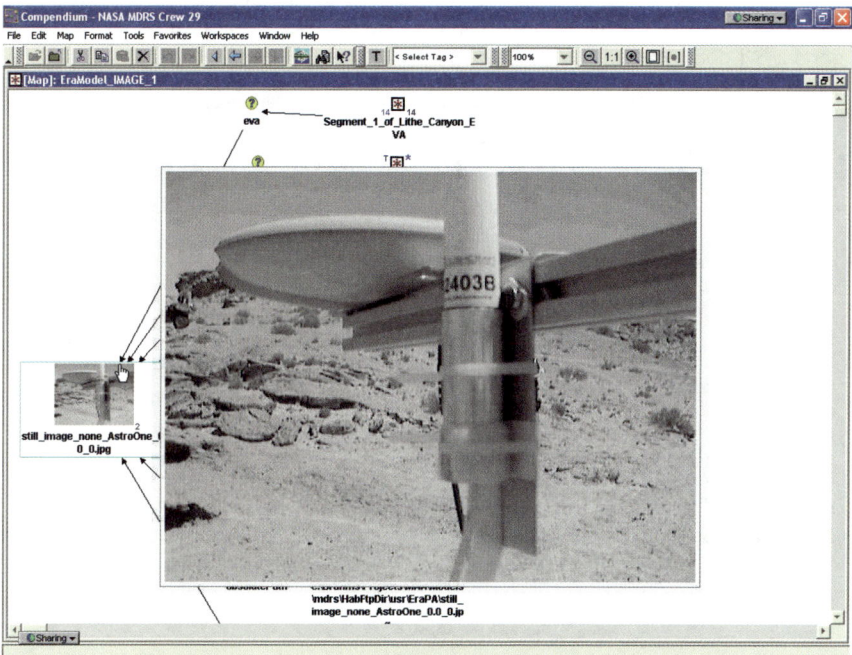

Fig. 11.2. Screen at 60:37 during FW1, showing the photographic image taken from the rover.

11.5.3 Detailed Analysis of Event FW6: Augmenting Guess Node with Diagnosis (61:45–63:12)

FW6 contains the first direct interaction between PRAC and RST participants in the Finding Waypoints episode. In its first moments, PRAC takes no actions while he waits for an opening in the RST's conversation about RST1's prior knowledge of the site the photo was taken from, so he can draw their attention to the "RST guessing" node he created in FW4. At 61:50 he attempts to interject: "There shouldn't..." but the participants are still engaged in their conversation and don't hear him. PRAC decides to wait until the conversation concludes, so he returns to making minor adjustments to the display, moving the node created in FW4 down a bit from 61:52 through 61:55. He then waits, with the node still highlighted, until there's an opening in the conversation. At 62:27 PRAC gets his thought out, saying "The RST shouldn't have to be guessing where this is taking ... should be quite..."

By doing this, he intervenes in the flow of the RST's discussion and returns it to the particular process point he is concerned with, mainly the way the science data had been imported into Compendium. RST1 and RST2 pick up this thread in their discussion (62:30–62:49): "No, you know what, yeah, they should definitely, I mean, since we're using waypoints for this? There should be somewhere that says what the waypoint..." "Waypoints... instead of just giving us GPS coords because it means basically" "I mean they put it in the name of the picture? I don't know if that's such a good..." "I don't know."

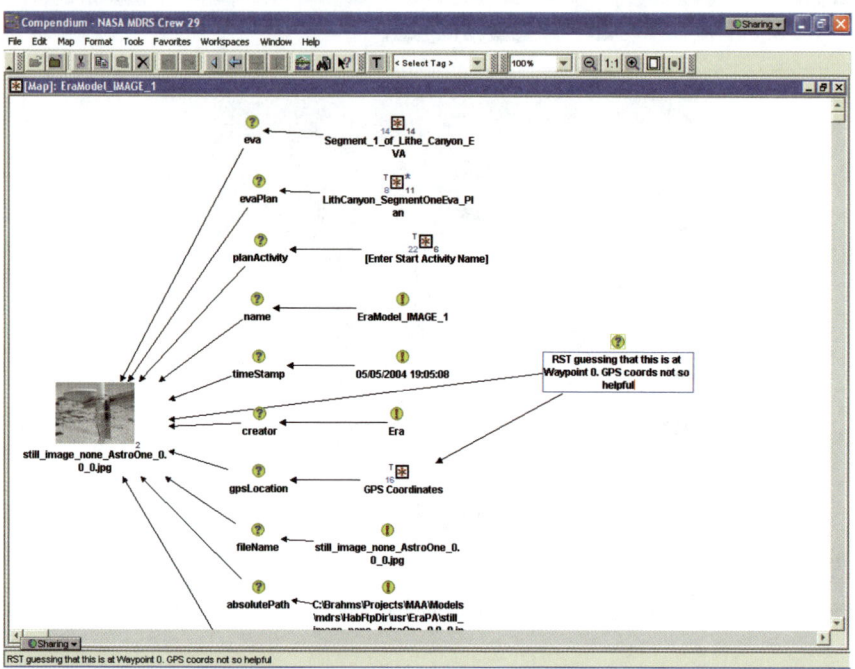

Fig. 11.3. Screen at 63:10 during FW6, showing the augmentation of the node label from FW4 with the RST's new observations, and the additional link to the "GPS Coordinates" map.

In response to these statements, PRAC launches a compound action to refine the "RST guessing..." node he had made in FW4 with the point about GPS coordinates that the participants just made. He first (at 62:49) creates a second link of that node to the map node containing the GPS coordinate information, indicating that the node is also commenting on the GPS coordinates, then clicks into the label of the "RST guessing..." node (at 62:50) and adds "GPS coords not so helpful," a paraphrase of RST1's comment above, to the end of the label (which now reads "RST guessing that this is at Waypoint 0. GPS coords not so helpful") (see Fig. 11.3).

At 62:52 RST1, who's been watching the moves, makes a direct response to PRAC's paraphrase as entered into the node (in italics below): "Y'know it should have, the, y'know, it should say Waypoint zero.... At this point it isn't helpful because we have to go back. So, um, ... what we put in here is "*RST guessing that this* is at Waypoint 0. GPS Coords not so helpful." The mention of "it isn't helpful" is a direct appropriation of a concept from the node that PRAC had introduced into the conversational flow (as opposed to a response to a verbal comment). This interchange also serves as a participant validation of the text PRAC had put into the node.

Table 11.8 summarizes the engagement, aesthetic, and ethical dimensions of the practitioner's moves during FW6.

Table 11.8. Practice dimensions in FW6.

Dimension	Description
Engagement	In FW6, PRAC's focus is on the participants and the process, directing their attention to the process point he had made and implicitly requesting they discuss and validate it (which they do). There is a short moment (61:52 through 61:55) when he shifts to focus on the map (and moves the node down) while he waits for an opening in the conversation
Aesthetics	In aesthetic terms, the making of the second link from "RST guessing...." can be characterized both formally and rhetorically. Formally: PRAC places the node in such a way that the link lines do not cross over any other nodes. His movement of the node downwards is to correct an earlier visual "mistake" from FW4, when the link from "RST guessing..." crossed over several of the pre-existing nodes. His choice in FW4 to set the new "comment" node in white space to the right of the rest of the nodes in the map, emphasizes its separateness from them and the nature of the comment it's making. He chooses to link the node to the main image node, drawing the link across all the other nodes in the view, which serves to make it more dramatic, and possibly more effectively emphasizing the disruptive quality of the missing information and the effect it had on the RST. Rhetorically: He makes a textual aesthetic choice in his use of the gerund "guessing" to imply the unfolding, transitive nature of the comment in the node. If he had used the past tense ("RST guessed") it would not have conveyed the same "process" sense of the moment
Ethics	PRAC makes several choices about when and how to intervene in the RST's discussion during this event. In the first, he makes the choice not to interrupt during the "prior knowledge of the area" discussion, waiting until the participants had apparently finished (for the moment) discussing that subject. He then chooses to interject his point about the data import issue, deciding that it was important enough to merit an interruption, and that he was justified in doing so. He then makes a further choice to allow the rest of the verbal comments in the event to belong to the RST, choosing to enshrine the most salient aspect of their conversation ("GPS coords not so helpful") as part of the node label. He makes the implicit choice not to direct their attention to his act of including those words, but their merit is shown in RST1's validation of them ("at this point it *isn't* helpful") when she describes what has been done on the screen to RST2. It is also interesting to note that she describes this as what "we" have done on the screen, though the creation of the node and its editing was solely at PRAC's initiative, without talking to the participants.

11.6 Discussion

What does the above approach offer to researchers and students of collaborative knowledge cartography? In this chapter I have provided a number of concepts and frameworks that begin to characterize what happens in instances of collaborative knowledge mapping practice, and shown, if only partially, how they can be applied to analyzing actual practice. In part, I have taken this approach because such concepts and frameworks are largely missing from research in hypermedia, concepts mapping, and related fields. At least, they do not presently exist in a form developed enough to pick up and use in either applied or research settings.

Beyond their potential research value, such analytical tools hold out promise to be used in reflective or experiential learning approaches for practitioners. Particularly, they seem to be applicable to the kind of expert coaching that Schön discusses in *Educating the Reflective Practitioner* (1987). He characterizes "design" as the common thread between professional practices, tracing design competencies in the work of psychotherapists and business students equally with architects and performing musicians. Learning the artistry of design is, for all these professions, best done through the experience of "doing" design (as opposed to learning abstract principles): "The student learns to recognize and appreciate the qualities of good design and competent designing in the same process by which she also learns to produce those qualities. She learns the meanings of technical operations in the same process by which she learns to carry them out." (p. 102)

The concrete experience of working through design problems in the medium and situation of the actual practice, if given the proper coaching, relies heavily on what might be termed meta-skills. For example, expert coaching relies not only on the application of proven coaching methods, but on the ability to devise new methods to match both new and existing methods to the needs of the particular student and situation. Schön advocates the conscious use of what he terms the "ladder of reflection." This provides for both students and coaches to ascend from direct experience of doing the practice, to a verbal description of what they did ("here's how I handled this situation, here are the moves I made"), to a characterization of the reasons for those moves ("here's what I was trying to do, here's *why* I did what I did, what did it mean to do that"), to reflection on what was learned by reflecting on the meanings behind the actions. Each rung of the ladder involves going up a level of abstraction and meta-reflection. Schön (1987:102) emphasizes that students must learn to be conscious of their actions as sequences of moves that are made for particular reasons, whose "consequences and implications cut across different domains," "helping a student break into manageable parts what had at first appeared to be a seamless flow of movement."

I propose that the frameworks I have described in this chapter will help provide scaffolding for learning interventions to help inculcate fluent and effective practice in collaborative knowledge cartography. The framework suggests questions that can be used to guide reflection on practice, such as: What coherence and values does the practitioner impose on the situation?

What is the narrative the practitioner is using to construct the situation? What obstacles to forward progress does the practitioner encounter? What resistance from participants and materials, etc. occurs? How does the practitioner respond in the face of these? How do the practitioner's actions and communication open up or close off dialogue in the situation?

In future work, I will report on research that is applying the model described above to both novice and expert practice. In these, I gave subjects a design task to carry out with the hypermedia software, such as creating a small documentary illustration of the neighborhood they work in. They then conducted short collaborative sessions in which they asked participants to make changes to the representation. I am currently analyzing the choices and trade-offs the subjects made during these activities. I believe this research will produce both practical and theoretical contributions. On the conceptual level, it will apply and extend the "technology as experience" framework, applying concepts of artistry and aesthetics to collaborative knowledge mapping. It will show to what extent these concepts can be useful in understanding situated experience with sensemaking support tools, like those of knowledge cartography. It will extend Schön's concepts of experiential learning and reflective practice into the education and development of collaborative knowledge mapping practitioners. On the practical level, this research will identify needed software support for fluid practice, particularly in knowledge mapping tools. It has already resulted in practitioner support improvements to Compendium, such as better support for incorporating imagery and fluid techniques for applying metadata to representational elements, supporting rich mapping on the fly.

References

Aakhus, M. (2001) Technocratic and design stances toward communication expertise: how GDSS facilitators understand their work. *Journal of Applied Communication Research*, 29(4):341–371

Aakhus, M. (2002) Design practice and transparency work in the technological facilitation of collaborative decision making. Unpublished manuscript

Aakhus, M. (2003) Neither Naïve nor Critical Reconstruction: Dispute Mediators, Impasse, and the Design of Argumentation. *Argumentation*, 17:265–290

Aakhus, M. (2004) Understanding the Socio-Technical Gap: A Case of GDSS Facilitation. In: G. Goldkuhl, M. Lind, and S. Cronholm (Eds.), Proceedings of the Second International Conference on Action in Language, Organisations, and Information Systems (pp. 137–148). Research Network VITS, Linköping, Sweden

Aakhus, M. and Jackson, S. (2004) Technology, Interaction, and Design. In: K. Fitch and R. Sanders (Eds.), *Handbook of Language and Social Interaction.* Mahwah: Lawrence Erlbaum

Arnheim, R. (1967) *Art And Visual Perception: A Psychology of the Creative Eye*. Berkeley: University of California Press

Bakhtin, M. (1990) *Art and Answerability: Early Philosophical Essays*. University of Texas Press

Barnes, S. (1994) Hypertext Literacy. In: *Interpersonal Computing and Technology*, 2(4):24–36. Available online at http://www.emoderators.com/ipct-j/1994/n4/barnes.txt

Bertelsen, O. and Pold, S. (2002) Towards the Aesthetics of Human–Computer Interaction. In: E. Frøkjær and K. Hornbæk (Eds.), Proceedings of the Second Danish Human–Computer Interaction Research Symposium. Copenhagen: University of Copenhagen

Bostrom, R.P., Anson, R., and Clawson, V.K. (1993) Group Facilitation and Group Support Systems. *Group Support Systems: New Perspectives*, New York: Macmillan, 146–148

Bromme, R. and Stahl, E. (Eds.) (2002) *Writing Hypertext and Learning: Conceptual and Empirical Approaches*. London: Pergamon

Bruner, J. (1990) *Acts of Meaning*. Cambridge: Harvard University Press

Buckingham Shum, S. (1996) Analyzing the Usability of a Design Rationale Notation. In: T. Moran and J. Carroll (Eds.), *Design Rationale: Concepts, Techniques, and Use*. Mahwah: Lawrence Erlbaum

Carr, C. (2003) Using Computer Supported Argument Visualization to Teach Legal Argumentation. In: P. Kirschner, S. Buckingham Shum, and C. Carr (Eds.), *Visualizing Argumentation: Software Tools for Collaborative and Educational Sense-making*. Berlin Heidelberg New York: Springer

Cohen, C. (1997) *A Poetics of Reconciliation: The Aesthetic Mediation of Conflict*. Unpublished PhD dissertation, University of New Hampshire, December 1997. Available online at www.brandeis.edu/ethics/coexistence_initiative/research_and_scholarship/reconciliation.pdf

Conklin, J. and Yakemovich, K. C. B. (1991) A Process-Oriented Approach to Design Rationale. *Human–Computer Interaction*, 6(3,4):357–391

Cross, N. (2003) The Expertise of Exceptional Designers. In: N. Cross and E. Edmonds (Eds.), *Expertise in Design: Design Thinking Research Symposium 6*. University of Technology, Sydney. ISBN 0-9751533-0-7. Available online at http://research.it.uts.edu.au/creative/design/papers/12CrossDTRS6.pdf

Dervin, B. (1983) An Overview of Sense-Making Research: Concepts, Methods, and Results to Date. Paper presented at the annual meeting of the International Communication Association, Dallas, TX

Dewey, J. (2005) *Art as Experience*. New York: The Berkeley Publishing Group

Emmet, L. and Cleland, G. (2002) Graphical Notations, Narratives and Persuasion: A Pliant Systems Approach to Hypertext Tool Design. In: Proceedings of the Thirteenth ACM Conference on Hypertext and Hypermedia. New York: ACM.

Engestrom, Y. (1993) Developmental Studies of Work as a Testbench of Activity Theory. In: S. Chaiklin and J. Lave (Eds.), *Understanding Practice: Perspectives on Activity and Context*. Cambridge: Cambridge University Press.

Fischer, G., Lemke, A., McCall, R., and Morch, A. (1996) Making Argumentation Serve Design. In: T. Moran, J. Carroll (Eds.), *Design Rationale: Concepts, Techniques, and Use*. Mahwah: Lawrence Erlbaum.

Fishwick, P., Diehl, S., Prophet, J., and Lowgren, J. (2005) *Perspectives in Aesthetic Computing. Accepted for Leonardo*. Cambridge, MA: MIT Press

Keller, C. and Keller, J. (1993) Thinking and Acting with Iron. In: S. Chaiklin and J. Lave (Eds.), *Understanding Practice: Perspectives on Activity and Context*. Cambridge: Cambridge University Press

Koskimaa, R. (2000) *Digital Literature: From Text to Hypertext and Beyond* (*Michael Joyce, Shelley Jackson, Stuart Moulthrop*). Unpublished PhD thesis, University of Jyväskylä. Available online at http://www.cc.jyu.fi/~koskimaa/thesis/

Landow, G. (1991) The Rhetoric of Hypermedia: Some Rules for Authors. In: P. Delany and G. Landow (Eds.), *Hypermedia and Literary Studies*. Cambridge, MA: MIT Press, pp. 81 103

Marshall, C. (2001) NoteCards in the Age of the Web: Practice Meets Perfect. *ACM Journal of Computer Documentation*, 25(3):96–103

McCarthy, J. and Wright, P. (2004) *Technology as Experience*. Cambridge, MA: MIT Press

Miles, A. (2003) Intent is Important: (A Sketch for a Progressive Criticism). *Journal of Digital Information*, 3(3)

Niederman, F., Beise, C., and Beranek, P. (1996) Issues and Concerns About Computer-Supported Meetings: The Facilitator's Perspective. *MIS Quarterly*, 20(1):1–22

Nissley, N. (1999) Aesthetic Epistemology: A Proposed Framework for Research in Human Resource Development. In: *Proceedings of the George Washington University, Center for the Study of Learning: Conference on Human and Organizational Studies*, pp. 306–356. George Washington University, Center for the Study of Learning, Washington, DC

Nnadi, N. and Bieber, M. (2004) Towards Lightweight Digital Library Integration. In: *Proceedings of the 2004 ACM Symposium on Document Engineering*, Milwaukee, pp. 51–53. Available online at http://web.njit.edu/~bieber/pub/nnadi-doceng04.pdf

Noll, J. and Scacchi, W. (1999) Supporting Software Development in Virtual Enterprises. *Journal of Digital Information*, 1(4):1–14

Okamura, K., Orlikowski, W., Fujimoto, M., and Yates, J. (1994) Helping CSCW Applications Succeed: The Role of Mediators in the Context of Use. In: *Proceedings of the 1944 ACM Conference on Computer Supported Cooperative Work*. North Carolina, TN: Chapel Hill.

Olson, G., Olson, J., Storrosten, M., Carter, M., Herbsleb, J., and Rueter, H. (1996) The Structure of Activity During Meetings. In: T. Moran and J. Carroll (Eds.), *Design Rationale: Concepts, Techniques, and Use*. Mahwah: Lawrence Erlbaum

Orr, D. (2003) *Aesthetic Practice: The Power of Artistic Expression to Transform Organizations*. Unpublished PhD dissertation, Benedictine University

Palus, C. and Horth, D. (2005) Aesthetic Competencies of Creative Leadership: Making Shared Sense and Meaning of Complex Challenges. Unpublished manuscript

Rogers, Y. (2004) New Theoretical Approaches for HCI. In: *ARIST: Annual Review of Information Science and Technology*, no. 38. Available online at http://www.asis.org/Publications/ARIST/vol38.html

Sawyer, K. (1996) The Semiotics of Improvisation: The Pragmatics of Musical and Verbal Performance. *Semiotica*, 108(3/4):269–306

Sawyer, K. (1999) Improvised Conversations: Music, Collaboration and Development. *Psychology of Music*, 27(2):192–205

Sawyer, K. (2004) Creative Teaching: Collaborative Discourse as Disciplined Improvisation. *Educational Researcher*, 33(2):12–20

Scacchi, W. (2002) Hypertext for Software Engineering. In: J. Marciniak (Ed.), *Encyclopedia of Software Engineering, 2nd. Edition*, New York: Wiley

Schmidt, K. and Bannon, L. (1992) Taking CSCW Seriously: Supporting Articulation Work. *Computer Supported Cooperative Work (CSCW)*, 1(1):7–40

Schön, D. (1983) *The Reflective Practitioner: How Professionals Think in Action*. London: Basic Books

Schön, D. (1987) *Educating the Reflective Practitioner: Toward a New Design for Teaching and Learning in the Professions*. San Francisco: Jossey-Bass

Selvin, A. (2005) *Aesthetic and Ethical Implications of Participatory Hypermedia Practice*. Technical Report KMI-05-17. Accessible online at kmi.open.ac.uk/publications/pdf/kmi-05-17.pdf

Strauss, A. and Corbin, J. (1990) *Basics of Qualitative Research: Grounded Theory Procedures and Techniques*. Newbury Park: Sage

Tripp, D. (1993) *Critical Incidents in Teaching: Developing Professional Judgement*. London, Routledge. Quoted in *Issues of Teaching and Learning* 2(8) November 1996. Available online at http://www.csd.uwa.edu.au/newsletter/issue0896/critical.html

Weick, K. E. (1995) *Sensemaking in Organizations*. Thousand Oaks, CA: Sage.

Weick, K. E. and Meader, D. (1993) Sensemaking and group support systems. In: L. Jessup and J. Valacich (Eds.), *Group Support Systems: New Perspectives*. New York: Macmillan

Yoong, P. and Gallupe, R. (2002) Coherence in Face-to-Face Electronic Meetings: A Hidden Factor in Facilitation Success. *Group Facilitation: A Research and Applications Journal*, #4:12–21

Yoong, P. and Pauleen, D. (2004) Generating and Analysing Data for Applied Research on Emerging Technologies: A Grounded Action Learning Approach. *Information Research*, 9(4) paper 195. Available online at http://InformationR.net/ir/9-4/paper195.html

12. Knowledge Cartography for Controversies: The Iraq Debate

Simon Buckingham Shum and Alexandra Okada

The Open University, Knowledge Media Institute, sbs@acm.org/a.l.p.okada@open.ac.uk

Abstract. In analyzing controversies and debates – which would include reviewing a literature in order to plan research, or assessing intelligence to formulate policy – there is no one worldview which can be mapped, for instance as a single, coherent concept map. The cartographic challenge is to show which facts are agreed and contested, and the different kinds of narrative links that use facts as evidence to define the nature of the problem, what to do about it, and why. We will use the debate around the invasion of Iraq to demonstrate the methodology of using a knowledge mapping tool to extract key ideas from source materials, in order to classify and connect them within and across a set of perspectives of interest to the analyst. We reflect on the value that this approach adds, and how it relates to other argument mapping approaches.

12.1 Introduction

In analyzing controversies and debates – which would include reviewing a literature in order to plan research, or assessing intelligence to formulate policy – there is no one worldview which can be mapped, for instance as a single, coherent concept map (Chap. 2). The cartographic challenge is to show which facts are agreed and contested, and the different kinds of narrative links that use facts as evidence to define the nature of the problem, what to do about it, and why. What support can we offer analysts for untangling this web, in order to provide helpful aerial views?

We will use the debate around the invasion of Iraq as a vehicle to demonstrate the methodology of using a knowledge mapping tool to extract key ideas from source materials, in order to classify and connect them within and across a set of perspectives of interest to the analyst.[1]

Our interest is in the support that knowledge cartography can provide to different stakeholders, for instance, to enhance public understanding and engagement with policy deliberations, or to provide specific groups of analysts (from students, to advocacy groups, to governments) in their struggle to manage the deluge of new information generated every day, and the historical sources that set the context.

---

[1] Hypertext maps from this analysis: www.kmi.open.ac.uk/projects/compendium/iraq

The specific hypothesis we set out to explore in this case study was that knowledge mapping tools could help as an analyst's tool for making sense of published contributions to the Iraq debate:

- For a given source article: mapping tools should help to clarify (at some level of granularity, dependent on the analyst) the contributions it claims to make and its argumentative structure.
- For the "gestalt" of the whole corpus: mapping tools should help to clarify the cross-connections and emerging themes which one would expect someone with a grasp of the debate (as expressed in the articles) to have, and communicate clearly.

We therefore introduce and reflect on:

- The product: a set of hypertextually linked knowledge maps of the Iraq debate, accessible via a specialist hypermedia tool, and via the Web
- The methodology: how this artifact was constructed
- Analytical support: how well the tools assisted the analyst
- Reading support: how well the tools assist the reader

First we set the context of the mapping exercise, introducing the debate and source materials. We then describe the methodology used to convert these into hypertextual maps of interconnected ideas, which are illustrated. We consider the extent to which we achieved our objectives, and the limitations of this exercise, which lead to open questions for further investigation.

12.2 The Iraq Debate

The 2003 invasion of Iraq is one of the most heated and complex public policy debates in recent times, with innumerable arguments on the legality, morality and prudence of the war being aired and analyzed in politics, academia and all quarters of the media. The issues are self-evidently complex, and the modes of argumentation deployed varied in type and quality. "Non-one" can claim to have mastered all angles on the issues, and the media reminds us daily of the chilling human cost of different policies.

The specific aim of this knowledge mapping exercise was to create an integrated overview of the debate as represented by a corpus of 25 articles written by leading commentators from different backgrounds. They were either in favor of, relatively neutral on, or opposed to the invasion of Iraq and the toppling of Saddam Hussein.[2] The initial reference for the analysis was the paper "One war, many theories" by Michael Cohen (2005). He reviews the fundamental positions of pro-war and anti-war commentators, and distills from these some themes and questions. Cohen asks

---

[2] This case study was conducted as part of *GlobalArgument.net*, a project we initiated in 2005 as a vehicle for systematically comparing computer-supported argumentation tools through argumentation experiments: participants agree on a topic for debate, a set of source documents from which everyone will work, and a schedule for modeling, publishing and analyzing the outputs. We are grateful to Peter Baldwin, co-founder of GlobalArgument.net, and Michael Cohen for collating these articles. http://kmi.open.ac.uk/projects/GlobalArgument.net

"How can we do justice to the multiplicity of positions on the war?" and proposes three concepts to organize the body of arguments:

- *Power*, defined as the capacity to produced intended effects;
- *Degree of institutionalization*, or the degree to which certain values and procedures stemming from them are embodied in a regulatory environment (impacting the role of organizations such as the UN);
- *Legitimacy*, the moral virtues of a certain act or value such that it finds affinities across a broadly defined populace or societal grouping.

We used these themes as part of our organizing structure since we were not experts in this field, but were able to follow his analysis, and could investigate what value a knowledge mapping tool could contribute to understanding and navigating the corpus when viewed through Cohen's analytic lens. As detailed below, we focused on two issues as a mini-template to organize the ideas:

- What were the causes of the Iraq invasion?
- What are the consequences of the war?

12.3 Knowledge Mapping Tool

Compendium is a hypermedia concept mapping tool, details of which are presented in Chap. 14.[3] It embodies, and extends, Horst Rittel's IBIS language for deliberation (Issue-based Information System) as proposed to support the "argumentative design" approach to complex societal dilemmas (Rittel, 1972). The mapping dimension that translates IBIS moves (raising Issues, Positions and Arguments) into a hypertext network of semantically classified nodes and links is based on *graphical-IBIS* (gIBIS: Conklin & Begeman, 1988). The methodological aspects to Compendium's use are threefold:

1. *Dialogue Mapping* (Conklin, 2006) which provides ways for a facilitator to map discussions in meetings (physical or online) in real time as gIBIS networks, on a shared display. We adapted this to analyze written contributions to an asynchronous discussion in the media.
2. *Conversational Modeling*, a model-driven extension to Dialogue Mapping (Selvin, 1999), for the systematic analysis of a problem by exploiting the tool's "T3" features: Templates, Transclusions and Tags (see below, Chap. 14).
3. *Concept Mapping*, as developed by Canas and Novak (Chap. 2) was used to the extent that we tagged relationships with whatever label seemed appropriate, extending the IBIS notation.

12.4 Mapping Methodology

As history reminds us, where boundaries are drawn in maps, and what is included, omitted or highlighted can be controversial. Like any symbolic representation, maps are not neutral, but are systematic ways to simplify the world in order to help focus

---

[3] Available from: Compendium Institute: http://www.CompendumInstitute.org

attention on specific phenomena – in the hope that in the process, one has not oversimplified. Making explicit one's mapping methodology, particularly in the nascent field of knowledge cartography where there are few shared conventions one can take for granted, illuminates how to read the map appropriately, how to account for its limitations, and how to repeat the mapping exercise on the same or other worlds.

As with any cartographic project, we were aiming to create a consistent visual language. Moreover, since we were creating interactive, hypermedia maps, we also needed to create a set of interaction design conventions (Fig. 12.1). These evolved through the analysis, and were summarized in the opening map to assist the reader.

We started by defining a top level node tagging scheme based on (i) Cohen's framework of *Power, Institutions, and Normsm* and (ii) our Issue-template focused on *Causes and Consequences* of the war. Over the course of the exercise, as in any

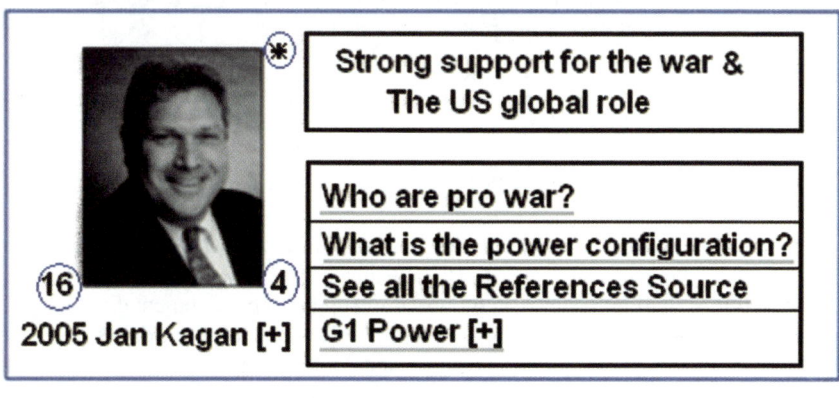

Fig. 12.1. Explanation of how to read and navigate nodes in maps. The map icon (*blue*) shows comments (*), number of connections to other maps (4) and total of nodes in the map (16). The node map (*pink*) shows tags and number of connections to other maps (4).

qualitative data analysis process, the tag-based coding scheme evolved as we engaged with the material, classifying and reclassifying it until the tag scheme was applied consistently (Table 12.1).

An article map for each of the 25 documents was constructed. Text fragments were dragged and dropped from the article into Compendium, classifying, linking and tagging each node (Fig. 12.2).

The discipline of using IBIS focuses attention on clarifying what the issue is at stake, and specific ways of addressing this, with their respective pros and cons. Isenmann & Reuter (1997) describe five steps to structure arguments using IBIS:

1. Identifying issues, positions and arguments
2. Activating external knowledge sources, select data, statistics, concepts
3. Creating relations
4. Navigating through the knowledge network
5. Reorganizing the issues network

Table 12.1. Specialization of top level themes into a set of classification codes used to "tag" nodes in the Iraq Debate maps.

Macro Themes (from Cohen)	Specialization into Tags		
C: Causes	C1: Weapons	C2: Terrorism	C3: Security
E: Effects	E1: Violence	E2: US Occupation	E3: Reconstruction
I: Institution	I1: United Nations	I2: Disarmament	
N: Norms	N1: Legitimacy	N2: Preemption	N3: Freedom
P: Power	P1: Control	P2: Democracy	P3: Oil

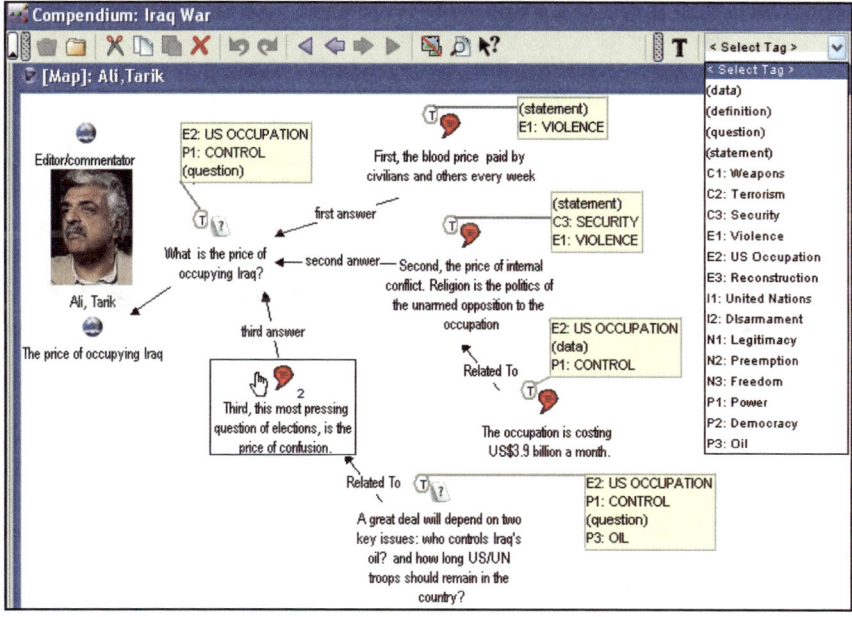

Fig. 12.2. Fragment of the article map for "*The price of occupying Iraq*" (Tariq, 2004) showing the tagging of nodes (tags are displayed on a mouse-rollover, but are shown for illustration).

However, these steps are not linear (e.g. relations may be made before sourcing related data. Moreover, in documents (as in speech), not all of these elements are either explicit, or occur in that order. Authors do not always start with focused questions. They may start with the main proposition, concept or data; and questions can arise during the document. It is the analyst's task to convert the prose into a map that shows the core issue(s), possible responses to them, and argumentation for and against them, drawing on data. We discuss later the variable levels of reconstruction that the analyst may bring to this mapping.

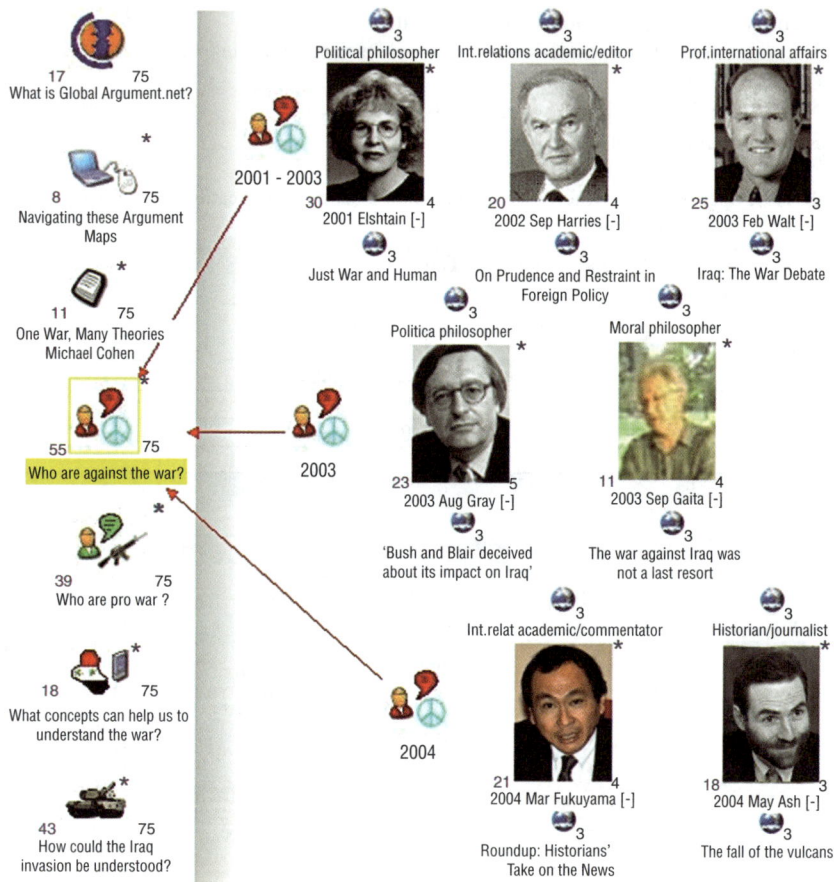

Fig. 12.3. Part of a top level navigation map to anti-war article maps.

We are now in a position to construct gestalt maps that connect the article maps. First, we cluster authors classified by Cohen as for and against the war (e.g. Fig. 12.3).

Next, we create gestalt maps to show connections across article maps around themes of interest: causes and effects of the war, and around Cohen's organizing themes. For instance, in order to create a map of *Pro-War* proponents on the theme of *Power*, we filter the database using Compendium's search tool to extract nodes tagged with *Pro-War* and the three types of *Power* tag (Fig. 12.4).

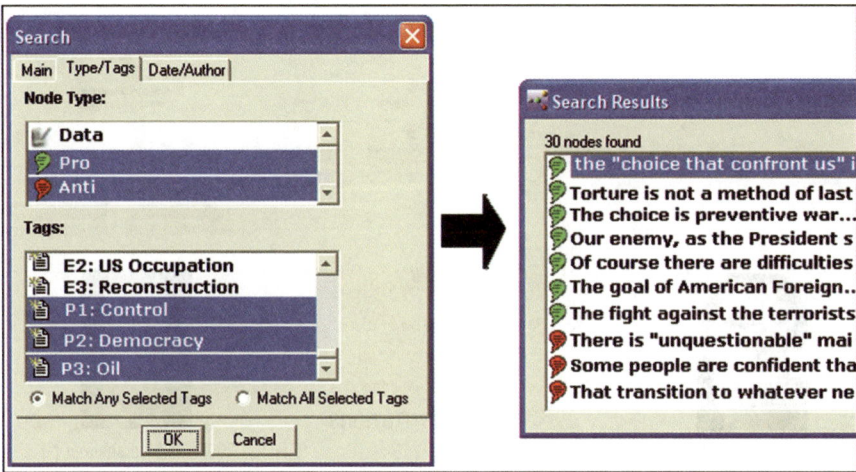

Fig. 12.4. Harvesting all nodes in Compendium through a search on specific node type(s) + tag(s): Find pro-war and anti-war positions with tags *P1: control*, *P2: democracy* and *P3: Oil*.

Once extracted from the database by a search, the nodes are pasted into a new map, and structured (Fig. 12.5).

Finally, we organized gestalt maps around the question *How could the Iraq invasion be understood?* in which we use issues around the war's causes and effects, and Cohen's Norms (ethics), Institutions and Power configurations (Fig. 12.6).

Thus, *What are the war's effects?* is answered by pro- and anti-war contributions tagged *E1: Violence; E2: Occupation* and *E3: Reconstruction*, while the issue *What ethical principles are at stake?* shows the different interpretations of this question by different writers (part of which is shown in Fig. 12.7).

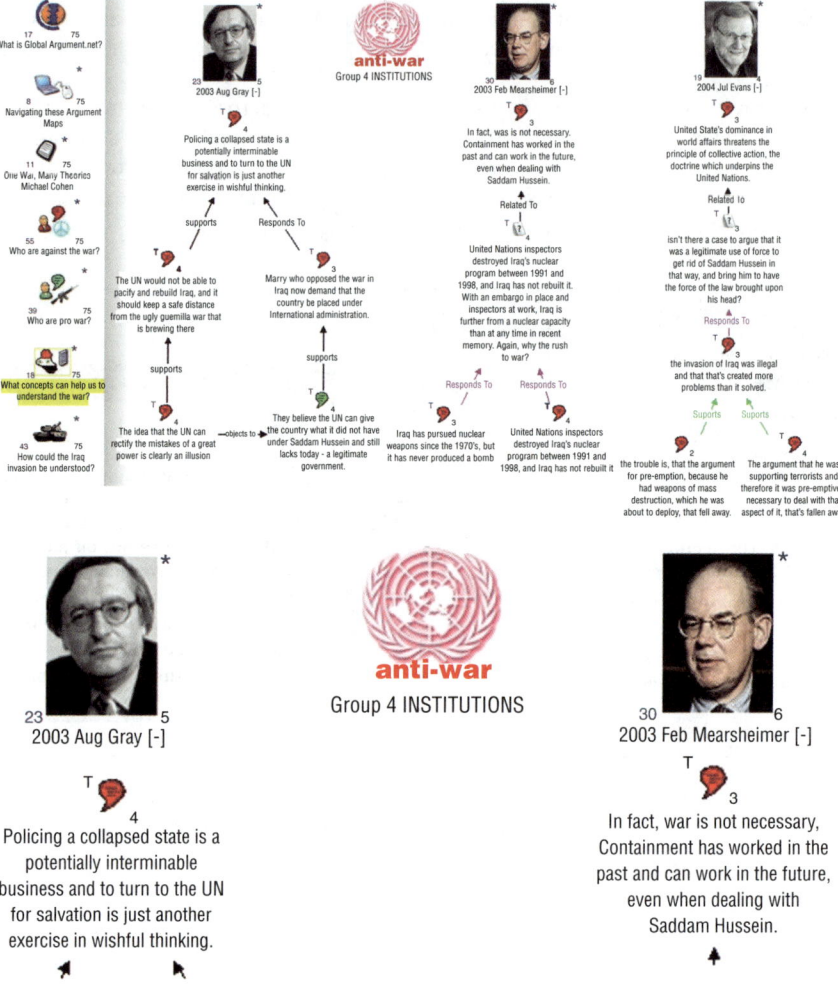

Fig. 12.5. (*Top*) Overview and (*bottom*) zoomed in fragment of a gestalt map across articles, with nodes tagged *Anti-War* and *Role of Institutions*.

12. Knowledge Cartography for Controversies: The Iraq Debate   257

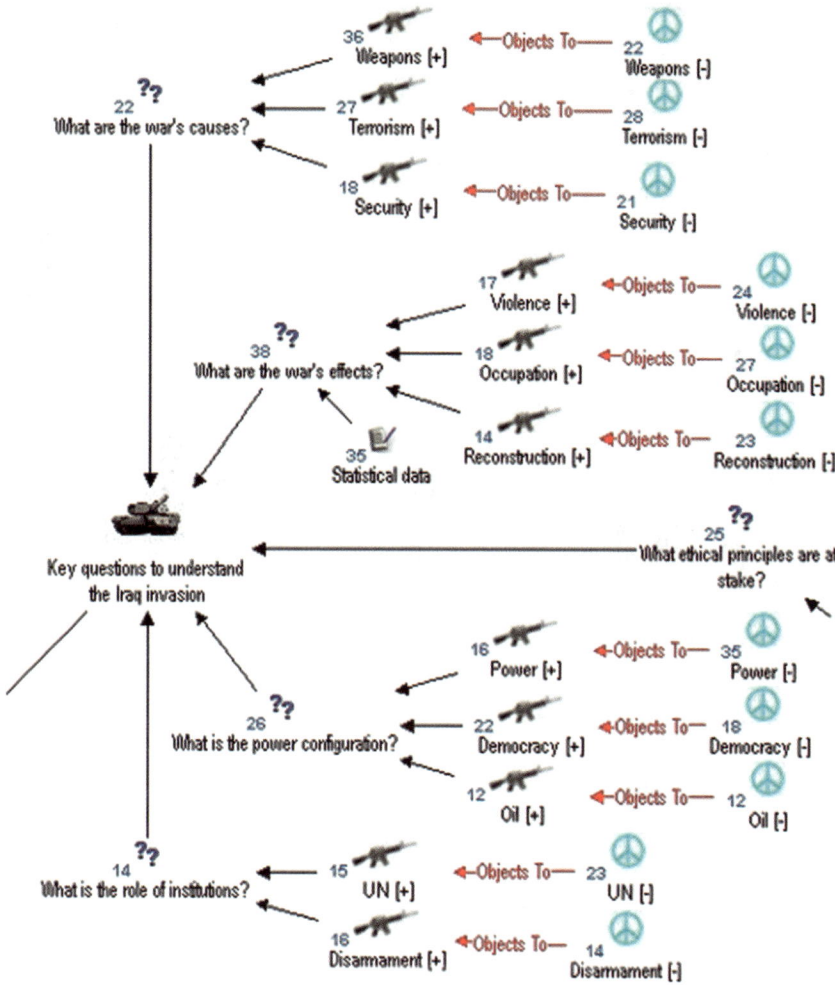

Fig. 12.6. Gestalt map around the question *How could the Iraq invasion be understood?*

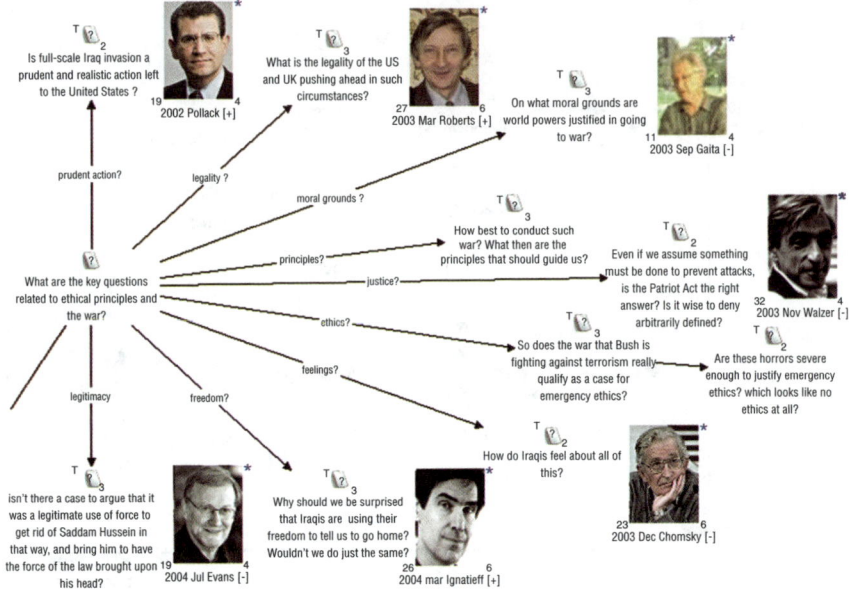

Fig. 12.7. A fragment of the gestalt map: *What ethical principles are at stake?*

12.5 Knowledge Mapping's Contribution

We turn now to consider the value of mapping a corpus in this way. What does one gain from constructing, and reading, hypertext maps of this sort? What do they offer beyond a conventional stack of annotated, printed articles, electronic notes on a digital version, or a set of tagged, bookmarked websites? Knowledge maps should add complementary value to the narrative richness of prose and the "marginalia" of direct physical/digital annotation.

In our view these knowledge maps have valuable *notational* properties (the visual language, whether on screen or paper) combined with *interactive* properties (the particularities of mapping within a specific software environment), a distinction made in various ways by Green (1989), Suthers (2008, Chap. 1) and many other diagrammatic reasoning researchers. We would highlight the following distinctive attributes for analysts and readers:

- *From text string to visualized, database object.* When we extract key sentences from articles, we collate them not merely as text strings (e.g. in a wordprocessor) but convert them into addressable nodes that can be spatially positioned, assigned an icon, linked, tagged, have other nodes placed inside them (if we make them a Map or List container node), and tracked by the system as they are pasted into multiple views. This is similar to qualitative data analysis tools for transcript analysis, but via a much stronger visual interaction paradigm.
- *From implicit to explicit structure.* As argued by many other proponents of visual modeling and argument mapping, there is value in making explicit and inspectable previously implicit structure in a piece of prose, if meaningful patterns can be perceived directly. One can immediately see the presence of different Issues, Positions and Arguments for/against, the presence of tags, the "weight" of a map (how many nodes inside it), and the level of node transclusion. The power of visual patterns increases with the systematicity of the map layout, which derives from greater formality in the modeling process – a theme to which we return below. Although we started from Cohen's principles, the mapping's contribution to grasping the *gestalt* of the debate rests on how we model *connections* between individual maps of articles. We are making an interpretive move that goes beyond Cohen's analysis when we extract a quote, and classify, transclude, tag or link it as a node, since this changes the shape of the digital space along one or more dimensions.
- *Multiple perspectives.* The new finer granularity of chunking ideas as nodes, combined with tagging of important facets, makes possible the easy extraction of different node clusters for the creation of gestalt maps that convey different dimensions to the controversy.

12.6 Improving the Rigour of Controversy Mapping

12.6.1 Granularity of Analysis vs. Cognitive Effort

As this book demonstrates, there are numerous approaches to mapping ideas. Focusing specifically on argument mapping, the work with *Araucaria* (Chap. 8) and *Rationale* (Chap. 6) is most relevant. Both of these visual languages promote a fine-grained analysis of statements, that requires extensive "normative reconstruction" (van Eemeren et al., 1993) of the spoken/written sources being analyzed, into more rational structures that complete the premises, warrants and moves that are invariably implicit, or missing, in normal speech/prose. In *Rationale*, the analyst teases apart the moves into a hierachical tree, ensuring that the claim being made does not "pull any rabbits out of the hat," to use their memorable phrase. In *Araucaria*, the analyst's attention is directed to identify the argumentation scheme that is being deployed, so that they can assess the argument's completeness with respect to the canonical visual pattern. In time, analysts learn to see these patterns without even explicitly mapping them, an explanation that the *Rationale* team use to explain their improved critical thinking results (van Gelder, 2003) and which lies at the heart of Conklin's (2006) Dialogue Mapping training to teach facilitators to hear – and make visible – the "deep structure" of contributions to discussions.

As with any structured modeling methodology, the point of investing this effort is to add rigor to the analysis. However, there is a cost/benefit tradeoff: mastering this intellectual discipline is a new literacy that takes effort – literally, "Lots of Argument Mapping Practice" (Chap. 6). In our view, the knowledge mapping of the Iraq Debate, whilst still requiring intellectual discipline and close reading, required less cognitive effort than detailed *Araucaria/Rationale* style argument analysis, to effect construction of a network with some valuable affordances. Nothing comes for free, of course. If IBIS-centric knowledge mapping is a rapid technique offering greater expressive *breadth* (anything can be captured in IBIS), it sacrifices *depth*. We help the analyst (especially the novice analyst, or a newcomer to the controversy) to bridge the cognitive formalization gulf in order to move from prose/speech to a network model, and thus offering a gentler learning curve. The tradeoff is that the arguments were not scrutinized as closely, hence the need to integrate finer grained argument mapping as deemed appropriate.

12.6.2 Who is the Analyst and What is Their Objective?

Although tools have different affordances, no tool is deterministic, guaranteeing a good job: tools can be used rigorously or opportunistically, and fluently or awkwardly. The maturity of the analyst wielding the tool is critical. Rider and Thomason (Chap. 6) discuss students' construction of poor argument maps. Conklin's (2006) work is devoted to improving the value added by Dialogue Mappers, and Selvin's work in Chap. 11 strives for frameworks that can cover fluency in collaborative knowledge cartography more broadly.

We can identify three factors that shape the knowledge maps. Firstly, our *task orientation* in this exercise was to map the contributions of the selected articles, with relatively little effort devoted to overlaying our own views – most nodes are grounded in quotes from the source articles. This was the first iteration, which could have been followed by further cycles where the analyst's own critique was added. Secondly, the quality of maps is unquestionably a function of the mapper's *subject matter expertise*: the analyst (Okada) was not an Iraq expert but playing the role of a student seeking to learn about the controversy. Thirdly, is *cartographic expertise* (tool plus language): she was learning to use both Compendium and IBIS, never having used them to analyze texts before, and never having used Conversational Modeling with its systematic use of tagging and translusion for information management. As such, this is a realistic use case scenario illustrating the kind of results one might get in an early knowledge mapping exercise with newcomers to the target domain and the mapping tool.

12.6.3 Going Deeper

Taking the current analysis as a first iteration, how could the next be more incisive? We would provide more "scaffolding" through the use of visual templates that interrogate more systematically an individual's viewpoint, or the state of the debate overall:

- *Dialogue Mapping template.* Conklin (2006) identifies seven issue types that we were using implicitly throughout the analysis in both article and gestalt maps, but which could be used more consciously and systematically to ensure balanced coverage of the whole debate (Fig. 12.8)

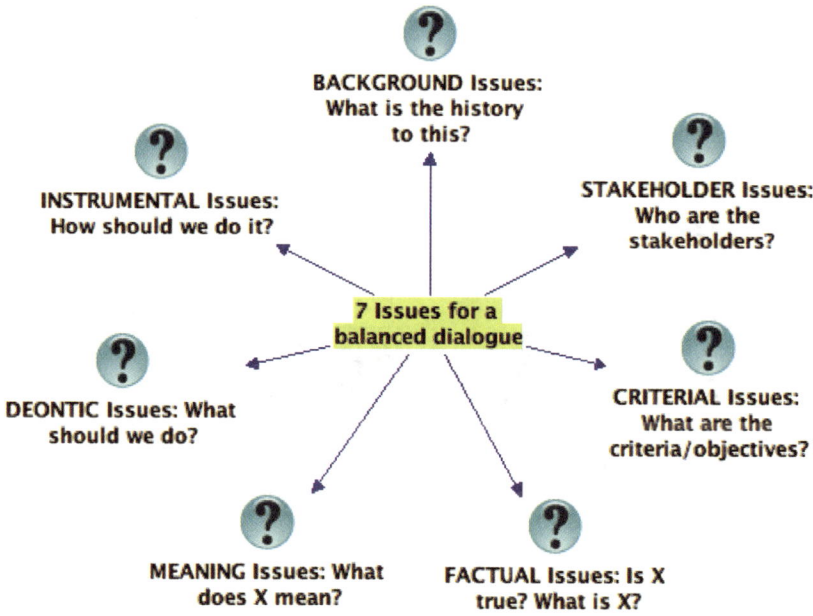

Fig. 12.8. Seven different kinds of Issue, each of which leads to different kinds of conversation (Conklin, 2006).

- *Expose the argumentation substructure.* We can build on the work of our argument mapping colleagues, as introduced above, by integrating aspects of their visual languages into the Issue-centric deliberation scheme at the heart of our approach. As shown in IBIS, we can link two nodes with a *supports* or *challenges* link, but this does not illuminate the sub-structure of the argumentation. What kind of argument is being made, and is this fallacious, or incomplete? When mapping another controversy, we have shown how *supports/challenges* links in a *Rationale*-like argument tree in Compendium, can be further expanded to show the argumentation scheme (Figs. 12.9 and 12.10).

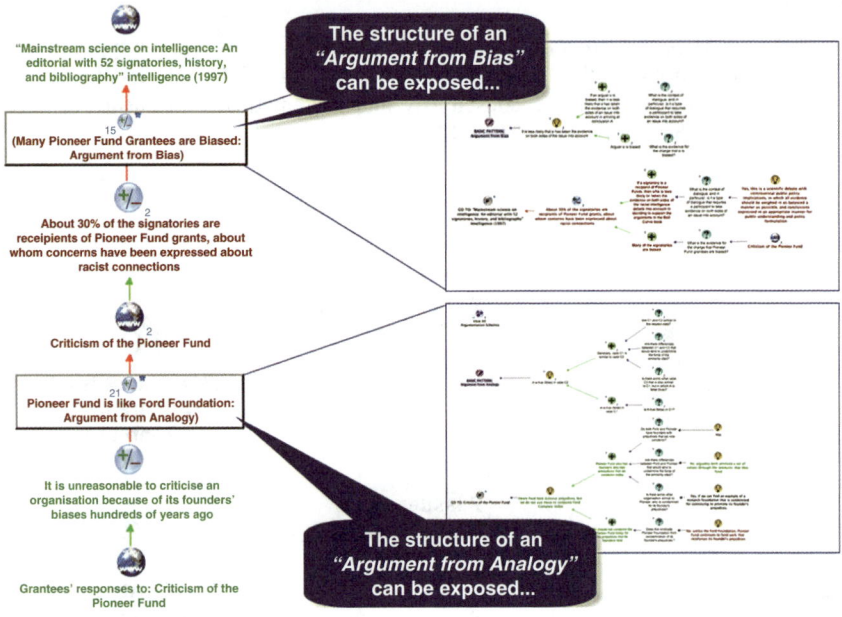

Fig. 12.9. Schematic overview, showing how the argumentative moves in a chain of nodes (*left*) can have a sub-structure behind them reflecting the argumentation scheme (*right*). See Fig. 12.10 for detailed view[4].

---

[4] Our thanks to Chris Reed and Doug Walton for the Araucaria XML library of argumentation schemes, which we simply imported into Compendium and converted to IBIS structures: http://compendium.open.ac.uk/compendium-arg-schemes.html

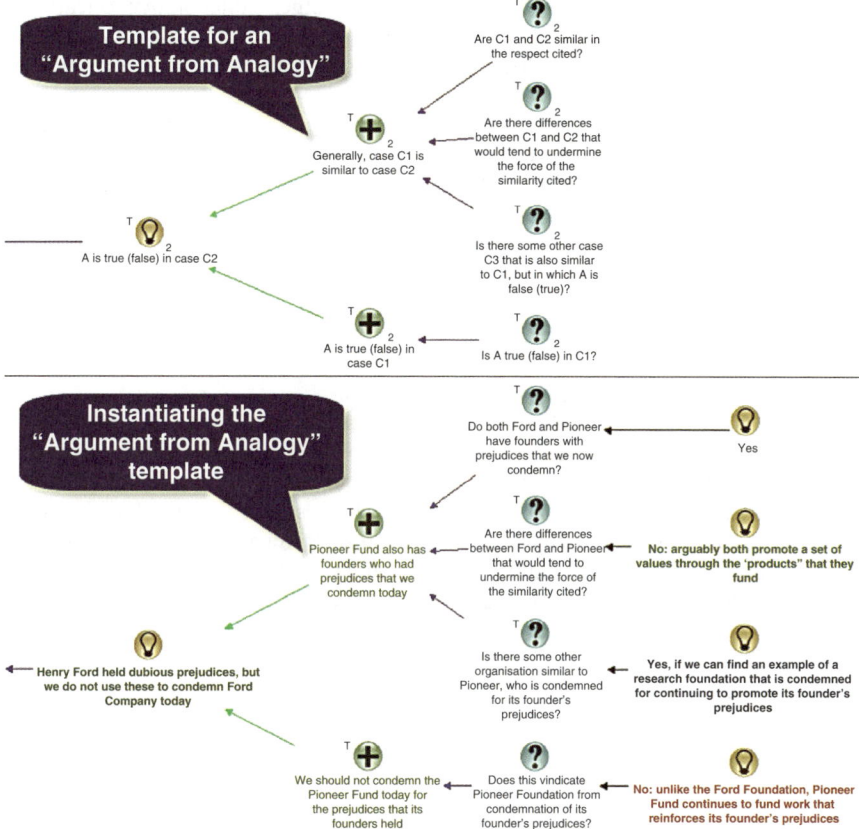

Fig. 12.10. The template for an Argument by Analogy, showing premises and relevant Critical Questions (*top*), instantiated with respect to the controversy (*bottom*).

12.7 Conclusions and Future Work

In this chapter we sought to demonstrate how knowledge mapping can scaffold the analysis of controversies and debates, using the Iraq Debate as an example. Our work continues on a number of fronts. Firstly, the maps have not yet been empirically evaluated with independent readers, so while we have proven the modeling methodology and implemented the maps technically, claims about the interactions between different views, users and tasks remain cautious. Readers can access the maps themselves to form their own opinions of course.

Secondly, we are developing Web-centric mapping tools that will make it simpler than at present for multiple analysts to contribute. This builds on and extends the tools developed in the Scholarly Ontologies project (Buckingham Shum et al., 2007).

Thirdly, we are integrating Compendium with other collaborative e-learning tools (Okada and Buckingham Shum, 2006), such as the *FlashMeeting* Web-video conferencing tool (Okada et al., 2007) and the *Moodle* virtual learning environment (OpenLearn, 2007).

Finally, while we are certainly interested in improving information management, sharpening critical thinking and promoting sound argumentation, at the same time, these are only part of the story if knowledge mapping tools are to go beyond fostering critical analysis (albeit a worthy end in its own right), and provide support for *shaping*, not just analyzing, the hardest kinds of policy deliberations. Those who are engaged in conflict resolution in the most strife-ridden communities and countries (not to mention the less extreme dynamics within our organizations), remind us that the key to making true progress is to establish the context for open dialogue in which stakeholders learn to listen to each other properly, and co-construct new realities (Isaacs, 1999; Kahane, 2004).

This chapter has focused somewhat on the rational, critical analysis of information and argument connections (see also Ohl, Chap. 13). However, the approach we are developing emphasizes a simple visual language that can be used effectively in real time to capture and reflect back a wide variety of deliberative moves, with its roots in facilitating dialogue that is owned by all stakeholders (Conklin, 2006; Selvin et al., 2002; Papadopoulos, 2004; Selvin, Chap. 11). The vision of our ongoing *Hypermedia Discourse* research program[5] is to create knowledge cartography tools and practices that integrate heart and mind. We need both critical thinking and open listening as we strive collectively to make sense of, and act on, the complexities and controversies now facing us.

References

Buckingham Shum, S.J., Uren, V., Li, G., Sereno, B. and Mancini, C. (2007). Modelling Naturalistic Argumentation in Research Literatures: Representation and Interaction Design Issues. In *International Journal of Intelligent Systems, (Special Issue on Computational Models of Natural Argument.* (Eds.) C. Reed and F. Grasso, 22(1), pp. 17–47.
Cohen, M. (2005). One War, Many Theories. GlobalArgument.net Experiment 1: http://kmi.open. ac.uk/projects/GlobalArgument.net/experiments/1/OneWarManyTheories.rtf
Conklin, J. (2006). *Dialogue Mapping: Building Shared Understanding of Wicked Problems.* Chichester: Wiley.
Conklin, J. and Begeman, M.L. (1988). gIBIS: A hypertext tool for exploratory policy discussion. *ACM Transactions on Office Information Systems*, 6, 303–331.
Green, T.R.G. (1989). Cognitive Dimensions of Notations. In *Proceedings of HCI'89 Conference: People and Computers V.* (Eds.) A. Sutcliffe and L. Macaulay, pp. 443–460. Cambridge: Cambridge University Press. http://www.cl.cam.ac.uk/~afb21/Cognitive Dimensions.
Isaacs, W. (1999). *Dialogue: The Art of Thinking Together.* New York: Doubleday.
Isenmann, S. and Reuter, W.D. (1997). IBIS: A Convincing Concept but a Lousy Instrument? In *Designing Interactive Systems: Processes, Practices, Methods and Techniques.* Amsterdam, The Netherlands: ACM Press, 163–173.

---

[5] Hypermedia Discourse project: http://kmi.open.ac.uk/projects/hyperdiscourse

Kahane, A. (2004). *Solving Tough Problems*. San Francisco: Berrett-Koehler.

Okada, A. and Buckingham Shum, S. (2006). Knowledge Mapping with Compendium in Academic Research and Online Education. *22nd ICDE World Conference*, 3–6 Sept. 2006, http://kmi.open.ac.uk/projects/osc/docs/KnowledgeMapping_ICDE2006.pdf

Okada, A., Tomadaki, E., Buckingham Shum, S. and Scott, P. (2007). *Combining Knowledge Mapping and Videoconferencing*. Open Education Conference: Localizing and Learning. Utah, USA.

OpenLearn (2007). Project OpenLearn, < http://openlearn.open.ac.uk>

Papadopoulos, N. (2004). Conflict Cartography: A Methodology Designed to Support the Efficient and Effective Resolution of Complex, Multi-Stakeholder Conflicts. ViewCraft White Paper, March 2004. http://www.compendiuminstitute.org/compendium/papers/conflictcartography42.03.pdf

Rittel, H.W.J. (1972) Second Generation Design Methods. *Interview in: Design Methods Group 5th Anniversary Report: DMG Occasional Paper*, 1, 5–10. Reprinted (1984) In *Developments in Design Methodology*, (Ed.) N. Cross pp. 317–327, Chichester: Wiley.

Selvin, A. (1999). Supporting Collaborative Analysis and Design with Hypertext Functionality. *Journal of Digital Information*, 1 (4), Article No. 16, 1999-01-14: http://jodi.tamu.edu/Articles/v01/i04/Selvin

Selvin, A., Buckingham Shum, S., Horth, D., Palus, C. and Sierhuis, M. (2002). Knowledge Art: Visual Sensemaking Using Combined Compendium and Visual Explorer Methodologies. The Art of Management and Organisation Conference, King's College London, (3–6 September). http://compendiuminstitute.org/compendium/papers/aomo2002Compendium.doc

Tariq, A. (2004). The price of occupying Iraq. *Green Left Weekly*, 3 March, http://www.greenleft.org.au/2004/573/32908.

van Eemeren, F.H., Grootendorst, R., Jackson, S. and Jacobs, S. (1993). *Reconstructing Argumentative Discourse*. Tuscaloosa, AL: University of Alabama Press.

van Gelder, T. (2003). Enhancing deliberation through computer supported argument visualization. In: *Visualizing Argumentation*. (Eds.) P.A. Kirschner, Buckingham Shum, S. and Carr, C. London Berlin Heidelberg New York: Springer, pp. 97–115.

13. Computer Supported Argument Visualisation: Modelling in Consultative Democracy Around Wicked Problems

Ricky Ohl

Griffith University, Department of Management, R.Ohl@griffith.edu.au

Abstract. In this case study, computer supported argument visualisation has been applied to the analysis and representation of the draft South East Queensland Regional Plan Consultation discourse, demonstrating how argument mapping can help deliver the transparency and accountability required in participatory democracy. Consultative democracy for regional planning falls into a category of problems known as "wicked problems". Inherent in this environment are heterogeneous viewpoints, agendas and voices, all built on disparate and often contradictory logic. An argument ontology and notation that was designed specifically to deal with consultative urban planning around wicked problems is the Issue Based Information System (IBIS) and IBIS notation (Rittel & Webber, 1984). The software used for argument visualisation in this case was Compendium, a derivative of IBIS. The high volume of stakeholders and discourse heterogeneity in this environment calls for a unique approach to argument mapping. The map design model developed from this research has been titled a "Consultation Map". The design incorporates the IBIS ontology within a hybrid of mapping approaches, amalgamating elements from concept, dialogue, argument, debate, thematic and tree-mapping. The consultation maps developed from the draft South East Queensland Regional Plan Consultation provide a transparent visual record to give evidence of the themes of citizen issues within the consultation discourse. The consultation maps also link the elicited discourse themes to related policies from the SEQ Regional Plan providing explicit evidence of SEQ Regional Plan policy-decisions matching citizen concerns. The final consultation map in the series provides explicit links between SEQ Regional Plan policy items and monitoring activities reporting on the ongoing implementation of the SEQ Regional Plan. This map provides updatable evidence of and accountability for SEQ Regional Plan policy implementation and developments.

13.1 Introduction

There is a growing body of literature on participatory democracy as a means of reinvigorating public involvement in policymaking (Coleman & Norris, 2005; Gordon et al., 2007; Vedel, 2006). There are many mechanisms being utilised for this purpose. The one that is the primary focus of this research is electronic consultation, also known as e-consultation. In e-consultation, elected representatives and government agencies use information and communication technologies and the Internet to consult citizenry on matters of democratic governance.

Consultative democracy has been defined as a wicked, ill-structured or messy problem due to the many disparate voices, viewpoints and agendas involved in such forums. OECD (2004, p. 52) proposes that *"wicked problems require deliberative discussion where consensus arises through debate with alternative options and competing interests being exposed"*. Computer supported argument visualisation (CSAV) provides a medium through which this can occur (Macintosh & Renton, 2004).

The field of CSAV consists of a range of tools where computer software is used to analyse and represent dialogue, discourse and argumentation, in diagrammatic form, using nodes and link lines. This medium can help establish common ground within diversity, understand positions, surface assumptions, and collectively construct consensus (Kirshchner et al., 2003).

The chapter first outlines the concept of consultative democracy and the issues currently being faced in this field. It then highlights the underlying notion of wicked problems in design contributing to the issue of emergent complexity in consultative democracy. A description of the draft SEQ Regional Plan Consultation and the consultation discourse analysis process employed by the government are then presented. Following this, cognitive support afforded via the use of CSAV in consultative democracy is introduced and, finally, the consultation map design extrapolated from the case study is discussed.

13.2 Consultative Democracy Defined

Disenchantment with representative democracy has led politicians to consider means of reinvigorating public involvement in public policy development (Bentivegna, 2006). In electronic (e) consultation, elected representatives and government agencies use information and communication technologies (including the internet) to consult the citizenry on matters of democratic governance. The OECD (2004), Coleman & Norris (2005), and Renton & Macintosh (2007) have proposed that there is a need for research that looks at tools and technologies that can aid in the analysis, synthesis and dissemination of the discourse in participatory democracy discourse. In addition, mechanisms to provide better transparency and accountability in participatory democracy and policy development are sought (United Nations, 2005). In such a fragmented, pluralistic forum it is a difficult task for *"representatives to make sense of the myriad of voices"*, and the desire for transparency places a greater onus on intermediaries to summarise contributions and represent the logic contributing to government decisions (Whyte & Macintosh, 2001, p. 196).

13.3 Issues in Consultative Democracy

A problem in consultative democracy is the potential for the communication of a very large volume of highly complex and ill-structured natural language information.

This imposes a difficult task for both analysts and public participants to interpret, comprehend, remember and retrieve pertinent information. In such a scenario, important relationships and inconsistencies (i.e. misinterpretation and ineffectual analysis) can go unnoticed. Furthermore, research in political psychology has revealed that citizens are cognitive misers who devote efforts to filtering, selecting and reducing information (Kuklinski, 2001). Hence, improved communication of critical consultation content in an easily digestible form, greater transparency in the interpretation and analysis of consultation content, and in the representation of resulting policy decisions and rationale, would enhance public consultation.

There are various argumentation schemes that can be mapped diagrammatically and modelled formally for computational analysis, but their focus is often on mapping legal, philosophical and scientific arguments, which are typically more rigidly structured than public consultations around wicked problems. A greater flexibility and informal style of logic is required to address the diversity of reasoning approaches and skills found in a large public.

The high probable volume of participants is a significant issue facing argument visualisation in participatory democracy. Consequently, some argumentation and representation approaches have focused designs toward this dilemma, for example, discourse maps (i.e. decision-trees), debate mapping and tree-mapping (Black et al., 1992; Shneiderman, 1992; Yoshimi, 2004). Yet, consultative democracy calls for the representation of both discourse context and detail, as it is the discernment of fine detail within the context of the consultation whole that enhances the perception of wickedness in participatory democracy and regional planning.

For public consultations to be seen as more than a token gesture, participants need to see that their contributions/issues have been considered (Coleman & Gotze, 2001). However, among the disparate information in public consultations and technically oriented language in government planning reports, this can be difficult for citizens to trace. Renton & Macintosh (2007, p. 125) state that *"argument maps have the potential to provide a readily accessible medium by which citizens can follow and join in public debates on policy issues"*. Using this method, participants can quickly identify whether their contribution has been considered.

It is, however, acknowledged that the notion of transparency in democracy is not as straight forward as one might wish. Although secrecy is a problem in politics, *"uncontrolled access coupled with excessive publicity might in fact be equally damaging to public welfare"* (Vedel, 2006, p. 233). Further, Vedel (2006, p. 233) argues that transparency can be used *"to hamper the information of citizens, when for instance so much information is supplied that the receivers cannot digest it"*.

13.4 Wickedness of Regional Planning and Design

Both urban design planning and participatory democracy have the nature of wicked problems. Buchanan (1992, p. 16) states *"design problems are indeterminate and wicked because design has no special subject matter of its own apart from what a designer conceives it to be"*. Buchanan (1992, p. 16) further explains that *"indeterminacy implies that there are no definitive conditions or limits to design problems"*.

In essence, design is imbued with individual creativity, which is conceptually a boundless activity. Solution options for a design problem are bounded only by the limitations of committed resources.

Accordingly, Rittel and Webber (1973) argued that most design problems fall into a category of social problems which Rittel termed "*wicked problems*". Included in this category are public policy issues (Rittel & Webber, 1973). Parsons (2006, p. 3) following the notion of wickedness, defines policy problems as "*malign*", "*vicious circles*", "*tricky*" and "*aggressive*" arguing that it is dangerous to deal with them as if they are "*benign*" or "*tame*".

Regional, urban and town planning incorporate the design and planning for the direction and management of social, economic, physical (i.e. building, infrastructure, ecology, geography), historical, and political development. When this planning design activity is performed in a consultative public arena with interested and concerned citizenry, the social element compounds complexity. Accordingly, regional planning is a wicked social design problem.

13.5 Draft SEQ Regional Plan Consultation

The Office of Urban Management, Queensland State Government released a draft Regional Plan for South East Queensland (SEQ) to its public in October 2004. From its release on the 27th of October until the 28th February 2005, the government conducted a public consultation programme in which the citizenry was invited to submit comments, concerns, and questions on any issues in relation to the draft SEQ Regional Plan. The public participated in an online forum, multiple offline forums and communicated in writing both digitally and in hardcopy form. Eight thousand, four hundred and sixty (8,460) formal written submissions were received via the ConsultQld online forum, email, post, and fax. This participation figure amounts to 0.30541 percent of the SEQ population in 2004–2005.

To illustrate that the draft SEQ Regional Plan (d-SEQ-RP) Consultation is a significant case study of inherent global interest, the following is presented. One of the mechanisms used for participatory citizen engagement in the d-SEQ-RP consultation was e-Consultation and is the primary focus of this case study. The United Nations' Global e-Government Readiness Reports present an assessment of the state e-government readiness and extent of e-participatory democracy worldwide. The United Nations' (2004) Global e-Government Readiness Report ranked Australia in first place, for (1) countries allowing citizen feedback on policy and (2) providing online consultant facilities. The following year, the United Nations' (2005) Global e-Government Readiness Report ranked Australia in first place for (1) indicating they will take citizen input into decision making and demonstrating this by providing receipt to citizens in a timely manner; and also for (2) providing feedback on issues. Clift (2002) also proposed that the Queensland Government was highly placed in the world rankings for e-Democracy and e-Consultation.

South East Queensland has a unique identity (i.e. natural and social factors and conditions) but is also fraught will issues that have international commonality and relevance such as:

- Natural Environment (i.e. biodiversity, atmosphere, waterways)
- Regional Landscape (i.e. scenic amenities, outdoor recreation)
- Natural Resources (i.e. management)
- Strong Communities (i.e. community engagement, social planning, disadvantaged, cultural heritage)
- Engaging Indigenous Peoples (i.e. traditional land owners, social and economic equity)
- Urban Development (design, residential development, transport planning, growth management strategies)
- Economic Development (growth strategies, industry and business development, innovation, skills and technology)
- Infrastructure (e.g. planning, co-ordination and funding, energy, ICTs)
- Water Management (water supply and planning, water quality)
- Integrated Transport (e.g. road, air and sea planning, accessibility, investment, efficiency) (Queensland Government: Office of Urban Management, 2005)

The current state of the art in e-Consultation platform tools use threaded discussion forums (i.e. prose discourse) which are limited for both discourse analysis and visualisation (Elliman et al., 2006). A tool that has been found to assist in the analysis and synthesis of complex discourse is computer supported argument visualisation (Renton & Macintosh, 2007). Furthermore, multimedia tools for information and argument visualisation have been found to improve on typical prose discourse (van Gelder in Kirschner et al., 2003; Mayer, 2005).

Macintosh (2006, p. 368) posits *"there is a need there is a need to enable scalable discourse capture and analysis with semantic (ontology-based) enrichment. Current research has not extended this to the eParticipation policy-making domain"*. In addition, Elliman et al. (2006, p. 2) state that *"the challenge of interactivity and scalability for eParticipation remains to be resolved"*. Accordingly, the challenges of scalability in participatory democracy due to the potential for high volume citizen participation, the emergent complexity in urban planning wicked problems, and lack of established standards for and research into an argument map approach and design applicable to regional planning consultations, denotes a gap in current knowledge.

Elliman et al. (2006) further assert that, prior to their own research on e-Participation over a policy initiative for traffic congestion in Edinburgh, Scotland which begun in 2006, there had been no in-depth research on how acceptable the use of CSAV is for providing visualisation of the substance (i.e. issues and arguments) that surfaces during e-participation for evidence-based policy-making. Past research on discourse analysis of e-participation for policy development has focused in quantitative analysis rather than the analysis of argument themes. To put a finer point on this line of reasoning, no research has been undertaken on the utility of IBIS-informed CSAV for discourse analysis and the visualisation of Regional Planning e-Consultation argumentation in evidence-based regional planning policy development.

13.5.1 Consultation Submission Analysis Process

There were 22 state government departments and 57 local interested groups who collaborated throughout the draft SEQ Regional Plan Consultation analysis process. Twenty two (22) analysts/planners manually analysed the public submissions. In addition, the process was audited by an independent auditor who performed spot checks to ensure the efficacy of analysis.

An early stage of the analysis process was to categorise submissions via topic and issue, which determined who (i.e. which specialist area) would perform further, more detailed analyses. Due to an unexpected high volume of public participation, additional members had to be engaged for the classification of submissions. Adding to the high volume of issues elicited from the consultation discourse was the complexity of fragmented natural language text submissions. Government analysts found it difficult to construct a synthesis of the range of content covered, let alone comprehend it all. How much more difficult would this be for a typical citizen, with little or no expertise in urban planning, to assimilate? Displaying a synthesis of content in a more easily digestible form is a benefit attributed to CSAV that the literatures bears out.

13.5.2 Human Cognition

Computer supported argument visualisation has been used to enable enhanced information extraction, analysts' cognition and transparency in decision-making (Mackenzie et al., 2005; Maguitman et al., 2004; Marshall & Madhusudan, 2004; Miller & Riechert, 1994). Englebart (1963, p. 54) concluded that the conceptual representation and structuring of content into a cognisant form that aligns with our mental models *"will significantly improve"* an individual's *"capability to comprehend and to find solutions within a complex-problem solving situation"*. Research respondent, expert 2, proposed that argumentation acts as a cognitive aid, making it easier to perceive the connectedness in submission content, and therefore relevance, to other topical areas of the consultation.

13.5.3 Cognitive Support

Working memory is a critical factor in complex cognitive tasks such as information processing, learning, reasoning and comprehension (Repovs & Baddeley, 2006). Working memory refers to information that is held at the forefront of the mind when performing a cognitive activity such as discourse analysis (Heuer, 1999). When dealing with novel information such as high volume, heterogeneous consultation discourse, it places heavy demands on the working memory, which has two severe limitations. (1) Miller (1956) indicated that working memory can only hold approximately seven pieces of information at one time. (2) Peterson and Peterson (1959) concluded that working memory has limited duration and without rehearsal all working memory contents can be lost within approximately 20 seconds. Therefore, unless information from working memory is chunked into meaningful units and transferred to long-term memory, it is believed to be transient. Mayer (2005) further proposes that we can only process (in the sense of combine, contrast, or manipulate) about 2–4 information elements at a given time. Therefore, failing knowledge for a particular problem, we perform a cognitive process which entails a search for problem-solving possibilities through randomly proposing a step and then testing it. The permissible random permutations of combining, contrasting, or manipulating four elements of information are significant and illustrate the additional load on an individual's cognition when dealing with novel information. Accordingly, working memory has critical implication in the assimilation and analysis of consultation discourse.

Heuer (1999) cites that the recommended technique for coping with such working memory limitations is problem externalisation. The use of a cognitive tool such as CSAV enables a user to externalise a problem and define relationships between component parts of the problem while providing a model to visualise the whole. CSAV functions to scaffold cognition by providing an external and asynchronous work space in which to manipulate and record complex discourse and scaffolds argumentation during problem solving by providing structure and notation (Buckingham Shum, 1997).

13.6 Consultation Mapping Design

The following discussion outlines the attributes of the consultation map model. This design has been derived from the iterative development and testing of map design features with research respondents. The findings were elicited from respondent data using qualitative research and a predominant grounded theory approach with selected elements from Glaser (1992), Strauss & Corbin (1998) and Charmaz (2006). This facilitated inductive theory building from an interpretive perspective. Strauss & Corbin (1990) propose that Grounded Theory emphasises the fit between data and emerging theory. Emerging concepts, propositions and theory were then contrasted with extant literature to identify and consider any similarities or contradictions.

13.6.1 Draft SEQ Regional Plan Consultation Maps

The e-consultation component of the draft SEQ Regional Plan (d-SEQ-RP) Consultation was a project within a programme (i.e. group of projects). E-consultation has been the focus because once consultation discourse is published and accessible to the public it then becomes public knowledge, whereas public discourse in other areas of the d-SEQ-RP Consultation are protected by confidentiality. Consequently, mapping of such discourse is not amenable to publicly released publication.

13.6.2 Draft SEQ Regional Plan Consultation Index Map

Map 13.1 below is an index map of the ten questions posted by the Queensland State Government for the d-SEQ-RP e-Consultation. The map displays (1) the root issue, (2) the thematic categorisation, (3) contextual information for questions, (4) the government questions to which the public were invited to respond and (5) icons that are a hyperlink to maps containing participant responses. All of the map content is verbatim as posted by the SEQ Queensland State Government. The orange boxing in the map has been added to segment each map hierarchy level and for discussion purposes only.

The node on the far left of the map generally represents the primary map topic (as in a Left-Right, IBIS, Dialogue Map) to which all following information on the map relates (Conklin, 2006). In this map, the principle node displays a graphic of the d-SEQ-RP cover. In IBIS-type discourse, the pinnacle of the argument hierarchy is usually an issue, posed as the root question (Rittel & Webber, 1984). Map 13.1 serves the purpose of the d-SEQ-RP e-Consultation map series *index* rather than a typical argument map but the IBIS form is still applicable.

Maroon text colour (a colour known nationally to be associated with Queensland) has been used to represent verbatim content posted by the government. Compendium note nodes [🗒] typically represent some non-specific, additional comment or notation. Thus, on the second level of the map hierarchy these were used to categorise (i.e. theme headers) their following connected threads of information. On the third level, note nodes [🗒] were again used to display the additional information posted by the Queensland Government with their online questions. The information in these nodes functioned to contextualise each of their associated questions. The fourth level of question nodes [❓] contains the actual questions posted by the Queensland Government. The final level on the far right displaying map nodes [🗺] and thumbnail graphs indicates access to additional hyperlinked maps which contain an analysis and representation of the d-SEQ-RP e-Consultation responses to each question. The underlying linked maps show all verbatim responses to the government questions posted relating to the subject environmental atmosphere. It was decided that the submissions content should be kept in the verbatim language to minimise the potential for misinterpretation and bias. Finally, a legend key has been added to communicate the meaning and application of the icons used.

Indexing is a navigational aid cited in Multimedia Learning Theory. Multimedia learning posits that multimedia systems "*call upon the same set of cognitive and language processes as traditional text processing*" (Mayer, 2005, p. 308). Hence, "*an information system comprising several pages should include a clear top-level content representation*" (Mayer, 2005, p. 308).

The d-SEQ-RP e-Consultation was a project within the d-SEQ-RP programme. This index map design could be applied to any programme, project or project segment. Users would have to be guided by the volume of task content in order to determine the map abstraction level.

13. Modelling in Consultative Democracy Around Wicked Problems   275

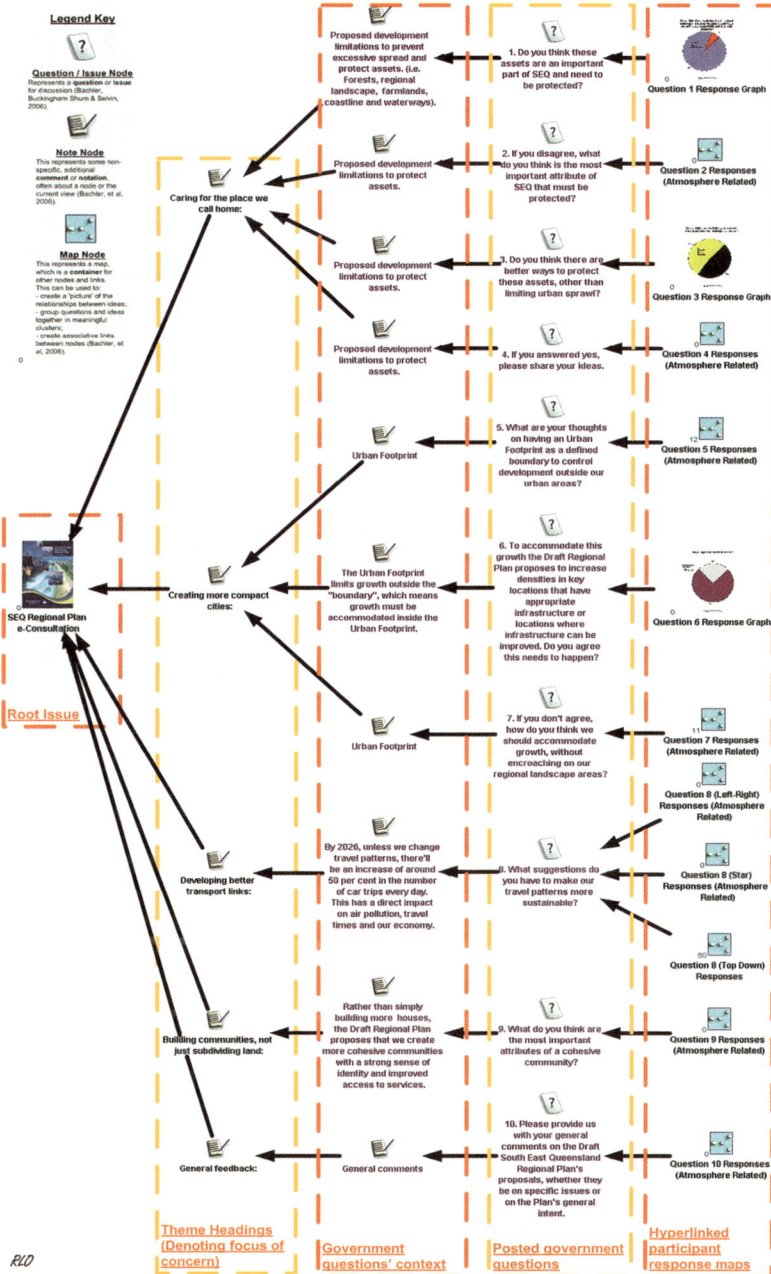

Map 13.1. d-SEQ-RP e-consultation index. Map 13.1 is a representation of all questions posed by the SEQ government for the online d-SEQ-RP consultation. This also functions as a macro level representation (i.e. index and access point) of the d-SEQ-RP e-Consultation maps series.

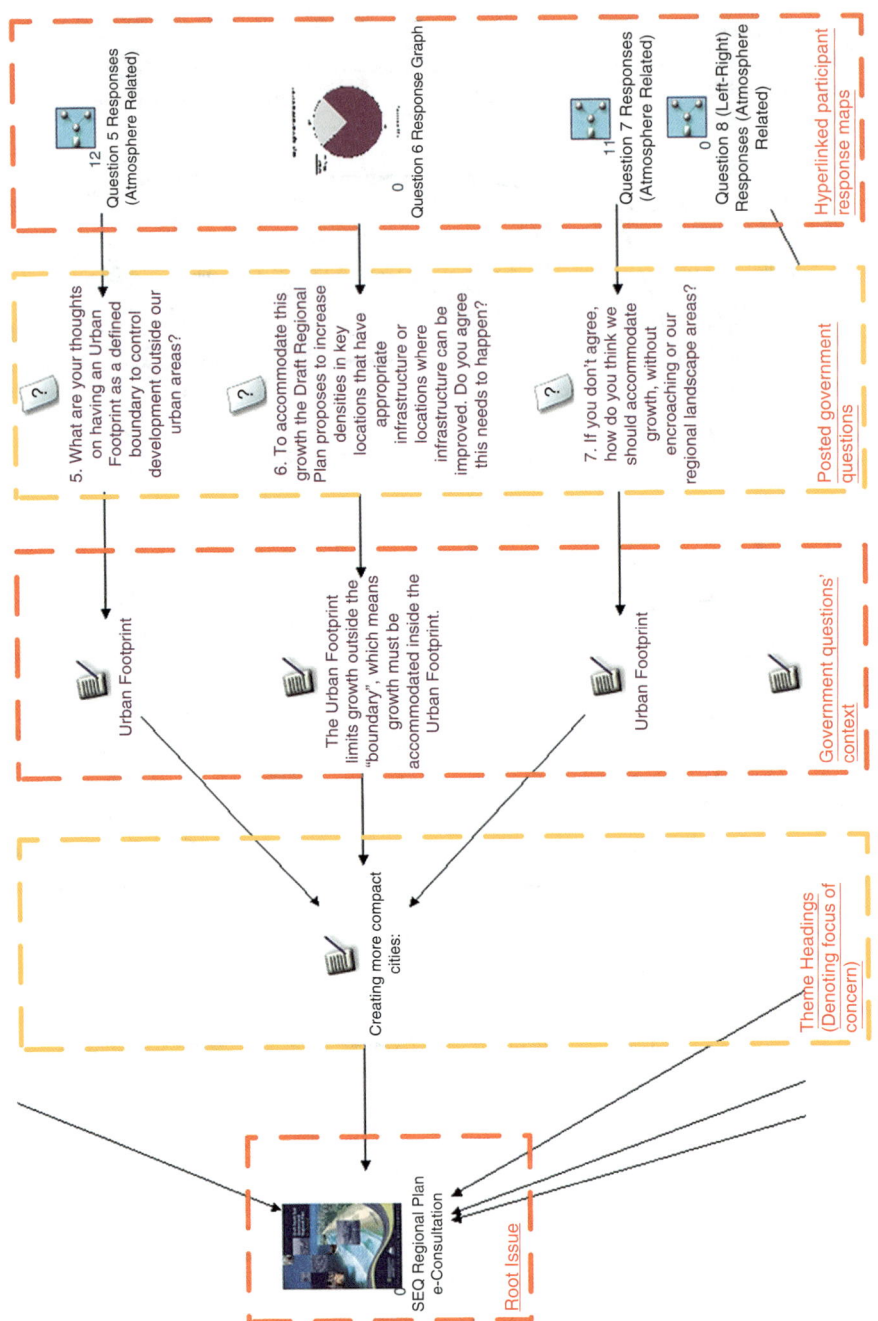

Map 13.1. (**a**) d-SEQ-RP e-Consultation Index (*Zoomed View*). Map 13.1a provides zoomed view of a cropped section from the full map to increase legibility.

13.6.3 Draft SEQ Regional Plan Consultation Graphs

Question 1 of the d-SEQ-RP e-Consultation was a closed-ended question with response options to either agree or disagree. This was represented in the SEQ e-Consultation Questions Index Map as a simple pie graph displaying the number of participants and the percentage of responses that agreed (93%) and disagreed (7%). Similarly, questions 3 and 6 were also closed-ended and thus their responses were represented in this fashion also.

13.6.4 Draft SEQ Regional Plan Consultation Tree-Map

Map 13.2 represents a sample of the maps that were constructed for this research programme that have been processed using a tree-map algorithm to create a tree-map display. A tree-mapping algorithm functions to visually represent high volume content in nested rectangle nodes, using 100% of available space. Exploration is enhanced by enabling users the flexibility to organise data in meaningful ways. In addition, dynamic filters to facilitate the exploration of data are built into some treemap technologies (Chintalapani et al., 2004). Treemapping provides the ability to visually compare relative node sizes of potentially thousands of nodes within a fixed space (Shneiderman, 2006; Zhao et al., 2005). For the functionality described, Shneiderman (2006) claims treemaps have unmatched utility.

Consultation map designs went through four major iterations guided by findings grounded in research respondent data. Maps corresponding to each project (i.e. map iterations) have been boxed and labelled within their project categories in the tree-map display. This approach creates an accessible programme library structure and map display. In addition, the tree-mapping software used enabled map enlargement when rolled over and zooming functionality, which provided focused and synthesised viewing. The storage of a high volume of argument maps in a searchable form for effective knowledge management is a current limitation of argument technologies identified in this research.

13.6.5 Draft SEQ Regional Plan Consultation Map Design

Map 13.3 above presents a single branch only (for discussion), of *question 8* discourse from the d-SEQ-RP e-Consultation. Once again, the orange boxing is for map hierarchy level segmentation and discussion only. Any logical *map structure* could be used dependent on preference and spatial requirements. For example, the top-down, left-to-right or star structure is commonly used. Research respondents generally preferred the top-down structure and left-to-right was the next preferred.

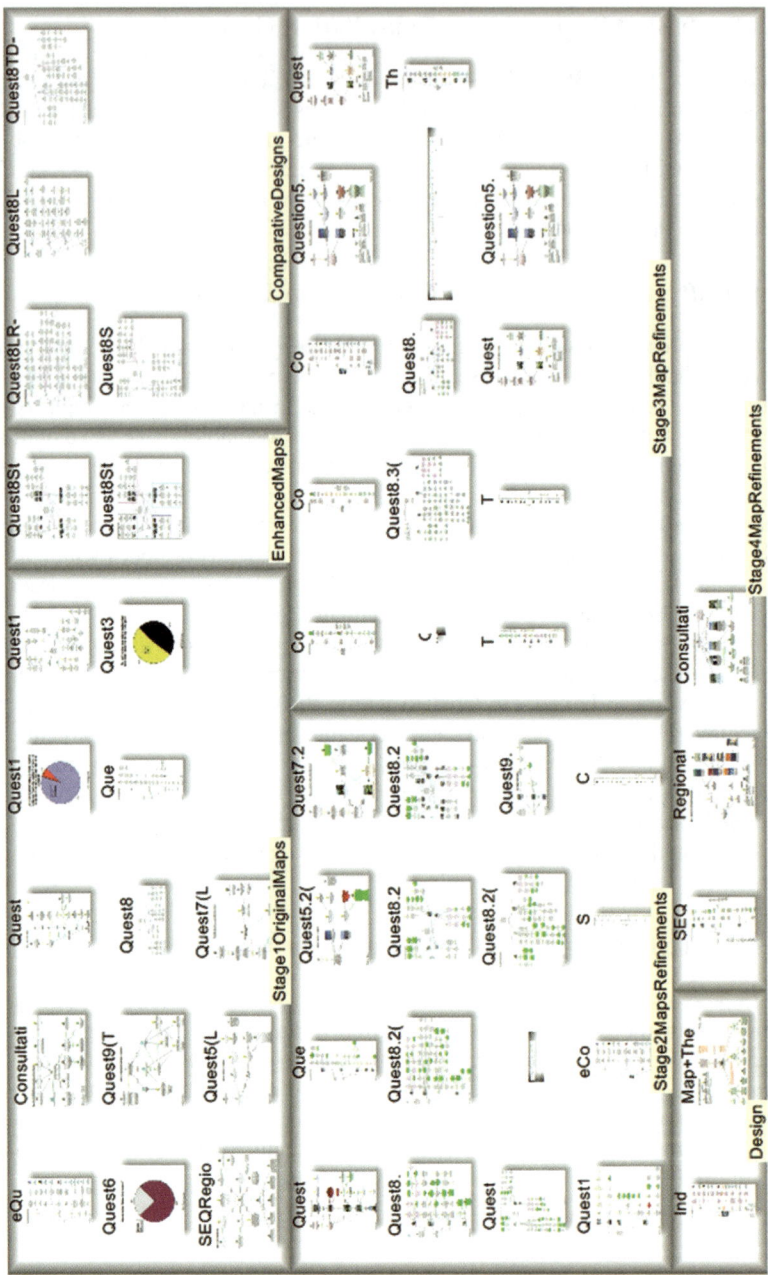

Map 13.2. Categorised tree-map design. Map 13.2 is an example of the application of tree-mapping to represent high volume content in meaningful categories such as the four stages of consultation maps from the d-SEQ-RP Consultation mapping project.

13. Modelling in Consultative Democracy Around Wicked Problems   279

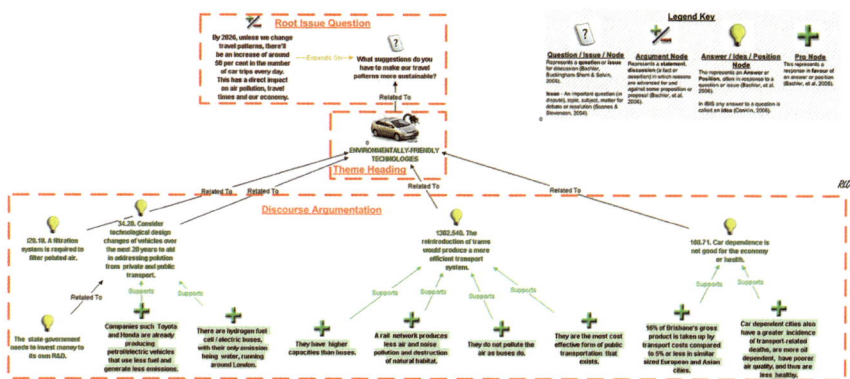

Map 13.3. Question 8 (themed branch). Map design schema. Map 13.3 is an example of the top-down consultation map schema used. It represents a single branch (i.e. theme) of the e-Consultation question 8 map. Map 13.3 is a cropped segment only of the full map theme.

(1) The first hierarchy level displays the *root map issue*. The node to the right is the issue, posed as a question, thus, a question node [?] has been used. As this is the key issue of the map, discourse focus and arrow direction point toward it. This particular question relates to sustainable travel patterns. The node to the left is displays the question context as posed by the government. The content in this node expands on the root question. In this instance, it has been framed by the government as a position statement. Thus, it has been represented with an argument node [✘]. The text colour maroon represent government wording.

(2) On the next hierarchy level below is a *theme heading*, labelled (Environmentally-Friendly Technologies) and represented graphically with an electric car. The Multimedia Learning Principle postulates that "*people learn better from words and pictures than from words alone*" (Mayer, 2005, p. 15). The thematic layout approach has been used to cluster themes of citizen concern. In multimedia learning Mayer (2005, p. 308) cites that "*thematic cues such as headings and introduction generally facilitate a reader's construction of consistent mental representations of the content*".

A distinct text colour was designated to the text in nodes for each theme, which aided in *chunking* information. Chunking is a principle cited by Miller (1956) that applies to the effective communication of information between human beings. Miller proposed a short-term memory heuristic which denotes that humans can more effectively receive, process and recall information if it is represented in seven, plus or minus 2, similarly classified chunks or units of information. The technique of utilising colour to distinguish themes is also used in thematic maps from cardiology to represent specific data patterns for geographic areas (Slocum et al., 2005).

(3) The third hierarchy level displays the *citizen submissions* responding to the root question. As these are submitted responses to a question, they are represented by answer/idea nodes [💡]. The nodes below display citizens' critical discussion. Node content here displays citizen rationale (premise(s)) from within their submission that elaborate upon their conclusion(s). The link labels display the type of interpreted

inference. The word interpreted has been used because the map represents the mapmaker's interpretation and perception of the citizens' submissions' meaning. In genuine public deliberation, as opposed to consultation only, each of these conclusions could be analysed further and potentially become the focus of additional critical discussion and argument maps. If any of these answers were deemed to be issues that needed further investigation, a critical question could be posed to probe further dialogue, thus creating a root question for further argument mapping.

However, it is important to determine and understand the objective of the particular consultation and to focus and scope the analysis and representation accordingly. Otherwise, the process can grow beyond the time and resource commitments. Moreover, past a certain point, the returns of the consultation, analysis and argument mapping will begin to diminish.

A background colour was assigned to pro (green) and con (red) nodes. This enables fast recognition of argument direction. Van Gelder in (Kirschner et al., 2003, p. 101) states, "*colour can be used to indicate in a matter of milliseconds whether a claim is being presented as reason or an objection. In prose, the reader has to interpret the claim and its context to figure out its role in the argument*".

(4) A fourth level of detail that can be added to consultation maps is the inter-theme relationships of discourse argumentation represented via the use of *cross-links* (See *Map 13.4*). This displays the inherent complexity and wickedness of public consultation on regional planning. Wicked problems are not linear, thus consultation map design should incorporate nonlinear relational design. It is the position of the author that cross-links make explicit, the emergent complexity in wicked environments and the consequential relationships required for a synthesised view and consideration of overall problem content. In support of this view, Dansereau (2005) proposes that gestalt features and content-specific structures should match the domain characteristics.

From concept mapping, cross-links act to represent nonlinear relationships (Novak & Canas, 2006). Relationships within a concept map that crossover from one topical segment or domain to another can be made explicit and represented visually via the use of cross-links. Furthermore, Novak and Canas (2006) suggest that identifying new cross-links can lead to creative insights. This highlights the non-linear complexity of consultation content and the potential multifaceted effect of policy decisions. Tillers (2007) posits that the generally proposed solution to problem complexity is to simplify it (i.e. reduce detail). Yet, he suspects that this is the wrong approach. Tillers (2007, p. 3) stated that "*effort should be made to develop tools that make it possible for human decision makers to increase (rather than decrease) the number of evidential premises and evidential inferences that decision makers should try to consider*".

A distinguishing design for cross-links in consultation maps is preferred. Link line colour in Compendium represents specific IBIS inference; therefore, the use of colour to distinguish cross-links is less effective. The use of *dotted lines* (carrying their genesis theme colour) is appropriate but not yet a feature in Compendium.

13. Modelling in Consultative Democracy Around Wicked Problems

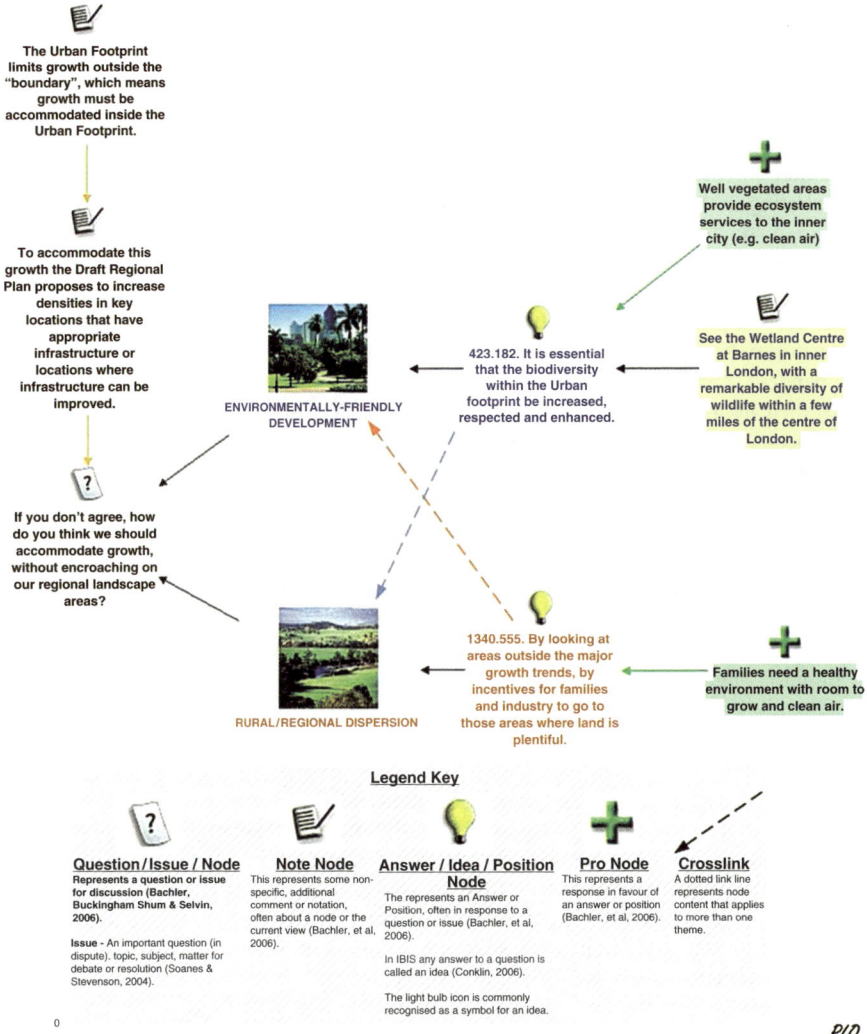

Map 13.4. Question 7. Map 13.4 shows the d-SEQ-RP participant submissions in response to the e-Consultation question 7. It provides a simple illustration of cross-links used to show inter-theme relationships between discourse argumentation.

Furthermore, including links for child nodes that cross to multiple parent nodes creates a *heterarchical* rather than a *hierarchical* map typology (Diaper, 2004). Heterarchical maps are also a space saving option because they eliminate the need to duplicate nodes if they apply to multiple themes and space saving is important for high volume content representation. Yet the added sophistication cross-links create can be a hindrance, especially for novices. Accordingly, the ability to turn cross-links on and off could be a useful feature.

13.6.6 Draft SEQ Regional Plan Consultation Analysis Findings

Using a CSAV tool (Compendium) and qualitative text analysis tools, an independent analysis of the d-SEQ-RP e-Consultation discourse drew out 11 major themes of public concern (PC) relating to the subject environmental atmosphere. Consultation maps presented explicit evidence of verbatim public responses contributing to themes, whereas the government reports did not.

Contrasting these 11 (PC) themes with themes in the atmosphere section of two primary government reports (i.e. the Consultation Report on the draft SEQ Regional Plan, and the SEQ Regional Plan), six of the (PC) themes were reported explicitly, three were implicit, two were not reported in the context of atmosphere, and one of these two was explicitly not supported by the government. This highlights that the independent analysis of the draft SEQ Regional Plan Consultation discourse, performed by a layperson (i.e. regional planning), was able to arrive at very similar conclusions (i.e. public issues determination) using CSAV as a government agency of experts. The consultation maps also made explicit all public themes as opposed to the selective representation provided in the government reports.

The consultation maps explicated the inter-theme relationships between public issues; the government reports did not. The maps explicitly align all atmosphere themes with related government policy; the government reports did not. The consultation maps also explicitly represented the ongoing reporting activities for monitoring the implementation of the SEQ Regional Plan, enabling interested citizens to monitor ongoing activities; again, the government reports did not.

13.7 Conclusions

Consultative democracy for regional planning falls into the category of wicked problems where there is the potential for a high volume of heterogeneous viewpoints and conflicting logic. The government planners and analysts in this case found this to be so. The emergent complexity in this environment dictates that tools and methods to assist in the analysis of discourse and enhance its representation are applicable. Research into the d-SEQ-RP Consultation found that CSAV and an appropriate mapping strategy aided in delivering an enhanced level of transparency and accountability.

The consultation-mapping model developed from this case study is based on the IBIS ontology and incorporates a hybrid of elements from concept, dialogue, argument, debate, thematic and tree-mapping. Using elements from concept mapping to present consultation discourse aided in conceptualising and visualising the interrelationships between disparate data using a node and link multimedia display. Together with elements of Jeff Conklin's dialogue map design informed the layout of consultation maps.

A subset of concept mapping, argument mapping, builds upon concept mapping providing argumentation structure and notation. This provides a cognitive tool to scaffold the consultation discourse analysis and representation and associated decision-making. The argument visualisation provides transparent evidence of policy rationale, or lack thereof, and can expose bias in discourse and policymaking. The particular argument schema used in Consultation Maps is based on the IBIS ontology, which was specifically designed to support urban planning argumentation around wicked problems. The Compendium notation and software used is also a derivative of the Issue Based Information System. Compendium provided a rich multimedia environment with a level of argumentation flexibility required in consultative democracy that is not afforded by many other argument visualisation approaches and technologies. The multimedia environment acted to enhance discourse assimilation beyond the typical prose discourse in threaded discussion forums currently used in e-Democracy engagement.

A thematic discourse display aids to chunk complex discourse into meaningful segments to assist content assimilation. It further functions to display evidence of the discourse analysis and synthesisation approach followed. Themes elicited from consultation discourse (i.e. representing patterns of citizen concerns) were then traced to policy decisions and these relationships were explicated in consultation maps.

Tree-maps and their derivatives are capable of displaying large amounts of information within a limited display space and therefore can be applied to visualise large hierarchies (Nguyen & Huang, 2005; Shneiderman & Wattenberg, 2001). This offers a tool with which to address the current knowledge management limitations (i.e. search functionality) in many argument visualisation technologies.

Consultation mapping provides a visual display of the heterogeneous viewpoints in a consultation in a detailed and synthesised representation so that focused detail can be assimilated within its context. It provides a visual display showing participants that their contributions have been acknowledged and recorded. It provided explicit evidence of consultation discourse analysis linked with ultimate consultation-related policies. This enables participants to follow rationale leading to policy decisions. Furthermore, a link between policy and implementation activities was made in the consultation maps, which would enable participants to monitor progress. Finally, the consultation maps provide a record available for reflection and reuse.

Contrasting the findings gained, from the independent analysis of the consultation discourse using CSAV and consultation mapping, with the government's findings recorded in the two primary reports from the draft SEQ Regional Plan Consultation revealed that the tool and map model was able to provide considerable benefits in both discourse analysis and representation. These findings represent benefits for government analysts/planners and the consultation citizenry.

References

Bentivegna, S. (2006). Rethinking Politics in the World of ICTs. *European Journal of Communication, 21*(3), 331–343.
Black, E., Jelinek, F., Lafferty, J., Mercer, R., & Roukos, S. (1992). *Decision tree models applied to the labeling of text with parts of speech.* Paper presented at the 1992 DARPA Speech and Natural Language Workshop.
Buchanan, R. (1992). Wicked Problems in Design Thinking. *Design Issues, 8*(2), 5–21.

Buckingham Shum, S. (1997, 24–26, March). *Representing Hard-to-Formalise, Contextualised, Multidisciplinary, Organisational Knowledge.* Paper presented at the AAAI Spring Symposium on Artificial Intelligence in Knowledge Management, Stanford University, Palo Alto: US.

Charmaz, K. (2006). Constructing Grounded Theory: A Practical Guide through Qualitative Analysis. New York, US: Sage Publications Ltd.

Chintalapani, G., Plaisant, C., & Shneiderman, B. (2004). *Extending the Utility of Treemaps with Flexible Hierarchy.* Paper presented at the Information Visualisation, Eighth International Conference on (IV'04) London, England.

Clift, S. (2002). E-Governance to E-Democracy: Progress in Australia and New Zealand toward Information-Age Democracy. Retrieved 15th April, 2004, from http://www.publicus.net/

Coleman, S., & Gotze, J. (2001). Bowling Together: Online Public Engagement in Policy Deliberation. London: Hansard Society.

Coleman, S., & Norris, D. (2005). *A New Agenda for e-Democracy.* Oxford, UK: Oxford Internet Institute (OII): Oxford University.

Conklin, J. (2006). Dialogue Mapping: Building Shared Understanding of Wicked Problems. Brisbane, Australia: Wiley.

Dansereau, D. (2005). Node-Link Mapping Principles for Visualizing Knowledge and Information. In S. Tergan & T. Keller (Eds.), *Knowledge Visualization and Information Visualization: Searching for Synergies.* (pp. 61–81). Berlin Heidelberg New York: Springer.

Diaper, D. (2004). Understanding Task Analysis for Human–Computer Interaction. In D. Diaper & N. Stanton (Eds.), *The Handbook of Task Analysis for Human–Computer Interaction.* (pp. 650). New Jersey, US: Lawrence Erlbaum Associates.

Elliman, T., Macintosh, A., & Irani, Z. (2006, July 6–7 2006). *Argument Maps as Policy Memories for Informed Deliberation: A Research Note.* Paper presented at the European and Mediterranean Conference on Information Systems (EMCIS), Costa Blanca, Alicante, Spain.

Englebart, D. (1963). Conceptual Framework for the Augmentation of Man's Intellect. In *Vistas in Information Handling* (pp. 1–29). Washington, DC: London: Spartan Books.

Glaser, B. (1992). *Basics of Grounded Theory Analysis.* Mill Valley, US: Sociology Press.

Gordon, T., Macintosh, A., & Renton, A. (2007). *Argumentation Support Systems.* UK: DEMO-net: The Democracy Network.

Heuer, R. (1999). Psychology of Intelligence Analysis. Retrieved 15 May, 2007, from http://www.odci.gov/csi/books/19104/index.html

Kirschner, P., Buckingham Shum, S., & Carr, C.E. (2003). *Visualizing Argumentation: Software Tools for Collaborative and Educational Sense-Making.* Berlin Heidelberg New York: Springer.

Kirshchner, P., Buckingham Shum, S., & Carr, C.E. (2003). *Visualizing Argumentation: Software Tools for Collaborative and Educational Sense-Making.* Berlin Heidelberg New York: Springer.

Kuklinski, J. (2001). *Citizens and Politics: Perspectives from Political Psychology.* Cambridge, UK: Cambridge University Press.

Macintosh, A. (2006). eParticipation in policy-making: the research and the challenges. In P. Cunningham and M. Cunningham (Eds.), *Exploiting the Knowledge Economy: Issues, Applications and Case Studies.* (pp. 364–369). Washington, US: IOS press.

Macintosh, A., & Renton, A. (2004, 27–29 October). *Argument Visualisation to Support Democratic Decision-Making.* Paper presented at the eChallenges e.2004 Conference, Vienna, Austria.

Mackenzie, A., Pidd, M., Rooksby, J., Sommerville, I., Warren, I., & Westcombe, M. (2005). Wisdom, decision support and paradigms of decision making. *European Journal of Operational Research, Article in Press*, 19.

Maguitman, A., Leake, D., Reichherzer, T., & Menczer, F. (2004, November 8–13). *Dynamic Extraction of Topic Descriptors and Discriminators: Towards Automatic Context-Based Topic Search.* Paper presented at the ACM International Conference on Information and Knowledge Management (CIKM '04), Washington, D.C., US.

Marshall, B., & Madhusudan, T. (2004, June 7–11). *Element Matching in Concept Maps.* Paper presented at the the fourth ACM and IEEE Joint Conference on Digital Libraries (JCDL-2004), Tucson: US.

Mayer, R. (2005). *The Cambridge Handbook of Multimedia Learning.* New York, US: Cambridge University Press.

Miller, G. (1956). The Magic Number Seven, Plus or Minus Two: Some Limits on Our Capacity to Process Information. *The Psychological Review, 63*, 81–97.

Miller, M., & Riechert, B. (1994). *Identifying Themes via Concept Mapping: A New Method of Content Analysis.* Paper presented at the the Theory and Methodology Division, Association for Education in Journalism and Mass Communication Annual Meeting.

Nguyen, Q., & Huang, M. (2005). EncCon: an approach to constructing interactive visualization of large hierarchical data. *Information Visualization, 4*, 1–21.

Novak, J., & Canas, A. (2006). *The Theory Underlying Concept Maps and How to Construct Them.*: Florida Institute for Human and Machine Cognition.

OECD. (2004). Promise and Problems of e-Democracy: Challenges of Online Citizen Engagement: Organisation for Economic Co-operation and Development.

Parsons, W. (2006). Innovation in the public sector: spare tyres and fourth plinths. *The Innovation Journal: The Public Sector Innovation Journal, 11*(2), 10.

Peterson, L., & Peterson, M. (1959). Short-term Retention of Individual Verbal Items. *Journal of Experimental Psychology, 58*, 193–198.

Queensland Government: Office of Urban Management. (2005). *South East Queensland Regional Plan 2005–2026.* Brisbane: Department of Local Government, Planning, Sport and Recreation.

Renton, A., & Macintosh, A. (2007). Computer-Supported Argument Maps as a Policy Memory. *The Information Society, 23*(2), 125–133.

Repovs, G., & Baddeley, A. (2006). The Multi-Component Model of Working Memory: Explorations in Experimental Cognitive Psychology. *Neuroscience, 139*, 5–21.

Rittel, H., & Webber, M. (1973). Dilemmas in a General Theory of Planning. *Policy Sciences, 4*, 155–169.

Rittel, H., & Webber, M. (1984). *Planning Problems are Wicked Problems.* New Jersey, US: Wiley.

Shneiderman, B. (1992). Tree visualization with tree-maps: 2-d space-filling approach. *ACM Transactions on Graphics (TOG), 11*(1), 92–99.

Shneiderman, B. (2006). Treemaps for space-constrained visualization of hierarchies. Retrieved 14 May, 2007, from http://www.cs.umd.edu/hcil/treemap-history/

Shneiderman, B., & Wattenberg, M. (2001). *Ordered Treemap Layouts.* Paper presented at the IEEE Symposium on Information Visualization., Los Alamitos, US.

Slocum, T., McMaster, R., Kessler, F., & Howard, H. (2005). *Thematic Cartography and Geographic Visualization. 2nd Edition.* New York, US: Prentice Hall.

Strauss, A., & Corbin, J. (1990). Basics of Qualitative Research: Grounded Theory Procedures and Techniques (1st ed.). Thousand Oaks, US: SAGE Publications.

Strauss, A., & Corbin, J. (1998). Basics of Qualitative Research: Techniques and Procedures for Developing Grounded Theory. Thousand Oaks, US: SAGE Publications.

Tillers, P. (2007). Introduction: Visualizing Evidence and Inference in Legal Settings. *Law, Probability and Risk, 6*(1–4), 1–6.

United Nations (2004). *United Nations Global E-Government Readiness Report 2004: Towards Access for Opportunity.* New York: Department of Economic and Social Affairs, Division for Public Administration and Development Management.

United Nations (2005). *United Nations Global e-Government Readiness Report 2005: From e-Government to E-Inclusion.* New York: Department of Economic and Social Affairs, Division for Public Administration and Development Management.

Vedel, T. (2006). The Idea of Electronic Democracy: Origins, Visions and Questions. *Parliamentary Affairs, 59*(2), 226–235.

Whyte, A., & Macintosh, A. (2001). Transparency and Teledemocracy: Issues from an 'E-Consultation. *Journal of Information Science, 27*(4), 187–198.

Yoshimi, J. (2004). Mapping the Structure of Debate. *Informal Logic, 24*(1).

Zhao, S., McGuffin, M., & Chignell, M. (2005). *Elastic Hierarchies: Combining Treemaps and Node-Link Diagrams.* Paper presented at the 2005 IEEE Symposium on Information Visualization, Washington: US.

14. Human-Agent Knowledge Cartography for e-Science: NASA Field Trials at the Mars Desert Research Station

Maarten Sierhuis[1] and Simon Buckingham Shum[2]

[1]Human-Centered Computing, NASA/Ames Research Center, Moffett Field, California, 94035, USA, Maarten.Sierhuis-1@nasa.gov
[2]Knowledge Media Institute, The Open University, Milton Keynes, Buckinghamshire, MK7 6AA, UK, sbs@acm.org

Abstract. This chapter describes the sociotechnical embedding of a knowledge cartography approach (*Conversational Modelling*) within a prototype e-science work system. This was evaluated over two 2-week field trials, simulating collaborative Mars-Earth geological exploration. We believe this work is the first demonstration of a knowledge mapping tool embedded within a human/software multiagent work system, with humans and agents reading and writing structures amenable to agent understanding and autonomous agent execution, and human understanding, annotation and argumentation. Secondly, in terms of the applied problem, we have demonstrated how human and agent plans, data, multimedia documents, metadata, discussions, interpretations and arguments can be mapped in an integrated manner, and successfully deployed in field trials which simulated aspects of mission workload pressure.

14.1 Introduction

At the time of writing, two NASA robotic rovers continue to explore the surface of Mars, over 3 years after landing in January 2004. While this and other missions astound us by what is possible with machine space exploration, there is much work already under way for human exploration. NASA is now planning to return to the moon, as the first step towards human exploration of Mars, a goal shared by the European Space Agency's Aurora programme. The work we report is part of NASA's human-centred computing programme whose research is to inform the creation of an effective and sustainable e-science work system between scientists on Earth and their astronaut colleagues on space missions. While interplanetary collaborative working is an extreme challenge with some unique features, the lessons we are learning are relevant to other projects confronting the challenges of distributed team working on one planet, such as simply Earth-based.

Our objective in this chapter is to describe how a particular form of knowledge cartography, called *Conversational Modelling,* has been used in realistic analogue simulations of collaboration between scientists on Mars and Earth referred to as

Mars-Earth scientific collaboration. We describe how the technical platform for Conversational Modelling, the *Compendium* tool (see also Chaps. 11, 12, 13) was embedded within NASA's broader Mobile Agents e-science work system, including people, robots, and software agents (Clancey et al., 2001, 2002, 2004, 2006). We are prototyping tools not only for information sharing, but also for key *sensemaking* activities in which the information is interpreted and reified in forms suitable for communication and interpretation by human colleagues and software agents.

To set the context, we first introduce Compendium as a knowledge cartography research platform, architected to support interoperability with other tools, and the Conversational Modelling approach. We then introduce the NASA *Mobile Agents* project that has been designing and testing a Mars-Earth scientific collaboration work system, and explain the workflow supported by Compendium and Conversational Modelling in the analogue Mars mission simulations conducted at the Mars Desert Research Station in Utah. Attention then turns to the different genres of knowledge maps that evolved to support this process, and various evaluation indices we can use to reflect on the impact of this work. We then draw together our conclusions to date, and future work.[1]

14.2 Compendium

14.2.1 User Interface

A technical objective of this work was to engage the tools and methods in their current state of development in non-trivial field tests, and from an action research perspective. The primary tool we used was Compendium [CompendiumInstitute.org] since (a) it has been designed from the start as a sensemaking-support environment and so in principle had the potential to support the mission, and (b) we had expert users who could support *both* the Mars crew (the Crew) and the remote science team on Earth (the RST). Providing Compendium as a sensemaking-support tool to expert users is core to the vision of integrated Mars-Earth knowledge management. Compendium is a hypermedia tool providing a virtual canvas (a "map") on which one can arrange and structure nodes (Fig. 14.1). Nodes may be *data* in any medium. Nodes may also correspond to *ideas* (e.g. open issues; scientific hypotheses; theories arguments; evidence; decisions) or *entities* in a domain being modelled (e.g. experiments; services; data; substances; devices). Nodes may simply be clustered spatially, or can be optionally *linked* using unclassified or classified arrows. Compendium provides, therefore, a visual environment for personal or group information management, scaling by embedding maps within maps.

Compendium maps are not flat drawings, but multi-dimensional views onto a relational database that can be rendered in multiple formats, and accessed directly by other services to read/write content. The hypertext "transclusion" feature (Nelson, 1987) enables a given node to appear and be updated in multiple views, that is, be given one or more meaningful contexts where it plays a role; as a result of

---

[1] Interactive web exports of the maps in this chapter, plus other materials, are presented on the project website: www.kmi.open.ac.uk/projects/coakting/nasa

transclusion, corrections or updates to a node are immediately updated in every context in which it appears.

Semantic richness (such as additional node typing or categorization) is added to nodes through user-definable *tags* (metadata keywords) assigned to any concept (node) in the database to show connections through membership in a common category. This form of open-ended classification has been popularised in recent years by social bookmarking "folksonomic" websites. Tags serve to specialize a node type with as many facets as required for it to play multiple roles in different contexts. At the end of the session all of the nodes so marked can be harvested, using a simple search algorithm. In modelling, nodes sharing a tag are often tracked as a library of nodes stored for future reuse. Tags may reflect generic meeting processes (e.g. *Action-Jane*), or may be driven by an underlying methodology that Compendium is being used to support (e.g. *Data-Provider*). Alternatively, ad hoc tags can be created on the fly, to reflect the emergence of a new theme. In short, tags are used to define meaning of a node in different contexts. Both, people and software agent can assign and use tags, based on specific rules that are in affect in different contexts.

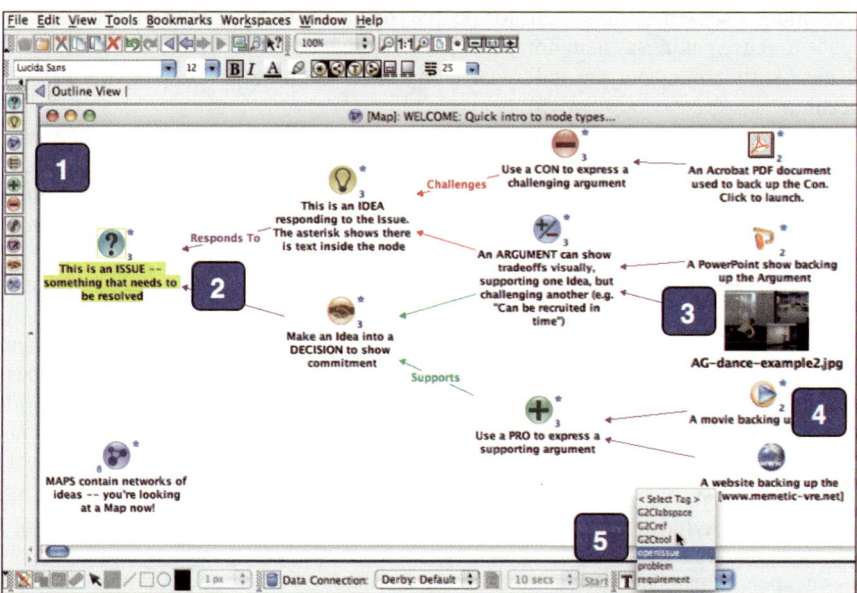

Fig. 14.1. Compendium's visual language for IBIS, the Issue-Based Information System. Key to the numbered elements in the image: (1) Drag and drop nodes from the palette on the left of the screen onto the map. (2) Question-, light-bulb-, and handshake icons with (named) links in order to capture and link key issues, ideas, arguments and decisions. (3) Relevant media resources/websites can be linked into this discussion. (Users can also create their own palettes of icons.) (4) A digit superimposed on a node means that it appears in more than one map, i.e. the same idea or document can play roles in multiple contexts and conversations, yet be linked. (5) User-defined keyword tags can be annotated onto nodes to help when searching for related material across multiple maps.

14.2.2 IBIS-based Conversational Modelling

Although it can be used for any kind of concept mapping, as shown in Fig. 14.1, Compendium comes "pre-loaded" with a visual language (icons, node types, and link types) for the Issue-Based Information System (IBIS) as proposed by Rittel (Rittel, 1972; Rittel et al., 1973) for tackling open-ended, ill-defined problems. IBIS provides a simple notation for connecting key *issues*, possible *responses* to these, and relevant *arguments*. Our previous work (Buckingham Shum et al., 2006a) has described how we have evolved a set of practices for using Compendium and IBIS, which extends the use of IBIS from capturing a free-form discussion in real time [a skill termed *Dialogue Mapping* – (Conklin, 2005)], to include more systematic domain modelling [termed *Conversational* Modelling – (Selvin, 1999)].

A modelling approach focuses attention on a specific subset of issues and information, it may constrain the kinds of options one considers, and it may also focus attention on how one assesses them. A modelling approach also provides a syntactic and semantic framework (context) of rules that the users of the approach must obey in order for them to reach common understanding. This is *useful* for developing a sensemaking system for people; however, it is *necessary* if we want to create a sensemaking system for people interacting with software agents. This is, because software agents can only deal with concepts (nodes) if they have a formal meaning.

Our hypothesis at the start of the project was that to bridge the gap between people, who need to mix informal and formal sensemaking representations, and software agents, using a modelling tool that integrates both approaches is a possible solution for human-agent sensemaking interaction. Compendium was selected as the tool, because it provides both informal and formal representation capability.

In Compendium, a modelling approach is translated into a set of linked *issue templates*, which can also be created to deal with any well understood situation where there is a recommended approach to proceed (for instance, from best practice or a standard operating procedure). Compendium templates typically structure nodes with predefined tags, creating formal structure, and formal node metadata. Node and link labels may be left informal, intended only for human interpretation, or constrained in content for agent interpretation.

14.2.3 A Knowledge Cartography Research Platform

As an open research platform, with freely available source code, Compendium is distinctive from other tools in the effort that has been invested in designing for integration with the "matrix" of other work system tools. Compendium is implemented as a cross-platform Java application that can swap between either the MySQL or Apache Derby relational databases. SQL and XML export/import assists data interoperability between clients and servers, and Semantic Web projects have added RDF compliant with different schemas (CoAKTinG, 2004; Memetic, 2006). Public Java application interface classes provide an interface for other systems to read and write to the database directly, so maps can be generated from another data source or interpreted for processing by another system. A shared MySQL database on a local area network supports rudimentary client-server architecture, but this is not optimised for internet access which can be slow. Data can be published to the Web as interactive image maps of concept/node networks or linear HTML outline documents (designed also to be accessible to screen-readers for visually impaired users). Web exports can be processed by extensions we have added to the open source *Moodle* e-learning content management system (OpenLearn, 2007).

Application-specific services (such as agent interoperability or map structure analysis) can be implemented over this substrate. For the Mobile Agents field trials, Compendium was linked into the Brahms multiagent infrastructure (Clancey, 1998; Sierhuis, 2001) by providing a Compendium software agent with access to read and write concept maps to the database. As illustrated below, issue templates – maps using predefined models of consistent concept network layout and tagging – could be interpreted by the software agents as Extra-Vehicle Activity plans,[2] and then populated by software agents or persons with captured science data over time, with metadata, as the science data was received from an EVA astronaut or from an EVA robotic assistant (i.e. a robot).

14.3 Embedding Conversational Modelling in e-Science Workflow

In a manned mission to Mars, the crew will necessarily be small, and must collaborate with scientists back on Earth, who themselves will work together in a distributed manner. NASA's Mars Exploration Rover mission[3] has demonstrated that it is not practical to co-locate all the experts needed for multi-year missions. Designing collaboration support between the *Crew* and *Remote Science Team* (RST) raises some basic questions for designing computer-supported distributed cognition for science teams. The key challenge in this scenario is to manage, under continuous time pressure and with a high cost of errors, the gathering of science data and metadata, followed by its interpretation on both Mars and Earth, in order to inform scientific reasoning and decision-making for timely subsequent explorations. Furthermore, long time delays for communication between Mars and Earth make it impossible to have instantaneous communication between the two parties, making sharing of contextual (semantic) concept maps an ideal tool for collaboration over time and space. Although interplanetary collaboration has unique demands, the planning, collection and interpretation of information across time an space are tasks common to many Earth-bound e-science contexts, indeed, to knowledge-intensive work across all organisational sectors.

NASA's *Mobile Agents Project* is a multi-year, multi-research team project bringing together human-centered work systems design, multi-agent systems, speech dialogue, robotics, networking, semantic web, and knowledge media. Throughout this process, the Mobile Agents Architecture (MAA) provides a means for modelling, simulating, implementing and managing a computer-supported Mars/Earth-based

---

[2] Extra-Vehicle Activity is work performed by an astronaut outside the space craft.
[3] NASA's Mars Exploration Rover (MER) Mission is an ongoing unmanned Mars exploration mission, commenced in 2003, which sent two robotic rovers Spirit and Opportunity to explore the Martian surface and geology.

science work system. It is implemented in the *Brahms* and Java programming languages. Brahms is an agent-oriented language (Wooldridge, 2002; Bordini et al., 2005) that provides a situated cognition perspective on the modelling of work practices (Clancey et al., 1998; Sierhuis, 2001; Clancey et al., 2005; Sierhuis et al., 2005). Every team in the Mobile Agents project integrates their research software and hardware with the Brahms MAA. The MAA is a multi-agent workflow engine that connects all systems together and enables the deployment of a holistic exploration workflow system (Clancey et al., 2004).

The Mars Desert Research Station (MDRS) provides a mission testbed for identifying requirements, competitively testing alternative technologies/protocols, and training astronauts. Figure 14.2 shows photos of the MDRS "Habitat", and astronauts on an EVA, gathering geological samples, and recording photos and voicenotes.

Fig. 14.2. The Mars Desert Research Station Habitat (the Hab) where the Crew lives, and the field geologist astronauts on an EVA to gather data.

The Mobile Agents 2004 field trial introduced a new research strand to MDRS analogue research, concerning collaboration with the RST who worked as a truly virtual team from offices and homes in California, New York state, and in two UK universities. Some members had never met physically (indeed, have yet to), simply being introduced by the project leader, and learning to work together via telephone, email, and shared documents via conventional office tools and a suite of collaboration tools. To explain the different roles played by the Compendium maps, it helps to have an overview of the workflow.

Figure 14.3 depicts the workflow of a typical EVA, explaining at what points Compendium is used:

1. The crew has a pre-EVA meeting in the habitat. This meeting is videotaped, and facilitated and captured via Compendium.
2. Both video and hypertext database is downlinked to Earth. A web-based MeetingReplay tool is automatically created from both the video and the Compendium database. The remote science teams (RST) watch the video on the web.

3. The RST have a teleconference facilitated in Compendium over the Web.
4. The RST's briefing is sent back to the crew in Compendium.
5. Based on the RST's Compendium map, the crew creates an EVA plan in Compendium.
6. When the crew is ready to start the EVA, the crew starts the Mobile Agents Architecture and asks the HabCom agent to load in the EVA plan directly from the Compendium database.
7. The Plan Manager Assistant agent distributes the plan to all Personal Agents that manage communications on behalf of the two astronauts (Astro1, Astro2) and the EVA Robotic Assistant (ERA). The system is now ready to start the EVA.
8. During the EVA the ERA and astronauts perform the EVA plan and collecting mission data (geological photographs and voicenotes). This data flows via their Personal Agents back to the Habitat and are stored in Compendium (and another NASA database called ScienceOrganizer). Not shown in the figure is that email alerts are also sent to the RST notifying them of new data, and that the Compendium database is then mirrored on Earth for the RST.

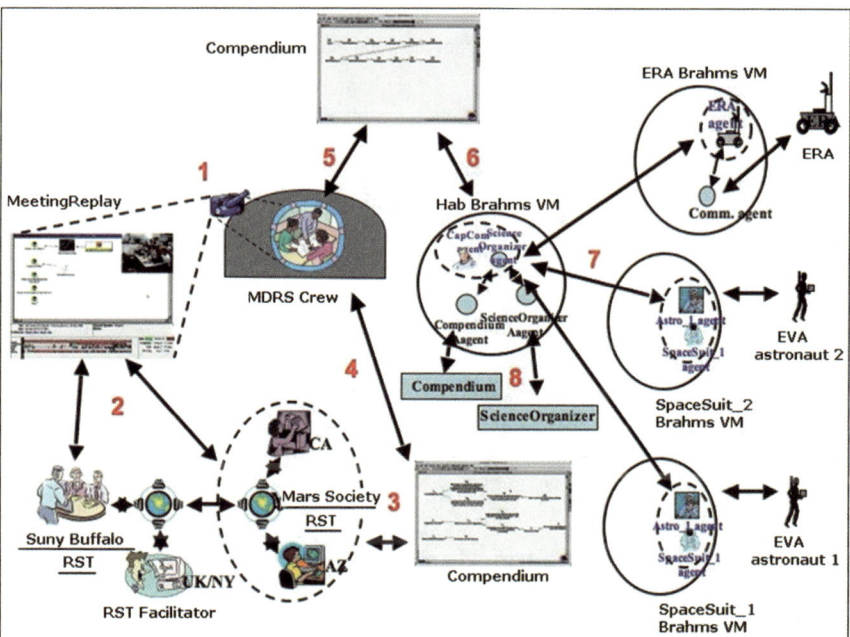

Fig. 14.3. Workflow to plan, gather and analyse geological data in an EVA using the Mobile Agents architecture.

This chapter provides answers to a number of questions with respect to Compendium's representational expressiveness and usability:

- Can the RST and/or Crew specify plans in Compendium that can be read and executed by software agents?
- Can the scientists in the Crew communicate their daily plans for an EVA to the RST via Compendium?
- Can Compendium enable the RST to propose EVA plans for the Crew?
- In what ways can Compendium support post-EVA analysis of the collected science data?
- Will the RST be able to provide useful feedback to the Crew via Compendium in a form that can be absorbed in a timely manner?

In the two field trials, all RST teleconferences were audio and screen recorded, resulting in an archive of digital screen movies. All Crew meetings were video and screen recorded for integration within the Meeting Replay tool, and again, providing raw data for analysis. Table 14.1 below summarises the number of EVAs and different data types, to give an indication of the datasets that scientists in each 2-week field trial generated and managed.

Table 14.1. EVAs and datasets from the 2004 and 2005 2-week field trials.

Field test	EVAs	Locations	Images	Image collections	Voicenotes	Panoramas	Sample bags
2004	4	20	140	15	19	12	21
2005	6	89	221	29	55	1	15
Total	10	109	361	44	74	13	36

To summarise, Compendium was used as both a personal and group knowledge mapping tool *within the RST*, *between the RST and the Crew*, and *between the Crew and software agents* supporting the planning and execution of EVAs.

14.4 Genres of Compendium Map

14.4.1 Mediating Between the Crew and Software Agents

In the 2004 field trial, the Crew used a set of interlinked issue-templates to plan the route of the next EVA (Fig. 14.4), constructing a visual map of the locations they wanted to visit and the activities to be conducted at each. These Compendium maps were then interpreted by the agents that coordinated commands and the flow of information during an EVA.

In the 2005 field trial, the RST took over the role of specifying the EVA plan. The RST worked through the templates, guided by their structure rather like completing a form, supported by the facilitator. However, an instance of the EVA plan template could be annotated using standard IBIS, e.g. with a rich description for the Crew of the activity to be undertaken, or to raise a query. The use of the EVA plan template enables the RST (or Crew) to formally communicate EVA plans for the software agent (formal in the sense that the EVA plan templates specifies the formal semantic of the EVA plan, using map-, question-, and position nodes using tags to specify EVA plan concept types). At the same time, the RST can use IBIS representations to communicate informally with the Crew (informal communication in the sense that Compendium does not force how to use IBIS formalisms).

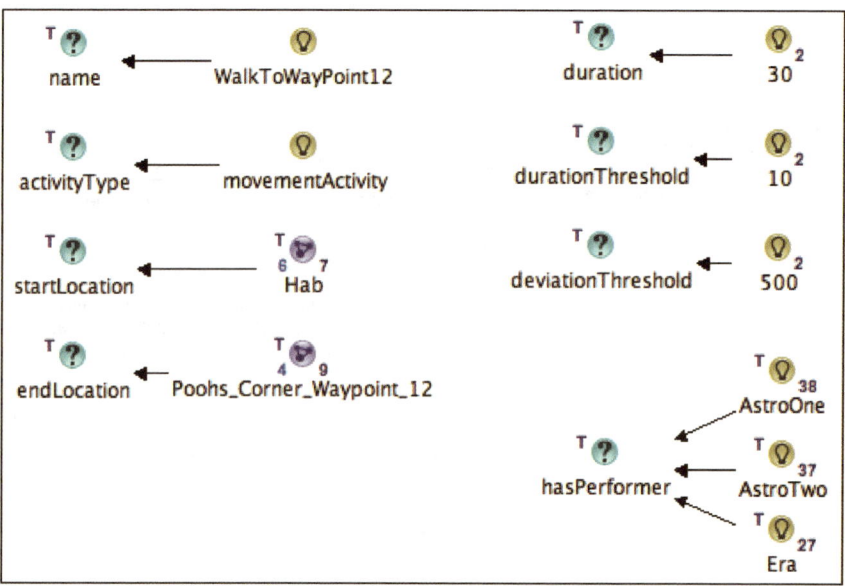

Fig. 14.4. An EVA plan constructed by the Crew in Compendium using a Conversational Modelling template (in this example the EVA Activity template). This plan is read by the Brahms software agents that coordinated the EVA work flow.

14.4.2 Viewing Science Data and Metadata

All the data generated during an EVA (360 degree panoramic photos taken by robots, plus photographs and voice annotations recorded by astronauts) are stored in the Compendium database by a software agent, using specific predefined Compendium templates. Compendium renders the data and metadata as maps with nodes, links and tags (Fig. 14.5), assisting the RST and/or Crew in seeing and navigating through the systematic use of tagging and transclusion. Thus, one could easily view all data from a given astronaut (tagged *astro1*), or all data associated with a particular work activity (a *workactivity* node transcluded by the software agent into multiple data maps).

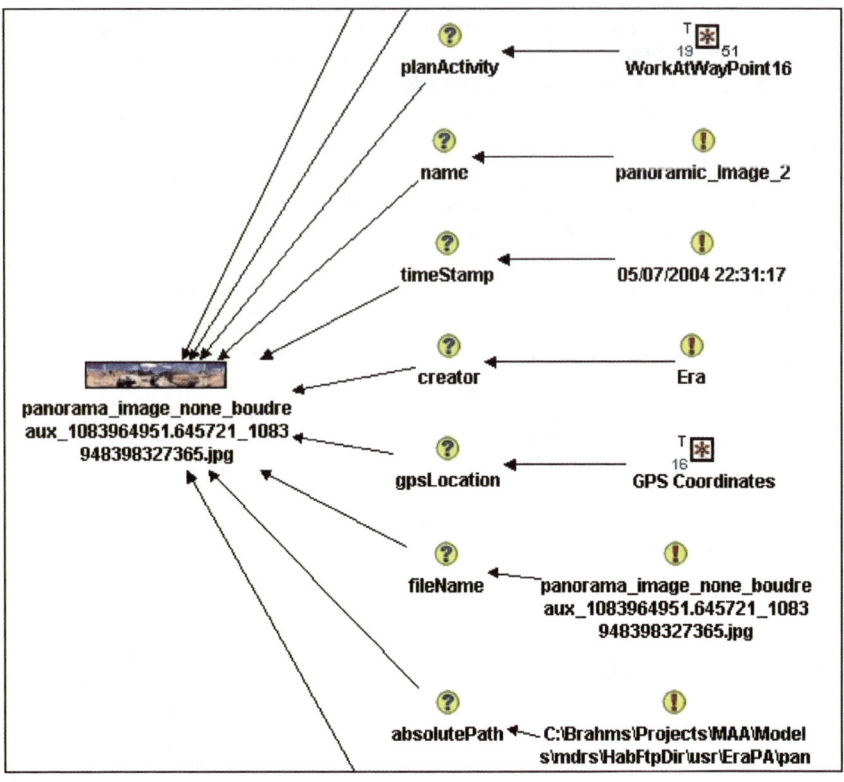

Fig. 14.5. Following the EVA, a map is created and populated in Compendium.

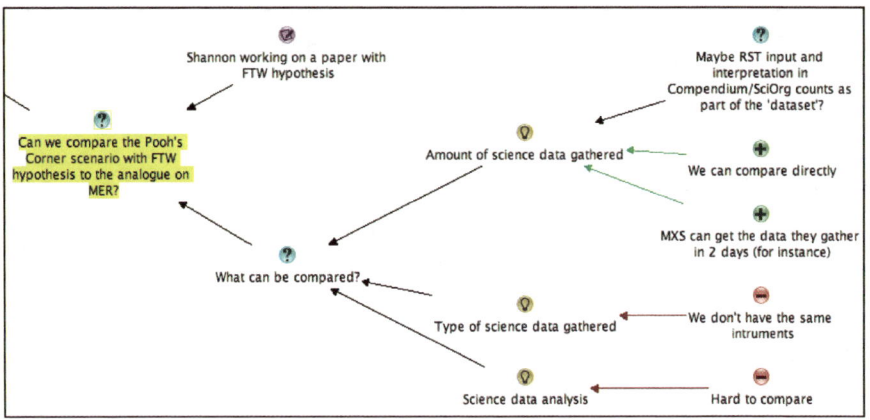

Fig. 14.6. Dialogue Mapping RST deliberation over the issues, options and tradeoffs in a methodological discussion about evaluating the field trial.

14.4.3 Crew and RST Data Analysis

As a team discussion unfolds, the contributions are simultaneously mapped on the screen (projected in the Hab in a crew meeting, or screen-shared over the internet during an RST teleconference using a desktop sharing tool). The Compendium Facilitator uses Dialogue Mapping to capture the team's discussions (e.g. Fig. 14.6).

14.4.4 Mediating RST Feedback to the Crew

Prior to the 2004 field test, the RST defined a Crew Feedback template to organise feedback to the crew. This template allows for grouping ideas as Key Feedback and Suggestions (Fig. 14.7). Every node is tagged accordingly, so that it is easy to find after a long (2+ h) meeting, and through Compendium's hypertext "transclusion" mechanism, the connection can be preserved to the original Dialogue Map in which the feedback idea had arisen. This provided traceability of the ideas for both RST and the Crew.

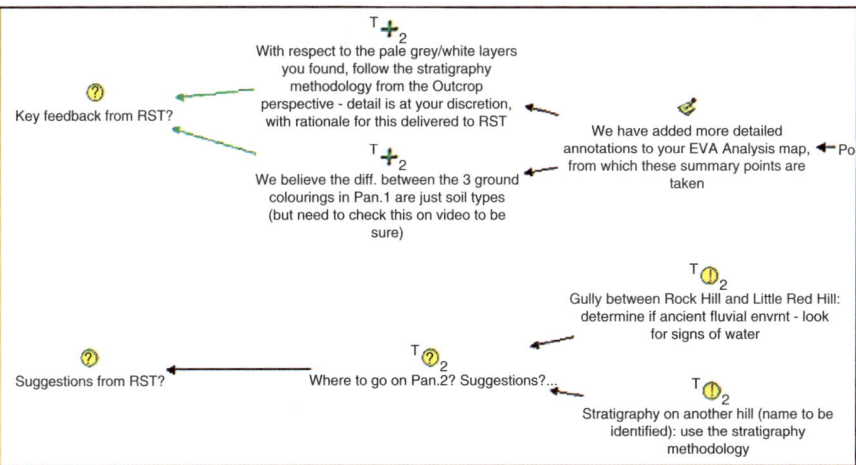

Fig. 14.7. Compendium map summarizing the RST's feedback to the crew. Each node is hyperlinked to the detailed dialogue map in which it was created, enabling recovery of the original context in which that node was recorded.

14.4.5 Knowledge Maps as Indices into Videos of Crew Meetings

The communication delay between Mars and Earth makes synchronous conversation and the sharing of computer screens impossible. In collaboration with the University of Southampton, we developed a Meeting Replay tool, which combines meeting materials within an interface structured to enable quick and easy indexing for future navigation of the meeting record. During the mission we recorded the Crew's daily EVA planning meetings and delivered a replay of the meeting over the web to the RST, within a few hours. By experimenting with these techniques we hoped to see if the RST could gain a better understanding not only what a crew is deciding, but why, and how, in order to provide the best kind of feedback.

Figure 14.8 shows the web-based Meeting Replay tool. The upper region shows the video of the meeting and the Compendium map as the discussion progresses. The lower region contains summary information about the meeting – who was there, who was speaking, the agenda, and an overview of the current topic (derived from the Compendium map). Some of this information is presented as a timeline, providing a visual index for an RST member to navigate the video, jumping to relevant or interesting parts of the discussion by clicking on the timeline or moving the slider.

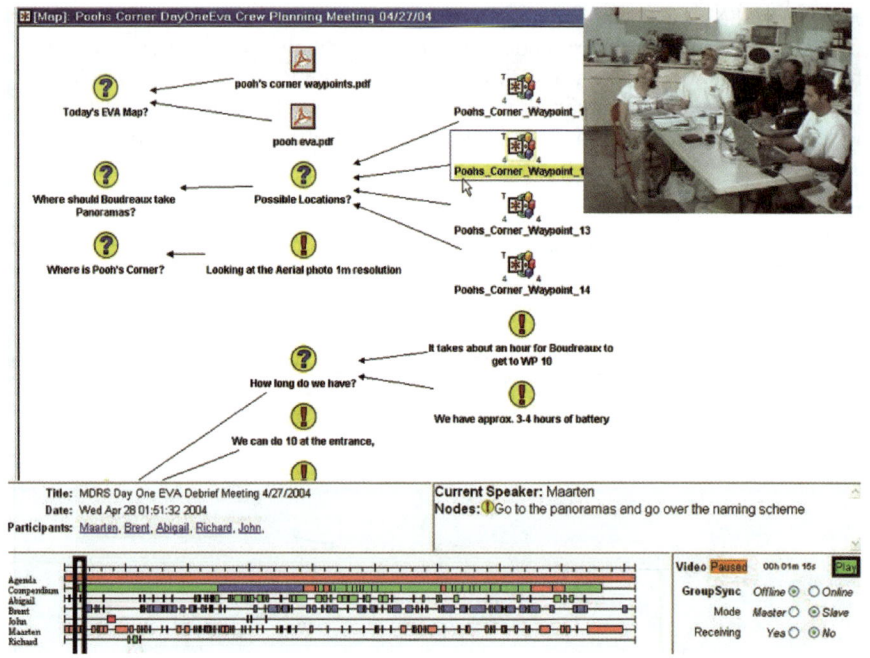

Fig. 14.8. Web-based Meeting Replay tool. When reviewing the meeting replay, Compendium has been extended so that it can be used as a "visual contents page" into the video. For instance, if the RST wants to see discussion prior to the recording of a particular decision, one can now click on this node in Compendium and the replay jumps to the point in the meeting where that node was recorded.

14.4.6 Communicating Crew Analysis to RST

During the first field test in 2004, the Crew geologists used Compendium to send back to the RST collages of photographs linked to notes and questions (Fig. 14.9). This proved to be an extremely productive way for the RST to understand how the Crew was thinking, as well as demonstrating the use of the tool in a way that the Crew geologists found intuitive.

14. Human-Agent Knowledge Cartography for e-Science   299

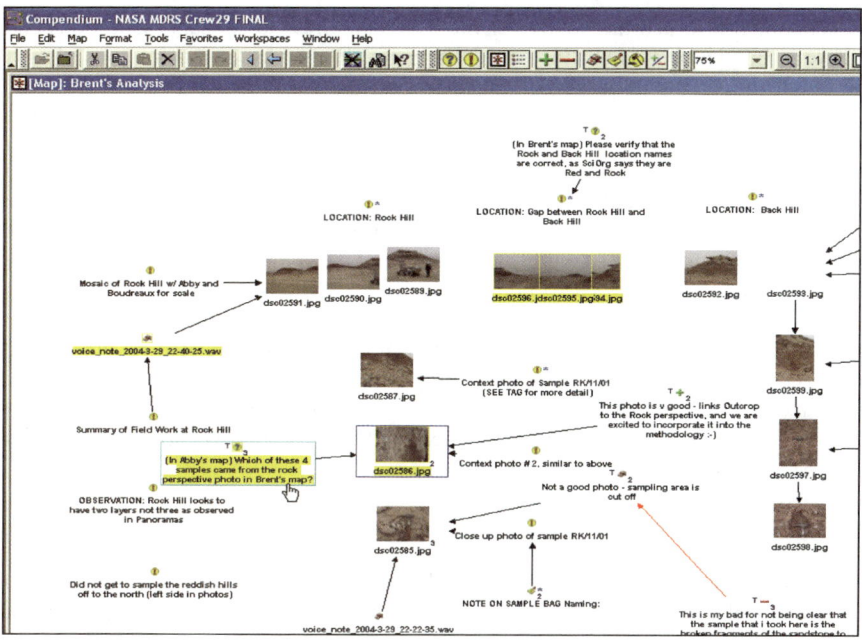

Fig. 14.9. A Crew geologist arranges and annotates his photos on returning to the Hab after an EVA, which he then sends to the RST.

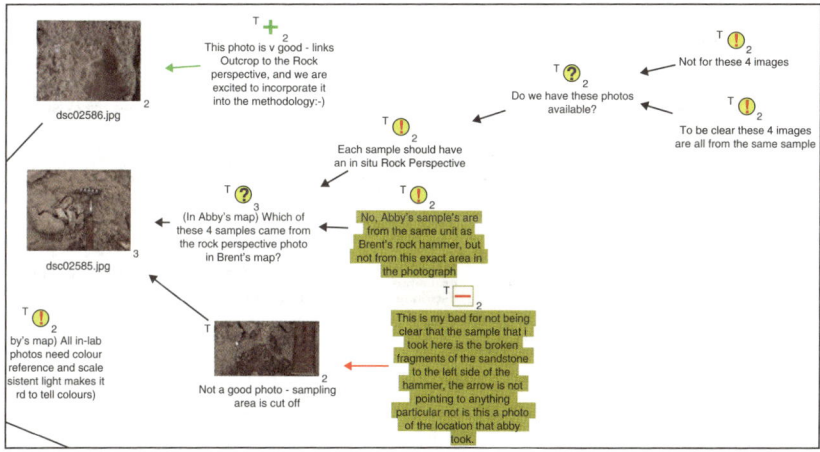

Fig. 14.10. Crew-RST exchanges about photographic data. Using Compendium as a shared canvas for collaborative analysis between the scientists on "Mars" and their remote support team on "Earth". First the scientists in the crew laid out photos of rock samples, and analysed them. The RST reviewed this and raised queries, linking them into the map, which accompanied another map containing their summary report. The crew then responded (*yellow highlighted nodes*).

This map afforded the ability for the RST and Crew to exchange questions and answers, but via a medium in which the target data under discussion was always present (Fig. 14.10).

14.4.7 RST Facilitator's Web Portal Maps

A new genre of Compendium map emerged early in the 2004 field trial, whose use became standard practice for the remainder of that field trial and into 2005. To expedite the pace at which the RST could assimilate new data as they awoke in different time zones (sometimes in the early hours), the RST Facilitator performed the lengthy EVA data download and published this to the Web as interactive image maps. The RST members then had to simply visit the URL that was circulated by email. The map highlighted the elements needed to prepare for the meeting that would otherwise be embedded in multiple emails: briefing notes from the RST Leader, the links to WebEx and the Meeting Replay, and critically, the web export version of the Crew's Compendium maps.

14.4.8 Scaffolding Scientific Methodology

With its dialogue/argument mapping capability, Compendium presented the opportunity to explore a flexible knowledge management environment for agreeing on

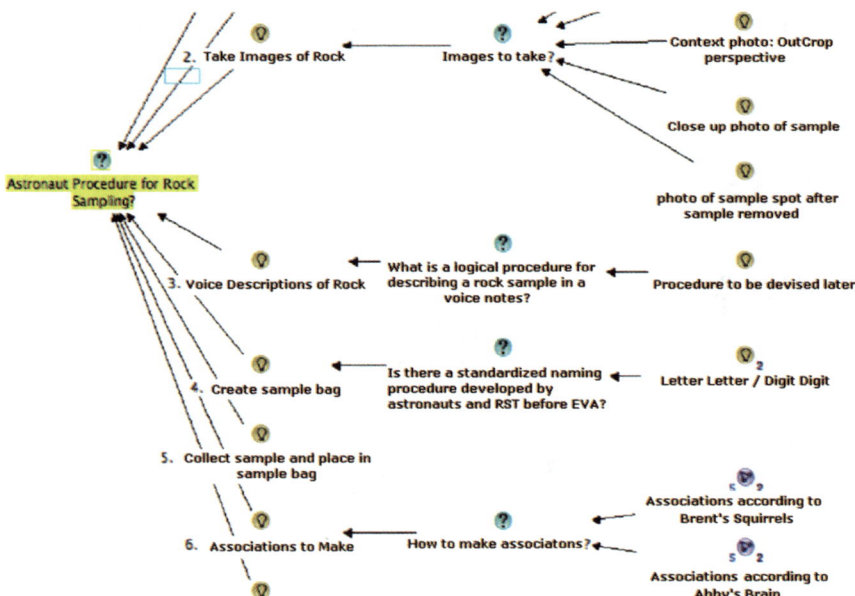

Fig. 14.11. In MDRS 2005, the rock sampling methodology, which the RST started to map in the 2004 field trial, was mapped and agreed in the Hab by the Crew Facilitator and scientist astronauts. This proved invaluable when the Crew had to operate autonomously without RST input, yet were able to collect data that was coherent to the RST.

hypotheses, and considering how incoming data might be linked as evidence. The RST Facilitator helped the RST to set up new templates to manage the links between hypotheses and data. The Crew Facilitator worked with all the scientists to map the methodology that had been started by the RST in 2004, with the result that all scientists went into the 2005 trial with agreement and ownership of how they would operate in this respect (Fig. 14.11).

14.5 Discussions and Future Work

We propose that the work reported in this chapter makes contributions with respect to the state of the art in knowledge cartography software infrastructures, and with respect to addressing a realistic distributed sensemaking problem. Firstly, we believe this work is the first demonstration of a knowledge mapping tool embedded within a human/software multiagent work system. This was sucessful due to the respective software architectures of Compendium and the Mobile Agents systems. Together, these tools assisted the creation of Compendium agents that could read EVA planning maps designed by humans, and write science data maps for human annotation and argument, through the systematic use of IBIS-based modelling templates that constrained and scaffolded different genres of Crew and RST conversation.

This was exemplified by the Crew constructing science *analysis* maps in the same Compendium database as the original EVA Plan, and by the software agent automatically stored science data. By using copy and paste (the Compendium functions to create translusions of nodes), the Crew created the analysis maps (a new information context), using the previously captured images by the software agents. This functionality, indeed, created the hypothesized human-agent collaboration capability that was envisioned at the start of the project. Formal representations were used by software agents (the EVA Plans) to capture science data automatically (software agent created maps of images, etc), which in turn were later on used by people (the Crew or the RST) to create informal representations of the science data analysis. Then people could add questions and answers to the same maps, effectively creating a shared understanding of the data and the analysis. The Compendium tool provides all these capabilities within one environment. This fluid movement along the formality continuum is central to the success of this approach, enabling transformations in all directions between informal notes, semiformal Concept and Dialogue Maps, and formal template-driven maps. We must support not only *formalization* but also *informalization*.

Secondly, in terms of the applied problem, we have demonstrated how exploration plans, science data, metadata, multimedia documents, discussions, interpretations and arguments can be mapped in an integrated manner, as a component of the larger distributed Mobile Agents work system. This human-agent work system was tested in two 2-week field trials and succeeded in simulating aspects of true mission workload pressure. The field trials demonstrated the synchronous and asynchronous media affordances of Compendium in a multiplicity of roles:

- As a way to create formal information structures for understanding by software agents, from informal discussions by people;
- As a way to navigate richly linked data and metadata in maps written by software agents;
- As a real time sensemaking environment for co-located (Crew) meetings, and for online (RST) meetings;
- as an asynchronous medium for Crew-RST exchanges;
- As an asynchronous medium for scientists (Crew and RST) to program software agents when planning EVAs;
- Combining planned, formal modelling, with interpretive scientific and project management discourse which could move in unpredictable directions.

Although the Mobile Agents Architecture is a research architecture using custom NASA technologies in part, all other collaboration tools used the standard internet and a mix of commercial software products (e.g. Microsoft and Apple applications, and WebEx for screen-sharing over the internet, though there are free alternatives such as VNC), plus freely available tools, some of which are also open source (Brahms, Compendium; instant messengers). Technically, therefore, more broadly, other collaborative e-science projects and distributed teams could benefit from the collaborative knowledge cartography described here.

What about the skill set required to use Compendium fluently? We have highlighted the role played by the *knowledge cartographer* within the Crew and RST; both people and software agents can do the knowledge cartography. We have shown that untrained scientists can use Compendium to collage and annotate photos, and to develop diagrammatic templates to scaffold a methodology. Moreover, anyone fluent in switching between multiple applications could perform this role in meetings. *Dialogue Mapping* freeform discussions as IBIS structures, in real time, is one of the highest-level skills, but one that can be learnt (and taught: www cognexus.org). Such maps can be constructed post-hoc, from meeting notes, if it is too demanding in the meeting, The particular focus in this chapter on the use of specialised templates for *Conversational Modelling* (e.g. for EVA Planning, or to structure the science data) demonstrates a hybrid approach, relieving the cognitive load on the dialogue mapper by scaffolding the discussion around a template "agenda" of issues, driven by a modelling approach or metadata scheme.

This work is being developed in a number of directions. As Chap. 11 by Selvin demonstrates, we are seeking to articulate the nature of the *knowledge cartography skill set* as revealed through the analysis of session recordings. Compendium has established a significant user base (~40,000 downloads of the tool, with >500 mailing list subscribers). Specifically, within NASA it continues to support the collaborative modelling of work systems (e.g. Sierhuis, 2006), while at the Open University, as a modelling tool providing visual templates for "Learning Design" (Chap. 10). On the technical front, we have integrated Compendium with the Access Grid, widely used in e-science/e-social science, to create a robust Meeting Replay environment (Buckingham Shum et al., 2006b). A Flash version of Compendium is being integrated into the Open University's FlashMeeting Web-videoconferencing tool (Scott et al., 2007), and we are now investigating its integration as a visual environment for Web 2.0 applications such as blogging (e.g. Eisenstadt, 2004) and semantic, social bookmarking (OSC, 2007). Compendium is funded from public research grants in the UK and US, and our aim is to continue to offer it as a freely accessible, open, knowledge cartography research platform. We welcome your collaboration in taking it forward.

Acknowledgment

Large scale e-science of this sort takes a lot of effort from many people. This project was funded in part by a NASA Research Announcement (NRA) through the Information Systems' program Human-Centered Computing project, Mike Shafto selecting officer. This work was part of NASA Ames' Mobile Agent Project, with William J. Clancey as overall Principal Investigator and Maarten Sierhuis as overall Project Lead. Project members are civil servants and contractors at NASA-Ames in California and Johnson Space Center in Houston, TX. Satellite network services were funded by the NASA Research & Education Network (NREN), and supported by researchers from NASA Glenn Research Center in Ohio. The United Kingdom's EPSRC funded the Advanced Knowledge Technologies consortium, of which the CoAKTinG Project is part: www.aktors.org/coakting. We are grateful to colleagues at the Open University's Knowledge Media Institute: Al Selvin for his contributions as an RST Facilitator and with assisting in our reflections on this role, and Michelle Bachler for programming Compendium. Our thanks to Kevin Page (University of Southampton) for support with the Meeting Replay tool. We are grateful to Shannon Rupert (MiraCosta College, now New Mexico State University), and the team at State University of New York at Buffalo: Stacy Sklar, Brent Garry, Abigail Semple, Melissa Farley, Brett Burkett, Kyle Fredrick, and Shannon Kobs. Our thanks also to the Northern California Mars Society mission support volunteers including especially Frank Crossman, as well the MDRS coordinator, Tony Muscatello, and the flight surgeon, Tam Czarnik, provided essential services during the 2 weeks at MDRS. Please see http://www.marssociety.org/MDRS/fs03/ (*Crew 29: April 25– May 8, 2004*) and http://www.marssociety.org/MDRS/fs04/ (*Crew 38: April 3–16, 2005*) for the complete listing of mission participants, daily log entries and photographs.

References

Bordini, R.H., Dastani, M., Dix, J. and Seghrouchni, A.E.F. (Eds). (2005). *Multi-Agent Programming: Languages, Platforms and Applications*, Berlin Heidelberg New York: Springer.
Buckingham Shum, S.J., Selvin, A.M., Sierhuis, M., Conklin, J., Haley, C.B. and Nuseibeh, B. (2006a). Hypermedia support for argumentation-based rationale: 15 Years on from gIBIS and QOC. *Rationale Management in Software Engineering*. A. Dutoit, R. McCall, I. Mistrik and B. Paech (Eds). Berlin Heidelberg New York: Springer, pp. 111–132.
Buckingham Shum, S., Slack, R., Daw, M., Juby, B., Rowley, A., Bachler, M., Mancini, C., Michaelides, D., Procter, R., De Roure, D., Chown, T. and Hewitt, T. (2006b).

Memetic: An Infrastructure for Meeting Memory. *Proceedings of 7th International Conference on the Design of Cooperative Systems*, Carry-le-Rouet, France, 9–12 May. [PrePrint: www.memetic-vre.net/publications/COOP2006_Memetic.pdf].

Clancey, W.J. (2001). Field science ethnography: methods for systematic observation on an expedition. *Field Methods*, 13(3), 223–243.

Clancey, W.J. (2002). Simulating "Mars on Earth" – A Report from FMARS Phase 2. *On to Mars: Colonizing a New World*. F. Crossman and R. Zubrin (Eds). Apogee Books.

Clancey, W.J. (2004). Roles for agent assistants in field science: understanding personal projects and collaboration. *IEEE Transactions on Systems, Man and Cybernetics – Part C: Applications and Reviews*, 34(2).

Clancey, W.J. (2006). Observation of work practices in natural settings. *Cambridge Handbook on Expertise and Expert Performance*. N.C. A. Ericsson, P. Veltovich, R. Hoffman (Eds).

Clancey, W.J., Sachs, P., Sierhuis, M. and van Hoof, R. (1998). Brahms: simulating practice for work systems design. *International Journal on Human–Computer Studies*, 49, 831–865.

Clancey, W.J., Sierhuis, M., Alena, R., Berrios, D., Dowding, J., Graham, J.S., Tyree, K.S., Hirsh, R.L., Garry, W.B., Semple, A., Buckingham Shum, S.J., Shadbolt, N. and Rupert, S. (2003). Automating CapCom using mobile agents and robotic assistants. *American Institute of Aeronautics and Astronautics 1st Space Exploration Conference*, Orlando, FL, Advanced Knowledge Technologies Project ePrint [http://eprints.aktors.org/375].

Clancey, W.J., Sierhuis, M., Alena, R., Crowford, S., Dowding, J., Graham, J., Kaskiris, C., Tyree, K.S. and Hoof, R.V. (2004). The Mobile Agents Integrated Field Test: Mars Dessert Research Station 2003. *FLAIRS 2004*, Miami Beach, Florida.

Clancey, W.J., Sierhuis, M., Damer, B. and Brodsky, B. (2005). The cognitive modelling of "day in the life" social behaviors using Brahms. *Cognition and Multi-Agent Interaction*. R. Sun (Ed). New York, NY: Cambridge University Press, pp. 151–184.

CoAKTinG (2004): *Collaborative Advanced Knowledge Technologies on the Grid*. EPSRC/e-Science UK Project: www.aktors.org/coakting

Conklin, J. (2005). *Dialogue Mapping: Building Shared Understanding of Wicked Problems*. Chichester, Wiley.

Eisenstadt, M. (2004). *More Dualling Blogs*. Blog Entry, November 9th, 2004, Knowledge Media Institute, Open University, UK: http://kmi.open.ac.uk/people/marc/2004/11/09/more-duelling-blogs

Memetic (2006): *Meeting Memory Technologies Informing Collaboration*. JISC UK Project: www.memetic-vre.net

Nelson, T. (1987). *Literary Machines* (Ed. 93.1).

OpenLearn (2007). *OpenLearn LabSpace*. Open University, UK: http://labspace.open.ac.uk

OSC (2007). *Open Sensemaking Communities* project, Knowledge Media Institute, Open University, UK: http://kmi.open.ac.uk/projects/osc

Rittel, H.W.J. (1972). *Second Generation Design Methods*. Interview in: Design Methods Group 5th Anniversary Report: DMG Occasional Paper, 1, 5–10.

Rittel, H.W.J. and Webber, M.M. (1973). Dilemmas in a general theory of planning. *Policy Sciences*, 4, 155–169.

Scott, P., Tomadaki, E. and Quick, K. (2007). The shape of live online meetings. *International Journal of Technology, Knowledge and Society*. [PrePrint: http://kmi.open.ac.uk/projects/osc/docs/Shape%20of%20Live%20Online%20Meetings,%20The.pdf]

Selvin, A. (1999). Supporting collaborative analysis and design with hypertext functionality. *Journal of Digital Information*, 1(4).

Sierhuis, M. (2001). Modelling and Simulating Work Practice; Brahms: a multiagent modelling and simulation language for work system analysis and design. *Social Science Informatics (SWI)*. Amsterdam, The Netherlands, University of Amsterdam, SIKS Dissertation Series No. 2001-10: 350.

Sierhuis, M. (2006). Collaboratively Modeling Mission Control at NASA. *Compendium Institute News*, 11th March 2006. http://news.kmi.open.ac.uk/rostra/news.php?r=55&t=2&id=20

Sierhuis, M., Clancey, W.J., Alena, R.L., Berrios, D., Shum, S.B., Dowding, J., Graham, J., Hoof, R.V., Kaskiris, C., Rupert, S. and Tyree, K.S. (2005). NASA's Mobile Agents Architecture: A Multi-Agent Workflow and Communication System for Planetary Exploration. *i-SAIRAS 2005*, München, Germany, European Space Agency.

Wooldridge, M. (2002). *An Introduction to MultiAgent Systems*, Wiley.

15. Template-Based Structured Argumentation

John Lowrance, Ian Harrison, Andres Rodriguez, Eric Yeh, Tom Boyce, Janet Murdock, Jerome Thomere, and Ken Murray

Artificial Intelligence Center, SRI International, Menlo Park, CA 94025, USA, firstname.lastname@sri.com

Abstract. A semiautomated approach to evidential reasoning uses template-based structured argumentation. A template captures best analytic practice as a hierarchically structured set of coordinated questions; an argument answers the questions posed by a template, including references to the source material used as evidence to support those answers. Graphical depictions of arguments readily convey lines of reasoning, from evidence through to conclusions, making it easy to compare and contrast alternative lines of reasoning. Collaborative analysis is supported via simultaneous access to arguments through web browser clients connected to a common argument server. This approach to analysis has been applied to a wide range of analytic problems and has been experimentally shown to speed the development and improve the quality of analytic assessments.

15.1 Introduction

We have been investigating the use of *template-based structured argumentation* as a means of capturing and guiding collaborative analysis. The idea is to capture best analytic practice for a given class of problems in a template and then use that template as the basis for collecting evidence and drawing conclusions about specific situations. Unlike our earlier work that focused on automating human uncertain reasoning (Lowrance et al., 1990, Lowrance, 1995), this approach focuses on recording and coordinating human reasoning. A key aspect of this has been the use of graphical depictions of arguments to rapidly convey the state of lines of inquiry, from evidence to conclusion, highlighting information needs as well as the evidence that drives the conclusion. To support this approach, we created a collaborative software tool called the Structured Evidential Argumentation System (SEAS) (Lowrance et al., 2001, Lowrance, 2006). Using this tool, contributing analysts directly manipulate depictions of arguments, adding and interpreting evidence relative to questions raised by the template, debate and draw conclusions based on the collective evidence, and finally use these depictions to convey their findings to decision makers.

Today most analytic efforts are conducted with minimal use of information technology. Analytic products are typically recorded in text documents with minimal structure, limited to the section headings that break up the document. As such, these analytic products are time-consuming to understand – one must read the text to find the conclusions and understand how the evidence supports them. It is difficult to determine how the conclusions should change with changes in the supporting evidence. Given two products on the same topic, it is difficult to compare and contrast the conclusions, what drives them, and how the lines of reasoning differ. Finally, it is up to the reader to extract the analytic method, if it is to be employed in doing future analyses; best analytic practice is difficult to glean from these products. At worst, the information technology employed is limited to word processing applications; at best, it is a collaborative document-authoring environment, with embedded links to documents used as evidence. While these collaborative environments are good in supporting the development of comprehensive narratives on well-understood topics, they do little to aid a group in collective reasoning, i.e., determining and recording how information should be collected and interpreted as evidence relative to an issue under active consideration.

Many prior attempts to inject information technology into analytic efforts (including our own) focused on capturing and automating the reasoning done by analysts. Complex belief networks were engineered that attempted to capture the detailed interactions among all the interrelated variables that impinge on the topic of interest. Since these models were based on formal theories (e.g., logic, probabilities), inference techniques could be used to automatically determine the ramifications of asserted new facts on related variables in the models. While such modeling techniques can be very usefully employed to address some analytic problems, they are not universally applicable. For some problems, they require more information than is available or obtainable, leading to the use of assumptions, estimates, and guesses that ultimately rob the models and their predictions of their legitimacy. Even in those situations where the information can be obtained to build well-founded models, these techniques have often failed to gain acceptance. The introduction of such automated models reduces the job of the analysts to that of data entry, which they resent; the amount of data that must be entered before the model produces a justified result can be overwhelming. Because the resulting lines of reasoning are difficult to understand or explain, decision makers are justifiably reluctant to act on the results; because of the opacity of the models, they cannot be created or modified directly by the analysts.

SEAS is our attempt to strike a middle ground between these two extremes. Our aim is to record the reasoning of analysts (not automate it), using simple structures, making the results easy to understand and explain, quick to compare and contrast, directly modifiable by analysts, and making it easy to separate the analytic method from the product. SEAS introduces more structure into the analytic environment than is in use today but not as much as belief networks. The analytic method is separated from the analytic products, resulting from its application. The analytic method is broken down into a set of smaller analytic tasks, with their interrelationships captured. Methods for acquiring information in support of these analytic tasks are also broken out. In structure, analytic results parallel the analytic methods on which they are based, with links to the information that supports the conclusions retained, and to the interpretations of that information relative to each analytic task. The type of situation for which a method was designed and for which a result was produced is also captured. However, much of the knowledge captured remains in natural language. In fact, when one compares an analytic product produced using SEAS with a contemporary analytic product expressed in a text document, one finds that most of the text in the document is within the structured argument. The structure has not replaced the words as much as it has augmented them, making it possible for the machine to aid analysts in new ways. In short, we are attempting to establish a division of labor where the analysts do the nuanced reasoning and the machine captures and presents that reasoning in ways that make it more accessible.

Our original focus was on aiding intelligence analysts addressing issues pertaining to national security. But we have since discovered that these same techniques have broader applicability. In particular, we have applied these techniques to assemble and draw conclusions from evidence pertaining to detecting workmen's compensation fraud, tax code compliance risk (Lowrance & Ragoobeer, 2004), information collection/sharing among emergency first responders, and other problems in government, industry, and the private sector.

15.2 Capturing Analytic Methods as Argument Templates

Our approach is based on the concept of a *structured argument*. While others before us were exploring structured argumentation concepts, particularly the notion of argument mapping (Wigmore, 1937; Toumlin, 1958; Kirschner et al., 2003), our approach generally departed from theirs in being template driven. Our structured arguments are based on a hierarchy of questions (a tree) that is used to assess a situation. This hierarchy of questions is called the *argument template* (as opposed to the *argument*, which answers the questions posed by a template). This hierarchy of questions supporting questions may go a few levels deep before bottoming out in primitive questions that must be directly assessed and answered. These primitive questions are multiple choice, with the different candidate answers corresponding to discrete points or subintervals along a continuous scale, with one end of the scale representing strong support for a given proposition and the other end representing strong refutation. Leaf nodes represent primitive questions, and internal nodes represent derivative questions. The links represent support relationships among the questions. A derivative question is supported by all the derivative and primitive questions below it. Figure 15.1 illustrates a thirteen-question argument template, with nine primitive questions and four derivative questions. Note that question 1 is answered based on the answers to 1.1, 1.2, and 1.3, and 1.3 is answered based on the answers to 1.3.1, 1.3.2, and 1.3.3.

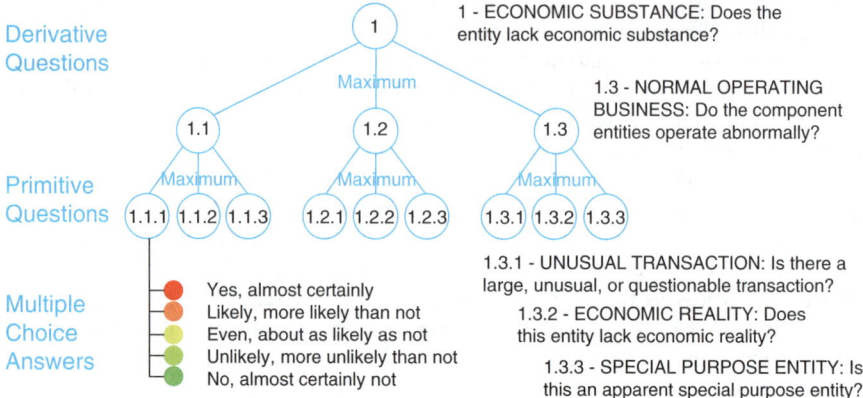

Fig. 15.1. Example argument template.

As pointed out by Morgan D. Jones (1995): "Structuring is to analysis what a blueprint is to building a house. Would you build a house without a blueprint? You could, of course, but there's no telling what you'd end up with. Building a house, building anything, without a plan is, to say the least, ill advised." An argument template serves as a blueprint for the construction of arguments. It reminds the analyst of the full range of factors that should be included and how they relate to one another. As such, it can guide a novice in addressing an unfamiliar assessment task and it can prevent an expert from jumping to a conclusion before all aspects of a problem have been fully considered. In addition, if two analysts independently construct arguments for the same problem based on a common template, they can be rapidly compared and contrasted, particularly through graphical renderings. Some templates are very abstract, serving more to organize a person's thinking than to guide it. Other templates are quite specific, posing detailed questions that can be used to guide a novice, imparting best practice. For example, a template originally developed by U.S. intelligence analysts, to assess the threat imposed by a particular terrorist group, was brought into our laboratory. There it was successfully generalized and applied by non-experts to assess the threat imposed by a different terrorist group, demonstrating how novices can be quickly brought up to speed on an unfamiliar problem, given a high-quality template.

Structuring of an argument template can be approached in two distinct ways: top-down and bottom-up. Using the top-down approach, one starts with the central question and attempts to break it down into a small set of supporting questions, each of approximately the same significance; then one breaks down each of those questions, attempting to break each into the same number of equally significant questions. An attempt is made to keep the number and significance of supporting question equal so that the eventual template encourages equal attention to equally significant aspects of the overall problem. This procedure continues until primitive questions are produced that can be directly answered or until the number of overall questions has become too numerous to include in a single template. In this latter case, the author might elect to limit the depth of the original template and then capture those elements that fell below that depth limit in their own templates; each of these *cascaded templates* would share its root question with one of the primitive questions in the original template. The relationship of these cascaded templates to the original template can be captured by adding these to the original template as *discovery tools* (more on this below). As such, an analyst who is developing an argument based on the original template, and is confronted with one of its primitive questions, can either elect to directly answer the stated question or invoke one of these discovery tools to further break down the question. The cascaded templates define useful subarguments that can support one or more higher-level arguments. The advantage of this approach is that the analyst determines which of these discovery tools to employ, thus choosing where and where not to spend additional effort. An analyst might choose to delve deeper, using a cascaded template because of not being able to directly answer the primitive question, and thus needing guidance in breaking it down to questions that can be answered. Or, the analyst, believing that this is central to the problem at hand, wants to engage in very deliberate reasoning.

Using the bottom-up approach, one starts by enumerating the detailed conditions that should be considered. Once these are enumerated, one begins to cluster these into coherent collections of roughly equal size and significance. One then clusters the clusters, again striving for clusters of equal size and significance, and continues this process until a single cluster remains. Each cluster should give rise to a question in the resulting template, with the nesting of the clusters captured as supporting questions.

In practice, neither the top-down nor bottom-up approach is typically employed in its pure form. Instead, both are employed at different times, one after the other, until a satisfactory result is achieved. Once the overall skeletal structure has been established, the analyst's attention should turn to writing the detailed questions and candidate multiple-choice answers for the template. In practice, we have found that analysts are capable of authoring templates after minimal training, but that authoring high-quality templates is challenging and requires additional experience.

An *inference method* completes an argument template. It is used to automatically answer some questions based on the answers to other questions. The analyst answers the primitive questions in the question hierarchy, and the answers to the derivative questions are automatically calculated. A typical inference method might take the maximum, minimum, or average (i.e., worst case or best case or average case) answer as the conclusion when combining the answers to several questions assessed along a continuous scale. We favor such simple inference methods over more complex methods (e.g., ones based on conditional probabilities) since they are easier to follow and explain. This reflects our goal to organize and record human reasoning rather than attempting to automate it.

To facilitate the rapid comprehension of arguments, we use a traffic light metaphor relating answers to colored lights along a linear scale, from green to red. The questions in a template are typically yes/no or true/false; the multiple-choice answers for primitive questions partition this range, associating an answer with each colored light. Typically, a five-light scale is used (green, yellow-green, yellow, orange, red). Here green might correspond to false, red to true, and the other three to varying degrees of certainty. No multiple-choice answers are associated with derivative questions; within arguments, answers are strictly summarized by lights indicating degree of certainty. Beside rapid comprehension, another advantage in the use of such a scale is the avoidance of false precision (i.e., fine distinctions being made in the inputs and outputs that are not justified by the available information).

A template author should establish a *situation descriptor*, for a new template, that describes the type of situations for which the template is intended to be used. Unlike the other information provided by the user in defining a template, much of the information in a situation descriptor is chosen from a situation ontology rather than being free text. The situation ontology serves much the same purpose as a card catalog in a library; it establishes indices and terms that are useful for retrieving objects based on the type of situation to which they are applied. For national security problems, these might include the part of the world being analyzed (e.g., the continent, region, or country under assessment), the principal actor (e.g., the leadership, the government, or its people), the event (e.g., political, economic, financial, or currency), and the time period. These descriptions, with the exception of time, are selected from hierarchies of terms that are established through traditional knowledge engineering techniques. By indexing objects according to this situation ontology, both exact and semantically close matches can be automatically retrieved based on a description of the situation of interest expressed in the same terms. These situation descriptors are augmented by free text fields where the specific aspects of the situation can be fully expressed; thus, the ontological terminology need not fully capture every distinction.

Discovery tools can be associated with primitive questions in a template. In general, they are recommended methods for acquiring information relevant to answering the associated question. These might be links to web pages, queries to databases or search engines, parameterized launches of other analytic tools, or references to cascaded templates. They capture an important aspect of an analyst's knowledge, namely, where and how to go about seeking information relevant to answering questions. Knowledge of this form is one thing that distinguishes an expert from a novice analyst. Discovery tools are captured on primitive questions within a template by storing the URLs that will launch them along with short textual citations used to reference them. As such, an argument template can be viewed as a complex query that breaks down a difficult question into simpler questions, coordinates multiple searches for information relevant to answering those simpler questions, and interprets the results as the basis for answering the difficult question.

15.3 Capturing Analytic Products as Arguments

Arguments are formed by answering the questions posed by a template. Answers are chosen from the multiple choices given in the template. If the available information does not allow the analyst to reduce the possible answers to a single choice, multiple choices can be selected bounding the answers that remain possible, given the available information. Upon answering each question, the template's inference method is applied, deriving the answers to derivative questions. Using the traffic light metaphor, arguments can be displayed as a tree of colored nodes. Nodes represent questions,

15. Template-Based Structured Argumentation   313

Fig. 15.2. Example argument.

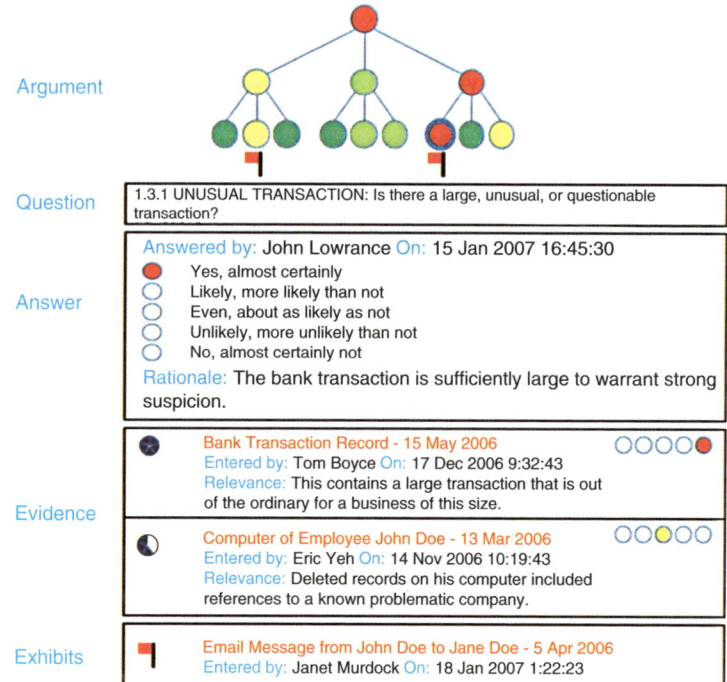

Fig. 15.3. Information supporting primitive question 1.3.1 in an argument.

and colors represent answers. Figure 15.2 shows one such tree. From such visualizations, one can quickly determine which answers are driving the conclusion. In this case, it is obvious that 1.3.1 is driving the answer to 1.3 and 1.3 is driving the answer to the root question (i.e., 1). Within SEAS, if the cursor is positioned over a node in such a visualization, a small pop-up window displays the associated question. Thus, by moving the cursor across the argument, the line of reasoning driving the conclusion can be quickly determined.

When answering a question in an argument, the *rationale* for answering in that way is recorded in text with attribution given to the answering analyst and the time that that answer was given (Fig. 15.3). Information used as evidence to support the answers given in an argument is recorded as part of the argument. When information that is potentially relevant to answering a question posed is first found, it is entered as an *exhibit*. This can be any kind of digital document (e.g., text, image, video, audio, spreadsheet) or a simple reference to a paper document. An exhibit assigns a unique identifier to the information, uploads the document for later access if it is in digital form, and records a *citation* (i.e., string of text) for referencing it (typically consisting of some combination of title, author, and date). When the *relevance* of the information to the question at hand is confirmed, the exhibit is promoted to *evidence*. The relevance is recorded in two ways: as text explaining the significance and as the answer(s) to the question that would be chosen if the answer were to be based solely on this evidence. The analyst making this assessment and the time of the assessment are recorded as well. When evidence is present, the rationale typically explains how the collective evidence supports the answer(s) chosen, explaining away that evidence that contradicts the answer and weaving together the supporting evidence to arrive at the stated conclusion. If the evidence is later explained away (e.g., an alibi is provided), it can be demoted back to an exhibit and retained along with the rationale for its demotion.

When a new exhibit is first attached to an argument, a red signal flag is raised to indicate that analyst attention is needed to determine its relevance. These flags are shown in the graphical visualization of arguments until the exhibits are promoted to evidence or until the flags are dismissed. Dismissing a flag on an exhibit indicates that the exhibit was found to not be relevant to answering the associated question. Retaining the exhibit with its lowered flag provides a record of this determination.

When discovery tools are present, they can be used to aid in the collection of evidence. If the discovery tools are of the *auto-populating* variety, when triggered they automatically turn all the "documents" that they return into exhibits with raised flags. Within SEAS, all such auto-populating discovery tools associated with an argument can be triggered at once; then the signal flags in the graphical depiction of the argument guide analysts to the locations within the argument where new information is waiting interpretation. When discovery tools are based on cascaded templates, cascaded arguments result from their triggering. In this way, the analyst can choose where to do a more thorough analysis, delving more deeply in a targeted way. A cascaded argument's conclusion can be automatically used as evidence in support of the higher-level argument.

The analyst also chooses a *fusion method* for combining all the evidence gathered supporting a single question. The fusion method can be manual (i.e., the analyst answers the question based on understanding of the evidence and its relevance) or automated (i.e., the answer is automatically reached by applying a fusion method to the relevance of the supporting evidence). When an automated method is in use, changes to the supporting evidence, including changes in supporting arguments, can ripple up through the argument that they support, changing the conclusions. Such changes are immediately visible in the graphical depiction of the argument. The simplest automated fusion methods correspond to worst-case, best-case, and average-case reasoning (Fig. 15.4). The consensus fusion method is similar to an arithmetic average, but it tends to favor the more emphatic answers over the less emphatic; emphatic answers are characterized by being precise (i.e., captured by few lights) and being at the extremes (i.e., green or red).

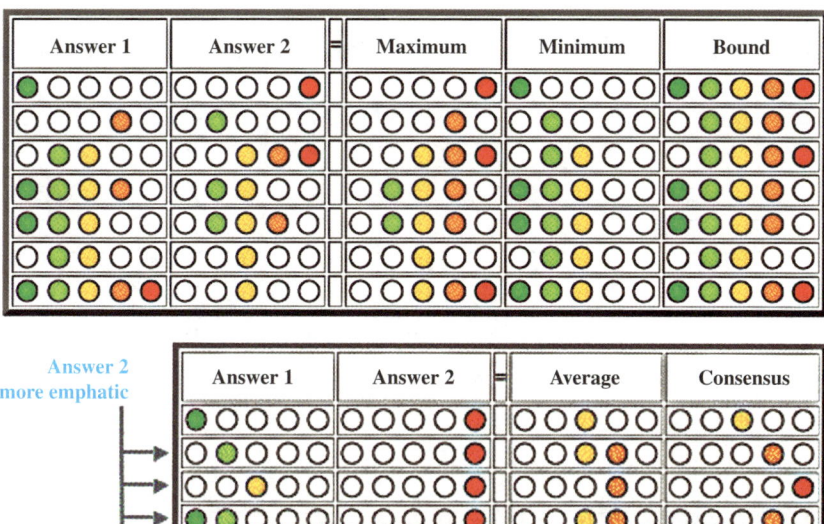

Fig. 15.4. Automated fusion methods.

Given that not all sources are equally credible, weights are useful in recording their presumed credibility. These are graphically depicted by circular symbols, filled to varying degrees, associated with each piece of evidence, the weight being proportional to the area filled (see Fig. 15.3). Within SEAS, clicking on one of these symbols permits one to choose from five different weights. In addition, some automated fusion methods are sensitive to these weights; those answers given less weight have less impact on their respective conclusions (Fig. 15.5). When these are in use, a change to the weight associated with a piece of evidence causes the answer to the question to be recalculated, along with all the derivative questions that depend on it. However, using weights to capture estimates of source credibility has proven to be extremely useful even when questions are answered manually. In addition, weighted fusion methods can be utilized within the inference methods of argument templates. Here they capture the idea that the answers to some supporting questions are more important than the answers to others when arriving at a conclusion. The weights associated with supporting questions are chosen by selecting from the same symbols used to weight evidence; if less than full weight is attributed to a question in an argument, its node is drawn proportionally smaller in the tree of nodes that depicts the argument (Fig. 15.14).

All the arguments and templates thus far discussed consist of a single hierarchy of questions, designed to arrive at the answer to a single overall question, the one uppermost in the hierarchy. In many applications, we have found it useful to employ

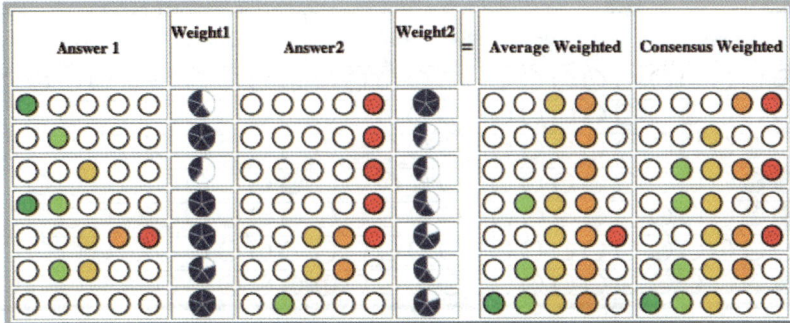

Fig. 15.5. Weighted automated fusion methods.

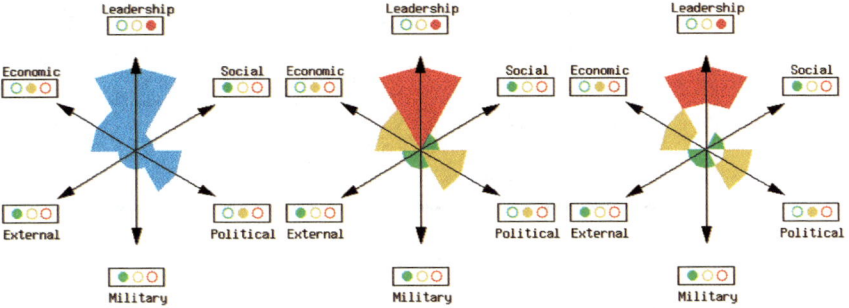

Fig. 15.6. Starburst depictions of multidimensional arguments.

a coordinated set of such *unidimensional* arguments, where each addresses a common topic from a different perspective, without attempting to roll these into a single overall answer. We refer to these as *multidimensional* arguments. For example, the assessment of the stability of a nation state might best be addressed by several independent assessments of the leadership, social, political, military, external, and economic situations.

In a *starburst* graphic (Fig. 15.6), the answers to the component arguments are organized in a pattern resembling spokes on a wheel. Each "spoke" corresponds to one answer; answers are displayed as "traffic lights" at the ends of the spokes; answers are also plotted as points along the spokes with the "hub" of the wheel typically corresponding to the green end of the linear scale and the "rim" typically to the red end; the points plotted on neighboring spokes are connected by lines, and the resulting polygon is filled. The result is a plot that visually conveys the argument, with the severity of the situation (typically) being proportional to the area of the plot. This technique invites rapid comprehension and comparison when multiple arguments are simultaneously displayed.

The starburst can be customized in a number of ways. One can specify whether each segment of the starburst should be depicted as a ray, beginning at the origin and extending out to the appropriate position, according to which lights are lit, or as

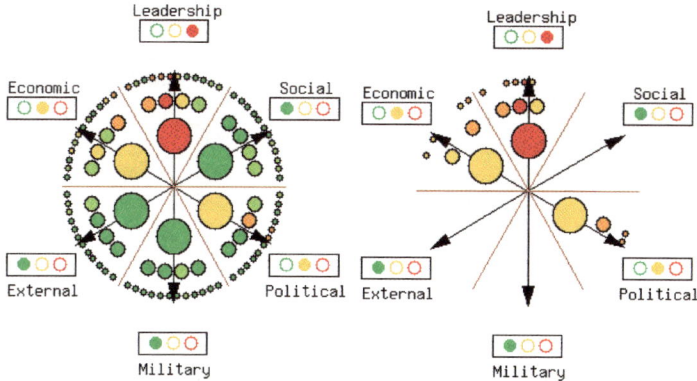

Fig. 15.7. Constellation depictions of multidimensional arguments.

sectors, having only those areas filled whose corresponding lights are lit. You also can specify how different parts of the starburst should be colored: mono in blue, max with the color corresponding to the highest-valued light, min with the color corresponding to the lowest-valued light, own with the color that corresponds to that portion on the starburst (i.e., green at the center, yellow in the middle, and red at the perimeter).

A *constellation* is another way of graphically depicting a multidimensional argument (Fig. 15.7). Using the same radial layout as for the starburst, it depicts the tree of lights corresponding to each component argument within the corresponding wedge, placing the root node/light nearest the origin and growing out from there. Larger nodes/lights are used nearer the origin. Although this can result in a cluttered display, it has the advantage of depicting every question/answer of a multidimensional argument within a single compact display. This is further enhanced by pop-ups, which appear when the cursor is positioned over any light, that display the corresponding question text. A further refinement allows one to filter out lights based on their corresponding color. Thus, for example, you might elect to show only the red, orange, and yellow lights, or just the red lights (i.e., the high-value information). Examples of this display appear in Fig. 15.7.

Yet another effect can be achieved by overlaying constellations on starbursts (Fig. 15.8). This allows the user to quickly grasp the overall argument through the starburst and the details through the constellation. While at first glance, these and the previous depictions of arguments might seem somewhat opaque, they have proven to be quite valuable, allowing one to quickly spot what is driving an argument, where one argument diverges from another, or what trend is developing across a sequence of arguments. This is particularly due to their compact nature, allowing multiple arguments to be viewed side by side, within a single screen/page.

While trees, starbursts, and constellations are particularly useful depictions for investigation online, where the corresponding question for each node/light is revealed upon positioning the cursor over it, these are less useful offline where no such

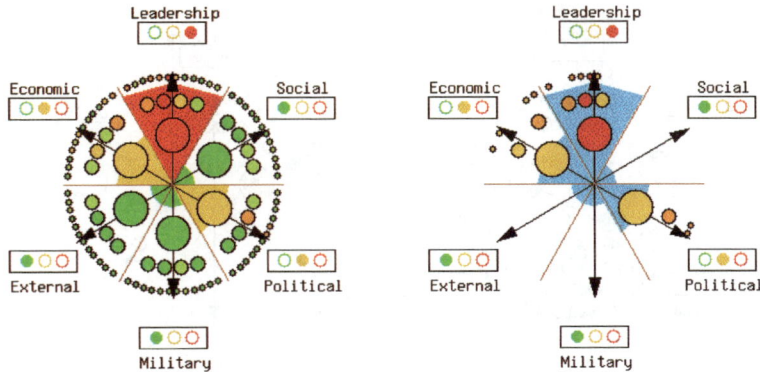

Fig. 15.8. Constellation overlaid on starburst.

ECONOMIC											
MACROECONOMIC STABILITY			FINANCIAL STABILITY			ECONOMIC HEALTH			INFRASTRUCTURE/ENVIRONMENTAL PROBLEMS		
BUDGET CRISIS	INFLATION	BALANCE OF PAYMENTS	BANKING SECTOR	CURRENCY	STOCK MARKET/INVESTMENTS	OUTPUT	KEY SECTOR	UNEMPLOYMENT	INFRASTRUCTURE	NATURAL ENVIRONMENTAL CATASTROPHE	MAN-MADE ENVIRONMENTAL CRISIS

Fig. 15.9. Table depiction of unidimensional argument.

information is available. To better convey the content of an argument offline, while striving to remain as compact as possible, we have developed a tabular argument summary (Fig. 15.9). In a tabular summary of a unidimensional argument, the root question is captured by a single cell at the top that spans the width of the table; the questions that support it are each represented by a cell in the next row of the table; the questions that support each of those are represented by cells in the next row of the table, below the cell of the question they support; and so on. Each cell is labeled with the topic of its corresponding question and is filled with a color corresponding to its answer. Multiple such tables are used to summarize a multidimensional argument, and can typically be printed on a single page.

Another very useful means for conveying the contents of an argument is through a textual summary (Fig. 15.10). Here questions are numbered and indented in outline style to reflect their position in the question hierarchy. The lights corresponding to the answer to each question are shown adjacent to each. Primitive questions also include answer rationale, along with the associated evidence and exhibits, and all their attributes. All are annotated with the contributing analyst and the time of the contribution. Thus, these capture the full contents of an argument, suitable for detailed review and as the starting point for a fully formatted textual report on the topic. Like constellations, one can choose to suppress the inclusion of questions whose answers are represented by certain colors. This provides a means to exclude the low-value information (e.g., near green) and focus on the high-value information (e.g., near red), allowing one to reduce the textual summary to those aspects that are driving the overall conclusions.

| 1 GOALS, INTENT, & STRATEGY : Does this terrorist organization intend to carry out a strategic course of action with the goal of harming the U.S. or its interests? | ○ ○ ○ ● ○ |

Analyst — SEAS Using Fusion Method Minimum (Closest to Green) on 18 May 2007 13:11:00

| 1.1 GOALS : Does this terrorist organization have goals focused on harming the U.S. or its interests? | ○ ○ ○ ● ○ |

Analyst — SEAS Using Fusion Method Maximum (Closest to Red) on 15 Nov 2004 10:41:33

| 1.1.1 LONG-TERM GOALS : Does this terrorist organization have long-term goals focused on harming the U.S. or its interests? | ○ ○ ○ ● ○ |

Analyst: Lowrance, John D., SRI International on 6 Jan 2006 16:15:34

Question Amplification:
- Eradicate U.S. presence from some part of the world
- Overthrow pro-Western governments
- Establish anti-US movement

Rationale: The most recent evidence suggest that Abu Sayyaf is evolving into a terrorist group with deeper Islamic roots and more connections to other Islamic terrorist groups. This likely indicates an alignment of Abu Sayyaf's goals with these other groups' goals, which do intend to harm the U.S. or its interests.

▶History (1)

Evidence: Analyst: Lowrance, John D., SRI International on 31 Aug 2004 16:00:38
TIME Asia Magazine: The Return of Abu Sayyaf – Aug. 30, 2004: Abu Sayyaf has evolved into a much more ferocious band. A new leadership has abandoned the kidnapping that brought in millions of dollars in ransom. Now, the group is returning to its Islamic roots and is using the familiar weapons of terror—bombing and assassination—in an attempt to achieve an independent Muslim republic in the southern Philippines. ● ○ ○ ○ ○ ●

Analyst: Lowrance, John D., SRI International on 31 Aug 2004 15:59:08
Naval Postgraduate School: Terrorist Group Profiles, Abu Sayyaf, 2003: Although from time to time it claims that its motivation is to promote an independent Islamic state in western Mindanao and the Sulu Archipelago—areas in the southern Philippines heavily populated by Muslims—the ASG has primarily used terror for financial profit. ● ○ ● ○ ○ ○

Exhibits: Sayyaf May Become International Terror Group– newsflash.org– STAR– by Marvin Sy, Manila, July 21, 2004

Fig. 15.10. Summary depiction of a portion of an argument.

Like argument templates, arguments too have associated situation descriptors. An argument's situation descriptor is like a template's situation descriptor except that it captures information pertaining to the prevailing situation for which the argument was developed. Like the situation descriptors associated with templates, they are used to find arguments that address related situations.

15.4 Supporting Collaborative Analysis

SEAS seeks to foster collaboration among analysts. In reviewing why analysts might seek out other analysts, we identified six reasons:

1. To learn from others by reviewing their analytic methods and products
2. To stimulate creative thinking by rapidly exchanging and generating ideas (i.e., brainstorming)
3. To gain insights by having others critique their work
4. To share the workload, and thus to get results quicker and to get superior results by having different people do what they do best
5. To improve their understanding by comparing and contrasting their results with the results of others
6. To improve the quality of their results by combining them with the results of others

Note that most of these activities stress the need for asynchronous collaboration aids. The most important capabilities for supporting collaboration in SEAS are through tools that aid argument or template understanding, argument or template comparison, argument or template merging, and argument or template critiquing, and that support division of labor regarding the creation and editing of arguments or templates.

From its inception, SEAS was designed as a collaborative tool aimed at supporting teams of analysts engaged in collective reasoning tasks. This is one of the reasons that it is architected as a web application, consisting of a web server with browser clients. All SEAS objects reside on the server. Users access these objects using a personal computer, equipped with an industry standard browser, connected to the server via a network (e.g., the Internet). In response, the server generates dynamic web pages that are rendered by the clients to provide depictions of SEAS objects, and/or modifies these objects based on client actions. SEAS provides asynchronous to near synchronous read/write access to all accumulated objects, which allows analysts to work together on common arguments, as their time permits.

Since SEAS is meant to support a community of analysts, it must address issues of privacy and access. An analyst in the early stages of argument development might not want work to be accessible by others. During development, an analyst might want certain individuals or groups to aid the process by reviewing or contributing to it. Even when an argument is complete, the analyst will want to control who will be allowed to see the results. Further, when an argument is used as evidence in support of another argument, then that argument serving as evidence must be guaranteed to persist in its current state to guarantee the integrity of the argument it supports. To address these issues of access control and stability of referenced objects, SEAS incorporates the concept of publishing. Three key attributes are related to the two states of publishing: unpublished and published. Published arguments and templates are guaranteed to persist, that is, they will continue to exist; no such guarantee is made for unpublished arguments or templates. As a consequence, only published arguments and templates can be reliably cited, much as only published works are (typically) included in bibliographies so that the reader has a real opportunity to obtain and read them. Unpublished arguments and templates are distinguished from published ones in that they are unstable, that is, likely to change in content. Published arguments and templates will not change. Finally, unpublished arguments and templates are distinguished from published ones in that their authors are given write access, while published ones restrict both their authors and audiences to read access.

All arguments and templates originate as unpublished works with a single author. While they remain unpublished, the author can add additional authors. Only the authors have access, and they are free to make modifications as they see fit. It is through this means that an analyst can enlist the help of other analysts in directly contributing to the development of an argument or template. An analyst can indirectly enlist the help of other analysts by linking arguments produced by them as evidence to support an argument, or by making use of templates developed by others as the basis for the arguments. Once a draft argument or template is ready for limited external review, the authors might add people or organizations to the audience. It is risky for this audience to link to this unpublished work since it might go away or be substantially changed in the future. When the authors decide that the argument is ready for external release, they publish it, giving read access to a specified audience in addition to themselves. These published arguments and templates can be reliably cited and referenced in other arguments since they are guaranteed to persist in an unchanging state.

Any author of an unpublished argument or template can change it at any time. In our most recent version of SEAS, the detailed history of changes is retained, allowing anyone with access to review the history of revisions. There is also a facility to spawn versions of an argument, that is, a copy of an argument in its current state, retained as a snapshot in its development. While the histories retain all the detailed changes, versioning provides a means to capture important waypoints in the development of an argument and, coupled with their graphical depictions, provides a convenient means to visualize the evolution of thinking, either by moving slowly from one depiction to the next or rapidly, producing an animation of its development.

When data is attached to an argument as an exhibit/evidence, if an individual has access to the argument, then SEAS will provide access to the attached data. However, if that data resides on an independent server from SEAS and has it own access controls, then those access controls will prevail. For example, assume that two companies wish to carry out a joint assessment that relates to a joint venture. One or more arguments might be established giving members of both companies read/write access. When data from the open Internet is attached via URL, then members from both companies can drill down to see it. However, when a company member attaches data using a URL that points to that company server, and that server is behind the company firewall, then although members of the other company can see the URL, along with the citation and any relevance given, if they attempt to follow the URL to see the data, the firewall will block them; of course, those in the home company that are behind the firewall will be able to open the URL and see the data. Those aspects of the data that need to be shared can be incorporated into the textual statement of relevance, without revealing those aspects of the data that make it proprietary. Should it be determined that the data should be fully shared, it can be moved to a server to which both companies have access (e.g., the SEAS server itself).

While the ability for co-authors to make direct changes to a developing argument is essential, at times they would like to annotate an argument with issues, without changing the argument itself. *Memos* are structured annotations that are attached to objects within the SEAS knowledge base, including exhibits, evidence, discovery tools, questions/answers, arguments, and templates. Each memo includes text for its subject and body and a type selected from a preestablished set, including comment, critique, for review, to do, summary, instruction, and assumption. Like arguments and templates, memos have a designated audience that restricts their access by others; only those who are members of the audience will know of their existence. One memo can be posted as a response to another, providing a means to imbed a threaded discussion regarding an element in an argument. As such, memos provide a means for private, semiprivate, or public discussion among analysts. Critiques are a way for contemporary analysts to contribute to each other's work. Assumptions might be added so that analysts in the future will better be able to interpret a historical analysis.

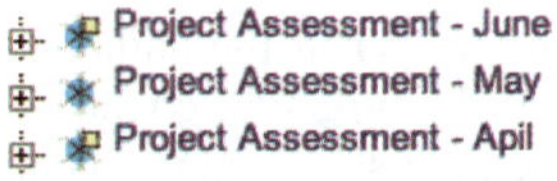

Fig. 15.11. Memos graphically portrayed in list of arguments.

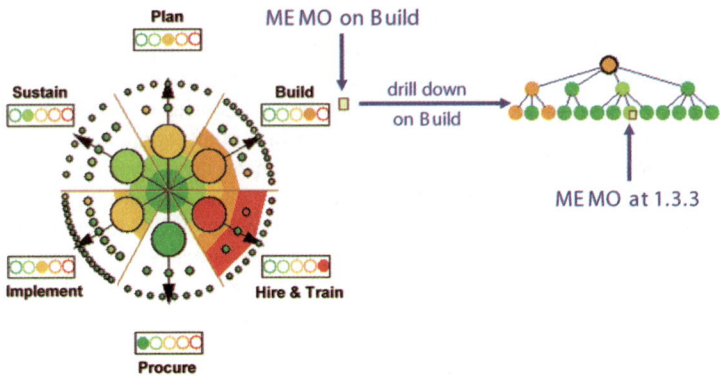

Fig. 15.12. Memos graphically portrayed within an argument.

Since collaboration in SEAS often proceeds asynchronously, analysts need to be made aware of memos that have been added, without having to actively search through argument or template details. SEAS makes the presence of memos known to analysts through its graphical annotation on its depictions of arguments and templates. The presence of a memo is indicated by the presence of a small yellow rectangle, meant to resemble a sticky note. Figure 15.11 shows memo annotations on argument icons in a list of multidimensional arguments. Drilling down on the third argument in the list displays the graphic on the left in Fig. 15.12, indicating that a memo is located in the Build component of the argument. Clicking on the Build component reveals the underlying unidimensional argument, depicted on the right in Fig. 15.11. The memo annotation indicates that a memo is attached to question 1.3.3. Drilling down on this question displays the contents of the memo along with the exhibits, evidence, rationale, and answers for question 1.3.3. Within SEAS, memos can be selectively filtered (or not) based on their type, with graphical depictions indicating where they can be found, allowing the user to go directly to such memos without searching.

SEAS includes another collaborative capability to handle the situation where multiple analysts have each developed their own independent assessment of a given situation, each capturing the assessment in a distinct argument based on a common template. Using starburst/constellation depictions of these arguments, one can quickly determine where there is agreement and disagreement in these assessments (Fig. 15.13), but this does not directly lead to a consensus. To do so, SEAS includes a technique for *joining* arguments, where a new argument is created, based on the same template, with each primitive question supported by one body of evidence for each of the constituent arguments. Each such body of evidence captures how that

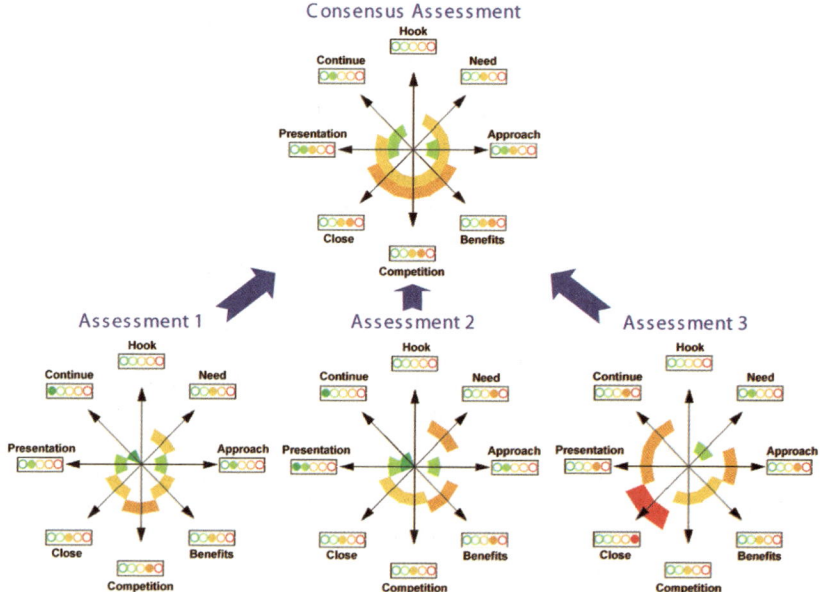

Fig. 15.13. Alternative assessments combined into a consensus assessment.

analyst answered the question with the rationale given as the relevance. When this joint argument is produced, a fusion method and optional associated parameters are provided that are used to combine the disparate answers. That is, the fusion method (e.g., weighted average) and parameters (e.g., source credibility weights) are used to combine the collective answers for each primitive question to arrive at a consensus answer, and these, in turn, determine the consensus conclusions for all the derivative questions. The result is a single argument that captures all the independent opinions as supporting evidence for a single consensus opinion (Fig. 15.13). Note that this form of collaboration takes advantage of the diversity of information and knowledge across a group, while limiting the risk of introducing bias or groupthink; no information is traded during deliberations, effectively eliminating the possibility of individuals influencing the thinking of others. The downside of this approach is that it is expensive, gaining no savings through division of labor.

When deployed, we have seen the collaborative capabilities of SEAS used in different ways, according to locally established business rules. For example, in one case, a group at a U.S. intelligence facility wanted to make a joint assessment of a potential threat. The group's members established a multidimensional template to drive the assessment and created an argument, with all members of the team as co-authors. However, they broke up responsibilities for creating the assessment according to experience. The junior members were tasked with searching for potential evidence that they would attach to questions as exhibits; more experienced members were tasked to determine the relevance/irrelevance of those exhibits and to promote the relevant to evidence and to lower the signal flags on the irrelevant. Even more senior analysts would answer the questions based on the collected evidence; the most senior member would review the overall result, using memos to identify problems that needed to be addressed. Although there is a linear progression implied in this division of labor, members of the team could work on their parts of the problem simultaneously. Coordination was achieved through signal flags and memos. However, it did suggest that SEAS might be enhanced to enforce such business rules, limiting the type of modifications that any analyst is allowed to make according to a specified plan of development.

In another case, SEAS was experimentally used to coordinate the collection and interpretation of information among first responders to a public health emergency. A template was developed that broke out the information and actions needed for a coordinated response among police, fire, hospitals, public health, and so on across city, county, state, and federal facilities. Upon a simulated discovery of a case of smallpox that could lead to an outbreak, an argument was established and made accessible over the Internet through a web portal. As various steps were taken (e.g., incident reported, communications established) and information acquired (e.g., identity and whereabouts of first and second contacts), entries were made in the argument, checking off accomplishments and attaching information. As such, the argument constituted a status board for the coordinated response, detailing the current situation status and highlighting what remained to be done.

In other applications, multiple templates have been used: some for coarse screening and others for detailed follow-up. For example, to address workers compensation fraud, one template was developed for use by store employees. It consisted of a very limited number of simple questions meant to quickly sort out likely legitimate claims from those that warrant further investigation. If this initial screening resulted in a red light, it was to be passed to professionals who would make a more detailed investigation. The initial argument would help the medical and legal professionals understand the reason for suspicion. They would then conduct an investigation, contributing their collective findings to a more detailed argument. Should a red light result from this more detailed analysis, it could be used as the basis for moving to litigation.

Another aspect for which business rules need to be established is to determine what actions are to be taken when lights of various colors come on. This helps directly in knowing how to respond given the current analytic results, but it also helps indirectly in better conveying the meaning of the lights. In one case, we found that in practice, only the green and yellow-green lights were being used. When we investigated, we found that the individual analysts did not want to appear alarmist. But while not appearing alarmist, they had effectively reduced the fidelity of the results to where there was almost no differentiation among situations. To improve fidelity, we established rules that would determine the action to be taken:

- Green: no action needed
- Yellow-Green: follow-up locally by revisiting the question and seeking additional information
- Yellow: reach out to sister organizations, asking them to contribute any information that they might have on the question

- Orange: conduct an in-depth study on the question, including a detailed trend analysis
- Red: report a warning condition up the chain of command

It is important to note that a red condition at one level in a hierarchically structured organization should not necessarily be a red condition nor interpreted the same way at another level. However, in this case, one could imagine that the same set of business rules might be applied at the next level in the organization, determining when to move an issue up another level within the hierarchy (or as Paul Simon once said, one man's ceiling is another man's floor). We often have found it useful to define the lights in terms of what form of communication/collaboration should ensue. For example, in a project management application, a yellow condition meant that a problem had been identified, but the project manager was able to resolve it without assistance, while a red condition meant that upper management assistance was needed to address the problem (i.e., a cry for help that guaranteed a follow-up meeting to discuss options for assistance). We have found it useful to record such information directly in the arguments or templates, included directly in the multiple-choice answers and/or attached as an instructional memo.

As arguments, templates, and other SEAS objects accumulate within a SEAS server, a means is needed to organize these objects for ready access. To fill this need, SEAS includes *collections* that are named containers into which one can place SEAS objects on a common theme. That theme is partially expressed by the name given a collection and by the situation descriptor associated with it. The type of the collection can be used to further express this theme. A *sequential collection* indicates that the items in the collection are linearly ordered and constitute a series. One element in the series does not replace a previous element, but adds to it, by addressing a different aspect of the theme, usually for a different time period. For example, a sequential collection is an ideal way to organize monthly arguments on a common topic, where each argument assesses the situation for a different month. On the other hand, each item in a *versioning collection* is meant to replace the previous item, typically correcting or enhancing it. Its items too are linearly ordered, but typically only the *current* item is in active use, while the items that came before it are retained to ensure the integrity of earlier assessments, and as a historical record.

Besides an item being designated as current, other items can be designated as the *previous* or *next* item. The next item is the one in line to become the next current item, at which time the present current item will become the previous. A versioning collection is ideal for tracking improvements and enhancements to a template over time. The initial version is established as the current one while the next one is under development. When the next one is ready to replace the current, the role of the current is changed to previous, the role of next changed to current, and a new copy of the next (now current) template is added to the collection and designated the next item. In so doing, arguments developed on earlier versions of the template are still based on the same versions, yet the versioning collection makes it clear that there are newer versions available and which is the best to build upon at the moment.

An *alternatives collection* captures the idea that its items are in competition with one another to be designated the best; the order in which the items are listed is of no consequence. This type of collection can be used to organize arguments that represent differing opinions on a common topic. If all such arguments are based on a common template, then a consensus argument can be automatically produced through a join. A *miscellaneous collection* indicates that there is no additional theme and that the order in which the items are listed is of no consequence. Such a collection might be used to collect exhibits on a common topic for later use in support of arguments.

In general, collections can be used to organize objects for easy access. Each user has a *home collection*. Opening this home collection immediately reveals all the items the user has placed in it. If it contains other collections, then those can be opened in hierarchy, revealing their contents. In this way a user's home collection plays a role similar to that of a user's home directory in a computer file system, with embedded collections acting much like subdirectories. Unlike directories, collections have situation descriptors, types, publication information, and (sometimes) roles making it even easier to find and share information. Further, if a signal flag is raised or a visible memo is attached to an object within the user's home collection, it is so annotated, as are the objects within it, making it easy for the user to quickly navigate to those objects needing attention.

15.5 The Argument Markup Language

The Argument Markup Language (AML) was designed as an XML interchange language for structured arguments. It was intended to be both human and machine readable, and capable of representing many different forms of structured arguments. Its design goals included the following:

- AML should support the representation of different types of structured arguments developed by different tools and methodologies.
- Argument viewing/browsing tools should visualize AML arguments that were developed using argumentation tools.
- Argument editing tools should import arguments, modify them, and export the results.
- AML arguments should be self-contained in that they should be able to contain data used as evidence within an argument (e.g., in base64 encoding),

The development of an XML schema for representing structured arguments was originally motivated by SRI's (SRI International) involvement in DARPA's Genoa program. This program included multiple structured argument development tools, argument viewers, and a corporate memory repository for retaining arguments, all to support the intelligence community in rapidly and systematically accumulating evidence, facilitating collaboration, and testing hypotheses that support decision making. While the structure of AML was influenced by SRI's structured argumentation tool, SEAS, it was our intent for it to support the other tools in Genoa and beyond. While our goal was to represent the concepts common to all structured argumentation tools, different argumentation tools, developed to support different classes of problems and technical approaches, invariably have some unshared concepts, making the interchange of arguments across tools necessarily imperfect.

The design of AML began by initially looking for common semantic concepts among argumentation tools and arguments, used to support different technical approaches and different fields of application. We captured these core semantic concepts in a common argument representation. This representation distinguished between uninstantiated argument models (argument templates in our terminology) and instantiated arguments (arguments in our terminology). In addition, templates combine a question hierarchy (or network in Bayesian net terminology) and an aggregation rule attached to each question (node) in the question hierarchy (network). AML also allows for collections of independent objects to be associated with one another (collection in our terminology), which has proved to be extremely useful in practical use, where arguments produced by different people or arguments about different aspects of the same issue can be grouped together.

Rather than use technical terms for the elements of AML (e.g., variable, condset, node), we decided to use legal terminology that is more readily understood (e.g., argument, evidence, exhibit, rationale, relevance). Thus, while AML can represent Bayesian networks, it does so using very different terminology than other popular schemas for Bayesian networks [e.g., Microsoft's XBN DTD (Microsoft, 2007)]. AML can represent the same things (and more), but is more easily understood by those not versed in Bayesian networks or probability theory. In addition AML is a relatively open XML schema that can be extended for use by other argumentation tools by incorporating tool-specific information.

The resulting schema went through several iterations, as we experimented in capturing different types of structured argument (e.g., capability model, Bayes net) using the schema. The latest version of the AML schema is available at the AML Home Page (Harrison & Lowrance, 2006), as is an example AML argument generated using SEAS. In addition, an experimental XSLT style sheet was developed, with the aim of providing a platform-independent way of visualizing AML files, outside of the tool that was used to create the AML file. SEAS fully supports both the import and export of AML.

SEAS's support of AML has provided additional opportunities for collaboration. In particular, the ability to export an argument template from one SEAS installation and then import it at another has been used to trade SEAS templates across government agencies. In this way, if one agency is about to begin working a problem that is related to a problem that has already been worked using SEAS at another agency, then rather than starting the template development process from scratch, the second agency can begin with the template developed by the first agency, and modify it as needed. We believe that such trading in templates is an important way to codify and promulgate the use of best practices.

15.6 Evaluation of SEAS

SEAS has been subjected to testing, in a number of experiments, by a number of different organizations, applied to a number of different problems. In general, the results have always suggested that the form of structured argumentation implemented by SEAS shows promise; at the same time, there have always been suggestions for improvements, primarily focused on usability issues. We have attempted to build on the promise and make the improvements as resources have permitted.

In experiments conducted by DARPA, the ability of analysts to work counterterrorism problems was assessed, with and without the aid of new information technology tools (Popp & Poindexter, 2006). SEAS was one of the tools employed. The experiment divided the analytic problem into three major steps broadly defined as research, analysis, and production. The results showed that analysts unaided by the tools spent far more time doing research and production than analysis; analysts aided by the tools were shown to reverse this, spending more time on analysis and less on research and production, allowing for more and better analysis in a shorter period of time. The significance is that analysts spend a greater percentage of their time doing what is most important, that is, critical thinking. The results also included an impressive savings in analyst labor and an increase in the number of reports produced – about half as many analysts created five times as many reports in the same amount of time. SEAS was credited with letting analysts explicitly represent their hypotheses for comparison and assessment, and identifying evidentiary data gaps for focused research.

The Internal Revenue Service (IRS) tested SEAS as a means to detect, classify, and quantify high-risk compliance patterns in tax filings from larger businesses (Lowrance & Ragoobeer, 2004). Some tax avoidance schemes use complexity to avoid detection and confuse IRS auditors, exploiting IRS stovepipes, cutting across multiple tax entities and multiple filing years. In this test, we worked with revenue agents on the analysis of a particular abusive tax avoidance shelter. A multidisciplinary team of IRS personnel was convened to analyze this current compliance issue and build an argument template for identifying its use. A prototype argument was later constructed for a particular case. Based on this, the IRS concluded that SEAS has good potential to assist in systematically assessing compliance risk, enabling collaboration among IRS experts to move rapidly in identifying and analyzing complex schemes, providing access to evidence from multiple sources for multidisciplinary teams to weigh and agree on an appropriate response, and providing auditors with access to more current and comprehensive knowledge about related entities and potential compliance issues that affect the entity that they are assigned to examine.

Other evaluations resulted in the following statements:

- "The decision maker is able to access all information, consider the validity of the information and of the analyst, check the date of information to make well-informed decisions using all of the information that is available and ensure that the information is germane and current to the problem set at hand."
- "Currently ... interactions between investigators, analysts, management and domain experts are ... telephone conversations, ... meetings, email correspondence etc. most of which is fragmented and lost over time. The SEAS system will provide a more convenient way to centralize this information and ... a record of ... our decision-making process."
- "SEAS, unlike many point-solution analysis tools, supports an extended analysis process with functions for problem formulation, information gathering, evidence handling, evidence assessment, and forming final conclusions. Overall, the analysts found the process clear and had no difficulty adapting to it."

While we firmly believe that structured argumentation and collective reasoning, as implemented by SEAS, has a significant role to play in the general areas of collective evidential reasoning, it is by no means a complete solution. Many aspects of the general problem require different approaches and supporting tools. Search engines, transaction analysis tools, natural language extraction and translation tools, link analysis tools, timeline analysis tools and statistical analysis tools, along with the more mundane email, instant messaging, teleconferencing, spreadsheets, word processing, and presentation development tools, all have a role to play. In addition, other approaches to structured reasoning need to be supported. SEAS is applicable when there is a given hypothesis that can be decomposed into its constituent elements, and that decomposition can be exploited to guide the finding and interpretation of evidence, to arrive at a conclusion regarding the validity of that hypothesis. In some situations, no hypothesis or too many hypotheses exist for this approach to be practical. Instead, hypotheses need to emerge as coherences in the available evidence are discovered (Pioch & Evertt, 2006; Rodriguez et al., 2005).

15.7 Other Applications of SEAS

While SEAS was initially developed to address problems of national security (e.g., nation state stability assessment, terrorist threat assessment, infrastructure security assessment), it has since been applied to a wide range of problems in other domains. The one constant has been that whenever we introduce a new group to SEAS as a proposed solution to one of its problems, the group's members identify several other problems that they think might benefit from its application.

Early on within SRI, we applied SEAS to R&D project management. The ideas were to capture in a template all those things that an experienced project manager knows are important to the long-term success of a project. While this included the usual elements of project management pertaining to how the project is progressing relative to plan, it also included elements pertaining to client satisfaction, the likelihood that the results will successfully transition into operational use, and the quality and interest in the general scientific results being produced. We found that even experienced project managers benefited because it provided them with a means to organize all the material that pertained to the project (e.g., financial reports, correspondence, technical reports, plans) and also alerted them to outstanding issues that they needed to address. For a junior project leader, the template served as an active tutor on project management best practice. In some cases, task leaders were assigned to complete portions of the assessment that pertained to their respective tasks, enabling the task leaders to communicate areas of concern to the project leader. When multiple projects were so managed, collections were established for upper management that included those projects for which they were acting as supervisors. When graphically depicted, these collections became personalized executive dashboards quickly illustrating projects that needed supervisory assistance.

In another set of applications, SEAS was used to assess the quality and potential of various entities pertaining to business. One such application involved the assessment of job candidates. A template was established that characterized the ideal candidate in terms of key attributes. Each person who interviewed a candidate assessed these attributes in an independent argument based on this template, carefully recording the basis for the assessment. For any given candidate, the independent arguments were graphically examined to determine if there were any substantial differences in the opinions; such differences in assessment might become the topic of a meeting where they could be resolved. Then the resulting arguments were joined to produce a consensus assessment. By comparing the graphical depictions of the consensus arguments across all the candidates, the stronger candidates could be easily identified, along with their potential weaknesses.

In a related application, a template was developed for doing employee grade assessment. Each light on the traffic light scale corresponded to a different job grade. The template characterized the performance for each grade across technical, interpersonal, and business development factors. Employees were asked to create an argument based on this template, where they assessed their own performance relative to all the factors. When possible, work products or correspondence were attached as evidence to back up their assessments. These assessments were reviewed by their managers and differences of opinion ironed out through meetings. Thus, the template became a communication channel between management and staff. The staff members commented that they thought this gave them a better understanding of career development paths within the company, where they stood within their selected paths, and what they needed to do to made progress.

Another application used SEAS to provide constructive feedback on business proposals. Here a template was developed that characterized the attributes of a high-quality business proposal. Given a proposal, multiple reviewers would independently assess it. The results were joined into a consensus assessment and provided to the authors. In some cases, such feedback was done in near real time: the proposal was pitched as a briefing. The reviewers each had a laptop connected to SEAS, and as the presentation progressed, they entered their remarks into their SEAS arguments. Time was available immediately after the presentation for the reviewers to complete their arguments, and the resulting arguments were joined to produce a consensus. A summary of the consensus was printed and handed to the presenter. While we found that this rapid style of assessment tends to be less comprehensive and thoughtful, there is compensatory value in the immediacy of the feedback.

Product assessment is another application of SEAS. Here we established a template that covered the various features that might influence the choice of automobile that a person would buy. We then assessed various automobiles against these criteria, making subjective assessments of things like "sex appeal" and objective assessments based on data for things like "safety" (Fig. 15.14). Once the assessments were complete, a prospective buyer could then set the weights in the template associated with the various attributes to reflect the importance of each criterion. As the weights were changed, SEAS automatically recalculated the conclusions for all the arguments (Fig. 15.15).

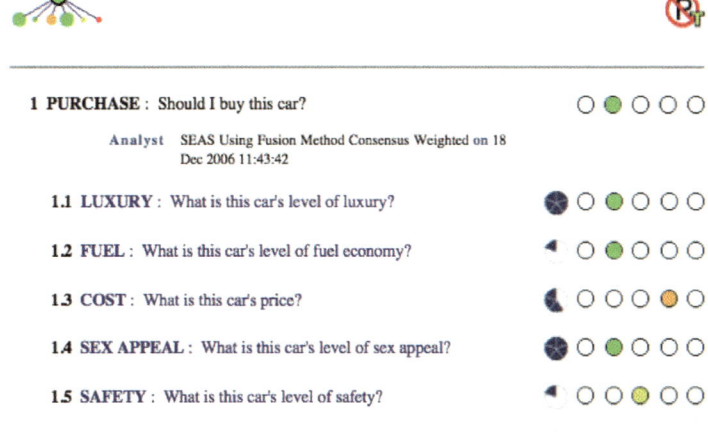

Fig. 15.14. Product assessment argument.

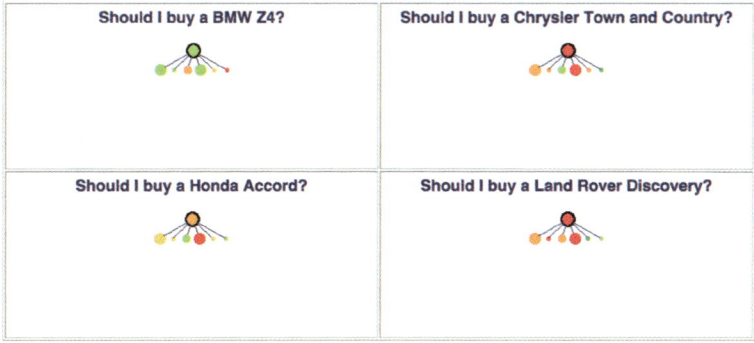

Fig. 15.15. Comparative product assessments.

Other applications have included:
- Scenario signpost monitoring
- Balanced scorecard
- Competitor intelligence
- Technology assessment
- Investment risk
- Partnership evaluation
- SEAS template quality
- Prospect for economic assistance assessment
- Business plan assessment

Many of the templates for these applications can be found in the "SEAS Template Library" collection that is available to all users. However, one of the most powerful aspects of SEAS is that users can develop their own templates for problems of their choosing. In this way, SEAS is similar to a spreadsheet program, but instead of focusing on supporting quantitative reasoning, SEAS supports qualitative reasoning.

15.8 Conclusions

The structured argumentation methodology and SEAS were developed to aid those performing analytic tasks. In particular, we were not looking to automate the analytical reasoning that they perform, but to facilitate it. This methodology

- Encourages careful analysis, by reminding the analyst of the full spectrum of indicators to be considered.
- Eases argument comprehension and communication by allowing multiple visualizations of the data at different levels of abstraction, while still allowing the analyst or decision maker to "drill down" along the component lines of reasoning to discover the detailed basis and rationale of others' arguments.
- Invites and facilitates argument comparison by framing arguments within common structures.

Today, intelligence analysts usually capture their knowledge in text documents. Typically, these documents have minimal structure, limited to section titles that break up the document. These intelligence reports are intended for human consumption. However, because of their limited structure they are time-consuming to read and understand. To compare one report with another requires that both reports be read, and it is up to the reader to find common and uncommon aspects of the underlying reasoning. It is also up to the reader to extract the analytic method if it is to be employed in doing related analyses. Searching a collection of such reports to find ones that might be related to the current problem of interest is also time-consuming. Of course, word processing and search engines can help to speed this process, but the level of aid is fundamentally limited.

We believe that our structured argumentation methodology, as implemented in SEAS, has shown that the addition of even minimal structure into the analytic process can aid analysts in developing, communicating, explaining, and comparing analytic results. An important aspect of this methodology is the retention of direct links to the source material and its interpretation relative to the conclusions drawn, allowing analysts to readily comprehend the thinking of others. This, coupled with a collaborative environment and a corporate memory of previously developed templates and arguments, allows analysts to leverage the thinking of others both past and present. Finally, even though our methodology was originally motivated by the desire to help intelligence analysts, it has been shown to be applicable to a wide array of problems in government, industry, and the private sector.

References

Harrison, I. and Lowrance, J. (2006) *AML Home Page*. SRI International, California: Menlo Park, http://www.seas.sri.com/aml/.

Jones, M.D. (1995) *The Thinker's Toolkit*. New York: Three Rivers Press.

Kirschner, P., Buckingham Shum, S., and Carr, C. (Eds.) (2003) *Argument Visualization*, Berlin Heidelberg New York: Springer.

Lowrance, J. (1995) *Gister Home Page*. California: SRI International, Menlo Park, http://www.ai.sri.com/gister.

Lowrance, J. (2006) *SEAS Home Page*. California: SRI International, Menlo Park, http://www.seas.sri.com.

Lowrance, J. and Ragoobeer, R. (2004) Designing a System for Structured Assessment of Compliance Risk. *Proceedings of SRPP Research Conference*, Washington, DC: IRS.

Lowrance, J., Garvey, T., and Strat, T. (1990) A Framework for Evidential Reasoning Systems. *Uncertain Reasoning*, Ed. Shafer, G. and Pearl, J., San Mateo, California: Morgan Kaufmann Publishers Inc., pp. 611–618.

Lowrance, J., Harrison, I., and Rodriguez, A. (2001) Capturing Analytic Thought. *Proceedings of the First International Conference on Knowledge Capture*. New York: ACM Press, pp. 84–91.

Microsoft (2007) *XML Belief Network File Format*. Microsoft Corporation, Redmond, Washington, http://research.microsoft.com/dtas/bnformat/.

Pioch, N.J. and Everett, J.O. (2006) POLESTAR – Collaborative Knowledge Management and Sensemaking Tools for Intelligence Analysts. *Proceedings of ACM Conference on Information and Knowledge Management*. New York: ACM Press.

Popp, R. and Poindexter, J. (2006) Countering Terrorism through Information and Privacy Protection Technologies. *IEEE Security and Privacy*, Vol. 4, Issue 6, Nov./Dec., pp. 18–27.

Rodriguez, A., Boyce, T., Lowrance, J., and Yeh, E. (2005) Angler: Collaboratively Expanding Your Cognitive Horizon. *Proceedings of the International Conference on Intelligence Analysis*, McLean, Virginia: The MITRE Corporation.

Toumlin, S. (1958) *The Uses of Argument*. Cambridge, UK: Cambridge University Press.

Wigmore, J. (1937) *The Science of Judicial Proof: As Given by Logic, Psychology, and General Experience and Illustrated in Judicial Trials*, 3rd ed. Boston: Little, Brown, and Co.

16. An Experience of the Use of the Cognitive Mapping Method in Qualitative Research

Mário Vasconcellos

University of Amazonia (UNAMA), Centre of Applied Social Studies, mariovasc@unama.br
Federal University of Pará (UFPA), Centre of Environment, mariovasc@ufpa.br

Abstract. This chapter aims to analyze the cognitive mapping method as a tool for supporting qualitative research, particularly to carry out literature reviews, concept analysis and qualitative data examination. The author uses his own experience in using the cognitive mapping method and in applying CmapTools software to understand the concept of partnership. The author highlights some advantages and disadvantages in employing cognitive mapping and CmapTools software. Speed, representation and consistency are advantages of this method. However, the author also shows that the possibilities of reductionism, simplification of ideas and misinterpretation may take place when the method is applied.

16.1 Introduction

The aim of this chapter is to share an experience in the use of the cognitive mapping method in qualitative research. Particularly, this chapter is based on the author's use of cognitive mapping methods (Okada, 2004) and CmapTools software for literature reviews, conceptual analysis and qualitative data interpretation. This chapter is part of the author's PhD research results on partnership between Local Organizations (community-based associations, co-operatives and workers' unions) and government in two areas of North-East Pará, Amazonia, Brazil. One of the research aims was to identify and to understand the meanings of partnership adopted by literature and by social actors involved in it.

The key questions raised in this chapter are: to what extent is the cognitive mapping method an effective tool for supporting qualitative research? What are its strengths? What are its weaknesses?

The chapter is divided in six sections. There are six sections to this chapter. It opens with a brief introduction, followed by an overview of the author's understanding of a literature review. It also creates a link between the literature review and the cognitive mapping. The author's literature review of the partnership concept is explained in the third section thru a mapping method. The fourth section outlines cognitive mapping in analyzing qualitative empirical research data. The fifth section highlights the advantages and disadvantages in the use of cognitive mapping and CmapTools software. Finally, the last section revises the three key questions raised above and reveals the author's conclusions.

16.2 Literature Review and Cognitive Mapping

It is generally accepted by PhD students and inexperienced social science researchers that the literature review is one of the most difficult research phases. This is due to two main reasons. First, the amount of literature is often extensive. Secondly, there are usually cross-cutting analysis perspectives that may cause difficulties in understanding ways of thinking. This is why there is a tendency, in many literature reviews, to emphasize "who said what," to trace the historical evolution of a debate without taking into account the changes of thinking, and/or to describe a subject supported by many quotations. In these cases, the researcher may lose his/her interpretive capacity to criticize the literature reviewed and to find a significant research question. The researcher tends to investigate a subject or theme rather than a research question. The quality of a literature review is based on the identification of books and articles, key ideas, a deep analysis of ways of thinking and concepts of interpretative consistency.

The key objective of a literature review should be an analytical summary of a question and the concepts involved in it. In order for this to be accomplished, it is necessary that the author analyzes the key bibliographical material ideas. Consequently, allowing the author to find correlations and differences between ideas and to understand the types and uses of books and statements in articles. Essentially, it is from the literature review that the researcher deals with subject discussions, identifies different ways in which a subject has been debated, distinguishes the key issues and the main theoretical and empirical criticisms. It is in the literature review that the researcher identifies knowledge gaps about a subject.

An effective literature review does not only depend on the researcher's intellectual capacity, but it also depends on the researcher's capacity and ability to apply suitable methods and techniques, which allow him/her to grasp ideas and knowledge. In addition to a high level of reading, the researcher needs to use techniques that allow him/her to visualize relationships among diverse debates, applied concepts and discussion fields.

While differences characterize the fields of a discipline, information systematization is a common field of ability necessary to all researchers. In any knowledge field, the volume of bibliographical material is often overwhelming. In order for information to be organized, section and subsections are required to connect the ideas from diverse articles, books, maps and others. Therefore, classification is an important phase of an analytical literature review.

Classification is essential because it facilitates the evaluation of ideas under a studied subject. It is difficult to systematically and progressively analyze a great volume of information without classification. The classification phase enables the researcher to visualize diverse contents, their peculiarities and relationships. Cognitive mapping is a useful tool to help the researcher classify and map out literature contents. Secondly, mapping out ideas from literature may take different ways, and different interpretative methods can be produced. This means that each researcher chooses and highlights connections between ideas and an author's thoughts which may be unlike connections done by other researchers. Moreover, the researcher builds connections between concepts from the existent cognitive structures and systematizes his/her own cognitive knowledge (Ausubel, 1968). Thus, classification is not an automatic action; conversely it is a technical activity that depends on the researcher decision makings. The researcher becomes able to assess set ways in which ideas about a subject have been organized, therefore is able to expand the horizons, and to examine the subject with different perspectives.

In the social sciences, classification is not just fixed categories. Ideas, theories, concepts and arguments are not objects of fixed and formal schemes of classification (Hart, 2001). On the contrary, they are part of the "research imagination" (Mills, 1970). They are part of a researcher's capacity and ability to form interpretative relations that introduce a new perspective of analysis. The cognitive mapping method brings together the researcher's imagination and a network of conceptual relations system. The process of building cognitive mapping is a researcher's way of thinking about a research question from knowledge already constructed by other authors.

Visual maps are interesting tools to support the literature review. These are mechanisms for knowledge acquisition and communication. Map building during the literature review is an interactive process that helps the researcher discover and make conceptual relations within the theoretical model that he/she is working on.

The map models comprise boxes and lines. The boxes have key words and the lines signify the relations between these key words. The lines can be unidirectional, bidirectional or multidirectional. The links may express causality, association, names and so on. The usual method is to describe themes from definitions of key words (sometimes a quotation from a text), and this facilitates a reduction of material into a matrix. The matrix helps the researcher identify from what fields the theory has been constructed and how the key concept has been dealt with. This is a tool which facilitates comparisons, contrasts and identification of interactions. The supporting software for building cognitive mapping is CmapTools. This is an interactive and accessible software that does not require extensive IT knowledge. The software brings flexibility to define central questions, to create key words and to create various links among theories, concepts and cognitive abstractions. The following sections will demonstrate some map examples.

16.3 Using Cognitive Mapping for Literature Reviews and Conceptual Examination

The reasons for using cognitive mapping as a tool for literature analysis and conceptual examination are linked to this research phase. A literature review often produces a great amount of bibliographical material which, in spite of the specific context in which it was produced, is presented in many different forms. An extensive bibliographical material may result on the dispersion of a research focus.

A graphical visualization of different forms which a concept takes may help a researcher identify and understand its forms within each discipline. The following example illustrates a conceptual examination. It uses the concept of partnership to demonstrate the complexity of a concept and its diverse meanings within its fields of disciplines.

16.3.1 The Meanings and Structures of Partnership

Similar to other concepts, the concept of partnership has also obtained a diversity of meanings which McQuaid (2000:10) suggests a range along an infinite spectrum). Literature about this subject indicates to have different notions about partnership. These notions are cooperation of (Robinson et al., 2000) trust (Harriss, 2000), complementarity (Lan, 1997) and synergy (Evans, 1997). They (notions) are associated with diverse perspectives in which the concept has been debated. Two spectrums are dominant in the case of Partnership (Box 16.1). The first spectrum is based on social actor and the second spectrum is based on institutional frameworks (Vasconcellos, 2005).

Box 16.1. A spectrum of partnership.

> At one end of the spectrum partnership is based on social actors. Partnership is debated as a form of organization in which the control of the partners enrolled depends on the existence of social actor trust (Brett, 1993; Postma, 1994; Fowler, 1997; Harriss, 2000; Dolny, 2000) and self-organization (Harriss, 2000). In this context, partnership motives are not shaped by ideas of material gain or coercion of the enrolled partners, but by a sense of common purpose supported by trust between its actors. Partnerships based on trust evoke the notion of partnership as a prolonged process and as the result of a long-term relationship between the actors (Lewis, 1998).
>
> At the other end of the spectrum, partnership in based on institutional frameworks and governments (Tendler, 1997; Evans, 1997; DFID, 2006; WB, 2004). This is because partnership is most commonly found in formal and political institutions (DFID, 2006; WB, 2004; Tendler, 1997; Evans, 1997; Lan, 1997; Heller, 1997). This perspective emphasizes partnership as shaped by the rules, regulations and governmental actions where it emerges (ibid.).
> (Vasconcellos, 2005)

In the literature based on social actor the discussion of the concept of Partnership range from the forms in which the concept is structured to the ideal type of partnership. Three themes are recurrent in the discussion that are: existence of trust, reasons that motivate formations of cooperation and types of partnerships. In the literature based on institutions and organizations, the debate about the concept of partnership is concentrated on political structure of public and private organizations (Public–Private Partnership), the structure of laws, norms and governmental regulations, complementarity of resources, and embebedness relationship between state and civil society for carrying out socio-economic programs and projects.

In rural development, partnership takes other various perspectives. However, at least two of them are more prominent. These are partnership as a form of participation (community/people participation and social participation) and partnership as a tool for development management. They, in their turn have been debated in diverse themes. In the debate of partnership as a form of participation, there are two streams: (1) community participation (equity, inclusiveness, power-sharing, mutuality) and (2) social participation (access to basic needs and basic human rights). In the management literature the discussion concentrates on (a) the relationships between Government and NGOs and also relationships between Donor and NGOs, (b) complementarity of resources, (c) business alliance and (d) inter-organizational relations. Table 16.1 and Boxes 16.2 and 16.3 illustrate differentiation between the themes and streams.

Table 16.1. Partnership perspectives for rural development.

Rural development meanings	
Participation	Management (efficiency, effectiveness and responsiveness)
Community participation (equity, inclusiveness, power-sharing, mutuality)	Relationships, Government–NGOs and donor–NGOs
	Complementarity of resources
Social participation (access to basic needs and basic human rights)	Business alliance
	Inter-organizational relations

Source: the author

Box 16.2. Partnership under participation meaning.

> In community participation, partnership is considered the most ethical approach to sustainable development and service delivery in rural areas (Chambers, 1983, 1997). This is because partnership seeks to promote community participation in decisions that affect themselves (ibid.). However, this perspective, which is extremely normative, reveals a simplistic understanding of community as one of harmonious unity within which people share common interests and needs, and conceals power relations within communities (Guijt & Shah, 1998; Cleaver, 2002). In spite of the key intention, to ensure the full and active participation of community members in the rural programmes that affect them, evidence suggests that partnership, as a mechanism of participation, has not worked effectively towards social inclusion and power sharing (Cleaver, 2002; Bowyer, 2005).

In partnership, social participation, which emerged in response to the previous normative understanding of partnership for inclusion of the powerless and power sharing, is recurrently used as an instrument to involve different sectors of society. Social participation is deemed important for promoting access to basic needs and basic human rights for poor rural people (OECD, 1997). Also under the rationale of participation, this perspective prioritizes enduring relationships for strategic issues such as combating poverty and creating sustainable livelihoods rather than "immediate problem solving" of issues such as water supply or combating diseases (DFID, 2006).

This perspective can be found in international donor, governmental and corporate materials: mission statements, annual reports, strategic planning efforts, special reports, programmes and project documentation (DFID, 2006; OECD, 1997). According to these organisations, partnership is an appropriate vehicle to address social and economic needs with the involvement of all sectors of society. It is the mechanism to promote the participation of the civil society in the planning and management of long term public programmes, minimising conflicts between divergent actors in favour of the society at large (DFID, 2006). (Vasconcellos, 2005)

Box 16.3. Partnership under the meaning of development management.

Under development management, partnership is an instrument to be used to reach more precise objectives typically correlated with effectiveness, efficiency and responsiveness (World Bank, 2004). The perspective of development management is generally treated under the theory of New Public Management. Partnership is treated not just as an instrument of people participation in public actions, or as a broad way of committing to society through social and economic needs. Instead, it is viewed as a method to conciliate public and private resources to carry out effectively and efficiently specific public programs. In spite of the instrumental view that partnership assumes under a development management perspective, there is a set of interconnected ideas that examine partnership in an analytical way.

One idea considers particular types of relationships and purposes. It focuses on relationships between governments, NGOs and donors, on advocacy-policy versus program implementation, and corporate citizenship (Lister, 2000; Ahmad, 2006). Its focus is on effective partnership. On a broader scale, it deals with the exercise of power and how it influences a partnership's success. The government's and donor's power are criticized suggesting the possibility of a zero-sum power relationship (Lister, 2000; Ahmad, 2006). In spite of insights about the influence of power on partnership, the pessimistic trend that this interpretation presents does not offer alternative ways to overcome negative issues in it or in any other development management approach. It suggests neutral power relationships that in fact do not happen in any reality.

A second concept deals with partnership efficiency. Here partnership is a strategic mechanism for resource complementarities between the public and private organizations (Sellgren, 1990) and is also a cost-efficient mechanism to carry out developmental projects with low costs and high performance (Bennet & Krebs, 1994). Partners seek out ties with others who can help manage strategic interdependencies efficiently. The rationales for a complementarity of resources and cost-efficiency assume narrow characteristics because partnership is only used for budget enlargement (Sellgren, 1990) or to balance economic costs with project outcomes. The rationales of complementarity focus on economic ends and view social aims as a consequence of resources efficiency.

Also concerned with economic outcomes, another concept is derived from business alliance literature. Partnership terminology in this context is evolving, and increasingly refers to less formal exclusive relationships, as opposed to the limited, historical application of legal structures, mergers and contracting relations. This concept addresses equality in decision making, the autonomy of the partner organizations and corporate citizenship to attain efficient and effective outcomes (Jacobs, 2000). However, it has a limited focus on the public–private relationship for market purposes. In spite of the importance of market orientation in partnerships with economic ends, the public sector is not pursuing purely commercial goals. A criterion for partnerships is that it involves public bodies in balance with social issues (McQuaid, 2000).

A fourth set of analysis includes political economics and networking theories. This thread examines inter-organizational relations, particularly between the public and private sectors, including civil society (Gilchrist, 2004). Although of a normative slant, this concept is the most analytic within partnership literature. It deals with the most rigorous identification and examination of inter-organizational coordination challenges, incentive systems, control mechanisms and structural alternatives (Kooiman, 1993; Kickert, 1997). These have emphasized the importance of the interrelationships between the political and the social context within networks. However, the theoretical and empirical validity of these views still need further analysis (McQuaid, 2000). So far, there is no clear understanding about the behavior and policies of organizations involved in partnerships for economic development. Also, the nature of their relationships with networks and partnerships between other actors that are not directly involved in partnership at local level (including the flows of resources, power and information within these networks) is not included in the analysis.
(Vasconcellos, 2005)

342   Mário Vasconcellos

Certainly the above quotations about partnership are incomplete. However, the quotations give insights about author's difficulties in defining bibliographical issues to follow and consequently to define precisely the concept used in his work. Despite various concepts of analytical views, these are not linear and do not exclude each other. For instance, at the same time that partnership is based on institutions and organization suggests cooperation, synergy and complementarity between institutions, partnership does not occur without trust between social actors. However, the debate on trust is part of discussion on partnership based on social actors. Any analysis of partnership in the organizational context that does not take into account social actors is incomplete. This is because there is no organization without social actors. From the other perspective, trust relations between people and/or institutions do not emerge isolated from a socio-institutional context. They are not apart from laws, societal norms of behavior and people's cultural background. Therefore, partnership analyses that do not take into account institutional aspects are also incomplete.

The map 16.1 shows that in spite of different analytical views, these are not isolated. On the contrary, they are interrelated. The map shows that there is not a bibliographical and/or conceptual hierarchy. At this point, the map shows that

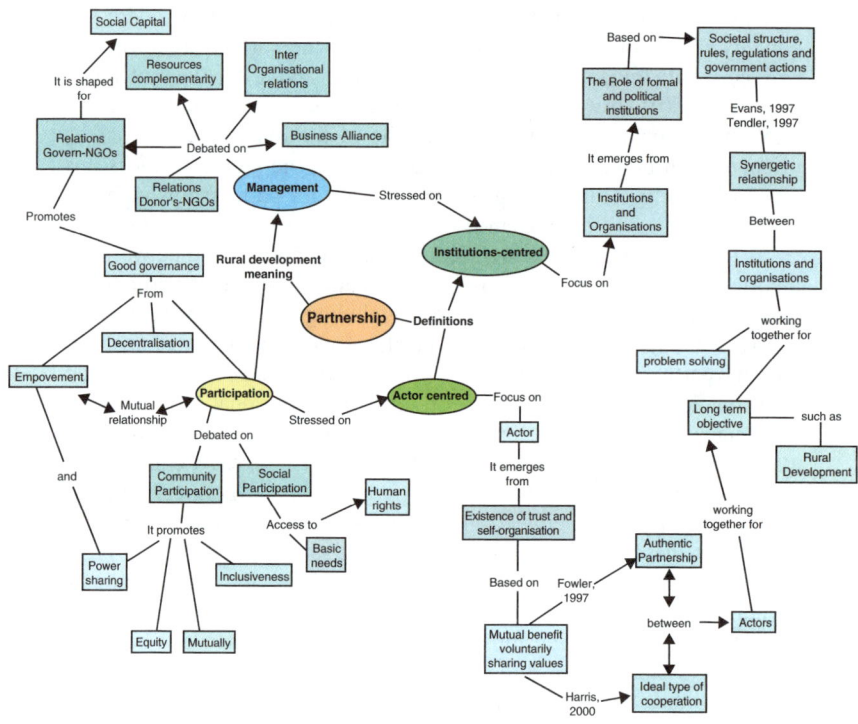

Map 16.1. Partnership in literature.

cognitive mapping is a helpful tool for visual perception of diverse cognitive analyses and constructs by other authors and to support the researcher to construct his/her own set of relations from previously produced knowledge.

Unlike the idea that hierarchical organizations facilitate concept understanding (Novak, 1998, 2005), this author's experience of building conceptual maps has shown that construction of non-sequential and multiple connection maps facilitate the organization of idea links that are not easily demonstrated. For instance, if the bellow map was built from a hierarchical model, it would not demonstrate the two ways in which the concept of partnership has been debated. From this point of view, a hierarchical deconstruction of the concept is more interesting to generate new subject interpretations. Although it is important to follow specialists' instructions in building cognitive maps from a "tree model," the technical orientations should not prevail over the researcher's intellectual abstractions. While certain authors' books and/or articles do not always clearly, coherently and consistently present their ideas, the researcher needs to identify the key issues in each piece of bibliographical material and these are contributions to knowledge. The map 16.1 shows that the concept of Partnership cannot be constructed in a hierarchical form and that there are interrelations between the diverse fields of analysis.

16.4 Use of Cognitive Mapping for Qualitative Data Analysis

The broad and diffuse spectrum on which a concept is debated in literature has automatic influence on a collection of empirical data. The researcher should have clear analytical discernment on how the data should be gathered. Otherwise, the data collection can be completely dispersed.

Despite the methodological advantages that qualitative research method offers for some fields and particularly to social sciences, this method contains difficulties for research validation. Here, research validation is different from validation in the natural sciences. In this latter, replication techniques in identical circumstances can be created in a laboratory. The social environment has elements that are generalized from relationships between facts that are specific to a particular phenomenon. The relationship between facts involves the inclusion of elements of interpretation that are not in the data; conversely they are part of the researcher's cognitive work.

A great concern of the qualitative method researcher is data validation (Bloor, 1997). Researchers look for tools that help them to collect and organize data that also enables interpretative insights. Triangulation has been used as an important method for qualitative data validation. In broad terms, triangulation is the use of different data gathering methods and cross-cut analysis (Bloor, 1997) to examine a sole research question. For instance, researchers use (at the same time) interview methods, document analysis and observation and cross the results achieved from each method to check similarities and differences in outcomes.

However, a serious issue in triangulation use is the amount of data generated. If the interview (structured and semi-structured) method is used, this generates a large amount of data that is difficult to deal with. One hour of tape transcription is around fifty transcription pages. Observation methods also generate a considerable number of notes, particularly ethnographic research. Documentary analysis needs to focus on data acquisition as documents have their own objectives and these are not like research aims. In addition, documentary analysis needs a context. Thus, the greatest qualitative research issue is data accuracy to confirm empirical evidences.

In the last 20 years different types of software have been created to support qualitative research data management such as NUD*IST and Inspiration. However, this software has also been criticized. If on the one hand they facilitate data organization, on the other hand they require an IT ability that is not many social researchers have (Durkin, 1997). In addition, such software is time consuming in organizing data before effective data analysis can be done (ibid). For instance, complete tape transcriptions are required, documents must be translated into the same software language, as well as prior elaboration of concepts and creation of codes and code catalogues. An analysis of this software is not part of this chapter; however what is stressed is that in the use of software, cognitive work is dependant and/or subordinate to technical ability in data organization.

CmapTools is an alternative tool for data organization without requiring extensive IT ability. It facilitates visual data organization that in its turn helps cognitive interpretation. CmapTools can be used in any language, does not require translation into a software language, and does not need prior elaboration of concepts. On the contrary, concepts emerge during the cognitive process of data interpretation. The issues considered here are CmapTools strengths and suggest an emphasis on cognitive interpretation rather than simply software techniques.

Field work research carried out by this author to understand two partnership relations between governments and rural communities showed that the CmapTools makes for easier data organization and facilitates cognitive interpretation. One of the field work research aims was to understand social actors' concepts of the partnerships in which they were involved. The analysis was based on partnerships between government agents (departments of agriculture, environment and planning) and local organization representatives (rural workers' unions, community based associations and cooperatives) in two *municípios* of Pará State, namely Ourém and Igarapé-Miri. These partnerships were established to create rural development committees and for the creation and execution of rural development planning. Research institutes' concepts of partnership were also considered because of their influence on local organizations.

The main field work research question was: what are the social actors' concepts of partnership? Thus, the researcher interviewed agriculturists, community leaders, government, leaders of rural workers, agents and researchers working in these areas. Thirty five interviews were carried out. These resulted in 1,500 transcript pages.[1]

The answers were multivariate as a result of the research information that involved different elements. The social actors' discourses were direct and indirect with connotative and denotative meanings. The examples below show some social actors' perspectives on partnership and multifaceted discourses.

---

[1] The interviews were copied prior researcher decision to use the CmapTools.

16.4.1 The Meaning of Partnership

Commitment to partnership is accompanied by a different operational understanding of the partnership concept. Consequently there is a self-evident problem to translate partnership into practice when there is a diversity of organizations and a diversity of understanding of the meaning of partnership. In both Ourém and Igarapé-Miri, the community-based development associations (CBDA) and the rural unions understand partnership as a coalition of interests between institutional actors as the quotations illustrate.

> (…) Partnership is established when everybody is together, when we build our project together (…).[2]
> (…) Partnership is a mutual relationship, where everybody speaks the same language for the achievement of a common aim (…) everybody is working for the same aim (…).[3]

However, community-based associations (CBA), cooperatives and agents of the state understand partnership only as the transference of financial resources from government to communities for the development of productive agricultural projects. Partnership is interpreted only as a method to maximize the use of resources to reach markets.

> (…) we wanted to improve our production and to put our produce directly to market (…) and then we looked for partners who could support our ideas (…) then we looked at POEMA, BASA, Banco do Estado do Pará [Bank of Pará State plc.] and other partners to carry out our ideas (…).[4]
> (…) what kind of partnership is that, where they [NGO and state] come along and talk, talk, talk but they do not give us anything [money, financing]? (…).[5]
> (…) this is the sort of partnership that does not work; when it is the time to put hands in the state pockets there is no money for the producers (…).[6]
> (…) they speak about partnership [state] but they do not ask us what we need, what projects we would like to create, if it is credit for coconuts, oranges … now they [regional state] have a project for cassava (…).[7]

The study identified that interpretations of CBA are linked to how most of them were created and how partnerships were established. The majority of the CBA came about as a result of credit policies. They were created with no clear understanding of the role of an association. In practice, this means that without a prior process of

---

[2] CBDA leader, Ourém.
[3] Member of the Rural Workers' Union, Ourém.
[4] Former head, Igarapé-Miri.
[5] CBA leader, Igarapé-Miri.
[6] CBA leader, Igarapé-Miri.
[7] CBA leader, Ourém.

capacity building, the creation of an association does not mean a creation for the collective.

> (...) Before the FNO there were just three associations in Igarapé-Miri (...) they were created with the support of the Catholic Church (...) we took account of the [socio-economic] situation, we would not go anywhere (...) then they [Church fathers] did a awareness-raising project (*conscientizacao*) (...) from 1993 to 1996 we had 28 associations, most of them created with local government support (...) local government invested in the creation of associations (...) the associations got money for the *município* (...) I think that around 15 associations were created by the local government (...) and you know, local government was not concerned about people's awareness (...) they [people linked to the new associations] do not even know the role of an association (...).[8]
> (...) in the last few years Ourém had many capacity building courses (...) there was a demand from the rural sector (...) we had many courses about associations (*associativismo*) and co-operation (*cooperativismo*) (...) we had many associations, but they [members of associations] did not know the meaning of an association (...) the trouble was that just a few people came along to attend the courses (...) I do not see a [positive] impact from the courses offered (...).[9]

Cooperatives' commitments to achieve market and economic growth are the main reasons for their interpretation of partnership as transference of financial resources from government to local organizations. However, what cooperative leaders call partnership was in reality, loans offered by the banks that have to be paid back.

> (...) the [co-operative] COOPFRUT was created to support small-scale rural producers to reach markets without the middleman (*atravessador*), it was to improve rural producers' income and eliminate the middleman (...) for that, we made partnerships with POEMA, BASA (Bank of Amazonia], Bank of Pará State (...) with this partnership we had access to credit and nowadays the cooperative is a reality (...).[10]
> (...) I do not think like that (...) people from [COOPFRUT] cooperative do not know the concept of partnership (...) the *prefeito* (mayor) paid R$48,000,00 to POEMA to create a project (...) the *prefeitura* (council) also paid for an office for POEMA (...) then they got loans from BASA and Bank of Pará State(...) nowadays they [associations] owe a great debt to BASA (...) and they call this partnership (...).[11]

Not surprising, it is a recurrent theme between external NGOs and research organizations that the use of partnership is to represent participation of the civil

---

[8] Former head of Rural Workers' Union, Igarapé-Miri.
[9] Former cooperative staff member, Ourém.
[10] Head of cooperative, Igarapé-Miri.
[11] Head of Farmers' Union, Igarapé-Miri.

society to discuss ideas for project support and for governance. This reinforces the interpretation that external institutional actors' comparative advantage lies in the quality of the relationships they can create (Fowler, 1990; Edwards & Hulme, 2002).

> (…) our concept of partnership is above all, to listen to everybody, to give an opportunity to everybody – all governmental and non-governmental organizations, business associations – in other words, to involve everybody in a broad debate to legitimate the process (…).[12]
> (…) partnership is when everybody works to reach a common aim (…) the objectives of the partners are the same or at least similar (…) there is a complement of resources, ideas (…) partnership helps in the management of projects (…).[13]
> (…) at that time, partnership was a way to combine efforts to carry out a collective project (…) this helped in the improvement of use of resources from the government (…) it was also to control the use of resources by the *prefeitura* (council) (…).[14]

Consequently, the CBDA and Rural Workers' Unions' collaboration with NGOs and research organizations has led to a much broader understanding of the concept of partnership.

> (…) certainly, their presence [GESPAN project] has been fundamental in changing the concept that we [farmers] are on the one side, rural producers [small-scale, family-based] are on the other side and the *Prefeitura* on another side (…).[15]
> (…) the job of PRORENDA was fundamental in expressing our [small-scale family-based, rural producers] relationship with the *prefeitura* (council) (…).[16]

In spite of the change of attitude of the local state agents in working more closely with the communities, the assimilation of the partnership concept has not modified the way in which the state interprets the communities' role in rural development. The historical use of a top-down planning approach makes quick change difficult especially when considering communities' participation in the entire system of rural planning and governance. The agents of the state still view communities as beneficiaries of public funds and projects.

> [How did the partnership work?]
> (…) from the ideas; the Department [*of agriculture*] asked them [associations, cooperatives, unions] what were their priorities and then we tried to build it up to a plan to meet their demands (…).[17]

---

[12] Head of POEMAR, Igarapé-Miri.
[13] Head of GESPAN, Igarapé-Miri.
[14] Head of PRORENDA, Ourém.
[15] Head of Farmers' Union, Igarapé-Miri.
[16] Head of Local Organisation, Ourém.
[17] Former head of the Department of Agriculture, Igarapé-Miri.

(…) many associations depend on the government (…) we must be their partner because they need support, for example to prepare land for production; they need equipment, seeds (…).[18]

This interpretation of the concept of partnership by the state representative is similar to a consultation or the provision of a service. In practice, this interpretation means that government is more concerned with the implementation of its programs and actions rather than the governance of rural systems.

This uncertain understanding of concepts of partnership indicates that there is a gap between what is said and what is done in terms of partnership. Actors involved in relationships that range from credit loans and public service delivery to consultation and project management, all reproduce a discourse of partnership that in practice is difficulty to identify in existence. To be carried out as a development tool for the achievement of collective goals in the rural sector, partnership requires at least an appropriate and common interpretation between all actors involved. Without an appropriate and common interpretation of partnership between all actors involved, it is difficult to promote. Equally, it is hard to gain conviction that partnership will work to conciliate interests and priorities and that it will also reach the historically excluded and powerless rural people.

Based on the various meanings that the concept adopted in the interviewees' words, the map 16.2 was elaborated. Methodologically, the creation of maps from interview discourses combined verbal communication and cognitive construction.

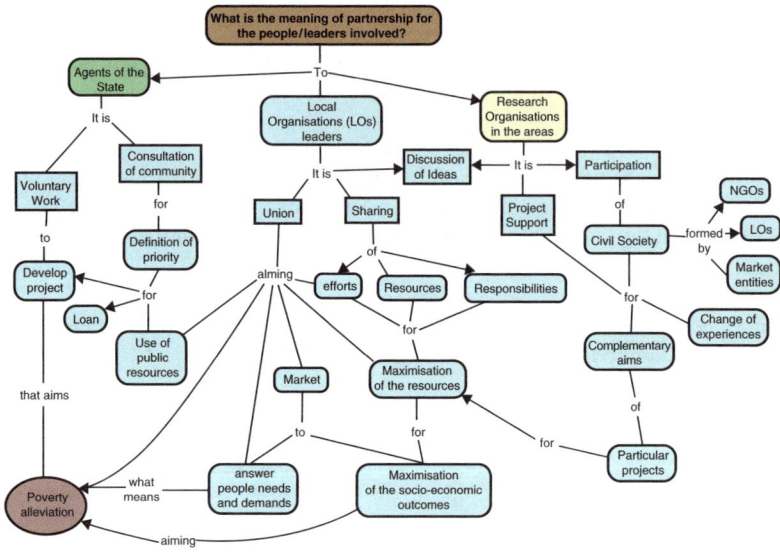

Map 16.2. The meaning of partnership for the people/leaders involved.

---

[18] Former head of Department of Agriculture, Ourém.

The mapping method helped the simplification of key ideas found in the long interviews. At the same time, the mapping method also linked empirical data with the theoretical model that was used in the research.

Natural expression is not the only form to give signifiers to discourse. On the contrary, as was shown above, metaphors and proverbs are usually used to give real meaning to speech. The author had to analyze carefully all interviews to identify the forms given to the partnership concept and the elements used to signify diverse concepts. Thus, the mapping method impelled the researcher to understand the real signification of partnership concepts without forcing the concepts into one sole model of interpretation.

There is no discourse out of historical, political and social contexts. Conversely, every discourse exactly reveals a historical, political and social influence on concept interpretation. The analysis of the partnership concept inside the diverse social actors' discourses corroborated with the researcher's previous assertion that the 1990s socio-political environment influenced partnerships formation. Partnerships between government and local organizations are the results of a financing public policy that was established in the 1990s. Before this decade, government and local organizations were placed on opposite sides. This is evidenced when the researcher created the map 16.3 with the historical, political and social factors that were subjacent to partnership formation in the rural development of Ourém and Igarapé-Miri.

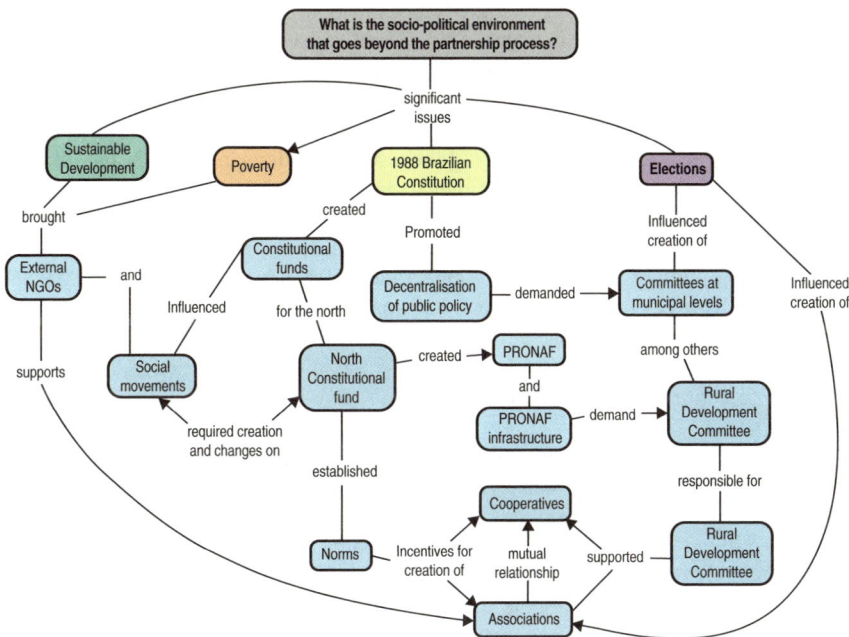

Map 16.3. Socio-political environment beyond the partnership process.

The mapping construction helped the researcher to link the empirical data and the two theoretical views about partnership identified in the literature review that are institution-based and social actor-based. For instance, the combination of maps facilitated the understanding that partnership may emerge in short time to respond to a particular demand of an institutional structure despite a need for mutual trust between the social actors. The research ratified that partnership is linked to institutional structure where it is established and suggests that partnership is a strategy which social actors can see advantages to it. This can occur despite the different social actors' meanings, aims and forms of collective work. Other conclusions emerged during the combination of maps and as such, are not within the scope of this article. However, it is important here to emphasize the interpretative possibilities that the combination of maps (those from the literature review, historical context, empirical data, and so on) afforded this research.

16.5 Cognitive Mapping Advantages and Disadvantages

Many advantages of cognitive mapping and CmapTools are introduced in this chapter. One of the strengths of using the concept of mapping is that it allows for a drastic reduction of data, thus extremely facilitating the process of cross analysis. The use of maps enables to display the various meanings of a single term, phrase or concept of all the interviews on a single map. It also allows a visual identification of linkages among the terms, concepts and events raised during the phase of the literature review, and/or events identified during the research process.

The reduction of data was also a critical issue. The possibility of reducing complex events and simplifying the respondents' views into a single word, phrase or concept during the data analysis, could cause misunderstandings in the overall picture of the event. The author sometimes had to reduce the respondents' views into phrases, in order to avoid misinterpretation.

Another strength of the use of concept mapping is that it permits a dynamic reassessment of interpretation in the appearance of a new event or fact. Concept mapping enables easy reconstruction of maps and consequently rebuilding of a concept's meaning, significance and relations over time. A problem arises when the researcher wishes to instantly reassess issues. In the author's experience, it is always necessary to return to the previous format, thus slowing down the progress of the data analysis.

The main difficulty in using concept mapping was its complexity in terms of the construction of linkages between events, terms and concepts. Some linkages were hard to build up when the maps got bigger and more complex in the cross analysis process. To overcome this bias, some maps had to be divided into two or three maps and regrouped later on.

As with any other research data management method, cognitive mapping should not be understood as faultless concerning literature reviews, conceptual understanding and qualitative data analysis.

During the literature review process and its conceptual understanding two issues emerged and challenged the researcher. First was how to build up non-hierarchical maps. The majority of the literature on cognitive mapping indicates the construction of hierarchical maps as the best way to organize ideas. There is an automatic tendency to create hierarchical maps. Although the author was aware that theories and concepts do not necessarily need to be hierarchical, the instructions for mapping indicate that under cross lines of linking should be avoided (Novak, 1998, 2005). This makes it more difficult to create complex relations between two or more key words. At this stage of map construction it is the technical aspect that dominates rather than the researcher's cognitive work. To overcome this difficulty, the author did not overemphasize map clarity or avoid complex matrices. When all the matrices were created, the author divided the complex matrices in smaller maps for better visualization. This initial difficulty resulted in the creation of a great number of maps thus making their management harder. Some time was used to find the best way to build up maps of complex topics.

Second, it took somewhat convoluted means to establish concept classification and sub classifications. These are frequently arbitrary and may not exactly represent what authors really mean. Additionally, concept classification and sub classification induce concepts (and/or discipline) separation that makes for difficult dialectic analysis. Complex concept classifications and sub classifications are part of the hierarchical model suggested by supporters of the method. However, in social sciences concept classification is not as valuable. Despite possible analytical consistency offered by the method, consistency is not in the maps but found in the researcher's explanations of his/her classification methods.

The main disadvantages in the use of cognitive mapping and CmapTools during examination of empirical data were definition of key words and linking words and also a tendency to build up cause–effect maps. Key words do not necessarily relate to the real significance of what the author wants to say. In some cases the same key word has different meanings on the same map. In other cases, the complexity of expression used by interviewees did not enable a reduction of his/her ideas into two or three key words. In this case, the author used the entire interviewees' sentences to keep interviewees' real expressions and meanings. As a consequence of this, long and full word maps were constructed that made understanding harder. However, the researcher should avoid the reductionism tendency that cognitive mapping instructions lean towards. If this tendency is not taken account there is a real possibility of idea simplification.

A similar difficulty was faced in the creation of linking words. These words took many forms such as verbs, preposition, names etc. Although linking words do not directly influence an author's interpretation, their creation demands an effort that does not necessarily enable understanding of this linking.

The greatest problem faced when using mapping on interview data analysis was a tendency to build cause–effect maps. Although cause–effect relations exist, the researcher should be aware that in many cases these relations do not occur. If the researcher builds a map with both cause–effect and non-cause–effect links, there is a tendency to read it in the same way and consequently leads to misinterpretation.

16.6 Conclusions

Unlike two decades ago, researchers that work with qualitative research method have many opportunities to use software for data management and analysis. Among other options, CmapTools is an alternative method to support the researcher in the use of the cognitive mapping method.

However, qualitative research does not only use cognitive mapping method and CmapTools software. Each piece of research is carried out from a particular research perspective that leads to a specific methodology. Research particularities are determined by the researcher's position and subjects. Cognitive mapping method and CmapTools software are options that may be applied with various perspectives and subjects.

In order to map out ideas, arguments and concepts of a body of literature are significant techniques for a literature review. The mapping facilitates the researcher in finding out his/her way inside the body of existent literature, to identify studies and key words and at the same time to build up a relations-based image of existing work. Although the mapping method is not the only form of idea acquisition, it encourages the researcher to deal with substantial literature without getting lost between various interpretations about his/her subject.

The cognitive mapping method facilitates field work data organization and reduction, particularly concerning data from interviews, documents, observation notes and ethnography. Three advantages were prominent in this author's experience. First, it provided flexibility in terms of data organization. This flexibility encouraged the researcher to conduct multiple relations between diverse research questions. CmapTools software also facilitated constant data reorganization and questions relations. Such changes occurred during this researcher's new reflections without changing the author's central ideas.

Second, the mapping method facilitated representation of ideas. The mapping made possible this researcher's idea representation with its own dynamic and in real time. This resulted in substantial researcher theorization. The mapping also facilitated representation of theories, concepts and data. This helped the researcher to visualize to what extent his thinking about theories, concepts or data were represented while keeping the researcher's trajectory and retaining information.

Third, the mapping method improved data consistency. The researcher could look back on representations from different times and in diverse ways and check the outcomes. In some cases, the researcher showed a set of maps to other researchers and they interpreted the maps in the same way. This made the researcher more comfortable with his research outcomes.

However, as with any other method that supports qualitative research, cognitive mapping has its limitations. The tendency towards hierarchical analysis and/or cause–effect examination exists and may cause inconsistency and interpretation errors during the literature review and/or data analysis. The possibility of reductionism and idea simplification also exists. In the literature review, the method instructions lean towards classification and sub classification of concepts. For data analysis, the method also suggests the creation of key words and linking words. These suggestions while aiming to reduce data volume may induce reductionism and a simplification of ideas. Finally, while flexibility may be a positive addition and a software benefit, this flexibility may be a problem for substantial researcher reflections on his/her subject.

List of Acronyms and Abbreviations

BASA	Bank of Amazonia plc.
CBA	Community-Based Association
CBDA	Community-Based Development Association
COOPFRUT	Igarapé-Mirí Co-operative of Small Rural Producers
GESPAN	Participatory Management of Natural Resources Management
POEMA	Poverty and Environment Program
POEMAR	Institute for Actions of Sustainable Development
PRONAF	National Support Program for Family-Base Agriculture
PRORENDA	Support Project for Small-Scale Rural Producers in the State of Pará

Acknowledgment

I am thankful to Alexandra Okada and Saburo Okada for their comments on an earlier version of this chapter. I am grateful to Sadhbh O'Dwyer and Roberta Pires for their proofreading. Thanks too to the Amazonia Development Institute (FIDESA) and Brazilian Education Ministry Agency (the CAPES Foundation) for supporting my PhD program.

References

Ahmad, M.M. (2006) The partnership between international NGOs (Non-Governmental Organisations) and Local NGOs in Bangladesh. Journal of International Development 18, 629–638.
Ausubel, D.P. (1968) *Educational Psychology: a Cognitive view.* New York and London: Holt, Rinehart and Winston.
Bennett, R.J. and Krebs, G. (1994) Local economic development partnerships: an analysis of policy networks in EC-LEDA local employment development strategies. Regional Studies 28, 119–140.
Bloor, M. (1997) Techniques of validation in qualitative research: a critical commentary. In: G. Miller and R. Dingwall (Eds.), *Context and Method in Qualitative Research.* London: Sage, pp. 37–50.
Bowyer, T. (2005) Public space, inequality and health: interaction and social welfare in rural Peru. International Relations 19(4), 475–492.
Brett, E.A. (1993) Voluntary agencies as development organisations: theorising the problem of efficiency and accountability. Development and Change 24(2), 264–303.
Chambers, R. (1983) *Rural Development: Putting the Last First.* London: Longman.
Chambers, R. (1997) *Whose Reality Counts? Putting the First Last.* London: IT Publications.

Cleaver, F. (2002) Paradoxes of participation: questioning participatory approaches to development. In: M. Edwards and A. Fowler (Eds.), *The Earthscan Reader on NGO Management*. London: Earthscan, pp. 225–240.

DFID (2006) Millennium Development Goals: Aid, Trade, Growth and Global Partnership. DFID, London. (www.dfid.gov.uk/mdg/aid.aso) [Accessed 10/10/2006]

Dolny, H. (2000) Building trust and co-operation: transforming the land bank. In: R. Dorcas, T. Hewitt and J. Harriss (Eds.), *Managing Development: Understanding Inter-Organizational Relationships*. London: Sage & The Open University.

Durkin, T. (1997) Using computer in strategic qualitative research. In: G. Miller and R. Dingwall (Eds.), *Context and Method in Qualitative Research*. London: Sage, pp. 92105.

Edwards, M. and Hulme, D. (2002) Making a difference: scaling up the development impact of NGOs – concepts and experiences. In: M. Edwards and A. Fowler (Eds.), *The Earthscan Reader on NGO Management*. London: Earthscan, pp. 53–73.

Evans, P. (1997) Government action, social capital and development: reviewing the evidence on synergy. In: P. Evans (Ed.), *State-Society Synergy: Government and Social Capital in Development*. Berkeley: University of California.

Fowler, A. (1990) Doing it better? Where and how NGOs have a comparative advantage in facilitating development. AERDD Bulletin 28.

Fowler, A. (1997) *Striking a Balance: A Guide to Enhancing the Effectiveness of Non-Governmental Organisations in International Development*. London: Earthscan.

Gilchrist, A. (2004) *The Well-Connected Community*. Community Development Foundation, Bristol.

Guijt, I. and Shah, M. (1998) *The Myth of Community: Gender Issues in Participatory Development*. London: IT Publications.

Harriss, J. (2000) Working together: the principles and practice of co-operation. In: D. Robinson et al. (Eds.), *Managing Development: Understanding Inter-Organizational Relationships*. London: Sage and The Open University.

Hart, C. (2001) *Doing a Literature Review: Releasing the Social Science Research Imagination*. London: Sage.

Heller, P. (1997) Social capital as product of class mobilization and state intervention: industrial workers in Kerala, India. In: P. Evans (Ed.), *State-Society Synergy: Government and Social Capital in Development*. Berkeley: University of California.

Jacobs, B. (2000) Partnerships in Pittsburgh. In: S.P. Osborne (Ed.), *Public–Private Partnerships: Theory and Practice in International Perspective*. London: Routledge.

Kickert, W. (1997) Public governance in the Netherlands: an alternative to Anglo-American managerialism. Public Administration 75, 731–752.

Kooiman, J. (1993) *Modern Governance*. London: Sage.

Lan, W.F. (1997) Institutional design of public agencies and coproduction: a study of irrigation associations in Taiwan. In: P. Evans (Ed.), *State-Society Synergy: Government and Social Capital in Development*. Berkeley: University of California.

Lewis, D.J. (1998) Partnership as process: building an institutional ethnography of an inter-agency aquaculture project in Bangladesh. In: D. Mosse, J. Farrington and A. Rew (Eds.), *Development as Process: Concepts and Methods for Working with Complexity*. London: Routledge.

Lister, S. (2000) Power in partnership? An analysis of an NGO's relationships with its partners. Journal of International Development 12(2), 219–225.

McQuaid, R.W. (2000) The theory of partnership: why have partnerships? In: S.P. Osborne (Ed.), *Public–Private Partnerships: Theory and Practice in International Perspective*. London: Routledge.

Mills, C.W. (1970) *The Sociological Imagination*. London and Oxford: Penguin.

Novak, J.P. (1998). Learning creating and using knowledge: concept maps as facilitative tools in school and corporations. Mahwah: Lawrence Erlbaum Associates.
Novak, J.P. (2005). The theory underlying concepts maps and how to construct them, http://cmap.coginst.uwf.edu/info/printer.html. [Accessed on 22/10/2005].
OECD (1997) Public–Private Alternatives to Traditional Regulations. Working Paper, 28.
Okada, A. (2004) *Cartografia cognitiva: tecnicas de mapeamento*. http://cursosonline.cogeae.pucsp.br/moodle/mod/resource/view.php?id=22 [Accessed on 22/03/2006].
Postma, W. (1994) NGO partnership and institutional development: making it real, making it intentional. Canadian Journal of African Studies 28(3), 447–471.
Robinson, D. et al. (Eds.) (2000). Why inter-organizational relationships matter. In: Robinson, D., Hewitt, T. and Hariss, J. (Eds.), *Managing Development: Understanding Inter-Organizational Relationships*. London: Sage & The Open University.
Sellgren, J. (1990) Local economic development partnerships: an assessment of local authority economic initiatives. Local Government Studies July/August, 57–78.
Tendler, J. (1997) *Good Governance in the Tropics*. Baltimore: John Hopkins.
Vasconcellos, M. (2005) *Parceria: conceitos e interpretações*. http://projeto.org.br/emapbook/ [Accessed on 22/03/2006].
World Bank (2004) *State-Society Synergy for Accountability*. World Bank, Washington.
tion: Neurobiological Bases of Hearing. New York: Wiley, pp. 385–430.

17. Collaborative Knowledge Modelling with a Graphical Knowledge Representation Tool: A Strategy to Support the Transfer of Expertise in Organisations

Josianne Basque[1], Gilbert Paquette[2], Beatrice Pudelko[3], and Michel Leonard[4]

[1]Tele-universite, LICEF Research Center, basque.josianne@teluq.uqam.ca
[2]Tele-universite, LICEF Research Center, paquette.gilbert@teluq.uqam.ca
[3]Tele-universite, LICEF Research Center, pudelko.beatrice@licef.teluq.uqam.ca
[4]Tele-universite, LICEF Research Center, leonard.michel@licef.teluq.uqam.ca

Abstract. This chapter presents a strategy for collaborative knowledge modelling between experts and novices in order to support the transfer of expertise within organisations. The use of an object-typed knowledge modelling software tool called *MOT* is advocated, to elaborate knowledge models in small groups composed of experienced and less experienced employees within organisations. A knowledge model is similar to a concept map, except that it is based on a typology of links and knowledge objects. This technique is used to help experts externalise their knowledge pertaining to concepts, principles, procedures and facts related to their work and to support the sharing of knowledge with novice employees. This chapter presents the rationale behind this strategy, the tool used, the applications of this method and the manner in which it can be integrated into a global knowledge management strategy within organisations.

17.1 Introduction

Over the last few years, economic and technological changes have sparked major challenges in the workplace. To remain competitive and efficient, organisations must rely upon the competencies of their human resources. Indeed, organisational know-how is often intrinsically linked to the tacit knowledge acquired by employees while working for the organisation. Hence, it is lost once the employees leave the organisation (Nonaka & Takeuchi, 1995; Polanyi, 1966). Jacob & Pariat (2001) claim that such tacit knowledge can represent up to 70% of the organisation's knowledge and competency assets. Since most Western societies will soon experience a substantial turnover of manpower, issues pertaining to the elicitation, representation, sharing, validation, re-use and evolution of knowledge has become particularly critical for organisations in recent years (Beazley et al., 2002; De Long, 2004). Consequently, many of them began to set up knowledge management (KM) strategies supported by information and communication technologies.

According to Apostolou et al. (2000), two approaches to KM can be distinguished. The first one, called a "product-oriented approach", focuses on the creation, storage and re-use of documents. Such an approach aims to create an "institutional knowledge memory". The second one, called a "process-oriented approach", addresses the social communication process and strives to transfer expertise directly among people: "in this approach, knowledge is tied to the person who developed it and is shared mainly through person-to-person contact. The main purpose of Information Technology in this approach is to help people communicate knowledge, rather than store it. This approach is also referred to as the 'personalisation approach'" (Apostolou et al., 2000, p. 2).

Traditional strategies used in the process-oriented approach to KM in organisations include formal training in groups, as well as informal training on a one-on-one basis. For example, an experienced worker who is about to leave the organisation is asked to train his successor over a period of a few days or weeks. Some other strategies include job sharing between senior and newer staff members, buddy systems, mentoring, sponsorships, and communities of practice (McDermott, 2001; Wenger, 1998).

However, transferring one's own knowledge to someone else does not constitute a simple task. Knowledge-transfer aptitudes and pedagogical competencies are not innate. Moreover, those who excel in their field are not necessarily aware of the manner in which they perform their work. Tacit knowledge is difficult to externalise. Most of the time, experts use their knowledge "live" and rarely have the opportunity to consciously reflect upon what they are doing. They basically find it hard to verbalise what they know or to explain their "action model" (Sternberg, 1999). Cognitive psychology research conducted within the "mental model" paradigm indicates that expertise consists of a highly organised structure of different types of knowledge (Chi et al., 1981; Ericsson & Charness, 1994; Glaser, 1986; Sternberg, 1997). A mental model is activated in the context of a specific task in an economical and situated fashion; specifically, the expert activates only the knowledge necessary to perform the task. Moreover, much expert knowledge becomes "encapsulated". Consequently, it is difficult to express it into words (Chi et al., 1988; Gentner & Stevens, 1983). Transferring one's expertise thus requires that the proficient practitioners delve deeper into their knowledge and spell out for others what seems clear and easy for them to understand. Many studies have shown that experts have difficulties formulating concrete and detailed explanations of a task, even if they are aware that their explanations are intended for novices (Hinds et al., 2001). The lack of means available to deal with these cognitive and metacognitive difficulties creates somewhat of a bottleneck for organisations that aspire to address expertise transfer.

A possible solution to approach this problem consists of creating situations where experts have to provide novices with a structured external representation of their knowledge of the field. This requires the integration of two aspects: (1) verbal interactions in the context of professional activity and (2) a means to trigger the externalisation of the expert's knowledge according to the novice's needs and knowledge level. The co-construction of graphical representations of knowledge offers great potential for this purpose. Indeed, many studies conducted in educational settings demonstrate that creating graphical representations in groups, such as concept maps, is beneficial to learning (Basque & Lavoie, 2006).

This chapter presents a strategy to support the transfer of expertise in organisations that consists of having small groups of experts and novices co-construct graphical knowledge models using an object-typed knowledge modelling software tool called *MOT* (Paquette, 2002). The strategy has some similarities to the concept mapping technique used by Coffey and his collaborators to elicit knowledge (Coffey, 2006; Coffey & Hoffman, 2003). However, our strategy differs in that (1) knowledge modelling here is jointly conducted with experts and novices (not solely with experts), (2) it is done within a KM perspective that is primarily *process*-oriented, although it can also be integrated into a product-oriented KM program as discussed further on and (3) it is completed using a semi-formal graphical representational language.

The remainder of this chapter is organised as follows. The knowledge modelling software tool is described in Sect. 2, followed by a presentation of the knowledge transfer strategy in Sect. 3. Then, in Section 4, the rationale behind the strategy is addressed. In Sect. 5, we report first applications of the strategy in two Canadian organisations. In Sect. 6, we explain how the strategy can be integrated into a more global knowledge management project within an organisation. Finally, to conclude, research issues emerging from our work are identified.

17.2 The Knowledge Modelling Tool

It is often said that a picture is worth a thousand words. This can be applied to sketches, diagrams and graphs used in various fields of knowledge. Concept maps are widely used in education to represent and clarify complex relationships between concepts (Novak & Gowin, 1984). Flowcharts serve as graphical representations of procedural knowledge or algorithms. Decision trees are another form of representation used in various fields, particularly in decision-making and expert systems. All these representation methods are useful at an informal level, as thinking aids and tools to communicate ideas, albeit with limitations. One of these is the imprecise meaning of the links represented in the model. Non-typed arrows can have various meanings, sometimes within the same graph. Another limitation consists of the ambiguity around the type of entities. Objects, actions performed on objects, conditions applied to actions and statements of properties about the objects are often not distinguished, which results in a missed opportunity to "disencapsulate" knowledge and makes graph interpretation imprecise and risky. Ambiguity can also arise when more than one representation is introduced into the same model. For example, concepts used in a procedural flowchart as entry, intermediate or terminal objects could be given a more precise meaning by developing them using part-whole or class-subclass relationships in sub-models of the procedure. This also applies to procedures included in concept maps that could be developed as procedural sub-models described by flowcharts along with decision trees.

In software engineering, many graphic representation formalisms have been or are used, such as entity-relationship models (Chen, 1976), conceptual graphs (Sowa, 1984), object modelling techniques (OMT) (Rumbaugh et al., 1991), KADS (Schreiber et al., 1993), or Unified Modeling Language (UML) (Booch et al., 1999). These representation systems were built for the analysis and architectural design of complex information systems. The most recent ones, such as UML-2, require the use of up to fifteen different kinds of models so that links between them rapidly become hard to follow without considerable expertise.

The initial goals of *MOT* developers were different. They intended to develop a graphical representation system that was simple enough to be used by individuals without a computer science background, yet sufficiently general and powerful to let them represent knowledge in a semi-structured way.

17.2.1 Background in Schema Theory

The syntax and semantics of the *MOT* graphical modelling language are based on the notion of schema. The concept of schema is the essential idea behind the shift from behaviourism to cognitivism. Cognitivism, a dominant theory in the field of psychology and other cognitive sciences for some years, is based on the pioneering ideas of Inhelder & Piaget (1958) and Bruner (1973). For Piaget, a schema is essentially a cognitive structure that underlies a stable and organized pattern of behaviour. In the early seventies, Newell & Simon (1972) developed a rule-based representation of human problem solving activities on the same basis, while Minsky (1975) defined the concept of "frame" as the essential element to understand perception as a cognitive activity and a means of reconciling the declarative and procedural views of knowledge.

Schemata play a central role in knowledge construction and learning. They guide perception, defined as an active, constructive, and selective process. They support memorisation skills seen as processes to search, retrieve, or create appropriate schemata to store new knowledge. They make understanding possible by comparing existing schemata with new information. Globally, through all these processes, learning is seen as a schema transformation enacted by higher order processes. Learning is seen as schemata construction and reconstruction through interaction with the physical, personal, or social world, instead of a simple transfer of information from one individual to another.

17.2.2 The Typology of Knowledge in MOT

In educational sciences, there is a consensus to distinguish between four basic types of knowledge entities (i.e., facts, concepts, procedures, and principles), despite some differences of opinion relative to the terminology and associated definitions (see for example, Merrill, 1994; Romizowski, 1999; Tennyson & Rasch, 1988; West et al., 1991). All four types of knowledge are also considered in the framework of schema theory. The distinction between conceptual and procedural schemata has long been accepted in the cognitive sciences. Later, the third category, conditional or strategic schemata, was proposed (Paris et al., 1983). These schemata have a component that specifies the context and conditions required to trigger a set of actions or procedures, or to assign values to the attributes of a concept. These categories map very well onto the existing consensus within educational sciences.

This categorisation framework has been retained as the basis of the *MOT* graphical language for representing knowledge entities. *Concepts* (or classes of objects), *procedures* (or classes of actions) and *principles* (or classes of statements, properties or rules) are the primitive objects of the *MOT* graphical language. These objects are visually differentiated from one another through different geometric figures, as shown in Fig. 17.1. Individuals from the three basic classes of knowledge objects are linked to them through an "instantiation" link (I), yielding three kinds of individuals (or facts): *Examples*, *Traces*, and *Statement*. Each set of individuals is obtained by providing precise values to the attributes that define a concept, a procedure or a principle.

Concepts can be object classes (country, clothing, vehicles, etc.), types of documents (forms, booklets, images, etc.), tool categories (text editors, televisions, etc.), groups of people (doctors, Europeans, etc.), or event classes (floods, conferences, etc.). *Procedures* are actions or operations performed by humans, systems or machines (add numbers, assemble an engine, complete a report, digest food, process students' records, etc.). *Principles* can state constraints on procedures (the tasks must be completed within 20 days), cause/effect relationships (if it rains more than 25 days, the crop will be jeopardised), laws (a sufficiently heated metal will stretch out), theories (economic laws), rules of decision (advising on an investment), or prescriptions (medicinal treatment, instructional design principles, etc.).

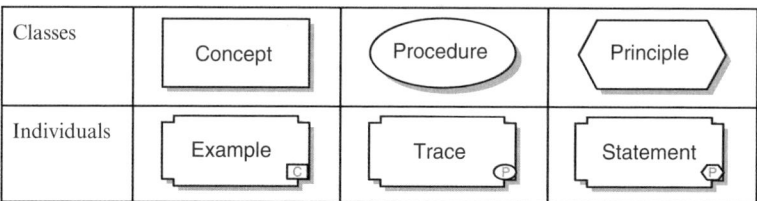

Fig. 17.1. Types of knowledge entities in *MOT*.

17.2.3 The Typology of Links in MOT

Graphs similar to UML object models could very well be used to represent the attributes that describe a schema with different formats according to their type. However, the graphical *MOT* language (Paquette, 2002, 2003) strives to improve the readability and the user-friendliness of graphs by externalising the internal attributes of a schema into other schemata with proper links to the original one.

For example, in Fig. 17.2, the link between the schemata "Triangle" and "Rectangular Triangle" is shown explicitly through a specialisation (S) link from the latter to the former concept. Links between the "Rectangle Triangle" concept and its sides or angles attributes are shown using a composition (C) link. The links from an input concept to a procedure and from a procedure to one of its products are both shown by an input/product (I/P) link. The sequencing between actions (procedures) and/or conditions (principles) in a procedure is represented by a precedence (P) link. Finally, the relation between a principle and a concept that it constrains, or between a principle and a procedure (or another principle) that it controls, is expressed by a regulation (R) link. Using these links, this simple example on the rectangular triangle concept becomes a *MOT* model, where relations between knowledge entities are made explicit and where the types of entities (procedural, conceptual and strategic) are amalgamated in the same model.

The *MOT* model such as this one includes different types of schemata whose attributes are all explicitly externalised and related to each other using six kinds of typed links that are constrained by the following grammar rules:

1. All abstract knowledge entities or classes (*concepts, procedures, principles*) can be related through an *Instantiation* (I) link to a set of *facts* representing individuals called *examples, traces,* and *statements*.
2. All abstract knowledge entities (concepts, procedures, principles) can be specialised or generalised using *Specialisation* (S) links.
3. All abstract knowledge entities (concepts, procedures, principles) can be decomposed using the *Composition* (C) link into other entities, generally of the same type.
4. Procedures and principles can be sequenced together using the *Precedence* (P) link.
5. Concepts can be inputs to a procedure using an *Input/Product* (I/P) link to the procedure or products of a procedure using an I/P link from the procedure.
6. Principles can regulate, using a *Regulation* (R) link, any procedure to provide an "external" control structure, to constrain a concept or a set of concepts by a relation between them, or to regulate a set of other principles (e.g., to decide on conditions of their application).

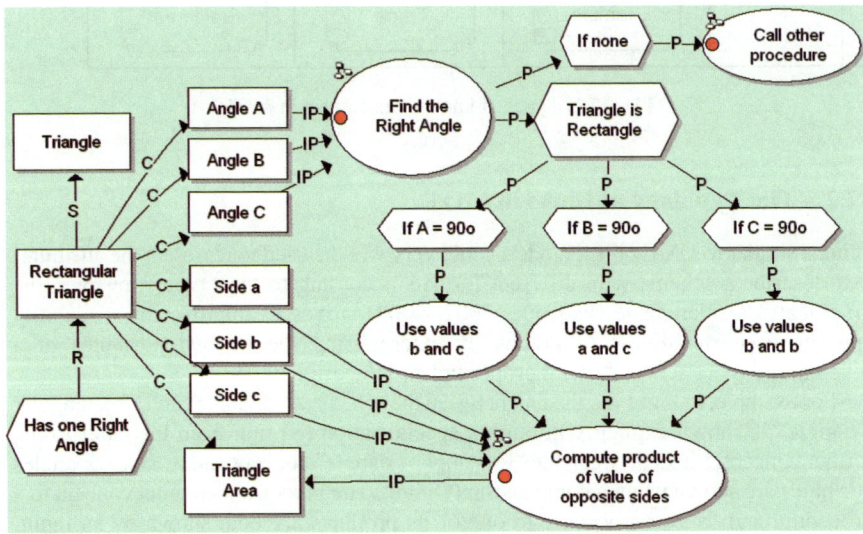

Fig. 17.2. A simple MOT model to provide a definition of the concept of a rectangle triangle.

The first three links are based on traditional distinctions in the field of Artificial Intelligence between instantiation (I: "is-a"), composition (C: "is part-of"), and specialisation (S: "a kind-of") links that are used to represent relationships between classes. The Input/Product (I/P) and Precedence (P) links are fundamental in procedural or algorithmic representations. The first one helps to represent data flows between information sources and operations, where they serve as input or product, while the second helps to represent sequences of operations or tasks. The Regulation (R) link consists of an essential innovation to relate principles to other types of knowledge. It is inspired by knowledge-based or expert systems where the control structure (usually conditional rules) is external to the task it controls. Typically, principles are processed by an inference engine that will apply these rules to trigger operations or to produce (other) objects.

Figure 17.3 summarises the grammar rules of the *MOT* graphical language in the form of an abstracted graph whose nodes illustrate types of knowledge objects with arrows that depict valid links between them. Based on these grammar rules, the *MOT* software restrains the types of links that users can create between two specific types of knowledge objects. For example, since a specialisation link can only be used between two objects of the same type, the user will be suggested a default link (the most probable valid one) if he tries to link two objects of different types with the "S" link. However, users can use the "untyped" links if they want to put their own labels on links. A specific shape is also provided for "untyped" knowledge objects.

With this set of primitive graphic symbols, it has been possible to build from simple to complex representations of structured knowledge in graphical models. For example, we can build representations that are equivalent to concept maps, flowcharts (including iterative procedures), decision trees and other types of models such as models of processes, methods and theories. All of these types of models have been elaborated in a number of projects conducted at the LICEF Research Center (Montreal, Canada) since the publication of the first version of *MOT* in 1996. Following are a few examples: a computerised school model (Basque et al., 1998), an assistance model

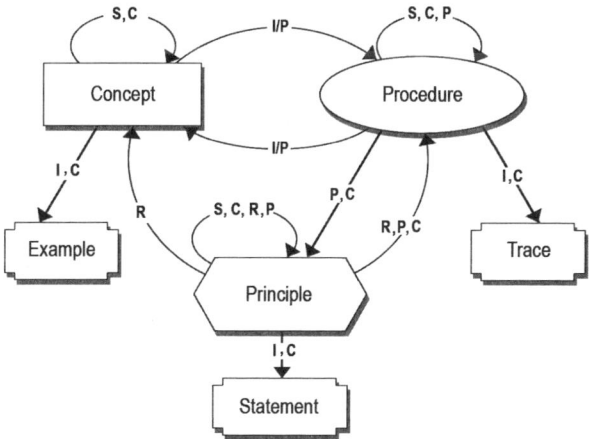

Fig. 17.3. The *MOT* metamodel.

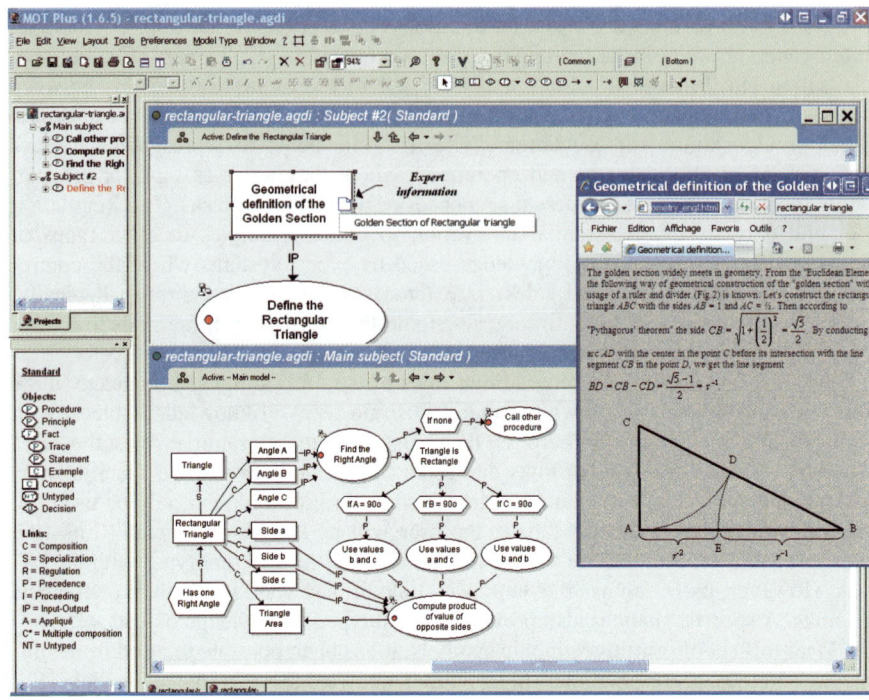

Fig. 17.4. The interface of the *MOT Plus* tool.

for distance learning (Dufresne et al., 2003), a troubleshooting model (Brisebois et al., 2003), a Web-based professional training model (De la Teja et al., 2000), a model of processes and methods in a virtual campus (Paquette et al., 2002), a knowledge base model (Henri et al., 2006), a learning objects' management process model (Lundgren-Cayrol et al., 2001), skills and competencies models (Basque et al., 2007; Paquette, 1999; Paquette et al., 2006), a self-management of learning model (Ruelland, 2000), etc.

Among other *MOT* functionalities, we find the possibility of creating a sub-model for each knowledge object[1] represented in the first level of the model and to link documents of different formats (with OLE or URL links) to each knowledge object. It is also possible to link a "comment" to a knowledge object or a link. The last version of the software, called *MOT Plus*, adds functionalities to depict specific types of models (ontologies, flowcharts, learning scenarios), enhanced exportation facilities (HTML, XML, OWL, IMS-LD, etc.), navigation improvements into sub-models with hierarchical menus, etc. The *MOT Plus* interface is presented in Fig. 17.4.

---

[1] Represented by the icon attached to knowledge objects developed further in a sub-model.

17.3 The Knowledge Transfer Strategy

As briefly defined above, the knowledge transfer strategy essentially consists of creating small groups of experts and novices for the purpose of co-constructing a knowledge model related to specific fieldwork using the *MOT* software. The entire procedure used to implement this strategy in organisations includes different steps that can be operationalised differently from site to site. The main steps are the following:

Specifying the domain to model: This decision usually stems from head managers' priorities. A systematic methodology can be used to identify, at a high-level, the most critical knowledge in the organisation (Ermine et al., 2006).

Selecting participants: This step consists of identifying the experts and novices who subsequently become involved in the project. Experts can be workers near retirement possessing strategic knowledge or individuals who possess rare knowledge. They usually are explicitly recognized as experts by their peers. The term "novice" is not automatically synonymous with new staff: this can be an employee who recently changed position within the organisation or an individual who needs to extend his knowledge on some work processes to be able to substitute other employees at times. In other words, the degree to which an individual can be considered a novice in a field varies significantly. Moreover, criteria other than degree of expertise (or apprenticeship) in the targeted field need to be considered to select participants: availability, willingness to share knowledge, familiarity with graphical representations, etc. This being said, the selected participants do need to be well-informed of the goal and the process of the knowledge modelling strategy. In order for the project to be a success, they must clearly be willing to become involved in the activity.

Knowledge modelling training session: Training will differ according to the role assigned to the experts and novices involved in the project. If they are to manipulate *MOT* in order to create their own knowledge models (even if this is done with the assistance of a knowledge modelling specialist), training relative to the *MOT* software and to its knowledge modelling language is necessary. In this case, an initial on-site 2-day session given to groups of 8–12 persons, followed by individual and group consultations with the instructor, have shown to be effective for basic training. If the organisation asks that the software be manipulated by a knowledge modelling specialist, participants' training for the *MOT* software will be minimal. Indeed, in such a case, a brief presentation of the typologies used in *MOT* suffices. Participants become quite easily and naturally familiar with the knowledge modelling language simply by observing a knowledge modelling specialist manipulate the software and use the representational language.

Collaborative knowledge-modelling sessions: The duration of the sessions can vary depending on the scope of the target field and the availability of the participants. In our case, we propose starting with an intensive 2- to 3-day session that allows participants to elaborate a global, relatively stable and consensual representation of the field. Additional sessions may be required in order to add details or submodels to the initial model. Such sessions can take place in small groups of 2–4 experts and novices. As already mentioned, two approaches can be used. In the first one, experts and novices co-construct the model at the same computer, with on-demand assistance of a knowledge modelling specialist whose role is essentially to provide feedback on the model and answer questions. Many small groups of experts-novices (dyads or triads) can work simultaneously in a computer room. In the second approach, two knowledge modelling specialists worked with a single group. The first one interviews participants in order to elicit overtly their knowledge, while another one creates the map on a computer. The map is projected on the wall so that all the members of the group could visualise it. In this second approach, it is important that, prior to the session, the knowledge modelling specialist who moderates the session read some documentation supplied by experts. With this information, he can even develop a sketchy first-level model, which will be suggested to participants in order to accelerate the knowledge modelling process and stimulate the negotiation of meaning at the beginning of the session. The first level of the model usually represents the main procedure and major sub-procedures used by the experts in their work. Then, the procedures and sub-procedures inputs and outputs (concepts) are added iteratively to the model, as are the principles that regulate the procedural knowledge. Sub-models are also developed progressively, if and as required. Throughout the process, knowledge modelling specialists help participants to elicit their knowledge at the appropriate level of granularity. They are also invited to be specific and consistent when labelling knowledge objects. Careful attention is paid to explicit redundancy. Indeed, when the same knowledge object is used at different levels of the model, it is to be copied and pasted with a special *MOT* function that adds a visual (red dot) on the graphic shape and that allows users to search all sub-models displaying the knowledge object and to propagate automatically any change made to its label. At any given moment during the session, participants or knowledge modelling specialists can suggest a complete restructuration of the entire knowledge model, a task that is facilitated by the use of a software tool.

Validation of the co-constructed knowledge model: Once the first version of the model is produced, a final validation can be performed by one or more experts who participated in the session and/or peer experts involved in the field. Also, the validation process can intertwine with the participants' real work practices. While "instantiating" the knowledge represented in the model based on actual work situations, modifications to the knowledge model can be more easily identified. Electronic documents or URLs can also be attached to knowledge objects in order to provide them with a more detailed and contextual meaning.

Presentation of the models by the participants to managers and colleagues: The participants usually appreciate presenting and explaining their co-constructed knowledge model to their managers and colleagues. This acts as a means of promoting their work, as well as allowing them to deepen their comprehension of the model.

Implementation of a maintenance strategy of the knowledge model: It is important to consistently continue to improve the model. This task can be performed by an individual or (preferably) a group of people endowed with a sufficient level of expertise in the field, while also being sufficiently familiar with the representational language used.

17.4 Rationale for the Knowledge Transfer Strategy

How can the collaborative knowledge modelling strategies conducted with groups of experts and novices promote the transfer of expertise to the latter? To answer this question, three aspects of the activity are examined: (1) the cartographic nature of the representational language used; (2) the semi-formal nature of this language and (3) the collaborative dimension of the activity. These three components are addressed in the following sections.

17.4.1 The Cartographic Nature of the Representational Language Used

The knowledge cartography strategy that we propose to support the transfer of expertise has some background in meaningful learning theory (Ausubel, 1968), which is at the origin of the seminal work of Novak & Gowin (1984) on concept mapping in education. It is also based on cognitivist work on hierarchical structures of knowledge and schemata (Kintsch, 1996; Rumelhart & Ortony, 1977; Schank & Abelson, 1977; Trabasso & van den Broek, 1985).

Significant learning is defined as an assimilation process of concepts in propositional networks (Ausubel, 1968). According to Novak & Gowin (1984), concept maps allow students to externalise personal knowledge in the form of significant propositional networks. Creating concept maps would then favour significant learning (Novak & Gowin, 1984), allowing learners to clarify links between concepts that they establish implicitly (Fisher, 2000; Holley & Dansereau, 1984) and involving them in deep knowledge-processing (Jonassen et al., 1997). This will lead them to "learn how to learn" (Novak & Gowin, 1984). Similarly, Holley & Dansereau (1984) argue that "spatial learning strategies" enhance deep knowledge-processing (Craik & Lockhart, 1972), hierarchical structuring of propositional representations and schemata, and inference making, especially causal inference making (Trabasso & van den Broek, 1985).

17.4.2 The Semi-formal Nature of the Representational Language Used

MOT can be described as a semi-formal knowledge representation tool. From an Artificial Intelligence perspective, a formal representation is defined as a representation that is machine-readable. Uschold & Gruninger (1996) describe four levels to formalisation of representations: "highly informal" (expressed in natural language), "semi-informal" (expressed in an artificial, formally defined language), "semi-formal" (expressed in a restricted and structured form of natural language) and "rigorously formal" (meticulously defined terms with formal semantics, theorems and proofs on properties such as soundness and completeness). It was stated above that knowledge models created with *MOT Plus* are machine-readable to a certain degree. For example, they can be exported in XML or into a relational database.

We also use the term "semi-formal" from a cognitive perspective to express the idea that, compared to typical concept mapping tools, *MOT* imposes some additional constraints on the representational activity based on schema theory that forms the set of grammar rules defining a formal grammar of graphic symbols.

Some authors argue that a constrained or semi-formal approach to concept mapping adds more precision, exhaustiveness and coherence to the knowledge representation, thus facilitating its interpretation and communication between humans (Gordon, 2000; Moody, 2000). Others warn about the danger of reducing the complexity of the knowledge domains. For example, Faletti & Fisher (1996) argue that "there are advantages in systematicity and ease of net generation associated with using a parsimonious number of relations [...], but the price of parsimony is the reduction of potentially valuable distinctions. On the other hand, a tendency toward profligacy can overwhelm" (p. 201).

However, although certain authors cite the flexibility of expressiveness as a major factor to consider in the design of concept map tools for learning (Hereen & Kommers, 1992), few studies have examined the specific contribution of the constraints associated with the use of semi-formal languages implemented in domain-independent digital tools dedicated to knowledge modelling (Alpert, 2004). Many hypotheses can be formulated in order to guide future research on this issue. A first hypothesis deals with the fact that typologies constitute some sort of meta-language which, if shared by members of a group, allows them to work on a common representation of the field. Knowledge modelling that uses typologies of knowledge and links would force participants to confront and recognise similarities and differences in their respective representation of the field, while offering the advantage of making the model subsequently easier to read for other individuals who are familiar with the typology.

A second hypothesis states that knowledge modelling that uses a finite set of categories of types of knowledge and links would help experts make their knowledge explicit and guide them in representing knowledge as typical schematic structures of work situations, that is, procedural models of production and of transformation of objects using artifact-mediated actions guided by rules, heuristics and norms.

In *MOT*, procedural knowledge is represented by nodes rather than links, as is the case with other concept mapping tools. Such a strategy seems an interesting solution for issues pertaining to distinguishing generic from specific links in a given field and to eliciting procedural knowledge.

Certain authors disagree with the use of canonical links by arguing that each field possesses its own set of relations and, therefore, they cannot be predetermined (Fisher, 1990). However, this researcher became more flexible after eight years of observing students creating biology concept maps with the SemNet software (Faletti & Fisher, 1996; Fisher & Moody, 2000). The data collected indicates that three of the relations used in the maps account for over 50% of all the relations in the field. These included "is composed of", "is a kind of" and "is a characteristic of". Other relations are specific to a field or a set of fields. For example, in the field of reproductive physiology, relations included "synthesises", "secretes", "stimulates", "inhibits", etc. For this reason, Faletti & Fisher (1996) compromised by distinguishing between the generic and specific relations of a field. According to this approach, Osmundson et al. (1999) include 21 predefined concepts and 14 predefined links in the menus of the concept mapping software developed for their research in the field of human biology (respiration, circulation and digestion). Experts in the field were consulted and the links that they identified are composed of links that are generic links to all fields (e.g. "is composed of") and links specific to the field (e.g. "absorbs", "digests", "pumps", etc.).

As mentioned above, in *MOT*, field-specific relations are represented in (procedural) nodes rather than in links. Therefore, the links used in the model only represent *generic* relations, resulting in a more economical and more parsimonious representational system.

It is noteworthy that, in *MOT*, users can also put their own labels on links using the "untyped link" category of the typology. However, we observed that often, these labels are used to express links that are already defined in the typology. For example, in a study conducted by Basque & Pudelko (2003), the label "results in" introduced by university students as an untyped link in their model corresponds to the Input/Product (I/P) link. The fact that users multiply labels for a single link type can actually indicate that it is difficult for participants to structure their own knowledge and recognize that similar meanings can be hidden behind words. It also makes it more difficult or time-consuming for others to read the map, obviously resulting in a limitation in cases where such maps are subsequently made available to other employees in the organisation.

We also believe that *MOT* language is a powerful tool to represent procedural knowledge (albeit in a declarative format)[2]. Current concept mapping tools essentially enhance representations of declarative knowledge, that is, representations of objects and their attributes (Fisher, 1992; Hereen & Kommers, 1992). *MOT* offers the possibility of representing actions as "knowledge objects" that can be decomposed into sub-actions. Actions (procedures) can be linked to each other with composition (C), precedence (P) or specialisation (S) links. The activity of representing knowledge can, therefore, be focused from the start on representing actions and, secondly, on representing objects and concepts used to perform actions and principles that guide actions. This is a value-added advantage because the experts' schemata imply much *procedural* knowledge (the *know-how*), along with knowledge regarding explicit conditions as to its applicability known as *conditional* or *strategic* knowledge (the *know-when* and the *know-why*) and with object schemata that can be instantiated at will (the *know-what* or *declarative* knowledge) (Chi et al., 1982, 1988; Ericsson & Charness, 1994; Glaser, 1986; Schmidt & Boshuizen, 1993; Sternberg, 1997).

Novice and experts then have the means to represent their field work as their own procedural model, with structures staying consistent no matter which level of the procedure is represented. This characteristic of the representational language can also bring the novice to interrogate experts during the co-construction of the knowledge model, the objects and principles linked to procedures in the model acting as anchors for interactions.

---

[2] The term "declarative" when applied to the term "knowledge" comprises two different meanings which are often confused. In a first sense, all knowledge that is overtly "verbalised" (that is, expressed with words) is said to have a declarative format. In a second sense, the term "declarative" defines a specific type of knowledge (declarative knowledge), that is, knowledge about objects and on properties of objects (the *know-what*), as opposed to "procedural" knowledge or knowledge on actions (the *know-how*). Procedural knowledge can then be represented in a declarative format.

17.4.3 The Collaborative Dimension of the Strategy

Finally, the proposed strategy implies that experts and novices interact during the elaboration process of the knowledge model. As mentioned previously, some studies conducted in educational settings have shown that, compared to individual concept mapping or other types of collaborative learning activities (e.g. producing an outline or a matrix representation), collaborative concept mapping is more beneficial to learning (see Basque & Lavoie, 2006, for a review). Different socio-cognitivist and socio-constructivist theories can be evoked in order to explain these results.

According to social cognitive theory (Bandura, 1986), observing an expert in action promotes learning. Learning cognitive skills can be facilitated by having human models verbalise their thought strategies out loud as they engage in problem-solving activities. The covert thoughts that guide actions are thus made observable through overt representation. "Modeling both thoughts and actions has several helpful features that contribute to its effectiveness in producing generalized, lasting improvements in cognitive skills" (Bandura, 1986, p. 74). Therefore, through *observation* and *modelling*, learners develop internal rules that help them self-regulate their own behaviour.

Other researchers, working with the Vygotskian paradigm (Vygotsky, 1978), emphasise the intrinsically social aspect of human cognition as well as the idea that cultural tools (symbols, rules, conventions, uses, etc.) mediate mental activities (Bruner, 1987; Cole & Engeström, 1993; John-Steiner & Mahn, 1996; Wertsch & Stone, 1985). An *internalisation* process takes place when a more competent person offers scaffolding to a less competent one.

Based on the piagetian theory, Doise & Mugny (1984) propose that situations most likely to generate *sociocognitive conflicts* between learners promote learning. The divergent points of view that emerge in social interactions may involve individuals making efforts to coordinate their personal perspectives, in order to maintain a "cognitive equilibrium" in their own cognitive structure. Certain educational studies show that collaborative concept mapping constitutes a situation where sociocognitive conflicts would actually occur through argumentative discussions (Osmundson et al., 1999; van Boxtel et al., 2000).

Justifications for the use of a collaborative knowledge modelling strategy to support the transfer of expertise can also be found in symbolic interactionist theories based on Mead's assumption that meaning is the result of a social negotiation process that is based on verbal interactions (Mead, 1934/1974). Basically, individuals are unable to interact in social situations when their mental representations differ too significantly (Clark & Wilkes-Gibbs, 1986). There is a need to establish mutual understanding, also called *common ground* or *intersubjectivity* (Rogoff & Lave, 1984), which is negotiated throughout the interactions. This shared understanding requires a common focus of attention and a set of common assumptions. A number of authors have emphasised the role of external representations, such as concept maps, to support the negotiation of meaning in learning contexts (Osmundson et al., 1999; Roth & Roychoudhury, 1993). Roth & Roychoudhury (1994) use the metaphor of "social glue" to describe how concept maps can lead learners to develop a shared vision of tasks and meanings that they attribute to concepts and relations between these concepts.

Finally, in the situated learning paradigm, the *legitimate peripheral participation theory* (Rogoff & Lave, 1984) states that novices should be given opportunities to participate regularly and actively in "communities of practice" in their field in order to promote the development of their competencies. Mentoring and apprenticeship as well as reflective discussions among practitioners in real-world or virtual spaces would be particularly beneficial to learning (Wenger et al., 2002). Collaborative knowledge modeling could well complement these strategies. Indeed, Roth & Roychoudhury (1992) observe that collaborative concept mapping promotes the development of a "culture of scientific discourse" in science classes.

17.5 Applications of and Research on the Knowledge Transfer Strategy

The collaborative knowledge modelling strategy was first used in 2002 at Hydro-Québec, the main producer, provider and distributor of electricity in the province of Québec, Canada (20,000 employees). By 2004, over 150 experts and 150 novices from various departments (management, electrical engineering, civil engineering, etc.) had already participated in a pilot project initiated by this large company (Basque et al., 2004). Experts and novices were first trained to use the *MOT* software. They were then asked to construct a knowledge model in dyads or triads. Based on anecdotal data collected by local representatives, Basque et al. (2004) report that, in general, both experts and novices tended to show a positive attitude towards the strategy. Many commented that this tool helped them "organise" their own knowledge. However, the authors noticed a certain amount of reticence, especially among experts who seemed to lack time to participate in these activities due to their heavy workload. Most participants found the software user-friendly, although few mentioned they had difficulties with the process of categorising knowledge, especially of identifying principles and of distinguishing them from procedures. Some experts lamented that collaborative knowledge modelling with novices slowed down their own modelling process; however, for others, the interaction with novices was essential to externalise what seemed obvious to them and *MOT* helped them capture a very large body of their knowledge in an economical fashion. Others recognised the inherent advantages of graphical representations while adding that they remained more comfortable sharing their knowledge by spelling it out in a written text or through live demonstrations. On the other hand, novices appreciated having a synthetic reference document that prevented them from constantly referring to the expert.

More recently, another public organisation in Québec began using this strategy. This time, a more rigorous research process was implemented, based on action-research methodology.[3] This ongoing project has the following objectives: (1) to evaluate the feasibility and efficiency of the strategy to transfer expertise, (2) to single out conditions that influence the efficiency of the strategy and (3) to identify

---

[3] This research project is supported by the CEFRIO (*Centre francophone de recherche sur l'informatisation des organisations*), which is a liaison and transfer centre that comprises university, industrial and governmental members and researchers in Quebec, Canada.

how the knowledge models can be exploited within the organisation in a global knowledge management perspective. A first group of four employees[4] participated in a 3-day session of collaborative knowledge modelling with the help of two knowledge modelling facilitators: one manipulating the software and one conducting the session, as described above. The knowledge model was projected on a widescreen. Participants included two experts and two "less expert" employees. These "novices" had already developed specific competencies in the targeted work field but lacked a global view of it. We videotaped the participants during the collaborative knowledge modelling session. Screen-captures of the work performed on the computer were recorded using the *Windows Media Encoder* software. Finally, individual interviews were conducted with each participant before and after the session. Although data analysis is still on-going, some results are briefly reported here, based essentially on the analyses of the model produced and the interviews conducted.

The first-level of a knowledge model produced during this 3-day session is reproduced in Fig. 17.5. Although the model was not totally completed at the end of the session, it comprised over 500 knowledge objects, which are distributed among 55 sub-models. All six types of links of the MOT typology were used. Procedures are the most numerous (217), followed by concepts (179), principles (123) and facts (11). These results confirm that a procedural perspective was used and that much strategic knowledge, which is usually tacit, was elicited. Interestingly, participants attached 29 comments to various knowledge objects, reminders for a future completion of the model. These reminders specify needs for future elaboration in sub-models, validation of information with other sources, addition of links to existing institutional documentation, development of new institutional documents or addition of illustrating examples. We also found self-questioning comments for future elucidation (e.g. *"Should we add this link here?" "Are these two terms equivalent?"*).

During the interviews and debriefings, participants declared that they were quite satisfied with this model considering the short time they devoted to its development. The knowledge modelling activity was also very positively evaluated by participants, even though they found it quite cognitively demanding. They mentioned that this activity (1) stimulated reflexive discussions and negotiation of meaning (2) lead them to simultaneously conceptualise the domain in "its totality and its components" and (3) lead them to elicit knowledge that they initially judged "trivial" but that they finally admitted as being central to expertise in their domain, or knowledge that they considered, before the mapping activity, as being "not elicitable". Indeed, some comments by the participants lead us to think that some tacit knowledge has actually been elicited. For example, one participant said: *"It is the first time that we illustrate the mechanics of this procedure. We used to refer to the 5 phases of the process, but now we clearly see that there are many other things which underlie the process"*. Another one commented: *"It was interesting to concretely describe things that were not defined anywhere else"*. It seems that the knowledge model is not a simple repetition or a collection of knowledge already documented in the organisation, but a real new creation that gives them new insight on the required expertise to perform the process described in the model.

---

[4] Two other groups recently participated in the study.

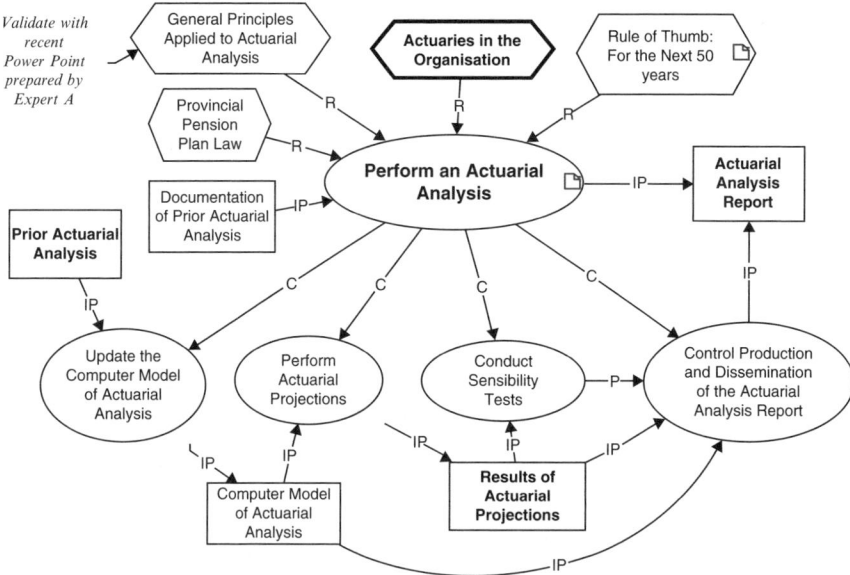

Fig. 17.5. A first-level of a knowledge model of the procedure "Perform an actuarial analysis" (translated from French).

Participants suggested that the model, when completed, would be useful as a complement to coaching techniques, by quickly introducing a new employee to the targeted knowledge domain. It would give him/her an integrated overview of the activities and actors engaged in the process delineated in the model, as well as the main principles that regulate the activities. One participant noted: *"The model will not tell new employees what they must do, but it helps them find their place in the larger process. When I began working for this organisation, it took me many years before I could situate my own activity in the whole picture. I think that maps can speed up the development of this knowledge."* An expert said that the model will help him transfer his knowledge to new employees: *"Instead of starting from scratch, at least, they would have a good basis from which to start. They can read documentation and study the knowledge model, providing them with a 'big picture'. Then, they can ask more specific questions. This prevents us from having to spell out everything and frees us to concentrate on specific activities"*.

Some participants noted that since the model gives a clear representation of activities performed by several different actors, it can prevent the "silo" effect often associated with strong specialisation of the workers in organisations. Thus, by providing the "big picture" of a contextualised professional knowledge, maps can be used as "boundary objects" (Star, 1989) in the organisation, that is, entities shared by different internal "communities of practice" but viewed or used differently by each of them. All actors do not necessarily fully understand the detailed knowledge represented in the common entity, but they can situate themselves within the larger organisational context and thus give new meaning to their own activities.

17.6 A Knowledge Management Perspective

The collaborative knowledge modelling strategy described so far is primarily a *process*-oriented strategy of KM. However, the knowledge models produced during this process can be subsequently integrated into a *product*-oriented approach to KM, with aims to share expertise with a larger audience within the organisation. Three types of usages can be identified in the product-oriented approach.

Firstly, as mentioned above, knowledge models created jointly by experts and novices can be made accessible to all employees within the organisation as reference documents. *MOT Plus* makes it possible to export the knowledge models in HTML format to facilitate sharing on the Web. Each model serves as a kind of interface for navigation within a knowledge network to which documents of various file formats can be attached (text, audio, video, etc.). All individuals in the organisation could also be invited to annotate models, suggest additions or discuss the models in virtual forums.

Secondly, knowledge models can be used to design training sessions for employees in the organisation. Indeed, the models provide instructional designers a clear idea of the targeted learning content to be addressed in training sessions. Several authors have already suggested using concept maps for instructional design (e.g. Coffey & Canas, 2003; Inglis, 2003). In his book entitled *Instructional Engineering in Networked Environments*, Paquette (2003) proposes a method called MISA[5], in which the object-typed knowledge modelling technique described in this chapter is proposed in order to specify the learning content and the target competencies of learning systems. This very technique is also suggested to instructional designers to help them elaborate the pedagogical (or instructional) model – which can take the form, in e-learning systems, of IMS-LD[6] compliant learning scenarios (Paquette et al., 2005) – , the media model, and the delivery model of learning systems.

Finally, the knowledge models co-produced by experts and novices can serve as input in the process of developing an "intelligent" digital knowledge management system that will hopefully be able to make inferences and be used with natural language queries. We believe that having experts and novices interact during the knowledge acquisition stage of the expert system development process, represents an interesting alternative to classical approaches of knowledge elicitation. However, as models co-constructed with *MOT* happen to be semi-formal, they cannot be interpreted by a machine. Indeed, ambiguities inherent to this level of knowledge modelling need to be removed. One way to achieve this is to transform the semi-formal models into ontological models. The advantage of formalising models as ontologies, using the standard OWL-DL format for example, is to make them available for computer-based processing. The resulting OWL-DL format is an XML file for which there are an increasing quantity of software components that can process a file for different

---

[5] MISA is a French acronym (*Méthode d'Ingénierie d'un Système d'Apprentissage*), which stands for "Engineering Method for Learning Systems".
[6] IMS-LD is a standardized language used for the specification of e-learning instructional scenarios (LD stands for "Learning Design"). These scenarios are machine-readable: they can be delivered on different elearning platforms that are compliant with IMS-LD.

purposes: describing documents in databases, searching for documents according to the classes of models, summarising or classifying documents, etc.

In the context of the *MOT* representation system, ontologies, particularly OWL-DL constructs, correspond to a category of models called "theories". Ontologies can thus be graphically modelled using the *MOT* syntax with certain extensions (see Fig. 17.6, for example). A new extension of the *MOT* editor introduces new graphic symbols acting as abbreviations, such as new links that replace one or two links plus a ruling principle or labels on knowledge objects that correspond to stereotyped properties: for example, stating that the relation is transitive or functional. Such an extension aims to simplify the graphic model when the goal is to build standardized models such as a learning design or an ontology (Paquette, 2006; Paquette & Rogozan, 2005).

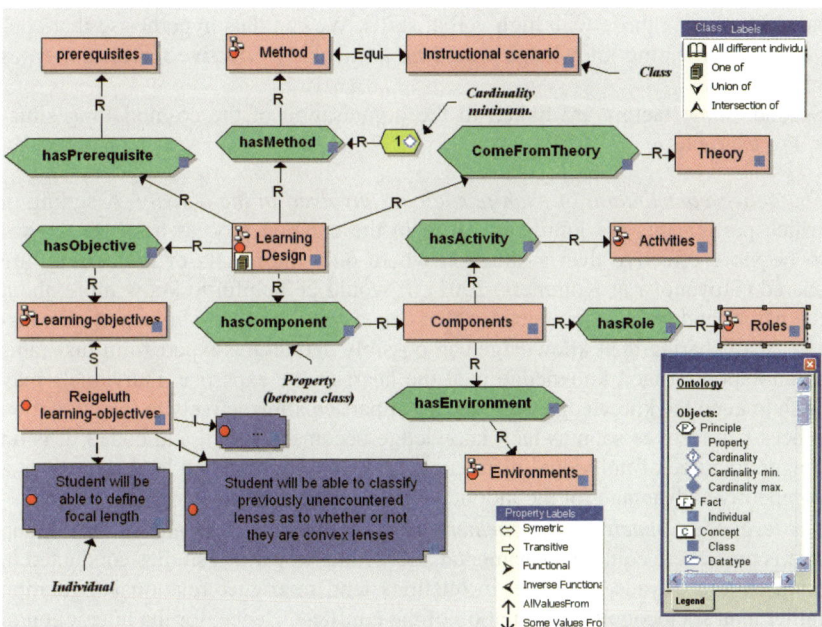

Fig. 17.6. First level of an ontological model representing knowledge from the Learning Design domain.

17.7 Conclusions

The collaborative knowledge modelling strategy described in this chapter seems promising for the transfer of expertise within organisations. However, it brings up numerous questions that need to be addressed with rigorous research. The first question is obvious: Is this strategy efficient? In other words, does it result in transfer of expertise?

Another concern involves the factors that are likely to influence the efficiency of the strategy. Briefly, here are some of the factors that need to be investigated according to our perspective.

First, a series of factors are related to the individuals involved. We wonder, for example, how individual variables, such as an expert's level of motivation to share his/her knowledge and/or the individual's spatial or verbal skills or his/her cognitive style affect the efficiency of such an activity. The few studies that investigated these topics were conducted in school settings (Okebukola & Jegede, 1988; Oughton & Reed, 1999, 2000; Reed & Oughton, 1998; Stensvold & Wilson, 1990). It would be valuable to conduct such research with adult participants in professional settings. For example, Stensvold & Wilson (1990) have shown, in a study conducted with Grade 9 participants, that creating concept maps was more beneficial to students with low verbal skills than to those with high verbal skills. We can thus hypothesise that concept maps representing knowledge would be particularly effective for certain types of employees.

Second, some factors are linked to the organisation of the co-modelling situations. For example:

- *The active contribution of each participant involved in the activity.* A setting in which participants are jointly involved in the creation process has been shown to be more effective than a situation where only the results of the activity are shared (Stoyanova & Kommers, 2002). It would be helpful to know more about the nature and types of interactions that correlate with successful expertise transfer. Also, sharing tacit knowledge can possibly detract the expert from his status as an expert. If tacit knowledge is at the heart of the expertise, individuals may wish to keep the knowledge tacit instead of participating actively to the elicitation process. Indeed, as soon as tacit knowledge becomes explicit and coded, it is no longer a source of individual differences and, consequently, no longer presents a competitive advantage for the individual (Sternberg, 1999).
- *The level of asymmetry of the partners' expertise paired up for the activity.* A gap that is too severe could be detrimental. According to various studies conducted in adult-children dyads, asymmetric relations tend to trigger relational regulation rather than sociocognitive regulation of the conflicts. Hence, for the interaction to be effective, problem-solving activities must be conducted on a sociocognitive level rather than on a social level (Doise & Mugny, 1984). Moreover, once aware of this asymmetry, the participants' representations of the relationship constitute a factor that can affect their partnership. Hence, participants with low self-esteem will tend to overestimate the competency of their partners, thus influencing their interactions.
- *The knowledge modelling training method.* Research conducted in the field of concept mapping provides little indication as to the most efficient method to train people for this type of activity. To what extent and how should people involved in collaborative knowledge modelling in a professional setting be trained in a knowledge modelling language in order to minimise the cognitive load of such an activity? How can we help them make links between knowledge in the most significant and useful manner, an activity considered very difficult by many researchers

(Basque & Pudelko, 2003; Faletti & Fisher, 1996; Fisher, 1990; Novak & Gowin, 1984; Roth & Roychoudhury, 1992)? Are there any aspects of collaboration that should be the target of specific training?

- *The representation language and the representation tool used.* Is the representation system suggested by the tool appropriate for all fields and sectors? Does it allow the representation of a variety of knowledge structures that can be organised into temporal script, in causal diagrams, procedural models, etc.? Is it best to impose the use of knowledge and link typologies? If strategic knowledge is at the heart of expertise, can we say that expertise is mostly represented in the "principles" included in a model? How do we promote the expression of this heuristic and often idiosyncratic knowledge? How can we guarantee sufficient freedom of expression to allow the representation of different knowledge structures to suit the needs of the knowledge modellers? How can we guarantee the convergence between the experts' words and actions, since they can distort their knowledge representations when they express it verbally? In other words, the externalised representation of actions may not reflect what actually occurs (Wilson & Schooler, 1991). It is difficult to separate tacit from explicit knowledge because these two types of knowledge are often tightly intertwined. An expert can describe rules which guide his action (explicit knowledge) without being able to describe which specific aspects of the situation triggered the application of the rules. However, he will be able to use the rule appropriately in context (tacit knowledge). How can constraints imposed by the representational language promote the elicitation of such situated strategic knowledge?

Third, there are factors related to the global organisational environment. Among those, we find, for example, the level of competition (between individuals or between various groups) that exists within the organisation, the level of hierarchy present in the organisation, the level of confidence and safety that employees feel towards the organisation, the manner in which knowledge is shared within the organisation, the existence of incentives associated with expertise transfer (tokens of recognition, rewards, release time), etc.

We hope that further research will shed some light on the contribution of any, or all, of these factors to the success of the knowledge modelling strategy.

References

Alpert, S. (2004). Flexibility of expressiveness: state of the practice. In P. Kommers (Ed.), *Cognitive Support for Learning: Imagining the Unknown* (pp. 253–268). Amsterdam: IOS Press.

Apostolou, D., Mentzas, G., Young, R., and Abecker, A. (2000). *Consolidating the Product Versus Process Approaches in Knowledge Management: The Know-net Approach.* Paper presented at the Conference Practical Application of Knowledge Management (PAKeM 2000) – April 12–14 2000, Manchester, UK.

Ausubel, D. (1968). *Educational Psychology: A Cognitive View.* New York: Rhinehart and Winston.

Bandura, A. (1986). *Social Foundations of Thought and Action: A Social Cognitive Theory.* Englewood Cliffs, NJ: Prentice-Hall.

Basque, J., Imbeault, C., Pudelko, B., and Léonard, M. (2004). Collaborative knowledge modeling between experts and novices: a strategy to support transfer of expertise in an organization. In A. J. Canas, J. D. Novak and F. M. Gonzalez (Eds.), *Proceedings of the First International Conference on Concept Mapping (CMC 2004), Pamplona, September 14–17, vol. 1,* (pp. 75–81). Pamplona: Universidad Publica de Navarra.

Basque, J. and Lavoie, M.-C. (2006). Collaborative concept mapping in education: major research trends. In A. J. Canas and J. D. Novak (Eds.), *Concept Maps: Theory, Methodology, Technology – Proceedings of the Second International Conference on Concept Mapping, vol. 1,* (pp. 79–86). San Jose, Costa Rica: Universidad de Costa Rica.

Basque, J. and Pudelko, B. (2003). Using a concept mapping software as a knowledge construction tool in a graduate online course. In D. Lassner and C. McNaught (Eds.), *Proceedings of ED-MEDIA 2003, Wold Conference on Educational Multimedia, Hypermedia and Telecommunications, Honolulu, June 23–28 2003,* (pp. 2268–2264). Norfolk, VA: AACE.

Basque, J., Rocheleau, J., Paquette, G., and Paquin, C. (1998). An object-oriented model of a computer-enriched high school. In T. Ottmann and I. Tomek (Eds.), *Proceedings of ED-MEDIA/ED-TELECOM 98.* Charlottesville, VA: Association for the Advancement of Computing in Education.

Basque, J., Ruelland, D., and Lavoie, M.-C. (2007). A Digital Tool for Self-assessing Information Literacy Skills. In T. Bastiaens & S. Carliner (Eds.), *Proceedings of the E-Learn 2007, World Conference on E-Leaning in Corporate, Government, Healthcare, & Higher education, Quebec City, October 16–19, 2007* (pp. 6997–7003). Chesapeake, VA: Association for the Advancement of Computing in Education (AACE).

Beazley, H., Boenisch, J., and Harden, D. (2002). *Continuity Management: Preserving Corporate Knowledge When Employees Leave.* Hoboken, NJ: Wiley.

Booch, G., Jacobson, J., and Rumbaugh, J. (1999). *The Unified Modeling Language User Guide.* Reading, MA: Addison-Wesley.

Brisebois, A., Paquette, G., and Masmoudi, A. (2003). Affective attributes in a distributed learning environments. In *9th International Conference on User Modeling.* University of Pittsburgh.

Bruner, J. S. (1973). *Beyond the Information Given.* New York: Norton.

Bruner, J. S. (1987). *Le développement de l'enfant: Savoir faire, savoir dire* (2nd ed.). Paris: Presses Universitaires de France.

Chen, P. P.-S. (1976). The entity-relationship model: toward a unified view of data. *ACM Transactions on Database Systems, 1*(1), 9–36.

Chi, M. T. H., Feltovitch, P. J., and Glaser, R. (1981). Categorisation and representation of physics problems by experts and novices. *Cognitive Science, 5,* 121–152.

Chi, M. T. H., Glaser, R., and Farr, M. J. (1988). *The Nature of Expertise.* Hillsdale, NJ: Lawrence Erlbaum Associates.

Chi, M. T. H., Glaser, R., and Rees, E. (1982). Expertise in problem solving. In R. Sternberg (Ed.), *Advances in the Psychology of Human Intelligence,* (pp. 7–75). Hillsdale, NJ: Lawrence Erlbaum Associates.

Clark, H. H., and Wilkes-Gibbs, D. (1986). Referring as a collaborative process. *Cognition, 22,* 1–39.

Coffey, J. (2006). In the Heat of the Moment... Strategies, Tactics, and Lessons Learned Regarding Interactive Knowledge Modeling with Concept Maps. In A. J. Canas and J. D. Novak (Eds.), *Concept Maps: Theory, Methodology, Technology,* (pp. 263–271). San Jose, Costa Rica: University of Costa Rica.

Coffey, J. W. and Canas, A. (2003). An Internet-based Meta-cognitive Tool for Courseware Development. In A. Rossett (Ed.), *Proceedings of E-Learn 2003, November 7–11, Phoenix, Arizona,* (pp. 909–912). Norfolk, VA: AACE.

Coffey, J. W. and Hoffman, R. R. (2003). Knowledge modeling for the preservation of institutional memory. *Journal of Knowledge Management, 7*(3), 38–52.

Cole, E., and Engeström, Y. (1993). A cultural-historical approach to distributed cognition. In G. Salomon (Ed.), *Distributed Cognitions: Psychological and Educational Considerations,* (pp. 1–46). Cambridge, UK: Cambridge University Press.

Craik, F. I. M. and Lockhart, R. S. (1972). Levels of processing: A framework for memory research. *Journal of Verbal Learning and Verbal Behavior, 11,* 671–684.

De la Teja, I., Longpré, A., and Paquette, G. (2000). Designing adaptable learning environments for the web: a case study. In *Proceedings of the ED-MEDIA Conference*. Montreal.

De Long, D. W. (2004). *Lost knowledge: confronting the threat of an aging workforce.* New York: Oxford University Press.

Doise, W. and Mugny, G. (1984). *The Social Development of the Intellect.* Oxford: Pergamon Press.

Dufresne, A., Basque, J., Paquette, G., Léonard, M., Lundgren-Cayrol, K., and Prom Tep, S. (2003). Vers un modèle générique d'assistance aux acteurs du téléapprentissage. *Sciences et Technologies de l'Information et de la Communication pour l'Éducation et la Formation, Numéro spécial: Technologies et formation à distance, 10*(3), 57–88.

Ericsson, K. A. and Charness, N. (1994). Expert performance: its structure and acquisition. *American Psychologist, 49*(3), 725–747.

Ermine, J.-L., Boughzala, I., and Tounkara, T. (2006). Critical knowledge map as a decision tool for knowledge transfer actions. *The Electronic Journal of Knowledge Management, 4*(2), 128–140.

Faletti, J. and Fisher, K. M. (1996). The information in relations in biology, or the unexamined relation is not worth having. In K. M. Fisher and M. R. Kibby (Eds.), *Knowledge Acquisition, Organization, and Use in Biology,* (pp. 182–205). Berlin, Heidelberg, New York: Springer.

Fisher, K. (1992). SemNet: a tool for personal knowledge construction. In P. Kommers, D. H. Jonassen, and J. T. Mayes (Eds.), *Cognitive Tools for Learning, Vol. NATO ASI Series, vol. 81,* (pp. 63–75). Berlin, Heidelberg, New York: Springer-Verlag.

Fisher, K. and Moody, D. E. (2000). Student misconceptions in biology. In K. Fisher, J. Wandersee, and D. E. Moody (Eds.), *Mapping Biology Knowledge,* (pp. 55–75). Dordrecht: Kluwer.

Fisher, K. M. (1990). Semantic networking: the new kid on the block. *Journal of Research in Science Teaching, 27*(10), 1001–1018.

Fisher, K. M. (2000). Overview of knowledge mapping. In K. M. Fisher, J. H. Wandersee and D. E. Moody (Eds.), *Mapping Biology Knowledge,* (pp. 5–23). Dordrecht: Kluwer Academic Publishers.

Gentner, D. and Stevens, A. (1983). *Mental Models*. Hillsdale, NJ: Erlbaum.

Glaser, R. (1986). On the nature of expertise. In H. Hagendorf (Ed.), *Human Memory and Cognitive Capabilities: Mechanisms and Performances,* (pp. 915–928). North Holland: Elsevier Science.

Gordon, J. L. (2000). Creating knowledge maps by exploiting dependent relationships. In *Applications and Innovations in Intelligent Systems,* (pp. 63–78) Berlin, Heidelberg, New York: Springer.

Henri, F., Gagné, P., Maina, M., Gargouri, Y., Bourdeau, J., and Paquette, G. (2006). Development of a knowledge base as a tool for contextualized learning. *AI and Society 20*(3), 271–287.

Hereen, E. and Kommers, P. A. M. (1992). Flexibility of expressiveness: a critical factor in the design of concept mapping tools for learning. In P. A. M. Kommers, D. H. Jonassen, and J. T. Mayes (Eds.), *Cognitive Tools for Learning (NATO Series, vol. F81)*, (pp. 85–101). Berlin, Heidelberg, New York: Springer.

Hinds, P. J., Patterson, M., and Pfeffer, J. (2001). Bothered by abstraction: the effect of expertise on knowledge transfer and subsequent novice performance. *Journal of Applied Psychology, 86*(6), 1232–1243.

Holley, C. D. and Dansereau, D. F. (1984). *Spatial Learning Strategies. Techniques, Applications, and Related Issues.* New York, London: Academic Press.

Inglis, A. (2003). Facilitating team-based course designing with conceptual mapping. *Distance Education, 24*(2), 247–263.

Inhelder, B. and Piaget, J. (1958). *The Growth of Logical Thinking from Childhood to Adolescence.* New York: Basic Books.

Jacob, R. and Pariat, L. (2001). *Gérer les connaissances: un défi de la nouvelle compétitivité du 21e siècle.* Montréal: CEFRIO.

John-Steiner, V. and Mahn, H. (1996). Sociocultural approaches to learning and development: a vygostskian framework. *Educational Psychologist, 31* 191–206.

Johnson-Laird, P. N. (1983). *Mental Models: Towards a Cognitive Science of Language, Inference, and Consciousness.* Cambridge, MA: Cambridge University Press.

Jonassen, D. H., Reeves, T. C., Hong, N., Harvey, D., and Peters, K. (1997). Concept mapping as cognitive learning and assessment tools. *Journal of Interactive Learning Research, 8*(3/4), 289–308.

Kintsch, W. (1996). Mental representations in cognitive science. In W. Battmann and S. Dutke (Eds.), *Processes of the Molar Regulation of Behavior.* Scottsdale, AZ, USA: Pabst Science Publishers.

Lundgren-Cayrol, K., de la Teja, I., and Léonard, M. (2001). *Modélisation d'un gestionnaire de ressources. Rapport interne de recherche.* Montreal, Canada: Centre de recherche LICEF, Télé-université.

McDermott, R. (2001). Designing communities of practice: reflecting on what we've learned. In *Proceedings of Communities of Practice 2001.* Cambridge, MA: Institute for International Research.

Mead, G. H. (1934/1974). *Mind, Self, and Society from the Standpoint of a Social Behaviorist.* Chicago: Chicago University Press.

Merrill, M. D. (1994). *Principles of Instructional Design.* Englewood Cliffs, NJ: Educational Technology Publications.

Minsky, M. (1975). A framework for representing knowledge. In P. H. Winston (Ed.), *The Psychology of Computer Vision.* New York: McGraw-Hill.

Moody, D. E. (2000). The paradox of the textbook. In K. M. Fisher, J. H. Wandersee, and D. E. Moody (Eds.), *Mapping Biology Knowledge*, (pp. 167–184). Dordrecht: Kluwer Academic Publishers.

Newell, A. and Simon, H. (1972). *Human Problem Solving.* Englewood Cliffs, NJ: Prentice-Hall.

Nonaka, I. and Takeuchi, H. (1995). *The Knowledge Creating Company: How Japanese Companies Create the Dynamics of Innovation.* New York: Oxford University Press.

Novak, J. D. and Gowin, D. B. (1984). *Learning How to Learn.* Cambridge: Cambridge University Press.

Okebukola, P. A. and Jegede, O. J. (1988). Cognitive preference and learning mode as determinants of meaningful learning through concept mapping. *Science Education, 72*(4), 489–500.

Osmundson, E., Chung, G. K., Herl, H. E., and Klein, D. C. (1999). *Knowledge Mapping in the Classroom: A Tool for Examining the Development of Students' Conceptual Understandings* (Technical report No. 507). Los Angeles: CRESST/ University of California.

Oughton, J. M. and Reed, W. M. (1999). The influence of learner differences on the construction of hypermedia concepts: a case study. *Computers in Human Behavior, 15*(1), 11–50.

Oughton, J. M. and Reed, W. M. (2000). The effect of hypermedia knowledge and learning style on student-centered concept maps about hypermedia. *Journal of Research on Computing in Education, 32*(3), 366–382.

Paquette, G. (1999). Meta-knowledge representation for learning scenarios engineering. In S. Lajoie and M. Vivet (Eds.), *AI and Education, Open Learning Environments. Proceedings of AI-ED 99*. Le Mans: France IOS Press.

Paquette, G. (2002). *Modélisation des connaissances et des compétences*. Sainte-Foy (Québec): Presses de l'Université du Québec.

Paquette, G. (2003). *Instructional Engineering in Networked Environments*. San Francisco: Pfeiffer/Wiley.

Paquette, G. (2006). *Building Graphical Knowledge Representation Languages – From Informal to Interoperable Executable Models*. Paper presented at the i2LOR-06 Conference, November 8–10, Montreal.

Paquette, G., De la Teja, I., Léonard, M., Lundgren-Cayrol, K., and Marino, O. (2005). An instructional engineering method and tool for the design of units of learning. In R. Koper, and C. Tattersal (Eds.), *Learning Design – A Handbook on Modelling and Delivering Networked Education and Training*, (pp. 161–184). Berlin Heidelberg New York: Springer.

Paquette, G., De la Teja, I., Lundgren-Cayrol, K., Léonard, M., and Ruelland, D. (2002). La modélisation cognitive, un outil de conception des processus et des méthodes d'un campus virtuel. *Revue de l'Éducation à distance, 17*(3), 4–25.

Paquette, G., Léonard, M., Lundgren-Cayrol, K., Mihaila, S., and Gareau, D. (2006). Learning design based on graphical knowledge-modeling. *Journal of Educational Technology and Society 9*(1), 97–112.

Paquette, G. and Rogozan, D. (2005). *Primitives de représentation OWL-DL – Correspondance avec le langage graphique MOT+OWL et le langage des prédicats du premier ordre. TELOS documentation*. Montreal, Canada: LICEF Research Center.

Paris, S., Lipson, M. Y., and Wixson, K. K. (1983). Becoming a strategic reader. *Contemporary Educational Psychology, 8*, 293–316.

Polanyi, M. (1966). *The Tacit Dimension*. London: Routledge and Kegan Paul.

Reed, W. M. and Oughton, J. M. (1998). The effects of hypermedia knowledge and learning style on the construction of group concept maps. *Computers in Human Behavior, 14*(1), 1–22.

Rogoff, B. and Lave, J. (1984). *Everyday Cognition: Its Development in Social Context*. Cambridge, MA: Harvard University Press.

Romizowski, A. J. (1999). *Designing Instructional Systems: Decision Making In Course Planning And Curriculum Design*. Sterling, VA: Stylus Publications.

Roth, W.-M. and Roychoudhury, A. (1992). The social construction of scientific concepts or the concept map as conscription device and tool for social thinking in high school science. *Science Education, 76*(5), 531–557.

Roth, W.-M. and Roychoudhury, A. (1994). Science discourse through collaborative concept mapping: new perspectives for the teacher. *International Journal of Science Education, 16*(4), 437–455.

Roth, W. and Roychoudhury, A. (1993). The concept map as a tool for the collaborative construction of knowledge: a microanalysis of high school physics students. *Journal of Research in Science Teaching, 305*, 503–554.

Ruelland, D. (2000). Vers un modèle d'autogestion en situation de télé-apprentissage. Université de Montréal, Montréal.

Rumbaugh, J., Blaha, M., Premerlani, W., Eddy, F., and Lorensen, W. (1991). *Object-Oriented Modelling and Design*. Englewood Cliffs, NJ: Prentice Hall.

Rumelhart, D. E., and Ortony, A. (1977). The representation of knowledge in memory. In R. C. Anderson, R. J. Spiro, and W. E. Montague (Eds.), *Schooling and the Acquisition of Knowledge*. Hillsdale, NJ: Erlbaum.

Schank, R. C., and Abelson, R. (1977). *Scripts, Plans, Goals, and Understanding*. Hillsdale, NJ: Erlbaum.

Schmidt, H. G. and Boshuizen, H. P. A. (1993). On acquiring expertise in medicine. *Educational Psychology Review, 5*(3) 205–221.

Schreiber, G., Wielinga, B., and Breuker, J. A. (1993). *KADS – A Principled Approach to Knowledge-based System Development*. San Diego, CA: Academic Press.

Sowa, J. F. (1984). *Conceptual Structures, Information Processing in Mind and Machine*. Reading, MA: Addison-Wesley Publishing.

Star. L. (1989). The structure of ill-structured solutions: boundary objects and heterogeneous distributed problem solving. In L. Glaser et M. N. Huhns (Eds.), *Distributed Artificial Intelligence, vol. 2*, (pp. 37–54). San Mateo, CA: Morgan Kaufman Publishers.

Stensvold, M. S. and Wilson, J. T. (1990). The interaction of verbal ability with concept mapping in learning from a chemistry laboratory activity. *Science Education, 74*(4), 473–480.

Sternberg, R. (1997). Cognitive conceptions of expertise. In R. R. Hoffman (Ed.), *Expertise in Context. Human and Machine*, (pp. 149–162). Menlo Park, CA/Cambridge, MA: AAAI Press/MIT Press.

Sternberg, R. (1999). What do we know about tacit knowledge? making the tacit become explicit. In J. A. Horvath (Ed.), *Tacit Knowledge in Professional Practice*, (pp. 231–236). Mahwah, NJ: Erlbaum.

Stoyanova, N. and Kommers, P. (2002). Concept mapping as a medium of shared cognition in computer-supported collaborative problem solving. *Journal of Interactive Learning Research, 13*(1/2), 111–133.

Tennyson, R. D. and Rasch, M. (1988). Linking cognitive learning theory to instructional prescriptions. *Instructional Science, 17*(4), 369–385.

Trabasso, T. and van den Broek, P. (1985). Causal thinking and importance of story events. *Journal of Memory and Language, 24*, 612–630.

Uschold, M. and Gruninger, M. (1996). Ontologies: principles, methods, and applications. *Knowledge Engineering Review, 11*(2), 93–155.

van Boxtel, C., van der Linden, J., and Kanselaar, G. (2000). Collaborative learning tasks and the elaboration of conceptual knowledge. *Learning and Instruction, 10*, 311–330.

Vygotsky, L. S. (1978). *Mind in Society: The Development of Higher Psychological Process*. Cambridge: Harvard University Press.

Wenger, E. (1998). *Communities of Practice: Learning, Meaning, and Identity*. Cambridge, UK: Cambridge University Press.

Wenger, E., McDermott, R., and Snyder, W. M. (2002). *Cultivating Communities of Practice*. Boston, MA: Harward Business School Press.

Wertsch, J. V. and Stone, C. A. (1985). The concept of internalization in Vygotsky's account of the genesis in higher mental functions. In J. V. Wertsch (Ed.), *Culture, Communication, and Cognition: Vygotskian Perspectives*, (pp. 146–161). Cambridge, MA: Cambridge University Press.

West, C. K., Farmer, J. A., and Wolff, P. M. (1991). *Instructional Design: Implications from Cognitive Science*. Englewood Cliffs, NJ: Prentice Hall.

Wilson, T. and Schooler, J. (1991). Thinking too much: introspection can reduce the quality of preferences and decisions. *Journal of Personality and Social Psychology, 60*, 181–192.

Author Biographies

Josianne Basque is a Professor in educational technology at Tele-universite, Montreal, a French Canadian Distance University. She designed online courses in the field of learning and cognitive science, technology in education, and instructional design. She is also a researcher at the LICEF Research Center, dedicated to research in the field of Cognitive Informatics and Learning Environments. Her current research interests include knowledge modeling applied to learning, knowledge management, and instructional design, the design of e-learning scenarios, collaborative learning, and self-evaluation of competencies.
email: basque.josianne@teluq.uqam.ca
Homepage: www.teluq.uqam.ca/~jbasque

Simon Buckingham Shum is a Senior Lecturer at the Knowledge Media Institute, Open University. BSc pyschology in University of York. MSc in ergonomics from University College London and Ph.D. from the University of York. He is interested in technologies for sensemaking, specifically, which structure discourse to assist reflection and analysis.
email: sbs@acm.org
Homepage: http://kmi.open.ac.uk/people/sbs/

Tom Boyce is an Emeritus Consultant in the Representation and Reasoning Program at SRI International's Artificial Intelligence Center. He has an engineering degree from Stanford and an MBA from Santa Clara University. He is interested in using AI software for corporate business intelligence applications, such as creating and tracking future scenarios. He has a long standing involvement in complex project management applications as well.
email: boyce@ai.sri.com
Homepage: http://www.ai.sri.com/people/boyce/

Alberto J. Cañas is a Co-Founder and Associate Director of the Institute for Human and Machine Cognition – IHMC. Bachelors degree in computer engineering from the Instituto Tecnologico de Monterrey, Mexico, and a Masters Degree in Computer Science and a PhD in Management Science, both from the University of Waterloo, Canada. He is interested in the theoretical aspects and in the implementation details of concept mapping in education. His research includes uses of computers in education, knowledge management, and human–machine interface.
email: acanas@ihmc.us
Homepage: http://www.ihmc.us/users/acanas

Gráinne Conole is a Professor of e-Learning at the Open University. BA in chemistry and Ph.D. in X-ray crystallography at North London University. Her interests are in the use, integration, and evaluation of Information and Communication Technologies and e-learning and impact on organizational change.
email: g.c.conole@open.ac.uk
Homepage: http://iet.open.ac.uk/pp/g.c.conole/biography.cfm

Liliane Esnault is an Associate Professor in Information Systems management, e-Business and Project Management at E.M. Lyon. BSc and Doctorate in Fundamental Molecular Physics from Ecole Supérieure de Physique et Chimie de Paris (ESPCI). She is currently involved in the European Research project PALETTE (Integrated Services for Communities of Practice), after several other European projects in the same area.
email: esnault@em-lyon.com
Homepage: NONE L I'm ashamed! The homepage for EM LYON is http://www.em-lyon.com

Ian Harrison is a Senior Computer Scientist with the Representation and Reasoning Program at SRI International's Artificial Intelligence Center. He received his PhD in engineering rock mechanics from Imperial College of Science, Technology, and Medicine, University of London, and his MSc in Artificial Intelligence from the University of Edinburgh. His research interests have primarily focused on the development and deployment of software tools to aid intelligence analysts.
email: harrison@ai.sri.com
Homepage: http://www.ai.sri.com/~harrison/

David Hyerle is the Developer of the Thinking Maps® model and the Founding Director of Thinking Foundation, a nonprofit research organization supporting participatory research on models for facilitating cognitive processes and critical thinking in schools. BA English literature on literacy. M.Ed. in Urban Education and Ed.D. in curriculum and instruction at U.C. Berkeley and Exchange Scholar at Harvard College. His research focuses on the areas of thinking, learning, and leadership.
email: designs.thinking@valley.net
Homepage: http://www.thinkingfoundation.org

Michel Léonard is a professional researcher at the LICEF Research Center. He worked in many areas: hospitals, industrial maintenance, video and audio RF, as a technician, coordinator, test and development engineer, production engineer, and manager. Since January 1994, he has contributed to the development and validation of instructional design methods and support systems. He also contributed to the development of the knowledge modeling software MOT. He is involved in the preparation and the delivery of training sessions on knowledge modeling and on instructional engineering with tools and methods developed at the LICEF.
email: leonard.michel@licef.teluq.uqam.ca

John Lowrance is the Director of the Representation and Reasoning Program at SRI International's Artificial Intelligence Center. He received his A.B. in Computer Science and Mathematics from Indiana University, and MS and Ph.D. in computer and information science from the University of Massachusetts. His research interests have primarily focused on evidential reasoning, a methodology for representing and reasoning from evidence (i.e., information that is potentially uncertain, incomplete, and inaccurate). His most recent work attempts to make evidential reasoning accessible to practicing analysts and decision makers.
email: lowrance@ai.sri.com
Homepage: http://www.ai.sri.com/people/lowrance/

Rita de Cassia Veiga Marriott is a Language Tutor at the University of Birmingham/ Department of Hispanic Studies & Centre for Modern Languages UK and a member of the Research Group on Education, Communication and Technology at the Catholic University of Parana (PUCPR)/Brazil. She was a lecturer in English as a Foreign Language and Meaningful and Collaborative Learning Online at the Postgraduate Education course at the Pontifical Catholic University of Paraná (PUCPR), where she attained her MA in Education. She was responsible for teacher development programs related to Computer Assisted Language Learning (CALL) providing support for the implementation of Distance Learning Courses at the Language Centre at the Federal University of Parana (UFPR) in Brazil. She is interested in methodologies for language teaching/learning, e-learning, collaborative learning, and concept mapping.
email: r.marriott@bham.ac.uk

Janet Murdock is a Computer Scientist in the Artificial Intelligence Center at SRI International. She holds BS and MS degrees in chemical engineering from Purdue and Massachusetts Institute of Technology. She also holds MS and Ph.D. degrees in computer science from Stanford University. Prior to coming to SRI International, she worked in industry (Design Power, Inc., Praxis Engineers, Inc., and GE Power Systems) creating artificial intelligence applications that solve engineering problems. Her research interests include representation and reasoning, evidence management, and multimedia-based user interfaces.
email: murdock@ai.sri.com
Homepage: http://www.ai.sri.com/people/murdock/

Ken Murray is a Senior Computer Scientist in the Representation and Reasoning Program at SRI International's Artificial Intelligence Center. He holds a Bachelors degree from the University of Iowa, and Masters and Ph.D. degree from the University of Texas at Austin. His interests include the design, construction, and application of large knowledge-based systems with particular focus on interactive methods for knowledge acquisition and knowledge integration.
email: murray@ai.sri.com
Homepage: http://www.ai.sri.com/people/murray/

Joseph D. Novak is a Professor Emeritus at Cornell University and a Senior Scientist at the Institute for Human and Machine Cognition, and President of the Joseph D. Novak Knowledge Consultants, Inc. BS in Science and Mathematics, MS in Science Education, Ph.D. at Science Education & Biology at the University of Minnesota. His interests focus on meaningful learning and concept maps in education and knowledge management.
email: jnovak@ihmc.us
Homepage: http://www.ihmc.us/users/user.php?UserID=jnovak

Alexandra Okada is a Researcher in Knowledge Mapping for Open Content Initiative at the Knowledge Media Institute, Open University. Visiting Lecturer at the Fundacao Getulio Vargas FGV Online and the Pontificia Universidade Católica PUCSP COGEAE Online. BSc Computer Science at the Instituto Tecnológico de Aeronáutica – ITA, MA and Ph.D. in Education at PUCSP. She is interested in how knowledge maps can be used to facilitate research, investigation and learning.
email: a.l.p.okada@open.ac.uk
Homepage: http://kmi.open.ac.uk/people/ale/

Ricky Ohl has gained broad experience from involvement in various businesses over 30 years. He holds degrees in Business Management and in Commerce with Honours. His earlier published research examined "The Implementation of an Internet Management System into a Virtual Private Network," a pioneering project with unknown risk factors. He is currently completing his Ph.D. research on "CSAV Modelling for Consultative Democracy around Wicked Problems." His teachings in both advanced Masters and undergraduate courses at Griffith University has focused on areas including knowledge management, business management, information visualization, information systems, informatics, and IT governance. He also performs corporate consulting in knowledge management, business systems, and Web presence.
email: rickyohl@gmail.com
Homepage: http://rickonneblue.awardspace.com/

Gilbert Paquette is a Professor at Tele-universite, Montreal, and the holder of the Canada Research Chair in tele-learning in cognitive engineering. He founded the LICEF Research Center in 1992 and initiated many strategic and large projects on instructional engineering of e-learning environments and on knowledge management. He is the main designer of the knowledge modeling software MOT. He is the author of three books and of hundreds of articles and communications in those fields. He is presently the director of the cross-Canadian project LORNET (Learning Objects Repositories Network).
email: paquette.gilbert@teluq.uqam.ca
Homepage: http://www.licef.teluq.uqam.ca/gp/

Béatrice Pudelko recently finished her doctoral studies in Cognitive Psychology at the University Paris VIII. In her thesis, she examined, with a Vygotskian approach, the epistemic mediations of a graphical knowledge representation tool during a text

comprehension activity. In the last years, she participated in many research projects at the LICEF Research Center. She is also a tutor in an online course on cognitive science and learning offered at Tele-universite. Her current research interests are related to the use of knowledge modeling for learning and for knowledge elicitation, to the development of cognitive skills and to artifact-mediated activity.
email: pudelko.beatrice@licef.teluq.uqam.ca

Chris Reed is Head of Research in School of Computing at the University of Dundee. He holds a doctorate in Computer Science from the University of Dundee. He is interested in Agent Computing, Argumentation Theory, Learning Technology.
email: chris@computing.dundee.ac.uk

Yanna Rider is a Consultant and Trainer at Austhink. She holds a Ph.D. in Philosophy from The University of Melbourne. She is interested in the conceptual underpinnings of Argument Mapping and its relationship to critical thinking, as well as in applying Argument Mapping in professional contexts.
email: yannarider@gmail.com
Homepage: http://www.austhink.com

Andres Rodriguez worked as a Computer Scientist with the Representation and Reasoning Program at SRI International's Artificial Intelligence Center until 2006. He is now an independent consultant. He holds a Bachelors in computer science from the University of Los Andes and a Master of Science in computer science from Stanford University. His research interests include machine-learning, reasoning under uncertainty, and Web enabled user interfaces.
email: rodriguez@ai.sri.com
Homepage: http://www.ai.sri.com/~rodriguez/

Glenn Rowe is a lecturer in Applied Computing at the University of Dundee and holds MSc in physics and astronomy from the University of British Columbia and PhD in physics from the University of Toronto. He is is devoted to walks in the country and the general pursuit of knowledge.
email: growe@computing.dundee.ac.uk

Albert M. Selvin is a Director in the Information Technology Group at Verizon Communications, USA, where he leads Web design, software development, and business process redesign teams. His research interests are on the practice of constructing hypermedia representations, practice in participatory hypermedia construction, and collaborative hypermedia authoring. He is the original developer and member of the ongoing core team for the Compendium approach and toolset and has facilitated over 500 sessions for industry, academic, and public groups. He received his BA in Film/Video Studies at the University of Michigan (1982), and an MA in Communication Arts from the University of Wisconsin (1984), and is currently a Ph.D. candidate at the Knowledge Media Institute, Open University, UK.
email: alselvin@gmail.com
Homepage: http://kmi.open.ac.uk/people/selvin/

Tony Sherborne is a Creative Director for the Centre for Science Education at Sheffield Hallam University, curriculum developer, and a NESTA Fellow Researcher. BSc and MA in science from Cambridge University. He is interested in using maps to enhance teachers' creativity in the design of curricula and pedagogical materials.
email: T.Sherborne@shu.ac.uk
Homepage: http://crackingscience.com

Maarten Sierhuis is a Computer Scientist and Senior Researcher at RIACS/NASA Ames Research Center. His research focuses on multiagent systems and artificial intelligence. His early work discusses about knowledge modeling and expert systems. His work area comprehends developing tools for modeling situated human behavior in organizations.
email: msierhuis@mail.arc.nasa.gov
Homepage: http://home.comcast.net/~msierhuis

Daniel D. Suthers is presently Associate Professor in the Department of Information and Computer Sciences at the University of Hawaii at Manoa, where he directs the Laboratory for Interactive Learning Technologies and is chair of the interdisciplinary Communication and Information Sciences Ph.D. program. He holds a B.F.A. from Kansas City Art Institute, and an MS and Ph.D. in Computer Science from the University of Massachusetts. His research focuses on the design of educational technologies for collaborative learning and online learning communities.
email: suthers@hawaii.edu
Homepage: http://lilt.ics.hawaii.edu/suthers/

Neil Thomason is Senior Lecturer in the Department of History & Philosophy of Science at The University of Melbourne and holds a doctorate in the Philosophy of Science from the University of California at Berkeley. He has taught Critical Thinking at Reed, Vassar, and The University of Melbourne. He is interested in everything except professional sport.
email: neilt@unimelb.edu.au
Homepage: http://www.hps.unimelb.edu.au/about/staff/neil_thomason/

Jerome Thomere is a Computer Scientist in the Representation and Reasoning Program at SRI International's Artificial Intelligence Center. He holds a Masters in Applied Mathematics from Ecole Centrale Paris and a Masters (DEA) in Artificial Intelligence from Universite Aix Marseille. His research interests include the representation of knowledge, techniques for approximate reasoning, and user interface design.
email: thomere@ai.sri.com
Homepage: http://www.ai.sri.com/people/thomere/

Patricia Lupion Torres teaches at the Masters and Research Degree Courses in Education at PUCPR (Pontifical Catholic University of Parana/Brazil) whilst is the Director of Distance Learning at the same institution. A pedagogue, she is a

Specialist in Psycho-pedagogy and in Sociological Theories, she holds a Masters in Education from PUCPR and a doctorate on Production Engineering from UFSC (Federal University of Santa Catarina/Brazil). She is also the Pedagogical Coordinator of the National Service on Rural Learning – SENAR-PR/Brazil. Her interests are e-learning, virtual universities, collaborative learning, and concept mapping.
email: patorres@terra.com.br

Mário Vasconcellos, is a Lecturer at University of Amazonia (Centre of Social and Economic Studies) and Federal University of Pará (Centre of Environment), both in Brazil. He holds a M.Phil. from the Centre of High Amazonian Studies, Federal University of Pará (Brazil), and Ph.D. from the Centre for Development Studies, Swansea University (United Kingdom). His research focuses on development management, local development, and sustainable development in Amazonia.
emails: mariovasc@unama.br; mariovasc@ufpa.br

Eric Yeh is a Software Engineer with the Representation and Reasoning Program at SRI International's Artificial Intelligence Center. He holds a Bachelors in Computer Science from the University of California at Berkeley. His interests lie in the use of artificial intelligence techniques, including machine-learning and natural language processing, to augment human decision making.
email: yeh@ai.sri.com
Homepage: http://www.ai.sri.com/people/yeh/

Romain Zeiliger is Computer Scientist and Research Engineer at GATE Groupe d'Analyse et de Théorie Economique at the Centre National de la Recherche Scientifique (CNRS-GATE) and Université Lumière Lyon2. He is the author of the Software Nestor Web Cartographer. He is also a researcher at the European Research project PALETTE. BSc in computer science at University Claude Bernard Lyon1. His interests are Navigation, CSCW, and Web-based Learning.
email: zeiliger@gate.cnrs.fr
Homepage: <http://www.gate.cnrs.fr/~zeiliger/>http://www.gate.cnrs.fr/~zeiliger/

Index

ALPHABETICAL INDEX [1]

A
Activity Theory, 19, 91
Actor Network Theory, 102
Aesthetics, 226, 229–231, 233–236, 243, 245
Affordance, 4, 12, 18, 133, 199, 213, 260, 301
AML, 164, 172, 176, 177, 179, 326, 327
Analysts, 174, 249, 258, 260, 263, 269, 272, 282, 308, 319, 332
Araucaria, 158, 163–179, 259, 260, 262
Argument Mapping, 113–116, 119, 122, 126, 128, 161, 223, 259, 260, 280, 282, 300, 309
Argument Structure, 137, 174, 175
Argument Visualisation, 268, 269, 271, 272, 282, 283
Argumentation Skills, 132, 133, 137, 161
Argumentation Theory, 171, 177
Artifacts, 1, 6, 7, 17, 19, 203, 204, 224, 226, 230, 238
Assessment, 6, 55, 61, 67, 68, 77, 86, 151, 270, 316, 330, 350
Authoring Skills, 127, 227

B
Belvedere, 2, 3, 5, 6, 7, 9, 11, 14, 17
Brainstorming, 53, 76, 77, 78, 79, 143, 145, 319
Business, 32, 114, 184, 223, 244, 329–331

C
CALL – Computer Assisted Language Learning, 51, 70
Case Scenario, 208, 261
Case studies, 133, 139, 158, 159, 161, 202–206, 218, 219

Categorisation, 7, 82, 274, 289, 361, 378
Challenges, 37, 58, 59, 66, 105, 227, 238, 271, 287
Circumstantial evidence, 169, 175, 176
Claims, 114, 117, 125, 136, 137, 140, 143
CmapTools, 29–33, 35, 38, 39, 44, 56, 194, 335, 336, 337, 344, 350–352
CMC – Computer Mediated Communication, 9–11, 13, 15, 51
Cognition, 74, 79, 91, 228, 272, 273, 291, 292
Cognitive Skills, 79, 81, 86, 113, 133, 121, 370
Cognitive Development, 78, 80, 86, 87, 186
Cognitive Learning, 27, 28, 51
Cognitive Mapping, 335–337, 343, 350–352
Cognitive Structure, 27, 28, 44, 51, 337, 360, 370
Collaborative Analysis, 299, 307, 319
Collaborative Analysis, 299, 315, 319
Collaborative Environment, 308, 332
Collaborative Inquiry, 1, 5, 6, 133, 134, 228
Collaborative Knowledge Mapping or Modelling, 224, 225, 234, 244, 245, 365, 367, 370–372, 375, 376
Collaborative Knowledge, 13, 14, 25, 26
Collaborative Learning, 2, 4, 17, 18, 49, 50, 68, 138, 228, 370
Collaborative Work, 106, 107
Communicative Skills, 52, 54, 61
Communities of Practice, 99, 358, 371, 373
Compendium, 33, 134, 135, 137–160, 189, 200, 207–219, 238–240, 245, 251, 253, 255, 260, 262, 264, 274, 280–283, 288–303

---

[1] This alphabetical index is followed by a categorised index which groups terms under broad categories that readers may find helpful.

Computerised Assessment, 117
Concept Mapping, 25–29, 33, 47, 48, 79, 86, 184, 192, 195, 251, 280, 282, 350, 359, 368, 370, 376
Concepts, 26, 48, 67, 361, 362
Conceptual Model, 14
Conceptual representations, 13, 17, 272
Conceptual Structure, 1, 13, 14, 382
Conceptualisation, 2, 13, 185,
Conectade Project - Panama, 36–44
Consistency, 6, 85, 100, 336, 351, 352
Constraints, 4, 185, 230, 361, 367, 368, 377
Constructivist Theory, 28, 40, 50, 68, 89–104, 108–110, 186, 190, 196
Convergence, 1, 13, 16, 18, 186, 377
Conversational Modelling, 251, 261, 287, 288, 290, 291, 295, 302
Corroborative Evidence, 169, 170, 172, 175, 176
Creative Skills, 66, 68
Criteria, 3, 5, 61, 68, 132, 133, 139, 140, 178, 189, 208, 330, 365
Critical Thinking, 118, 119, 121, 122, 125, 128, 132, 133, 161, 163, 171, 178, 179, 260, 264, 328
Cross-links, 48, 66–68, 280, 281
Curricula(um), 33, 131, 183–185

D

Decision Maker, 280, 308, 328, 332, 385
Decision-making, 76, 200, 203, 216, 227, 231, 270, 272, 282, 291, 326, 328, 337, 359
De-constructing, 98
Deliberation, 33, 132, 159, 251, 262, 280
Designer (Curriculum), 186, 188, 197
Designer (Hypermedia Software or System), 18, 227, 386
Designer (Learning), 200, 201, 203, 205, 213, 219, 374
Designer (VLE), 12, 13, 18
Designers (Architet / Urban), 226, 269
Diagnosis, 185, 186
Diagramming, 77, 163–171
Diagrams, 2, 79, 122, 125, 165, 169, 172, 175
DialogPlus, 203, 208, 209, 213, 216
Dialogue Mapping, 127, 134, 139, 145, 147, 151, 156, 158–161, 260, 261, 297, 302

Difficulties, 55, 59, 68, 86, 90, 119, 140, 140, 145, 153, 342, 343, 358, 371
Disorientation, 90

E

e-assessment, 205
Engagement, 100, 109, 229, 230, 231, 239, 243, 249, 270, 271, 283
Ethics, 226, 230, 235, 255
Evaluation, 6, 18, 28, 66, 68, 70, 117, 124, 129, 167, 168, 174, 177, 185, 190, 194, 336
Evidence, 169, 170
Evidence based dialogue map, 133, 136, 137
Evidence-based regional planning, 272
Evidence map, 2, 5, 7, 9, 11, 12, 14, 16
Expertise, 73, 118, 133, 223, 260, 272, 358–360, 365–367, 370, 372–377
Explanations, 6, 63, 132, 137, 151, 351, 358
Explanatory Evidence, 170, 172, 175, 176

F

Facilitator, 36, 39, 42, 134, 227, 231, 232, 251, 260, 294, 297, 300, 303, 372
Familiarity, 37, 132, 133, 224, 365
Feedback, 30, 50, 58, 79, 85, 93, 113, 117, 118, 122, 156, 159, 270, 297, 298, 366
Field work, 344, 352, 369
FlashMeeting, 264, 302
Format, 193, 201, 209, 350, 369
Formative Assessment, 55, 70, 138, 151

G

Generalisations, 136
GlobalArgument Project - Iraq Debate, 250
Government, 25, 38, 183, 268, 270, 271, 272, 274, 282, 283, 335
(post)Graduates, 206
(under)Graduates, 8, 118, 134, 158, 178, 134
Grammar, 134, 362, 363, 367
Granularity, 13, 158, 208, 250, 259, 366
Graphic Organisers, 76–80
Graphical Visualisation, 155, 185, 223, 313, 314, 332, 338
Grids, 96
Grounded Theory, 238, 273
Guidance, 6, 9, 49, 92, 146, 200, 203, 205, 212, 213, 216, 219, 311

H

Heuristics, 115, 116, 158, 159, 196, 279, 368, 377
Holding Hands, 115, 124
Hypermedia, 3, 90, 134, 226, 227, 245, 250, 252
Hypermedia Discourse, 264
Hypertext, 3, 90, 93, 96, 226, 227, 240, 251, 258, 288, 292

I

IBIS or gIBIS, 33, 134, 136, 147, 148, 157–59, 227, 251, 253, 260, 262, 272, 274, 280, 282, 283, 289, 290, 295, 301–302
Improvisation, 226, 228, 230, 233, 234
Inconsistency, 6, 7, 352
Inquiry, 2, 3, 6, 132, 133, 225, 229, 307
Inquiry Skills, 2
Inspiration, 208, 344
Interdisciplinary curriculum, 185
Interdisciplinary Learning or problem, 77
Interdisciplinary problem, 83, 185
Interpersonal Skills, 47
Interpretation, 74, 85, 117, 135, 151, 174, 190, 193, 196, 269, 288, 290, 324, 329, 332, 335, 343–344, 349–352, 359, 368
Interviews, 200, 205, 344, 349, 352, 366, 372

K

Knowledge Management, 108, 109, 277, 283, 288, 300, 357, 359, 372, 374
Knowledge Model, 30, 31, 33, 34, 35, 365, 366, 369–373
Knowledge Structure, 26, 48, 73, 86, 377

L

LAMP, 113, 116–119, 121–129
Language Acquisition, 49, 55, 70
Language Fluency, 52, 63, 66, 69, 157
LAPLI, 47, 48, 49, 51–53, 55, 59, 64, 68–70
Leader, 76, 77, 79, 86, 205, 228, 292, 300, 312, 316, 329, 344, 346, 327
Learning Design, 199–219, 302, 374, 375
Learning or pedagogical Scenario, 105, 205, 364, 374
Learning Skills, 36, 138, 157
Lecturers, 117

Legal (Cases or Practice), 172, 178, 179, 226, 269, 324
Lexical List, 59, 60
Linguistic Skills, 49, 53, 55, 58, 61, 68, 70
Literacy, 76, 131, 133, 134, 139, 226, 260

M

Manager, 230, 325, 329, 330, 365, 366
Mapmaker, 28, 83
Mapping Skills, 140, 145, 157, 224
Mars Mission - NASA, 238, 287, 288, 291, 292, 297
Matrix, 5, 7, 8, 9, 17, 337, 370
Meaningful Learning, 26, 27, 40, 47, 48, 50, 70, 367
Media, 4, 12, 16, 75, 78, 109, 133, 157, 206, 228, 250, 291
Memorisation Skills, 360
Mental Fluency, 73
MetaCognition, 67, 85
MindManager, 208
Mind Mapping, 73, 89, 96, 98, 106, 199, 207, 208
Misunderstanding, 156, 350
Mobile Agents Project - NASA, 238, 291, 292, 303
Moodle, 135, 138, 139, 156, 159, 160, 205, 264, 291
MOT, 359–375
Multidisciplinary teams, 328
Mutual or Group Awareness, 4, 12, 82, 103, 234

N

Navigation experience, 89, 90, 98, 102
Navigation Visualisation, 93
Negotiation, 4, 18, 34, 63, 78, 99–103, 107, 108, 366, 370, 372
Nestor, 89, 93–95, 102–110
Network, 29, 105, 196, 251, 253, 260, 291, 327, 337, 374
Networking, 73, 75, 78, 199, 291
Notations, 1–5, 19, 133
Novices, 85, 186, 224, 226, 281, 310, 358, 359, 365–367, 371–374
Nud*ist, 344

O

Objective Assessment, 330
Obstacles, 196, 224, 232, 244

One laptop per Child, The USA, 43
OpenLearn Project, UK, 160, 161, 219, 264, 291
Oral or Verbal Skills, 51, 55, 62, 63, 70, 376

P
Palette, 100, 289
Participatory Democracy, 267–271
Participatory Design, 90, 110
Phoebe, 203, 213, 216
Portfolio, 29, 44, 206
Practitioners, 2, 75, 86, 145, 199, 223, 224–228, 235, 244, 245, 358, 371
Premises (convergent or linked), 164–166, 171–176
Premises (Explicit), 114, 116, 259, 263, 280
Premises (Hidden or unstated), 114–115, 121, 123, 128
Problem Solving, 10, 15, 50, 59, 86, 185, 272, 273, 360, 370, 376
Pupils / Children, 2, 26, 36, 41, 75, 76, 131–161, 184, 192

Q
Qualitative research, 139, 273, 335, 343, 344, 352
Questioning, 54, 120, 124, 143, 151, 120, 124,

R
Rationale, 113, 262
Reading, 49, 52–53, 62, 68, 86, 94–96, 110, 113, 120, 123, 126, 142, 158, 178, 226–227, 232, 250, 258, 260, 336
Reason!Able, 86
Reassement, 350
Reduction, 74, 337, 350, 351, 352, 368
Refutation, 165–168, 171, 174, 177, 309
Repository, 204, 205, 326
Representational Guidance, 5, 7, 9, 10, 16, 17, 18
Researchers, 82, 86, 119, 132, 134, 157, 161, 184, 201, 208, 216, 227, 244, 258, 336, 337, 343, 344, 352
Reusability, 67
Rubrics, 6, 7, 18, 42

S
Salience, 4, 5, 9
Schemata, 79, 360, 361, 362, 367

Science Education, 36, 131, 134, 188, 191
SEAS, 307–309, 313–315, 319–332
Second Life, 70
Self Assessment, 77, 82, 151
Sensemaking or Making meaning, 17, 134, 223, 224, 228, 230, 232–234, 238–240, 245, 288, 290, 301–302
SEQ Regional Plan, 267, 268, 270, 272, 277, 282, 283
Shared Visualisation, 196
Shared understanding, 134, 227, 249, 301, 370
Social bookmarking, 289, 303
Stakeholder, 189, 190, 231, 234, 235, 249, 264, 267
Stella, 77, 86, 192
Students understanding, 25, 26, 31, 33–35, 44, 48, 50, 53, 55, 59, 66, 68, 77–78, 82, 114, 120–121, 132–134, 151, 156
Students, 48, 73, 75, 104, 117
Subjective Assessment, 330
Summative Assessment, 61, 66, 67
Surf map, 98, 99, 106

T
Taxonomy, 5, 42, 203, 209, 218, 219
Teachers, 36–44, 49, 51, 70, 80, 104, 108–109, 119, 131, 132, 136, 143, 145, 151, 158, 189–193, 196, 200, 203, 205
Templates, 159, 208, 213, 251, 261, 290, 291, 294, 295, 301, 302, 309–312, 314, 320, 321, 332
Testimonial evidence, 169, 170, 177
Thinking Maps, 75, 78–87
Thinking Patterns, 79, 81, 82
Thinking Skills, 59, 81, 82, 119, 125, 131, 224
Tools Fluency, 86, 133, 157, 224
Totally Wild Science Course, UK, 135, 137, 138
Toulmin Model, 136, 137, 139, 163, 167, 168, 171–180
Training, 38–44, 78, 80, 91, 99, 116, 117, 119, 128, 226, 260, 311, 358, 364, 365, 374, 376, 377
Tree maps, 77, 83, 269, 277, 282, 283
Triangulation, 343
Tutors, 104, 105, 108, 201, 203

U
Urban / Regional / Social Planning, 269, 270, 271, 272, 280, 282, 283

V
Visual Patterns, 159, 259

W
Web Maps, 89, 93, 94, 209
Wicked problems, 134, 268–271, 280, 282, 283
Wigmore Model, 169–172, 175–179
Writing, 68, 121, 125, 140

CATEGORISED INDEX

APPLICATIONS
Business, 32, 114, 184, 223, 244, 329–331
Curricula(um), 33, 131, 183–185
Knowledge Management, 108, 109, 277, 283, 288, 300, 357, 359, 372, 374
Language Acquisition, 49, 55, 70
Learning Design, 199–219, 302, 374, 375
Legal (Cases or Practice), 172, 178, 179, 226, 269, 324
Science Education, 36, 131, 134, 188, 191
Urban / Regional / Social Planning, 269, 270, 271, 272, 280, 282, 283

ARGUMENTATION CONCEPTS
Claims, 114, 117, 125, 136, 137, 140, 143
Premises (convergent or linked), 164–166, 171–176
Premises (explicit), 114, 116, 259, 263, 280
Premises (hidden or unstated), 114–115, 121, 123, 128
Refutation, 165–168, 171, 174, 177, 309

ARGUMENTATION NOTATIONS
AML, 164, 172, 176, 177, 179, 326, 327
IBIS or gIBIS, 33, 134, 136, 147, 148, 157– 159, 227, 251, 253, 260, 262, 272, 274, 280, 282, 283, 289, 290, 295, 301–302
Toulmin Model, 136, 137, 139, 163, 167, 168, 171–180
Wigmore Model, 169–172, 175–179

ASSESSMENT
Assessment, 6, 55, 61, 67, 68, 77, 86, 151, 270, 316, 330, 350
Formative Assessment, 55, 70, 138, 151
Computerised assessment, 117
e-assessment, 205,
Self Assessment, 77, 82, 151
Objective Assessment, 330
Reassement, 350
Subjective Assessment, 330
Summative Assessment, 61, 66, 67

CHALLENGES / ISSUES
Challenges, 37, 58, 59, 66, 105, 227, 238, 271, 287
Consistency, 6, 85, 100, 336, 351, 352
Difficulties, 55, 59, 68, 86, 90, 119, 140, 140, 145, 153, 342, 343, 358, 371
Familiarity, 37, 132, 133, 224, 365
Inconsistency, 6, 7, 352
Misunderstanding, 156, 350
Multidisciplinary teams, 328
Obstacles, 196, 224, 232, 244
Reduction, 74, 337, 350, 351, 352, 368

EVIDENCE
Circumstantial evidence, 169, 175, 176
Corroborative Evidence, 169, 170, 172, 175, 176
Evidence, 169, 170
Evidence based dialogue map, 133, 136, 137
Evidence-based regional planning, 272
Evidence map, 2, 5, 7, 9, 11, 12, 14, 16
Explanatory Evidence, 170, 172, 175, 176
Testimonial evidence, 169, 170, 177

FRAMEWORKS / THEORIES
Activity Theory, 19, 91
Actor Network Theory, 102
Argumentation Theory, 171, 177
CALL – Computer Assisted Language Learning, 51, 70
CMC – Computer Mediated Communication, 9–11, 13, 15, 51
Cognitive Learning, 27, 28, 51
Collaborative Environment, 308, 332

Collaborative Inquiry, 1, 5, 6, 133, 134, 228
Collaborative knowledge mapping or Modelling, 224, 225, 234, 244, 245, 365, 367, 370–372, 375, 376
Collaborative Learning, 2, 4, 17, 18, 49, 50, 68, 138, 228, 370
Collaborative Work, 106, 107
Communities of Practice, 99, 358, 371, 373
Constructivist Theory, 28, 40, 50, 68, 89–104, 108–110, 186, 190, 196
Conversational Modelling, 251, 261, 287, 288, 290, 291, 295, 302
Grounded Theory, 238, 273
Meaningful Learning, 26, 27, 40, 47, 48, 50, 70, 367
Participatory Democracy, 267–271
Participatory Design, 90, 110

LEARNING & MAPPING/SKILLS
Argumentation Skills, 132, 133, 137, 161
Authoring Skills, 127, 227
Cognitive Skills, 79, 81, 86, 113, 133, 121, 370
Communicative Skills, 52, 54, 61,
Creative Skills, 66, 68
Expertise, 73, 118, 133, 223, 260, 272, 358–360, 365–367, 370, 372–377
Inquiry Skills, 2
Interpersonal Skills, 47
Language Fluency, 52, 63, 66, 69, 157
Learning Skills, 36, 138, 157
Linguistic Skills, 49, 53, 55, 58, 61, 68, 70
Literacy, 76, 131, 133, 134, 139, 226, 260
Mapping Skills, 140, 145, 157, 224
Memorisation Skills, 360
Mental Fluency, 73
Networking, 73, 75, 78, 199, 291
Oral or Verbal Skills, 51, 55, 62, 63, 70, 376
Thinking Skills, 59, 81, 82, 119, 125, 131, 224
Tools Fluency, 86, 133, 157, 224

LEARNING & TEACHING ISSUES
Cognition, 74, 79, 91, 228, 272, 273, 291, 292
Cognitive Development, 78, 80, 86, 87, 186

Critical thinking, 118, 119, 121, 122, 125, 128, 132, 133, 161, 163, 171, 178, 179, 260, 264, 328
Explanations, 6, 63, 132, 137, 151, 351, 358
Diagnosis, 185, 186
Feedback, 30, 50, 58, 79, 85, 93, 113, 117, 118, 122, 156, 159, 270, 297, 298, 366
Guidance, 6, 9, 49, 92, 146, 200, 203, 205, 212, 213, 216, 219, 311
Interdisciplinary Learning or problem, 77
Interdisciplinary problem, 83, 185
Interdisciplinary curriculum, 185
Interpretation, 74, 85, 117, 135, 151, 174, 190, 193, 196, 269, 288, 290, 324, 329, 332, 335, 343–344, 349–352, 359, 368
Learning or pedagogical Scenario, 105, 205, 364, 374
Inquiry, 2, 3, 6, 132, 133, 225, 229, 307
Problem Solving, 10, 15, 50, 59, 86, 185, 272, 273, 360, 370, 376
Reading, 49, 52–53, 62, 68, 86, 94–96, 110, 113, 120, 123, 126, 142, 158, 178, 226–227, 232, 250, 258, 260, 336
Students Understanding, 25, 26, 31, 33–35, 44, 48, 50, 53, 55, 59, 66, 68, 77–78, 82, 114, 120–121, 132–134, 151, 156
Training, 38–44, 78, 80, 91, 99, 116, 117, 119, 128, 226, 260, 311, 358, 364, 365, 374, 376, 377
Writing, 68, 121, 125, 140

MAPPING AND MODELLING
Brainstorming, 53, 76, 77, 78, 79, 143, 145, 319
Categorisation, 7, 82, 274, 289, 361, 378
Conceptualisation, 2, 13, 185
Criteria, 3, 5, 61, 68, 132, 133, 139, 140, 178, 189, 208, 330, 365
De-constructing, 98
Diagramming, 77, 163–171
Navigation experience, 89, 90, 98, 102

MAPPING IN GROUPS
Collaborative Analysis, 299, 315, 319
Collaborative knowledge, 13, 14, 25, 26
Engagement, 100, 109, 229, 230, 231, 239, 243, 249, 270, 271, 283
Improvisation, 226, 228, 230, 233, 234

Mutual or Group Awareness, 4, 12, 82, 103, 234
Negotiation, 4, 18, 34, 63, 78, 99–103, 107, 108, 366, 370, 372
Shared understanding, 134, 227, 249, 301, 370

MAPPING/SENSEMAKING

Decision-making, 76, 200, 203, 216, 227, 231, 270, 272, 282, 291, 326, 328, 337, 359
Deliberation, 33, 132, 159, 251, 262, 280
Evaluation, 6, 18, 28, 66, 68, 70, 117, 124, 129, 167, 168, 174, 177, 185, 190, 194, 336
Generalisations, 136
MetaCognition, 67, 85
Questioning, 54, 120, 124, 143, 151, 120, 124
Sensemaking or making meaning, 17, 134, 223, 224, 228, 230, 232–234, 238–240, 245, 288, 290, 301–302
Wicked problems, 134, 268–271, 280, 282, 283

MAPPING TECHNIQUES

Argument Mapping, 113–116119, 122, 126, 128, 161, 223, 259, 260, 280, 282, 300, 309
Cognitive Mapping, 335–337, 343, 350–352
Concept Mapping, 25–29, 33, 47, 48, 79, 86, 184, 192, 195, 251, 280, 282, 350, 359, 368, 370, 376
Conversational Modelling, 251, 261
Dialogue Mapping, 127, 134, 139, 145, 147, 151, 156, 158–161, 260, 261, 297, 302
Graphic Organizers, 76–80
Mind Mapping, 73, 89, 96, 98, 106, 199, 207, 208
Surf map, 98, 99, 106
Thinking Maps, 78–87
Tree maps, 77, 83, 269, 277, 282, 283
Web Maps, 89, 93, 94, 209

MAPPING TOOLS

Araucaria, 158, 163–179, 259, 260, 262
Belvedere, 2, 3, 5, 6, 7, 9, 11, 14, 17
CmapTools, 29–33, 35, 38, 39, 44, 56, 194, 335, 336, 337, 344, 350–352
Compendium, 33, 134, 135, 137–160, 189, 200, 207–219, 238–240, 245, 251, 253, 255, 260, 262, 264, 274, 280–283, 288–303
Inspiration, 208, 344
MindManager, 208
MOT, 359–375
Nestor, 89, 93–95, 102–110
Rationale, 113, 262
Reason!Able, 86
SEAS, 307–309, 313–315, 319–332
Stella, 77, 86, 192
Thinking Maps, 75, (79–, 87)

MAPPING & VISUALISATION

Argument Visualisation, 268, 269, 271, 272, 282, 283
Graphical Visualisation, 155, 185, 223, 313, 314, 332, 338
Navigation Visualisation, 93
Shared Visualisation, 196

METHODS & TECHNIQUES

Heuristics, 115, 116, 158, 159, 196, 279, 368, 377
Holding Hands, 115, 124
LAPLI, 47, 48, 49, 51–53, 55, 59, 64, 68–70
LAMP, 113, 116–119, 121–129

MODELS & STRUCTURES

Argument Structure, 137, 174, 175
Cognitive Structure, 27, 28, 44, 51, 337, 360, 370
Conceptual Model, 14
Conceptual representations, 13, 17, 272
Conceptual Structure, 1, 13, 14, 382
Knowledge Model, 30, 31, 33, 34, 35, 365, 366, 369–373
Knowledge Structure, 26, 48, 73, 86, 377

REPRESENTATIONAL ISSUES

Aesthetics, 226, 229–231, 233–236, 243, 245
Affordance, 4, 12, 18, 133, 199, 213, 260, 301
Artifacts, 1, 6, 7, 17, 19, 203, 204, 224, 226, 230, 238
Concepts, 26, 48, 67, 361, 362
Constraints, 4, 185, 230, 361, 367, 368, 377

Convergence, 1, 13, 16, 18, 186, 377
Cross-links, 48, 66–68, 280, 281
Diagrams, 2, 79, 122, 125, 165, 169, 172, 175
Disorientation, 90
Ethics, 226, 230, 235, 255
Format, 193, 201, 209, 350, 369
Grammar, 134, 362, 363, 367
Granularity, 13, 158, 208, 250, 259, 366
Grids, 96
Hypermedia, 3, 90, 134, 226, 227, 245, 250, 252
Hypermedia Discourse, 264
Hypertext, 3, 90, 93, 96, 226, 227, 240, 251, 258, 288, 292
Lexical List, 59, 60
Matrix, 5, 7, 8, 9, 17, 337, 370
Media, 4, 12, 16, 75, 78, 109, 133, 157, 206, 228, 250, 291
Network, 29, 105, 196, 251, 253, 260, 291, 327, 337, 374
Notations, 1–5, 19, 133
Palette, 100, 289
Portfolio, 29, 44, 206
Repository, 204, 205, 326
Representational Guidance, 5, 7, 9, 10, 16, 17, 18
Reusability, 67
Rubrics, 6, 7, 18, 42
Salience, 4, 5, 9
Schemata, 79, 360, 361, 362, 367
Social bookmarking, 289, 303
Taxonomy, 5, 42, 203, 209, 218, 219
Templates, 159, 208, 213, 251, 261, 290, 291, 294, 295, 301, 302, 309–312, 314, 320, 321, 332
Thinking Patterns, 79, 81, 82
Visual Patterns, 159, 259

RESEARCH METHODS
Case Scenario, 208, 261
Case studies, 133, 139, 158, 159, 161, 202–206, 218, 219
Collaborative Analysis, 299, 307, 319
Field work, 344, 352, 369
Interviews, 200, 205, 344, 349, 352, 366, 372
Qualitative research, 139, 273, 335, 343, 344, 352
Triangulation, 343

ROLES
Analysts, 174, 249, 258, 260, 263, 269, 272, 282, 308, 319, 332
Decision Maker, 280, 308, 328, 332, 385
Designer (VLE), 12, 13, 18
Designer (Curriculum), 186, 188, 197
Designer (Learning), 200, 201, 203, 205, 213, 219, 374
Designer (Hypermedia Software or System), 18, 227, 386
Designers (Architet / Urban), 226, 269
Facilitator, 36, 39, 42, 134, 227, 231, 232, 251, 260, 294, 297, 300, 303, 372
Government, 25, 38, 183, 268, 270, 271, 272, 274, 282, 283, 335
(post)Graduates, 206
(under)Graduates, 8, 118, 134, 158, 178, 134
Leader, 76, 77, 79, 86, 205, 228, 292, 300, 312, 316, 329, 344, 346, 327
Lecturers, 117
Manager, 230, 325, 329, 330, 365, 366
Mapmaker, 28, 83
Novices, 85, 186, 224, 226, 281, 310, 358, 359, 365–367, 371–374
Practitioners, 2, 75, 86, 145, 199, 223, 224–228, 235, 244, 245, 358, 371
Pupils / Children, 2, 26, 36, 41, 75, 76, 131–161, 184, 192
Researchers, 82, 86, 119, 132, 134, 157, 161, 184, 201, 208, 216, 227, 244, 258, 336, 337, 343, 344, 352
Stakeholder, 189, 190, 231, 234, 235, 249, 264, 267
Students, 48, 73, 75, 104, 117
Teachers, 36–44, 49, 51, 70, 80, 104, 108–109, 119, 131, 132, 136, 143, 145, 151, 158, 189–193, 196, 200, 203, 205
Tutors, 104, 105, 108, 201, 203

SCENARIO & PROJECTS
Conectade Project - Panama, 36–44
GlobalArgument Project - Iraq Debate, 250
Mars Mission - NASA, 238, 287, 288, 291, 292, 297
Mobile Agents Project - NASA, 238, 291, 292, 303
One laptop per Child, The USA, 43

OpenLearn Project - UK, 160, 161, 219, 264, 291
SEQ Regional Plan, 267, 268, 270, 272, 277, 282, 283
Totally Wild Science Course - UK, 135, 137, 138

SOFTWARE SYSTEMS/ TECHNOLOGIES
DialogPlus, 203, 208, 209, 213, 216
FlashMeeting, 264, 302
Moodle, 135, 138, 139, 156, 159, 160, 205, 264, 291
Nud*ist, 344
Phoebe, 203, 213, 216
Second Life, 70

Printed in the United States of America